CHANHU- DARO EXCAVATIONS

1935-36

CHANHU- DARO EXCAVATIONS
1935-36

BY

ERNEST J.H. MACKAY

GYAN

Published by

Gyan Publishing House
5, Ansari Road
Daryaganj, New Delhi-110002
Phone: 011-47034999, 9811692060
E-mail: books@gyanbooks.com

Distribution Network
gyanbooks.com
India, USA, Canada, UK, Australia

ISBN: 978-93-6280-091-6 (PB)
First Published, 1943

2nd Impression 2024

Printed at: Gyan Press, Delhi.

CHANHU- DARO EXCAVATIONS
Author: ERNEST J.H. MACKAY

Painted by Suzanne E. Chapman

Painted by Nina de Garis Davies and Suzanne E. Chapman

CHANHU-DARO EXCAVATIONS
1935-36

BY

ERNEST J. H. MACKAY

Published for

AMERICAN SCHOOL OF INDIC AND IRANIAN STUDIES

AND

MUSEUM OF FINE ARTS, BOSTON

BY

AMERICAN ORIENTAL SOCIETY

NEW HAVEN, CONNECTICUT

1943

PREFACE

The three ancient mounds of Chanhu-daro are situated a little over half-a-mile south of the modern village of Jamal-Kirio, near Sakrand in the Nawābshāh District of Sindh. The left bank of the river Indus is now twelve miles distant, but in the third millennium B.C., the river, or a branch of it, flowed close beside the city; more than once, indeed, it threatened its total destruction. The Khīrthar Mountains, in Baluchistan, some thirty-seven miles distant from the mounds, are crossed by a pass which is used by caravans to this day, as there is a plentiful supply of fresh water. The ancient city was therefore very favourably situated for trade both by land and sea.

In February, 1931, the late Mr. N. G. Majumdar, Assistant superintendent of the Archaeological Survey of India, came upon the site in the course of his survey of the ancient sites of Sindh for the Government of India. After three weeks' examination of the mounds, he left in March, satisfied as to their date and their importance. From his admirable report on this and other ancient sites of Sindh,[1] Professor W. Norman Brown and I selected Chanhu-daro for excavation by the first American Archaeological Expedition to India.

Plate I shows the relative extent and position of the three mounds (I-III) of the ancient city, whose original name we do not know. The largest (No. II) is some 1,060 feet in circumference and stood 23.5 feet high from datum level before excavation. The smallest (No. III), to the north-west of Mound II, is only 450 feet in circumference and is now 12.5 feet in height. Mound I lies to the south-west of Mound II and is separated from it by a gap about 150 feet wide. This last mound, being more compact in shape, is more impressive than Mound II, though its height (22.2 feet) and circumference (about 950 feet) are actually somewhat less. All three mounds are of the same date and were originally one and undivided, but many winter and summer rains have enhanced the effects of floods of ancient days; indeed, the present wide separation of Mounds I and II was originally caused by a cataclysmic flood which cut through the heart of the city.

According to a resident of the little village of Jamal-Kirio, who is a Professor at the Sind College, Karachi, the name *Chanhu-daro* is derived from the names of two sisters, Chanhiyun and Bohiyun, of whom nothing else is known; *daro* in Sindhi means a " place." Which mound is Chanhiyun and which Bohiyun I was unable to ascertain, and these names are probably much older than their Sindhi equivalents. There is no fixed tradition in the neighbourhood as to the origin of the mounds, but a great black snake, said to have been many yards long, is associated with them in village legend. It is quite possible that this serpent was simply a king cobra magnified by tradition, for snakes are quite commonly found among the ancient mounds of Sindh. In the course of our excavations we came upon several snakes, all of normal size, hibernating deep in the ruins.

Between Mounds II and III there lies the simple tomb of a local saint, Khalil Pir.[2] This tomb is regarded as sacred in the immediate neighbourhood, but nothing is known of

[1] *Explorations in Sind* [*Mem. Arch. Surv. Ind.* No. 48, 1934].

[2] Pl. I, square 4/E.

the saint except that he was a stranger and was buried there about a hundred years ago. Placed on slightly rising ground (Pl. IX, e) and orientated north to south, the tomb measures eight feet in length by four feet wide. Over its rough superstructure of bricks taken from the ancient mounds, a coarse white cotton sheet had been laid with its edges held down by pieces of brick, the whole giving a realistic impression of a dead man laid upon a bier. About nine feet to the north-west of the tomb stands a very old *jhal* tree; another to the south-west of the tomb is now dead. On our arrival at the site we found the tomb surrounded by a low zareba of dead thorn branches in order to keep the cattle away, and we substituted a circular bank of earth to protect it more effectively.

Two brushes of ordinary village make hang from the adjacent tree and are used by petitioners to sweep the shroud and the surrounding ground. Women do not visit the tomb; it is the men who bring a thank-offering there after the birth of a son. When the child is about seven months old, his hair is ceremonially cut near the tomb and is then placed upon it in a triangular bag ornamented round the edges with little coloured tufts of wool. An old villager told me that many years ago a man who was in urgent need of a hundred rupees prayed at the tomb that this sum might be granted to him. After spending the night there, he saw a large bag of money on the tomb, but when he picked it up and turned to go an invisible wall prevented his departure and the money vanished. He prayed throughout the second day and again saw the bag of money. This time he opened it and took out the hundred rupees for which he had asked. He was then permitted to return to his home with it.

On the arrival of my Indian assistants and myself at the site on October 23rd, 1935, the preparation of the camp was begun. For the first few days, however, until October 27th, it was more convenient to live in the P. W. D. dak bungalow at Sakrand and to travel to and fro by train until the camp and equipment were ready. I have to thank Mr. S. A. Maybury Lewis, I. S. E., for permission to occupy the bungalow and for much valuable assistance. Mr. S. B. Rege, Executive Engineer, Nawābshāh, and Mr. D. Bilani, Assistant Engineer, P. W. D., Sakrand, were also very ready with their help; I am grateful to them for their many courtesies.

After making a survey of the mounds and marking out the whole area into squares of 50 feet, we commenced the actual excavation on November 2nd. A suitable datum level had to be chosen and this was marked by a solid structure of brick and cement close to our camp. By the help of the P. W. D., this datum level was later correlated with an official bench-mark in the village of Jam Dahri, about three miles away. The level there, *95.45 feet above low-water ordinary Spring Tide* at Karachi, was marked at our camp by a concrete floor in a small brick-lined pit; but as we had to start levelling before the correlation could be made, our working datum-level was five feet higher, and was thus 100.45 feet above sea-level.[3]

It had been my practice at Mohenjo-daro to give a number, or numbers, to each room or find-spot. These numbers were carried down to the lowest levels of the excavations

[3] Sunk to the east of Mound II, just outside our zareba.

and, as it happened, the system was simplified by the fact that buildings of the various levels had been erected one above the other with little alteration in alignment. At Chanhu-daro, however, the walls of one occupation seldom rested on the walls of the occupation beneath, so that the greatest care had to be taken that our numbers were not shifted as we removed one stratum to examine another. I am satisfied, however, that even in open ground the deviation of our numbered pegs was very slight and there was practically none at all where brick walling was found below brick walling. Such few deviations as have been necessitated in the numbering on the plans for the need of clearness are in no case of actual importance.

The numbering of the squares will assist the reader to find his place on the plans. These should be read to the right and upwards.

The system of field-cards which I introduced and used for several years at Mohenjo-daro was employed again at Chanhu-daro. These cards were filled in with the locus and level of each object before its removal from the find-spot. The cards were then brought with the finds to our workroom where the records were completed by my wife or myself. In all we had some 5,000 cards, referring to an equal number of finds to be classified at the end of the season.[4]

We had so many visitors that we had eventually to put a thorn hedge round the camp in order to avoid breakage of the larger finds, particularly pottery spread out to dry after washing. On holidays only we admitted a few people at a time. Our Sindhi visitors were always very welcome, but it was sometimes difficult to convince them that we had a large amount of work to do and little time in which to do it.[5]

For our Indian staff I have nothing but praise. Mr. Ghulam Mohi-ud-Din, our draughtsman, was especially valuable as he had already worked with me at Mohenjo-daro. Mr. Gulzar Muhammed Kahn, who was responsible for the photography, was also a valued friend from the same site; and a third, Mr. Kadir Bux, was once more in charge of the labour and pay-sheets.

Mr. H. D. Sankalia, a student under Father Heras, Director of the Indian Research Institute, Bombay, worked with me at the latter's request from November 29th to December 20th, 1935. On January 14th, 1936, my wife arrived at the camp from England, and the line plates in this book will testify to the skill with which she drew most of the smaller objects that we found. From January 19th till the 28th, we had the pleasure of the company of Dr. M. B. Emeneau from America. During this time he studied certain peculiarities of the Brāhūī language with the willing assistance of our Brāhūī headman, Daud Muhammed.

Mr. M. S. Vats, Superintendent of the Archaeological Survey of India, visited the excavations from December 11th until the 13th, 1935, and Mr. J. F. Blakiston, Director

[4] Some of the finds were of little importance, and they were reburied in a pit after they had been inspected by the officials of the Archaeological Survey of India.

[5] The local Sindhis, even the simple peasants, took a very welcome interest in our work, far greater, indeed, than anything I have experienced before in an eastern country.

General of Archaeology in India, was with us from January 21st until the 23rd. We closed down actual excavation work on March 26th, 1936.

It had been arranged that the division of the finds with the Archaeological Department should be made on the spot in order to avoid unnecessary transport costs. Accordingly, Dr. C. L. Fabri came to Chanhu-daro from Mohenjo-daro on March 14th, and was followed on the 16th by Mr. K. N. Dikshit, then Deputy Director General (now Director General). With the friendly cooperation of all concerned, the division of the finds, with the exception of small objects like seals and beads, was accomplished in four days. After Mr. Dikshit had returned to Delhi, Mr. K. N. Puri, from Mohenjo-daro, started packing up those objects which were to be retained by the Government of India. We ourselves had the double task of packing the finds allotted to the Museum of Fine Arts, Boston, which were to go to America via Karachi, and the smaller finds, which were to be taken to Delhi for division.

On March 31st, my wife and I closed down the camp; we arrived in Delhi on April 2nd. In addition to the smaller finds we had brought with us, there were also several hundred bronze and copper objects to be divided between the Government of India and Boston. These had been sent some weeks ahead and had been chemically cleaned by Khan Bahadur Muhammed Sana Ullah, the Archaeological Chemist in India, who with great skill and patience had separated them out from the corroded masses in which many of them were found. When the division had been completed, my wife and I were engaged for some time in making drawings of these metal objects, for the heavy crust on them had made it impossible to do this in the field. After packing and despatching the share allotted to the Museum of Fine Arts, we left for England on April 23rd.

We should like to express here our very sincere thanks to the Government of India and to the Director General of the Archaeological Survey for the great interest shown in this first archaeological expedition to India under the amended Monuments Act. They assisted us in many and various ways and in fact could not have done more to promote the success of this American expedition—a very happy augury for further archaeological work in India.

Lastly, we wish to thank the Director of the Museum of Fine Arts, Boston, and his staff for their devoted interest throughout the excavations and since. To Miss Ardelia Ripley Hall especially we are indebted for the attention and thought she has bestowed to our many needs, which have included the photographing and expert examination of many objects after they had been cleaned. Mrs. N. de G. Davies and Miss Suzanne E. Chapman are responsible for the clever fac-simile copies of sherds shown in colour in the Frontispiece and Pl. XXIII, for which we are very grateful. The valuable assistance of those American experts who have so kindly made scientific reports on the finds is gratefully acknowledged elsewhere.

My wife was responsible for most of the line drawings of small objects other than the pottery forms, and she rendered invaluable assistance in recording the many objects brought into the camp.

Throughout this book I have used the term "Harappā Culture" in place of "Indus Valley Culture." It was at Harappā in the Montgomery District of the Panjab that the remains were first discovered of this civilization whose cities some five thousand years ago were scattered over a wide area of north-west India, and whose influence was probably felt over the greater part of the then Indian world. In thus associating a civilization with the site at which evidences of it were first unearthed, we are following the established custom of modern archaeology. " Indus Valley Culture " is too elastic a term to be any longer used; since it was first employed three entirely different cultures have been revealed by the spade and named after the places in the Indus Valley at which they were found: namely, " Amri," " Jhukar," and " Jhangar."[6] The first of these, the Amri Culture, is definitely earlier than the Harappā civilization, and the second and third, the Jhukar and Jhangar Cultures, followed the Harappā Culture after a considerable lapse of time. Traces of these last two cultures were found in the upper levels of Mound II and are described in Chapters VII and VIII of this book.

If we were not so well acquainted with the craftmanship of the people of the Harappā Culture as it is exemplified at Mohenjo-daro and Harappā, we might have found it difficult to distinguish between the products of the Jhukar people and those of the Harappā people in the Chanhu-daro mounds. The upper part of Mound II has been considerably disturbed in the search for building material; for successive occupations took toll not only of the bricks scattered about on the surface, but of those that could be dug up from the débris of previous occupations. The fillings were cleared from older houses and their walls demolished for their bricks, with the result that comparatively few objects were found in their original positions. The Jhukar people, it is suspected, even kept as souvenirs certain of the objects of Harappā date that they found in these forays into the lower levels of the mound. For instance, the pins with coiled heads (1630, 1659) illustrated in Pl. LXXII, 21, 22 were found as high as 16.7 feet above datum level;[7] unless this type of pin was also made by the Jhukar people, which seems unlikely, despite its simplicity, we can only suppose that somebody of the Jhukar people found it at a lower level and reused it for their clothing or their hair. Fortunately this uncertainty does not effect the pottery or the seals. Though there was, of course, a certain amount of overlapping in the case of the pottery, very few specimens of the Jhukar ware—and especially of the painted ware—could not be easily distinguished from the earlier Harappā wares, as we shall show later on in this book. The stratum which produced the Jhukar pottery varied somewhat in level, for by the time of the Jhukar occupation the top of Mound II was far from being flat; it ranged from 13.7 feet above datum on the east to 17.8 feet above datum on the west.

[6] N. G. Majumdar, *Explorations in Sind* [*Mem. Arch. Surv. Ind.* No. 48].

[7] Another mutilated specimen of the same type occurred at the level + 21.0 feet.

TABLE OF CONTENTS

LIST OF PLATES

Chapter I

TRENCHES

Mound II was selected for our most extensive operations but before beginning work there it was necessary to find a suitable place on which to deposit our débris. A fairly extensive area of uncultivated ground on the north-eastern side of the mound was finally chosen, but it had, of course, first to be examined to see what lay beneath before dumping took place. With twenty-one Brāhūi and fifteen Sindhi diggers a series of trenches was accordingly begun on November 2nd, 1935, and the number of the diggers rapidly increased as the work became known in the surrounding villages.

Mound II stood 23.5 feet above our datum level and about 28 feet above the surrounding plain, and it was roughly 3,850 square feet in area (Pl. III). Its northern and eastern slopes were fairly steep (Pl. IX, a), but the southern and western sides inclined more gently (Pl. IX, b). It was everywhere cut by ravines, which had been gradually scored by the waters of countless winter and summer rains. Like its fellows, Mound II was light red in colour, owing to the abundance of fine brick dust formed by the action of salt on the masonry within. This gradual disintegration must have reduced considerably the height of the mound in the four thousand years or more during which it has lain derelict.

It was difficult at first to account for the large number of over-baked bricks lying on the slopes of the mound. Their presence suggested that there had been a brick-kiln near by, but it was later discovered that their preservation was due to the fact that they had not fallen to powder like the bricks of more moderate hardness.

Our first Trench, A(o) in Pl. III, was begun near the edge of the cultivated ground. After running for some distance north to south, it was then diverted to the southwest. In this trench were discovered the foundations of a massive wall which in size and excellence of masonry more closely resembled that of Mohenjo-daro than any other wall found during the season's work. After tracing this great wall for about 80 feet, we found that its northern end was broken, and here the presence of crops prevented us from searching further. We then followed the wall in the opposite direction until it took a right-angled turn to the west. We were soon again brought to a standstill, this time by a zareba of thorn bushes surrounding the tomb of the local saint. This massive wall, which is seen in Pl. X, c, d, measured 5 feet 4½ inches wide at the northern end and 4 feet 9 inches at the south. The bricks were laid as shown in Pl. X, c, and were of two sizes, 10¾ x 5½ x 2½ inches and 11 x 5¾ x 2¼ inches, mud being used as mortar. The eastern side of the wall was smooth and level, but its western face was rough, indicating that it was not intended to be exposed. It must be remembered, however, that this is a description of the foundations; the real wall above no doubt had both faces equally well finished.

Projecting from the eastern face of the wall at its northern end was a footing at the level -6.9 feet (Pl. X, d). This footing extended 22 feet along the wall and narrowed in width from 6 inches at the north to 3 inches at the south, suggesting either that at some time alterations had been made or that the alignment of the wall had been rectified. A mass of broken masonry, 12 feet long and 13½ inches thick, which had subsided badly in places, lay against the eastern face of the wall at its eastern end (Pls. VI, 1; X, c).

A slightly curved drain (Pl. VI, 1), with a channel 4½ inches wide by 5¼ inches deep, was unearthed near the southern end of the great wall.[1] Above this was a short section of another drain, which is shown in Pl. III. Apart from these two drains, no other masonry was found in the immediate neighbourhood of the wall.

Its level at the northern, and better preserved, end was — 4.7 feet, or 3 feet below the surface of the ground. The southern face[2] of the westward arm had a slight batter, but the other faces were vertical.

It would be idle to suggest the purpose of this wall until further portions of it have been uncovered. Its presence at some distance from the main mound definitely proves that the city covered a much larger area in the earlier stages of its history than we at first suspected, and that, during this period, buildings were erected whose masonry rivalled in excellence that of some of the finest buildings at Mohenjo-daro.

Trench A(1) was cut on the eastern side of the wall just described in the hope of finding masonry connecting with it, but the few remains unearthed seemed to bear no relation to it at all. At loci 2, 3, 4 was a rectangular structure, measuring 3 feet 1½ inches by 1 foot 11 inches inside. Its walls, which averaged over 4 feet in height, were one brick thick, and there was a paved floor at the level — 8 feet. This structure was probably the cess pit of a house of which a corner was unearthed at locus 5; the house wall was 2 feet thick and less than 1 foot high, with its base at the level — 5.7 feet.

Little of interest was found in the trench. Close to locus 3 the skeleton of an adult was discovered 2 feet below the surface of the ground, but it was undoubtedly of late date and nothing was associated with the bones.

Trenches A(2) and A(3) were cut in a south-westerly direction from the southern end of the great wall, and in alignment. Close to locus 35 a broken fragment of wall stood some 16 inches high with its foundations at the level — 4.6 feet. Just below this level was unearthed the pottery cylinder (No. 1056) seen in P. XCI, 49, and south-west at locus 36, a copper razor (525, Pl. LXXIII, 31) and two curry-stones (1496, Pl. XCI, 33, 40) were unearthed at — 2.7 and — 3.4 feet respectively. West of this wall and at the same level as its base we found the lower portion of a large storage jar. At locus 40 in the further end of the trench was another badly preserved wall, standing 2½ feet high, reaching to a little below the surface of the ground, which at this point began to rise steeply.[3] The little pottery figure of a dove (757), seen in Pl. LVII, 12, came from just in front of this wall at the same level as its foundations.

A second line of trenches was then dug parallel with, and east of, those already

[1] Its foundations were 8.5 ft. below datum.

[2] At this point the wall stood over 5 ft. high with foundations at — 8.1 ft. The base was remarkably level throughout its length.

[3] The base of this wall was 7.7 ft. below datum.

described, and one [B(4)] at right angles. In Trenches B(1), B(2), and B(4) only a few fragments of very rough masonry were revealed, i. e., between loci 19 and 20. In Trench B(3) a thin wall was uncovered north-east of locus 22, with its foundations at − 3.9 feet. A little south-west of this last wall were unearthed the fragments of the finely painted storage jar (503) seen in Pl. XXXV, 1, at the level − 6.5 feet. In the vicinity of locus 22 in Trench B(3) a copper awl (197, Pl. LXXII, 9), a little bronze jar (172, Pl. LXXIII, 34), and some painted sherds (3922, Pl. XXXII, 1, 1a) were found at levels between − 4. 3 and − 10.3 feet.

Trench B(5), which approached the lower slopes of Mound II, proved more interesting. At locus 59 there were the remains of a thick wall about 2 feet high, with foundations at the level + 0.2 feet. South of this were other, thinner, walls in a very badly weathered condition.[4] Below the wall at 59 was a small length of covered-in drain with a recess, 18 inches square, on its south-eastern side (Pl. VI, 2), and alongside this a collection of pottery vessels (995-997, Pl. XXVIII, 42-44) was found at the level − 2.0 feet. An opening in this recess, 10 inches high by 7 inches wide, served as an outlet for the drain. At locus 55 the remains of a large storage jar (No. 506) were unearthed together with a copper razor (496, Pl. LXXIII, 28), the frame of a model cart (3708, Pl. LVIII, 6), a clay food-stand (3704, Pl. XXV, 20), and a pottery cone (3707, Pl. LX, 23), all between − 0.5 and − 2.2 feet. A few bricks round the base of the storage jar had probably formed part of a pavement at the level − 0.3 feet. West of the jar, but at lower level, the drainage system illustrated in Pl. XI, d was unearthed. The upper drain was an open channel, 6 inches wide by 5 inches deep, made of bricks 11 x 5 x 2½ inches in size.[5] About 2 feet below again was a drain of quite another type consisting of tapered pottery segments (Pl. VI, 4) laid with a considerable slope towards the south-east, the fall being 1 foot in the total length of 11 feet.[6]

Other interesting structures (illustrated in Pl. XI, b) in this trench lay between loci 41 and 56. The inside diameter of the round brick bin, which stood 18 inches high and may have been used for grain, was 2 feet 1½ inches,[7] and close by was a large storage jar which had, however, been removed for safety before the photograph was taken. South of the jar was a cess pit, 20 inches square and 29 inches deep, with a paved floor.[8] An opening near the top of the north-western side of the cess pit showed that a drain with a channel 5 inches wide and 3 inches deep had formerly emptied into it. South of this pit was a pavement at the level − 0.8 feet, roughly constructed of broken brick, which had been drained by a water-channel, 3 inches wide and 4½ inches deep. Only 9 feet of this drain remained, with a drop of some 10 inches in that length.[9]

Locus 43 to the north-west produced a painted bowl (3702, Pl. XXVII, 59) at the

[4] Their foundation levels were between + 1.2 and − 0.2 ft.
[5] The level of its floor was − 1.7 ft.
[6] Its northern end was at the level − 3.7 ft.
[7] The level of its highest portion was − 1.9 ft.
[8] The surface of this was 1.8 ft. below datum.
[9] The eastern end of this drain was 5 in. below the pavement.

depth of — 5.9 feet and from lower still came the clay figure of an antelope (3852, Pl. LV, 13) at — 10.2 feet.

The round brick construction was built of slightly curved bricks, 4¾ inches wide by 3 inches thick, and 8½ and 10½ inches in length on inner and outer sides respectively. These bricks must have been made for special purposes, such as the building of bins and the lining of wells, but their shape was hardly suited to the small radius of this particular structure. Apparently this is the first known occurrence of curved bricks. They have not been found at Mohenjo-daro, nor have I heard of any from Harappā. The wells at both these sites were lined with wedge-shaped bricks, but ordinary bricks were also made to serve this particular purpose.

A curious feature was the amount of stone that had been mixed with this brickwork; no less than six unfinished saddle-querns of varying sizes were found in it. One of these is clearly discernable in the photograph in Pl. XI, b.

After the removal of the bin and cess pit, the two drains shown in Pl. VI, 5 were found below. Both were 5 inches wide by 3 inches deep, but their remains were too scanty to show the direction of the flow.[10]

South-west of the pavement at locus 56, came the trial inscription in steatite (518, Pl. LI, 4), a pottery kohl-jar (852, Pl. XXVII, 71), two copper awls (636, 637, Pl. LXXII, 7, 10), a pottery figurine (621, Pl. LIII, 10), and an unfinished seal (594, Pl. LI, 3) at levels ranging from + 0.8 to — 5.7 feet.

Trench B(5) was excavated to a depth of — 10.7 feet at its south-western end,[11] but nothing further was found in the way of masonry save a few patches of sun-dried brick whose shape and size it was impossible to determine. With some difficulty we extracted a few whole bricks which proved to be of two sizes: 12½ x 5¾ x 3½ inches and 13¼ x 6½ x 4 inches respectively. It is probable that these bricks had formed part of one of the platforms on which houses had been raised above flood level.[12]

In Trench C(1) there was no trace of any building, though it was carried to an average depth of 6.3 feet below the surface of the plain. At the north-eastern end a skeleton of late date was found at the level — 5.5 feet; it faced south-east and lay in an extended position on its back with the arms close to the sides. No objects were associated with the body.

A considerable amount of masonry was unearthed in Trenches C(2) and C(3). A blocked-up doorway, 2 feet 8 inches wide, in a section of wall at the north-western end of Trench C(3), had a well preserved sill at the level 5.5 feet below datum.[13] The jambs of this doorway averaged 2 feet 4 inches in height, with their foundations at — 6.4 feet. South-east of this wall a little square patch of brickwork may once have formed part of a pavement,[14] one brick thick, although, from its angle, it clearly had no connection with a

[10] Their average level was 4.3 ft. below datum.

[11] The surface levels were + 3.4 ft. here and + 0.3 ft. at the north-western end of the trench.

[12] The highest part of this unburnt brick-work was 8 ft. below datum.

[13] The thickness of the wall was 1 foot 9½ inches, and the bricks were 10.9 x 5 x 2.25 ins. in size.

[14] Level — 5.5 ft.

very much larger area at locus 31. Here a piece of pavement, roughly 4 feet long by 3 feet wide, was built of two courses of bricks laid on their flats.[15]

The short wall at the end of this floor stood slightly over 1 foot in height, with its foundations 7.6 feet below datum.

At locus 26, to the east, we came upon masonry which must have formed part of an important building. A wall, 4 feet 5 inches wide, built of bricks 11 x 5½ x 2 inches in size, still stood about 4 feet 6 inches high. A little to the north of it and level with its upper portion was another fragment of wall at a different angle. This last, which was also of quite respectable thickness (4 feet), stood only four courses high.[16] When it was removed, immediately below it we came upon another wall (Pl. VI, 3) abutting on, though not bonded with, the lower part of the 4 feet 6 inches high wall at right angles to it, thus forming the corner of a room or, more probably, a courtyard, for the second wall was supported by a buttress, measuring 2 feet wide by 11 inches thick.[17] A large pottery bowl (825, Pl. XXVII, 63) and a clay whistle (467, Pl. LIX, 5) came from locus 26 at the levels – 5.0 and – 12.1 ft. respectively. The food-stand dish (3968) illustrated in Pl. XXVII, 36 was unearthed in locus 36, where it was found lying at the depth of – 5.6 feet.

Trench D(1) was cut close beside Trench B(3), the space between them being cut away later to expose fully the long, well-built drain crossing the north-eastern end of the first mentioned trench. This drain, which we picked up again when excavating Trench J(1), had a channel 4¾ inches wide by 3 inches deep, and its sides were built of bricks laid on their longer edges.[18] At its north-western end it was at the level – 2.8 feet, and it sloped very gradually some 27 feet to the south-east. Below this drain, at – 8.1 feet, was found the base of a large painted storage jar with an unusual *pipal*-leaf design (662, Pls. XXXVI, 37, XXXVII, 20).[19]

At locus 38 in Trench E(1), considerably further west, was a badly damaged pavement which had originally been surrounded by walls, but only the north-western portion of the walls remained and the masonry was poor (Pl. XI, c). This floor, which is shown as square in the plan, was 5 feet 6 inches in width, but its original length could only be guessed at, because of denudation. It was built of two courses of bricks laid on their flats with the surface level of the pavement at – 2.8 feet. The front wall of this little building faced north-west and had a slight batter. In it was a water-chute, which was 4½ inches in width at the base and narrowed to 1½ inches at the top. Immediately below this chute was a large jar whose rim was 2.9 feet below datum.[20] The bricks used for both wall and pavement were 9¾ x 5¼ x 2¼ inches. A foot below the north-western corner of the pavement was a second large jar (No. 1002) at the level – 6.2 feet and close to this lay the pottery cone

[15] The top of this floor was at – 6.1 ft.

[16] Its foundation level was – 7.6 ft.

[17] The bases of these two walls averaged – 13.7 ft.

[18] The bricks were 9.4 x 4.4 x 2.5 ins. in size.

[19] The surface levels of this trench were: – 0.5 ft. at the north-western and + 0.9 ft. at the south-eastern end.

[20] The highest part of the wall here was 2 ft. above this level.

(3933) seen in Pl. LX, 33 and the clay figurine (3585) illustrated in Pl. LIII, 4. The painted jar (3654) in Pl. XXVIII, 59 was recovered from locus 32, where it lay at 2.3 feet below datum. Locus 33 to the west produced a pottery ring (1278, Pl. LXXXIX, 8) at – 4.9 feet and the little kohl-jar (499) illustrated in Pl. XXVII, 76. The seal (926) in Pl. LI, 18 came from locus 34, level – 7.1 feet.

With the exception of a third storage jar (No. 233) in the north-western corner,[21] nothing else in the way of walling was discovered in Trench E(1), which was carried to an average depth of – 9.7 feet.

Trench F(1) was at first a separate pit, but the complex series of pavements and drainage channels found here necessitated widening it to meet the trenches on either side. The structures unearthed in the higher levels of this pit are shown in the general plan in Pl. III and also in Pl. XI, e, f. The upper channel in Pl. XI, f drained a pavement at the level – 1.6 feet,[22] which was in a very bad state of preservation and was removed to reveal a much better preserved floor below. The water from the upper pavement ran into a large storage jar,[23] which when full overflowed into the drain.

The sides of the drain were built of bricks set on their longer edges and the channel was 3 inches in width by 4½ inches deep. This was traced for about 13½ feet towards the north, in which distance there was a drop of about 14 inches. It was then joined by another drain at right angles to it, of which about 12 feet remained in fairly good condition.

The lower, better preserved pavement in the foreground of Pl. XI, e and in the distance in Pl. XI, f was 2.1 feet below datum level. It was drained by a poorly constructed channel which we traced for about 24 feet northwards (Pl. VI, 8), where it was a foot below the level of the pavement.

Below again, we came upon a third badly denuded floor and water-channel, a plan of which appears in Pl. VI, 6 and a photograph in Pl. XI, f (the lower drain on the left-hand side). It was impossible to discover the original dimensions of this last pavement, but the few bricks that remained were 3.4 feet below datum level. The channel also ran almost due north. About 23 feet of it were cleared and at the broken northern end we found a large jar into which the water ran before overflowing into another drain.[24] This last channel had formed part of a fourth system lying below the other three (Pl. VI, 7), with a much better preserved pavement than any of them.[25] Here the original skirting of bricks set on edge round the pavement and projecting above it for 3½ inches was complete on its eastern side and partly preserved along its northern and southern ends. A photograph of the drain is seen in Pl. X, a, and the large jar is the one mentioned in connection with the third system of drainage immediately above. This fourth channel ran from north-west to south-east, but disappeared after about 22 feet of it had been cleared. It was 4 inches

[21] At the level – 2.4 ft.

[22] This pavement must not be confused with the lower paving in the foreground of the photograph.

[23] Just seen in Pl. XI, f.

[24] There was a drop of 6 ins. to this jar from pavement level.

[25] At the level 4.1 ft. below datum.

wide by 2½ inches deep and, unlike those above, its sides were built of bricks laid on their flats.[26]

It is difficult to estimate the length of the periods marked by these four entirely separate drainage arrangements, but the fact that a depth of only 2 feet 6 inches lay between the uppermost paving and the lowest showed that no period could have been of great duration. It must be remembered that these floors with their drains were situated on the lower slopes of Mound II, and it is possible that the natural rise in level was greater there than it was higher up, for much material must have been washed down the mound even during the time when it was covered with houses.[27] When Mound II has been excavated to the level of these trenches, we shall perhaps be able to sort out this jumble and link them up with the occupation levels we shall discover in the mound itself.

Locus 42 in Trench F(1) produced an inscribed sherd (4789, Pl. XXXVIII, 5), a foodstand (4854, Pl. XXV, 29), and the pottery group (866, a-f) seen in Pl. XXVIII, 24-29, the last coming from as low as — 10.5 feet. Mention may also be made of several objects found in locus 65 in Trench F(2). These comprise a group of pebble-weights (No. 1095), one of which is shown in Pl. XCI, 26, two pottery rattles (1074, Pl. LIX, 9, 10), and a pottery figure of a dog (883, Pl. LVI, 6), at depths ranging from — 3.4 feet to — 7.2 feet.

At locus 49 in Trench G(1) a corner of a wall was discovered. This was 2 feet 3 inches broad at the thickest part, but only three courses of brick remained and there was nothing else in the vicinity save the base of a large storage jar,[28] a kohl-jar (1875, Pl. XXVII, 81), and a clay cylinder (1140, Pl. XCI, 48), the two last being at — 1.0 and — 2.9 feet respectively. Two pebble-weights (881, 1072, Pl. XCI, 23, 24) and a pottery model of a dove (1402, Pl. LVII, 6) were taken from locus 47 in the north-eastern corner of this trench at the levels — 5.6 and — 6.1 feet. Some distance to the south-west, however, well preserved brickwork was unearthed at loci 58 and 75. This proved to be a long, thin wall which turned eastwards at one end. This wall, which was 28 feet in length and 1 foot 5 inches in thickness, was peculiarly constructed—four courses of burnt brick were interspaced with courses of sun-dried brick, both kinds of bricks being 11 x 5½ x 2½ inches in size.[29] The height of the wall was 1 foot 8 inches and it rested on débris at the level + 0.6 feet.

On the south-western side of this wall was a brick-lined pit with a paved floor, 6 feet 4 inches long by 2 feet 7 inches wide. Its eastern end was the best preserved, and here the top was 2.1 feet above datum, the floor being a little over 2 feet lower. It is difficult to say for what purpose this pit was used. It seems much too large to be a soak-away or cess pit; moreover, there were no openings for drains in its walls, which were one brick thick and not absolutely vertical.[30]

[26] The north-western end of this drain was 6 ins. below the level of the pavement.

[27] The length of the interval between the construction of the upper and lower systems of drainage in this trench, I should put at not more than fifty years.

[28] At the same level as the base of the wall which was 2.1 ft. above datum.

[29] Very similar masonry was found in several parts of Mohenjo-daro: *F. E. M.*, p. 164, pl. XX.

[30] The bricks used in its construction were 10¼ x 5¼ x 2¼ ins. in size.

The surface level at the north-western end of Trench G(1) was — 0.6 feet, and at the south-eastern end + 4.6 feet; it was excavated to an average depth of 8 feet.

The most westerly of our trenches [H(1)] presented one solitary item of interest, an isolated pipe drain running from north-west to south-east, where it ended in a pottery gutter, one end of which was inserted into the pipe and the other closed by a pottery sherd (Pl. X, b). As the photograph shows, this drain was constructed of tapered pottery segments, two of which are illustrated in Pls. LXXXVIII, 18 and XC, 30, and the gutter (1545) in Pl. XCI, 19. Eight portions of the drain remained, but the pavement or other masonry once associated with it had been removed in ancient times.[31] A little north-east of this drain, a stone door-socket(?) (1308, Pl. XCII, 22), a stone mace-head (3608, Pl. LXXXIX, 25), and a pottery gamesman (3871, Pl. LX, 6) were found in locus 51, all except the first being about 8 feet below datum.

The surface level of this trench was — 0.0 feet at the north-western end and at the south-west + 5.8 feet.

Trench I(1), towards the eastern end of the series, contained no masonry of any kind save only a short stretch of roughly built drain at locus 62. The channel of this was 4 inches wide by 4¾ inches deep, and flowed to the north-east, the average level of its bed being + 0.8 feet.[32] This trench was dug to the level of — 9.0 feet, its surface levels at north-east and south-west respectively being — 1.5 and + 2.4 feet. Locus 61 on the north-eastern edge produced the handled cup (670, Pl. XXV, 55) at — 6.5 feet.

At the north-eastern end of Trench J(1), immediately west of Trench I(1), quite a thick wall was encountered, but only a little over 12 feet of it remained. Some 3 feet 3 inches in thickness, it stood only a foot high, as the greater part of it had been removed anciently by quarriers for bricks.[33] This trench also contained the broken south-eastern end of the brick drain mentioned in the description of the adjoining Trench D(1). At locus 79 the corner of another wall was uncovered. This stood only 1 foot 4 inches high,[34] and though not quite so thick may once have formed part of the same building as the other wall found in this trench. Close to here the two animal figures (952, 948, Pls. LV, 10, LVII, 1) and a stone palette (1122, Pl. XCI, 43) were recovered at fairly high levels. Locus 73 on the north-eastern side of this trench contained a seal (950, Pl. LII, 9) at — 0.1 feet and the interesting painted sherd (1558) illustrated in Pl. XXXIII, 15 at — 3.4 feet. Trench J(1) was cut to a depth of 9 feet below datum; its surface levels at the north-east and south-west being — 1.5 and + 5.9 feet respectively.

No masonry was discovered in the most easterly of the series of trenches, K(1), though it was carried down to the level of — 8.5 feet. The pottery dove (889, Pl. LVII, 8) and a clay pellet (1334, Pl. LIX, 26) were among some unimportant articles cleared in the vicinity of locus 77. The ground level here was — 1.2 feet at the north-eastern and + 2.0 feet at the south-western end.

[31] The gutter at the end of the pipe was 10.8 ft. below datum; the trench was carried down a foot deeper but nothing else was found.

[32] The bricks were 9¾ x 4½ x 2¼ ins. in size.

[33] Its top was 2.2 ft. below datum.

[34] Its broken top was 1.5 ft. below datum.

I have already mentioned that none of the structures found in these trenches can be definitely correlated at present with any that have been discovered in the main part of Mound II. They lie at a considerably lower level than any of the buildings exposed on that mound and, until we have reached the trench levels in our systematic paring of the mound, it would be unsafe to assign them to any particular occupation level. The work done in these trenches has, however, produced sufficient evidence to show that there are at least three or four occupation strata lying below the buildings cleared by our extensive operations on the mound itself. At the same time, every object found in the trenches was already familiar through the work done at Mohenjo-daro and Harappā. As we had the same experience in the deep "Cutting" that was made later in the season on the other side of Mound II, there seems no hope of finding at Chanhu-daro a culture of earlier date than that which we have named the "Harappā Culture."[35] Any vestiges that there may be of the "Amri Culture" must now lie too far below the present water-level in the soil to be attainable.

Below is a list of some more interesting antiquities found in these trenches:

Trench A

Section (1)

No. 135, Pl. XCII, 2. Level: — 5.5 ft. Drill-head.
No. 868, Pl. XXIX, 9. Level: — 5.6 ft. Pottery tumbler.

Section (2)

No. 1023, Pl. XXVII, 91. Level: — 8.6 ft. Kohl-jar.

Section (3)

No. 1008, Pls. LIX, 7; LXI, 1. Level: — 3.6 ft. Pottery rattle.
No. 998, Pl. XCI, 6. Level: — 3.7 ft. Pottery table.
No. 1000, Pl. LVIII, 19. Level: — 3.8 ft. Model cart-frame.
No. 1003, Pl. XXXIX, 21. Level: — 3.8 ft. Pottery feeding-cup.
No. 1062, Pl. LVIII, 24. Level: — 4.2 ft. Model cart-wheel.
No. 1004, Pl. XXXIX, 27. Level: — 4.4 ft. Insect cage.
No. 3804, Pl. LVII, 7. Level: — 7.8 ft. Pottery dove.

Section (4)

No. 1216, Pl. XXXVI, 16. Locus 69. Level: — 0.3 ft. Painted sherd.
No. 1219, Pl. LIX, 4. Locus 67. Level: — 0.7 ft. Pottery marble.
No. 1269, Pl. LI, 21. Level: — 4.1 ft. Seal.
No. 1811, Pl. XXV, 23. Locus 69. Level: — 4.9 ft. Footed bowl.
No. 1126, Pls. LXXXIX, 23; XCIII, 35. Locus 69. Level: — 5.3 ft. Mace-head.
No. 1013, Pl. LIX, 1. Locus 67. Level: — 6.1 ft. Pottery animal.
No. 3795, Pl. LX, 21. Locus 67. Level: — 6.1 ft. Pottery cone.
No. 3787, Pl. XXV, 59. Locus 69. Level: — 7.9 ft. Handled cup.

Trench B

Section (1)

No. 108, Pl. LXXII, 24. Level: — 2.7 ft. Arrow-head.
No. 100, Pl. XXXIV, 2. Level: — 4.2 ft. Painted sherd.
No. 773, Pl. LIX, 38. Level: — 4.7 ft. Pottery gamesman.

---

[35] Originally termed "Indus Valley Culture."

No. 87, Pl. XCI, 1. Level: – 4.7 ft. Pottery stand.
No. 95, Pl. LIX, 22. Level: – 5.1 ft. Pottery gamesman.
No. 90, Pl. XXVI, 21. Level: – 5.2 ft. Pottery jar-cover.
No. 89, Pl. XXVI, 19. Level: – 6.1 ft. Pottery jar-cover.

Section (2)

No. 188, Pl. XCII, 19. Locus 22. Level: – 5.3 ft. Stone pestle.
No. 565, Pl. XXVI, 61. Level: – 10.1 ft. Corrugated pottery sherd.

Section (3)

No. 918, Pl. XCIII, 24. Level: – 4.2 ft. Flint flake.
No. 503, Pl. XXXV, 1. Level: – 6.5 ft. Storage jar.
No. 533, Pl. LV, 6. Level: – 7.7 ft. Pottery horn of animal.
No. 544, Pl. XXXVII, 12. Level: – 7.7 ft. Painted sherd.
No. 564, Pl. XXXVIII, 8. Level: – 7.7 ft. Incised sherd.

Section (5)

No. 275, Pl. LX, 12. Level: + 0.3 ft. Ivory die.
No. 488, Pl. LXXIII, 6. Locus 44. Level: – 0.7 ft. Fish-hook.
No. 487, Pl. LV, 2. Level: – 0.7 ft. Pottery model of bull.
No. 3706, Pl. LIII, 9. Level: – 1.7 ft. Pottery figurine.
No. 968, Pl. XC, 29. Level: – 2.7 ft. Pottery bangle.
No. 804, Pl. XCIII, 26. Level: – 3.2 ft. Flint flake.
No. 3878, Pl. XXXIII, 12. Level: – 3.3 ft. Painted sherd.
No. 364, Pl. LXXIII, 13. Level: – 3.9 ft. Arrow-head.
No. 806, Pl. LX, 22. Level: – 3.9 ft. Pottery cone.
No. 783, Pl. LIX, 28. Level: – 4.4 ft. Pottery gamesman.
No. 784, Pl. LIX, 25. Level: – 4.4 ft. Pottery gamesman.
No. 967, Pl. XC, 28. Level: – 4.9 ft. Pottery bangle.
No. 337, Pl. LV, 3. Level: – 4.2 ft. Animal figure.
No. 3702, Pl. XXIII, 2. Level: – 5.9 ft. Painted jar.
No. 835, Pls. LXXI, 7; LXXVI, 8. Locus 63. Level: – 6.0 ft. Copper knife.
No. 3797, Pl. XXXIII, 2. Locus 43. Level: – 6.8 ft. Painted sherd.
No. 3802, Pl. LVIII, 3. Locus 44. Level: – 10.2 ft. Pottery cart-wheel.

Trench C

Section (2)

No. 355, Pl. XCI, 13. Level: – 2.5 ft. Paste cylinder.
No. 203, Pl. XXV, 54. Level: – 5.0 ft. Handled cup.

Section (3)

No. 470, Pl. XXV, 21. Level: – 5.8 ft. Stem and base of food-stand.
No. 465, Pl. LIV, 7. Level: – 7.9 ft. Pottery figurine.
No. 3568, Pl. LVIII, 8. Level: – 7.9 ft. Pottery model bull.

Trench D

Section (1)

No. 3907, Pl. LXXXVIII, 5. Level: – 0.7 ft. Pottery button.
No. 339, Pl. LXX, 3. Level: – 1.9 ft. Chisel.
No. 431, Pl. XXV, 8. Level: – 2.0 ft. Food-stand.
No. 1157, Pl. LX, 29. Level: – 2.1 ft. Pottery cone.
No. 713, Pl. XXXVI, 20. Level: – 2.5 ft. Painted sherd.
No. 714, Pl. XCI, 39. Level: – 2.6 ft. Hone.
No. 1039, Pl. XCI, 21. Level: – 8.1 ft. Paste plaque.

No. 723, Pl. LVIII, 10. Level: – 4.1 ft. Pottery cart-frame.
No. 1069, Pl. XXXIII, 1. Level: – 6.5 ft. Painted sherd.
No. 3381, Pl. XXXVI, 12. Level: – 7.5 ft. Painted sherd.

Trench E

No. 1276, Pl. LVII, 9. Level: – 3.2 ft. Pottery dove.
No. 3588, Pl. XCII, 21. Level: – 4.8 ft. Pottery plaque.
No. 926, Pl. LI, 18. Locus 34, Level: – 7.1 ft. Seal.

Trench F

Section (1)

No. 1100, Pl. XC, 27. Level: – 3.4 ft. Pottery bangle.
No. 3619, Pl. LIV, 12. Level: – 4.1 ft. Pottery figurine.
No. 3621, Pl. XXXIII, 3. Level: – 4.5 ft. Painted sherd.
No. 1031, Pl. XCIII, 25. Level: – 5.1 ft. Flint flake.

Section (2)

No. 3720, Pl. XXXVII, 28. Level: – 3.6 ft. Painted sherd.
No. 3721, Pl. LXXXIX, 27. Level: – 3.6 ft. Stone rubber.
No. 3714, Pl. LVIII, 17. Level: – 3.6 ft. Model animal.
No. 3668, Pl. XXXVI, 25, 41. Level: – 4.2 ft. Painted sherds.
No. 1469, Pl. XXXIV, 1. Level: – 4.6 ft. Painted sherd.
No. 1467, Pl. XXXIII, 11. Level: – 4.6 ft. Painted sherd.
No. 3754, Pls. XXIII, 5; XXXVII, 40. Locus 66. Level: – 6.6 ft. Painted sherd.
No. 3855, Pl. XXVI, 9. Locus 64, Level: – 8.9 ft. Jar-stand.

Trench G

No. 1348, Pl. LXX, 22. Level: – 2.3 ft. Copper knife.
No. 1139, Pl. XCI, 47. Level: – 2.6 ft. Pottery cylinder.
No. 592, Pl. LXX, 21. Level: – 3.1 ft. Copper knife.
No. 3660, Pl. LXXXIX, 29. Level: – 3.8 ft. Unfinished mace-head.
No. 1687, Pl. XC, 40. Level: – 4.2 ft. Faience bangle.
No. 882, Pl. LVI, 5. Locus 50. Level: – 5.3 ft. Animal figure.

Trench H

No. 3865, Pl. XC, 39. Locus 53. Level: – 1.7 ft. Faience bangle.
No. 1206, Pl. LVIII, 7. Locus 52. Level: – 4.1 ft. Pottery model bull.
No. 3724, Pl. LIX, 12. Level: – 7.6 ft. Pottery marble.

Trench I

No. 1178, Pl. LX, 25. Level: – 3.2 ft. Pottery cone.
No. 3592, Pl. XXX, 1. Level: – 5.8 ft. Painted sherd.

Trench J

No. 1301, Pl. XXVII, 74. Locus 71. Level: – 5.9 ft. Painted kohl-jar.
No. 1354, Pl. LX, 39. Locus 73. Level: – 7.8 ft. Pottery cone.

Trench K

No. 3745, Pl. XXXII, 9. Level: – 4.4 ft. Painted sherd.
No. 3667, Pl. XXXVI, 21. Level: – 4.4 ft. Painted sherd.
No. 3743, Pl. LV, 1. Level: – 4.4 ft. Pottery animal's head.

Chapter II

THE CUTTING

On February 18th, 1936, a deep exploratory cutting was commenced close to and partly embracing the south-western slopes of Mound II, its object being to examine the remains of any earlier cultures that might lie below the two Harappā strata, of which Mound II was principally composed. On March 24th, we reached a depth of 25.1 feet below datum level, or 28.2 feet below the average surface of the ground, and found that owing to the presence of water we could go down no further.[1] At the very bottom of this deep cutting, objects attributable to the Harappā Culture were found, and there seems every reason to believe that the lowest strata of that culture will never be reached at Chanhu-daro without the aid of expensive pumping equipment.[2]

Because the Cutting was begun in loose alluvial soil, an area of about 90 feet square was first cleared to a depth of about 4 feet below datum. In so doing, we unearthed a group of buildings (Pl. VI, I) which proved to be of the greatest interest, for all were out of alignment with those of Harappā II occupation. These new buildings (Pl. XII, c, e) definitely constituted a Harappā III occupation and I have no doubt that they will eventually be found to link up with others, as yet uncleared, which lie beneath the Harappā buildings already excavated (Pl. XIII, d).

As far as could be seen, there was no evidence of any continuity between the Harappā II and Harappā III Periods; no wall of the former occupation was built on a wall of the earlier period as foundation, and there was a considerable layer of débris between the two. The average level of the foundations of the Harappā II occupation (background of Pl. XII, c) was + 8.7 feet; that of Harappā III (foreground of the same illustration and Pl. XII, e) was more than 7 feet lower.[3]

From the state of the buildings of this Harappā III occupation, it is apparent that they had been left derelict and were never re-occupied; a flood had undermined them and left many walls ready to fall (Pl. XII, c, e). Indeed, we had to remove the upper portions of several before their foundations could be properly examined. This flood was quite as destructive as the one which at a later date brought the Harappā I occupation also to an end. We have, indeed, definite proof that two, if not three, floods wrought havoc in the ancient city.

The plans and photographs of Harappā I and Harappā II occupations (Pls. III, IV, XV) show marked divergences in their layouts, while the remains of Harappā III occupation are differently orientated from both. As we have seen, definite layers of débris, composed of broken brick, brick-dust, and potsherds, separated these three superimposed strata; nor was any wall of an upper level aligned on one of the occupation below save by accident.

[1] On March 25th, the surface of this sub-soil water was 25.5 feet below our datum level.

[2] It will be remembered that water also prevented us from examining the earliest levels of Mohenjo-daro.

[3] + 1.1 feet.

The remains of Chanhu-daro were, in consequence, far easier to understand than those of Mohenjo-daro, where walls were continually raised in the self-same alignment as the levels of the city rose.

The plan (Pl. VI, I) of Harappā III explains itself, but reference should be made to the photographs on Pl. XII, b, c, e. The large chamber 421, 423, whose northern corner is missing, was estimated to have been a little under 27 feet long and rather over 10 feet wide. It must have been entered from the north-west through a doorway that had been demolished anciently. Pl. XII, e shows the dilapidated state of the north-eastern wall; when found, it stood considerably higher than in the photograph,[4] but had to be partly dismantled for safety's sake.

Apart from its size and the one-time excellence of the masonry, there was little of interest in this room. Noticeable, however, was a footing along its south-eastern wall at the level + 5.8 feet, the present top of the wall being about a foot higher. The south-western wall was exceptionally well preserved and was higher than any near by.[5] The middle of this chamber (locus 423) yielded the dish of a food-stand (3958, Pl. XXV, 2) and a sherd of perforated ware (4384, Pl. XXVI, 2), the first being found just above the top level of its walls at + 7.7 feet and the second on a level with the foundations. Locus 421 produced the stone pendant (No. 4005) illustrated in Pl. LXXXIX, 6, the clay whorl (4383) seen in Pl. XCII, 4, a sherd of the interesting corrugated ware (4989) shown in Pl. XXVI, 67, and a drill socket (4990) pictured in Pl. XCII, 10. The first was unearthed at the level + 4.3 feet and the last three at + 0.5 feet. A pottery jar-cover (5109, Pl. XXIX, 57) was recovered from here also at the depth of 1 foot below datum level.

Room 470 was about 20 feet long by 14 feet wide,[6] and its north-eastern wall was one brick thinner than the south-western wall of room 421, 423 (2 feet 4 inches in thickness), against which it abutted with a space between varying from 2 to 4 inches in width; the foundation levels and heights of these walls were practically the same. In the north-western corner of this room was a circular pavement, 9 feet 10 inches in diameter and one brick in thickness, which was made of both whole and broken bricks. In the middle of this pavement, but separated from it by a thin layer of rubbish, stood a brick column 22 inches square and 18 inches high.[7]

Similar circular brick pavements have been found at Mohenjo-daro and Harappā: sometimes a large pottery jar had been sunk in the centre,[8] and it is possible that these pavements were used in some way in the hulling of grain. There was, however, no place for a jar in the centre of this particular pavement and the little column was evidently built when the pavement was no longer in use.[9]

[4] Its foundations were 3.5 ft. above datum.

[5] The foundations were 0.6 ft. above datum, and most of it was a little under 5 ft. high.

[6] It could not be measured with accuracy because of curvature due to subsidence of the south-western wall.

[7] Its base was 5.3 ft. above datum.

[8] A second example may be seen in Pl. IV, sq. 7/E, loc. 306.

[9] F. E. M. (E. Mackay, *Further Excavations at Mohenjo Daro*. 2 vols. Delhi, 1938), p. 167. Circular pavements are also known at Ur, for which see Woolley, *Ur Excavations*, vol. V, p. 10, pls. 3(a); 66.

The remains of another pavement, one brick thick, were found in the south-eastern corner of the same room. This floor, which had subsided very badly, was 9 feet 2 inches long by 4 feet 8 inches wide, with an average level of + 3.9 feet. It may have been used as an ablution floor, or possibly the whole room had at one time been paved. The circular floor already mentioned was at a slightly lower level.

Beneath the middle buttress supporting the south-western wall of this room lay an elephant's tusk (No. 3815), 26 inches long and about 5 inches in diameter at one end, which was in a very friable condition (Pl. XVI, d). The buttress measured 26 inches by 19 inches and 24 inches high, its base being 2 feet above datum. As there were no indications that this room had been used for ivory working—in fact it was singularly bare of objects—the care that had been taken to conceal this tusk suggests that it was stolen property.

A doorway, 3 feet 4 inches wide, at the north-western corner of room 470 led into room 466, which was 18 feet 7 inches long. This room also was in a very ruined condition, except for its north-western and south-eastern ends. In the latter wall was a niche, 34 inches wide and 19 inches deep, with its base at the level + 3.9 feet, from which the height of the wall was 26 inches. Two unusual clay models of bulls (3838, Pl. LV, 9 and 3839, Pl. LV, 4), which are possibly of Jhukar date, and a fossil shell (3844, Pl. XCIII, 23) were found in front of this niche at the level + 2.3 feet. The fossil had probably been valued as a curio. Some two feet lower the copper or bronze axe (4313) illustrated in Pl. LXX, 29 was unearthed at practically datum level.

A round brick structure near the door of this same room, 21 inches in diameter inside and standing 15 inches high,[10] had been used either as a kiln or as a fire-place; its bricks showed slight marks of burning and a little wood ash was found in it. Of the doorway into room 482, the south-eastern jamb was very indefinite and might well have been a later addition. The north-western corner of this room (481) yielded the pottery bowl (4932, Pl. XXVII, 57) at + 1.7 feet. Other antiquities found here include a hone (5095, Pl. XCI, 44) and the jar stopper of unusual type (4844) shown in Pl. XXIX, 69. Both come from the level of − 2.2 feet, which is some three feet below the foundations of this badly wrecked apartment.

There is little to say about rooms 482, 484, and 487. They were irregular in shape, as will be seen on the plan (Pl. VI), and their walls varied in thickness, while their foundations were at about the same level.[11] Some of the masonry in these Harappā III buildings was fairly massive, notably the north-western wall of room 481, which was 4 feet thick.

Room 482 provided no objects, but chamber 484 contained the pottery tube (4804) seen in Pl. LXXXVIII, 10 and a fragment of cut pottery (4749) illustrated in Pl. XXXVIII, 6, both at + 1.3 feet, or about foundation level. A clay model of a bull (4175, Pl. LV, 12), possibly of Jhukar date, was found also in this room about 18 inches lower. Room 487 yielded little of interest.

[10] Its base level was − 0.1 ft.

[11] + 1.4 ft.

These remains of the Harappā III occupation that we cleared in making the "Cutting," represent three, if not four, separate houses, all of them quite small but evidently the homes of fairly well-to-do people. A careful search by their owners for objects of value after the flood which had wrecked these dwellings had subsided, unfortunately left little for us to find. But unfinished beads and broken stone drills in some of the rooms show their occupants to have been bead-makers, as were the people who lived in the houses of the next or Harappā II occupation, some 7 feet higher.

In the northern corner of the "Cutting" we exposed the upper part of an immense mud-brick structure (408, 420, 473). This platform averaged 13 feet 6 inches wide and we traced it for a distance of about 30 feet to the north-west, where it was lost in the side of the Cutting. When work is resumed at Chanhu-daro, we hope to clear this mass of masonry completely. The part examined was near the edge of the mound; it was consequently badly weathered. It was possible to trace it to a depth of about 12 feet,[12] and there can be no doubt that this was part of a mud-brick platform, similar to many unearthed at Mohenjo-daro, on which houses were raised to keep them above flood level. These platforms are usually so compacted by their weight and damp that it is difficult to detect their artificial nature. In this case we were unable to extract single bricks for measurement until the platform had dried out sufficiently to allow the courses to become clearly visible. Two sizes of bricks had been used, namely, 11¾ x 6 x 3 inches and 11¼ x 5½ x 2¾ inches.

On this mud-brick mass, at its western end, were the remains of a drain, 4 inches wide and 2½ inches deep, constructed of burnt brick. A fragment of a toy cart (5282, Pl. LVIII, 18), a stone palette (4335, Pl. XCI, 34), and a dish from a food-stand (5332, Pl. XXV, 9) were also lying on this platform at levels from 0.9 to − 4.6 feet below datum.

Near this mud-brickwork were three brick columns (468, 475), evidently portions of one or two houses, whose foundation levels ranged from + 0.3 to − 2.1 feet. The "L"-shaped pier to the south-east was 24 inches long from north-east to south-west and 18 inches high. A clay model cart-frame (5159, Pl. LVIII, 9) and a pottery animal (4718, Pl. LV, 11) were lying in the vicinity of the columns in locus 475 at the depth of − 0.6 feet.

At locus 469 part of the corner of a room still stood about 14 inches high (Pl. XII, e, middle distance).[13] Here just below foundation level, was found the copper fish-hook (3812) seen in Pl. LXXIII, 8 and lower still a seal (4852, Pl. LII, 5) at − 2.8, and three painted sherds (5312-14, Pl. XXXVII, 4, 34, 36) 2 feet lower. The curious pottery stand (5316) illustrated in Pl. XCI, 7 came from not far away and from the same level.

The broken masonry (474, 483, 489, and 479) probably once formed part of the corner wall referred to. The best preserved portions of the remains of a washing pavement (loc. 483; Pl. XII, e), 4 feet 6 inches long by 3 feet 3 inches wide, was edged with a skirting 2¼ inches high. The surface of this pavement, which was constructed of three courses of brick, was at the level + 2.9 feet. Near by stood a wall, one brick thick, several openings in which were obviously designed to allow the water from the pavement to drain away.

[12] Its average upper and lower levels were + 0.7 and − 11.6 ft. and its upper surface was concave

[13] This corner wall was 11 inches thick and its base was 3.4 ft. above datum.

In this wall was also a doorway, 2 feet 4 inches wide, with the sill at the level + 2.6 feet and the jambs only standing a few inches higher.

A long wall (483), only half a brick thick, which ran north-eastwards from the pavement was like the other walling close by in being only two courses high.[14] A few feet of drain (474), 3¾ inches wide by 2 inches deep, which ran north-west to south-east, together with a wall parallel to it, formed the end of this little complex of masonry. This latter wall was 21 inches thick, about 18 inches high, and a length of nearly 8 feet remained: in it were two drain-holes, 5½ inches wide and 9 inches high.[15] No objects, except the pottery tumbler (4801) seen in Pl. XXIX, 6, were to be found at this comparatively high level.

All this Harappā III masonry had to be removed in order that we might go deeper. A plan of the still earlier masonry (Harappā IV) found below is seen in Pl. VI, 11, and photographs in Pl. XII, a, b, d. A high wall (477, 479) with a right-angled turn was the chief feature of this Harappā IV occupation. A depth of some 12 feet separated the foundations of Harappā III and Harappā IV.

Commencing at locus 477, this wall, which was one brick (or 10¼ inches) thick, ran in a north-westerly direction for about 15 feet; here its north-eastern face was badly preserved.[16] It then turned at right angles to the north-east, running a further distance of nearly 18 feet, where it met a thicker wall which projected from the side of the Cutting at locus 479. The top of this wall averaged 1.8 feet below datum, and a footing or ledge, 4½ inches wide, was about 3 feet lower. At the level −9.3 feet, the foot of the wall rested on débris composed of broken bricks and sherds and the fragmentary remains of a still older wall. An extensive break in the longer section suggested that there had once been a doorway; indeed, its north-eastern jamb[17] was still recognisable though there was no trace of the other.[18] It was impossible to discover the sill level of this doorway, but it could hardly have been much higher than the ledge mentioned above, which was 5.2 feet below datum.

Locus 477 produced the pottery kohl-jar (5126) illustrated in Pl. XXVII, 89, which was found in the rubbish just above this wall. A pottery jar (5275, Pl. XXVI, 71) came from just below its summit. The débris on which this wall was standing yielded several objects of interest, particulars of which will be found in the list at the end of this chapter.

The thicker masonry which projected from the side of the Cutting at locus 479 was 1 foot 9 inches thick and down its south-western face ran two vertical channels, 8½ inches wide and 1 foot 4 inches deep with a distance of 6½ inches between them. This wall with its two water-chutes (left-hand corner of Pl. XII, b) stood some 2 feet higher than the long wall, and its foundations, at the level −6 feet, were also considerably higher.[19]

[14] Its base was 3 ft. above datum.

[15] The bases of these were at + 2.9 feet, i. e., 3 ins. above the foundations of the wall.

[16] The bricks of this wall measured 10¼ x 5¼ x 2 inches.

[17] In the middle foreground of Pl. XII, b.

[18] The break allowed for a doorway of the usual width (3 ft. 4 ins.) or even larger.

[19] The top of this wall was 0.3 ft. above datum, and the bases of the two chutes were at the level −3.7 ft. The bricks measured 10¼ x 5 x 2 inches in size.

It is probable, therefore, that the thicker wall was built by the people of Harappā III and that the long, thin wall, as already suggested, belonged to Harappā IV.

Close to the southern end of the long wall, near locus 477, traces were found of a third and wider wall, standing only a few inches high,[20] whose position and level showed that it had no connection. At locus 489, a block of seven courses of masonry stood 18 inches high; a portion of a wall demolished in ancient times, which was estimated to have been 2 feet 8 inches thick.[21] From the level of its foundations we inferred that it was the work of the people of Harappā IV.

A fragment of a wall (locus 468) in the south-eastern corner of the Cutting was 2 feet 8 inches thick and 1 foot 3 inches high. This also appeared to be a relic of the Harappā IV occupation, although its foundations, at -4.1 feet, were rather high for that period. From here was taken the dish of a food-stand (5330, Pl. XXV, 4) at about foundation level, and a foot lower (-5.3 feet) lay the painted sherd (5302) seen in Pl. XXXVII, 11.

The well at locus 478 was found at a considerably lower level, as the photograph (Pl. XII, d) shows. Its inside diameter was 2 feet 10 inches, and it was built of wedge-shaped bricks, 9½ inches long, 3¼ inches thick, 4½ inches wide at one end and 3½ inches wide at the other. The top of the well was uncovered at the level -16.3 feet, but there seems every reason to believe that the upper part of its lining had been carried away by a flood and that the existence of the well was unknown to the next occupants of Mound II.[22]

This well was the only one found at Chanhu-daro, save for the one discovered by the late Mr. Majumdar in a trial trench in Mound III.[23] Mr. Majumdar's well had an inside diameter of 3 feet 6 inches and was also built of wedge-shaped bricks. The top, which was badly broken, was 6.8 feet below datum, and on January 1st, 1936, the water-level in it was at -28.8 feet. On setting up camp at Chanhu-daro we raised the steening of this well and brought it into use again after an interval of some 4,500 years. It also now supplies water to the inhabitants of the near-by village of Jamal-Kirio.

Plate XII, a shows the excavation of this Cutting in progress. The work had to be done with care to ensure that the sides did not fall in. Wide ledges were left all round as paths for the basket boys, with stairways to the ledges below. Not only did we prove that traces of the Harappā Culture existed below water-level, but we also found convincing evidence of more than one flood.

The few objects that were unearthed in the lower levels of this Cutting are given in the list at the end of this Chapter; in the main they are not particularly associated with any structural remains.

Pl. VII (I and II), are scale plans of the Cutting to illustrate the various levels that were dug through. These are briefly described below.

[20] Its top was 2 ft. below datum.

[21] The top of this wall was 7 ft. below datum.

[22] Sub-soil water prevented us from clearing more than a few feet of the interior. It probably is very deep.

[23] *Explorations in Sind*, p. 36.

Taking first No. II which shows the stratification of the northern side of the pit, we have at the surface a layer (G), varying in thickness, of rubbish, pottery, and pulverized brick, which had been washed down the sides of the mound during numberless rainy seasons. Beneath, a thick layer (F) is composed of water-deposited silt mixed with a little rubbish; this stratum averages 5 feet 5 inches in thickness. Below again (E) is a thick layer of débris of all kinds, mixed with a great deal of broken brick, which had been left by people who robbed the place of its bricks to build again after a great flood. It was this flood which deposited the thick layer of silt marked (D) in the section. Below this flood silt is a thin stratum (C) of débris, beneath which another layer (B) of silt marks a third flood period. The base of stratum (B) at an average depth of 19.9 feet below datum, was remarkably level, never rising or falling more than a few inches. Stratum (A) is a very thick layer of water-logged rubbish, and continues below the water-level at 25.5 feet below datum.

On the right-hand side of this section will be seen the remains, actually about 12 feet high, of the mud-brick platform already mentioned, whose base was an average of 11.6 feet below datum. The top of this platform had been much denuded. The remains of similar mud-brick platforms were found in several parts of Mound II (Pl. IV), and to judge from the level at which they were unearthed it is probable that they were all built by the people of Harappā III occupation.

No. I in Pl. VII is a section of the middle of the western side of the Cutting. The same three flood strata (B, D, F) appear again, but as this part of the pit was situated in flatter and lower ground, certain differences were observable between this and the northern face. Since this lower ground is less subject to denudation than the actual mound, we find two more flood strata (H and J) above level (G), which represents the Harappā II occupation. The layer (I) of different disintegrated brick and potsherds between is from its level clearly débris washed down from Harappā I occupation. An interesting feature is that below stratum (B) is a thin, but quite perceptible, line of ash which did not appear in the northern section. It will be noticed that the tilt of this line of ash is in a direction opposite to that of the strata above, and it seems justifiable therefore to assume that the people of Harappā V had their little town on a site that was overlapped by the later site. This would account for the non-appearance of the layer of ash in Pl. VII, II. In other words, the people of Harappā IV shifted their little township rather off the site of their predecessors.

The intervening strata prove that the several floods which surrounded the little city must have been separated by considerable intervals of time. It is difficult to say whether these floods coincided with those at Mohenjo-daro. Both Chanhu-daro and Mohenjo-daro were, at the height of their prosperity, close to the river Indus; but the two cities were eighty miles apart, so that they need not always have been affected by the same bursting of the river banks. At the present day, the Indus is always liable to break its banks at bends during the flood season, and this may happen in just one place after a long period of comparative quiescence. Personally, I am inclined to the view that in the past major floods in the Sindh valley were not always confined to one small part of it. Extreme weather conditions in Sindh are known to correspond with similar conditions in Mesopotamia. In the 14th Century, A. D., and again in 1929, both the Indus and the Tigris and Euphrates rivers rose to unusual heights and did much damage.

It would be most helpful in the question of dating if we could equate at least one major flood stratum in the two cities Chanhu-daro and Mohenjo-daro. This could be done with any degree of safety only by comparing the base levels of the various layers of river silt with the level of the sub-soil water at the same date in both cities. Even the latter must vary, however, with the season and the situation of the site; and reluctantly I feel bound to postpone even the most tentative suggestion until further excavation provides us with other and more reliable data for comparison.

As yet the pottery and other objects found at Chanhu-daro give insufficient guidance for us to correlate the occupation levels of Chanhu-daro with those of Mohenjo-daro. The following data might here be put on record against the time when other information can be added:

January 13, 1931. Level of sub-soil water at Mohenjo-daro, 34.2 feet below datum, i. e., 144.5 feet above mean sea level (datum = 178 feet above mean sea level).

January 1, 1936. Level of sub-soil water at Chanhu-daro, 28.8 feet below datum, i. e., 66.6 feet above mean sea level (datum = 95.4 feet above mean sea level).

March 24, 1936. Level of sub-soil water at Chanhu-daro, 25.5 feet below datum, i. e., 69.9 feet above mean sea level.

OBJECTS OF THE JHUKAR PERIOD FROM CUTTING

Square 9/F

No. 4203, Pl. XLIX, 8. Locus 468. Level: + 1.3 ft. Bronze seal.
No. 5281, Pl. XLVIII, 1. Locus 475. Level: − 2.5 ft. Incised sherd.
No. 5024, Pl. LX, 4. Locus 469. Level: − 4.9 ft. Shell gamesman.

Square 10/F

No. 4269, Pl. XLVI, 38. Locus 467. Level: + 4.0 ft. Painted sherd.
No. 3957, Pl. LV, 5. Locus 378. Level: + 5.3 ft. Clay model bull.
No. 3917, Pl. XLIX, 14. Locus 470. Level: + 3.2 ft. Pottery amulet.
No. 3918, Pl. XLVIII, 2. Locus 424. Level: + 3.2 ft. Lugged sherd.
No. 3919, Pl. LIX, 36. Locus 424. Level: + 3.2 ft. Bobbin or gamesman.
No. 4302, Pl. XLVI, 11. Locus 466. Level: + 2.9 ft. Painted sherd.
No. 3498, Pl. XCII, 38. Locus 465. Level: + 2.9 ft. Painted head-rest.
No. 3130, Pl. XLVI, 14. Locus 472. Level: + 2.8 ft. Painted sherd.
No. 4610, Pl. XLI, 39. Locus 471. Level: + 2.8 ft. Pottery bowl.
No. 4512, Pl. XLVI, 22. Locus 379. Level: + 2.7 ft. Painted sherd.
No. 3768, Pl. XLIX, 12. Locus 465. Level: + 2.7 ft. Pottery amulet.
No. 4003, Pl. L, 10. Locus 472. Level: + 2.6 ft. Faience amulet.
No. 3497, Pl. L, 4; LXXXVII, 1. Locus 464. Level: + 2.5 ft. Stone amulet.
No. 4567, Pl. XLIII, 1. Locus 466. Level: + 2.4 ft. Painted sherd.
No. 3840, Pl. L, 14. Locus 465. Level: + 2.3 ft. Pottery amulet.
No. 4814, Pl. XLVI, 8. Locus 472. Level: + 1.9 ft. Painted sherd.
No. 4707, Pl. LX, 13. Locus 464. Level: − 1.5 ft. Bobbin or gamesman.
No. 5164, Frontispiece (b), 2. Locus 484. Level: − 1.4 ft. Painted jar.

No. 4808, Pl. XLVI, 15. Locus 464. Level: + 1.3 ft. Painted sherd.
No. 4746, Pls. Frontispiece (b), 3; XLII, 13. Locus 464. Level: + 1.3 ft. Painted sherd.
No. 4745, Pl. XLVI, 30. Locus 464. Level: + 1.3 ft. Painted sherd.
No. 5132, Pl. XLVI, 2. Locus 466. Level: − 1.2 ft. Painted sherd.
No. 5131, Pl. XLVI, 31. Locus 466. Level: − 1.2 ft. Painted sherd.
No. 4802, Pls. XXXIX, 11; XL, 23. Locus 465. Level + 1.1 ft. Lugged vessel.
No. 4213, Pl. XLIX, 7. Locus 470. Level: + 0.3 ft. Pottery amulet.
No. 4792, Pl. XLII, 23. Locus 475. Level: + 0.6 ft. Painted sherd.
No. 4942, Pl. XLV, 36. Locus 472. Level: + 0.6 ft. Painted sherd.
No. 4941, Pl. XLVI, 45. Locus 472. Level: + 0.4 ft. Painted sherd.
No. 4227, Pl. L, 1. Locus 484. Level: + 0.1 ft. Stone amulet.
No. 4212, Pl. LX, 14. Locus 464. Level: + 0.1 ft. Bobbin or gamesman.
No. 4795, Pl. XLV, 32. Locus 464. Level: + 0.1 ft. Painted sherd.

Square 10/G

No. 4731, Pls. Frontispiece (b), 1; XLII, 17. Locus 477. Level: + 0.8 ft. Painted sherd.
No. 4731, Pl. XLII, 17. Locus 477. Level: + 0.8 ft. Painted sherd.
No. 4729, Pl. XLI, 46. Locus 477. Level: + 0.8 ft. Pottery jar.
No. 4582, Pl. XLII, 2. Locus 481. Level: + 0.4 ft. Painted sherd.
No. 4422, Pl. XLVII, 6. Locus 480. Level: + 0.4 ft. Painted sherd.
No. 4174, Pl. LX, 15. Locus 482. Level: + 0.3 ft. Bobbin or gamesman.
No. 4799, Pl. XLVIII, 23. Locus 483. Level: − 0.9 ft. Large pottery pan.
No. 5061, Pl. XLVI, 20. Locus 486. Level: − 1.3 ft. Painted sherd.
No. 5035, Pl. XXXIX, 12. Locus 480. Level: − 1.4 ft. Lugged vessel.
No. 5041, Pl. LX, 18. Locus 482. Level: − 1.4 ft. Bobbin or gamesman.
No. 5295, Pl. XLVI, 23. Locus 477. Level: − 4.6 ft. Painted sherd.
No. 5311, Pl. XLVI, 35. Locus 477. Level: − 5.8 ft. Painted sherd.

It will be noticed that in the above list of objects practically all come from above datum level. Their original place was on the summit of Mound II, from which they have rolled or have been washed down.

OBJECTS OF THE HARAPPĀ PERIOD FROM CUTTING

Square 9/F

No. 5045, Pl. XXIX, 24. Locus 407. Level: + 10.8 ft. Pottery tumbler.
No. 4016, Pl. XXVI, 59. Locus 404. Level: + 4.9 ft. Pottery bowl.
No. 3811, Pl. LII, 29. Locus 468. Level: + 3.8 ft. Seal.
No. 4504, Pl. XXXVIII, 16. Locus 468. Level: + 3.8 ft. Inscribed sherd.
No. 3949, Pl. LXX, 5. Locus 410. Level: + 3.6 ft. Copper chisel.
No. 4737, Pl. LXI, 6. Locus 409. Level: + 3.1 ft. Pottery rattle.
No. 4063, Pl. LXX, 4. Locus 420. Level: + 2.9 ft. Copper chisel.
No. 3938, Pl. LXX, 2. Locus 410. Level: + 2.1 ft. Copper chisel.
No. 5049, Pl. XXVII, 75. Locus 409. Level: + 0.5 ft. Pottery kohl-jar.
No. 5048, Pl. XCII, 6. Locus 409. Level: + 0.5 ft. Bobbin.
No. 4950, Pl. XCIII, 32. Locus 407. Level: + 0.6 ft. Stone mace.
No. 5046, Pl. XXIX, 15. Locus 407. Level: + 0.8 ft. Pottery tumbler.
No. 4222, Pl. XCII, 5. Locus 474. Level: + 0.8 ft. Clay whorl.
No. 5055, Pl. XXVII, 32. Locus 407. Level: + 0.8 ft. Pottery bowl.
No. 4779, Pl. XXVIII, 57. Locus 428. Level: − 1.0 ft. Painted jar.
No. 4770, Pl. LI, 5. Locus 410. Level: − 1.1 ft. Seal.
No. 4776, Pl. XCI, 20. Locus 428. Level: − 1.1 ft. Paste cylinder.

No. 4844, Pl. XCI, 9. Locus 481. Level: — 2.2 ft. Jar-stopper.
No. 5117, Pl. XXX, 21. Locus 474. Level: — 2.3 ft. Painted sherd.
No. 5280, Pl. XXXIII, 7. Locus 475. Level: — 3.1 ft. Painted sherd.
No. 5020, Pl. LIX, 13. Locus 408. Level: — 5.3 ft. Faience marble.
No. 5192, Pl. XXXVI, 14. Locus 469. Level: — 6.7 ft. Painted sherd.
No. 5387, b, Pl. XXIX, 18. Locus 468. Level: — 6.8 ft. Pottery tumbler.
No. 5342, Pl. XXXVIII, 12. Locus 475. Level: — 6.9 ft. Incised sherd.
No. 5356, Pl. XXXVIII, 20. Locus 469. Level: — 8.2 ft. Incised sherd.
No. 5193, Pl. XCI, 8. Locus 469. Level: — 8.5 ft. Pottery stand.
No. 5361, Pl. XXXVII, 24. Locus 475. Level: — 9.0 ft. Painted sherd.
No. 5393, Pls. XXXVII, 47; XXIII, 4. Locus 469. Level: — 11.0 ft. Painted sherd.
No. 5191, Pl. XXXVI, 17. Locus 473. Level: — 12.3 ft. Painted sherd.
No. 5372, Pl. XXXII, 6. Locus 473. Level: — 12.5 ft. Painted sherd.
No. 5372, Pl. XXXVI, 1. Locus 473. Level: — 12.5 ft. Painted sherd.
No. 5383, Pl. LXXII, 6. Locus 469. Level: — 15.1 ft. Copper awl.
No. 5442, Pl. XXXI, 11. Locus 469. Level: — 18.3 ft. Painted sherd.

Square 10/F

No. 4176, Pl. LXX, 18. Locus 484. Level: + 10.3 ft. Copper awl.
No. 4916, Pl. LIX, 24. Locus 484. Level: + 0.1 ft. Pottery ball.
No. 3957, Pl. LV, 5. Locus 378. Level: + 5.3 ft. Pottery animal.
No. 4916, Pl. LIX, 16. Locus 484. Level: + 0.1 ft. Pottery ball.
No. 4381, Pls. LXIX, 10; LXXVI, 22. Locus 379. Level: + 0.05 ft. Copper pin.
No. 3816, Pl. LXXII, 20. Locus 379. Level: + 0.05 ft. Copper pin.
No. 5385, Pl. XXVII, 46. Locus 466. Level: — 6.9 ft. Large bowl.

Square 9/G

No. 5300, Pl. XXXVI, 11. Locus 483. Level: — 4.9 ft. Painted sherd.
No. 5298, Pl. XXXVII, 1. Locus 483. Level: — 4.9 ft. Painted sherd.
No. 5440, Pl. XXXI, 2, 3. Locus 469. Level: — 18.3 ft. Pottery sherds.
No. 5442, Pl. XXXI, 5. Locus 469. Level: — 18.3 ft. Painted sherd.

Square 10/G

No. 5062, Pl. XXVI, 13. Locus 485. Level: — 0.5 ft. Pottery jar-cover.
No. 5032, Pl. XXXVIII, 3. Locus 480. Level: — 1.4 ft. Inscribed sherd.
No. 5036, Pl. XXXVIII, 2. Locus 480. Level: — 1.4 ft. Pot-mark.
No. 5146, Pl. LXXIII, 9. Locus 478. Level: — 6.6 ft. Copper ring.
No. 5204, Pl. LVIII, 14. Locus 481. Level: — 6.9 ft. Pottery cart-frame.
No. 5390, Pl. XXVII, 52. Locus 478. Level: — 7.2 ft. Pottery bowl.
No. 5378, Pl. XXXVIII, 28. Locus 478. Level: — 8.2 ft. Incised sherd.
No. 5201, Pls. XXXI, 10; XXXVII, 3. Locus 478. Level: — 9.3 ft. Painted sherd.
No. 5373, Pls. XXIII, 1; XXX. 24. Locus 478. Level: — 9.4 ft. Painted sherd.
No. 5205, Pl. XXXVI, 13. Locus 481: — 11.4 ft. Painted sherd.
No. 5395, Pl. LVII, 15. Locus 477. Level: — 12.5 ft. Pottery animal.
No. 5398, Pl. XXVIII, 61. Locus 481. Level: — 13.4 ft. Perforated vessel.
No. 5392, Pl. XXXVII, 37. Locus 478. Level: — 13.4 ft. Painted sherd.
No. 5404, Pl. XXXVIII, 29. Locus 481. Level: — 15.1 ft. Reserved slip ware.
No. 5403, Pl. XXXVIII, 15. Locus 481. Level: — 15.1 ft. Incised sherd.
No. 5416, Pl. XXXVIII, 22. Locus 481. Level: — 15.1 ft. Painted sherd.
No. 5318, Pl. XXXVIII, 27. Locus 477. Level: — 15.2 ft. Reserved slip ware.
No. 5418, Pl. XXXVII, 14. Locus 481. Level: — 15.7 ft. Painted sherd.

No. 5417, Pl. XXXVI, 2. Locus 481. Level: — 15.7 ft. Painted sherd.
No. 5405, Pl. LXXXVIII, 9. Locus 477. Level: — 16.2 ft. Pottery tube.
No. 5448, Pl. XXXII, 5. Locus 481. Level: — 18.0 ft. Painted sherd.
No. 5447, Pl. XXXVIII, 24. Locus 481. Level: — 18.0 ft. Incised sherd.
No. 5445, Pl. XXXI, 12. Locus 481. Level: — 18.6 ft. Painted sherd.
No. 5408, Pls. LXXXVIII, 6; XCI, 10. Locus 481. Level: — 20.5 ft. Pottery handle.
No. 5436, Pls. XXXI, 7; XXXVI, 38. Locus 481. Level: — 20.5 ft. Painted sherd.
No. 5451, as Pl. LXXXI, 2. Locus 481. Level: — 20.5 ft. Cylindrical wire beads.
No. 5430, Pl. XXXVII, 25. Locus 481. Level: — 22.0 ft. Painted sherd.
No. 5427, Pl. XXXVII, 43. Locus 481. Level: — 22.0 ft. Painted sherd.
No. 5441, Pl. XXXIV, 7. Locus 481. Level: — 22.0 ft. Painted sherd.
No. 5410, Pl. XXIX, 13. Locus 481. Level: — 23.8 ft. Pottery tumbler.
No. 5435, Pl. LX, 2. Locus 481. Level: — 23.8 ft. Pottery gamesman.
No. 5450, Pl. XC, 19-21. Locus 481. Level: — 25.1 ft. Shell object.

CHAPTER III

MOUND II (UPPER LEVELS)

Scattered over the summit and upper slopes of Mound II, as shown in Pl. III, were a few graves of early Muhammadan date, each a long, narrow, brick-lined vault, orientated north to south and roofed either with bricks set pent-wise or with a row of pottery jars, mouth downwards (Pl. XVII, d). These tombs ranged from 4 to 6 feet in length and from 12 to 15 inches in width and depth;[1] they were found at levels ranging from + 15 to + 23.5 feet.[2] The bricks used to line them were mostly taken from the ancient buildings of the Jhukar and Harappā levels, but in one or two the bricks were of much later date and measured 9½ x 4½ x 2 inches, 11 x 9 x 1¾ inches, 14 x 9 x 2¼ inches, and 8 x 6 x 2 inches. Most of these later bricks had one side deeply cut in chevrons or a wavy pattern; others had decorated edges; evidently they once had an ornamental purpose. Towards the end of the season we discovered their provenance, namely, an ancient cemetery at Malu Sand, half-a-mile south of Chanhu-daro, where are large numbers of graves, some of them shown by inscriptions to be several centuries old. When the graves of this deserted cemetery had fallen into decay, carved bricks that had decorated their superstructures were carried off to Chanhu-daro to be used for graves of a humbler order.

Most of the skeletons in these Muhammadan graves were in a very fragmentary condition, owing to their nearness to the surface of the mound. Where we were able to ascertain the position of the body, it was always extended on its back with the hands close to the sides and the head to the north. Usually the face was turned to the west. Nothing was found with the bones save two globular carnelian beads close to the right wrist of a woman and a small piece of copper (1528) in a man's mouth.[3]

The pottery jars that served to roof these graves were of two types (Pl. XL, 1-3). Some were roughly painted; and several had been holed, but, I think, not purposely. The tomb (No. 83) that we illustrate in Pl. XVII, d, e, was 6 feeet 10 inches long by 1 foot 5 inches wide and was found at the level + 15.0 feet. Bricks of both the Muhammadan and Harappā Periods had been used for its slightly corbelled lining.

Jhangar Culture

When these few Muhammadan burials had been cleared and the bones suitably re-buried, we found at various levels between + 18.9 and + 22.8 feet, jars of a polished grey ware, some of which had been ornamented with simple incised designs (Pls. XXXIX, 1-8, XL, 5-11). With the exception of the bead illustrated in Pl. LXXXVII, 22 there was nothing associated with this ware, which seems to have been left on the mound by small

[1] One grave was 8 ft. long.

[2] The summit of the mound was + 23.5 ft., i. e., 28.5 ft. above the surrounding plain.

[3] This was square and very thin and not a coin.

groups of people whose habitations had entirely disappeared.[4] As this ware is fully described in Chapter VIII on the Pottery, we need only mention here that similar pottery has been unearthed in other parts of Sindh; it has been named "Jhangar Ware" after the site at which it was first found by the late Mr. N. G. Majumdar.[5] The two examples of this pottery that were found at low levels had evidently been washed down from above. The other pieces were found in Squares 8/D, locus 82; 8/E, loci 86, 87, 93; 9/D, locus 95; in all of these positions there was no association with brickwork. Unfortunately, we are unable definitely to term this well made, but primitive-looking pottery; a fuller discussion of its most likely date will be found in Chapter VIII.

Jhukar Culture

Almost immediately below these relics of the "Jhangar Culture" there came to light quantities of painted pottery which bore no resemblance either to the Jhangar ware above or to the earlier pottery of the Harappā Period beneath, now so familiar to us from Harappā, Mohenjo-daro, and allied cities. Similar pottery had also been found by Mr. Majumdar elsewhere in Sindh. The first occasion was at Jhukar, which place has, therefore, the honour of giving it its name.[6] The makers of this interesting Jhukar ware occupied Mound II at Chanhu-daro after it had been deserted by the Harappā people; indeed, they took up residence in some of the deserted houses of the Harappā I Period, after raising the walls in many cases with generally indifferent masonry constructed with Harappā bricks. The poorer people, however, seem to have lived in square or rectangular huts of matting which they paved with broken brick (Pl. XIX, a); their fire-places they made outside their huts with low roughly built walls to protect them from the wind (Pl. XVI, b).[7] One of the most extensive floors left by these Jhukar people (north-western corner of Square 8/D) was roughly 8½ feet square and made of broken bricks.[8]

There was a somewhat more elaborate fire-place (Pl. XVII, f) in one of the re-occupied houses (Square 8/E, room 46, 91); indeed, it was made as a recess in the upper part of an ancient doorway and measured 2 feet 1½ inches long by 1 foot 8½ inches deep. In it there still remained the three bricks on end that had supported the cooking-vessels,[9] and there were ashes both on the floor of the recess[10] and on the earth pavement in front of it. The room in which this interesting fire-place was found is seen in Pls. XVIII, b, XIX, b.

There were other recessed fire-places of this type, which seems peculiar to the people of the Jhukar Period,[11] in the following rooms all in Square 9/E, namely, room 85, north-western wall; room 93, south-eastern wall and room 112, south-eastern wall. Their levels

[4] Probably these were simple huts of grass or reeds.

[5] *Explorations in Sind*, pp. 68-70, 78-79, 154, 156, 158.

[6] *Ibid.*, pp. 5-7, 9-18.

[7] These are indicated on the plan in Pl. III, Sqs. 8/C, loci 169, 307; 9/C, locus 215; 8/D, locus 202; 9/D, loci 130, 209.

[8] At the level + 15.8 ft.

[9] These bricks were cut down from a larger size and measure 5¼ x 4 x 3 ins. in size.

[10] At the level + 17 ft. The wall behind this recess was 3 ft. higher.

[11] The Harappā people preferred simple platforms of brick.

ranged between 17 and 18.2 feet above datum. That these niches were actually used as fire-places and not as cupboards or the like is proved by the thick bed of ashes found on the floors of three of them.

The floors and fire-places of the humbler matting dwellings were situated on the eastern and rather lower side of the mound between the levels 13.7 and 15.8 feet above datum, i. e., an average of 2 feet lower than the brick built houses.

Where this Jhukar People came from and how far their influence extended we do not as yet know. They had a well defined culture of their own in spite of apparent poverty, for they used painted wares (Chapter VII) which in make and style of decoration differ radically from the pottery of the Harappā I people who preceded them. They also used head-rests (Pl. XCII, 38), again foreign to the custom of their predecessors, and their beads (Pl. LXXXVII), seals (Pls. XLIX, L), and other possessions are quite unlike anything found in the Harappā levels. That they were great mat-makers is shown by the large number of bone-awls that they left (Pl. XCII, 28, 30, 31, 33). In short, they were a civilized though impoverished people; they knew enough of the crafts to practise glazing. The date at which these Jhukar People occupied Mound II would seem to have been round about 1700 B. C., possibly a little earlier if our estimate be correct that Chanhu-daro was finally deserted by the Harappā I People about 2300 B. C.

Below are some more important Jhukar objects found in these high levels, many more, as already stated, had been washed down the sides of the mound.

Square 6/F

No. 1726, Pl. XLIX, 11. Locus 159. Level: + 16.6 ft. Pottery amulet.

Square 7/C

No. 1548, Pl. LIX, 34. Locus 101. Level: + 16.2 ft. Bobbin or gamesman.
No. 2240, Pl. XLI, 41. Locus 102. Level: + 15.5 ft. Pottery jar.
No. 1756, Pl. XLIII, 3. Locus 102. Level: + 14.9 ft. Painted sherd.
No. 1798, Pl. XLI, 47. Locus 102. Level: + 14.1 ft. Pottery jar.

Square 7/E

No. 3399, Pl. XLVIII, 21. Locus 100. Level: + 14.6 ft. Pot-mark.
No. 2130, Pl. XL, 20. Locus 88. Level: + 14.3 ft. Footed bowl.
No. 1652, Pl. XLIX, 1. Locus 121. Level: + 13.2 ft. Pottery amulet.

Square 8/C

No. 1937, Pl. XLIV, 11. Locus 152. Level: + 16.6 ft. Painted sherd.
No. 1939, Pl. XLIV, 4. Locus 153. Level: + 16.5 ft. Painted sherd.
No. 1594, Pl. L, 16. Locus 109. Level: + 16.5 ft. Stone amulet.
No. 1938, Pl. XXXIV, 18. Locus 153. Level: + 16.0 ft. Painted sherd.
No. 2251, Pl. XLV, 23. Locus 152. Level: + 14.8 ft. Painted sherd.
No. 2273, Pl. XLVIII, 6. Locus 153. Level: + 14.1 ft. Incised sherd.
No. 1788, Pl. XL, 24. Locus 109. Level: + 14.0 ft. Pottery bowl.
No. 2334, Pl. XL, 26. Locus 151. Level: + 13.1 ft. Painted bowl.

Square 8/D

No. 2091, Pl. XLI, 28. Locus 82. Level: + 22.7 ft. Pottery jar.
No. 4788, Pl. XL, 30. Locus 82. Level: + 22.6 ft. Pottery jar-stand.
No. 1281, Pl. LX, 19. Locus 82. Level: + 21.8 ft. Bobbin or gamesman.
No. 2065, Pl. XL, 14. Locus 82. Level: + 21.4 ft. Pottery Bowl.
No. 2070, Pl. LIX, 43. Locus 82. Level: + 21.0 ft. Knuckle-bone.
No. 2066, Pl. XL, 21. Locus 82. Level: + 20.8 ft. Pottery bowl.
No. 1754, Pls. Frontispiece (b), 10; XLV, 20. Locus 84. Level: + 20.7 ft. Painted sherd.
No. 2068, Pl. XLII, 9. Locus 82. Level: + 20.7 ft. Painted sherd.
No. 1776, Pl. XLVIII, 3. Locus 84. Level: + 20.0 ft. Incised sherd.
No. 2121, Pl. XLVI, 12. Locus 89. Level: + 15.3 ft. Painted sherd.
No. 1957, Pl. LXXVIII, 15. Locus 183. Level: + 15.3 ft. Faience button.
No. 3175, Pl. XLI, 19. Locus 178. Level: + 15.0 ft. Stem of food-stand.
No. 1982, Pl. LXXII, 19. Locus 196. Level: + 14.5 ft. Copper pin.
No. 1988, Pl. XXXIX, 14. Locus 108. Level: + 14.4 ft. Pottery lamp.
No. 2610, Pl. XLVI, 1. Locus 107. Level: + 14.3 ft. Painted sherd.
No. 3065, Pl. XLVII, 1. Locus 84. Level: + 13.7 ft. Painted sherd.
No. 2250, Pl. XLVII, 16. Locus 89. Level: + 13.0 ft. Painted sherd.
No. 2052, Pl. XCII, 32. Locus 89. Level: + 12.3 ft. Bone awl.

Square 8/E

No. 1279, Pl. XLVI, 36. Locus 87. Level: + 21.2 ft. Painted sherd.
No. 1345, Pl. LX, 20. Locus 87. Level: + 19.0 ft. Bobbin or gamesman.
No. 2099, Pl. XLI, 18. Locus 93. Level: + 18.0 ft. Jar-cover.
No. 1292, Pl. LIX, 40. Locus 83. Level: + 17.9 ft. Bobbin or gamesman.
No. 1575, Pl. L, 3. Locus 86. Level: + 17.3 ft. Faience amulet.
No. 1507, Pl. XXXIV, 24. Locus 90. Level: + 17.0 ft. Painted sherd.
No. 1453, Pl. L, 7. Locus 90. Level: + 16.8 ft. Faience amulet.
No. 1659, Pl. LXXII, 22. Locus 92. Level: + 16.3 ft. Copper pin.
No. 3385, Pl. XLVIII, 10. Locus 94. Level: + 16.2 ft. Incised sherd.
No. 1758, Pl. XLIII, 7. Locus 90. Level: + 15.3 ft. Painted sherd.
No. 2086, Frontispiece (b), 5. L ocus 146. Level: + 15.0 ft. Painted sherds.
No. 2086, Pl. XLII, 4. Locus 146. Level: + 15.0 ft. Painted sherd.
No. 2116, Pl. XLV, 28. Locus 146. Level: + 14.2 ft. Painted sherd.
No. 2111, Pls. Frontispiece (b), 4; XLVI, 33, 34. Locus 91. Level: + 13.5 ft. Painted sherds.
No. 1748, Pl. LXXVIII, 12. Locus 146. Level: + 13.5 ft. Faience button.
No. 2153, Pl. XL, 13. Locus 113. Level: + 13.2 ft. Pottery jar-stand.
No. 4033, Pl. XL, 28. Locus 185. Level: + 12.9 ft. Pottery bowl.
No. 3141, Pl. XLVII, 15. Locus 114. Level: + 12.9 ft. Painted sherd.

Square 9/D

No. 1817, Pl. XLI, 37. Locus 95. Level: + 19.8 ft. Pottery jar.
No. 1394, Pl. XCII, 33. Locus 95. Level: + 19.3 ft. Bone awl.
No. 1395, Pl. LX, 28. Locus 95. Level: + 19.1 ft. Grey pottery cone.
No. 2060, Pl. XLV, 22. Locus 130. Level: + 16.8 ft. Painted sherd.
No. 1935, Pl. XLIII, 10. Locus 133. Level: + 16.7 ft. Painted sherd.
No. 1630, Pl. LXXII, 21. Locus 130. Level: + 16.7 ft. Copper pin.
No. 1535, Pl. LIX, 33. Locus 133. Level: + 16.5 ft. Bobbin or gamesman.
No. 1551, Pl. LIX, 35. Locus 133. Level: + 16.1 ft. Bobbin or gamesman.
No. 1886, Pl. L, 8. Locus 136. Level: + 15.6 ft. Faience amulet.
No. 1962, Pl. XCII, 30. Locus 130. Level: + 15.0 ft. Bone awl.
No. 3177, Pl. XLVI, 7. Locus 192. Level: + 15.0 ft. Painted sherd.

No. 1963, Pl. XCII, 28. Locus 106. Level: + 14.9 ft. Bone awl.
No. 1918, Pl. XLIX, 4. Locus 179. Level: + 14.9 ft. Faience amulet.
No. 2373, Pl. XXXIV, 19. Locus 180. Level: + 14.8 ft. Painted sherd.
No. 2018, Pl. XCII, 31. Locus 106. Level: +13.5 ft. Bone awl.

Square 9/E

No. 2224, Pl. XXVI, 73. Locus 85. Level: + 20.0 ft. Pottery jar.
No. 1505, Pl. XLII, 14. Locus 85. Level: + 19.1 ft. Painted sherd.
No. 1846, Pl. XLVII, 13. Locus 123. Level: + 18.1 ft. Painted sherd.
No. 2510, Pl. XL, 19. Locus 137. Level: + 17.6 ft. Painted bowl.
No. 1849, Frontispiece (b), 9. Locus 123. Level: + 17.5 ft. Painted sherd.
No. 3937, Pl. XLI, 42. Locus 124. Level: + 17.0 ft. Storage jar.
No. 1936, Pl. XLV, 39. Locus 152. Level: + 16.6 ft. Painted sherd.
No. 1815, Pl. L, 12. Locus 124. Level: + 14.9 ft. Pottery amulet.
No. 3143, Pl. XLVIII, 20. Locus 161. Level: + 14.4 ft. Incised sherds.
No. 2920, Pl. XLII, 18. Locus 131. Level: + 13.7 ft. Painted sherd.
No. 2015, Pl. XLV, 24. Locus 127. Level: + 13.3 ft. Painted sherd.
No. 2079, Pl. XCII, 29. Locus 181. Level: + 13.1 ft. Bone awl.
No. 2604, Pl. XLIX, 2. Locus 219. Level: + 9.6 ft. Faience amulet.

Square 9/F

No. 4191, Pl. XLII, 10. Locus 401. Level: + 18.3 ft. Painted sherd.
No. 1958, Pl. LXXII, 18. Locus 187. Level: + 13.7 ft. Copper pin.

Harappā Occupation I

The buildings of the uppermost Harappā level (Harappā I) were well preserved only on the south-eastern side of Mound II. Elsewhere a great deal of denudation had taken place, and as the plan in Pl. III shows, on the rest of that mound only isolated walls were found.[12] A much larger area was covered by the houses of the last Harappā occupation than by those of their Jhukar successors, but in the course of many centuries a large proportion of the masonry round the periphery of the mound had been washed down to its foot. Even some of the Jhukar remains lay round the base of Mound II, occasionally with Harappā sherds overlying them.

Even on the eastern side of the mound only isolated walls remained from the Harappā I occupation. To judge from their thickness and their lay-out, the houses were mainly small and unimportant, though the pavement (169) in Sq. 8/C suggests a house with some degree of comfort. This would seem to have been the floor of a room some 17 feet long by 8 feet wide; the base of the surrounding wall, 11 inches or one brick thick, still remained—though only one brick high—on the south and east. The pavement itself was one course thick, with the bricks laid on their flats and orientated east to west.[13] At locus 151 in this square lay part of a stag's antler (1732), whose ends had been severed with a saw, and close by was an unfinished weight (1631). Two painted sherds (4299, 4298; Pls. XXXII, 2, XXXVII, 9) and the large pottery bowl (3345) seen in Pl. XXVII, 66 were in the close

[12] For instance, the large storage jar (Pl. XVII, c) found in Sq. 7/C, locus 98, was no longer connected with any building.

[13] At the level + 13.8 ft.

vicinity. All these objects were a little over 12 feet above datum. The seal (2467) illustrated in Pl. LII, 26 was found in the same place about 2 feet deeper.

A small house, apparently of only two rooms (179, 193, Sqs. 9/C and 9/D), could only be conjecturally restored. As will be seen in Pl. XVIII, f, the remains of its walls stood only a little over a foot high; their foundations were at the level 10.8 feet above datum.[14] The more substantial masonry south-west and west of this house is shown by the photograph in Pl. XVIII, a to have been built on foundations of débris and not on the remains of earlier walls.[15] A carved shell ball (2050, Pl. LIX, 15) was found at locus 215 close to the base of the wall here. In the vicinity of the thick and isolated wall at locus 174 a shell cone (1928, Pl. LX, 37) was lying just below its summit,[16] and not far away at locus 216 the pottery jar-stand (1922) seen in Pl. XXVI, 10 was unearthed at the level + 11.8 ft. From locus 211, at about a foot below the corner wall here,[17] came an unfinished shell ladle (4308, Pl. XC, 6). The presence of these three shell objects implies that there was once a shell factory in the near vicinity. Locus 95 produced a copper pin (2193, Pls. LXIX, 8, LXXVI, 23) which has a coiled head and was lying at the depth of + 12.1 feet.

Still further in the same direction the masonry is better preserved. Room 140 (Sq. 8/D; Pl. XVIII, b) was either a single-roomed house or part of a larger building that has disappeared. The remains of its substantial wall, 2 feet 10 inches in width and only 2 feet high,[18] show it to have measured 9 feet 2 inches across; its length we can only guess. That this room had no connection with room 86, 176 to the south-west of it is proved by the two walls that separate them with a narrow space between. The solid wall, 3 feet 6 inches thick, on the north-western side of room 176 was, however, practically at the same level as the walls of room 140. These rooms are seen in the background of Pl. XVIII, d, and again it will be noticed that their bases rest on rubbish and not on other walls.

Room 140 contained nothing of interest except a badly broken jar in its south-western corner. A painted sherd (3133, Pl. XXXVII, 31) and a red ochre stick (2690, Pl. XCII, 27) were unearthed in chamber 176 to the south-west, the first just above the foundations of the walls of this room and the second a little over two feet below. Locus 82 produced the very curious faience object (2188) seen in Pl. LXXXIX, 1, at the level + 13.4 feet. The pin with a coiled head (1859) illustrated in Pls. LXIX, 9 and LXXVI, 24 was taken from locus 107 at the level + 12.6 feet. Exactly the same type of pin (1349) was found at locus 84, where it was evidently an intrusion; for it lay as high as 21.0 feet above datum. Locus 108 which was close to 107 yielded a pottery jar-stopper (1980, Pl. XXIX, 52) at + 14.6 feet. South-westward at locus 223, lay an unfinished seal (2000, Pl. LI, 9) at the level + 12.2 feet, and close by and about a foot deeper was a large sandstone block (4728, Pl. XCIII, 10), which had been used in bead-making. At locus 196 to the east a third copper pin (1982, Pl. LXXII, 19) was recovered from the level + 14.5 feet and close to the thin

[14] Low as it is, I cannot place this house as belonging to the Harappā II occupation.

[15] The level of their foundations was + 13.5 ft.

[16] This was standing 2 ft. 8 ins. high, its base being 12 ft. above datum.

[17] About a foot high with its base at + 12.7 ft.

[18] Its foundations were at the level + 13.4 ft.

wall[19] at locus 138 was a copper or bronze knife (2028, Pls. LXX, 23, LXXVI, 26) at the level + 13.2 feet. Here also was a copper jar (1800, Pls. LXXIII, 38, LXXV, 16) lying mouth downwards at the high elevation of + 16.5 feet. There is some uncertainty as to whether this particular object is of Harappā or Jhukar make. High above these walls, and centering round locus 82, a number of Jhukar objects were unearthed at levels ranging from + 22.7 to + 14.9 feet. These include the storage jar (1799) seen in Pls. XLI, 49 and XLVII, 34; a pottery amulet (2488, Pl. L, 13), and the stem of a food-stand (3429, Pl. XLI, 13).

We may perhaps regard the complex of walls that fills the greater part of Square 9/E as one building; its south-eastern side has been conjecturally restored. Room 93, 96, the partly cleared north-western wall of which is seen in Pl. XIX, d, was fairly well preserved, with walls averaging 6 feet 6 inches high.[20] The upper parts of these walls, however, had been removed before the photograph was taken, owing to the danger of their falling; in places the north-eastern wall of this room and of room 46, 92 beyond had been as much as 9 feet high. The danger was partly due to subsidence, partly to the inferior masonry of the Jhukar Period which composed the upper portions of these walls.

In the south-eastern wall of room 93, 96 was a blocked-up doorway, 3 feet 9 inches wide, with its sill at the level + 16.9 feet. High up along this wall further south-west was a niche, 3 feet 8 inches wide by 1 foot 5 inches deep,[21] which appears to have been a fire-place of the Jhukar Period. The lower 3 feet of this wall is of Harappā I date. In this chamber the tine of an antler (1604) was found on a level with the base of the niche and from below in the Harappā I stratum came a painted sherd (3277, Pl. XXXVII, 13) at the depth of + 12.6 feet.

Room 85, south-east of room 93 and entered from it, averaged 8 feet 6 inches long by 6 feet wide.[22] A niche, 2 feet 9 inches long by 1 foot 7 inches deep,[23] high in the north-eastern wall of this room was certainly a Jhukar fire-place, for wood ashes were found both in the niche and in its close vicinity. Well above the walls of this room was found the fine Jhukar jar (2224), at the level + 20 feet, which has been included by mistake in Pl. XXVI, 73 amongst some pottery of the Harappā Period.

A carefully blocked-up doorway in the western wall of this chamber was originally 5 feet 6 inches wide and was subsequently narrowed to 3 feet 6 inches wide.[24] This doorway gave access to room 112 in the Jhukar Period, and most probably in the Harappā I Period also, for the wall here goes down to the level + 13.6 feet.

Room 112 was 9 feet 7 inches long by 5 feet 4 inches wide, and a recess in its south-eastern wall appears to have been another fire-place of Jhukar date.[25] A buttress on

[19] This wall stood about a foot high; its base was 11.7 ft. above datum.

[20] Their bases average 12.3 ft. above datum.

[21] Its base was at the level + 17.3 ft.

[22] The wall between these rooms stood over 5 ft. high.

[23] Its base was 15.3 ft. above datum.

[24] Its upper sill was at the level + 18.3 ft. and the lower one + 15.6 ft., the top one being certainly of Jhukar date.

[25] It measured 2 feet 5 inches wide by 13 inches deep, and its floor at the level + 17 ft. was covered with ashes.

the eastern side of this room had been built to support the wall, but with indifferent success, for both had given way. A storage jar (1781) lay against the eastern wall of this room at the level +14.5 feet and close to a filled up doorway which had communicated with room 85. A second jar (2225, Pl. XXVII, 68) lay also on this side at a slightly lower level. The interesting socketed axe (1655, Pls. LXXII, 25; LXXVI, 37) of apparently Jhukar workmanship was found in this room as high as 17.6 feet above datum, yet well below its highest wall.

The long narrow chamber 126, 150, 219 was no less than 23 feet 7 inches long by 7 feet 6 inches wide. In places its walls stood 8 feet high,[26] and the poorness of the masonry of the upper Jhukar addition at the level + 15.0 feet was very noticeable. Apparently the only entrance to this room was at its south-eastern end; it was only 2 feet 9 inches wide and had been blocked up. The level of its sill (+ 12.5 feet) marks it as being Harappā I work, and it was probably blocked up in Jhukar times. Through this doorway the somewhat irregular enclosure 128, 172 was reached (Pl. XVIII, e). In clearing the northern corner of room 126 the faience cone (1600) of Jhukar workmanship seen in Pl. XXIX, 68, was found at the level + 16.7 feet, and a second one of the same make (1671, Pl. XXIX, 67) was unearthed in the western corner of room 132 at about the same level. Close to the south-western wall of the former room was a large painted pan of Jhukar make (1779).[27] This important object is illustrated in Pl. XLI, 50 and again in Pl. XLVII, 35, where it is shown lying in situ at the level + 16.7 feet. About 2 feet higher came the Jhukar dish (1861) which appears in Pl. XL, 31 and a sherd in Pl. XLII, 24. There was a surprising absence of Harappā material at the appropriate level in this same room and a Jhukar amulet (1993, Pl. XLIX, 15) found here at the low depth of + 12.8 feet, was an unexpected find and should be regarded as an intrusion.

The south-western wall of courtyard 128, 172, for such it probably was, was 1 foot 11 inches thick and still stood some 2 feet high. The foundation levels of this wall and others in the vicinity were very irregular because this part of the mound had subsided. They all slope from north-east to south-west and vary between 11.6 and 12.7 feet above datum. The curious mass of brickwork immediately in front of the doorway from room 219 is difficult to understand. It is some 3 feet high and its hollow interior was much too small to serve as a cess pit. Possibly it was a buttress with an earth filling intended to support the very thin wall that it abuts against; it would also have been useful as a kind of bench to the people who used this courtyard in Jhukar times, and it effectually blocks the Harappā I doorway against which it lies.[28] Alongside it was a bin-like construction, about 8 inches deep inside and 5 feet long by 2 feet 2 inches wide. A large storage jar found in this bin suggests its domestic use.[29] This bin and the possible buttress alongside it are seen in the middle distance of Pl. XVIII, e. A jar of the Jhukar Period (3057, Pl. XL, 22) was unearthed in this enclosure at the level + 11.5 feet.

[26] Foundation level + 11.2 ft.
[27] Its exact position is marked on the plan in Pl. I.
[28] Its foundations were at the level + 11.7 ft.
[29] Its base was 13.4 ft. above datum.

South-west of this courtyard is a large room (220, 221), divided into two portions by a thin partition wall. Both parts had been roughly paved and, as Pl. XVIII, e shows, floors and walls had subsided very badly. The paving of the floors was very rough and may conceivably be Jhukar work. Because of their collapse they vary in level as much as 14 inches.[30] The walls around certainly belonged to the Harappā I Period and like the floors inside vary much in level owing to unequal settling.[31] Subsidence was a very prominent feature of this part of the mound and was undoubtedly due to floods penetrating the base of the mound and causing it to drop very considerably. Lying in the débris well above the floor of room 220 was a bead-amulet (1911, Pl. L, 5) and close to the outside angle of the wall at locus 201 was a copper or bronze axe (1994) seen in Pls. LXX, 30, LXXVI, 4, together with the fine bronze kohl-jar (1977, Pls. LXXIII, 39, LXXVI, 32). The axe was at the level + 11.2 feet and the kohl-jar some two feet higher; both are of Harappā workmanship.

The two rooms 124, 162 evidently belonged to another house, which may once have extended well to the south-west; two rooms remained, fortunately, in a good state of preservation, and of their very substantial walls one was 2 feet 11 inches thick. Room 124, 125 was 11 feet 6 inches long by 9 feet wide, and most probably there was once a doorway between it and the adjoining room 162, 187. This latter room, of very much the same size as No. 124, 125, had a large bin or storage place in its north-western corner, enclosed by a wall one brick thick.[32] Just above this bin a quantity of wheat and other seeds (2345, 2347, 2348) was found in a badly carbonized condition; its high level (+ 15.4 ft.) suggests that it was deposited here by a Jhukar inhabitant. A small store of grain (2344) was also found in the adjoining room (124, 125) at the same level.[33]

At the south-western end of room 162, 187, a copper pin (1958, Pl. LXXII, 18) and a copper bangle (1959, Pl. LXXVI, 20) were found at the level 13.7 feet above datum. Room 125 contained a jar (3343, Pl. XXIX, 1) some three feet lower. The last object is undoubtedly of Harappā workmanship.

The outer faces of the north-eastern and north-western walls of these two rooms, which ranged from 6 to 8 feet high, had a pronounced batter which can be clearly seen in Pl. XIX, b. This batter was formed by inclining the bricks of each course slightly downwards to the inside and thus forming a slope a little over 5 degrees from the vertical. It is difficult to conceive of these sloping walls being of Jhukar work, whereas this method of building was a prominent feature in the architecture of the Harappā people; at Mohenjo-daro it was common in both private and public buildings. This house, therefore, from its foundations[34] to the top of its walls belonged solely to the Harappā I Period, though it is certain that the Jhukar people re-occupied it later.

[30] Their highest level was + 12.5 ft.

[31] The base of the south-western wall of room 220 was 9.7 ft. above datum, whereas the same wall in room 181 was as high as 13.6 ft. above datum.

[32] This was 1 ft. high and its base was at the level + 13.4 ft.

[33] For a full description of these seeds see Chap. XV.

[34] An average of 10.2 ft. above datum.

We could not expect to find intact buildings in Square 9/F, owing to the steep slope of the mound here. From the remains of room 184 we recovered the handled amulet (1946) seen in Pl. XLIX, 3, and a painted jar (2242, Pl. XLI, 29), both being of the Jhukar Period and coming from the levels + 13.7 and + 13.0 feet respectively. Close to these were the singular pottery mould (2012) illustrated in Pls. LXXXVIII, 11, XCI, 35 and the hone (3278) shown in Pl. XCI, 37. The mould was quite possibly used by the Jhukar people, as objects of this kind are strangely rare in Harappā times, but the hone, which was buried 2½ feet deeper (+ 10.7 feet), is undoubtedly of the earlier period.

The two rooms (104, 91 and 146) in Square 8/E were in a good state of preservation; their lofty walls are seen at the back in Pl. XVIII, b. That they belonged to a separate house and not to the building south-east of them is proved by the fact that there are no vestiges of a doorway in the high wall between (Pl. XVIII, c).[35] Room 104 was entered from the north-west and was 8 feet 5 inches long by 7 feet wide. Its doorway (Pl. XVIII, c), which was found blocked up, was 4 feet 3 inches wide and its sill and jambs had sunk very badly.[36] A small buttress placed against the south-eastern wall of this room had possibly supported a roof beam.

In the upper levels of room 104 were found a painted sherd (1869, Pl. XXXIV, 17), a spouted jar (2098, Pl. XLI, 44), a second sherd (1847, Pl. XLV, 38), and the stem of a food-stand (2995, Pl. XLI, 22). These Jhukar objects ranged in level from + 18.5 to + 15.5 feet. Lower down were recovered the pottery jar-stopper (1721) seen in Pl. XXIX, 49, a fragment of a steatite bowl (2178, Pl. XCIII, 30), and a copper chisel (1805, Pl. LXX, 12), at levels from 14.9 to 12.5 feet above datum. These last three objects belong to the Harappā Period.

The long apartment 91, 92, 146, was also in good condition, but before it could be cleared the Jhukar masonry which formed the upper part of its north-eastern wall had to be removed for the safety of the diggers;[37] this was not so much due to faulty building as to subsidence. The room, 20 feet 8 inches long by an average of 8 feet 9 inches wide, was entered from the court 185 by a doorway 3 feet 9 inches wide at the north-western end of its south-western wall. This entrance was subsequently blocked up in the Jhukar Period and converted into a fire-place, of which Pl. XVII, f is a photograph. As in room 104 a buttress or beam-support had been placed against the south-eastern wall. This, which was some 18 inches square, had sunk with the wall. The masonry of the Jhukar Period which formed the upper part of the walls of this room was very poor with little care taken to break the joints in the brickwork. Nevertheless, the height of these walls and of those adjacent to them was quite impressive, as is seen in Pls. XIII, a, b, XIV, a, XV, a, and XIX, b. The south-western, north-western, and north-eastern walls of this room had an

[35] This wall was heightened in the Jhukar Period and when excavated stood 8 ft. 6 ins. high with its foundations at the level + 10.6 ft.

[36] The sill was 13.7 ft. above datum and had been raised from an original level of + 12.6 ft. The height of the right-hand jamb in the photograph is + 17 ft., and its foundations stood at the level + 11.8 ft.

[37] This wall is also seen in Pl. XVIII, b.

average height of 7 feet, some 4 feet of their upper portions from about the level + 15.9 feet being of Jhukar work.[38]

A portion of a stag's antler (1725) was found in this room at the level + 13.5 feet; one end of this was burnt, a fact suggesting that it had been used as a poker. A fine pottery bowl (2112, Pl. XXVII, 29) also came from here and was lying at the level + 13.7 feet. Higher up and belonging to the Jhukar Period were two pottery amulets (1574, 1582) seen in Pls. L, 9 and XLIX, 10, at the level + 17.9 feet. At the depth of 16.3 feet above datum there was found the copper pin (1659) shown in Pl. LXXII, 22, of a type that is also known in the Harappā Period. A great number of Jhukar sherds, which are illustrated in Pls. Frontispiece (b), 4, 8, XLV, 42, XLVI, 16, 33, 34, 42, 43, XLVII, 14, 33, were also taken from this room at levels ranging from 17.9 to 13.4 feet above datum.

In the courtyard 185 to the south-west was a rectangular bin which had been built up against the doorway in its north-eastern corner after the latter had fallen into disuse (Pl. XIX, d, right-hand side). The bin, which was 6 feet 2 inches long by 1 foot 4 inches wide inside, was only a few inches deep.[39] With walls only one brick thick and its earthern floor, it was undoubtedly made by Jhukar people. The thin wall of the north-western side of this court was also built in Jhukar times.[40] On a level with this wall at locus 114 was found the Jhukar sherd (1848) that appears in Pl. XLII, 8, and from lower down came a jar-cover (2155, Pl. XLI, 33) at the level + 15.9 feet. There were also a few Harappā objects found in this court, of which a pottery bowl (3073, Pl. XXVII, 55), a jar-cover (3064, Pl. XXXIX, 19), and a copper ring (1908, Pl. LXXIII, 21) are examples.[41]

North-west of these rooms and courtyard were the remains of two houses, whose thin walls stood two feet high.[42] A possible doorway led from the north-east into room 103 (Square 7/E), but both jambs had disappeared, or the break in the wall may have been due to brick-robbing. A part of the south-eastern wall of this chamber is seen in Pl. XX, a, standing some 3 feet higher than a privy and drain built in the Harappā II Period.[43]

An unfinished shell dish of Harappā workmanship (3155, Pl. XC, 22) was found below room 103 at the level + 12.0 feet, and in the room itself was the Jhukar amulet (1426) seen in Pl. XLIX, 5, lying at + 15.4 feet. Locus 83 to the west produced another amulet of the same period (1266, Pl. XLIX, 9) at the depth of + 12.9 feet, and near-by lay an Harappā seal (1393, Pl. LII, 16) at the high level of + 15.4 feet, as well as a pottery spoon (1357, Pl. XCII, 25) and a painted sherd (4973, Pl. XXXVI, 34) at the levels + 13.5 and + 11.6 feet respectively. At locus 149 (middle of Sq. 8/F) a pottery rattle (1599, Pls. LIX, 8, LXI, 4) and a clay model animal (1971, Pl. LV, 15) were unearthed at about 11.0 feet above datum. North-east of room 103 at locus 121 a pottery figurine (1602, Pl. LIII, 3) was recovered from the level + 13.5 feet and from about the same depth and a

[38] The average level of their bases was 13.2 ft. above datum.
[39] Its floor level was 16.0 ft. above datum.
[40] It stood only 6 ins. high with its base at the level + 17 ft.
[41] The levels of these ranged from + 14.5 to + 12.6 ft.
[42] The bases of these averaged 13.7 ft. above datum.
[43] Its foundations were at the level + 14.1 ft.

little to the north-west came the bead-hone (1561) seen in Pl. XCIII, 15 and a pottery bowl (2163, Pl. XXVII, 24).

Little remained of room 97 (Square 7/E), outside which was a well constructed cess pit, 2 feet by 1 foot 2 inches inside and only 9 inches deep, denudation having removed most of its upper portion. Here was found a steatite seal (1293, Pl. LI, 31) at the level 14.9 feet above datum and a pottery bowl (3287, Pl. XXVII, 58) about 4 feet deeper. Both these objects can be dated to the Harappā Period.

Only a corner remained of a third or adjoining room (83, 443) to the south-west, standing some 2 feet high.[44] The copper finger-ring (1621) seen in Pl. LXXIII, 20 was found close to this at the level + 11.2 feet. The two massive walls, ranging from 2 feet 4 inches to 3 feet thick, that straddle Squares 7/E and 8/E[45] were relics of a most important building. Room 122, 143 measured 14 feet 6 inches long by 6 feet 6 inches wide; the restoration of the other rooms is conjectural. A chisel (1634, Pl. LXX, 20) found in room 122 at the level of its foundations must be ascribed to the Harappā I Period, and another (1989, Pls. LXX, 17, LXXVI, 11) was unearthed three feet lower and from under the adjoining chamber 142. This last room also yielded a bobbin or gamesman(?) (1638, Pl. LIX, 42) at the level + 14.7 feet, an object that was largely used by the Jhukar people but in what way is uncertain. Two Jhukar sherds (1755, 5264, Pls. XXXIV, 21, XLVII, 28) were recovered from outside the south-western wall of room 100 (locus 99) at the levels + 17.7 and + 16.8 feet respectively.

All these buildings of the Harappā I Period had been heightened from time to time. And the Jhukar people, as already mentioned, also made additions to them when in turn they occupied the mound. The base levels of the walls built by the people of the Harappā I occupation range from 10.2 to 14.9 feet above datum. The Jhukar additions and restorations, as far as we could trace them, had an average base level about 3 feet higher. The apparent low levels of certain of the foundations of Harappā I occupation, e. g., 10.2 feet, are to be traced to subsidences and sometimes to the fact that the upper part of the mound was by no means level when it was occupied. There was no difficulty at all in discriminating between the remains of the Harappā I and II occupations; practically no buildings of the former period rested on the remains of the latter, and as can be clearly seen in Pls. XVIII, a, d, f, XIX, b, XX, a, and especially the sections in Pl. V, a very considerable depth of débris lay between the two strata.

The sizes of the bricks used in the Harappā I Period, all of which were burnt, were 11 x 5¼ x 2¾ inches, 10¾ x 5½ x 2¾ inches, and 10½ x 5¼ x 2¼ inches. These same bricks were used by the Jhukar people, who like their predecessors took their toll of the ruined buildings round about them.

The following objects all belong to the Harappā I occupation; some of them had been thrown out of buildings that had been robbed of their brickwork in later times.

Square 6/E

No. 3164, Pl. XCI, 32. Locus 431. Level: + 10.1 ft. Stone weight.

---

[44] Its base was 13.9 ft. above datum.

[45] These averaged 1 ft. 6 ins. high and their foundations were 15.2 ft. above datum.

Square 7/C

No. 1810, Pl. LXX, 28. Locus 135. Level: + 13.6 ft. Copper razor.
No. 2349, Pl. XXVIII, 1. Locus 98. Level: + 12.4 ft. Pottery jar.
No. 2280, Pl. XXXI, 14. Locus 134. Level: + 12.2 ft. Painted sherd.
No. 2318, Pl. LVIII, 21. Locus 98. Level: + 12.1 ft. Toy cart-frame.
No. 2265, Pl. XXVII, 43. Locus 98. Level: + 12.0 ft. Large pottery bowl.
No. 1895, Pl. LXXXVIII, 3. Locus 98. Level: + 12.0 ft. Pottery bulla.
No. 1803, Pl. LXX, 31. Locus 165. Level: + 11.8 ft. Lance-head.
No. 2517, Pl. LXXXVIII, 13. Locus 134. Level: + 11.6 ft. Pottery tube.
No. 4401, Pl. XXXVI, 32. Locus 135. Level: + 11.3 ft. Painted sherd.

Square 7/E

No. 2020, Pl. LVII, 4. Locus 204. Level: + 12.9 ft. Model bird in paste.
No. 1441, Pl. XC, 26. Locus 88. Level: + 11.2 ft. Pottery bangle.

Square 8/B

No. 2780, Pl. XXVI, 53. Locus 234. Level: + 11.1 ft. Pottery jar-cover.

Square 8/C

No. 2271, Pl. XXVII, 87. Locus 153. Level: + 14.1 ft. Pottery kohl-jar.
No. 2308, Pl. XCII, 24. Locus 170. Level: + 11.9 ft. Pottery jar-cover.
No. 2198, Pl. XC, 32. Locus 226. Level: + 11.7 ft. Drain-pipe.
No. 2358, Pl. LII, 21. Locus 152. Level: + 11.1 ft. Seal.

Square 8/D

No. 2188, Pl. LXXXIX, 1. Locus 82. Level: + 13.4 ft. Faience object.
No. 3140, Pl. XXXVII, 38. Locus 202. Level: + 12.8 ft. Painted sherd.
No. 2030, Pl. LIX, 17. Locus 108. Level: + 12.7 ft. Pottery ball.
No. 2177, Pl. LX, 8. Locus 217. Level: + 12.0 ft. Faience gamesman.

Square 8/E

No. 1481, Pl. LIX, 31. Locus 90. Level: + 14.1 ft. Pottery gamesman.
No. 2176, Pl. XXIX, 50. Locus 94. Level: + 12.1 ft. Pottery jar-stopper.
No. 3155, Pl. XC, 22. Locus 103. Level: + 12.0 ft. Shell dish.

Square 8/F

No. 1617, Pl. XXIX, 51. Locus 144. Level: + 12.9 ft. Pottery jar-stopper.
No. 2157, Pl. XCI. 38. Locus 145. Level: + 11.9 ft. Hone.
No. 4655, Pl. XXX, 20. Locus 163. Level: + 11.5 ft. Painted sherd.
No. 2506, Pl. XXV, 18. Locus 144. Level: + 11.4 ft. Dish of food-stand.

Square 9/C

No. 2007, Pl. XC, 35. Locus 212. Level: + 11.7 ft. Frag. faience bangle.
No. 2199, Pls. LXVI, 6-21; LXXV, 11-13. Locus 227. Level: + 11.3 ft. Copper group.
No. 1991, Pl. LXXXVIII, 14, 15. Locus 212. Level: + 11.2 ft. Two drain pipes.
No. 2200, Pl. LXXI, 10. Locus 228. Level: + 11.1 ft. Copper adze.
No. 2361, Pl. LI, 32. Locus 227. Level: + 10.9 ft. Seal.
No. 2693, Pl. XCIII, 33. Locus 228. Level: + 10.8 ft. Mace-head.

Square 9/D

No. 2516, Pl. XXVI, 66. Locus 192. Level: + 14.3 ft. Pottery bowl.
No. 2039, Pl. LIII, 1. Locus 216. Level: + 11.2 ft. Pottery figurine.
No. 2288, Pl. XXXIV, 4. Locus 195. Level: + 11.0 ft. Painted sherd.
No. 2295, Pl. LXXVI, 10. Locus 262. Level: + 10.7 ft. Copper chisel.

Square 9/E

No. 1912, Pl. LVII, 10. Locus 171. Level: + 14.6 ft. Clay model bird.
No. 2977, Pl. XXVII, 48. Locus 137. Level: + 14.3 ft. Pottery bowl.

Square 9/F

No. 2004, Pl. LIX, 37. Locus 187. Level: + 12.8 ft. Knuckle-bone.

Chapter IV

MOUND II: SECOND HARAPPĀ OCCUPATION

On comparing the plans III and IV with the sections in Pl. V, it will be seen that as far as the alignment of their walls is concerned Harappā occupations I and II bear no relation to one another. Between the two periods the mound had clearly been deserted for a considerable interval of time which it is difficult to estimate, and hardly a wall of the Harappā I Period rests directly on one of the level below.

The remains of Harappā II were hidden beneath an accumulation of dust and débris, which on some parts of the mound was no less than 4 feet thick, and the newcomers (Harappā I) planned their buildings as if the site were entirely new.

Plate XV gives panoramic pictures of the remains of these two periods taken from the dump to the north-east of the mound; by the end of the season this dump had reached the height of 26.5 feet above datum level, i. e., 3 feet higher than Mound II before we began to excavate it (Pl. XXI, c). It should be pointed out that many of the ruined walls in the lower picture are not so high as they appear; at the close of the season's work we left them standing high on their foundations of débris, which had been trimmed in alignment with the walls (Pl. XXI, a, b, e, f). Thus it is seen that Harappā II occupation also was by no means in alignment with Harappā III below; after the former period also, the site had been temporarily abandoned and our deep "Cutting" (Chapter II) showed that Harappā III occupation was differently orientated from the two occupations above it.

The bases of the walls of Harappā II range between 7.7 and 9.8 feet above datum and, though we have only cleared a small area of Harappā III, over 7 feet of rubbish in places appears to divide it from Harappā II above.[1]

In the excavation of Harappā II we came upon the upper portions of solid platforms of unburnt brick (shown by hatching in Pl. IV). Platforms such as these are well known at Mohenjo-daro, where they were expressly constructed to raise buildings beyond the reach of floods. Only in the "Cutting" did we penetrate low enough to ascertain the base level of one of these platforms; it was found to be 11.6 feet below datum (Pl. VI, I).

The tops of these mud-brick platforms range from 6.8 to 9.8 feet above datum, an average of + 8.3 feet. Their construction must have entailed a considerable expenditure of energy and wealth, for there is reason to think that they extended over most of the site. Probably all its inhabitants gave either labour or money to ensure the safety of the city against the menace of floods. Even so, it was destroyed yet again by a flood which cut great gaps through it and divided it into three separate parts.

In face of the formidable task of elevating their city above flood-level, the people of Harappā II Phase fortunately found plenty of excellent material for this purpose in the plain around; indeed, it is possible that the ground was in places so sodden by water that

[1] The average level of H. III is 1.1 ft. above datum.

this only needed to be shaped for conversion into bricks. Owing to the difficulty of separating these sun-dried bricks from the platforms to measure them, it looks as if a large proportion were not really dry before being used, so that they had become compacted together. The few bricks that we could extract measured 11¼ x 5½ x 2¾ ins., 11¾ x 5½ x 3½ ins., 11¾ x 6 x 3 ins., and 12½ x 6½ x 4 ins.

The burnt bricks used for the houses and other buildings of Harappā II occupation vary little in size from those made in the following period; they range from 10½ x 5¼ x 2¼ to 11 x 5½ x 2¾ inches. The most usual size was 10½ x 5¼ x 2¼ inches. All were well shaped and properly fired. The larger sized bricks, 11 x 5½ x 2¾ inches, were only sparingly used; they were far more common in the Harappā I Period above.[2] A size of brick very frequently used in Sindh to-day is 11¾ x 5¾ x 2¾ inches, and I am told that bricks of this size are used nowhere else in India. As this size approximates very closely that of the larger bricks of the Harappā Period, it is conceivable that long ago, when the sites of ancient Sindh were being stripped of their usable bricks, these large sized bricks were copied for their convenience of size and shape.

Though so much of the masonry of Harappā II had been removed by brick quarriers,[3] for obvious reasons material was rarely taken from the pavements of bathrooms and privies or from the drainage systems that served them. The survival of the drains, which were always carefully built, enabled us to determine the lay-out of a street even when the walls of the houses on either side had disappeared. The paved floors of other rooms, however, had rarely been left intact.

The brick floors of privy and bathroom were customarily laid somewhat above the general floor level of the house to accord ease of drainage, and they were always edged all round to a height of 2½ to 3 inches to protect the bases of the walls from moisture. In all cases, the privy was constructed against the street wall of the house to be as close as possible to a main drain (Pl. XX, a, f).

Although Chanhu-daro was a much smaller city than Mohenjo-daro and populated chiefly by artisans, as proved by the plentiful evidence of crafts that were practised there, its drainage system was as well thought out and doubtless quite as effective as that of the larger city. The long lines of the drains are clearly seen in the lower picture of Pl. XV, which also illustrates the heavy toll of bricks that had been taken from the buildings that once lined the streets.

On reference again to Pl. IV it will be seen that the principal buildings were grouped about a wide thoroughfare whose direction was north-west to south-east. Another street, at whose width we can only guess, crossed this thoroughfare at right angles (it runs diagonally through Squares 7/C, 8/D, 8/E). A lane parallel to this street (see Sq. 7/E) was detected only because of the 32 feet or so of drain that ran down it. A fourth street ran westwards from the south-eastern end of the main street (Sqs. 9/D and 10/E) and then turned at right angles towards the north-west; traces of the covered drain in this street are indicated in Sq. 9/E.

[2] At Mohenjo-daro also, the bricks tended to become slightly larger towards the upper levels.
[3] The buildings in this stratum were nothing like so well preserved as those in the level above.

The arrangement of these streets shows that some attention had been paid to town-planning, a feature which we did not find in the Harappā I level above. Nor did we find any drainage system of importance in the latter stratum. A very considerable decline in the amenities of life had evidently taken place in the interval between the two periods. This decline was also noted in the uppermost strata at Mohenjo-daro. Allowances, however, should be made for the respective size and standing of the two cities; a poorer and less cultured community would deteriorate much more quickly than a richer and more educated one.

In the little group of fragmentary pavements and badly dilapidated walls in Sq. 7/C, room 238, 460 was a probable 17 feet 8 inches long by a certain 14 feet 8 inches wide. Its substantial north-western wall, 2 feet 3 inches thick, still stood one foot high.[4] In it were found a steatite seal (3495, Pl. LI, 17) and a bronze or copper knife (3496, Pl. LXXII, 4), also a very interesting pottery head of a figurine (2427, Pl. LIII, 11, 11a), but this little piece lay a few inches above the foundations of the walls. North-west of this room was a smaller one (240) of which only one wall remained. Some 18 square feet of pavement, whose bricks were laid on their flats, show this room to have been a bathroom or privy; its floor sloped to the north-east for the water to flow into a small brick channel of which only enough remained to identify its use.[5] This floor is seen in the middle foreground of Pl. XXI, a, left high on a foundation of débris. At its north-eastern edge was a large storage jar (3489, Pl. XXIV, 3) with its top slightly below the level of the pavement, which it was perhaps intended to drain. Close to the western corner two seals (3493, Pl. LI, 12; 2389, Pl. LII, 30) were unearthed and a large jar (3490, Pl. XXIV, 9) lay just where its owner had left it.

A pavement in room 239, four courses thick and at the level + 9.7 feet, drained into a channel in the street outside,[6] and this was 4 inches wide and deep and covered with bricks laid on their flats.[7] The walls of room 237, which was 10 feet 8 inches wide, averaged 2 feet high, their base level being + 8.8 feet. In the rubbish well above its ruined walls the food-stand dish (3272, Pl. XXV, 28) was found and a little to the northwest a pottery figurine (2257, Pl. LIII, 8) and a model dove in clay (3204, Pl. LVII, 11) were unearthed. At locus 101 in this same square a remarkably well preserved toy cart of bronze with wheels complete and a driver holding a goad (2463, Pl. LVIII, 1, 1a) was found lying at the level of + 9.7 feet, well below the bases of the walls in its vicinity. Close to this was the model of an antelope (2652) illustrated in Pl. LVI, 10 at about the same level.

We were unable to ascertain the width of the street south-west of the rooms described above, owing to the disappearance of the walls. At locus 273 (7/D), however, the street was nearly 8 feet wide.

The isolated remains of walls in Square 8/C were of little interest, being too thin for buildings of any importance, and our restorations are, of course, only conjectural.

[4] The base of this wall was 9.7 ft. above datum.

[5] The average level of this pavement was 9.5 ft. above datum.

[6] The street wall was 16 ins. thick and stood some 4 ft. high.

[7] The floor of this drain was 9.8 ft. above datum.

These remains ranged from 9 inches to 2 feet 4 inches in height.[8] Some of them rested on the mud-brick platform shown by hatching in Pl. IV, whose average level was + 9.8 feet, but it is very doubtful whether solid platforms like these could really have been intended to support such insignificant masonry. In all probability the buildings for which this and other similar platforms were erected had been pulled down for the sake of their bricks and later on unimportant houses were built in their place.[9] The little pavement, 5 feet 8 inches each way, near the south-western corner of the platform, was 9.8 feet above datum and built of one course of brick. The surrounding walls had disappeared, but its use can safely be surmised by the fact that it had been left untouched. A large pottery jar (2524) with its mouth close to, and practically level with, the pavement had perhaps served to drain it.

The little patch of flooring at locus 442 in Square 9/B measured 44 inches square and sloped towards its north-eastern corner, where there were the remains of a little drain, 5 inches wide by 2½ inches deep.[10] Close by was a large pottery pan (3209, Pl. XXIV, 2), which was possibly a bath and was at the same level as the floor. Two steatite seals (3215, 3207, Pl. LI, 14, 22) came from the same vicinity and near the same level. In the open space north-west of this ruined house several finds were recorded. Locus 289 at the depth + 8.6 feet provided a large storage jar (3491, Pls. XXIV, 6, XXXV, 3) and a seal (3492, Pl. LII, 32). Inside room 231 was a second seal (3485, Pl. LI, 11). Room 109 contained the pottery animal (2583) seen in Pl. LVI, 1 and just outside it was a large jar (2464) at the level + 9.5 feet. At locus 295 a model figure of a duck in pottery (2892, Pl. LVII, 3) was unearthed and not far from here came an unfinished shell dish (4366, Pl. XC, 9) and a sandstone block (3564, Pl. XCIII, 9), the grooves on which show that it had been employed for bead making. Stone drills of the kind used in bead manufacture (as Pl. LXXXVI, b, 8) were also picked up here.

Owing to the close proximity of the edge of the mound, the house in Square 8/B had practically disappeared. But there still remained part of the walls of a room standing as much as 3 feet high in places, with the floor-level 8.6 feet above datum. A small assembly of metal objects (2365, a-q, Pls. LXVIII, 1-16, LXXV, 1-10) found buried at the level + 9.5 feet at locus 284, included several unfinished castings. This hoard was clearly the property of a metal-worker and is shown as in situ in Pl. LXXV, 1. Close to this group was a clay model of a duck (2396, Pl. LVII, 2) and a pottery figurine (3347, Pl. LIII, 12). At locus 235 near by, a seal was found (2390, Pl. LII, 6) at the depth of + 9.9 feet.

Of the various buildings that line the north-eastern side of the main street, mostly in Square 9/C, that one marked 179, 190, 207, 208 was very dilapidated. Part of the south-eastern end of the narrow room 179 (extreme left of Pl. XXI, f) stood only 8 inches high,[11] though the walls were as much as 2 feet 3 inches thick. Though one wall had gone, room

[8] Their foundation levels averaged + 10.2 ft. and they were built of bricks 10½ x 5¼ x 2½ ins. in size.

[9] The same wholesale clearance of building material occurred at Mohenjo-daro, where we found the impressions against the sides of these platforms of the brickwork that formerly encased them.

[10] This was 6.7 ft. above datum.

[11] Its base was 9.1 ft. above datum.

207 had clearly been 9 feet 10 inches long by 6 feet wide. The remaining walls still stood 18 inches high.[12]

The wide doorway leading from the north-east into 190 suggests that, small as it was, this was once a courtyard. A number of unfinished disc-shaped steatite beads (No. 2301), similar to those illustrated in Pl. LXXXIII, 36-39, lay on the floor of this court at the level + 10.4 feet. Outside the 22 inch-thick north-eastern wall of this court at locus 212 was a pavement, 3 feet 8 inches square, with the usual edging of brick around it standing some 2½ inches high;[13] and two pottery drain-pipes (1991, Pls. XVI, e, LXXXVIII, 14, 15) found in the close vicinity possibly once drained this little bath or privy. Just north-east of this pavement and about a foot lower, we came upon a group of copper and bronze tools and utensils (2593, Pls. LXIV, 1-11, LXV, 1-9, LXVI, 1-5, LXXIV, 10-17), including a casting, all so corroded together as to be inseparable until they had been chemically cleaned. The fine clay figure of a rhinoceros (2701) in Pl. LVI, 8 also came from the same spot, but another foot higher. Near by, at locus 213, another hoard of metal objects (2360, a-g, Pl. LXVII, 13-19) had been buried at the level + 10.4 feet, and a bronze model cart (2291, Pl. LVIII, 2), together with the dish of a food-stand (2815, Pl. XXV, 3), was found at the same level. The toy cart was not so well preserved as the specimen found in Square 7/C, but is valuable for being of a different type.

A large storage jar (3323, Pl. XXIV, 1) was unearthed at the level + 7.2 feet at locus 296, and an axe and a knife near by, of either copper or bronze (2382, Pl. LXVII, 20, 21), lay at about the same level as the hoard described above. A seal (2559) illustrated in Pl. LII, 20 was also found at locus 296, about 2 feet above the jar that was also unearthed there.

The long, thin wall 291, 294 must have had some special purpose. It was only three bricks high, but at its north-western end there was the lower part of a blocked-up doorway, 2 feet 3 inches wide,[14] with an earthern sill. Beside this wall there were a number of finds. At locus 291, a pottery kohl-jar (3484, Pl. XXVII, 92) and a copper knife (3486, Pl. LXXII, 1) lay on the mud-brick platform here at the level + 7.1 feet. A shell cone (3533, Pl. LX, 31) was recovered at locus 208, and near locus 292 some flint drills (3457, 3526), like those illustrated in Pl. LXXXVI, b, 8, lay at the level + 7.0 feet. The finely painted jar (3011) shown in Pls. XXIII, 6 and XXXIX, 23 was unearthed just west of locus 208 at the level + 9.6 feet and formed a group with two less important pieces.

In this vicinity also, these ruined walls stood on part of an extensive mud-brick platform, whose average level was 9.2 feet above datum.

Bead Factory with Furnace

Farther along the main street towards the north-west (Square 9/D) was a remarkable building (215, 286, 287, Pl. VIII) with several unusual features.

The main portion of this very intriguing building is some 33 feet long by 12 feet 6

[12] Their base level averaged 9 ft. above datum.

[13] At the level + 10.2 ft. This floor was constructed of two courses of brick.

[14] Its base was at + 9.1 ft.

inches in width on the outside; the varying thickness of its walls shows that they had been reconstructed.

The small and very carefully built room 215, 9 feet 2 inches long by 7 feet wide, was entered from the east by a doorway, 3 feet 3 inches wide on the outside, whose well rabbeted jambs show that it was once closed on the inside by a substantial door.[15] A second doorway, 4 feet 7 inches wide (Pl. XX, d, foreground) on the opposite side, had been altered considerably. The original sill was 6.6 feet above datum and the door it served had been blocked up leaving at its north-western side a narrow aperture, 2 inches wide, which served for the drainage of water into the lower jar seen in Pl. XVII, i. Later, as the ground level rose, this aperture was filled up some 2 feet from the sill, and to catch the drainage another jar was placed on top of the first.

From the north-western side of room 215 (Pl. XX, d) a series of well-built flues, averaging 5½ inches wide by 8 inches high, ran to the other end of the building where they had been destroyed. Five of these flues have survived, and there may have been two or three more. That three other flues at right angles communicated with them had been revealed by the removal of bricks from here in ancient times. Pl. XX, c, shows two of these cross-flues clearly.

The flues were covered by a single course of bricks and on this pavement there were three compartments (Pl. VIII) of varying size with walls only half-a-brick thick, and standing some 18 inches high. These compartments may once have had doorways on their south-western sides, whose jambs were demolished later by brick robbers. Along the other side was a passage (286), which narrowed from 2 feet 3 inches to 1 foot 11 inches in width at the other end, where two broad, shallow steps, each 3 inches high, led to a pavement (287) at the north-western end of the building.[16]

As is seen in Pl. XX, d, the two courses of brick below the line of flues rested on a thick layer of débris at the average level of 9 feet above datum,[17] which is also the foundation level of some of the walls.

The thinness of the walls of the compartments above the flues together with their small size precludes the possibility of this building having been a *hammam*, or sweat-house. Moreover, the absence of any signs of a great temperature in the flues is strong evidence that the heat used was very moderate. There was no ash anywhere in the flues and the heat can hardly have come from room 215, where there was no trace of a furnace. The purpose of this building is an interesting problem. A possible clue to its use is presented by the number of beads, many unfinished, that lay scattered about on the earthern floor of room 215.[18] Among them was a concreted mass of minute steatite beads (2391, B, Pl. XCIII, 5). It had evidently been intended to glaze these, and this curious arrangement might have been built for this purpose and then never used. Among the beads found in room 215

[15] Its sill was 10.3 ft. above datum and its jambs stood some 2 ft. high.

[16] Its level is 10.7 ft. above datum and that of the south-eastern end of the passage 9.6 ft. above datum.

[17] The level is averaged because there had been a subsidence of the middle of the building.

[18] At the level +9.3 ft.

there were a number of copper tools (2384, a-f, Pl. LXIII, 12-14, LXXVI, 14), three copper or bronze knives (2290, a-c, Pls. LXIX, 1, 2, LXXVI, 7), a copper pin (2294, Pl. LXIX, 7), a seal (2285, Pl. LI, 15), a flake drill (2326, Pl. XCIII, 6), a faience gamesman (2326, i, Pl. LX, 7), a queer shell object (2326, k, Pl. XC, 18), and some carnelian nodules (2326, u, Pl. XCIII, 17-20). All these were found at the level of + 10.4 feet. About a foot lower and in the same room was a shell feeding cup (2408, Pl. XC, 2), the copper canister (2449) seen in Pl. LXXV, 15, a shell cone (2401, Pl. LX, 36), and the flint core (3012) which had been used as a rubber and is illustrated in Pl. XCIII, 28. Two large shells (2991), one of which is shown in Pl. XC, 1, appear to indicate that shell working was also practised in this workshop.

On the floor of the passage 286 was a brown steatite seal (2428, Pl. LII, 19) which, from its colour, was apparently unfinished.

The courtyard 297 on the north-eastern side of this building may one day supply the clue to the source of the heat conducted or intended to be conducted through the flues; for it appears to have communicated with the interior of the building by an opening just under 2 feet wide that was blocked up at some later date.[19] The very wide entrance into this courtyard could easily have admitted carts and pack-animals with supplies of fuel.

In this courtyard some most interesting and illuminating finds were made. In the middle of its wide entrance, a large pottery jar (2528, Pl. XXVII, 53) was found set in the ground at the level + 10.1 feet with its rim well below the foundations of the walls. A large pan (2596, Pl. XXIX, 37) in the north-eastern corner contained a number of copper and bronze tools, an ingot of bronze, and bangles and razors (2596, Pls. LXVII, 1-12, LXXIII, 29, LXXIV, 1, LXXVI, 19), all of them products of the metal-worker's craft. The top of this pan was well below the base of the adjacent door-jamb and it seems to have been buried here for safety. A very miscellaneous assortment of most interesting material (2529, a-z; aa-jj, Pls. LXII, 1-23, LXIII, 1-5, LXXIV, 2-9) lay spread over the floor of the court at the average level + 10.4 feet, and it looks as if the occupants of this unique building had had to leave the place hurriedly and had never returned. These objects include a seal (2529, cc, Pl. LII, 23) and an unfinished carved shell ball (2556, Pl. LIX, 14). A copper chisel (2575, Pl. LXX, 15) also came from here and from the same level.

On the south-eastern side of the court at locus 227, more copper was unearthed at the level + 11.3 feet (2199, a-o, Pls. LXVI, 6-21, LXXV, 11-13). But this hoard may have been buried here by someone in the occupation mentioned above. Beneath this was another collection of copper and bronze (2525, a-g, Pl. LXIII, 6-11) at the level + 9.4 feet. The pottery figurine (2527) seen in Pl. LIII, 13 lay near by, together with a seal (2361, Pl. LI, 32), a copper razor (2359, Pls. LXXIII, 33, LXXVI, 33), and a copper knife (2523, a, Pl. LXXII, 2). Close by, at locus 228, a fine elephant seal (2594, h), shown in Pl. LI, 20, was unearthed and an interesting assortment of metal objects, together with miniature pottery (2594, a-p, Pls. XXVIII, 38-41, LXXVI, 29-31), all at the level + 9.9 feet. From this place there also came a stone mace-head (2693, Pl. XCIII, 33) and an unfinished shell dish (2624, a, Pl. XC, 10). With these lay the strange-looking shell object (2379) illus-

[19] The sill of this aperture (+ 9.1 ft.) is 16 ins. below the floor level of the passage 286.

trated in Pl. XC, 16, whose use we do not know. At locus 263 we found a copper razor (3044) of the type shown in Pl. LXXIII, 25 and also a copper axe (2296, Pl. LXXI, 6), which may have been dropped by one of the occupants of this building at the time of leaving it.

Just outside the north-eastern entrance to room 215, a stone hone of animal shape (2364), like that in Pl. XCIII, 11, had been left.

If the excavation of Chanhu-daro is one day resumed, the upper part of this very curious building should be removed in order to ascertain exactly how it was used, and whether it was for the purpose that we have surmised, though the unfinished beads found both in room 215 and the courtyard 297 leave little doubt of that.

This heating system is in no way comparable with the possible hypocaust found at Mohenjo-daro. The latter was quite different in design and its decoration alone proved that it was for man's own use.[20]

Room 183 (Square 8/D), which was only 8 feet 9 inches long by 7 feet, 3 inches wide (Pl. XX, e, foreground), was entered from the street by a doorway, 4 feet wide, that was blocked up at a later date. This entrance had two sills, the upper one at the level + 9.6 feet, and the other 7 inches lower, with a single course of mud-brick and one of burnt brick between the two. A second doorway with its sill a little higher up than the upper one of the street entrance opened from this small room to the courtyard 297 (Pl. XX, e, left-hand side). This doorway appears to have been about 4 feet 8 inches wide. On the present evidence, it seems not unlikely that this room was occupied by the man in charge of what appears to have been a factory for beads and seals.

Room 196 was separated from room 183 by a partition wall only half a brick thick, and it looks as though the two were originally one large room. Save where a rectangular bin, 4 feet square inside,[21] had been built against this unbonded partition wall, room 196 was paved with two courses of bricks sloping gently towards the south-east corner.[22] This room had two doorways, one to the street and the other at its further end opening into room 310, whose walls were in a ruinous condition and nowhere over a foot high.[23] This latter doorway was originally some 4 feet wide, but it was subsequently narrowed to 15 inches and perhaps then served as a cupboard niche.[24] The street doorway was 4 feet 6 inches wide and its sill at the level + 8.5 feet.

Unfortunately, nothing was found in this fine, large room to provide a clue to its use. The pottery elephant (3483) seen in Pl. LVI, 9, which lay on the paved floor, was probably a treasured toy of a child who lived in this part of the building.

Rooms 138, 310, 311 could only be conjecturally restored, but the walls of the better preserved room 178, which was 15 feet long by an average of 5 feet 8 inches wide, still stood from 7 inches to 14 inches in height.[25] No. 310 contained a jar-stopper made in

[20] *Mohenjo-daro and the Indus Civilization*, p. 237, pl. LXIX, b.

[21] About 1 ft. high, with its floor at the level + 9.8 ft.

[22] + 9.5 ft. above datum.

[23] Their foundations stood at the level + 9.1 ft.

[24] Its sill was 9.6 ft. above datum.

[25] Their foundations were at the level + 9.0 ft.

shell (2626), which is pictured on Pl. LXXXIX, 13. In room 178 were two bird-whistles (2822-3) of the kind shown in Pl. LIX, 5, 6, a seal (2531, Pl. LII, 15), and a pottery animal (2658, Pl. LVI, 2), which lend support to the suggestion that this part of the building was a dwelling house.

Pl. XXI, b shows the little room 203 across the side street which passed beside the factory. This room was 7 feet 4 inches wide and its probable length 9 feet or so. The smaller apartment adjoining it was probably entered from the north-east, but brick-robbing has made this uncertain.[26] A small, badly preserved cess pit connected this little room with a drain in this side street, whose channel (Pl. XXI, b) here was 9.7 feet above datum. At locus 274 a pottery bulla (2633), seen in Pl. LXXXVIII, 1, was lying at the level + 9.6 feet.

As the plan in Pl. IV shows, the main street was irregular in width and its alignment far from straight. Near locus 197 (Square 8/D) it was only 15 feet 6 inches wide; a view of this end is seen in Pl. XXI, e, whereas Pl. XXI, f shows its widest part, 18 feet 8 inches, at locus 193. The objects found in this street included, at locus 211, a poorly preserved seal (3051, Pl. LI, 24) at the level + 8.1 feet; at locus 341, a dish with two compartments (4140, Pl. XXXIX, 17); at locus 209, two storage jars (3212 and another) shown in position in Pl. XVII, i, both used as cess pits. Between loci 209 and 447 lay a seal (3206, Pl. LII, 11). Close to the drain at locus 130 was a sandstone block (3634), used in shaping beads. At locus 290 in Square 8/D, a copper jar-cover (2522, Pl. LXXIII, 36) lay between the drain and the house wall at the level + 9.8 feet. Locus 84 contained the large storage jar (2598) illustrated in Pl. XVII, b, with its rim level with the sill of the very wide doorway leading into room 196. An unfinished shell dish (2973, Pl. XC, 3) was taken from locus 197 at the level + 8.9 feet and a copper fish-hook (2542) from locus 108 at about a foot higher.

As was usual in the ancient cities of the Harappā Period, most of the buildings on either side of this street were served by very efficient street drains. But for some reason or other not all the houses were connected with them. Of the bead factory only room 215 was drained—and then into the two large cess jars already mentioned (Pl. XVII, i).

On both sides of the main street, the direction of flow was to the south-east. The drain which passes two sides of the house attached to the factory commences near locus 314 (Square 7/C), some 60 feet or so along the side street, receiving the outfall of houses on either side which had practically disappeared. The floor of the channel at locus 314 was 9.7 feet above datum, and 5 inches lower where it turned into the main street (Pl. XXI, e). After passing some distance down the street, this drain received a tributary from the well paved room 196;[27] the junction is seen, partly excavated, in Pl. XVIII, d. A large jar (2598, Pl. XVII, b) was unearthed beside this tributary at locus 84. At this point of junction (locus 223), the drain and its tributary turn across the main street to enter the long sewer on its other side (Pl. XX, e, extreme right-hand side).

The long sewer on the other side of the main street also began in the narrower street at right angles, at locus 87 in Square 8/E, where its broken end rested on a large pottery

[26] The walls stood about 2 ft. high with their bases at + 9.5 ft.

[27] Its level here was 8.9 ft. above datum.

jar (3047, Pls. XVII, a, XXIV, 5).[28] It turned at right angles into the main street at locus 108,[29] and sloping gently passed down the further end of the street to locus 341, where we could find no further trace of it.[30] In all, this sewer had a fall of 17 inches in about 148 feet. It is seen not fully excavated in Pl. XVIII, a, f.

Towards its end an important tributary from another side street enters the long main sewer at locus 211 (Pl. XIX, e).[31] This branch apparently originated from a house at locus 218 (Square 10/E). Curiously enough the declination of this branch drain is towards the north-east, but this is entirely due to a subsidence, as the photograph in Pl. XXI, d clearly shows. A finely painted jar (4656, Pl. XXXV, 4) was found at locus 195 at the level + 7.0 feet.

The channels of this very extensive and well planned drainage system range from 4½ to 5½ inches wide and deep in the side streets; in the main street they are 7½ inches deep. As is seen in Pls. XVIII, d, f, XIX, e and XX, f, the channel was always covered with bricks laid on their flats, these bricks being exactly the same in size and shape as those used for the houses.

Great care was exercised in laying these drains. The inner angle of one of the turns at locus 223 (Square 8/D) was carefully rounded off to impede the flow of sewage as little as possible. The same had been done at the junction at locus 211 (Square 9/D), where one of the rounded bricks is seen in the centre of the photograph Pl. XIX, e.

We were able to detect various places along these drains where the covering bricks had been lifted off in order to remove stoppages, and many of these bricks were not put back as carefully as they might have been.

Despite the better preservation of the buildings on the opposite side of the main street from the bead factory, we were frequently in doubt as to the ground plans of the rooms. The inner rooms 136, 139, 264 of the large house in Square 9/D were very dilapidated, and only the south-western and south-eastern walls of the house remained. The latter, which was 2 feet thick and still stood 3 feet high, is seen in Pl. XXI, d.[32] The south-western wall was of about the same height, but, curiously enough, its foundations were about a foot higher.

The small room 174, which was 7 feet 7 inches long by 3 feet 2 inches wide, may possibly have been a little workshop, for many unfinished beads were found there at the level + 6.8 feet and also a seal (2297, Pl. LI, 29) at a slightly lower level. This room must have been entered from the north-west, but owing to the removal of bricks from the wall, all traces of an entry had been lost. In room 264 was the fish-hook (2943) seen in Pl. LXXIII, 5; and a multiple pottery bracelet (3002, Pl. XC, 34) comes from room 139. In the street outside to the south a pottery figurine (2039, Pl. LIII, 1) was lying with a pottery drain-pipe (2292, Pl. XC, 33).

[28] The base of its channel here was + 9.9 ft.

[29] Here its level was + 9.3 ft.

[30] At this point it was 8.2 ft. above datum.

[31] At locus 218 its level now is + 6.7 ft. At locus 211 it was the same level as the street drain here, namely, + 8.2 ft.

[32] Its base was 8.6 ft. above datum.

Room 95, which was a little over 14 feet long by 10 feet wide, appears to have been an annex to this house, despite the double wall between. On the inside of the street wall was an exceptionally well preserved ablution place or privy, with a floor 4 feet 1 inch by 3 feet 1 inch in size, constructed of three courses of brick, of which the upper one was 9.6 feet above datum. As is seen in Pl. XX, f, this pavement was surrounded by the usual skirting of brick, though in this case the bricks were set on their longer edges instead of on their ends. The walls that had enclosed this pavement had all been removed for the sake of their bricks. The water from this convenience ran out, as the photograph shows, through an aperture in the base of the street wall, which here was 19 inches thick, and then through a short channel into the street drain. This arrangement is seen from another view-point in the right-hand bottom corner of Pl. XVIII, f. A footing, projecting from the base of the street wall and apparent on the inside only showed that the wall had been built up on an earlier and wider one.[33]

In a later wall at the back of this room, which still stood some 17 inches high, the bricks had been laid in an unusual manner (Pl. XX, f). The foundations of this wall (+ 9.8 feet) were 2 feet higher than those of room 95, but the bricks used for both the room and the later wall were exactly the same size, 10¾ x 5 x 2½ inches.

Room 95 could be entered from the small courtyard 82 by a doorway 3 feet 4 inches wide.[34] Though small, 82 must have been either a courtyard or a blind alley; there was no trace of a wall on its south-western side. The side walls of a brick bin in this court or alley, do not meet the wall behind, and we must presume that it was a stall for fodder rather than a grain bin. A fine seal (2462, Pl. LI, 33) was found here at the level + 9.5 feet.

Room 176, 217 (Pl. XX, e), in the house next door, was 14 feet 8 inches long. In its south-eastern corner a well preserved ablution place had the usual skirting of bricks standing 4 inches above its pavement,[35] the water from which ran out through the street wall and then through a short channel into the main drain. The level of a footing 4 inches wide, on the inside of the street wall, was 8.5 feet above datum.[36] This room was entered from the north-west by a doorway, 4 feet 4 inches wide, which at some later date was narrowed to 2 feet 6 inches wide by the addition of a new jamb on its northern side. Subsequently, this opening was entirely blocked up.[37]

Little more than the outline of room 425 remained, with the foundations of the south-western corner 7.7 feet above datum.

A narrow lane, averaging 3 feet 10 inches wide, ran behind these two houses, parallel with the main street; the south-eastern end of this lane is seen in Pl. XXI, d. Unfortunately, most of the house or houses on the other side of this lane had been demolished by brick-robbers. Only three walls of room 137 remain, averaging only 1 foot high;[38] the small

[33] This footing was at + 10.2 ft., and its base at + 8.2 ft.

[34] The sill of this was 9.8 ft. above datum.

[35] At the level + 9.1 ft.

[36] The street wall here was 3 ft. high.

[37] Its sill was 7.9 ft. above datum, and the new jamb stood 2 ft. high.

[38] Their bases were at + 8.1 ft.

aperture, 1 foot 8 inches wide, in the south-eastern wall is far too narrow to have been a doorway. In this room a spear-head (2602, Pl. LXXI, 12) was found at the level + 8.3 feet and the open space at locus 171 contained a copper platter (2844, Pl. LXXIII, 35) and a bronze adze (2843, Pl. LXXI, 9) at the level + 7.7 feet. The interesting vase inscribed in black paint (3419) and shown in Pl. XXXIX, 24 came also from this place. At locus 224 beyond, there was a faience jar (2936, Pl. LXXXIX, 2), and locus 172 yielded an unfinished weight (2380) at the level + 9.4 feet. This last object, together with some stone drills found at locus 253 on the other side of Square 9/E, suggests that lapidaries once occupied the houses on this part of the site. Some paste plaques and cylinders were present in a stratum of ashes and dark-coloured soil near locus 171.[39]

Very little was left of room 132 except for a privy that averaged 4 feet long by 2 feet 10 inches wide and was roughly built of two courses of brick.[40] An outfall, 2¾ inches wide, led to the street drain in the lane outside.[41]

Two isolated houses on the edge of the mound beyond (Sq. 10/E) had almost disappeared. In room 252, 261 of the further one a steatite seal (2293, Pl. LI, 28) was found. Room 218 in the nearer house was better preserved and its 2 foot-thick south-western wall stood in places 1 foot 6 inches high.[42] One jamb of the doorway in the north-western wall was missing, but the sill was still well defined.[43] From just outside this doorway came a steatite seal (2426, Pl. LII, 14) from the level + 9.0 feet.

Between these two houses was a fire-place, whose walls, half-a-brick thick, stood 1 foot 6 inches high, and near by, at locus 251, a painted jar of the Jhukar Period (3182, Pl. XLI, 38), which had rolled down the side of the mound, was found in close proximity at the level + 7.2 feet. South of locus 250 we also came upon a large painted sherd (3671, Pl. XXXVI, 23) at the depth of + 6.8 feet. This sherd is especially noteworthy because it is painted in polychrome, a technique that was rarely used in the pottery of the Harappā Culture. At locus 225 a second article of Jhukar workmanship was recovered, namely, a pottery bead-amulet (2289, Pl. L, 15) which lay at the higher level of + 10.3 feet.

Locus 181, near the middle of Square 9/E, revealed a remnant of a drainage channel, 5 inches wide and deep,[44] probably part of a sewer that ran down a once existing lane. A small tributary leading to this drained a privy that stood some 10 inches higher than the drain itself. The pavement here was 5 feet long by 3 feet 6 inches wide, constructed of two courses of brick but without the usual edging of brick around it. The short channel that drained this floor was partly supported on a large jar (Pl. XVI, c), which may have received the outfall before the sewer was laid in the lane. Near by and at about the same level, several unfinished shell bangles were found (2871, Pl. XC, 15), and at locus 219 a faience

[39] These lay at the level + 6.8 ft. See Pl. XCI, 12, 13, 20-22, for some of these curious objects.

[40] At the level + 10.4 ft. Some of the bricks in this pavement had been sawn.

[41] The walls here were only a foot high with their bases at + 8.1 ft.

[42] Its foundations were at + 8.6 ft. and stood on mud-brick, which was probably part of the platform north-east of it.

[43] This sill was + 9.0 ft.

[44] At the level + 8.2 ft.

amulet (2604, Pl. XLIX, 2) of Jhukar make. This last was certainly an intrusion, lying as it did at the level + 9.6 feet. Locus 201 yielded a mace-head (2972, Pl. XCIII, 34), which lay between the privy and the thin wall of another room.

A second convenience in room 125 clearly belonged to another house. This privy (Pl. XIX, f) had the usual edging around it standing 2¾ inches high above the surface of the pavement.[45] Its doorway, 3 feet 8 inches wide, was well preserved with its sill at the level + 9.1 feet.[46] Below this platform was a larger pavement of two courses of brick-work; as the photograph in Pl. XIX, f shows, there was a 5-inch layer of débris between the two.[47] The earlier floor was part of a room whose walls had practically disappeared, but other isolated bits of paving showed that the room could not have been less than 10 x 9 feet in size. Despite being carefully laid, this paved floor had subsided badly in places.[48] The south-western mud-brick wall of this room is of later date; its foundations were 9.7 feet above datum.[49] From just north of locus 125 came an irregular block of amethyst (2865, Pl. XCIII, 2). That bead-making was carried on in the immediate neighbourhood is suggested by this find and the number of stone drills that were lying close by.

Northwards from here in Square 8/E there were only very fragmentary remains of houses. At locus 141 a small irregular pavement, some 2 feet 6 inches square,[50] drained into the important street drain already mentioned, that emptied in turn into the main street sewer. Close to this pavement was a little pottery ink-pot (?) (2466, Pl. XCI, 3), and from locus 155 close by came the pottery figurine (3205) seen in Pl. LIV, 5. In the area 92, 146 a copper or bronze adze (2847, Pls. LXXI, 11, LXXVI, 16) was found together with a clay model of an antelope (3234, Pl. LVI, 11). Locus 430 yielded a seal (3043, Pl. LI, 26), and another one (3148, Pl. LI, 13) of better workmanship came from locus 113 in the north-western corner of the square. A third seal (3045, Pl. LI, 27) was unearthed at locus 177 and near the edge of the mound at locus 142 (Sq. 8/E, right hand bottom corner) lay a large painted sherd of Jhukar date (2666, Pl. XXXIX, 15), which had evidently been washed down to its level of 9.4 feet above datum. At locus 115 (Square 8/F) a brick pavement, 3 feet 2 inches long by 2 feet 5 inches wide and surrounded by an edging,[51] had drained, by a short channel of which only a few bricks remained, into a large storage jar (3317) which served as a cess pit. Adjacent to this pavement was a shell cone (1929). A stag's antler (4471) was found at locus 418 at the level + 8.7 feet, and from 117 came a copper chisel (3211, Pl. LXX, 10).

Several brick columns in this neighbourhood (Squares 8/F, 7/E, and 7/F), appear to have supported the roofs of workshops open to the air.[52]

[45] This was 3 ft. 6 ins. in extent and its level + 9.1 ft.
[46] The base of the wall was + 8.3 ft.
[47] To avoid confusion this lower pavement is not shown on the plan in Pl. IV.
[48] Its highest level was + 8.6 ft.
[49] The bricks in this wall measured 12½ x 6½ x 4 ins.
[50] Level was 8.3 ft. above datum.
[51] Level: + 8.8 ft.
[52] These ranged from 9 ins. to 3 ft. high and their base levels averaged + 8.1 ft.

A platform at locus 119 (Square 7/F) was surrounded by walls only one brick high.[53] It was drained by a hole in its north-eastern wall. Near this privy was a copper or bronze chisel (3149, Pl. LXX, 13), and from not far away, at locus 439, came the stone hone in animal shape (3151) illustrated in Pl. XCIII, 16. At locus 443 a little toy ram (3301, Pl. LVIII, 15), once fitted with wheels, was lying near some broken walling. This last area also yielded a number of agate nodules (5178) at the level + 6.6 feet, being raw material for another bead-maker whose workshop had entirely disappeared. Close to the edge of the mound and east of 189 was a seal (2468, Pl. LII, 27) at + 9.8 feet.

A fine storage jar (3153, Pl. XXIV, 8) was found at locus 110, and close to a thin wall, one brick high, whose base was 8.2 feet above datum. From locus 158 (north-eastern corner of Square 7/F) came a pottery jar-stand (4295, Pl. XXVI, 7) and west of locus 189 and near the edge of the mound a figurine (4069, Pl. LIV, 9). The copper bangle (3210) seen in Pls. LXXIII, 30 and LXXVI, 21 came from locus 299.

A 29 feet length of drain with a fall of 7 inches marked a long forgotten street in Square 7/E, once parallel with the more important street crossing the main thoroughfare of the city at right angles. This drain served a privy at locus 121, but whether it communicated with the main sewage system we can never know, as it disappears at the edge of the mound at locus 157 (Pl. XVI, f). The privy (Pl. XX, a) was probably 3 feet 8 inches square. Though the walls are missing, the brick-quarriers had left its skirting nearly intact and standing 2¾ inches high.[54] As is seen in the photograph, the water reached the drain by a sloping gutter. The wall, 15 inches high, behind this privy belongs to the Harappā I occupation; its base is some 3 feet higher than the pavement in front of it.[55] This convenience appears to have been part of a seal-maker's house, for no less than three unfinished seals were found in its close vicinity (3198, 3052, 3159, Pl. LI, 1, 1a, 2, 2a, 8, 8a). A drill-cap (4537, Pl. LXXXIX, 28) was also found here.

Room 122, 154, in the house between the parallel side streets (Square 7/E), was 8 feet 6 inches wide, with its three remaining walls having an average height of 13 inches.[56] In this room was found a rare type of round seal (2532, Pl. LI, 23) and also a painted wheel belonging to a large model cart (2723, Pl. LVIII, 20). This last is of especial interest, in that it proves that in ancient Sindh wheels were made of three main pieces just as are the wheels of the carts used in that province today.

The walls of the house across the street were nearly 2 feet thick and stood a little over a foot high.[57] The circular pavement seen in Pl. XVI, h was in this house (Locus 306, sq. 7/E) in the vicinity of the privy. It measured 3 feet 7 inches in diameter, but possibly it was originally much larger. It was constructed of radially arranged bricks round a small

[53] The level of this pavement was + 7.8 ft. and the bricks composing it measured 10½ x 5¼ x 2½ ins. in size.

[54] The pavement was + 11.8 ft. the floor of the channel below it was 1 ft. lower.

[55] + 14.9 ft.

[56] Their bases were at the level + 9.7 ft.

[57] The average level of their foundations was + 9.8 ft.; they were built of bricks 10½ x 5¾ x 2½ ins. in size.

sunken jar to whose mouth they sloped down from the circumference.[58] Very similar circular pavements have been found at Harappā and Mohenjo-daro;[59] their use is still uncertain. At Harappā grain was found at the bottom of the jar set in one of these pavements, suggesting that they may have been used for hulling or mealing grain. Unfortunately, there was nothing of interest in the jar at Chanhu-daro. The foundations of the walls that appear in the plan on two sides of this circular floor were at a higher level and clearly had no connection with it.[60] At locus 97 there were found six pottery bangles similar to those seen in Pl. XC, 26-29, a type of bracelet commonly worn by the women of Chanhu-daro.

A well conditioned pavement of two courses of brick (locus 302; sq. 7/E) seems to have been the floor of a bathroom in the house beyond to the west. This measured 7 feet 10 inches long by 5 feet wide, but the walls around it had been removed for the sake of their bricks and the room itself may actually have been larger.[61] A large storage jar (3324, Pl. XXIV, 4) on its eastern side served to drain this floor (Pl. XVII, g), and in it we found a human skull, a large shell, a copper or bronze ring, and a few implements of copper or bronze, some of which were broken (Pls. LXIX, 11-15, LXXVI, 5, 6). Very rarely is anything of value found in a drainage jar, save objects that have been washed in accidentally, and this notable exception has proved of the greatest interest, as the report on this skull by Drs. W. M. Krogman and W. H. Sassaman in Chapter XVI will show. Why this skull, shown in position in Pls. XVII, h and XCIV, 2, 3, was buried here without the rest of the skeleton, and whether it had any connection with the objects found with it, must be left to the imagination of the reader.

The peculiar masonry to the right of this jar (Pl. XVII, g) and partly resting on it, is a rectangular column, 2 feet 7 inches by 1 foot 6 inches, which stood 2 feet high with its base at the level + 9.0 feet.

At locus 88 in the same square (7/E) were the remains of the only staircase found at Chanhu-daro, possibly many others had been demolished for the sake of their bricks. This flight (Pl. XX, b) was but 2 feet wide with treads 8½ inches broad and rising 11½ inches.[62] Unluckily, there was nothing to show to what it led, but it was more probably to a roof than to an upper storey, for the walls of the house behind it were very thin.

Near the foot of this stairway, at locus 164, a seal (2595, Pl. LII, 22) and a pottery figurine (3334, Pl. LIV, 6) were found. In room 88 behind was another figurine (4070, Pl. LIII, 2) and a gamesman (1780, Pl. LIX, 21). This little chamber was some 11 feet long and its walls stood only 8 inches high except for the portion abutting against the staircase.[63] West of and near locus 300, a second seal (2530, Pl. LII, 31) was unearthed at the level + 9.5 feet.

[58] The edge of this pavement was at + 8.6 ft. and there was a fall of 6 ins. to its centre.

[59] *Ann. Rep. Arch. Surv. Ind.*, 1928-29, p. 79; pl. XXX, a.

[60] They stood only a brick high with their bases at the level + 10.2 ft.

[61] Its surface level was + 9.5 ft.

[62] Its foot was 7.4 ft. above datum and its top-most tread was a trifle over 3 ft. higher.

[63] Their bases were at + 8.0 ft.

Room 159 of the house opposite (square 6/F) was entered by a well preserved doorway, 4 feet wide, on its north-eastern side, whose northern jamb still stood 2 feet 8 inches high.[64] From this room we recovered a seal (2605, Pl. LII, 24) and a small storage jar (3321, Pl. XXIV, 7); the latter had probably been used to store valuables, for its rim was set 6 inches below the foundations of the walls. The remains of a massive mud-brick wall immediately north-west of this room has yet to be examined. Near it at locus 434 we unearthed a copper or bronze razor (3319, Pl. LXXVI, 28) at + 7.1 feet.

The excavation of this Harappā II stratum has produced interesting evidence that many, if not most, of the inhabitants of this portion of the site were artisans. It is safe to infer from the many tools and implements, some of them unfinished castings, scattered about the squares 8/B, 8/C, and 9/C,[65] that this quarter of the city was occupied by metal-workers. In addition to isolated tools, considerable hoards of copper and bronze tools and utensils, all compacted together by corrosion, were found in several places, and, though very similar groups have been unearthed in the residential parts of Mohenjo-daro, where they were probably the outfits of carpenters and the like, these hoards at Chanhu-daro are shown by the presence of castings to have been the property of actual metal-workers.

Whether the two little bronze carts found in this quarter at loci 101 and 213 (Squares 7/C and 9/C) had already been used as toys, it is impossible to say. No furnaces that could have been used for smelting and metal-casting have yet been found; it is quite possible that this kind of work was carried on well outside the city and brought in to be finished.

Bead-making was an important source of revenue. Large numbers of unfinished beads, together with the stone drills used for boring them, were taken from Squares 8/C, 9/C, 9/D, and 9/F.[66] The north-eastern side of the "Great Cutting" yielded also many specimens. Supplies of the raw materials for bead-making were also unearthed; in several cases nodules of agate showed signs of having been treated with heat.[67] There were also lumps of amethyst, crystal, and carnelian. The principal focus of bead-making seems to have been the southern quarter of the city, though this craft was also practised elsewhere.

Closely associated with bead-making was the manufacture of stone weights, many of which are so highly finished that we suspect that they were used for testing purposes. Specimens of unfinished weights, which we must presume were left in the places where they were made, were unearthed in Squares 8/C, 8/E, 9/D, 9/E, and 9/F.[68]

Eight unfinished seals of the Harappā Period were found in Squares 7/C, 7/E, 8/D, 8/F and Trench D(1),[69] which suggests that the northern quarter of the city was engaged in this craft; unfinished seals have been found nowhere else save one example in the Cutting.

Another possible industry which seems, however, not to have been closely localized,

[64] The sill of this entry was + 8.1 ft., and its foundations some 4 ins. lower.
[65] Loci 297, 228.
[66] Loci 450, 293, 190, 215, 174, 85, 253.
[67] Loci 237, 443, 215, 139, and 124 in squares 7/C, 7/F, 9/C, and 9/D.
[68] Loci 151, 103, 215, 172, 427, 187, at levels ranging from + 6.6 to + 12.7 ft.
[69] Loci 459, 121, 223, 344, 56.

was bone working, though very few finished articles in this material have been recovered. Perhaps it would be more correct to accept the view of Colonel Sewell that the horns of the sambar deer were used in medicine,[70] in which case the places at which these horns were found at Chanhu-daro, some of them bearing saw-cuts, may have been the positions of druggist shops.[71] Very few ivory objects were found, and the working of this material does not appear to have been extensively practised.

Shell-working was certainly carried on, but only in a small degree, most of the evidence coming from the northern part of the mound. Four unfinished bangles (Pl. XC, 15) were found at locus 181 in Square 9/E, and unfinished shell dishes came from Squares 7/D, 8/C, 8/D, 8/E, and 9/C.[72] Two shell balls (Pl. LIX, 14, 15), apparently unfinished, were unearthed in Squares 8/C and 9/D.[73] The raw material for this work, the untouched shell (Pl. XC, 1), was often found; univalve shells with marked protuberances appeared in room 215 and other parts of Square 9/D. Shell was also used, though not in large quantities, for beads of the wafer type.

The white paste plaques (as Pl. XCI, 21, 22) that came from near locus 137 in Square 9/E show signs of being used in the process of glazing; it will be noted that they were found in the bead-making quarter of the city. Similar plaques which had evidently been washed down were unearthed in Trenches C(2), D(1), G(1), and E(1). Judging from the number of glazed beads that were found, the art of glazing must have been extensively practised at Chanhu-daro.

Square 6/C

Animal figure (2721, Pl. LV, 7). Locus 266. Level: + 9.0 ft.
Drain-pipe (2720, Pl. LXXXVIII, 17). Locus 266. Level: + 8.5 ft.

Square 6/E

Weight (3164, Pl. XCI, 32). Locus 431. Level: + 10.1 ft.
Scale-beam (2601, Pls. LXXI, 1; LXXVI, 18). Locus 330. Level: + 9.2 ft.

Square 6/F

Copper ring (3411, Pl. LXXIII, 10). Locus 434. Level: + 7.1 ft.

Square 7/C

Pottery bulla (1895, Pl. LXXXVIII, 3). Locus 98. Level: + 12.0 ft.
Pottery jar (4398, Pl. XXIX, 4). Locus 102. Level: + 9.6 ft.
Pottery group (3489, Pl. XXVIII, 30-32). Locus 461. Level: + 9.1 ft.
Pottery bowl (3490, Pl. XXVII, 64). Locus 461. Level: + 9.1 ft.
Knife (3496, Pl. LXXII, 4). Locus 238. Level: + 8.8 ft.
Chisel (3494, Pl. LXX, 8). Locus 238. Level: + 7.5 ft.
Shell ornament (3685, Pl. LXXVIII, 13). Locus 461. Level: + 7.5 ft.
Pottery table (3740, Pl. XCI, 2). Locus 98. Level: + 7.2 ft.

---

[70] *Mohenjo-daro and the Indus Civilization*, p. 672.
[71] Squares 8/C, 8/E, 8/F, and 9/D.
[72] Loci 321, 153, 197, 142, 103, 228; from levels ranging from + 6.9 to + 10.1 ft. Pl. XC, 3, 4, 9, 10.
[73] Loci 215, 297.

Pottery rattle (4300, Pl. LXI, 2). Locus 267. Level: + 7.2 ft.
Toy ram (4134, Pl. LVIII, 12). Locus 267. Level: + 7.2 ft.
Steatite seal (3737, Pl. LI, 6). Locus 459. Level: + 7.0 ft.
Cut brick (4310, Pl. XCII, 34). Locus 134. Level: + 6.9 ft.
Frag. incised dish (4272, Pl. XXXVIII, 25). Locus 134. Level: + 6.8 ft.
Oval pottery dish (4468, Pl. XXXIX, 18). Locus 102. Level: + 6.8 ft.
Painted sherd (4474, Pl. XXXIII, 17). Locus 269. Level: + 6.7 ft.
Net weight (4565, Pl. XCII, 14). Locus 463. Level: + 6.4 ft.

Square 7/D

Pottery jar (2709, Pl. XXIX, 42). Locus 272. Level: + 9.6 ft.
Pottery jar (2708, Pl. XXIX, 41). Locus 272. Level: + 9.4 ft.
Painted sherd (3472, Pl. XXX, 3). Locus 271. Level: + 9.2 ft.
Painted sherd (2710, Pl. XXXVI, 19). Locus 272. Level: + 9.0 ft.
Animal figure (3513, Pl. LV, 8). Locus 319. Level: + 8.0 ft.
Painted sherd (4410, Pl. XXXVII, 34, a). Locus 271. Level: + 7.2 ft.
Painted sherd (4363, Pl. XXXVI, 3). Locus 321. Level: + 7.1 ft.
Pottery handled cup (3700, Pl. XXV, 58). Locus 321. Level: + 7.1 ft.
Shell dish (4359, Pl. XC, 4). Locus 321. Level: + 7.1 ft.
Pottery ram's head (4271, Pl. LVIII, 16). Locus 271. Level: + 6.8 ft.
Pottery bulla (3779, Pl. LXXXVIII, 2). Locus 271. Level: + 6.7 ft.

Square 7/E

Pottery draughtsman (1780, Pl. LIX, 21). Locus 88. Level: + 10.8 ft.
Pottery bowl (3287, Pl. XXVII, 58). Locus 97. Level: + 10.6 ft.
Decorated carnelian bead (2485, Pl. LXXIX, 3). Locus 278. Level: + 9.8 ft.
Pottery group (3283, Pl. XXVIII, 18-23). Locus 276. Level: + 9.4 ft.
Pottery group (3150, Pl. XXVIII, 35-37). Locus 306. Level: + 8.0 ft.
Pottery figurine (4070, Pl. LIII, 2). Locus 88. Level: + 7.9 ft.
Pottery cone (3414, Pl. LX, 35). Locus 302. Level: + 7.7 ft.
Pottery toy (3303, Pl. LIX, 2). Locus 300. Level: + 7.6 ft.
Decorated carnelian bead (3354, Pl. LXXIX, 6). Locus 278. Level: + 7.5 ft.
Pottery figurine (3454, Pl. LIV, 4). Locus 324. Level: + 7.5 ft.
Toy chariot (4533, Pl. LVIII, 13). Locus 121. Level: + 6.9 ft.
Shell cones (3262, a, b, Pl. LX, 24, 30). Locus 121. Level: + 6.9 ft.

Square 7/F

Painted sherd (3183, Pl. XXXVII, 19). Locus 119. Level: + 10.6 ft.
Pottery bowl (3109, Pl. XXVII, 51). Locus 147. Level: + 10.0 ft.
Pottery figurine (2423, Pl. LIII, 7). Locus 118. Level: + 9.8 ft.
Copper knife (2663, Pl. LXXII, 5). Locus 189. Level: + 8.8 ft.
Bone paddle (3031, Pl. XC, 23). Locus 147. Level: + 8.7 ft.
Storage jar (3153, A, Pl. XXXV, 2). Locus 110. Level: + 8.7 ft.
Pottery bowl (2829, Pl. XXVII, 60). Locus 147. Level: + 8.7 ft.
Pottery jar-stand (4296, Pl. XXVI, 8). Locus 158. Level: + 8.6 ft.
Painted jar (4975, Pl. XXVI, 82). Locus 298. Level: + 8.1 ft.
Copper chisel (3149, Pl. LXXVI, 9). Locus 119. Level: + 8.0 ft.
Pottery jar (5007, Pl. XXIX, 43, a). Locus 188. Level: + 7.9 ft.
Pottery feeding-cup (4880, Pl. XXXIX, 21). Locus 440. Level: + 7.7 ft.
Pottery figurine (3201, Pl. LIV, 1). Locus 440. Level: + 7.6 ft.
Pottery jar-cover (4810, Pl. XXVI, 54). Locus 331. Level: + 7.5 ft.
Pottery whistle (4680, Pl. LIX, 19). Locus 158. Level: + 7.2 ft.
Steatite seal (3359, Pl. LII, 3). Locus 110. Level: + 7.1 ft.

Pottery figurine (3366, Pl. LIV, 10). Locus 331. Level: + 7.0 ft.
Pottery figurine (3739, Pl. LIV, 11). Locus 240. Level: + 7.0 ft.
Painted sherd (3213, Pl. XXXVI, 24). Locus 331. Level: + 6.9 ft.
Painted sherd (4525, Pl. XXXI, 22). Locus 346. Level: + 6.9 ft.
Copper arrowhead (3309, Pl. LXXIII, 14). Locus 346. Level: + 6.7 ft.
Pottery cosmetic jar (3302, Pl. XXVII, 70). Locus 443. Level: + 6.7 ft.

Square 8/B

Pottery bowl (4403, Pl. XXVII, 49). Locus 232. Level: + 9.7 ft.
Faience gamesman (2400, Pl. LX, 10). Locus 285. Level: + 9.6 ft.
Metal hoard (2365, Pl. LXXV, 1-10). Locus 284. Level: + 9.5 ft.
Bronze knife (2365, K, Pl. LXXVI, 25). Locus 284. Level: + 9.5 ft.
Bronze knife (2931, Pl. LXX, 25). Locus 285. Level: + 8.2 ft.
Net-weight (4367, Pl. XCII, 9). Locus 235. Level: + 7.7 ft.
Steatite button (3673, Pl. LXXVIII, 9). Locus 233. Level: + 7.6 ft.
Pottery tube (4238, Pls. LXXXVIII. 12; XC, 24). Locus 449. Level: + 7.6 ft.
Decorated carnelian bead (3506, Pl. LXXIX, 11). Locus 451. Level: + 7.5 ft.
Arrowhead (3446, B, Pl. LXXIII, 3). Locus 447. Level: + 7.0 ft.
Arrowhead (3444, A, Pl. LXXIII, 2). Locus 447. Level: + 7.0 ft.

Square 8/C

Painted sherd (3280, Pl. XXXVI, 22). Locus 152. Level: + 10.9 ft.
Pottery jar-stand (2665, Pl. XXVI, 4). Locus 167. Level: + 10.9 ft.
Steatite seal (2467, Pl. LII, 26). Locus 151. Level: + 10.5 ft.
Stone gamesman (2573, Pl. LX, 5). Locus 170. Level: + 10.3 ft.
Frag. stone dish (2984, Pl. XXIX, 47). Locus 308. Level: + 10.0 ft.
Decorated carnelian bead (2513, Pl. LXXIX, 14). Locus 226. Level: + 9.6 ft.
Copper ornament (2596, Pl. LXXVIII, 2). Locus 297. Level: + 9.3 ft.
Tube-drill (2596, O, Pl. LXXX, 9). Locus 297. Level: + 9.3 ft.
Large pottery pan (2596, Pl. XXIX, 37). Locus 297. Level: + 9.3 ft.
Painted jar (4362, Pl. XXVIII, 69). Locus 152. Level: + 8.5 ft.
Copper knife (3322, Pl. LXXI, 8). Locus 297. Level: + 8.0 ft.
Mace-head (3684, Pl. LXXXIX, 22). Locus 394. Level: + 7.9 ft.
Pottery bowl (4571, Pl. XXVII, 65). Locus 394. Level: + 7.5 ft.
Pottery gamesman (3694, Pl. LX, 3). Locus 308. Level: + 7.5 ft.
Animal figure (3781, Pl. LVI, 12). Locus 289. Level: + 7.4 ft.
Painted sherd (4301, Pl. XXXVII, 42). Locus 289. Level: + 7.4 ft.
Perforated pottery jar (3536, Pl. XXVIII, 62). Locus 295. Level: + 7.4 ft.
Hone (3563, Pl. XCI, 36). Locus 393. Level: + 7.3 ft.
Pottery whistle (4355, Pl. LIX, 18). Locus 170. Level: + 7.3 ft.
Steatite seal (3485, A, Pl. LI, 30). Locus 231. Level: + 7.2 ft.

Square 8/D

Sherd (2886, Pl. XXVI, 67, a). Locus 290. Level: + 9.9 ft.
Copper arrowhead (2571, Pl. LXXIII, 15). Locus 129. Level: + 9.6 ft.
Toy ram (2937, Pl. LVIII, 11). Locus 288. Level: + 8.7 ft.
Painted sherd (4848, Pl. XXXI, 8). Locus 176. Level: + 8.1 ft.
Painted sherd (4677, Pl. XXXVII, 33). Locus 176. Level: + 8.0 ft.
Pottery tube (4564, Pl. XC, 25). Locus 89. Level: + 7.5 ft.
Pottery jar-stand (1795, Pl. XXVI, 5). Locus 311. Level: + 7.2 ft.
Pottery feeding-cup (4351, Pl. XXV, 56). Locus 311. Level: + 7.2 ft.
Fish-hook (3641, Pl. LXXIII, 17). Locus 311. Level: + 7.1 ft .
Whetstone (3693, Pl. LXXXIX, 21). Locus 311. Level: + 7.1 ft.

Square 8/E

Painted sherd (2895, Pl. XXX, 10). Locus 113. Level: + 10.1 ft.
Pottery figurine (2683, Pl. LIV, 2). Locus 91. Level: + 10.0 ft.
Painted sherd (3434, Pl. XXXVII, 17). Locus 185. Level: + 9.8 ft.
Jar-stopper (2897, Pl. XXIX, 73). Locus 155. Level: + 9.8 ft.
Bronze chisel (2842, Pl. LXX, 6). Locus 114. Level: + 9.1 ft.
Steatite seal (2848, Pl. LII, 2). Locus 425. Level: + 8.0 ft.
Copper razor (2850, Pl. LXXVI, 34). Locus 177. Level: + 8.0 ft.
Pottery cup (3481, Pl. XXXIX, 16). Locus 103. Level: + 7.9 ft.
Pottery figurine (3190, Pl. LIII, 6). Locus 280. Level: + 7.1 ft.
Weight (3189, Pl. XCI, 29). Locus 280. Level: + 7.0 ft.
Pottery figurine (3186, Pl. LIV, 3). Locus 280. Level: + 7.0 ft.
Pottery jar-cover (3080, Pl. XXIX, 53). Locus 425. Level: + 6.8 ft.

Square 8/F

Animal figure (1971, Pl. LV, 15). Locus 149. Level: + 10.7 ft.
Frag. faience bangle (1961, Pl. LXXVII, 5). Locus 117. Level: + 9.9 ft.
Painted sherd (3338, Pl. XXX, 23). Locus 145. Level: + 9.9 ft.
Pottery cosmetic jar (4093, Pl. XXVII, 72). Locus 115. Level: + 8.0 ft.
Animal figure (3989, Pl. LVI, 7). Locus 259. Level: + 7.0 ft.
Clay model axe (3170, Pl. LXXXIX, 30). Locus 418. Level: + 7.0 ft.
Metal objects (3145, Pl. LXXVI, 1, 2). Locus 417. Level: + 7.1 ft.
Steatite seal (3200, Pl. LI, 7). Locus 344. Level: + 6.9 ft.
Copper razor (3214, Pl. LXXIII, 22). Locus 148. Level: + 6.8 ft.
Pottery net-sinker (3171, Pl. XCI, 16). Locus 115. Level: + 6.8 ft.
Feeding-cup (4074, Pl. XXXIX, 20). Locus 116. Level: + 6.7 ft.
Pottery perforated jar (4073, Pl. XXVI, 3). Locus 116. Level: + 6.6 ft.
Pottery toy-cart (5008, Pl. LVIII, 5). Locus 115. Level: + 6.6 ft.
Steatite seal (3049, Pl. LI, 16). Locus 115. Level: + 6.5 ft.
Flint saw (3162, Pl. XCIII, 27). Locus 115. Level: + 6.4 ft.
Copper knife (3147, Pl. LXXII, 3). Locus 260. Level: + 6.2 ft.
Brick runnel (4609, Pl. XCI, 18). Locus 414. Level: + 4.2 ft.

Square 9/C

Ivory object (2351, Pl. LXXXIX, 15). Locus 190. Level: + 10.5 ft.
Ornament (2385, Pl. LXXVIII, 1). Locus 263. Level: + 10.4 ft.
Pottery cup (2816, Pl. XXVI, 60). Locus 228. Level: + 10.3 ft.
Bronze casting (2495, Pl. LXX, 27). Locus 208. Level: + 9.9 ft.
Pottery group (2594, Pl. XXVIII, 38-41). Locus 228. Level: + 9.9 ft.
Bead-hone (3013, Pl. XCIII, 11). Locus 208. Level: + 9.7 ft.
Pottery bowl (2694, Pl. XXVII, 67). Locus 205. Level: + 9.3 ft.
Copper arrow-head (2540, Pl. LXXIII, 4). Locus 208. Level: + 9.1 ft.
Pottery bowl (2775, Pl. XXVII, 30). Locus 208. Level: + 9.1 ft.
Bronze chisel (2469, Pl. LXX, 9). Locus 294. Level: + 8.9 ft.
Bronze chisel (2645, Pl. LXX, 1). Locus 292. Level: + 8.6 ft.
Steatite seal (3154, Pl. LII, 18). Locus 395. Level: + 7.7 ft.
Pottery rattle (4978, Pl. LXI, 3). Locus 395. Level: + 7.3 ft.
Pottery kohl-jar (3484, Pl. XXVII, 92). Locus 291. Level: + 7.1 ft.
Bronze axe (3697, Pl. LXXI, 4). Locus 205. Level: + 7.1 ft.
Pottery insect cage (4230, Pl. XXVII, 79). Locus 291. Level: + 7.1 ft.
Ivory comb (3488, Pl. LXXXIX, 12). Locus 205. Level: + 7.1 ft.
Fish-hook (3487, Pls. LXXIII, 18; LXXVI, 15). Locus 292. Level: + 7.0 ft.

Painted jar (4229, Pl. XXVI, 58). Locus 291. Level: + 7.0 ft.
Stone drill-head (4687, Pl. XCII, 3). Locus 206. Level: + 6.8 ft.
Pottery whistle (4646, Pl. LIX, 20). Locus 389. Level: + 6.7 ft.

Square 9/D

Bronze chisel (2295, Pl. LXXVI, 10). Locus 262. Level: + 10.7 ft.
Decorated carnelian bead (2326, Q, Pl. LXXIX, 13). Locus 215. Level: + 10.4 ft.
Lump of crystal (2326, E, Pl. XCIII, 1). Locus 215. Level: + 10.4 ft.
Bead-tool (2375, Pl. LXXX, 3). Locus 215. Level: + 10.3 ft.
Bead-tool (2304, Pl. LXXX, 6). Locus 215. Level: + 10.2 ft.
Pottery jar (4406, Pl. XXVI, 72). Locus 264. Level: + 10.0 ft.
Faience gamesman (2419, Pl. LX, 11). Locus 287. Level: + 9.9 ft.
Shell ladle (Pl. 2453, Pl. XC, 13). Locus 179. Level: + 9.8 ft.
Drain-pipe (3464, Pl. LXXXVIII, 16). Locus 95. Level: + 9.5 ft.
Copper knife (2408, Pl. LXX, 24). Locus 215. Level: + 9.4 ft.
Decorated carnelian bead (2434, Pl. LXXIX, 2). Locus 215. Level: + 9.4 ft.
Ivory peg (2405, Pl. LXXXIX, 7). Locus 215. Level: + 9.3 ft.
Pottery bangle (3002, Pl. XC, 34). Locus 139. Level: + 9.1 ft.
Steatite seal (2597, Pl. LII, 1). Locus 192. Level: + 8.9 ft.
Steatite seal (2558, Pl. LII, 12). Locus 106. Level: + 8.8 ft.
Pottery jar (2988, Pl. XXVI, 69). Locus 264. Level: + 8.5 ft.
Mace-head (2838, Pl. LXXXIX, 26). Locus 139. Level: + 8.4 ft.
Bronze chisel (2642, Pl. LXX, 7). Locus 174. Level: + 8.3 ft.
Steatite seal (3168, Pl. LII, 4). Locus 211. Level: + 8.1 ft.
Copper ring (3167, Pl. LXXIII, 12). Locus 211. Level: + 8.1 ft.
Painted sherd (4047, Pl. XXXI, 15). Locus 174. Level: + 8.0 ft.
Copper arrowhead (3208, Pl. LXXIII, 16). Locus 209. Level: + 7.6 ft.
Round pottery plaque (3500, Pl. XCII, 18). Locus 287. Level: + 7.1 ft.
Animal figure (4252, Pl. LVI, 3). Locus 133. Level: + 7.0 ft.
Painted sherd (4656, Pl. XXXIII, 8). Locus 195. Level: + 7.0 ft.
Cut sherd (4340, Pl. XXXVIII, 11). Locus 133. Level: + 6.9 ft.
Fish-hook (3038, Pl. LXXIII, 7). Locus 139. Level: + 6.9 ft.
Pottery cone (3461, Pl. LX, 27). Locus 283. Level: + 6.8 ft.
Painted-sherd (5429, Pl. XXXVII, 44). Locus 95. Level: + 6.7 ft.
Pottery group (4657, Pl. XXVIII, 45-48). Locus 209. Level: + 5.9 ft.
Frag. incised dish (4414, Pl. XXXVIII, 18). Locus 192. Level: + 4.2 ft.

Square 9/E

Decorated-carnelian bead (2797, Pl. LXXIX, 10). Locus 125. Level: + 9.7 ft.
Pottery bowl (4402, Pl. XXVII, 56). Locus 254. Level: + 9.6 ft.
Copper razor (2608, Pl. LXXIII, 25). Locus 126. Level: + 8.5 ft.
Cut sherd (4036, Pl. XXXVIII, 7). Locus 201. Level: + 8.4 ft.
Spear-head (2602, Pl. LXXI, 12). Locus 137. Level: + 8.3 ft.
Frag. pottery bangle (2747, Pl. LXXVII, 11). Locus 128. Level: + 8.3 ft.
Weight (2867, Pl. XCI, 31). Locus 127. Level: + 8.3 ft.
Frag. incised dish (4465, Pl. XXXVIII, 19). Locus 111. Level: + 7.5 ft.
Flint drill (2941, Pl. XCIII, 7). Locus 85. Level: + 7.4 ft.
Shell ladle (4046, Pl. XC, 17). Locus 171. Level: + 7.2 ft.
Round pottery plaque (4541, Pl. XCII, 23). Locus 111. Level: + 7.2 ft.
Copper razor (2846, Pl. LXXVI, 36). Locus 224. Level: + 6.9 ft.
Faience jar (2936, Pl. LXXXIX, 2). Locus 224. Level: + 6.9 ft.
Scale-beam (2964, Pl. LXXI, 3). Locus 171. Level: + 6.9 ft.
Copper razor (2846, Pl. LXXIII, 26). Locus 224. Level: + 6.9 ft.

Faience bangle (2924, Pl. XC, 37). Locus 198. Level: + 6.8 ft.
Pottery jar (3419, Pl. XXIX, 46). Locus 171. Level: + 6.5 ft.

Square 9/F

Hone (3278, Pl. XCI, 37). Locus 184. Level: + 10.7 ft.
Painted sherd (3435, Pl. XXXVII, 22). Locus 265. Level: + 10.1 ft.
Brick runnel (4608, Pl. XCI, 17). Locus 410. Level: + 9.5 ft.
Pottery cone (4520, Pl. LX, 26). Locus 258. Level: + 8.6 ft.
Triangular plaque (4521, Pl. XCII, 26). Locus 258. Level: + 8.5 ft.
Pottery tube (4196, Pl. LXXXVIII, 7). Locus 401. Level: + 8.2 ft.
Cut brick (4021, Pl. XCII, 8). Locus 406. Level: + 8.0 ft.
Steatite seal (2845, Pl. LI, 19). Locus 405. Level: + 8.0 ft.
Flint drill (2957, Pl. XCIII, 8). Locus 255. Level: + 6.9 ft.
Animal figure (3120, Pl. LV, 14). Locus 407. Level: + 6.4 ft.
Decorated carnelian bead (3999, Pl. LXXIX, 7). Locus 473. Level: + 3.2 ft.

Square 9/G

Bronze chisel (3152, Pl. LXX, 11). Locus 439. Level: + 7.5 ft.

Square 10/C

Steatite seal (3326, Pl. LII, 10). Locus 385. Level: + 6.9 ft.
Pottery cosmetic jar (4232, Pl. XXVII, 78). Locus 385. Level: + 6.9 ft.
Pottery figurine (3418, Pl. LIV, 8). Locus 381. Level: + 6.8 ft.

Square 10/D

Painted bowl (4666, Pl. XXVIII, 64). Locus 248. Level: + 6.9 ft.
Steatite seal (2603, Pl. LII, 13). Locus 362. Level: + 6.8 ft.
Pottery jar-cover (2756, Pl. XXIX, 62). Locus 362. Level: + 6.7 ft.

Square 10/E

Bone pulley (2457, Pl. XCI, 5). Locus 230. Level: + 8.8 ft.
Pottery jar-cover (3409, Pl. XXIX, 66). Locus 261. Level: + 7.5 ft.
Ivory die (2670, Pl. LX, 16). Locus 359. Level: + 7.1 ft.

Square 10/F

Steatite seal (3318, Pl. LII, 28). Locus 423. Level: + 6.7 ft.

CHAPTER V

MOUND I

Mound I is only a little over 150 feet south-west of Mound II (Pl. II), and, though it covers a smaller area, it was only a foot under the height of the latter mound.[1] Its sides, like those of Mound II, are steep and deeply fissured by rains on the north and west (Pl. IX, f), but inclined gently on the south and west, though here, too, deep furrows have been cut by water.

Except for several exploratory trenches cut by Mr. Majumdar in 1931, the mound was untouched when we commenced work upon it late in the season. Our own examination of it was necessarily very brief and confined to a portion of the summit only. There appears to be no doubt that Mound I was originally a part of Mound II and that a flood, or a series of floods, separated them from one another.[2] The deep cutting that we made close to the south-western side of Mound II and extending into that mound itself revealed traces of buildings obviously connected at one time with masonry lying on the outskirts of Mound I. These buildings had been partly swept away and then covered beneath a thick layer of alluvium.

We commenced our examination of this mound on the morning of February 19th, 1936, but as it was closely surrounded by private land we were not able to deposit the spoil earth far enough away; for this reason we could not employ as many men for the work as we should have wished. In another season arrangements could be made with the owner of the adjacent land to allow us to use part of it as a dumping ground, thus giving us plenty of space in which to work.

It would appear that the mound was occupied solely by people of the Harappā Culture. A few sherds of the Jhukar people were unearthed,[3] but so few in number compared with the large quantities found on Mound II that they had probably been left there by casual visitors. It is, however, impossible to be certain on this point until more extensive digging has been done.

On reference to the plan in Pl. II, it will be seen that one house occupied most of Square 12/K with, as shown by the drainage system, a lane on both its eastern and southern sides. The entrance from the street on the south was 3 feet 7½ inches wide and each of its well made jambs still stood 2 feet 6 inches high.[4] The door-way led into room 27, which averaged 7 feet 11 inches in length by 5 feet 6 inches in width. The well preserved eastern wall of this room still stood 4 feet 4 inches high (Pl. XXII, a, e).

An unbonded partition wall separated room 27 from room 44, which was nearly square though inaccurately built. A doorway on the northern side of this room was 3 feet 2 inches

[1] It was 22.2 ft., above datum at its northern end.

[2] For the relation of this mound to Mound II, see Majumdar, *Explorations in Sind*, pl. IV (b).

[3] Pls. XXXIX, 9, 13; XL, 18, XLI, 4, 35, XLII, 15, 21, 22, XLIII, 9, XLV, 21, XLVI, 3, 9, 29, XLVIII, 4.

[4] Its sill was 15.5 ft. above datum.

wide, and its sill, which was still in excellent condition, stood 15 feet above datum. The walls here averaged 3 feet in height and were in a strikingly good state of preservation, considering that they were only one brick thick and lay but a few inches below the surface of the mound.

Room 15, 29 was not so well preserved, especially on the western side, although the northern and eastern walls averaged 2 to 4 feet in height. This room opened into the large room 20 through a doorway estimated to have been 4 feet wide; both the northern jamb of the door and its sill were in a ruinous condition. As far as we could tell the sill seems to have been at about the same level as the other door-sills in the house. The centre of this last room yielded a pottery stand (5029, Pls. LXXXIX, 4, XCII, 36), a large round stone (4754, Pl. XCI, 45) like some found in Mound II, and a fragment of a faience bangle (4429, Pl. XC, 38). All these were at the level + 14.0 feet. A pottery grating (5030, Pl. XCII, 20) came from the south-eastern corner of this room at the same level.

Pl. XXII, f (extreme right hand side) shows how badly denuded was the large chamber 20, 30, 60. No definite doorways could be traced save the one leading from room 29 and another, a very narrow one, entering the paved room 58 on the east. This room was possibly divided at one time into two apartments by a wall one brick in thickness. The eastern end of this partition wall when cleared stood a little under a foot high, but it petered out towards the west. Its foundations were at the level + 14.2 feet, and part of it rested on another thin wall, not in alignment with it, which has yet to be examined. Broken fragments of paving at locus 60 in the south-eastern corner of the room lay 14.3 feet above datum, i. e., only a few inches above the foundations of the near-by walls.[5]

The small room 58 was much more interesting. It must have been entered from the west and through or over a wall which had been destroyed to below pavement level, for no other entrance could be found. It measures 6 feet 10 inches long by 5 feet 5 inches wide, and was at one time paved all over with one course of bricks laid on their flats. These bricks were of various sizes and had evidently been taken at random from other buildings, possibly from some distance off. The pavement itself was 14.8 feet above datum, and the walls surrounding it stood for the most part nearly 2 feet high.[6] The cell-like room 14 contained a wheel from a model cart (5059, Pl. LVIII, 23) and a gamesman (4430, Pl. LX, 9), both lying at the level + 14.1 feet. The western wall of room 58 was not shared by the eastern wall of room 60, although it is difficult to see any reason why it should not have been.

In the north-western corner of room 15 was a block of masonry of nearly solid construction, which, in all probability, had been built to support a heavy roof beam.[7]

West of room 20, 30 were the remains of a large courtyard whose walls were rather more substantial than those of the house itself. As will be seen in Pl. XXII, c (distance on left), little of this courtyard remained, but there was enough to show that it had been about 18 feet square.

[5] These averaged 14.8 ft. above datum.

[6] Their foundations were 13.9 ft. above datum.

[7] The top of this was 16.1 ft. above datum; its foundations were 2 ft. deeper.

Another house (Sq. 12/J) lying to the east of the one just described and separated from it by a narrow street was so close to the edge of the mound as to be in a very ruinous condition (Pl. XXII, f). Even in its original state this house must have been a ramshackle affair. The little patch of paving, one brick thick, at the level + 13.9 feet in the north-western corner of room 25 was all that remained of a privy. It had formerly been surrounded by a wall, about 5 inches thick, enclosing a space 3 feet 4 inches square. The owner of this house evidently kept an animal or two, for a round manger was unearthed near locus 54. This was 16 inches in diameter and built of bricks 10½ inches long, set on their ends (Pls. XVI, g, XXII, b).[8]

Pl. XXII, a, b show the condition of the masonry on this north-eastern side of the mound.

In a narrow street along the southern side of this house was a brick drain, with a channel 8½ inches wide by 6 inches deep. But the width of the street was uncertain, because there was no wall on the opposite side. The drain, and presumably the street as well, turned southwards at right angles and then again at right angles to the west. This latter part of the street was better preserved; it was 3 feet 8 inches and 4 feet 8 inches at its eastern and western ends respectively. Here the channel of the drain was 7¼ inches wide by 5½ inches deep, the sides being of bricks laid on their longer edges and covered by bricks laid on their flats. The western end of this water channel could not be traced; both it and the ground in which it lay had subsided badly owing to floods. The walls of the houses on either side of this little street were only a brick thick (10½ inches) and averaged 3 to 4 feet higher than the cover of the drain, which, when in use, must have been a few inches below the earthen surface of the street.[9]

Room 21, 47 of the house on the southern side of this street was very dilapidated. Its western and southern sides measured 9 feet 8 inches and 3 feet 5 inches respectively, and in the shorter side there was a wide entrance into room 36, 49 (Pl. XXII, c, centre). This second room was only 4 feet 8 inches wide at its southern end, but the western wall, which was roughly built of bricks laid on their longer edges as headers and their flats as stretchers, was 18 feet 5 inches in length (Pl. XXII, d). In this wall was a doorway, about 4 feet in width, whose sill was missing. The length of room 36, 49 makes it probable that it had originally been divided into two parts with an entry through the partition. A narrow, projecting footing inside the remains of the eastern wall was only three bricks high and possibly marked the presence of an earlier wall.[10] In front of the wrecked doorway here a brick, used as a door-socket (5060, Pl. XCI, 14), was unearthed in locus 23.

Room 46 averaged 8 feet 8 inches long by 7 feet wide, but though the walls surrounding it reached an average of 2 feet in height, no doorway could be seen in them (Pl. XXII, c, background). Possibly this little enclosure had been filled up to make a sleeping platform, like those used in modern Sindhi villages, but in this case it was difficult to see why its

[8] The top of this manger was 14.6 ft. above datum.
[9] The bricks used in these walls measured 10½ x 5¼ x 2½ ins.
[10] The wall here stood 12 ins. high above this footing which was at the level of + 15.9 ft.

foundations should be 13.4 feet above datum and agreeing with the same level as that of the other walls near-by.

It is difficult to say whether rooms 38, 45 and 61 (Pl. XXII, c, left middle distance) formed part of one or two houses, for only about 12 feet remained of the long wall bounding them on the south (Sq. 12/K) and this was only one brick high.[11] Room 38 contained an unfinished mace-head (5218, Pl. LXXXIX, 19) at the level + 13.0 feet.

Locus 62 was, perhaps, another sleeping platform; its walls, also one brick thick, showed no signs of a doorway. They stood, however, only three courses high, and it is possible that an entrance may have existed above this level.[12]

The long wall at locus 61, a brick in thickness, stood a little under 2 feet high with foundations at + 14.4 feet level. East of this wall at locus 40 was a large stretch of pavement, 11 feet in length, E.-W., and 7 feet 7 inches wide. It had been enclosed by a skirting of bricks laid on their longer edges[13] and was probably used as an ablution platform. The walls around it had long been removed to serve other building purposes.[14]

On the north-western corner of this last feature lay a curious structure, a brick pit, 3 feet 3½ inches long inside, 1 foot 4 inches wide, and 1 foot deep. It was still partly covered with two courses of brick set corbel-wise, the bricks overlapping about an inch. This may have been filled in and used as a seat by the bather or as a cess pit of a later date than the pavement on which it stood.

The short length of drain at the same corner of this pavement had no connection with either floor or pit; it was at a different level, with its flow towards instead of away from the paving. Its channel was 5 inches in width and depth,[15] and it evidently formed part of a system of drainage awaiting clearance at a lower level.

Immediately east of the long room 36, 49 (Sq. 13/K, locus 23) described above, the remains of an elaborate drainage system were disclosed. Here was a cess pit in the street, 2 feet 10 inches long by 1 foot 4 inches wide inside, with walls half-a-brick thick.[16] Beneath this sump, but evidently associated with it, was a brick channel, 5 inches wide and deep, with its southern end curving towards the south-east (Pl. XXII, c). This drain sloped considerably from its southern end and doubtless drained the ruined structures whose remains are situated in loci 64, 65. A small pavement, also badly preserved, lay close to the eastern side of this drain and immediately adjacent to the cess pit. It was 3 feet 10 inches in width but only 2 feet remained of its original length,[17] and the traces of a low brick skirting around it showed that it had been used as a bathroom or privy. From locus 11 here came the shell ladle (4698) illustrated in Pl. XC, 14, together with a copper or bronze ring (4312, Pl. LXXIII, 11), both from the level + 14.1 feet.

Further south again, between loci 10 and 12 (Sq. 13/K), another short length of drain

[11] 13.3 ft. above datum.
[12] The top of these walls were 13.3 ft., above datum.
[13] Level + 14.9 ft.
[14] Possibly the pavement itself was not removed as the bricks were considered impure.
[15] The floor of this drain averaged + 13.7 ft.
[16] It was 2 ft. deep and its foundations were 13.2 ft. above datum.
[17] Its surface was 14.2 ft. above datum.

was unearthed, evidently a continuation of the system already described.[18] Locus 10 produced a small painted jar (5214, Pl. XXXIX, 25) and a copper or bronze axe (4898, Pl. LXXI, 5) at + 14.0 and + 12.9 respectively. From a higher level (+ 16.2 feet) came the fossil shell (4619) shown in Pl. XCIII, 22.

Better built and thicker walls were encountered as we proceeded eastwards from this lane, but they were all in a grievously ruined condition. None the less, it was evident that this had been an important quarter on this mound. All these walls rested on débris of considerable thickness and were nowhere over 2 feet high, as will be seen in the photographs in Pl. XXII, c, e.[19] Other buildings undoubtedly lie beneath these remains, belonging to a separate and earlier occupation of this part of the site by the Harappā people.

Among these walls we found the remains of a privy at locus 57 (Sq. 13/J), consisting of a brick pavement, two courses thick, at the level + 15.6 feet. This pavement was drained by a small channel running to the east, of which only a length of 6 feet remained. In the close vicinity of these walls, two pieces of shell inlay (4831, 4602, Pl. XC, 7, 8), and a painted pottery rattle (5065, Pl. LXI, 5) were unearthed at levels between + 13.4 and + 14.2 feet.

From this preliminary survey of the uppermost occupation level of Mound I, we have come to the conclusion that the majority of the buildings on it could hardly have been higher than one storey. At the same time it is unlikely that the people who inhabited these houses were in the habit of sleeping on the roof, for not a single stairway was discovered. Yet despite their humble nature, these houses were as well drained and provided with the same conveniences as those of the better class dwellings on Mound II.

From the evidence afforded by objects unearthed in and outside their houses, there is no doubt that the summit of Mound I was occupied to the last by people of the Harappā Culture. These people probably lingered here until they gradually died out or left, family by family, to join more prosperous communities elsewhere. It is not impossible that the flooding of the country by the Indus was so extensive, so frequent, and so prolonged each time that the later inhabitants of Chanhu-daro were forced to make their way to lands of higher elevation, where they lived until their identity was lost and they became merged with people of a lower status of civilization. I am inclined to think that they retreated towards the east, for the hilly regions to the north and west would have had little attraction for an urban people accustomed to the comparative security of the plains.

Other parts of the excavated portion of Mound I yielded interesting objects which had evidently been thrown out of dismantled buildings by quarriers. The number of mace-heads found, some of which are unfinished, show that stone working was one of the crafts that were practised here. Another craft carried on in this part of Chanhu-daro was the making of faience objects such as buttons, nose or ear-plugs, and the like.

Square 12/J

Mace-head (5219, Pl. LXXXIX, 17). Locus 18. Level: + 13.3 ft.

---

[18] The channel of this was at + 13.7 ft.

[19] The average level of the foundations of these walls was + 13.7 ft.

Square 13/J

Weight (3882, Pl. LXXXIX, 11). Locus 6. Level: + 16.4 ft.
Weight (3822, Pl. LXXXIX, 10). Locus 3. Level: + 15.8 ft.
Seal (4596, Pl. LII, 25). Locus 2. Level: + 14.4 ft.
Stone stand (4589, Pl. XCII, 13). Locus 2. Level: + 14.3 ft.
Pottery cone (5242, Pl. LX, 32). Locus 3. Level: + 14.5 ft.

Square 13/K

Pottery cone (5320, Pl. LXXXVIII, 4). Locus 51. Level: + 12.6 ft.
Seal (3819, Pl. XLIX, 6, 6a). Locus 34. Level: + 13.6 ft.
Pottery whorl (5071, Pl. XCII, 7). Locus 34. Level: + 14.2 ft.
Chisel (5019, Pl. LXX, 14). Locus 34. Level: + 13.9 ft.
Mace-head (4775, Pl. LXXXIX, 20). Locus 37. Level: + 13.1 ft.
Gamesman (5307, Pl. LX, 1). Locus 67. Level: + 13.0 ft.
Kohl-jar (5199, Pl. XXXIX, 26). Locus 34. Level: + 12.9 ft.
Mace-head (5198, Pls. LXXXIX, 16; XCIII, 36). Locus 51. Level: + 12.8 ft.

CHAPTER VI

POTTERY OF THE HARAPPĀ CULTURE

This and the two following chapters deal with the pottery found in and around Mounds I and II at Chanhu-daro. The pieces are dealt with chronologically (i. e., finds from the lowest, and earliest, levels are described first) while, to avoid unnecessary detail, the specimens illustrated are set out in the catalogue at the end of this book, with the locus and level of each one, the colour of the clays, slips and paints, and other information.

No traces of an earlier occupation than that of the Harappā Culture have been discovered at Chanhu-daro, although in one part of the site,[1] as we have seen, a special search was being made for evidences of a still older civilization when the level of the sub-soil water, some 28 feet below the surrounding plain, was reached. It was obvious, however, that this level had risen very considerably since the Harappā people had inhabited the city at least 4,600 years ago, for their burnt brick buildings were still standing far below the surface of the water. Nevertheless, in spite of this difficulty, there remains a chance that evidences of the earlier culture already discovered by the late Mr. Majumdar at Amri in Sindh[2] may come to light at Chanhu-daro when work is resumed there under more favourable conditions. We have, at any rate, been fortunate enough to find traces of three distinct cultures which succeeded that of the Harappā civilization. This discovery is of some importance, for it throws light, to some small extent, on the dark period between the decline and fall of the Harappā Culture and the arrival in India of the Āryan speaking peoples,[3] who were destined to exercise such an enormous influence on the country of their adoption.

The earliest pottery of the Harappā Culture unearthed at Chanhu-daro is illustrated in Pls. XXV, 37, 38, 41, 50, XXVII, 1, 2, XXIX, 13, 32, XXXI, 2, 3, 5, 7, 11, XXXII, 5, XXXIV, 6, 7, XXXVI, 2, 38, XXXVII, 14, 25, 43, XXXVIII, 15, 22, 24, 27, 28. All these pieces were found at depths ranging from 15 to as much as 24.8 feet below datum level. Nos. XXV, 50 and XXIX, 13 are new to us. The incised dishes of food-stands seen in Pl. XXXVIII, 15, 23, 25 are very like specimens from low levels at Mohenjo-daro.[4]

The sherds of early date shown in Pl. XXXVIII, 26, 27, 29 are of particular interest and will be described more fully later. Reserved slip wares, to which type these three sherds belong, only occur in the lowest levels at Mohenjo-daro,[5] and they were similarly low down at Chanhu-daro. At the former site, however, only one slip was used, the contrast

[1] Known as the "Cutting" and situated on the south-western side of Mound II (Chap. II).

[2] *Explorations in Sind* (*Mem. Arch. Surv. Ind.*, No. 48).

[3] Estimated by some to have taken place about 1200-1500 B.C., but thought by others to have been even earlier.

[4] *F. E. M.* (Mackay, *Further Excavations at Mohenjo-daro*), pl. LXVII, 17, 18, 22, 25.

[5] *F. E. M.*, pp. 45, 184, 188, 652, 668. I have explained here how this reserved slip ware is related to that found in other countries.

being obtained by exposing the natural colour of the clay. At Chanhu-daro the effect was produced by superimposing one slip on another of a different colour.

Some of the painted sherds found in the lower levels bear unusual patterns as, for example, the disconnected motifs appearing on the rim of the broken vessel in Pls. XXXI, 7 and XXXVI, 38. This sherd was originally part of a carefully made dish or bowl of exceptional thinness; its section is shown just below the drawing in Pl. XXXI. The young pīpal plants, painted in a semi-conventionalized manner on the sherds in Pl. XXXI, 2, 3, 5, 11, are also quite unlike other representations of this favourite motif which have come to light either in the upper levels of Chanhu-daro or elsewhere.

The differences that it has been possible to point out, however, are too few to allow us to say with certainty at present that the wares from the lower levels are radically different from those of the upper strata, though there is no doubt that they are, in the main, superior in finish and painting. Apart from pottery, objects taken from the lower levels seem to be identical in form and workmanship with others found higher up, but when more of this early material has come to light it may then be possible to compare it closely with that of later date and to get some idea of the differences between the arts and crafts of the various periods. The culture as a whole will then appear in better perspective.

Clays and Materials

The clays used by the Chanhu-daro potters resemble those employed at Mohenjo-daro and Harappā. One is an alluvial material, tempered with mica, sand, and lime, which becomes pink or light red in colour when burnt. Mica is more often than not found naturally associated with sand in Sindh, but the lime was purposely added to the clay by the potter and occurs in appreciable quantities. In some cases the lime particles have swelled and made cavities in the surface of a jar.

Sometimes a clay that burnt a grey colour was used, although something may have been added to the raw material to produce this effect. The grey ware found at Chanhu-daro is frequently gritty to the touch and is often overloaded with lime and sand.[6] It is sometimes coated with a thick black slip (Pls. XXV, 9, XXVII, 25, XXIX, 3, XXXVIII, 12, 15) or with a dark grey one (Pls. XXV, 16, XXVI, 83). The dish in Pl. XXVII, 25 is dark grey outside and black within. The wares in Pls. XXV, 18, XXVII, 64, 92 have a polished surface. The last example, a kohl-pot, is again illustrated in Pl. XXXIX, 22. This particular type of ware was, however, far from common at Mohenjo-daro. At Chanhu-daro only a few specimens have been found, and, up to the present, none of them have appeared at a level lower than — 15.1 feet.

A dirty-looking, drab clay was used for the vessels in Pls. XXV, 24, XXVII, 4, 10, 11, 28, 32, XXIX, 39.

Slips

The slip usually employed is yellowish white or cream in colour and, when applied too thickly, is apt to scale. Some of the pottery has no slip at all, but the painted wares are

[6] Much more so than with the grey wares of Mohenjo-daro. This grittiness was particularly noticeable in the pottery shown in pls. XXVI, 33, 48, XXVII, 20, 21, 47, XXVIII, 48, 50.

normally coated with a red slip bearing an appreciable polish. Red-coloured slips are often found on otherwise undecorated pottery.

A pink-coloured slip was seen on the pieces illustrated in Pls. XXVII, 30, 39, 50, 51, 54, 71, 83, XXIX, 22, 33, XXXII, 7, XXXIV, 6, 10, 22, XXXIX, 19, and a brown one on the vessels and sherds in Pls. XXVII, 32, 86, XXIX, 16, 28, XXXVI, 24, XXXVIII, 5, 11. In Pl. XXVI, 72 this brown slip is applied over a red one, while in Pl. XXVIII, 60 a purple slip is used in the same way. The vessels in Pls. XXXI, 9 XXXVII, 27 have buff coloured slips. It is possible that the pink tint of some of the slips may have been due to excessive firing, but it is usually easy to see when this has occurred, for the colouring then tends to be very uneven.

Red and cream-coloured slips sometimes appear together on a jar, the red on the upper portion and the cream below. As a rule, the whole jar has been coated with the lighter slip while it was still on the wheel, and the red was added later.

Bright yellow and white slips decorate the sherd illustrated in line in Pl. XXXIII, 6 and in photograph in Pl. XXXVI, 23. This sherd, however, originally formed part of a jar painted in polychrome and is the only one of its kind and period unearthed at Chanhu-daro. It will be described later in the section dealing with painted pottery of this period.[7]

The pottery of the Harappā Period is adequately baked and fairly hard. Very few over-baked pieces have been found, proving that the Chanhu-daro potter knew how to manage his furnace. The great majority of the wares are wheel-made, but a considerable number of hand-made pieces were also unearthed. Some of these are of careful workmanship; others were obviously made and baked by children.

Trimming

Much of the pottery has been trimmed with some instrument before being fired. For some reason which is not yet clear the potter was not able to smooth the lower part of a jar while it was on the wheel and consequently this portion had to be scraped, sometimes very roughly, after the vessel was thrown. The wares of Mohenjo-daro show traces also of the same unequal work.[8]

A broken jar has often been trimmed by grinding down the rough edges so that it may be fit for use again. The tops of the small vessels seen in Pls. XXVI, 60, XXVII, 13, 16, 23, XXVIII, 67 and the base of the dish snapped from a food-stand in Pl. XXVII, 36 have all been treated in this way. Despite the obvious cheapness of the pottery, it was evidently thought worth while to spend some time and trouble on renovating these small pieces, rather than to throw them away as useless.

Repairs

Examples of more orthodox repairs have also been noted. For instance, the polychrome sherd in Pl. XXXVI, 23 has a small hole close to one of its edges, proving that the jar of which it once formed a part had been riveted or tied together with thongs. A large storage

[7] With this exception, yellow slips are only found on the Trihni and modern Sindhi wares.

[8] *F. E. M.*, pp. 179, 180.

jar, two pieces from which are illustrated in Pls. XXXVI, 4 and XXXVII, 20, had also been repaired in this way.[9]

Suspended Vessels

Small jars with holes bored in their rims so that they can be hung up are as well known at Chanhu-daro as they were at Mohenjo-daro. The specimens illustrated in Pls. XXVII, 84, 89, 92 and XXXIX, 22, have each a minute hole drilled on either side. These little vessels no doubt once contained some kind of cosmetic, and it was thought necessary to hang them up to protect their contents from mice and ants. Larger vessels, unless they were kept in slings, were never suspended in this way.

Ring-bases

Most of the pottery had flat substantial bases. Some specimens, however, must have had a stand to hold them upright. Ring-bases were rare at Chanhu-daro and found only on the two large bowls or pans illustrated in Pls. XXVII, 53 and XXIX, 43 and on the little jar in Pl. XXVI, 59, which type of vessel at Mohenjo-daro is seldom without a base of this kind.

Rims

Bowls with wide, flat rims sometimes have this portion decorated. For example, the pieces in Pl. XXVII, nos. 39 and 41 are painted with a series of concentric hemispheres in red, very like the pattern on No. 19 in Pl. XXXIX. Transverse lines in the same colour appear round the rims of the bowls in Pl. XXVII, 8, 44. In the latter specimen these lines are linked together at the ends, forming a continuous ladder pattern.

Potmarks and Inscriptions

Marks and inscriptions were found on several jars and sherds. These are illustrated in Pls. XXXIV, 2-4, XXXVII, 5, XXXVIII, 1-3, 5, XXXIX, 24, and described in detail below. The seal impressions sometimes appearing on the Mohenjo-daro pottery are, however, unknown at Chanhu-daro.

Plate XXXIV. No. 2, a sherd 2.4 inches long, bears an unintelligible sign painted in black on a dark red slip.

No. 3 shows more clearly the two signs painted in black on the small jar in Pl. XXXIX, 24. This little vessel is 6.1 inches high and is coated with a cream slip. The first sign here often occurs on the seals of the Harappā Culture and was also found scratched on the shoulder of a badly broken storage jar unearthed in Trench F(1) at the level of — 13.1 feet. The second sign is still untraced.

No. 4 (see also Pl. XXXVII, 5) shows a sherd, 3.32 inches long, with two signs painted in black on the natural surface of the pottery. The first, a solar motif, frequently appears on the painted wares of the Harappā civilization (Pl. XXXI, 9, XXXII, 7, etc.) and at Mohenjo-

[9] The rivet holes were biconical and about 0.15 in. in diameter. They were drilled at unequal intervals along the sides of a crack in the base of this jar.

daro occurs in the form of a faïence ornament.[10] The second sign is apparently a slight variation of a well-known character on the seals.

Plate XXXVIII. No. 1, a round pottery plaque, 2.8 inches in diameter and 0.5 inch thick, has a slightly concave upper surface and a flat base. On the former is scratched a pentacle—the first known appearance of this sign on an object of the Harappā Culture. This still serves as a magic symbol in India to-day,[11] and one authority states that it is derived from one of the *Euphorbias*, which has pistils of similar form.[12] Any motif in which a triangle may be traced is regarded with special favour in India. The goddess Māriyamma is said to have one of her dwellings in a triangle,[13] while Abbott states that the pentacle itself is used in India as a charm against the Evil Eye.[14] It may, therefore, be assumed with some authority that the pentacle incised on this plaque had some magic or religious significance, although it is impossible to say how the plaque itself was used.

The pentacle occurs occasionally on Sumerian seals,[15] and it appears several times on clay tablets from Jemdet Nasr and is painted also on a jar from the same site.[16] It is portrayed as a five-pointed star with the interior filled in at Tepe Giyan,[17] and, in its strictly linear form, is a symbol which has been used in Palestine from ancient times down to the present day.[18] It has come to light in countries as widely separated as Nubia [19] and Greece.[20]

The extreme rarity of this symbol as regards the art of the Indus Valley leads us to assume that it was borrowed from another country, probably Mesopotamia, where, as has been pointed out, it was fairly common. Again, it may have entered India from Baluchistan (although it occurs rarely on the pottery of that country [21]), and have become identified later with part of a sacred plant.

The pentacle is very common in China where it is regarded as one of the many symbols of longevity, perhaps because the design, when properly executed, has no beginning or end. Its efficacy against the Evil Eye is said to be thwarted if it is not drawn without a stop.

Plate XXXVIII. No. 2 is a sherd 7 inches long. This came from a large jar and has a double triangle motif which was deeply incised upon it while the clay was wet. It is unlikely that this particular mark had any connection with the double-axe cult object of Minoan

[10] *F. E. M.*, pl. CXI, 11, 23, 24.

[11] The symbol occurs on punch-marked silver coins: J. Allen, *Ancient Indian Coins (Cat. Brit. Mus.)*, 1936, Index IV, p. 7.

[12] Various species of this plant are regarded as sacred in many parts of India.

[13] Oppert, *Original Inhabitants of India*, p. 483.

[14] *The Keys of Power*, p. 136.

[15] Ward, *Seal Cylinders of Western Asia*, p. 134, fig. 377; Legrain, *Ur Excavations*, vol. III, pl. 37, figs. 105, 227, 239, 398, 400.

[16] Langdon, *Oxford Editions of Cuneiform Texts*, vol. VII, pls. I, III, VI, etc.; Mackay, *Anthropology Memoirs*, Field Museum, Chicago, vol. I, pl. LXVIII, 11.

[17] Contenau et Ghirshman, *Fouilles du Tépé Giyan*, pl. 66.

[18] It is scratched on a potsherd from Ezion-Geber, *Illust. Lon. News*, Aug. 5, 1939, p. 247, fig. 5.

[19] *Liv. Ann. Arch. and Anthrop.*, vol. VIII, pl. XIV. It is also found as a potmark on a prehistoric jar from Egypt; see Petrie, *The Making of Egypt*, pl. XXXI, 64.

[20] Swindler, *Ancient Painting*, fig. 210.

[21] Stein, *Mem. Arch. Surv. Ind.*, No. 37, pl. XI.

Crete, for the same design often appears on the painted pottery of the Harappā Culture (see Pl. XXXVII, 7), where triangular devices are very common. An exactly similar double triangle was found scratched on the base of a badly broken jar from Chanhu-daro,[22] and the same motif also appears on some of the seals from Mohenjo-daro;[23] it is, therefore, not surprising to find it used as a pot-mark. It also served the same purpose on prehistoric Egyptian pottery.[24]

No. 3 shows a sherd from a jar-stand, 6.6 inches in length. This also bears a true pot-mark for the signs were impressed upon it when the clay was damp. Three devices are now visible, two of which are familiar as they appear on the Mohenjo-daro seals,[25] but the third, on the right, is far from clear and looks like an animal. We may have in these three pictographs and others that possibly followed them the name of the owner of this piece of pottery.

No. 5 comes from the side of a large pottery jar and the signs upon it were scratched after it had been fired. The "V"-shaped device on the left often precedes inscriptions both on seals and pottery;[26] its meaning is unknown. It is followed by groups of upright strokes numbering twelve in all, but here again it is impossible to say what they represent. Below all is an oval motif, which may be an unfinished form of a common type of sign that appears on the seals of the Harappā Culture.

Kilns

No kilns that could have been used for pottery have as yet come to light at Chanhu-daro, probably because they were placed well outside the city. Should they be discovered later, however, they are almost certain to be of the same type as those already found at Mohenjo-daro.[27]

INCISED WARES

Most of the examples of incised work consist of fragments of the dishes of food-stands, of the kind illustrated in Pl. XXV, 1-6. In the specimens shown in Pl. XXXVIII, 12-21, 23, 25, the incised patterns have rather the effect of being in relief, but no raised work of any kind occurs on any of the Harappā wares, except on one particular type of vessel which has not yet appeared at Chanhu-daro.[28]

The patterns on the sherds Nos. 14, 16, 21 in Pl. XXXVIII are made up of thin, spiral lines whose regularity suggests that they were cut before the dishes were removed from the wheel. The spaces between the spirals were then filled in with short strokes so as to form a number of cells or partitions. The most carefully executed design is that on sherd No. 14,

[22] No. 1249. Unearthed at the level of − 5.3 ft. in Trench K(1).
[23] Smith and Gadd, *M. I. C.*, pl. CXXIII (cxxxix, cxl).
[24] Petrie, *The Making of Egypt*, pls. VII, 30, XVIII, 88, XIII, 56.
[25] *M. I. C.*, pls. CXXIII (clix), CXXVI (cclxxix).
[26] *F. E. M.*, pl. LXIII, 3, 4.
[27] *Op. cit.*, p. 177; pl. L, b, d.
[28] *Op. cit.*, pl. LXVI, 54.

where the pattern resembles the interior of a large shell of the ammonite type;[29] it is hardly angular enough to have been copied from a spider's web.

No. 15 in Pl. XXXVIII, which measures 5.1 inches across, bears a curious ornament consisting of a number of small semi-spirals arranged rather irregularly in concentric circles. These appear to have been impressed either with the end of a tube having overlapping edges or with the mouth of a small univalve shell.

The simple design on No. 12 consists of several crescent-shaped markings set in circles. The same markings appear again on No. 25, where they are associated with a spiral line.

The only painted example of this shell-like pattern occurs on a sherd from Mohenjo-daro.[30] The ornament is peculiar to the time of the Harappā Culture and is, therefore, of great assistance when material has to be dated, but it is difficult to explain why it should appear only on the dishes of food-stands. The device may, of course, be a sacred one and the stands on which it alone appears have been reserved for religious use. The patterns obviously bear a close relationship to one another and must have taken some time to execute; each stroke was put in separately by hand.

Similar incised designs on fragments of the dishes of food-stands come from the lower levels of Mohenjo-daro,[31] and Mr. Majumdar has discovered sherds marked in the same way in other parts of Sindh.[32] A few sherds marked in the same way have even appeared in Baluchistan,[33] where their presence may denote the existence of trade relations between the people of that province and those of the Harappā Culture. On the other hand it is equally possible that this pottery formed part of the personal belongings of merchants from India, who would include in their baggage any objects needed for their religious observances.

These incised dishes were also embellished with colour. Nos. 13, 14, 19, 20, 23 in Pl. XXXVIII have red bands painted round their inner margins, while Nos. 19 and 23 are edged with black. A cream-coloured slip improves the appearance of No. 25, while the backs of Nos. 13, 14, 16-18, 21 are washed over with red. Nos. 12 and 15 are of grey-coloured ware.

Incised dishes of this type occur solely in the Harappā II and III occupations at Chanhu-daro, whereas, as already stated, they have been found in the lower levels of Mohenjo-daro only. This appears to indicate that Chanhu-daro was deserted by the Harappā people some time before the same fate overcame the sister city to the north-west. This question of the relative age of the two cities will be referred to later when objects other than pottery are being discussed.

Nos. 8 and 9 in Pl. XXXVIII are portions of the bases of two large pans, similar to the specimen illustrated in Pl. XXIV, 2. The first, which measures 16.5 inches across, bears a series of intersecting circles deeply incised with a notched tool. The circles are so carefully

[29] A particular fossil shell of ammonite form (saligram) is revered by many Brahmans today.

[30] F. E. M., pl. LXX, 39. This once formed part of a dish of a food-stand.

[31] *Op. cit.*, pl. LXVII.

[32] *Explorations in Sind*, pls. XXII, 48, XXXI, 7-10, 14-16.

[33] Stein, *Mem. Arch. Surv. Ind.*, No. 43, pls. XXI (Kul. I), XXX (Mehī. II, 4. 4). The Mehī-damb example makes the fossil origin of this pattern almost a certainty.

drawn that it is probable that the design was sketched in beforehand. The roundels in the centre of each were possibly impressed with the rim of a small jar. The simpler pattern on No. 9 again shows careful work. Here the impressions, each 2.1 inches in diameter, have been stamped with some round object.[34] Other sites in Sindh have also produced this curious pan decoration.[35]

It is not known why these large pans were thus decorated, or to what use they were put. Clothes may have been washed in them: the rubbing of the garments on the rough surface made by the pattern on the base of the pan would perhaps help to remove the dirt. Again, they may have been used for hulling grain or for preparing wafer bread, which would thus become impressed with a pattern.

No. 22 in Pl. XXXVIII is part of the lower portion of a storage jar which was thickly coated with a mixture of sand and clay. This coating was then removed in sections, so as to leave a series of thick lines in slight relief. Water vessels still retain in Sindh today this sandy layer which is supposed to help keep the contents of a jar cool.

No. 24, which measures 4.2 inches long, is part of the neck and shoulder of a large jar impressed with shallow zig-zag lines made with a blunt point. No. 28, a portion of a storage jar, is decorated in the same way.

RESERVED SLIP WARE

At Mohenjo-daro several pottery sherds were found which could be compared with certain wares from Kish and Ur in the treatment of their slips.[36] Three specimens of the same kind of pottery were found, two in early levels at Chanhu-daro, and are illustrated in Pl. XXXVIII, 26, 27, 29. The first sherd, a very thin one, 3.6 inches in length, has been coated with a pink slip which has then been removed in places with a comb-like tool to allow the body colour of the pottery to show through. The contrast here is not very marked, but it appears to greater advantage in No. 27. This piece was covered first with a dark, almost black, slip and then with another of a light grey colour. The top slip has been partly removed in lines to reveal the darker one beneath. No. 29 comes from a jar that has been over-fired. The upper slip is purplish-black, but the one below it is now of a somewhat indefinite shade. In places it is light green, though originally it may have been cream-coloured. The dark slip here has been removed in two directions, the regularity of the lines showing that a notched instrument was used for this purpose.

The great rarity of this reserved slip ware suggests that it was imported from other countries. Sir Leonard Woolley has stated that some specimens found by him in the lowest levels at Ur[37] may have come from Anatolia. Reserved slip ware, carried out in glaze, has been unearthed at Mohenjo-daro,[38] but no examples are known from other sites.

[34] Compare this pattern with those in *F. E. M.*, pl. LXVII, 21, 24.

[35] Majumdar, *Explorations in Sind*, pl. XXXI, 17, 18.

[36] *F. E. M.*, pp. 45, 184, 188, 652, 668; pl. LXVII, 3, 4.

[37] *Antiquaries Journal*, vol. X, pp. 331, 339. There is, however, a slight difference between the Ur and the Indian wares. At Ur only one slip was used, whereas at Chanhu-daro and at Mohenjo-daro two slips are, with one exception, always employed.

[38] *M. I. C.*, pp. 578, 692; pl. CLIX, 1.

CUT WARE

Nos. 6, 7, 10, 11 in Pl. XXXVIII are portions of pottery vessels or stands in which triangular holes have been cut. This form of decoration is also known at Mohenjo-daro,[39] but neither there, nor at Chanhu-daro, have anything like complete specimens been found. Examples from Mesopotamia, however, may provide some clue to the shape of the objects from which our sherds have come. The tall pottery stands, some of hour-glass shape ornamented with triangular holes, which have appeared at Kish[40] and other Sumerian sites,[41] may well be the prototypes of this Chanhu-daro pottery. The sherds we illustrate are all slightly curved and cannot, therefore, be parts of ventilators or gratings. No. 7 is coated with a cream-coloured and No. 11 with a brown slip; the remaining two have no slip at all.

The holes in all four sherds have been cut with some sharp instrument, but this has not always been carefully done, in spite of the fact that in some cases guiding marks are still visible lightly incised on the surface of the pottery.[42]

This particular form of ornamentation was not confined to India or Mesopotamia. It was practised at Susa,[43] appears on very early jar-stands and altars from Egypt,[44] while various pottery objects from Palestine have also been treated in the same way. In Mesopotamia, however, the practice was especially common. Here specimens have come to light which are contemporary with the Harappā Period, while others have been found which antedate it.[45] In some cases the holes appear to be purely ornamental, but where they occur in stands for water-jars, they would also serve for ventilation.

PLAIN AND SIMPLE PAINTED POTTERY

In the following description of the pottery from Chanhu-daro, I shall continue to use the same system adopted in the Mohenjo-daro reports, i. e., each jar is classified under a letter according to its form and under a double letter if the type is divergent. This procedure will, I hope, assist the reader to compare the wares from the two cities as far as it is possible to do so. Certain types found in one city, however, have no counterparts in the other and potters often appear to have been influenced by purely local fashions.

We have yet to find a Chanhu-daro, for instance, a very coarse type of pottery (Type B) which was very common at Mohenjo-daro. The vessels in Pls. XXVI, 73, a and XXIX, 36, a

[39] F. E. M., pl. LXVII.

[40] Watelin, *Excavations at Kish*, vol. IV, pls. I, XVI, 6: Langdon, *Journ. Roy. As. Soc.*, 1930, pl. IX, 4.

[41] The triangular incisions on some stands from Tell Asmar do not pierce the pottery and were, perhaps, intended to hold inlays; Frankfort, *Orient. Inst. Communications*, Chicago, No. 20, pl. II, 12, 13.

[42] These can be clearly seen in No. 11, which measures 3.8 ins. across.

[43] *Mém. Dél. en Perse*. ts. VIII, pp. 80, 137; XX, p. 114.

[44] Quibell, *Hierakonopolis*, I, pl. XXXV, 4. For other Egyptian examples see De Morgan, *La Préhistoire Orientale*, II, p. 285.

[45] Herzfeld, *Samarra V.*, pp. 37-39; pl. XXI.

bear some resemblance to it, although they are far superior in workmanship. Both these vessels come from the top of Mound I, the last area of the city to be occupied by people of the Harappā Culture. Again the tall conical cups shown in Pl. XXIX, 5-11 cannot be paralleled at Mohenjo-daro, where another type of vessel took its place.

Type A (Pls. XXV, 1-42, XXVII, 36, XXVIII, 31, XXXVIII, 12-21, 23, 25)

Few of these pottery food-stands have been found intact, the thin-stemmed variety with a broad base being especially subject to damage. We have found more dishes and bowls belonging to these food-stands than the stems and bases that supported them, for the reason that the former could be put to other uses, whereas the latter on separation became worthless. The dish illustrated in Pl. XXVII, 36 is a case in point, for after it had become parted from its stand, its base was ground down smooth and it was set to other purposes. The tall stands were exceptionally weak at the junction of dish and stem, for these two parts had to be made separately and then luted together with clay. Various attempts were made, such as roughening the surfaces to be joined to strengthen this weak spot but not always with satisfactory results.[46]

This type of utensil was probably used to hold special foods, fruits, and so forth, like its modern counterpart. On the other hand it may have been used in marketing, for vessels of exactly similar form are carried about on the head in Bali at the present time, for which see the photograph in Pl. XCIII, 31. The hollow base of the stand fits the crown of the head very comfortably.

The stands from Chanhu-daro fall naturally into two groups:

(a) Tall stands with slender stems as in Pls. XXV, 1, 3, 7, 9, 10, 13-16, 19, 21, 22, 26, 27, XXVII, 36.

(b) Stands of squat form as in Pl. XXV, 2, 4-6, 8, 11, 12, 17, 18, 20, 23-25, 29.

The latter type, being the more substantial, is the one most frequently found complete.

Tall Stand. A carefully polished red slip, light or dark in colour, covers the tall stands (or parts of them) illustrated in Pls. XXV, 1, 10, 19, 21, 27, XXVII, 36, while a red pigment is spread rather more roughly over the surfaces of Nos. 3, 7, 15 in Pl. XXV and of No. 31 in Pl. XXVIII. The dishes shown in Pl. XXV, 9, 16 are of grey ware, the first being coated with a polished black slip and the second with one of very dark grey. A cream-coloured wash improves the appearance of No. 26 in Pl. XXV, but No. 22 in the same plate has no slip at all.

Various differences can be observed in the stems of the taller stands. No. 19 in Pl. XXV seems to have been severely plain, but Nos. 15, 16, 21, 27 have their upper portions moulded.

It is unusual to find traces of painting on these tall stands, apart from the coloured slips and washes already described. No. 15 in Pl. XXV is ornamented with black lines, while No. 14 has the inside of its rim decorated with three equidistant groups of multiple loops in black.

[46] For an example of such roughening, see *F. E. M.*, pl. LXVII, 14.

The shapes of the dishes themselves vary considerably. The bowl-like forms in Pls. XXV, 9, 14, 26, XXVIII, 31 could have held but little and may have been used for incense. The carination of No. 9 suggests that it may once have had a cover.

Squat Stands. These are finished in various ways. Most of them are covered with a red slip, which is sometimes highly polished. Others are cream-coloured and two (Pl. XXV, 8, 20) are without a slip at all. The exceptionally fine specimen in Pl. XXV, 23 is coloured red outside and partly so within and thin black lines further ornament its foot. No. 18 in Pl. XXV is of grey ware showing horizontal polish markings. No. 20 is quite plain except for a red circular band inside the dish and red lines round its rim and the edge of its base.

Incised patterns appear on what are left of the dishes that surmount the stands in Pl. XXV, 11, 16, 17. The designs on Nos. 11, 16 take the form of a series of radiating lines cut jerkily with some sharp point and producing a notched effect very much like that on a similar dish in Pl. XXXVIII, 18. No. 17 in Pl. XXV is decorated inside with a spiral line made up of semi-circular markings. Mention has already been made in the preceding section on "Incised Wares" of the patterns that are so frequently found on these food-stand dishes.

More decoration appears on the squat food-stands than on the tall variety. The outside of No. 5 in Pl. XXV is ornamented with the sun-motif illustrated in Pl. XXXIII, 15. This is painted in black and contrasts well with the red slip covering the dish. No. 25 in the same plate has a light red slip which is embellished with grouped lines in black and a narrow band of leaf-like motifs. No. 29 is decorated on the outside with roughly executed lines, loops, and ladder patterns, carried out in black on a red slip. The sherds seen in Pls. XXX, 12, XXXIII, 7, 15, XXXIV, 7, all painted in black on red, are portions of food-stands, probably of the squat type.

The model stand No. 24 in Pl. XXV is hand-made and from its rough workmanship was apparently made by a child.

Type B (Pls. XXVI, 73, a, XXIX, 36, a)

The late, degraded form of this type, so common at Mohenjo-daro[47] is unknown at Chanhu-daro. The two specimens illustrated here come from the summit of Mound I. They are ornamented with scored spiral lines and can only just stand on their narrow bases.

Type C (Pls. XXVIII, 42, XXIX, 16, 25-36)

This type of cup with its thick walls and base was far more common at Mohenjo-daro. No. 16 in Pl. XXIX is thinner than most specimens, especially in its lower part. It is coated with a brown-coloured wash which extends well down inside it. No. 32 is uncommon on account of its red slip, cream being the colour most often met with on these vessels.

Type D (Pl. XXVI, 59)

No. 59 in Pl. XXVI resembles very closely those found at Mohenjo-daro except that it lacks a beading round the base. It has a ring base and has been washed over with a light red paint.

[47] F. E. M., pl. LX, 14-17.

Type DA (Pl. XXVII, 52)

The single example of this type is coated with a light red slip on the upper part only Jars of this shape were also rare at Mohenjo-daro.

Type E (Pls. XXVI, 65, 68, XXVIII, 1, 10, 11, 37, 45, XXIX, 4)

The shelf at the junction of neck and shoulder is characteristic of this type of pottery, otherwise the specimens differ slightly in form. The moulded foot of No. 68 in Pl. XXVI marks a new departure from the plain bases of these rather uninteresting vessels. The same shelf formation appears in the storage jars illustrated in Pl. XXIV, 3, 4, 6, 7.

Type EA (Pl. XXVIII, 3)

This jar resembles the preceding type closely, except that the shelf is missing. The jar we show is extremely well made and is ornamented with thin, black lines on a light red slip.

Type F (Pls. XXVII, 62, 66, 67, XXVIII, 13)

The main features of this type are the beading at the junction of neck and shoulder and the differently coloured upper and lower portions. All the jars illustrated are painted red above and, with the exception of No. 62, cream below. The red slip on No. 67 still bears traces of its original polish.

Type G (Pls. XXVI, 88-91, XXVIII, 4, 6, 19, 21, 24, 29, 36, 46, 50, 53, 54, XXIX, 1-3)

Jars belonging to this type are full-bodied, with wide mouths and substantial flat bases. The two jars in Pls. XXVIII, 50 and XXIX, 3 are grey in colour, the last bearing traces of a black slip. Nos. 4 and 6 in Pl. XXVIII are decorated with incised spiral lines. Vessels of this shape must have had a great many uses and were probably turned out in large quantities.

Type H (Pl. XXVIII, 15-17, 20, 26, 27, 30, 51, 52)

These vessels in general resemble Type C but are squatter in form. The smaller sizes are found in such numbers that it seems likely they were stocked by shop-keepers who used them as containers for small purchases of cooking oil, etc. They are always of rough workmanship and usually have no slip. Their flat bases nearly always show the marks of the string that was used to sever them from the wheel.

Type I (Pl. XXVII, 89, 90)

These little jars with their flared mouths and curious bases are rare. No. 89 which is without a slip has two holes in its rim and is one of the "Suspended Vessels" already described. No. 90 is decorated with black lines on a dark red slip and the usual flared lip is missing.[48]

[48] I have not been able to examine this jar again but I suspect that its rim had been broken and the rough edges then rubbed smooth.

Type J (Pls. XXVII, 69, 70, 74-87, 91, 92, XXVIII, 9, XXXIII, 4, XXXVII, 6, XXXIX, 22, 26, 27)

Many of these small, narrow-mouthed jars are ornamented with simple black or red lines. They differ considerably in shape.

No. 69 is hand-made and has four small openings instead of one. Nos. 73 and 92 are also illustrated in photograph in Pl. XXXIX, 22, 26. The first is a beautiful little vessel decorated in black on a cream-coloured slip and the latter is a hand-made jar of grey paste, the surface of which shows vertical polish marks. Its carinated top is pierced with two small holes by which it was suspended.

No. 9 in Pl. XXVIII comes under this type letter owing to its narrow mouth, though it is hard to say whether our restoration of its rim and neck is a correct one. No. 4 in Pl. XXXIII is a rim of one of these small mouthed vessels whose aperture is only 0.24 inch. It is quaintly ornamented with four fishes. A similar top is shown in Pl. XXXVII, 6. The motif here may represent a five-petalled flower or the jar painter may have likened its concave top to one of the *Convolvulacea* and added the dark markings to heighten the resemblance. These two last pieces are painted in black on a polished red slip.

The hand-made vessel No. 79 in Pl. XXVII is probably a model cage. It bears a lattice pattern in red painted on the natural surface of the pottery and the only opening is a small hole, 0.55 inch in diameter, on one side of the knob on the top. No. 27 in Pl. XXXIX is a photograph of an almost identical article. This last is 3.2 inches high (about half-an-inch higher than the first specimen) and is also hand-made. Its ornamentation is similar to the first except that a cream slip has been used.[49]

Very similar cages have been unearthed at Mohenjo-daro,[50] and a specimen containing the model of a bird is known from the same site.[51] The Chanhu-daro objects may, therefore, be only models of bird-cages. On the other hand, the apertures in their tops are just wide enough to admit an insect about the size of a cricket, and they may have been used to accommodate this musical creature.

The ordinary narrow-mouthed jars appear to have been mostly used for eye-paints. Some contained a black powder which, on analysis, proved to be some kind of soot.[52]

Type JA (Pl. XXVII, 71-73)

This sub-type with its bulbous, almost carinated body and deeply recessed mouth is rare. No. 71 is roughly ornamented with wavy lines carried out in red on a pink slip. A red wash covers No. 72 and No. 73 is crudely painted in black on a cream-coloured slip.

Types K and KA

No examples of these rare types have, as yet, come to light at Chanhu-daro.

[49] Certain cracks in the cage suggest that it was made on the coil system.

[50] *M. I. C.*, pl. LXXXIV, 1, 2.

[51] *F. E. M.*, pl. LXXXI, 6.

[52] See Chap. XV.

Type L (Pl. XXVII, 61)

Possibly this squat carinated vessel may belong to this type, but it is difficult to classify owing to its missing upper portion. The jar is well made and is decorated with dark red bands on a light red slip.

Type LA (Pl. XXIX, 38-40, 43, a)

These curiously formed vessels with narrow mouths and bases are well represented at Chanhu-daro. The first three are coated with a red and the last with a cream slip. Their narrow apertures indicate that they were made to contain liquids and their bases are too unstable for them to have held anything safely without the support of a stand.

Type M (Pl. XXV, 30, 50, 57)

Bowls set on a short foot, either solid or hollow, were fairly common at Mohenjo-daro, but do not appear to have been popular with the Chanhu-daro inhabitants. The hand-made example No. 30 has no slip and is possibly the work of a child. No. 50 is roughly finished and also has no slip on the outside. Inside it is coated with red, and a ladder pattern in dark red decorates the top of its rim. The upper portion of the fine bowl No. 57 is unfortunately missing. It had been washed over with a cream-coloured slip and bears inside an incised pattern of lunar-shaped markings arranged in concentric circles. Incised work of this kind is usually confined to Type A wares.

Type MA (Pls. XXV, 43-49, 51-53, XXVIII, 59, 65)

These vessels generally have hollow feet, but unlike Type M their upper parts are taller and resemble jars rather than bowls; moreover, they vary considerably in shape. This type was common at Mohenjo-daro.

Nos. 43, 46, 48, and 53 in Pl. XXV are decorated with red bands, either on a cream slip or on the natural surface of the pottery. The last-named is hand-made. No. 59 in Pl. XXVIII has lost its foot, but there appears to be no doubt that it belongs to this type. It is roughly painted with intermixed black and red lines laid directly on the surface of the pottery.

Type N

A rare jar from Mohenjo-daro has the lower part of its body strongly incurved to enable it to sit securely on a stand.[53] No duplicate of this type has yet appeared at Chanhu-daro, though, as Pl. XXIV shows, incurved bases do occur on some of the storage jars.

Types P and Q

These types are not represented at Chanhu-daro.

[53] *M. I. C.*, pl. LXXXI, 32.

Type R (Pls. XXIX, 41, 42, 44-46, XXXIX, 24)

The examples found of this graceful and distinctive type are not so well finished as those from Mohenjo-daro. At that city they were sometimes painted in polychrome and also copied in silver and copper. There is reason to believe that vessels of this type were used for ritual purposes.[54]

Type S

This type is unknown at Chanhu-daro.

Type SA (Pls. XXVI, 69, 70, XXVIII, 22)

A very uncommon type. The three specimens we show have their lower portions extensively trimmed and are covered with cream-coloured slips.

Type SB (Pl. XXVI, 72)

As this jar has lost its rim there is a little uncertainty whether it should be included under this type letter or not. It had evidently been used as a water-jar, for it is coated first with a red and then with a brown slip, evidently to make it water-tight.[55]

Type U (Pl. XXVII, 1-6, 22, 24, 27)

These shallow dishes, all of rough workmanship, and, with one exception, without slips, are very similar to many from Mohenjo-daro. No. 22 is wheel-made, despite its small size, and No. 24 is coloured red inside and out; its interior is also ornamented with thin, black lines.

Type UA (Pls. XXVI, 60, 62-64, XXVII, 13-19, 23, XXVIII, 7, 8, 38, 40, 41, 43, 44, 47, 56, 57, 68, 69, XXXIX, 25)

A number of cups greater in height than in diameter are included under this type letter. They are of various shapes and sizes.

Nos. 15, 17 in Pl. XXVII and Nos. 39-41 in Pl. XXVIII are hand-made. A red slip covers the two cups in Pls. XXVI, 63 and XXVIII, 42. Those illustrated in Pls. XXVI, 62, XXVII, 19, and XXVIII, 39, 44, 56, 57, 69 are all roughly ornamented with red lines applied to the natural surface of the pottery. No. 43 is an exception, for it is coated with a cream wash.

No. 38 in Pl. XXVIII is only 2.1 inches high and bears a rough decoration of irregular black lines on a light red ground.

The two small vessels in Pl. XXVI, 60 and Pl. XXVII, 23 were originally taller, but their broken tops had been rubbed down smooth and in the case of the first even carefully bevelled.

The cup in Pl. XXXIX, 25 measures 2.8 inches high. Its lower third is cream-coloured and the upper two-thirds red and ornamented with three black lines. A minute jar was found fixed in this cup to serve as a stopper.

[54] F. E. M., p. 227.

[55] This same brown coating is found on some of the storage jars.

Type UB (Pl. XXVII, 34, 35)

These cups with their straight, sloping sides are represented by one from Mohenjo-daro, but this had rather a wider base.[56] Neither of the two vessels illustrated has a slip, and No. 35 is more carefully finished than No. 34.

Type V (Pls. XXIII, 2, XXVII, 7-12, 20, 21, 25, 26, 28-32, 38-51, 54-61, 63-65, XXVIII, 32, 48, 60, 64, 67)

Many of these bowls, of various sizes and shapes, will have to be sub-divided later when fresh material is available. Some are of better finish inside than out and pared exterior surfaces are very common.

No. 8 in Pl. XXVII has a red spot in the middle of its base and red transverse lines in groups ornament its rim. No. 26 has an inside decoration of concentric circles in light red. The curious bowl shown in Pl. XXVII, 39 is covered with a pink-coloured slip inside and out. Groups of looped lines in dark red decorate the flat rim and wavy lines in the same colour are painted round the outside. No. 41 has its flat rim decorated in much the same way. A ladder pattern in red is just distinguishable on the edge of No. 44.

The large bowl No. 46 is very smoothly finished inside and is undecorated save for five cord lines round its outside. No. 50 bears purplish-black lines on a pink slip, and the upper portion of No. 51 is pink and the lower cream-coloured.

A red wash that has dripped in places covers the rim and neck of No. 58, the rest of this vessel being cream-coloured. Solar motifs and thick and thin borders in black paint on a light red slip are a feature of the decoration of the little bowl No. 59, which is also shown in colour in Pl. XXIII, 2. The rim of No. 61 is missing; its body is ornamented with dark red lines on a light red ground.

A red slip is used on Nos. 31, 65, in Pl. XXVII and also on No. 32 in Pl. XXVIII. A brown slip covers No. 32 in Pl. XXVII. Nos. 25 in Pl. XXVII and 48 in Pl. XXVIII are both of grey ware, the former having a black slip on the inner and a dark grey one on the outer side.

Nos. 21, 28, 29, 48, 49, 55 in Pl. XXVII are all hand-made.

Type W (Pl. XXVII, 36, 37)

No. 36 has been included here because, although originally the top of a food-stand, it was later used as a platter. Its ragged base had been carefully rubbed down flat to serve as a foot, though a most inadequate one. A light red slip covers this dish inside and out.

No. 37, a platter with a wide base, is roughly finished on the outside; inside it is exceptionally smooth and coated with a red wash.

Type X (Pls. XXIII, 4, XXVI, 12-55, XXVIII, 66, XXIX, 49-53, 57-62, 69-73, XXXVII, 47, XXXIX, 19)

A considerable number of jar-covers in perfect condition were found; their substantial make prevented them from being easily broken. The most common form is the simple lid

[56] *F. E. M.*, pl. LVI, 52.

shown in Pls. XXVI, 36, 37, 40, 43, XXVIII, 66, XXIX, 59-61, 70, 71. These are all hand-made and but few are covered with a slip. No. 66 in Pl. XXVIII differs from the others in having a red wash on its upper surface and also a small slanting hole on each side of the projection that serves as a handle.

A peculiarity of many of these covers is the presence of a shallow hole on the top of the knob-handle (Pl. XXIX, 58, 59, 61). A possible explanation for it is that it once held a small twig for steadying the cover while it was being fashioned.

The notched edge of the lid in Pl. XXIX, 57 is also strange, but would allow of a certain amount of air to enter the jar it covered. No. 70 in the same plate has a converging hole on each side of the handle, possibly for the same reason.

Decorated jar-covers of this period are rare, a fact that makes No. 4 in Pl. XXIII (see also Pl. XXXVII, 47) of especial interest. This lid, which once had a knob, measures 7.7 inches in diameter and is finely painted with a circle and leaf motif in black on a highly polished red slip. The jar to which this cover originally belonged was probably equally beautiful.

Nos. 64-66 in Pl. XXIX are made of shell and will be referred to again further on in this book.

The bowl-like type of lid with knob handle inside (Pl. XXVI, 12-34) is much more common than at Mohenjo-daro. In most cases the handles are below the rims, which make them difficult to grasp. Beyond the very occasional use of a red wash or slip this type of jar-lid is never ornamented. I have mentioned elsewhere that jar-covers of this type occur in Baluchistan, Sumer, Palestine, and even the south of Italy.[57] Practically all these bowl-shaped specimens have a better finish on the inside than on the outside, for the reason that little of the latter could be seen when the jar was in position.

The exceptionally large lid, No. 22 in Pl. XXVI, comes from the summit of Mound I and was probably made to fit a storage jar. The top of its handle bears a spot of red paint, evidently a distinguishing mark. Nos. 32, 41, 55 in Pl. XXVI are painted red inside and out, while Nos. 49, 51, 53 are decorated with that colour on the outside only. No. 39 is hand-made and its upper surface is ornamented with concentric circles in red. The lids in Pls. XXVI, 29, 33, 48 and XXIX, 71 are made of a coarse grey paste.

A very unusual lid, or rather stopper, with a flanged top is shown in Pl. XXVI, 54. A small hole pierces its shank, by which it was once tied to the vessel it fitted. No. 69 in Pl. XXIX (see also Pl. XCI, 9) has been treated in the same way. These two objects may have belonged to water-skins.

No. 57 in Pl. XXVI closely resembles two lids found at Mohenjo-daro, except that it has a longer shank.[58] The stoppers pictured in Pl. XXIX, 49-52 are of an entirely new shape. They are all hand-made, very regular in form, but with rather rough surfaces. Nos. 53, 62, 73 in the same plate may be either plumb-bobs or jar-stoppers, probably the latter. Each one is hand-made, ruddled, and perforated for a cord. The base of No. 71 is square in form, measuring 1.2 inches each way.

A small jar used as a stopper can be seen in Pl. XXXIX, 25.

[57] *F. E. M.*, p. 204.

[58] *M. I. C.*, pl. LXXXII, 51, 55.

Type Y (Pl. XXVI, 61, 67, 67, a)

This type of vessel was rare at Mohenjo-daro; at Chanhu-daro only three sherds were found which could be identified with it. It is characterised by its broad, flat base and horizontally fluted sides.[59]

Type Z (Pl. XXVI, 72)

It is uncertain whether the tall jar with missing neck and rim in Pl. XXVI, 72 belongs to this type or should come under the heading SB, where it has been mentioned.

Type AA

This type has not been found at Chanhu-daro.

Type AC (Pl. XXV, 54, 55, 58, 59)

Handled cups of this type were plentiful at Mohenjo-daro. Its ear-like handle is always perforated. Nos. 54, 58, 59 are hand-made, the last two being without the usual cream slip. No. 9 in Pl. XXVII is almost certainly one of these cups that has lost its handle.

Vessels like these were probably used to ladle out water from a large jar to which they may have been tied to prevent loss.

Type AD (Pl. XXVI, 74-87)

These squat, open-mouthed jars, greater in diameter than in height, are also plentiful at Mohenjo-daro. Some are quite presentable in appearance, others are very roughly made. A cream-coloured slip is the usual finish. Nos. 79 and 82, however, are coloured red, the latter being further ornamented with a hatched border and lines in black paint. No. 83 is of grey clay coated with a darker slip of the same colour.

Type AE (Pl. XXVI, 4-11)

Jar stands in several new varieties have come to light at Chanhu-daro. No. 6, which comes from the summit of Mound I, has a very unusual carinated base. The curious form in Pl. XXVI, 7 also comes from Mound I and is similar to one unearthed at Mohenjo-daro.[60] No. 10 is entirely new and appears to be a copy in clay of a ring of rope or straw, the simplest form of jar-stand.

None of the examples shown are ornamented; painted or incised stands of this period are very rare.[61] The reversibility of these stands should be noted, and Nos. 8 and 11 were evidently made to seat jars of various sizes.

Type AF (Pls. XXVI, 1-3, XXVIII, 61-63)

It has not yet been settled what purpose these perforated vessels served, but Sir Aurel Stein's suggestion that they may have been braziers at present holds the field.[62] Some

[59] *M. I. C.*, pl. LXXXIII, 1, 2; *F. E. M.*, pl. LIII, 21.

[60] *F. E. M.*, pl. LIII, 53. [61] *F. E. M.*, p. 185. [62] *Mem. Arch. Surv. Ind.*, No. 43, pp. 64, 130.

features of their workmanship, however, still need explanation; for example, the significance of the large hole punched in the base of nearly every specimen.[63] These objects have recently been compared to the ritual vessels that are used by devotees in Madras at the present day for burning camphor.[64] The suggestion to my mind is quite plausible, but for camphor we should perhaps substitute incense.

This type of vessel is always wheel-made and rarely covered with a slip. The sides are pierced irregularly with a number of small holes, made with a stick pushed through from the outside. A larger hole, as already said, is almost invariably present in the centre of the base.

Plate XXVI. No. 1: 4.53 inches high. Upper portion missing. Holes irregularly placed and averaging 0.3 inch in diameter.

No. 2: 2.1 inches high. Holes 0.07 inch in diameter. Six holes in base of same size as those in sides.

No. 3: 2.43 inches high. Hole in base 0.3 inch in diameter. Other holes average 0.1 inch in diameter. Dark red line painted round rim.

Plate XXVIII. No. 61: 1.3 inches high. Roughly made, perhaps by a child. One small hole in centre of base and others of the same size distributed irregularly round the sides.

No. 62: 1.84 inches high. Hole in centre of base 0.1 inch in diameter. Holes in sides averaged 0.06 inch wide and have their rough edges inside more or less smoothed.

No. 63: 1.23 inches high. Minute holes in sides and base. Evidently a model for a great part of its interior is solid.

Types AG, AH

These two types are at present unknown at Chanhu-daro.

Type AI (Pl. XXIV, 3)

Only one example of this globular type of vessel has been found and this has been included among the storage jars on account of its large size. It has no slip but is otherwise well made.

Type AJ (Pl. XXVIII, 12, 35, 55)

The height of this type of jar seldom exceeds its width. It is distinctly rare, though a variation of it (Type E) is much more common. The second jar illustrated is without a slip. The lower portions and bases of all three have been pared. Vessels of this type from Mohenjo-daro are sometimes ornamented.

Group AK (Pls. XXV, 24, 30, XXVI, 60, 63, XXVII, 13-19, 75, 76, 82, 84-88, XXVIII, 25, 43, 56-58, 60-69)

Excluding low vessels, such as dishes and the like, there have been found in the cities of the Harappā Culture numbers of jars under two inches in height. Owing to their varied

[63] This, I take it, was to support the vessel on a rod. If so, these jars may have been used as torches. The miniature ones could have been used by children in play.

[64] Aiyappan, "Pottery Braziers of Mohenjo-daro," *Man*, 1939, sect. 65.

forms some of these have been described under other headings; they evidently served as containers for eye-paints, scented fats, and cosmetics of various kinds. Many of them are gaily ornamented with painted lines, sometimes carefully drawn but more often ragged and uneven.[65] The plainer specimens are usually roughly made, but so regular are some of them in size and make that it is suspected that they were expressly fashioned to hold a fixed quantity of liquid. No. 84 in Pl. XXVII, of very small capacity, has two holes in its rim by which it could be suspended. Only three examples have red slips (Pls. XXVI, 63, XXVII, 18, XXVIII, 65), the second of these having a dark red line round its rim as well. Roughly painted lines in red, applied to the natural surface of the pottery, ornament Nos. 56, 57, 64, 69, in Pl. XXVIII.

A dark brown slip covers the little vessel in Pl. XXVII, 86. This piece is evidently a model of a storage jar; similar miniature replicas of storage vessels have been found at Mohenjo-daro.[66]

It is doubtful whether Nos. 13 and 16 in Pl. XXVII should be included in this group, for their tops had been accidently broken and then rubbed down smooth.

Type AL (Pls. XXV, 56, 60, XXXIX, 20, 21)

Feeding cups of this kind are common also at Mohenjo-daro. No. 56 in Pl. XXV is coated with a dark brown wash superimposed on a red one, a process which made it milk-tight and also helped to keep it clean. Its spout is missing, the hole at the fracture here is 0.1 inch in diameter. No. 60 is also illustrated in Pl. XXXIX, 20. It is somewhat roughly made and the narrow hole through its spout (0.09 inch) is just big enough to allow thick milk to flow through. The spout of No. 21 in Pl. XXXIX is missing. This last little cup measures 3 inches in length and is exceptionally well made, with thin walls and a polished red slip inside and out.

Type AM (Pls. XXVI, 56, XXXIX, 17)

Partitioned trays of this kind are uncommon. Five examples have appeared at Mohenjo-daro[67] but one only at Chanhu-daro. The specimen we illustrate is hand-made and has two compartments. It is without a slip, but its interior has been so carefully smoothed over with the fingers that an almost polished surface has thereby been produced. The flat base of this article, which most likely was used for condiments, shows that it was either shaped or laid to dry upon a bed of sand.

Types AN, AO, AP

These three types are not represented at Chanhu-daro.

Type AQ (Pl. XXVIII, 49, XXXIX, 23)

This beautifully made and finished jar, which is shown in photograph in Pl. XXXIX, 23 and again in colour in Pl. XXIII, 6, is of a rare type. An unpainted vessel, originally of

[65] This decoration appears in some cases to have been done when the vessel was on the wheel.
[66] *F. E. M.*, p. 209.
[67] *F. E. M.*, pl. LXVI, 12, 15, 21, 27, 34.

the same form, is known from Mohenjo-daro.[68] The various motifs which appear on the present specimen are in black on a highly polished light red slip. In the upper register of this jar the motifs differ on opposite sides, as can be seen by comparing the drawing with the photograph.

Type AR

Not yet known at Chanhu-daro.

Type AS (Pls. XXIV, 1-9, XXIX, 37, 43, XXXV, 1-4)

A considerable number of storage jars was unearthed. These ranged in height from 16 inches to over 3 feet.[69] Some of them were found serving as cess pits, others supported drains.

Nos. 1 and 3 in Pl. XXIV are shapes that are well known at Mohenjo-daro.[70] No. 2 is a large pan which is shown in situ in Pl. XVI(a). Its base inside bore an incised pattern that was much like that on a fragment of a pan seen in Pl. XXXVIII, 9. The deep groove round the neck of No. 4, which is again illustrated in Pl. XVII(g), was perhaps provided to hold a cord to tie down a lid or cloth cover. This jar contained a skull, a large shell, and some metal objects (Pl. LXIX, 11-15), and its discovery is described in p. 25.[71]

The cordoned jar, No. 5, is a new variety and had been pressed into service to support the brick drain shown in XVII(a). Its well finished surface is coated with a cream-coloured slip, and the ribs are formed of thin strips of clay, which were carefully placed in position and then smoothed over with the fingers to effect a close adhesion to the jar. Whether this method of strengthening a jar was an independent invention or borrowed from contemporary Sumer, where it was common, is not yet known.[72] No ribbed jar of this type is known from Mohenjo-daro.

No. 6 in Pl. XXIV (see also Pl. XXXV, 3), is much like No. 4, except that the lower part of its body has a pronounced inward curve designed to make it rest more securely on its stand. No. 7, with its high neck and flat base, upon which it stands well, is a most unusual jar.

A photograph of a very graceful jar common at Mohenjo-daro, may be seen in Pl. XXXV, 2. This vessel is coated outside with a brown and inside with a red slip, a very rare procedure. No. 9 in Pl. XXIV, of a common form, was discovered lying close to, and level with, the large pan (No. 2) described above.

A noticeable feature of some of these storage jars is the concave base, formed, it may be,

[68] *F. E. M.*, pl. LXIV, 42. Its original hollow foot is missing, and all traces of it have been removed by grinding.

[69] Two large jars from an earlier excavation are pictured in Majumdar, *Explorations in Sind*, pl. XX, 26, 28.

[70] *F. E. M.*, pl. LVIII, 4, 8.

[71] A description of the skull will be found in Chapter XVI.

[72] Several ribbed jars have been found in the Kulli mound in Baluchistan. These, it would seem, are contemporary with the Chanhu-daro vessel: Stein, *Mem. Arch. Surv. Ind.*, No. 43, p. 124, figs. 41, 42. At Nāl, cordoned jars were very common: Hargreaves, *Mem. Arch. Surv. Ind.*, No. 35, pl. II (b, c).

by setting the vessels on a pivoted stand while their surfaces were being finished. The final touches have been given to these jars so carefully that it is difficult to decide exactly how they were made. Several large vessels from Mohenjo-daro appear to have been built up of coiled strips of clay and then completed on a turn-table.[73] Certainly no paddle was ever used on their surfaces.

All these jars are adequately baked, and the same materials were used in their manufacture as for the rest of the pottery. They are frequently decorated, sometimes with elaborate designs, sometimes only with thin lines of black, as in Pl. XXXV, 3. The finely painted jars in Pl. XXXV, 1, 4 are painted in black on rather rough red slips.[74] Other painted jars of this type from Chanhu-daro appear in Mr. Majumdar's Report,[75] and many of the sherds shown in Pls. XXX, XXXI, XXXII, XXXIV, etc. are portions of jars of the storage type.

A plain red slip is used on Nos. 2, 6, and 8 in Pl. XXIV and a cream-coloured one on Nos. 4, 5, and 7. Nos. 1, 3, and 9 appear to have had no slip at all. As already mentioned, No. 2 in Pl. XXXV is coated with a brown wash, possibly in an attempt to render it water-tight.

Except for the objects found in Pl. XXIV, 4 and a bone implement (Pl. XC, 23) from No. 2 in Pl. XXXV, these jars yielded little of interest. The three pieces of pottery numbered 30-32 in Pl. XXVIII were found inside No. 3 in Pl. XXIV. The cordoned jar No. 5 contained no less than nine small vessels, eight of which are shown under numbers 10-17 in Pl. XXVIII; the ninth jar of this group was of the same shape as No. 12. Lastly, the grey bowl shown in Pl. XXVII, 64 came from the inside of No. 9 in Pl. XXIV.

A very unusual variety of storage vessel is illustrated in Pl. XXIX, 37. It measures 15.5 inches in diameter and 11 inches high and is coated with a cream slip. The projecting ledge around it shows that it must have been fitted with a lid, but this was never found. This pan is encircled by a double row of ventilation holes, each 0.25 inch in diameter, and it may be assumed, therefore, that its original purpose was to hold food. When it was found, however, it contained a number of copper and bronze implements and tools, some of which are illustrated in Pls. LXVII, 1-12, LXXIII, 29, LXXIV, 1, LXXVI, 19.

A smaller pan in Pl. XXIX, 43 has a ring base and is ornamented with purplish-black lines applied on a red-coloured wash.

From its position high up on the summit of Mound I, the storage jar shown in Pl. XL, 4 is thought to belong to the Late Harappā Period. In shape, especially in regard to its incurved lower portion, it is not unlike some of the jars in Pl. XXIV, but it differs from them in being covered with a thick sand deposit almost up to the neck. This coating has been grooved with the fingers to form a rough pattern.

[73] F. E. M., p. 212. Some of the large Jhukar jars appear to have been made in the same way, as witness the face of the large sherd in Pl. XLVII, 15.

[74] Nos. 1 and 4 in this plate are 21.2 and 21.75 ins. high respectively.

[75] *Explorations in Sind*, pl. XX, 26, 28.

NEW TYPES OF POTTERY

Type AT (Pls. XXIX, 5-11, XXXIX, 16)

A strange-looking vessel is the tall conical cup of which examples may be seen in Pl. XXIX, 5-11. At Chanhu-daro this new form largely takes the place of the roughly made cups (Pl. XXIX, 28) which have appeared in such quantities at Mohenjo-daro. These narrow vessels could have held but a minimum of liquid and would have had to be emptied before they could be set down again; some of them can hardly stand on their inadequate bases. Taking their instability into account and also the fact that Sumerian priests are represented as holding libation vessels of much the same shape,[76] we may infer that at Chanhu-daro this particular type of pottery served a similar religious purpose.

Most of this pottery is of rough workmanship and heavily pared. Sometimes the latter is very carefully done and the facets left by the knife are almost regular, as is seen, for example, in the little cup 3.4 inches high in Pl. XXXIX, 16. Very few of these vessels have a slip, although No. 7 in Pl. XXIX has one of cream. The type has been found at levels ranging from − 6.6 to + 11.0 feet.

Type ATA (Pl. XXIX, 12-15, 17-24)

This is a slight variation of the preceding type and embraces cups with concave sides, a feature especially pronounced in Nos. 23, 24. Like those of Type AT these little vessels have been heavily trimmed, and in consequence their small flat bases show slightly rounded edges. No. 13, which is hand-made, comes from a level as low as 23.8 feet below datum level. A pink-coloured slip covers No. 22, but the remainder are of little interest apart from their shape.

The pottery vessels described below cannot at present be included under any type letter, until we know whether or not their forms are accidental.

Plate XXVI. No. 66, a cup-like vessel, is thin for its size and is without a slip. It can barely stand on its very narrow base. No. 71, with its thin flared mouth and narrow neck, has a very graceful shape. It is ornamented with broad bands of purplish-black on a light red slip.[77]

Plate XXVII. No. 33 in this plate is illustrated again in photograph in Pl. XXXIX, 18. It is an oval, hand-made dish with its rim overhanging its interior and suggesting that it had been made to hold a liquid. It has no slip but is otherwise of careful work. No. 39, with its markedly concave sides, is a curious vessel. Its flat, wide rim bears a decoration of a series of loops in dark red, and wavy lines of the same colour encircle its body, which is coated with a pink slip. From the style of its decoration this bowl could belong to the Jhukar Period. It was found at the foot of Mound II, but may have rolled down from a higher level.

[76] C. Zervos, *L'Art Mesopotamie*, pl. 83. Vessels of very similar form in metal, stone, and clay have been found on many Sumerian sites: Frankfort, *Oriental Institute Communications*, Chicago. No. 20, p. 7 (6); Woolley, *Royal Cemetery*, pls. 235 (42, 43), 251 (7c, 16).

[77] It is possible that this jar may be of Jhukar work.

No. 53 is not unlike in shape the vessels of Type Y,[78] but lacks the deeply grooved sides of that type and, moreover, has a ring base. It is extremely well made and is ornamented with four pairs of purplish-black lines on a light red slip.

The decoration of No. 68 consists of a number of thick and thin lines in purplish-black on a smooth red coating. Its tall neck, which may once have possessed a flared lip, is coloured a warm black and its high foot is thickly covered with a pink-coloured slip.[79]

Plate XXVIII. The deep, overhanging rim of No. 2 distinguishes it from the vessels of Type AJ. Heavy for its size and without a slip the lower portion of this jar is ragged and badly trimmed. A thin spiral line decorates the body of No. 14, which somewhat resembles Type SA, but nothing quite like this specimen has been found at Mohenjo-daro.

No. 18 is a very large version of Type C. It has a red-coloured slip and its lower portion shows considerable trimming. The deep groove round the middle of No. 29 is a most unusual feature. This jar is without a slip and its sides below the groove have been heavily scraped. No. 34 is a well-made flask which bears very pronounced string grooving on its flat base and should have been included with the Jhukar pottery.

PAINTED POTTERY OF THE HARAPPĀ PERIOD

Polychrome Ware

The fragment of a bowl, illustrated in line in Pl. XXXIII, 6 and in photograph in Pl. XXXVI, 23, is the only specimen of polychrome ware of this period that has appeared at Chanhu-daro. On it is painted the figure of a squirrel, facing to the right with paws held to its mouth and tail carried aloft.[80] The body of the animal is white with the outlines and markings in black. Behind it is a roundel, also in black and white, followed by an indefinite object that looks like a tree. Facing the squirrel is a bird with head turned backwards and coloured a dark red outlined with black. All these motifs are set on a light yellow ground. The lower register shows a row of bright red spots encircled with black on a white base. This multi-coloured bowl was evidently a valued possession, for attempts had been made to repair it. One of the rivet-holes used, 0.1 inch in diameter, may be seen on the right hand edge of the sherd in Pl. XXXVI, 23. In its original condition this bowl must have been of exceptional excellence for it is carefully painted, the squirrel, in particular, being a very realistic piece of work. It is worth noting that the painter has avoided using bright tones for an animal whose natural colouring in India is grey and black. It is indeed possible that grey was the colour used for the squirrel in the first place, and that this, in the course of time, has faded to white. The bird next to the squirrel is perhaps intended for a peacock, a favourite subject for the decoration of the monochrome pottery, as we shall presently see.

[78] *F. E. M.*, pl. LIII, 21.

[79] Compare the shape of this vessel with one of Jhukar date in pl. XLI, 38.

[80] This is the first appearance of this animal on painted pottery, though models of it in faience have appeared at Mohenjo-daro: *M. I. C.*, pl. XCVI, 7; *F. E. M.*, pl. LXXVII, 20.

Monochrome Wares

Monochrome painting is nearly always carried out in black, or purplish-black, on a red slip, and in this respect it does not differ from the monochrome wares of Harappā and Mohenjo-daro. Occasionally, a cream-coloured slip is used in place of the red one, or, rarer still, the natural surface of the pottery is employed as a ground. The black or purplish-coloured paint is a manganiferous haematite, ground down in water, which when applied to a non-porous slip, such as a red one, remains slightly in relief and has a matt appearance. When painted on a cream slip or on a jar with no slip at all, it is more rapidly absorbed and consequently looks thinner and inclines to dark purple in hue.

Designs

No human figures occur on any of the painted wares of the Harappā Period.[81] Animals and birds, especially the latter, are, however, quite common, but geometrical and floral designs are the most frequent and were evidently held in high regard. The large storage jars are very often extensively decorated, practically the whole of a jar being covered with a maze of design, except for the base which normally would be hidden by a stand or by the earth in which it was sometimes set. Floral sprays with birds among the branches (Pl. XXXVI, 7, 9), peacocks amid trees and undergrowth (Pl. XXXVI, 14, 16), goats nibbling at trees (Pl. XXXVI, 25), all find a place in the delightful scenes painted on the larger jars. Conventionalized plant forms are popular, the pipal tree being the favourite subject (Pl. XXXVI, 37), but formal geometric patterns are somewhat infrequent, if an exception is made in the case of the intersecting circle design (Pls. XXIII, 4, 5, XXXVII, 40-42, 47, 48). So few painted vessels are without some traces of this pattern that it might well be called the hall-mark of the Harappā Culture.

Simple bands and borders suffice to decorate the smaller pieces of pottery, so that much of the surface is left bare, but great trouble was taken to avoid blank spaces on the larger wares. This *horror vacui* often led a jar-painter to over-elaborate his work (Pls. XXXIII, 8 XXXV, 4, XXXVI, 14, 19), rather than to rely on simple forms and back-grounds. On the other hand, this confusion does give an idea of the way the colouring and markings of animals in the Indian jungle melt, by a natural process of camouflage, into the surrounding foliage.

In describing this painted pottery it will be convenient to group together the various forms and patterns that decorate it. The animals will, therefore, be dealt with first.

Ibex. Though this beast is frequently depicted on the Mohenjo-daro pottery, it occurs but once on a sherd from Chanhu-daro, where it is shown in an alert position against a background of trees or bushes (Pl. XXXVI, 24). The body of the animal is filled in with cross hatching and it appears to stand in an enclosure, if we may so regard the curved line that shuts this scene in. Despite the stick-like legs and the unnatural curves of the body this ibex still retains a certain amount of realism, in striking contrast to the inanimate objects that

[81] I exclude a certain type of pottery found at Harappā which is definitely of a later date than that now under survey.

fill in the rest of this border.[82] Possibly this wild goat was not very familiar to the jar-painters of Chanhu-daro, for the city lies on the eastern side of the Indus and well away from the rocky heights of Baluchistan where this animal still abounds.

Antelope. Two antelopes, painted in black on a thick red slip, appear on the sherd in Pl. XXXIII, 1. The beasts are very crudely drawn, and the long straight horns of one of them terminate in tufts, which add to its bizarre appearance. Each animal has a long tail ending with a plume and arranged to fill in an empty space. The bodies are carefully hatched, and to avoid monotony, one beast looks to the front and the other has its head turned round.

The hind-quarters of what may be another antelope may be seen on the right hand side of the large sherd in Pl. XXXII, 7.

Goat. This animal was domesticated in very early times in India. It is clearly depicted on the two sherds shown in Pls. XXXIII, 5, XXXVI, 25, but for want of space the beast on the first sherd has no forelegs, though the horns and beard are plainly indicated. The shape of the former rather suggests the markhor, a species which wanders in large herds in Baluchistan and has been repeatedly bred in confinement with the domestic goat.[83]

The head of the animal in Pl. XXXVI, 25 has a bird-like appearance, perhaps because the jar-painter intended to draw a peacock, but then changed his mind and added the body and limbs of a goat. The awkward position of the legs seems to confirm this impression.[84]

Animals arranged *en file* seldom appear on the wares of the Harappā Culture, but the sherd in Pl. XXXVII, 27 provides an interesting example of this disposition which again appears on a second fragment from Chanhu-daro.[85] The style of decoration on these two sherds precludes them from being of Indian work and we must look somewhere to the west for the source of their manufacture.[86] This *en file* arrangement frequently appears on Elamite pottery, although in some cases the figures have become so degraded that they are hardly recognizable as animals.[87] A geometric motif derived from the same source is commonly found on wares from Nāl.[88] The same distorted figures of animals are also known on two sherds from Mohenjo-daro;[89] the painter of them possibly had no idea of their original meaning.

Squirrel. This animal only appears on the polychrome sherd in Pl. XXXVI, 23, already described.

[82] This is a fragment of a medium-sized jar painted in black on a light brown and rather thin slip.

[83] *Capra Falconeri,* Hugel.

[84] Cf. the head of this animal with those of the birds in Pl. XXXVI, 16.

[85] Majumdar, *Explorations in Sind,* pl. XX, 9. The animals here are described as stags, which they may well be.

[86] These rows of animals, each resembling the other, occur quite frequently on the wares of Baluchistan: Stein, *Mem. Arch. Surv. Ind.*, No. 43, pls. XXII (Kul. IV. I), XXVIII (Mehī. I. I. 7), XXIX (Mehī. III. 4. 2), XXXII (Maur. I. 2).

[87] *Mem. Dél. en Perse*, t. XIII, pls. XVIII, 3, 5, XLII, 2.

[88] Hargreaves, *Mem. Arch. Surv. Ind.*, No. 35, pls. XVII, 57, XVIII, 12.

[89] *M. I. C.*, pl. XC, 21; *F. E. M.*, pl. LXVIII, 7.

Hare. A hare is undoubtedly depicted in Pl. XXXVI, 19, though its ears are so merged with the background that it was at first difficult to identify. This is the first known appearance of this animal on pottery of the Harappā Culture, although it is well known on certain copper tablets which come from Mohenjo-daro.[90] It is hard to say whether any particular religious significance was attached to the hare in ancient India; many of the inhabitants of that country see a hare amongst the markings on the moon.[91] It was worshipped as a deity in Egypt and appears in the art of that country as early as predynastic times. It was also used as a motif on seals up to the time of the Sixth Dynasty[92] and occurs among Egyptian hieroglyphs as well as in the Hittite script.

Serpents. Representations of serpents on the pottery of this period at Chanhu-daro are always associated with the cone-like objects depicted on the sherds in Pls. XXX, 5, XXXVI, 14, 32, XXXVII, 30, 35, 36, the last specimen being a particularly good example.[93] It is impossible to determine the species of snakes as badly drawn as these, but they are certainly not cobras, which reptiles sometimes appear on amulets from Mohenjo-daro.

Fishes. Two pieces of pottery illustrated in Pl. XXXVI, 17, 21 show fishes nibbling at water-weeds. Both scenes are too roughly drawn, however, to show their species; in all probability they are river rather than sea fish. It has been suggested that these fishes are to be considered hooked, but, if so, the lines would surely be taut instead of wavy. In Pl. XXXIII, 4 four fishes are arranged round the narrow mouth of a kohl-pot, a very uncommon decoration for a jar of this type. The strange animal in Pl. XXXVI, 20 may be a mud-fish from the shape of its head, and the short chevron-like markings that surround it may here be an attempt to represent water.[94]

Although there are many fish signs in the script, fishes seldom appear on the painted wares of the Harappā Culture. At Mohenjo-daro one fish appears on a polychrome sherd,[95] but on no other piece of pottery. Elsewhere, it is quite a common motif, occurring on the wares of Nāl and Mehī-damb in Baluchistan,[96] the early pottery of Elam,[97] and the early painted wares of Samarra.[98]

Birds. Birds of many kinds are depicted on the Chanhu-daro pottery (Pls. XXXII, 2-9, XXXIII, 2, 3, 7, 12, XXXV, 1, XXXVI, 1, 2, 4, 5. 8-16, 18, 22, 23). The peacock, a sacred bird in many parts of India to-day, was the favourite subject and is easily recognisable by

[90] *M. I. C.*, pl. CXVII, 5, 6. A faience model of this animal is also shown in *F. E. M.*, pl. LXXIV, 20. At Harappā it appears on a small paste seal: *Ann. Rep. Arch. Surv. Ind.*, 1927-28, pp. 84, 85.

[91] Crooke, *Folklore of Northern India*, II, p. 50.

[92] Petrie, *Buttons and Scarabs*, p. 2.

[93] Serpents associated with the same objects occur on a sherd from Mohenjo-daro: *M. I. C.*, pl. XCII. 23.

[94] Cf. with the fish shown in Stein, *Mem. Arch. Surv. Ind.*, No. 43, pl. XXIX (Mehī. III, I, 5).

[95] *F. E. M.*, p. 219, pl. LXX, 10.

[96] Hargreaves, *Mem. Arch. Surv. Ind.*, No. 35, pl. 62; Stein, *Mem. Arch. Surv. Ind.*, No. 43, pls. XXI. XXIX.

[97] *Mém. Dél. en Perse*, t. XIII (117, 174, 175); t. XX (19, 20).

[98] Herzfeld, *Samarra V*, figs. 5-7, etc.

its crest and spreading tail (Pls. XXXII, 3, 4. XXXIII, 2, 12, XXXV, 1, XXXVI, 4, 12, 16, 22). Birds identical in shape with these are sometimes shown without a crest, the omission being perhaps due to hurried work (Pl. XXXII, 2, 4, 8, 9).

The peculiar exaggeration of the crests of the birds in Pls. XXXII, 3, XXXIII, 2, 12, XXXV, 1 shows an exuberant imagination. A plant-form actually takes the place of the crest in Pl. XXXIII, 2, while the two are combined in Pl. XXXIII, 12.[99] This close association of a plant-form with this bird is of special interest, for peacocks are definitely connected, in some parts of India, with earth worship or with an earth goddess; they figure, for instance, in the great earth festival held by the Khonds of Southern India.[100] The solar emblems surmounting the tall crest of the peacock in Pl. XXXIII, 12 are also of particular importance. Here there certainly seems to be an association with the sun as well as with the earth, the latter being represented by the two leaves on either side.[101]

The little scene in Pl. XXXII, 3 possibly depicts the same bird standing over a nest. The head of a young one appears just above the edge of it and the parent bird either is arranging the home or has brought food to the fledgling. The parent bird, it will be noted, has a crest similar to that of the peacock in Pl. XXXIII, 2.

The peacock does not figure elsewhere on ancient pottery, probably because it is a native of India;[102] in very early days it was possibly unknown to other countries.[103]

The bird in Pl. XXXII, 6 (see also Pl. XXXVI, 1) is possibly confined in a cage or trap,[104] but so much is missing from this scene that its interpretation is difficult. A model pottery cage and bird from Mohenjo-daro proves that birds were kept in cages by the people of that city.[105]

It is difficult to say to what species the two birds in Pl. XXXII, 7 belong. Their strong legs and outstretched wings suggest that like the ostrich they represent a kind more accustomed to running than to flying. A water-hen was perhaps in the mind of the painter of Pl. XXXIII, 3. Although the curious attitude is rather that of a bittern, the tail is against any such identification unless this part is a separate motif that became mixed up with the bird. No. 7 in the same plate may be the common coot,[106] large flocks of which are found in Sindh, especially near the lakes.

Insects. The figure in Pl. XXXVI, 26 is obviously an insect; the curved leg or filament on each side of the body strongly suggests a water boatman. The objects surrounding it also look to me to be water-plants.

[99] Compare pl. XXXIII, 2 with another sherd from Chanhu-daro: Majumdar, *Explorations in Sind*, pl. XX, 6.

[100] Hopkins, *Religions of India*, pp. 528, 536.

[101] This will be readily understood by those who have seen a peacock in erect plumage in the glaring sun.

[102] Though still found in Sindh, the bird is thought by some to have been introduced there by human agency.

[103] This will have to be amended if the bird painted on a bowl from one of the Khurāb burials in S. E. Persia be accepted as a peacock: Stein, *Archaeological Reconnaissances*, pl. XXXIV, 5.

[104] It is not unlike a bul-bul in appearance.

[105] *F. E. M.*, pl. LXXXI, 6.

[106] *Fulica Atra*, Linn.

Trees and Plants. A painted jar or sherd without some floral or plant design upon it is a rarity. The most common plant motif is the pipal tree, either represented in a natural manner, as in Pl. XXXVI, 9, or conventionalized, as in Pl. XXXII, 1, a. Sometimes, as will be seen in Pl. XXXIV, 5, the leaves of this plant are barely distinguishable from those of other plants, but when arranged in a stylized way, as in Pls. XXXI, 2, 3, XXXVI, 37, this pipal design forms a very striking decoration. Here the jar-painter has made the most of his skill and carefully avoided all extraneous details. It will be noticed that in Pl. XXXVI, 37 and again in Pl. XXXV, 4 he has been careful not to commit the common fault of allowing the hatching to overlap the outlines of the leaves, and one gets the feeling that he (or she) thoroughly enjoyed painting these two storage vessels and that more time than usual was spent upon them.

Many of the plants appearing on the pottery are represented as growing in the ground. Examples of these may be seen in Pls. XXXI, 2, 3, XXXII, 1, a, XXXVI, 29, 37, where a little mound of earth is shown at the bases of some of them.[107] In India it is still a praiseworthy act to plant and nourish one of the sacred trees, and it may be that some of the painters of this pottery derived their inspirations from actual sacred trees growing in their own compounds.

A very common motif is the chain of leaf-like objects to be seen on the sherds in Pls. XXX, 7, XXXI, 16, 20, XXXII, 1, 1, a, XXXIII, 12, XXXVI, 16, 21, 26, XXXVII, 20, 26, 29, some of which have filaments projecting from them on one side. Rows of these linked together appear conspicuously on the large storage jar in Pl. XXXV, 1 and on the sherd in Pl. XXXVII, 24. As the motif is associated with water-animals in Pl. XXXVI, 21, 26, it may be derived from some kind of water-weed. Sometimes each element in the chain has a dot in the centre, making it not unlike that of a bird's head (Pl. XXXII, 1, 1, a). Occasionally the elements are separate and scattered about the field as in Pl. XXXII, 4.[108] This motif, whether connected or detached, is rarely seen on the pottery from Mohenjo-daro.

Neither the broad-leafed tree or bush in Pls. XXXIII, 8 and XXXV, 1, 4, nor the plant shown in Pl. XXXIV, 1 can at present be identified. The shrub or tree with fringed leaves in Pls. XXXIV, 9 and XXXVII, 17, 22, which also appears on the Mohenjo-daro pottery,[109] may be a representation of the nim tree.[110] This tree is regarded as sacred by the Hindus, its leaves being held to possess, among other magical qualities, the power to prevent disease. The carefully drawn branches and leaves on the sherd in Pl. XXXIV, 9 look rather like mimosa, but they may represent the khair tree,[111] whose sprigs are used in India to protect the wearer against the Evil Eye.

[107] The same little heap of soil is also associated with a tree cut on a seal from Chanhu-daro: Majumdar, *Explorations in Sind*, pl. XVII, 34.

[108] Cf. with the bird's heads on pottery from Luristān: Contenau et Ghirshman, *Fouilles du Tépé-Giyan*, pl. 67. On the other hand is this particular motif a variation of the guilloche pattern that so often appears on Sumerian and Cappadocian seals and also on the pottery of Persia?

[109] F. E. M., pl. LXIX, 11; LXX, 25.

[110] *Azidirachta Indica.*

[111] *Acacia Catechu.*

In some cases it would appear that the jar-painter had no particular tree or bush in mind and let his hand wander freely over his work. His chief concern seemed to have been to cover the surface of a jar as quickly as possible so as to start work on another vessel. Many of the designs on the pottery show evidence of this hurried labour, and comparatively few pieces have had sufficient time spent upon them.

Festoons. The festoon ornament on the sherd in Pl. XXXVII, 24 is made up of vertical chains of the leaf-like motif described above, linked together by ribbon loops. This pattern has been carefully drawn, but another example from Chanhu-daro has not been so well carried out.[112]

Intersecting Circle Patterns. Patterns of this kind were as common at Chanhu-daro as at the other cities of the Harappā Culture. Various examples of them will be seen in Pls. XXIII, 4, 5, XXX, 11, 16, 17, 22, XXXIII, 8, 11, XXXVII, 34, a, 40-42, 47, 48. Their delineation in Pl. XXXVII, 40, 47 (see also Pl. XXIII, 4, 5) is particularly careful. Rougher work may be seen in Pl. XXXVII, 42. On the large storage jars in Pl. XXXV, 1, 4 a circle motif takes a prominent place, and in vessels of this kind about half the painted area is usually occupied by this pattern. No other decoration is as a rule placed below it, but a wide register above it is generally reserved for other forms of decoration.[113]

The extreme regularity of the design in Pl. XXXVII, 40 (see also Pl. XXIII, 5) suggests that it was not drawn free-hand, although no marks have been left to prove this. A sherd from Mohenjo-daro bearing the same pattern has faintly incised lines, carefully spaced out, to serve as a guide to the jar-painter.[114] The large jar-cover illustrated in Pl. XXXVII, 47 and in colour in Pl. XXIII, 4 is ornamented with a circle design painted in black on a burnished red slip, the most carefully finished example of this type of decoration yet discovered.

Patterns of this kind are not often found outside India. At Arpachiyah in Northern Iraq Mr. Mallowan unearthed a bowl covered with a pattern composed of four-petaled rosettes, so regularly drawn that intersecting circles must have been used as a guide for them by the painter.[115] The same design has been found on pottery of very early date from the Brak mound in North-west Syria,[116] while at Chagar Bazar, also in Syria, a sherd decorated in this same manner has come to light, which, if it had been found in Sindh would have been readily accepted as belonging to the Harappā Culture.[117] These examples from Iraq and Syria are, however, considerably earlier than any of the wares of the Harappā Culture, and Mr. Mallowan tentatively suggests that "perhaps these early potters of Assyria and Syria moved eastwards and in some region yet unexamined carried on that tradition for

[112] Majumdar, *Explorations in Sind*, pl. XX, 24.
[113] Majumdar, *Explorations in Sind*, pl. XX, 26, 28.
[114] *F. E. M.*, p. 22; pl. LIV, 6.
[115] Mallowan and Rose, *Prehistoric Assyria*, fig. 60(3).
[116] Mallowan, *Illust. Lon. News*, Oct. 15th, 1938, p. 699.
[117] Mallowan, "Excavations at Tall Chagar Bazar," *Iraq*, vol. III, pl. II, 2. Mr. Mallowan was the first to note the resemblance.

which we seem to find comparatively late evidence in India."[118] With this statement I am fully in accord, for as I shall point out later some very close resemblances exist between a later (Jhukar) pottery found at Chanhu-daro and the Tall Halaf wares from Mr. Mallowan's excavations.

A very interesting intersecting circle pattern covering a large part of a pavement in the palace of Ashur-bani-pal, Nimrôd, provides a good example of this type of ornament in use at a much later date.[119] The Egyptians never used circles freely in decoration and apparently not at all before the Eighteenth Dynasty. At this time and later, however, an intersecting circle pattern was in use which resembles very closely the Indian examples.[120]

Rayed Solar Motifs. These very striking motifs, which were so popular with the Chanhu-daro people, are not represented at Mohenjo-daro and rarely occur on wares of contemporary date from other parts of Sindh and the Panjāb. They take various forms and positions on the pottery. Especially prominent specimens will be seen on the sherds in Pls. XXXI, 1, XXXIII, 10, 13, 14, XXXVI, 40, 41, and its use as a repetition motif in wide borders will be observed in Pls. XXXIII, 11, 17.

The centre of the device is either a plain circle with a spot in the middle or an annulus divided into four quarters, each of which is filled in with some form of ornamentation (Pls. XXXIII, 10, XXXVI, 41). The rays issuing from the centre may be either straight with oblique ends, as in Pl. XXXI, 1, or set at a tangent, as in Pl. XXXIII, 10, 14, 15, 17, etc., this last being by far the most common. Each ray terminates in a leaf-like form, pipal leaves being used in Pl. XXXIII, 16.[121]

This combination of plant-form and orb perhaps symbolizes the close connection between vegetation and sunshine, and the tangential forms successfully convey a belief that the sun was a rotating body, It should be noted, however, that, as in the case of the svastika (an allied solar emblem) the direction of the revolution, whether clockwise or anti-clockwise, did not trouble the artist.

It has been said that this solar sign does not occur on pottery from Mohenjo-daro, but something akin to it has been found there carved on a seal. This is a six-rayed object with one ray terminating in the head of a horned animal.[122] A sun-symbol with seven rays, each ray terminating in a pipal-leaf and closely resembling the emblem in Pl. XXXIII, 16, appears on one side of a faience sealing from the excavations at Harappā.[123] Very elaborate and complex examples of the same motif combined with leaves and buds are used in Madras and Bengal to-day to decorate thresholds and floors on special occasions.[124] They also occur on the ancient punch-marked coins of India.[125]

[118] *Op. cit.*, p. 42.

[119] H. R. Hall, *Babylonian and Assyrian Sculpture in the British Museum*, p. 49, pl. LIV.

[120] Petrie, *Egyptian Decorative Art*, pp. 47, 48, figs. 87, 88.

[121] Cf. a third sherd from Chanhu-daro in Majumdar, *Explorations in Sind*, pl. XX, 12.

[122] F. E. M., pl. C(g). Dr. Legrain has already pointed out that horned animals are frequently associated with sun symbols. On Lycian coins we find the horse and birds occupying the same position: *Culture of the Babylonians*, pl. LV; see also P. E. Dumont, *Journ. Amer. Orient. Soc.*, vol. 53, pp. 331-2.

[123] *Ann. Rep. Arch. Surv. Ind. 1928-29*, pl. XXXII (b, 10, b).

[124] H. G. Durai, *Man*, 1929, sect. 60. See also *Man*, 1933, sect. 168.

[125] J. Allen, *Ancient Indian Coins (Cat. Brit. Mus.)*, 1936.

Further afield a seven-rayed object with spatulate ends is painted on the inside of a bowl from Arpachiyah, dated to the Late Tell Halaf Period.[126] The same symbol also occurs on an early steatite seal from Crete, but here ball-like appendages take the place of the leaves at the end of the rays.[127]

No examples of this radiant form of the sun-disc appear on Sumerian or Elamite pottery, through it is known on Sumerian seals from Tell Asmar and Kish[128] and again on seals from Susa.[129] In Egypt, buttons belonging to the period covered by the Ninth to the Twelfth Dynasties bear this motif,[130] and a very curious form of it, not found elsewhere, may be seen on a predynastic bowl.[131] It appears appropriately enough on the ceilings of some tombs at Thebes.[132] In Crete these radiant sun motifs are carved on Early and Middle Minoan seals, besides being painted on the pottery. In Baluchistan the symbol frequently is found on certain funerary wares from Shāhī-tump, but these may be of later date than the Harappā wares from Chanhu-daro.[133]

The fact that this rayed form of the sun motif is common to the art of so many countries makes the land of its origin a matter of conjecture.[134] Anatolia, perhaps, is the most suitable choice, for the symbol has been found there on Early Hittite pottery as well as on the later seals.

One of the most common motifs occurring on the pottery of the Harappā Culture is the roundel with deckled or serrated edges seen on the sherds in Pls. XXX, 1, 10, XXXI, 9, XXXII, 1, 1, a, 7, etc. This very simple form of the sun-motif was copied in faience and was frequently worn at Mohenjo-daro as a dress ornament.[135] Its place on pottery is to fill in empty spaces (Pls. XXXI, 2, XXXII, 1, 1, a, etc.) or to serve as a border pattern (Pls. XXIII, 2, XXXI, 9, XXXII, 7, XXXIII, 8, 11, XXXV, 4, etc.), while its appearance in the fish scene in Pl. XXXVI, 17 may possibly be an attempt to depict the reflection of the sun in the water.

Though so common on the pottery of the Harappā Culture, this motif is not included among the signs on the seals. The position is reversed in Crete,[136] for though it does not appear on the pottery of that island it occurs as a sign in the Minoan script.[137] The same

[126] Mallowan and Rose, *Prehistoric Assyria*, fig. 53.

[127] Evans, *Palace of Minos*, II, p. 218, fig. 123(a). The same form is to be found on M. M. I. vases, for which see Bosanquet and Dawkins, "Palaikastro Excavations," *Journ. Brit. Sch. Athens*, Suppl. Pap. No. 1, 1902-06, pl. X.

[128] Frankfort, *Orient. Inst. Comm.*, No. 19, fig. 29. The seal in question is more clearly reproduced in Woolley, *The Development of Sumerian Art*, fig. 21(c); Mackay, *Anthrop. Mem.*, Field Mus., Chicago, vol. I, pl. XLII, 5, 7.

[129] Childe, *New Light on the Most Ancient East*, p. 243, fig. 93.

[130] Petrie, *Buttons and Design Scarabs*, pl. VII, 1, 2.

[131] *Journ. Eg. Arch.*, vol. XIV, p. 262.

[132] Petrie, *Decorative Patterns of the Ancient World*, pl. LI.

[133] Stein, *Mem. Arch. Surv. Ind.*, No. 43, pls. XV, XVI.

[134] It is also represented in the early art of Cappadocia, Greece, Cyclades, Danube basin, Sweden, America, and China.

[135] *M. I. C.*, pl. CXLV, 14, 15, 19; *F. E. M.*, pl. CXI, 23, 24.

[136] Evans, *Palace of Minos*, I, p. 282.

[137] Its association with a sign which also does not appear on the seals should be noted in pl. XXXIV, 4.

symbol is frequently depicted on the painted wares of Northern and Southern Persia; at Tepe-Giyan it was especially popular,[138] A possible variation of the symbol with dots around the circumference in place of the usual serrations occur on several bowls from Arpachiyah.[139]

Svastika. This four-limbed symbol of the sun finds no place on the pottery of the Harappā Culture though it frequently appears on beads and amulets. Possibly the jar-painters refrained from placing such a lucky sign on objects that were liable to breakage. It is of interest to note in this connection that the svastika is only portrayed on special burial pottery in Baluchistan, which normally would stand in little danger of being broken.[140]

Scale Patterns. Scale patterns of a simple type were especially popular with the people of Chanhu-daro, who sometimes used the device to cover large areas of their vessels, thereby creating a very monotonous effect. Examples of the various uses of this motif will be seen in Pls. XXX, 4, XXXI, 12, 14, 15, XXXII, 1, 1, a, XXXIII, 1, XXXIV. 15, XXXVII. 25. As a rule scale patterns are roughly executed, but particular care was taken in the case of Pl. XXXI, 12, which is unusual in its regularity and unique in the manner in which the middles of the loops are thickened. Lines of lunar markings are thus formed, each being put on separately and giving the finished work the effect of continuity.

An unsightly design appears in Pl. XXXI, 14. This at first sight seems to be made up of a number of minute circles, each with a dot in the centre, but closer inspection will show that it really consists of a number of loops, forming a most unusual scale pattern.

The more elaborate scale patterns that were so favoured at Mohenjo-daro have no counterparts at Chanhu-daro.

Chequer Patterns. This type of ornament is only represented on three sherds from Chanhu-daro (Pls. XXIII, 1, XXX, 24, XXXVII, 8); at Mohenjo-daro it was much more common. The pattern is without doubt derived from basket work and examples of it are to be seen on most ancient wares. It occurs as early as the Tall Halaf Period.

Ladder Patterns. Quite large areas were occupied with this pattern as the sherds in Pls. XXXI, 18, 19, 22, XXXVII, 28, 44 will show. When carefully executed, as in Pl. XXXI, 18, 22, the effect produced is not unpleasant, but when the ratlines are fine and closely spaced, as in Pl. XXXVII, 28, the result is most unpleasing. This type of decoration is also known on the Mohenjo-daro pottery; it is possibly derived from the rope sling in which some of the larger jars were carried.

Hemispherical Motifs. The significance of the linked hemispherical objects portrayed on the sherds in Pls. XXXI, 8, 17 and XXXVI, 10 is unknown. They are always arranged

[138] Contenau et Ghirshman, *Fouilles du Tépé-Giyan*, pls. 21, 24, 65, etc.; *Mém. Dél. en Perse;* t. VIII, pp. 112, 128, 134; t. XX, p. 122.

[139] Mallowan and Rose, *Prehistoric Assyria*, figs. 65, 67.

[140] Stein, *Mem. Arch. Surv. Ind.*, No. 43, pls. XV, XVI, XVII. On some pieces of this burial pottery from Shāhī-tump, the svastikas have five and even six arms and should perhaps be rightly termed rayed sun-motifs.

in parallel rows and in one case (Pl. XXXVI, 10) appear to enclose the figure of a bird. They may, therefore, be nets or traps of some kind, a supposition borne out by the trap-like objects alongside the apparently imprisoned ibex in Pl. XXXVI, 24. At Mohenjo-daro single motifs of hemispherical shape occupy the vacancies of a loop pattern,[141] but at Chanhu-daro they are never used in this way.

Comb Motif. Examples of this queer motif are illustrated in the upper registers of the sherds in Pls. XXIII, 3, XXXI, 12, XXXII, 1, XXXIV, 15, and similar objects appear on the pottery of Mohenjo-daro.[142] Those who doubt the fact that combs can be used as motifs on pottery should refer to particularly distinct examples on vessels of the Tell Halaf Period from Northern Mesopotamia.[143] Combs are also painted on an early bowl from Susa.[144] Why such objects are represented at all on pottery raises a question that cannot be easily answered. That they formed part of the equipment of a potter is shown by the incised patterns on the two sherds in Pl. XXXVIII, 26, 29, but it seems unlikely that he regarded this one tool as important enough to be embodied in the designs on his wares. Special combs are used for the hair of deities in many Indian temples to-day, and it is not impossible that one of these articles, reserved for this purpose, was actually venerated in centres of the Harappā Culture.

Hide Motif. This name has been given to the motif on the sherd in Pl. XXXVII, 13, though whether the jar-painter had a hide in mind when he pictured it is open to question. A motif not unlike it was in common use at Mohenjo-daro set vertically or horizontally in broad borders.[145] The same form of ornament is sometimes found on Elamite wares.[146]

Pedestal Motifs. This peculiar device though common at Chanhu-daro, appears but once at Mohenjo-daro.[147] It consists of a row of objects shaped like hour-glasses (Pl. XXX, 2-4, 6) which closely resemble the cane stands in general use in India to-day, frequently carried by food-vendors at railway stations. Their Indian name is *modhā* and the clay stands found on many Sumerian sites are thought to be copies of the same form.[148]

It is possible that the cut fragments of pottery shown in Pl. XXXVIII, 6, 7, 10, 11 were originally parts of stands resembling and almost contemporary with the tall pottery stands of Sumer.[149] It is, however, difficult to explain why objects of this description

[141] F. E. M., pls. LXIX, 21; LXX, 7, 40, 41.

[142] *M. I. C.*, pls. LXXXVII, 6, LXXXIX, 9, XCI, 13, 14, 16.

[143] Mallowan and Rose, *Prehistoric Assyria*, fig. 78 (28); Von Oppenheim, *Tell Halaf*, pl. LIII, 1.

[144] De Morgan, *La Préhistoire Orientale*, III, fig. 70.

[145] *M. I. C.*, pls. LXXXIX, 5, XCI, 1-6. Other examples of it will be found in Majumdar, *Explorations in Sind*, pls. XV, 33, XVI, 21, XXII, 6. Childe regards it as being derived from the intersecting circle design, *Ancient Egypt and the East*, 1933, pts. I, II, p. 17.

[146] *Mém. Dél. en Perse*, t. XX, p. 106.

[147] F. E. M., pl. LXX, 34. Similar objects are portrayed on two sherds from Kohtras Buthi: *Explorations in Sind*, pl. XXIX, 31, 35.

[148] "A Sumerian Representation of an Indian Stand," *Journ. Roy. As. Soc.*, 1933, pp. 335-338, pl. IV.

[149] For Sumerian examples of this cut ware see Frankfort, *Oriental Institute Communications*, No. 20, 1934-35, pl. II, 12-14; Watelin, *Excavations at Kish*, IV, pls. I; XVI, 6.

should serve as motifs on Indian pottery. Possibly the real articles were used to support sacred vessels, a suggestion which is corroborated by the fact that their Sumerian counterparts have been found in at least one temple.[150] The Sumerian word for these clay stands is *masab*, indicating that their prototypes were of reed form.

The significance of the cone-shaped objects appearing on the sherds in Pls. XXX, 5, XXXIV, 15, XXXVI, 32, XXXVII, 30, 35, 36 is unknown. On the pottery they are always divided from one another by vertical wavy lines resembling serpents and particularly so in Pl. XXXVII, 30. The same motif, associated also with snake-like forms, is a prominent feature in the decoration of a large jar from Susa.[151]

Linked Ball Motifs. The type of decoration shown on the lower parts of Pls. XXXI, 20-22, XXXVI, 4, 29, 39, XXXVII, 20, 37 invariably appears on a jar at the basal junction of the ornamented and unornamented portions. It is found only on large storage jars and may be a survival of the rope slings in which some of these vessels were carried. If this be so, the balls in the pattern may stand for the knots in the sling. The same device is commonly found on the Mohenjo-daro jars and on pottery of the same period from other parts of Sindh.[152] It usually runs all round the jar, but occasionally, as in Pl. XXXVI, 4, alternates with simple loops.

Scrabble Markings. The markings illustrated on the sherds in Pl. XXXIV, 13, 16 are used to cover considerable areas of large jars. They are generally arranged parallel to one another and may be set vertically, horizontally, or obliquely; the rough way in which they are painted is in effect good. A similar mode of decoration occurs also on the Mohenjo-daro pottery.

Cruciform Motifs. Motifs in the form of a cross are decidedly infrequent. A St. Andrew's cross may be seen on the painted jar in Pl. XXXIX, 23 (see also Pl. XXIII, 6), and a large storage jar previously found by Mr. Majumdar at Chanhu-daro also bears the same design.[153] This form of cross, besides appearing among the signs of the Harappā script,[154] and on seals and amulets from Mohenjo-daro,[155] also occurs on two early painted sherds from Samarra.[156] With the exception of this last ware it does not appear to occur on Sumerian and Elamite pottery, though other forms of crosses are quite common. A St. Andrew's cross from Tal-i-Pir, Haraj, in south-eastern Persia forms part of a very effective and unusual design.[157] On Indian pottery the motif is painted in black with a square white

[150] For instance the Abu Temple at Tell Asmar.

[151] De Morgan, *La Préhistoire Orientale*, III, p. 75, fig. 110. For other examples from Chanhu-daro see Majumdar, *Explorations in Sind*, pl. XX, 20, 25, 28.

[152] *Ann. Rep. Arch. Surv. Ind.*, 1927-28, pl. XXVIII, 22; *Explorations in Sind*, pls. XXII, 29, XXVI, 14, XXVIII, 16. Compare this motif with one from Tepe Giyan: Contenau et Ghirshman, *Fouilles du Tépé-Giyan*, pl. 58.

[153] *Explorations in Sind*, pl. XX, 28. See also pl. XXVI, 5 for an example from the site of Ghazi Shah.

[154] *M. I. C.*, pl. CXXVI (cclxxxiii).

[155] *F. E. M.*, pl. XC, 14.

[156] Herzfeld, *Samarra V*, p. 92; pl. XXI, 85.

[157] Stein, *Archaeological Reconnaissances*, pl. XXIX (vi. 25).

centre, whereas on the Samarra and Persian wares it is depicted the other way, namely, the centre only is black or red.

A variation of the design is seen in Pl. XXXVII, 12, composed of four triangles with the corners of their bases touching. This form is unknown at Mohenjo-daro.

Double Triangle Motif. This motif is frequently used as a border design on the wares of the Harappā people, and that it was in common use at Chanhu-daro the sherds in Pls. XXX, 18, 20, 21, XXXVII, 7, 9-11 will show. The triangles in Pls. XXX, 18 and XXXVII, 11 differ from the others in not being completely filled in, while in Pl. XXXVII, 9-11 solar motifs are used to fill the voids between them. The same association of a solar motif with the double triangle is present on at least one piece of Elamite pottery from Susa.[158]

The setting of the motif is usually vertical at Chanhu-daro. At Mohenjo-daro it is sometimes horizontal or in alternate positions.[159] When horizontal, as on the sherd in Pl. XXXVIII, 2, it can be likened to the double-axe symbol of Crete,[160] but no claim to relationship can be made, considering the purely geometric nature of the motif and the ease with which it can be drawn.

Rosettes. The four-petalled rosette which is used as a border pattern in Pl. XXXVII, 14 is also well known at Mohenjo-daro.[161] Outside India, this motif is particularly well represented on the wares of Tell Halaf and Samarra,[162] but it is not found in Elam, except on the early seals of Susa.[163] Here, however, it is set upright and not in the usual *saltaire* position. The rosette rarely appears on the pottery of Baluchistan, although one very unusual example of it was unearthed at Moghul-ghuṇḍai, painted in two colours on a black ground.[164]

It seems unquestionable that the motif was evolved, as Childe has pointed out, in India[165] as well as in Early Assyria, from the intersecting circle pattern, of which Pl. XXXVII, 41 is a good example. One bowl in particular from Arpachiyah is almost covered with these rosettes arranged in such a way as to show the origin of the pattern.[166] This use of the rosette motif extended down to the Jhukar Period as the sherds on Pls. XLVI, 3, XLVIII, 21 will prove.

Rhomb Motifs. This simple pattern, although common on the painted wares of Sumer and Elam, is seldom found on the pottery of the Harappā Period. One example from Chanhu-daro is illustrated in Pl. XXXVII, 15, the rhombs being hatched in two direc-

[158] *Mém. Dél. en Perse*, t. XX, p. 125.

[159] *M. I. C.*, pl. XCII, 10, 14-17.

[160] In this position it appears amongst the signs on the seals: *M. I. C.*, pl. CXXIII (cxxxix).

[161] *M. I. C.*, pl. XCI, 9-11.

[162] Mallowan and Rose, *Prehistoric Assyria*, fig. 60 (3); pls. XV, XVI, etc.; Von Oppenheim, *Tell Halaf*, pl. LII, 3; Herzfeld. *Samarra V*, pls. XV, 29, XIX, 78, XX, 53-55, XXXII, 219, 224, XL, 272.

[163] Delaporte, *Catalogue des Cylindres*, I, pl. 18 (17, 20).

[164] Stein, *Mem. Arch. Surv. Ind.*, No. 37, pl. XI (MM. N. 26), XIV (D. 4).

[165] *Ancient Egypt and the East*, 1933, pts. I, II, pp. 16, 17.

[166] *Prehistoric Assyria*, fig. 60 (3). I have already referred to an intersecting circle pattern on a sherd from Tall Chagar Bazar: Mallowan, *Iraq*, vol. III, pl. II, 2.

tions and enclosed by border lines. At Mohenjo-daro it is known on only two sherds.[167] It was a favorite motif in the preceding Amri Period[168] and it often appears on the modern painted wares of Sindh.

Single Hatched Borders. The vertical lines used for the hatching of this variety of border are wavy in Pl. XXX, 14 and straight in Pls. XXXIV, 12 and XXXVII, 33, but the effect is much improved when thick lines are employed as in Pls. XXX, 8, XXXIV, 12. The leaf-like markings in the last example are particularly attractive, but none of these simple methods of filling a border is very common.

Double Hatched Borders. Pls. XXIII, 6, XXVI, 82, XXVII, 81, XXX, 9, 10, 15, 19, XXXVI, 24, XXXVII, 30, 33, 43, 48 are all examples of a favourite method of border decoration. It is found most frequently on the smaller pieces of pottery, but the hatching, though always oblique, varies very much in appearance, being in some cases carefully executed and in others roughly.

Bead Borders. This common pattern is most often found on the necks of large vessels at Mohenjo-daro[169] and appears to be derived from a string of beads. Curiously enough, the example illustrated in Pl. XXXII, 7 is the only one that has come to light at Chanhu-daro.

Simple Loop Patterns. These, as a rule, are used to decorate the inside edges of bowls and dishes (Pls. XXX, 19, XXXIII, 7, 15, XXXIV, 7, XXXVI, 13, XXXVII, 39), although they are sometimes seen on the lower parts of storage jars (Pl. XXXVI, 4).

A distinctive form of the loop pattern is often employed for borders (Pls. XXIII, 2, 6, XXXI, 11, XXXIII, 7, 11, 17, XXXIV, 8, 12, 15, XXXV, 4, XXXVI, 11, 16, 21, 22, 32). The loops have been converted into rows of panels with curved tops or bases by filling in the requisite spaces; the compartments so formed are generally occupied by solar emblems. On one sherd from Mohenjo-daro hatching has been used in place of solid colour.[170]

Loop patterns form a link between this early pottery and the later painted wares of the Jhukar Culture, where they are used in multiple form to decorate the edges of food-stands, as will be seen in Pls. XLII, 1, 7, XLIII, 5, 7, 8, etc. It is interesting to note that the edge of a dish was still the favourite place for them.

Unusual Motifs. It is difficult to identify the curious ball-like objects with a line through them which appear on the sherds in Pls. XXXI, 14, XXXVII, 1-3. They certainly suggest some form of basket-work and may be traps or cages of some kind. On the other hand they may perhaps be compared to the cult object of basket form which appears before the urus animal on some of the seals.

Summary. From this brief description of the various motifs used on the pottery of the Harappā Culture at Chanhu-daro, it will be noticed how plant forms predominate in the

[167] *M. I. C.*, pl. XCI, 21; *F. E. M.*, pl. LXVII, 6.
[168] Majumdar, *Explorations in Sind*, pl. XVIII, 25, 26, 30, 31, etc.
[169] *M. I. C.*, pl. LXXXVII, 6, XC, 21, XCI, 13, XCII, 3, 24; *F. E. M.*, pls. LXVIII, 3, 5, 23, LXX, 13.
[170] *M. I. C.*, pl. LXXXIX, 12.

scheme of decoration. Even the common intersecting circle pattern may, on occasion, be so elaborated as to convey the impression of a climbing plant. Although the plant motifs are, in many cases, roughly executed, the effect produced is always natural and lively, even when a design is over-shadowed by a wealth of detail in the background. When animals are present, they are, it is true, sometimes crude and wooden in appearance, but this cannot be said about many of the birds, for the realism with which they are drawn is seldom equalled on ancient pottery. A great deal of imaginative feeling has also gone into their composition, the curious crests of some of the peacocks being cases in point.

It will be observed, too, that comparatively few of the animals are in stereotyped positions. In most cases they are performing natural actions—the insect is swimming, the fishes nibbling, the squirrel foraging, while the birds are shown in their natural surroundings and even feeding their young. This is even more remarkable when the disadvantages of pottery as a medium of decoration are taken into consideration. Though few alterations were possible and faulty work could not be erased, the jar-painter none the less performed his task with confidence and skill.

In present-day Sindh it is the men who make and the women who paint the pottery,[171] and we shall not be far wrong in thinking that the credit for the decorating of the Chanhu-daro and allied wares should be given to the women.

It is interesting to compare the purely geometric style of decoration so popular on the wares of the earlier Amri and the later Jhukar Periods with the free designs on the Harappā pottery of Chanhu-daro and other sites. From this alone we may perhaps assume that the people of the Harappā Culture temporarily imposed their civilization and their art on another and distinct people who were already in occupation of North-western India. When in time the Harappā people disappeared or, possibly, assimilated in the older population, their art would have given place once more to the earlier ideas and geometric decoration, though applied to pottery of improved shapes and types.

[171] Harrison remarks that in the case of hand-made pottery the potter is nearly always a woman, while the opposite holds good in the case of pottery made on the wheel, *Pots and Pans*, p. 34.

CHAPTER VII

POTTERY OF THE JHUKAR CULTURE

This class of pottery takes its name from the site in Sindh where it was first discovered. Early in 1928, the late Mr. N. G. Majumdar commenced a tentative investigation of the two mounds of Jhukar situated about six miles west of the town of Larkana,[1] and was rewarded by the discovery of pottery and other objects belonging to several cultures. Remains characteristic of the Harappā Period were found in the lower levels of Mound "A" at Jhukar, but above them lay other buildings, together with a new kind of pottery which Mr. Majumdar termed "Late Jhukar."[2] Still higher up the mound evidences of a third culture, the "Indo-Sassanian," first came to light, but are not the concern of this book.

The makers of the "Late Jhukar" wares unearthed by Mr. Majumdar lived in houses constructed of burnt brick similar to those built by the people of the earlier Harappā Culture. It would seem, therefore, that they either reoccupied deserted dwellings of their predecessors or re-used old material taken from the levels below. In all probability they did both, as their fancy or circumstances dictated.[3]

Soon after the excavation of Mound II at Chanhu-daro was commenced, convincing evidence came to light that it had been occupied by a people using the same class of pottery that had been found in the second, or middle, stratum at Jhukar. On both sites the pottery was discovered in levels just above those containing remains of the Harappā Culture, and there remains, therefore, no doubt that the makers of this Jhukar pottery were the immediate successors of the Harappā people, whose buildings and other remains lay below.

The pottery and other objects of the Jhukar period unearthed at Chanhu-daro did not, however, come exclusively from the upper levels of Mound II. In some cases the weathering of the mound had caused material to be washed down its slopes and sometimes Jhukar material actually lay below later deposited Harappā remains. These facts must be borne in mind when the catalogue at the end of this book is consulted as they explain why objects belonging to the same culture come from such different levels. It is only when a mound has been well penetrated or sliced that a true perspective of its contents can be obtained.[4]

Some Differences Between the Jhukar and Harappā Wares

(1) The Jhukar painted pottery is usually decorated in two colours, red and black,

[1] *Explorations in Sind (Mem. Arch. Surv. Ind.)*, No. 48, pp. 5-18.

[2] Mr. Majumdar's "Early Jhukar" pottery is now identified with that of the Harappā Culture.

[3] At Chanhu-daro they acted in the same way.

[4] The lowest level at which a piece of Jhukar pottery was found (Pl. XLVI, 35) was 5.8 ft. below datum in the "Great Cutting."

excluding the slip, while the Ḥarappā pottery is always in monochrome, i. e., black on a red slip.[5]

(2) The designs and motifs on the Jhukar pottery are entirely different from those of the earlier wares. In the case of the Jhukar the style is geometric, in that of the other, naturalistic.

(3) The fabrics of the Jhukar people are coarser and more porous than those of their predecessors. The firing of the pottery is also inferior.

(4) The red slips employed on some of the Jhukar pottery are not always polished; when a polished slip is used, it has not the careful finish of the earlier wares, while the pigment used is of a much brighter tint. The cream-coloured slips, which are always thickly laid, have a peculiar straw-pitted surface, a feature entirely absent on the Harappā wares.

Clays

The Jhukar pottery is made from a clay that burns pink in the furnace and in this respect it resembles most of the Harappā fabrics. Mica and lime were the principal tempering materials, the latter occurring in quite large particles. Sometimes a drab-coloured body is found, the sherds and vessels in Pls. XXXIX, 14, XL, 13, 15, 16, 21, 24, 25, XLI, 33, XLVI, 38, XLVIII, 65, all being of this colour. No grey ware seems to have been manufactured in this period.

Hand-made Pottery

Hand-made vessels were found in some numbers and formed about the same proportion of the total number of finds as in the preceding period. They are mainly of specialized types, as Pls. XXXIX, 11-14; XL, 15, 16, 18, 23-25, 27, 32, XLI, 18, 23, 32, 33, 43, XLVIII, 2 show, and were probably made in the homes of their owners. The remainder of the pottery, both painted and unpainted, was raised on a quick wheel. A cord, as in the previous period, was sometimes used to separate a vessel from the wheel, the marks it made being particularly noticeable in the vessels shown in Pls. XL, 29, XLI, 27, 31.

Firing

It is possible that the Jhukar pottery was baked in trenches or pits heaped over with brushwood or straw. This is still a common practice in Sindh to-day, and it would account for the curious straw-marks that disfigure some of the slips. The firing is sometimes very indifferent. The sherds illustrated in Pls. XXXIV, 21, XLI, 10, 33, XLV, 35, 37, XLVI, 31, XLVII, 15, and XLVIII, 20, all have dark, underbaked cores, a fault which is rarely encountered in the Harappā pottery.[6]

[5] I exclude certain polychrome wares which otherwise bear no resemblance to the Jhukar pottery.

[6] Similar under-baked interiors have been noted in vessels from Periāno-ghuṇḍai. The pottery from this site somewhat resembles Jhukar work: Stein, *Mem. Arch. Surv. Ind.*, No. 43, p. 34, pl. V.

Trimming

The lower portions of some of the vessels show signs of having been trimmed. This is especially noticeable in the specimens shown in Pls. XXXIV, 22, XL, 14, XLI, 28, 34, 40, 44, 45, while the upper part of the large jar seen in Pl. XLVIII, 1 was heavily pared when the clay was almost dry. It is difficult to say, however, whether this procedure was followed as extensively as it was in the Harappā Period, for so few pieces of Jhukar work have been found intact.

Make

The greater number of sherds and vessels are of substantial thickness, although no heavier than some specimens of Harappā pottery. Quite thin vessels were also manufactured, the pieces illustrated in Pls. XLI, 41, XLII, 4, 19, 20, XLIV, 5, XLV, 36, 39, XLVI, 24, 33, 34, XLVII, 6, and XLVIII, 1 all being examples of this description. No. 39 in Pl. XLV is a photograph of part of a large storage jar. This is an unusual sherd, not only because of its surprising thinness, but also because, as its inner side clearly shows, a paddle was used to consolidate the clay. A thick deposit of sand, a portion of which is just visible in the photograph, had originally been laid over the lower part of the jar to help keep its contents cool.[7]

Plain Wares

An examination of the catalogue at the end of this book will show that a great deal of this pottery is unpainted; indeed, about two-thirds of the Jhukar vessels and sherds found at Chanhu-daro are undecorated. Hand-made vessels are never painted, though they are commonly covered with a slip of some kind.

Slips

Slips are not always present on the unpainted pottery, specially in the case of the hand-made specimens. The sherds illustrated in Pls. XLIV, 6, XLVII, 24, 27 are also without a slip, though painted in one or two colours.

Cream-coloured Slips. Slips of this colour are the most common of all and occur on painted as well as on unpainted pottery. They never seem to have been polished and have sometimes been applied so thickly that they are inclined to scale. They are also very absorbent, for sometimes paint applied to them has penetrated to the pottery underneath. Examples of this slip appear in Frontispiece (b), 1, 3, 4, 8, 9, 10.[8]

Red Slips. Red slips are also common, but the shades of this colour are not quite the same as those used on the wares of the Harappā Culture. Sometimes the slip is polished, sometimes unpolished, although in the latter case it is not always easy to say whether the lack of this finish is deliberate or caused by the action of the soil. These red slips vary in

[7] It has already been pointed out that a similar sand coating is present on some of the storage jars of the Harappā Period.

[8] Even the ink used to mark our finds in the field had a tendency to run on this kind of slip.

tint between an orange and a cherry red, and the fact that they differ from those on the older pottery may be because of imperfect baking or because the ochre used came from another source.

The broad horizontal red bands decorating so much of the Jhukar pottery are applied on top of the body slips. For this reason they are included among the paints in the catalogue, although they cover considerable areas on much of the pottery.

Red slips are the sole decoration of the vessels illustrated in Pl. XLI, 34, 39, 40, 46. In the first two examples, this slip extends only as far down as the carinated portion; below this the surface has been left bare. No. 48 in the same plate has been similarly treated, but here the base bears a cream-coloured wash. As a general rule the red slips serve as a ground for linear markings or designs painted in black, purplish-black, or purple. The bowls in Pl. XL, 22, 31 are ornamented in this way, the first very irregularly. Two examples in colour of the same black on red are shown in Frontispiece (b), 5, 6, both pieces illustrated belong apparently to the same bowl.

The fragments of food-stand dishes seen in Pls. XLI, 2, XLIV, 12, 15, XLV, 22, 31, XLVI, 1, 4, 7, 17, 39, 43, XLVII, 5, 16, 30 bear a red slip on their inner faces only and are coloured pink outside. Other sherds from similar dishes and also the small bowl in Pl. XLVII, 25 have cream-coloured exteriors and red interiors.[9]

Two slips, a red and a cream, are found beside each other inside the fragments of dishes shown in Pls. XLIII, 8, XLVI, 16. The outside of these pieces bears the second colour only and the same combination occurs on the two jars in Pl. XLI, 28, 36, the last having three black spots painted on one side. A red and a pink slip are found on the sherd in Pl. XLV, 33, both serving as a ground for various motifs in a purple-coloured paint. Slips of the same two shades appear on the almost perfect jar illustrated in colour in Frontispiece (b), 2.

Pink Slips. These slips are very numerous, the tint being particularly decided on the vessels and sherds in Pls. Frontispiece (b), 2, 7, XLI, 27, XLV, 27. Sometimes this coloured slip apparently covered the entire jar or dish,[10] while in other cases it is applied to the interior only, the outside being of another colour.[11] Of the reverse procedure only three examples have come to light, namely the base of the food-stand in Pl. XLI, 15 and the fragments of dishes in Pls. XL, 26, XLV, 37.[12]

A pink-coloured slip is used on the inside of the dish in Pl. XXXIV, 18, the exterior of this piece bearing no slip at all.

Grey Slips. The fragments of painted pottery seen in Pls. XLV, 30, 41, XLVII, 3 appear at first sight to be covered with a grey slip, but closer examination will show that the grey is caused by accidental burning.

[9] Pls. XXXIV, 17, 21, XLI, 12, 14, 25, XLII, 25, XLIII, 4, 7, 10, XLIV, 13, XLV, 25, 26, XLVI, 6, 8, 12, 16, 27, 41, XLVIII, 23.

[10] Pls. XXXIV, 22, XXXIX, 9, XL, 28, XLI, 13, 19, 20, 27, 35, 45, XLII, 12, 19, XLIII, 9, XLV, 24, 28, 29, 42, XLVI, 3, 23, 28, XLVII, 8, 10, 13. No. 24 in Pl. XLV is reproduced in colour in Frontispiece (b), 7.

[11] Pls. XL, 20, XLIV, 10, XLV, 27, XLVI, 5, 9, XLVII, 7, 17. The exterior slip is cream-coloured.

[12] The interior of these dishes is cream-coloured.

Yellow Slips. A slip of a decided yellow colour decorates the large storage jar in Pl. XLI, 49, which piece is shown in situ in Pl. XLVII, 34. Although the colour may be due to accident, it may be remembered that slips in this colour are sometimes found on the polychrome pottery of the Harappā Period, one example being illustrated in Pl. XXXVI, 23.

Paints

Red and black are the two main colours used in the decoration of the Jhukar pottery; red for the broad horizontal bands so characteristic of this ware and black for edging these bands as well as for the motifs and patterns. Sometimes the black has a distinct purple tinge, while in other cases a decided purple is employed. The designs in Pls. XXXIX, 9, XLI, 4, 35, XLII, 6, 13, XLV, 20, 36, XLVI, 23, 26, XLVII, 7, 9 are executed in a brown-coloured paint.[13]

Only two of these colours are used to decorate a single vessel, though three or more shades of the same colour frequently appear.[14] For instance, the red used for a pattern may differ slightly in tint from that of the bands on a jar.[15] Again, the motif on the sherd in Pl. XXXIV, 21 is painted in dark red on a light red slip, while the light red chequers in Pl. XLII, 20 are outlined in a darker shade.

Examples of bichrome ware are far more numerous than those ornamented in monochrome, principally because highly decorated foodstands were very popular with the Jhukar people. Storage jars painted in two colours were also preferred to the plainer kinds. The decoration of the monochrome pottery is usually simple, consisting of plain lines and borders in red,[16] purple, black, or brown.[17]

Earth colours only were employed; red ochre for making the various shades of red and a manganiferous haematite for the blacks and purples. The browns may have been prepared from another haematite or by mixing two colours together.

In some cases the colours were applied with mops of various sizes. Sometimes the jar-painter used a fine brush, probably made from the teased-out end of a twig, although it is not impossible that proper brushes of hair were expressly made for this purpose. The absorbent nature of some of the slips made it necessary to use a liberal quantity of paint and this sank into the ground, so that the slight relief effect so common on the Harappā wares is seldom present on the Jhukar vessels. All the paints have a matt surface and there are no indications that any binding substance was mixed with them.

The red bands that make this pottery so distinctive are, in many cases, so regularly drawn that there is reason to think each jar must have been set on a turn-table for the purpose. The wheel that was used to raise the vessel may have been employed for this purpose. The women who paint the decorated pottery that is still made in various parts of Sindh use a wooden block pivoted on a stone or piece of brick, and so great is their skill

[13] No. 20 in Pl. XLV is illustrated in colour in Frontispiece (b), 10.

[14] The slip colour is excluded in every case.

[15] Noticeable in Pls. XXXIX, 15, XL, 26, XLI, 2, XLII, 16, Frontispiece (b), 9.

[16] Pls. XXXIX, 9, XL, 12.

[17] Pls. XL, 19, 20, 22, 28, 31, XLI, 35, 36, 41, XLII, 4, Frontispiece (b), 5, 6.

with this simple apparatus that they can draw a line round a jar so that its ends meet exactly.[18]

It seems likely that some of the designs on the Jhukar pottery were carefully measured, if not outlined beforehand, before they were painted. No. 12 in Pl. XLIII looks much too regular to have been entirely free-hand work and the same applies to No. 6 in Pl. XLVII. This process is, however, not a new departure, for some of the painted designs on the Harappā pottery are also extraordinarily regular, as, for instance, the pattern on the sherd in Pl. XXXVII, 40.

Potmarks

Potmarks are rare. On the back of the dish in Pl. XLVII, 12, a rough cross (shown in No. 31 in the same plate) is painted in purplish-black. The three irregular black spots on the jar in Pl. XLI, 36 seem in this case to be identification marks, though similar spots on the small vessel shown in colour in Frontispiece (b), 2 are arranged in four sets at equal distances round the jar and here obviously intended as an ornament.[19]

A very conventional tree is deeply scratched on the base of the food- or jar-stand shown in Pl. XLVIII, 4, but this may have been meant as a decoration. A cross-like marking, part of which is missing, is heavily incised on the side of the vessel in Pl. XLVIII, 19, but as the edge and interior of this broken specimen are deeply scored, the symbol, apparently a Greek cross, is a decorative feature and not a true potmark.

One can be more definite concerning the incised markings shown in Pl. XLVIII, 20. These were placed opposite to one another inside the dish of an unpainted stand, which appears in line in Pl. XLI, 10. The four-petalled rosette cut on the sherd in Pl. XLVIII, 21 also seems to be a true potmark.

Incised and Relief Work

The incised work carried out in the Jhukar Period is entirely different from that of the earlier material. No complete examples have yet been found and the majority of the sherds shown in Pl. XLVIII come from jars of varying sizes. With the exception of No. 2, all the sherds shown come from wheel-made pottery.

The jar-cover appearing in Pl. XL, 17 has its rim and knob handle roughly incised, the first with a wavy line and the second with crossed lines similar to those scored on the knob handle in Pl. XLVIII, 13. The top of the rim of the large jar-stand in Pl. XL, 30 is ornamented with wavy parallel lines made with some toothed instrument, while the interior of the same vessel is vertically partitioned with similar lines set at intervals with about 4.7 inches between each group. The sherd in Pl. XLVIII, 19, is incised in the same way on the top edge, and inside it has been scored all over in a very regular and careful manner with some tool resembling a comb.

Nos. 11, 13, 17, 22 in Pl. XLVIII are knobs from jar-covers of the type illustrated in Pl. XLI, 18, 23, which seem to have been expressly made for large jars only. The star with

[18] "Painted pottery in Modern Sind," *Journ. Roy. Anthrop. Inst.*, Vol. LX, pp. 127-135.

[19] This jar (No. 5164) was found at locus 484 in the "Great Cutting" at the level — 1.4 ft.

five rays cut on No. 17 is reminiscent of the solar patterns so common on the painted Harappā wares (Pl. XXXIII, 10, 11, 15, 17, etc.), and the spiral on No. 11 recalls some of the incised patterns found on the dishes of food-stands belonging also to the earlier period (Pl. XXXVIII, 19, 21, 25).

Plate XLVIII. No. 1 in Pl. XLVIII is thinly made and was once part of the rim and neck of a large storage jar. The surface of the clay has been roughened by paring when it was almost dry and the surface thus formed has been impressed with a series of oblique strokes more or less regularly arranged. A deep zig-zag line also ornaments the neck.

The only example of relief decoration is illustrated in No. 2. This is a portion of a hand-made bowl with an unpierced lug projecting from one side.[20] The neck of this interesting fragment which measures 3.4 inches long is roughly ornamented with flat overlapping pellets of clay, a mode of decoration foreign to any other Indian pottery of early date.[21]

The four sherds, Nos. 3, 10, 18, 24, come from different jars. The first and last of these have a portion of the surface horizontally divided into ledges, which, in the case of No. 24, average 0.32 inch in depth. They are pitted at regular intervals with blind holes, which produce a most curious effect. Nos. 10 and 18 are also decorated with a row of metopes made with some serrated instrument. No. 24 was probably once ornamented in the same way.

The fragments of the large storage jars No. 5-9, 12, 14-16, all bear incised patterns of various kinds. The strange motif appearing on Nos. 6 and 16, is, perhaps, intended to represent fish. No. 25, part of a coarsely made jar, has no less than three kinds of ornamentation; a cord impression, two lines of deeply incised zig-zags, and, above and below these, ribbing.

Round the outside of the pan No. 23 are no less than eight spiral cord impressions. These are so carefully arranged that they must have been intended as a decoration, for it would have been unnecessary to bind this vessel so regularly merely to guard against its cracking while being dried. The spouted jar in Pl. XLI, 44, which is not of large size and therefore unlikely to have cracked, bears four similar lines of cord impressions.

The marks of a cord may also be seen on the lower portion of the medium-sized jar illustrated in colour in the Frontispiece (b), 8 and again in photograph in Pl. XLVI, 33, 34. Sometimes the vertical edges of food-stand dishes bear such cord impressions, No. 4 in Pl. XLI and two similar dishes not illustrated being examples of this technique.[22]

In some cases, therefore, it seems likely enough that cord markings were intended to be decorative and in others they served their original utilitarian purpose. Cord impressions sometimes appear on the pottery of the Harappā Culture, but always on those of large size which did need a certain amount of binding to prevent fissures in the drying process.[23]

[20] There was probably a second lug on the opposite side of this bowl like that in Pls. XL, 23.

[21] The nearest approach to this type of decoration is to be found on sherds from North Baluchistan, which, however, appear to be of later date: Stein, *Mem. Arch. Surv. Ind.*, No. 37, pls. I, XIV, XV.

[22] Nos. 2088 and 2141.

[23] *M. I. C.*, p. 291; *F. E. M.*, p. 212.

Ring-bases

A vessel with a ring-base is as rare in the Jhukar Period as in earlier times. In the case of the three examples that we are able to illustrate (Pls. XL, 19, 31, XLI, 17) the base has been made separately and the joining has been done so carefully that it is difficult to detect it. The foot of the fine chalice in Pl. XLI, 26 hardly comes in this category nor do the lower portions of the food-stands so popular with the Jhukar people.

Pottery Types

A fair proportion of the Jhukar fragments were sufficiently preserved to allow us to ascertain the original shape of the vessels of which they once formed a part. The forms we were able to restore in Pls. XXXIX, XL, and XLI are, however, too few in number for anything but a rough classification and a more systematic arrangement must wait until further material of the same culture has come to light.

Food-stands and their Dishes (Pls. XL, 12, 13, 26, XLI, 2-6, 10-16, 19-22, 24, 25, XLII, 1, 7, XLIII, 1, 3, 5-8, XLV, 35, XLVI, 40, 42, 45, XLVII, 30, 31, XLVIII, 20, 23)

The Jhukar people at Chanhu-daro used both the tall and squat type of food-stand, but, unfortunately, not a single specimen has survived intact.[24] Fragments of the dishes belonging to these stands were found scattered about the upper levels of Mound II and one or two sherds lay high up on Mound I. Most of the painted sherds seen in Pls. XLII, XLIII, XLIV, XLV, XLVI, XLVII are parts of food-stand dishes whose sturdier stems and bases have more or less survived injury. As explained in the previous chapter the dish of a Harappā stand was always made separately from the stem and base and then joined together before the parts had dried. This technique was also adopted by the Jhukar potter and explains the reason why, when breakage did occur, the dish nearly always came away from the lower part of the stand.

These Jhukar utensils were elaborately decorated in several colours, the bulk of the ornamentation being confined to the interior of the dish. The exterior parts of the latter and the stems and bases are painted with simple lines in monochrome (Pl. XLI, 21, 22) or with broad bands of red paint, edged with black or purple lines (Pls. XLI, 13, 19, 20, 24, 25, XLVII, 30, 31).

Similar red bands, indicated in the line drawings by stippling, frequently divide the inside of a dish into two or three zones, as in Pls. XLII, 1, 7, XLIII, 1, 3, 6, XLVI, 42, 45. The band or bands on the exteriors are always situated close to the margin of the dish (Pls. XL, 26, XLVII, 30, 31); sometimes they do not appear at all, thin lines in purple or black being substituted for them.[25] The dish in Pl. XLI, 10, is remarkable for its lack of decoration, there being substituted for it two incised markings (shown in Pl. XLVIII, 20)

[24] This was also the case at Jhukar and Lohumjo-daro where fragments of these stands were found: Majumdar, *Explorations in Sind* (*Mem. Arch. Surv. Ind.*, No. 48), pls. XVI, 22, XXII, 28.

[25] This was the case with the dishes illustrated in Pls. XLIII, 5, XLV, 35, XLVI, 40, 45.

cut on opposite sides of its interior. As mentioned before, the sole decoration of the dish in Pl. XLVIII, 23 consists of string markings round its outer surface.

Pls. XL, 12, 26, XLI, 2-6, 10-12, 14, XLVIII, 23 show how the dishes of these food-stands vary in shape. Those having wide, flat, or nearly flat rims have this portion decorated with multiple loops, as shown in Pl. XLIII, 5-8, etc.

A very curious type of dish appears in Pl. XL, 12, the upper part of which is missing. Its exterior is decorated with a cream-coloured slip upon which is painted a chequer pattern in dark red, each red square alternating with one the colour of the ground. Underneath this dish is a break, showing where the stem had once been, and this is surrounded with twelve painted concentric circles.

It is a moot point whether these food-stands were inspired by the earlier Harappā specimens, for they are common to many cultures.[26] As I have said before, the Jhukar examples bear a resemblance, as far as shape is concerned, to some of the Harappā stands, but the way in which they are decorated is entirely different. It is as yet impossible to say whether they were in ordinary household use or reserved for religious purposes; the fact that not a single specimen has been found complete may have had nothing to do with any ritual aftermath.[27]

Footed Vessels (Pls. Frontispiece (b), 2, XXXIX, 10, XL, 19, 20, 31, XLI, 26, 27, 38)

This type of vessel occurs in various forms. No. 19 in Pl. XL is coated with a cream slip. On the outside a dark purple band decorates its rim, while inside are three irregular lines in the same colour. This interesting bowl was found resting on top of the wall at the South-western corner of room 137 in Square 9/E.

No. 20 in Pl. XL is coloured pink inside, and on the outside is decorated with thin purple lines on a cream slip. It is not particularly well finished, both surfaces being rather rough. No. 31 in the same plate is coated with a polished red slip and further ornamented with lines in black paint.

The cup in Pl. XLI, 26, a beautiful specimen with rather a high base, is undecorated; even the customary slip is absent. No. 27, beside it, is covered with a bright pink slip, which has trickled down in places over the foot. The base of the latter bears the marks left by the string used to sever it from the wheel. Similar chalice forms appear among the pottery of the Harappā Period and are illustrated in Pl. XXV, 44, 45.[28] Frankfort and Speiser suggest that the chalices found on Mesopotamian and Assyrian sites have an Anatolian-Transcaucasian origin,[29] but it is a matter of surmise how this type of vessel reached India, although it is significant that chalices have come to light on sites in Baluchistan and are

[26] See Fleure and Peake in *Journ. Roy. Anthrop. Inst.*, 1930, p. 52. They mention Egypt, Mesopotamia, Asia Minor, Crete, Sicily, Bosnia, and Spain as countries where such stands have been found.

[27] I hint at the ancient and modern custom in India and elsewhere, of breaking vessels that have served any religious purpose, to avoid being later put to improper use.

[28] See also *F. E. M.*, pls. LXI, 74, LXVI, 29, 49.

[29] E. A. Speiser. The Pottery of Tell Billa, *Museum Journ.*, Univ. Mus., Philadelphia, Vol. XXIII, p. 267.

there classed among the early wares.[30] It seems probable, therefore, that the type found its way to the Harappā people through South-eastern Persia and Baluchistan, if, indeed, the Harappā folk did not bring it with them. Whether the type was handed down to the Jhukar people or re-introduced by them must await further investigation.

The curious specimen in Pl. XLI, 38 (also shown in photograph in Pl. XXXIX, 10) is ornamented with a wide band of loops and spots in dark purple on a cream-coloured ground, while above and below this bold pattern are wide strips of red edged with purplish black. Unfortunately, the rim of this jar is missing, but it was probably coloured the same shade of purple as the neck. Vessels of similar shape have been found on the Jhukar mound,[31] and another came to light in one of the Harappā levels at Chanhu-daro (Pl. XXVII, 68). This last example, however, differs entirely from the Jhukar jar described above in style of decoration.

The small jar, 2.5 inches in height, shown in colour in Frontispiece (b), 2, probably once had a base resembling that of Pl. XLI, 38. It was unearthed from locus 484 in the "Great Cutting" at the level − 1.4 feet.

Spouted Vessels (Pl. XLI, 44, 45)

Both these interesting vessels have lost their rims. No. 44 is well made but is without a slip and its lower portion shows signs of having been pared. Four spiral cord markings round its widest part may be an attempt at decoration; a jar of this size would hardly have needed protection while drying. Part of the spout is missing, the hole through it at the break measuring 0.3 inch in diameter. No. 45 is covered with a pink slip and, as in No. 44, the lower portion and base have been trimmed. The upper portion is exceptionally well finished.

These two pieces are the only examples of their kind found at Chanhu-daro and have been assigned to the Jhukar Period because No. 44 was found at a high level in Mound II.[32] They may, of course, have been importations, but in shape they do not resemble those of contemporary Sumer, nor can they be compared with the spouted vessels discovered by Sir Aurel Stein in Baluchistan.

Jar-covers (Pls. XXXIX, 9, XL, 17, XLI, 18, 23, 32, 33, 35, XLVIII, 11, 13, 17, 22)

Thanks to their substantial construction, most of the jar-covers of the Jhukar Period have been found in more or less perfect condition, with the exception of one type which was hand-made and indifferently baked. The covers are occasionally painted or incised with patterns, and, though one or two examples resemble some of Harappā work, the majority are quite different from those made in the earlier period.

[30] Stein, *Mem. Arch. Surv. Ind.*, No. 43, pls. VIII, XVI, XXX.

[31] Majumdar, *Explorations in Sind*, pl. XVI, 17-19.

[32] Spouted vessels are practically unknown at Mohenjo-daro, only one example being recorded from that site: *M. I. C.*, p. 228. Fragments of such vessels have been found at Jhangar, but the forms of these differ from the Jhukar specimens. Majumdar, *Explorations in Sind*, pl. XXXI, 6, 11.

No. 9 in Pl. XXXIX, which appears in line in Pl. XLI, 35, measures 2.4 inches in diameter and is roughly decorated with concentric lines in purplish-brown paint on a pink-coloured slip. These lines are too faint to photograph. A rough hole pierces the handle of this cover, and a number of small holes, averaging 0.09 inch in diameter are arranged round the circumference. These were possibly provided for ventilation purposes like the notches round the edge of a cover of the Harappā Period illustrated in Pl. XXIX, 57.

The shape of the cover in Pl. XL, 17 is not unlike that of the Harappā specimens shown in Pl. XXVI, 12-34, but it differs in having an incised line on top of the rim and wavy crossed lines on the handle like those on the knob in Pl. XLVIII, 13. This cover bears a cream slip and, though well finished on the inside, has a rough and dragged exterior surface.

Nos. 18, 23, 32, 33 in Pl. XLI are simple, flat lids with broad strap-like handles. No. 33 is of drab ware, the remainder are of ordinary pottery. All are hand-made, badly baked and of rough workmanship. No. 18 has marks of burning on its base as if it had been used to stop a flue. In spite of their home-made appearance these covers, excluding No. 23, are coated with cream-coloured slips.

The four incised objects in Pl. XLVIII, 11, 13, 17, 22 are the tops of knob handles that once belonged to large covers. No. 22 is the best preserved of the four and is attached to what remains of a flat, round base like those in Pl. XLI, 15, 23, which they closely resemble except in the shape of their handles. They are all wheel-made and quite unlike covers that were used by the Harappā people.

Jar-stand (Pl. XL, 30)

This is the only jar-stand of Jhukar make so far discovered and is a particularly large one, measuring 17.7 inches in diameter. It is without a slip and around the top of the upper edge run a series of continuous wavy lines scratched with a comb or notched flint. Vertical lines of the same description are arranged in groups on the inside with intervals of about 4.7 inches between them. Possibly the interior incised lines, which would in the ordinary way be hidden by a jar, were provided to prevent the latter from shifting about on the stand.

Handled Vessels (Pls. XXXIX, 11, 12, XL, 23, XLVIII, 2)

Handles only occur on hand-made vessels. No. 11 in Pl. XXXIX, which appears in line in Pl. XL, 23, has a flat base and vertical walls, from which protrude two roughly formed, pointed lugs on opposite sides of the vessel. No. 12 in the same plate is a fragment of a bowl 2.1 inches high. A thick, flat handle projects from the side and probably a second was once opposite to it. The surface of this particular piece is very rough and retains traces of a cream-coloured slip. The curious fragment, also of a bowl, shown in Pl. XLVIII, 2 is 2.7 inches high and bears a vertical lug which is slightly different in shape to the other examples mentioned.

All the above handles are unpierced and were used to lift or support the vessels on which they were found, and which, likely enough, were used for cooking purposes.

Lamp (Pl. XXXIX, 14)

This specimen is 1.8 inches high and roughly made of a drab coloured clay. It seems to be a model made by a child, for the spout to hold the wick is set much too low for any but the minimum of oil to be contained in the vessel. No lamps of this type are known either at Chanhu-daro or Mohenjo-daro in the Harappā Period.

Storage Vessels (Pls. XXVI, 73, XLI, 1, 7, 8, 42, 49, 50, XLVII, 34, 35)

Many fragments of storage jars were found scattered about the summit of Mound II and in the débris round its base. Few perfect examples were unearthed, but even so there was quite enough evidence to show that both in shape and style of decoration they differ radically from the jars used in the preceding period.

Nos. 1, 7-9 in Pl. XLI show the contours of the rims and shoulders of four such jars; the painted face of No. 1 appears in Pl. XLIII, 12. No. 42 in Pl. XLI is a fine specimen, decorated in unusually simple manner with two bands of light red edged with purple with a thick purple line below. The narrow neck of this jar suggests that it had been used for water or some other liquid.

No. 49 in Pl. XLI is also illustrated in Pl. XLVII, 34 where its appearance when found and its type of decoration are shown. Four broad red bands divide this vessel into three registers and these are filled in with various motifs painted in purple. The ground is a yellow slip inclining to pink in places.

The large round pan in Pl. XLI, 50 is shown in its original position in Pl. XLVII, 35, but, unfortunately, the designs it bore were so obscured by lime deposits that they could not be copied in the field. Two wide bands of red, edged thickly with purple, decorate this curious vessel, and between the bands a pattern of hatched triangles can just be made out. A reddish-purple band on the top edge of this pan extends down inside for some distance and a ledge round it once accommodated a close fitting cover.[33] This particular type of pan was probably expressly made to hold bread or flour.

Some of the larger Jhukar vessels have a slight ribbing between the neck and shoulder as will be seen, for instance, in Pls. Frontispiece (b), 7, XLI, 1, 8, XLVI, 20, 44, XLVII, 4, 32, XLVIII, 16, 24.[34] The large incised fragment in Pl. XLVIII, 25 has two ribs instead of the usual one. This feature appears on but one storage jar of the Harappā Period (Pl. XXIV, 5), but this is an unique specimen with several ribs that were obviously applied for strengthening purposes. The ribs on the Jhukar jars are, on the contrary, intended merely for ornament; they are not prominent and are situated where they would afford but little protection to the vessel.

The small storage jar in Pl. XXVI, 73 has been erroneously inserted there. It is of Jhukar manufacture, is undecorated, and coated with a cream-coloured slip.

Globular Vessels (Pls. XXXIX, 15, XLI, 29, 36, 41)

No. 15 in Pl. XXXIX bears a pattern of oblique and horizontal lines in light red set

[33] Compare this pan with one of earlier date in Pl. XXIX, 37.

[34] This ribbing is also present on the sherds shown in Pls. XLIII, 3, 12, XLV, 24.

between groups of vertical lines in black on a cream-coloured slip. Broad red bands border this ornamental strip, while the loops and lines below are in black. The rim and neck are coloured a purplish-black, which has trickled down a little way inside. Unfortunately, the base of this interesting jar is missing but it would appear to have been rounded.

The vessel in Pl. XLI, 29 is coated with a light red slip on which a simple pattern of vertical and horizontal markings in black has been drawn. The lower portion of this jar has no slip, the junction between the red and natural surface of the pottery being very irregular.

The neck and rim of No. 36 in the same plate has been washed over with red, the rest being coloured cream. Three black spots of irregular size, placed on only one side of this vessel, may be identification marks. The same grouping of spots occurs on the vessel illustrated in colour in No. 2 of Frontispiece (b), but in this case they are repeated four times at equal distances round the body of the jar.

No. 41 in Pl. XLI is well made and thin for its size. Its sole decoration consists of thin purple lines painted in groups of three on a smooth, dark red slip.

Jars with Low-centered Bodies (Pls. XXVIII, 34, XLI, 28, 34, 40, 46-48)

The little jar in Pl. XLI, 28 has lost its rim, which was possibly flared. It is well made and covered with a thick red slip, as far down as its greatest girth, which has dripped in places on to its cream coloured lower portion. No. 34 in the same plate is of the same type and, except for the fact that it has no slip at all below its carination, is similarly coloured. A light red coating showing signs of polish covers the whole of No. 40; its neck and rim are missing, and its base has been trimmed with some sharp instrument.

The rather rough surface of No. 46 bears a red slip, while No. 47, which is markedly striated inside and out, is coloured cream. The portion below the angle of the base of the coarsely finished No. 48 is particularly thick, with a surface that looks as if it had been pared when its clay was very dry. This part of the jar has a cream wash, the remainder being painted red.

The jar illustrated in Pl. XXVIII, 34 has been inadvertently included with some Harappā pottery. It has no slip or decoration and was found, together with its little hand-made companion, at the high level of + 17.5 feet.

Round-based Jar (Pl. XLI, 37)

This particular jar was found in many pieces and it was just possible to restore it. It has an almost rounded base and must therefore have been kept on a stand or on loose soil. Moderately baked, it is thin for its size and its slipless body is rough in texture and bears straw-markings.

Ordinary Bowls and Dishes (Pls. XXXIX, 13, XL, 14-16, 18, 21, 22, 24, 25, 27-29, 32, XLI, 39)

The rough-looking bowl in Pl. XXXIX, 13 (see also Pl. XL, 18) is hand-made and much blackened by smoke. It is encrusted with a grey substance which may be the remains of food. No. 14 in Pl. XL is a well made specimen, part of which has been roughly trimmed on the outside. It contained a thick grey deposit when found and this, coupled with the shape of the vessel and the fact that it is without a slip, suggests that it had been used for cooking. Nos. 15 and 16 are two small hand-made bowls, both of a drab paste and obviously manufactured at home.

The striated, coarse-looking bowl in Pl. XL, 21 has a smooth interior. It is a badly baked specimen, drab in colour, whose paste is plentifully mixed with sand and mica. No. 22 is coated all over with a light red wash and is roughly decorated, both inside and out, with irregular lines of a purple hue. The deep, hand-made vessel No. 24 is small in size and made of a drab-coloured paste without a slip. The same applies to No. 25.

No. 28 is ornamented on the outside only with bands of purplish-black applied on a pink slip. The small bowl No. 29 has cord markings on its wide base and is of rough work, with marks of secondary burning here and there. No. 32 is hand-made and of rough workmanship.

The curious specimen illustrated in Pl. XLI, 39 is coloured red as far down as its carination; below, the surface is left bare. It is an interesting type and one regrets the missing rim.

Cups (Pls. XLI, 30, 31, 43)

No. 30 is an unusually thick and heavy cup coated with a cream-coloured slip. The clay of No. 31 contains a large proportion of lime particles and mica. It has no slip and its base is heavily scored by the cord used to remove it from the wheel. No. 43 is not only inadequately fired but is of the roughest workmanship.

Designs and Patterns

A brief description will now be given of the designs and patterns appearing on the Jhukar pottery. It has already been explained that the broad red bands that divide so many examples of this painted pottery into horizontal registers, in combination with the blacks, purples, or browns used for the motifs and patterns, place this pottery in the category of bi-chrome, if the colours of the slips are not also taken into account. Sometimes a red of a slightly different tint from that of the bands, is employed in the decoration of a jar (Pls. XXXIX, 15, XLII, 6, 8, 9, 11-17, 19, XLV, 20),[35] this colour being denoted in the line drawings by stippling.

Red Bands. The bands that render this Jhukar pottery so distinctive vary in width from 0.75 to sometimes as much as 2.5 inches. They are nearly always edged with a black or purple line, probably for the reason that the red was applied with a very coarse brush or mop and it was necessary to hide its uneven margins.

The number of bands vary. Large vessels such as the storage pieces in Pl. XLI, 42, 50 have only two. Four appear on the large jar in Pl. XLVII, 34 and three are sometimes used on the smaller wares (Frontispiece (b), 4, 8). They serve also to decorate the interiors of most of the dishes of food-stands, singly as in Pl. XLV, 25, 37 and repeated as in Pls. XLVI, 42, 45, XLVII, 19, etc. One band generally decorates the outside of such dishes and the same

[35] Some of these examples are again illustrated in colour in Frontispiece (b).

kind of ornamentation is present on the bases of the stands as, for example, in Pl. XLI, 13, 19, 20, 24, 25.

These broad red bands are in most cases plain; that they were sometimes ornamented is shown by the two food-stand dishes in Pls. XLIV, 12, XLVI, 8. Occasionally a line of loops or other kind of pattern has trespassed upon them because of careless or hurried work.

Coloured bands as a pottery decoration came first into use in India in the Amri Period,[36] a culture that preceded the Harappā civilization. As we have already seen, this form of ornamentation was never used by the Harappā people, but it appears again on the Jhukar pottery. Later on, as we shall presently see, these red bands re-occur on the Trihni and still later Muhammadan wares (Pl. XL, 1, 2); they even persist down to the present day in Sindh.

Similar red bands are a feature of some of the Jemdet Nasr wares in Sumer and are especially prominent on some pieces of pottery from Tepe Ali Ābād in Persia.[37] It is, however, on the wares of the latter part of the Tell Halaf Period that they are most conspicuous, a fact which provides another instance of the apparent close relationship existing between this North Assyrian and Jhukar pottery, notwithstanding the great interval of time that separated these two cultures.[38] To this and other points of resemblance I shall allude later.

Animal Motifs. Animal figures have been found on only two pieces of Jhukar pottery, in contrast to the earlier Harappā material, on which, as we have seen, animal and more particularly bird motifs are extremely common.

The sherd in Pl. XLV, 21 bears the figure of a running ibex. This fragment, part of a large storage jar, is coated with a cream slip, upon which the scene is painted in purple. The only other representation that I know of this animal in a running attitude occurs on a sherd from Periāno-Ghuṇḍai in Northern Baluchistan. This last example, together with other pieces of pottery associated with it, can be regarded as being either of, or closely related to, Jhukar work.[39]

The same species of goat will be seen on the broken dish in Pl. XLV, 22. This silhouette is very carefully drawn in a purplish-black paint on a light red ground. The angle of its body indicates that the missing forelegs were resting upon the plant device in front of it, quite in the Sumerian manner. This particular plant motif, as we shall later see, forms a common repetition motif on much of the Jhukar pottery.

Plant-forms. One of the chief differences between the painted wares of the Jhukar and Harappā Periods is to be found in the manner in which plant forms are depicted. With two possible exceptions (Pl. XLV, 19, 42) the Jhukar artist is content to portray his floral

[36] Named after the site where this very distinctive pottery was first found; cf. Majumdar, *Explorations in Sind*, pp. 24-33.

[37] *Mém. Dél. en Perse*, t. VIII, pl. VII.

[38] Mallowan and Rose, "Excavations at Tall Chagar Bazar," *Iraq*, vol. III, pl. II, 4-6. Mallowan suggests also a possible relationship between the Tall Halaf and Jemdet Nasr wares, for which see *Prehistoric Assyria*, p. 177.

[39] Stein, *Mem. Arch. Surv. Ind.*, No. 37, pp. 35, 36; pl. V (P. 36).

devices in a conventional manner; indeed, motifs of this description are frequently so geometric that their origins are scarcely apparent at all. It will be remembered that the Harappā jar-painter showed considerable enterprise in his plant arrangements on a jar, but at the same time never lost sight of the identity of the plant on which he based his theme. One has only to compare the Harappā work illustrated in Pls. XXXIV, 1, XXXVI, 7, 9, 28, 37, etc., with the Jhukar designs in Pls. XLV, 20, 24, 32, XLVI, 32, etc., to see the dissimilarity of the ceramic art of the two periods.

The pipal tree, which appears so frequently on the Harappā wares, finds no place at all on the Jhukar pottery, and the acacia, with its long thin leaves (Pl. XXXVII, 17, 19), is also absent. The most favoured motif employed by the Jhukar artist was a highly conventionalized plant motif, possibly derived from the lotus,[40] and was made to serve either as a continuous pattern round a jar or dish (Pls. XLIII, 7, 10, 12, XLIV, 13, XLVII, 6, etc.) or to alternate with other patterns, as for example in Pls. XLII, 3, 10, XLVI, 27, etc. The clever and economical way in which this form of frieze is arranged, so as to enable each portion to form an integral part of a continuous pattern, indicates that the artist knew something of the principles of design.[41]

The next most popular design was a leaf or bud form with a long curved stem generally arranged in parallel rows (Frontispiece (b), 7, Pls. XLII, 10, XLIII, 1, XLIV, 7, XLV, 24, 32, XLVI, 32, XLVII, 1, 2, 4, 15). The peculiar filaments that are sometimes associated with this last form of decoration (Pls. XLIII, 1, XLV, 32, XLVII, 1, etc.) suggest a water plant and bring to mind the curious root-like processes that sometimes appear on the Harappā pottery.[42] This leaf and stem motif forms, in combination with other devices, wide borders round the larger jars.

Both the sherds shown in Pl. XLV, 19, 42 once belonged to tall vessels of the storage type. The plants depicted on them cannot at present be identified, but it appears that an attempt was made in both cases to break away from convention and portray the natural form. Both motifs are painted in purple, the first on a cream and the second on a pink-coloured slip, while No. 42 also bears the red band characteristic of the Jhukar Period.[43] What appears to be the same species of plant is pictured on early sherds from Tepe Giyan and Tepe Sialk in North-western Persia.[44]

The sherd illustrated in Pl. XLV, 20, and again in colour in Frontispiece (b), 10, bears a very conventional tree form which was, no doubt, repeated at intervals round the jar.

[40] The lotus does not appear on the Harappā pottery, though its seed-vessels were sometimes copied in faience to serve as pin-heads: *M. I. C.*, pl. CLVIII, 4, 6. It grows in many parts of Sindh, especially in the Manchhar Lake.

[41] This same motif appears on certain vessels from Baluchistan, all of which appear to be of Jhukar make: Stein, *Mem. Arch. Surv. Ind.*, Vol. 37, pls. VI (p. 48), VII (P. SW. 4), VIII (P. SW. 4), XI (M. M. E. 15).

[42] As seen in Pls. XXXI, 23, XXXVI, 41.

[43] The level and locus of No. 19 in Pl. XLV cannot be given in the catalogue at the end of this book, because its original label was eaten by white ants.

[44] Contenau et Ghirshman, *Fouilles du Tépé-Giyan*, pl. 60; Ghirshman, *Fouilles de Sialk*, Vol. I, pls. LXII, LXIII, LXV, LXVI.

This tree and other designs associated with it are painted in red and brown on a cream-coloured slip, the effect produced being a very striking one.

Ball and Stem Motif. This motif, peculiar to the Jhukar Period (Pl. XLV, 25, 28, 30, 31, 35, 37), may be intended to represent a bud or seed-vessel with a long stem, the latter being always gracefully curved and the former carefully hatched. Up to the present, this device has been found only on the dishes of food-stands, where it usually appears in black or purple on a cream-coloured ground. On the sherd in Pl. XLV, 31, however, it is set on a light red slip and forms a continuous and compact pattern round the interior of this dish. With the single exception of a sherd from Jāī-damb in Southern Baluchistan, the employment of this particular device is unknown to me on pottery from sites outside India.[45] A variation of it, however, has been adapted to form part of a solar symbol on a Cretan seal.[46]

Chevron Patterns. This simple, yet effective, decoration is used on all classes of vessels, though somewhat rarely on the dishes of food-stands (Pls. Frontispiece (b), 1, 3, 5, 6, 7, 9, XLII, 4, 11, 12, 15-18, XLVII, 13, 17-19, 24, 27, 33). Examples of it painted in monochrome are, however, distinctly rare. In the case of Nos. 4 (see also Frontispiece (b), 5, 6) and 18 in Pl. XLII the design is painted in black, the slip being in the first specimen red and in the second cream-coloured. In Pl. XLVII, 33 the motif is executed in red on a cream slip. In most cases this chevron pattern is in two colours, red and black, so arranged that the down strokes are of one colour and the up of the other (Pls. XLII, 11-13, 15, 17, XLVII, 13, 17-19, 24). The sherd in Pls. XLII, 4, 11, 15-18, XLVII, 13, 17, 24 show this pattern enclosed in compartments separated by groups of vertical lines or other arrangements; in some cases it forms an unbroken border round a jar or dish (Pls. XLII, 12, XLVII, 19, 23).

Chevron patterns were very rare at Mohenjo-daro, their colouring being in every case black.[47] It was not a common motif on the pottery of Sumer and Elam, except in the Jemdet Nasr Period, where the up and down strokes are always of the same colour and frequently separated by a vertical line.[48] A device appearing on the very early Tall Halaf wares of North Assyria resembles the Jhukar type of chevron most closely, the method of using two colours for the alternate markings being the same in both cases.[49] A sherd from the Zayak valley in Southern Baluchistan also bears a chevron pattern painted in black and red, but this differs slightly from the Jhukar examples both in the placing of these two colours and in the arrangement of the motif.[50] There seems no doubt that these chevron patterns were originally derived from basketry.

[45] Stein, *Mem. Arch. Surv. Ind.*, No. 43, pl. III (J. D. 2). It is impossible to ascertain what relationship this sherd bears to Jhukar pottery without handling it.

[46] Evans, *Palace of Minos*, II, p. 218, fig. 123(a).

[47] *F. E. M.*, pl. LXX, 15.

[48] Frankfort, *Oriental Institute Communications*, No. 20, pl. VI.

[49] Von Oppenheim, *Tell Ḥalaf*, pls. I, 6, LII, 5, LIII, 2. Specimens of this ware found at Arpachiyah also bear this motif, but here it is painted in monochrome on the exterior of certain bowls: Mallowan and Rose, *Prehistoric Assyria*, figs. 70 (5), 71 (3); Mallowan, "Excavations at Tall Chagar Bazar," *Iraq*, vol. III, fig. 24 (4).

[50] Stein, *Mem. Arch. Surv. Ind.*, No. 43, p. 33, pl. I (Z. N. 7).

Chequer Patterns. The chequers in Pls. XLII, 25, XLIV, 1, XLVI, 1, 2, 4, 6, 7, 27 are hatched in black or purplish black on a red-coloured slip. In Pl. XLII, 20 the ground is cream-coloured and the squares filled in with red and outlined with the same colour in a darker shade. The squares in Pl. XLVI, 5 are alternately brown and pink, the latter being the ground colour. A very unusual combination occurs on the sherd in Pl. XLII, 19, where the colours used are black and dark red on a pink coloured slip. The chequers in this particular example and also those in No. 20 are completely filled in, but this form of treatment is rare, the usual method being to cross-hatch them and thus allow the colour of the ground to show through. The lighter squares in Pl. XLVI, 1, 2, 6, are partly filled in with crossed lines, perhaps to render them less obtrusive. This use of crossed lines in this particular form of pattern is also to be found on some of the Tell Halaf wares, but, as far as can be ascertained, on no other pottery than the Jhukar.[51] These chequer devices are to be found on all types of vessels, but are used chiefly to decorate the dishes of food-stands in association with other motifs.

Rhombs. Rhombs are used on the Jhukar pottery to fill in single and double horizontal borders, as in Pls. XLIV, 3, and XLVI, 14, 15, or arranged vertically panel-wise, as in Pl. XXXIV, 24, or set in massed groups (Pls. XLIV, 2, XLVI, 8). Except in the two last cases the rhombs are invariably hatched. The curious lines projecting from the top and bottom angles of the rhombs in Pl. XLVI, 14 are also to be seen on some painted wares from Dāmīn and Khurāb in Persian Baluchistan, though in other respects these have nothing in common with our Jhukar material.[52] Rhombs, similarly furnished, appear on some vessels from Samarra,[53] but this complex form does not appear to have been used elsewhere.

This rhomb device is associated with a plant motif in Pl. XLIV, 13. Here the central petal of the lotus, if it be a lotus, is lozenge-shaped instead of having the usual bud-like form.

The massed rhomb pattern in Pls. XLIV, 2, XLVI, 8 is found also on wares from Jemdet Nasr[54] and Nineveh.[55] Used in several lines to fill in horizontal borders, these rhombs are quite frequently used on the Al-'Ubaid[56] and Tell Halaf pottery;[57] on the last it often forms the sole decoration of a bowl or jar.

Rhombs with Incurved Sides. Pl. XLVI, 12, 17. This type of rhomb is rare and appears only on two Jhukar sherds. It was not used in the Harappā Period. It occurs on a sherd from Sistan[58] and on another from Northern Baluchistan.[59] The Tell Halaf and

[51] Von Oppenheim, *Tell Ḥalaf*, pl. II, 2; Mallowan and Rose, *Prehistoric Assyria*, figs. 32, 37, 78.

[52] Stein, *Archaeological Reconnaissances*, pls. XI (A. 68), XIII (200), XXXIII (13).

[53] Herzfeld, *Samarra V*, pls. XXXV, 221, XXXVI, 234, a, 239. In these examples the couplings are doubled.

[54] *Anthropology Memoirs*, Field Museum, Chicago, vol. I, pl. LXVIII, 2.

[55] Thompson and Mallowan, *Illust. Lon. News*, 1931, p. 1121 (9).

[56] Hall and Woolley, *Ur Excavations*, vol. I, pl. XVIII (1769).

[57] Mallowan and Rose, *Prehistoric Assyria*, figs. 71, 72; *Iraq*, vol. III, fig. 22.

[58] Andrews, *Burlington Magazine*, 1925, pl. I, fig. 26.

[59] Stein, *Mem. Arch. Surv. Ind.*, No. 37, pl. V (P. 2).

Al-'Ubaid wares also furnish examples, though here, too, the form is as scarce as the straight-sided type is common.[60]

Spot Decoration. Large spots, sometimes curiously situated, take their share of Jhukar decoration. A very unusual example is illustrated in Pl. XXXIV, 22, where spots are used to fill in the spaces of a multiple loop pattern, and again in Pl. XLVI, 12, 17, where they serve the same purpose in quite a different pattern. The jar shown in Pl. XXXIX, 10 and again in Pl. XLI, 38 is decorated with large purple spots set between loops of the same colour, the combination forming a simple and yet pleasing pattern.[61] Another unusual spot device is depicted on the large sherd in Pl. XLII, 6, which once formed part of a storage jar. Here red spots are placed between partitions of brown-coloured paint. In Pl. XLII, 13 one red and one brown spot are irregularly set in a petal-shaped motif (shown more clearly in Frontispiece (b), 3). No. 2 in Frontispiece (b), is a small jar ornamented on all four sides with three black spots in a row.[62] A similar three-spot pattern is also present on the vessel shown in Pl. XLI, 36, but there it is probably an identification mark as it is not repeated elsewhere on the jar.

This very unusual use of the spot device has few parallels elsewhere. On a sherd from Southern Baluchistan a row of spots is painted very like those on the jar in Pl. XLI, 36.[63] Spots are an important feature in the decoration of the Tell Halaf pottery, as well as on the wares of the Al-'Ubaid Period and also on certain Persian fabrics.[64] In the main, however, the spots are minute in size and, moreover, distributed over considerable areas.

Spot motifs do not appear exclusively on the Jhukar wares from Chanhu-daro; they are also to be found on pottery of the same culture from other parts of Sindh,[65] and on the later Trihni ware (Pl. XLV, 1, 4, 5, 13). The large spots used on the Harappā pottery, linked together by lines as in Pl. XXXVI, 29, form an entirely different motif.

Loops, Single and Multiple. Single loops are used either for a border pattern, as in Pls. XXXIX, 10, 15, XLI, 38, XLII, 22, XLV, 39, XLVII, 28, or to break a sudden transition between the painted and unpainted portions of a vessel as in Pls. XLII, 2, XLIV, 13, XLV, 25, XLVI, 14, 37, 41-43. In this connection the loops sometimes stray on to the red bands so characteristic of the Jhukar pottery (Pls. XLV, 25, XLVI, 37).

An exceptional double row of loops appears on the sherd in Pl. XLVI, 38, the arrangement forming a perhaps unintentional scale pattern. Occasionally the loops are roughly hatched as will be seen in Pl. XLVII, 20, 21, 23, 29, all these examples being fragments of large storage jars. No. 22 in Pl. XLVII, which is part of the rim of a food-stand dish,

[60] Mallowan, "Excavations at Tall Chagar Bazar," *Iraq*, vol. III, fig. 22 (1); *Prehistoric Assyria*, pl. V (f), Fig. 34 (6).

[61] This combination of the spot and loop occurs also at Mohenjo-daro, but there the loops are in multiple rows and form a kind of scale-pattern: *M. I. C.*, pl. XCI, 32.

[62] Compare this jar with a second from Chanhu-daro: Majumdar, *Explorations in Sind*, pl. XXI, 21.

[63] Stein, *Mem. Arch. Surv. Ind.*, vol. 43, pl. X (Naz. 19).

[64] A single row of large spots form a continuous border round the neck of a jar from Tepe Gawra: Speiser, *Excavations at Tepe Gawra*, pl. LXVIII, 118.

[65] Majumdar, *Explorations in Sind*, pls. XVI, 16, 19, XXII, 17, 18.

shows a contracted form of a multiple loop pattern, which, when expanded, is the most common marginal decoration of all the dishes (Pls. XXXIV, 22, XLIII, 5-8, etc.).

Simple loop patterns are to be found on most ancient wares and were especially favored by the Tell Halaf people, where they were employed to fill in wide and sometimes very monotonous borders.[66] The multiple loop variety, however, is not so well known; it is occasionally found on vessels of the Harappā Period, decorating the rims of certain kohl-jars (Pl. XXXIX, 19). Double and triple rows of loops are frequent on the Susian pottery,[67] and multiple rows on the early Samarra wares,[68] but these are arranged in continuous lines round the jars and not grouped concentric-wise as in Pl. XXXIV, 22, etc. The latter must, therefore, be regarded as a characteristic type of Jhukar decoration.

Crescent-shaped Motifs. This conspicious motif (Pls. XXXIV, 18, XLIV, 4, 9-11, 14, XLVI, 29, XLVII, 12, 16, 26) is most frequently found on the dishes of food-stands and is sometimes associated with the lotus pattern (Pl. XLIV, 4, 10, 14), to which reference has already been made. A curious variation of it appears on some fragments of storage jars in Pls. XXXIV, 18, XLIV, 4, where it resembles somewhat a jelly-fish seen in profile.

The hatched crescentic markings in Pl. XLVI, 29 may be part of a continuous pattern. They appear to bear no relation to the crescents described above, which are never set in this vertical position.

Crescent motifs are rarely found on prehistoric pottery. A mark of this shape is incised on the base of a bowl of the Tell Halaf period from Arpachiyah, but this, of course, was not intended to be an ornament.[69] A group of five crescents, set one below the other, is painted on a sherd of Al-'Ubaid date from Ur,[70] and two examples of this motif appear on an early painted sherd from Zhōb-Thāl in Southern Baluchistan,[71] and three on the inside of a bowl from Nāl.[72]

It is difficult to say, however, whether all the forms mentioned above were inspired by the moon; indeed, the jar painters may have had something quite different in mind. One is less doubtful with regard both to the Arpachiyah example and also to a row of crescents which serve as a border on a sherd from Mohenjo-daro.[73]

Triangular Patterns. In view of the geometric nature of the designs and patterns on the Jhukar pottery, it is somewhat surprising to find that the simpler triangular motifs were far from popular. They appear on two sherds only (Pl. XLVI, 18, 23). In the first two, triangles are linked together in horizontal and vertical positions alternately, and in the second they are placed in a row side by side. Possibly the triangles depicted on this last

[66] Mallowan and Rose, *Prehistoric Assyria*, pl. XXII, 3; figs. 68-70, etc.
[67] *Mém. Dél. en Perse*, t. VIII, fig. 147; t. XIII, fig. 9.
[68] Herzfeld, *Samarra V*, figs. 155, 161.
[69] Mallowan and Rose, *Prehistoric Assyria*, fig. 69 (6).
[70] Hall and Woolley, *Ur Excavations*, vol. I, pl. XVII (1536).
[71] Noetling, *Zeitschrift für Ethnologie*, 1898, p. 467, fig. 24.
[72] Hargreaves, *Nāl* (*Mem. Arch. Surv. Ind.*, No. 35), pl. XVIII, 3.
[73] *M. I. C.*, pl. XC, 16.

sherd were joined to inverted ones above them, thus forming the well-known double-triangle motif that appears in No. 18.

This double-triangle, or hour-glass motif, as it is termed by some, frequently occurs on ancient pottery, though the single form is perhaps more common still. The single variety was the most favoured by the Harappā people at Chanhu-daro; at Mohenjo-daro the exact opposite was the case.[74]

Joined triangular patterns, somewhat resembling butterflies in shape, are illustrated in Pls. XLIV, 9, XLVI, 7. I do not suggest that there is an attempt here to represent the actual insect, though butterflies actually appear on some Cretan wares, especially in the Early Minoan Period.[75] As far as can be ascertained, butterflies have not been identified on any other pottery of this or earlier date.[76]

On our Jhukar pottery the triangle is sometimes employed to compose the cross-like figures that ornament the centres of many of the food-stand dishes (Pls. XLIII, 7, XLIV, 6, 8, XLVI, 19, 22, 39). When so used the triangles are often irregular in shape and have one or more curved sides.

Triangles with concave sides form very effective borders in Pls. XLIV, 12, XLVI, 13, XLVII, 34 or parts of a border in Pl. XLVI, 16. The pattern in Pl. XLVI, 13 is almost an exact duplicate of one on an early sherd from Sistan.[77]

Cruciform Designs. Cross-like patterns (Pls. XLIII, 7, XLIV, 6, 9, XLVI, 19, XLVII, 31) are frequent but appear in the centres of dishes only. A six-armed cross will be seen in Pl. XLIV, 6, and a four-armed one in Pl. XLIV, 9, the voids round this last example being filled in with crescent-shaped motifs. Whether this association of the cross with the crescent has any significance or is merely accidental, is difficult to say. Ancient cross patterns are thought by some to represent the sun and it is therefore not impossible that this particular device on this Jhukar fragment is an attempt to combine lunar and solar emblems in one design.[78]

A motif resembling a Maltese cross, which apparently was repeated four times, appears on the dish in Pl. XLVI, 19, and a similar cross filled the centre of the dish in Pl. XLIV, 8. This type of cross is rarely found on Mohenjo-daro wares,[79] but exceptional use of it is to be seen on the early pottery of Samarra, where it is usually converted by the addition of animal figures and the like into elaborate svastikas, thus emphasizing its solar character.[80]

The Maltese cross is not uncommon on early pottery from other sites. Its first appearance is on the Tell Halaf pottery,[81] and it also occurs on a very early sherd of the Highland

[74] *M. I. C.*, pls. XCII, 10, 14-17; *F. E. M.*, pl. LXVIII, 1.

[75] Evans, *Palace of Minos*, vol. I, pp. 42, 75, 166.

[76] They sometimes appear on glazed hippopotami figures of the Twelfth Dynasty of Egypt and also on tomb walls, but never on the pottery.

[77] Andrews, *Burlington Magazine*, 1925, pl. I, 44.

[78] For another combined cross and crescent device, which appears on a Late Minoan amphora, see Rostovtzeff, *History of the Ancient World*, pl. XXV, fig. 4.

[79] *M. I. C.*, pl. XVI, 7.

[80] Herzfeld, *Samarra V*, figs. 23, 25-27, 30; pl. XII, 24.

[81] Mallowan and Rose, *Prehistoric Assyria*, pls. XVIII, XXII, 10.

Culture from Persia.[82] It adopts several forms at Susa and Musyān,[83] and is depicted on two sherds of Al-'Ubaid date from Ur.[84] Much later it is met with on Kassite seals and again on a certain type of pottery discovered in Palestine and believed to be Cilician.[85]

Nearer India, the motif is found on early wares from Southern Persia[86] and from Sistan, where it is as elaborately treated as it is in Elam,[87] and in Baluchistan, where it is very prominent on a certain type of vessel from Shāhī-tump.[88]

The Maltese cross appears to have originated in North Syria. Thence it reached Mesopotamia and Persia at an early date and later arrived in India, by way of Sistan and Baluchistan. Its appearance, first in the Harappā and later in the Jhukar Period has been described, but it was never really popular with either of these cultures and on the Jhukar pottery takes a form which differs considerably from the simpler older pattern.

Other cross motifs, such as the Greek and St. Andrew types, occur fairly frequently on the seals and amulets of the Harappā people. The former, however, is never used on the pottery and the latter only occasionally.[89]

Bead Motif. In Pl. XXXII, 7 this motif is shown appropriately ornamenting the neck of one of the Harappā vessels, but only two examples of it have so far come to light on the Jhukar pottery. One of these appears in Pl. XLVII, 32, the other is to be seen on a sherd found by Mr. Majumdar at Lohumjo-daro.[90]

Excluding the rather similar rhomb motif, a true bead pattern occurs but once on the Amri pottery.[91] The Harappā people, who were particularly fond of the device, do not appear then to have borrowed it from the culture immediately preceding their own. Baluchistan has so far produced only two examples of this motif,[92] and it was just as rarely used in Sistan.[93] Roughly drawn representations are to be seen on sherds from South-eastern Iran.[94]

This bead pattern appears most frequently on the Tell Halaf pottery and is used there in rows of two or more as a border pattern; sometimes it is the only motif used on a dish or bowl.[95] It rarely appears on Al-'Ubaid wares and is absent on the Samarra pottery as well as being strangely scarce elsewhere.

[82] Herzfeld, *Illust. Lon. News*, 1929, p. 893, fig. 11.
[83] *Mém. Dél. en Perse*, t. VIII, figs. 175, 177; t. XVI, figs. 4, 7.
[84] Hall and Woolley, *Ur Excavations*, vol. I, pl. XVI (1650, 1652).
[85] Petrie, *Ancient Gaza*, vol. IV, pl. XXX, figs. 23-26.
[86] Stein, *Iraq*, vol. III, no. 2, pls. XIX, 2, XXI, 45, XXII, 43, etc.
[87] Andrews, *Burlington Magazine*, 1925, pl. I, nos. 34-36, 38.
[88] Stein, *Mem. Arch. Surv. Ind.*, No. 43, pls. XV, XVI.
[89] For example Pls. XXIII, 6, XXXIX, 23. The crossed lines on the exterior of the dish in Pl. XLVII, 31 cannot be regarded as a decorative motif.
[90] *Explorations in Sind*, pl. XXII, 16.
[91] *Op. cit.*, pl. XXXIX, 10.
[92] Stein, *Mem. Arch. Surv. Ind.*, No. 37, pl. XXI (S. J. 23); No. 43, pl. XII (Sh. T. ii. 5).
[93] Andrews, *Burlington Magazine*, 1925, pl. I, 23, pl. II, 74.
[94] Stein, *Archaeological Reconnaissances*, pls. XIV (Khur. B. ii. 204), XVII (B. i. 119).
[95] Mallowan and Rose, *Prehistoric Assyria*, pls. XIII, XIV, XXIII, etc.

Criss-cross Bands. The uninteresting feature of cross-hatched bands as a mode of decoration was as common in the Jhukar as it was in the Harappā Period. Such bands are, however, not so unsightly if the hatching is oblique as in Pl. XLVI, 24, 30, 32. When the crossed lines are vertical and horizontal or nearly so, the effect produced is far from pleasing, as will be seen in Pls. XLV, 39, XLVI, 6, 10, 28, XLVII, 28. In Pl. XLVI, 6 the margin of a dish has been decorated in this manner, in striking contrast to the more lively patterns generally painted on this part of a dish.

Bands and borders filled in with vertical and horizontal hatching are commonly found on the Tell Halaf wares,[96] the more attractive oblique hatching being comparatively rare. The exact opposite is the case as far as the Al-'Ubaid and Samarra wares are concerned. On a sherd from Arpachiyah oblique and horizontal lines are used together with fairly satisfactory results.[97]

Oblique hatching was alone employed to fill in borders on the Harappā wares. In some cases it is very roughly done but is none the less effective on this account.

Hide Motif. This pattern, so common on the Harappā pottery,[98] appears only on the Jhukar sherd illustrated in Pl. XLVI, 11, where it encircles the neck of a storage jar. The same device occurs on an Elamite sherd,[99] but does not seem to have been employed elsewhere.

Rosettes. Four-petalled rosettes, so popular with the Harappā people, appear much less frequently in the succeeding Jhukar Period. On the sherd in Pl. XLVI, 3 this motif is set in compartments and probably formed a continuous border round the jar. In Pl. XLVIII, 21 a rosette is deeply incised on the surface of a storage vessel fragment and was, no doubt, intended as an identification mark.

Irregular Lines and Markings. Irregular lines and markings arranged in an orderly manner play an important part in the decoration of the Jhukar pottery. Their association with carefully drawn patterns of various kinds (Pls. XLII, 10, XLIII, 10, 12, etc.) shows that the irregularities are intentional and not due to hurried or careless work.

A favourite arrangement is a group of notched stripes in parallel rows which alternates with panels composed of a number of vertical lines (Pls. XLII, 2, 8, 9, XLIII, 12, XLV, 23, 33, 34, XLVI, 13) or with some other form of decoration, as in the case of the sherds illustrated in Pls. XLII, 3, 5, 7, 10, 13, XLIII, 10, XLV, 24, 26, 29, 41, XLVII, 4, 9. The more abbreviated markings, especially those on the fragments in Pl. XLV, 23, 29, appear at first sight rather like badly drawn figures of animals, but a comparison between them and other examples shows that the resemblance is accidental. Some of the lines used are so short that they might almost be termed spots, but even then they have a certain decorative value as Frontispiece (b), 4, 8, Pls. XLI, 29, XLVI, 33, 34 will show.

[96] *Op. cit.*, pls. XIII, XVIII, XIX (4), XX; figs. 55, 57.
[97] *Op. cit.*, fig. 33 (4).
[98] *M. I. C.*, pl. XCI, 1-6; *F. E. M.*, pl. LXVIII, 1; see also Pl. XXXVII, 13 of this book.
[99] *Mém. Dél. en Perse*, t. XX, p. 106.

In Pl. XLII, 8, 9, 13, 17, two colours, red and black, are used to accentuate the markings, as will be more clearly seen in the coloured Frontispiece (b), 1, 3.

The metopic arrangement seen in Pl. XLII, 1, 2, is to be seen on one sherd of the Harappā Period,[100] and occurs again on sherds from Baluchistan and Sistan;[101] the relationship between the two last wares and the Jhukar pottery is, as yet, uncertain.

Roughly painted wavy lines in single, double, or even triple rows often encircle a jar or dish (Pls. XXXIV, 18, 19, 23, XLVI, 36, 44). It will be noted that each line is bordered by a straight one.

Vertical lines of serpent form, painted in red and separated from each other by black divisions, provide a unique decoration on the sherd in Pl. XLII, 14.

Rare Motifs. The leaf-like motif appearing on the large fragment of a storage jar in Pl. XLV, 38 is painted in thin purple on a cream-coloured slip. It seems to be identical with the strange motif depicted on a large jar unearthed at Damb Buthi in Sindh.[102] Both these motifs should be compared with the curious objects on each side of the sherd in Pl. XLII, 14, but it is impossible to say what they are intended to represent.

The border pattern on the three fragments illustrated in Pls. XLII, 24, 26, XLVI, 10 do not appear, as far as I am aware, on any other ancient pottery. At first sight it would seem that these three sherds come from one vessel. As a matter of fact, they were unearthed not only in different parts of Mound II, but also at different levels. All are painted in black on a polished red slip and were originally parts of large dishes, possibly of the food-stand type.

The sherd in Pl. XLV, 39, which belonged to a large jar of surprising thinness, bears a figure-of-eight motif drawn in black on a smooth red slip. In shape this motif closely resembles a Minoan shield, or one of the queer incised clay amulets that are found on the site of Harappā and apparently nowhere else.[103] A very similar device is seen among the pictographs on a seal of the Harappā Period from Chanhu-daro and here its resemblance to a shield is very marked.[104] The same figure is quite common on the Late Tell Halaf pottery, but there, as Mr. Mallowan points out, it is undoubtedly derived from the conjoined *bucrania* motif, which, at the end of its development, became so stylized that it took the form of a simple eight-shaped ornament.[105]

If the view is taken that this particular device on an Indian jar is taken from a shield, it must be assumed that some of the inhabitants of that country used a guard familiar to the Libyans, the Greeks, the Hittites, the Cretans, and the Scythians.[106] This would imply

[100] *M. I. C.*, pl. LXXXIX, 14.

[101] Stein, *Mem. Arch. Surv. Ind.*, No. 37, pls. VI (P. 57), XI (M. M. N. 10); No. 43, pls. XXV (Nun. 12), XXVII (Nun. III, 1), XXIX (Mēhi, III, 4, 3); Andrews, *Burlington Magazine*, 1925, pl. I, 1.

[102] *Explorations in Sind*, p. 115; pl. XXV, 34. Mr. Majumdar found this jar in a burial deposit, but the pottery accompanying it seems to be of earlier date than the Jhukar Period.

[103] *Ann. Rep. Arch. Surv. Ind.*, 1924-5, pl. XXVIII, 9.

[104] Majumdar, *Explorations in Sind*, pl. XVII.

[105] Mallowan and Rose, *Prehistoric Assyria*, pp. 154-163, figs. 74, 75.

[106] For reasons why the Minoan and probably other shields were eight-shaped, see J. L. Myres and A. E. H. Love, *Man*, 1939, sects. 37, 38.

connections, or relations, with the Near East, but, as yet, no evidence has been found in India to support such a theory.[107]

It seems unlikely, therefore, that the motif on this particular Jhukar sherd is derived from a shield. Indeed, it is so like the abstract forms of the *bukranium* on the Tell Halaf pottery that the resemblance can hardly be an accidental one. The backgrounds, too, are strikingly similar, that on the Jhukar specimen being apparently a copy of the fine stippled ground so popular with the Tell Halaf and Arpachiyah potters.[108]

It may be that the artist who decorated this Jhukar vessel had no idea of the original meaning of this motif. It most probably reached him through very devious channels from a remote past and he simply adopted it to suit his own purpose. His setting of the motif in a vertical and disconnected position is different from the Arpachiyah arrangement, which is horizontal and forms a chain-like border pattern.

The linked, six-sided pattern in Pl. XLVII, 28 is possibly a variation of the incurved rhomb pattern. It has been found only on this one sherd—a fragment of a large jar—and is painted in purplish-black on a dark red slip. The motif has some relation to a border pattern that is often seen on the Tell Halaf wares,[109] and another point of resemblance, to which attention has already been drawn, is the curious way in which the bands on either side of it are hatched.[110]

The simple method of dividing a border into panels by the use of groups of vertical lines[111] is common to most ancient pottery, but the pattern used to fill in the compartments on the jar in Pl. XXXIX, 15 is unique. Here horizontal lines in red bridge the oblique black lines in the design; the effect, despite its extreme simplicity, is very pleasant.

Groups of oblique lines in reverse directions are used to form a running border in Pl. XLII, 22. The resulting pattern is unusual, but closer inspection will show that it is derived from a zig-zag motif with the upper and lower portions removed. Although it only occurs occasionally on the Jhukar pottery, several examples of it have been found on sherds of Al-'Ubaid date from Ur;[112] it also appears, though rarely, on certain wares from Baluchistan, Sistan, and South-eastern Persia.[113]

Comparisons and Relations

Comparisons between the Jhukar and Harappā Wares. The differences, between these two wares considerably outweigh the resemblances, for, as already stated, there is a

[107] Bedrich Hrozny sees many resemblances between the Harappā and Hittite scripts: *O Nejstaršim Stěhování Národu A O Problému Civilisace Proto-Indické.*

[108] Mallowan and Rose, *Prehistoric Assyria*, fig. 76 (3-5). It should be noted that Pl. XLV, 39 is the only example of a Jhukar sherd with a ground of this description.

[109] Oppenheim, *Tell Halaf*, pls. I, 6; II, 6; Mallowan and Rose, *Prehistoric Assyria*, fig. 54(4).

[110] *Op. cit.*, fig. 55; pls. XIII, XVII, XX.

[111] Frontispiece (b), 4-6, 8, 10; pls. XXXIX, 15, XLI, 29, XLII, 15, 21, XLV, 23, 33, XLVI, 25, 33, 34, 40.

[112] Hall and Woolley, *Ur Excavations*, vol. I, pl. XIX (2012, 2025, 2168).

[113] Stein, *Mem. Arch. Surv. Ind.*, No. 43, pl. XXIV (Baz. 8); Andrews, *Burlington Magazine*, 1925, pl. II, 85; Stein, *Archaeological Reconnaissances*, pl. XX (Kal. 1). For a similar pattern from Mohenjo-daro, see *M. I. C.*, pl. XCI, 17.

marked dissimilarity between the fabrics, the style of decoration, and most of the motifs and patterns used. Yet it appears possible that a certain amount of borrowing did take place. The shape of the Harappā jar in Pl. XXVII, 68, for instance, is singularly like that of the Jhukar vessel in Pl. XLI, 38, though each is ornamented in quite a different manner. Again, the careful arrangement for a cover to fit the pan in Pl. XXIX, 37 is almost exactly duplicated on the Jhukar vessel in Pl. XLI, 50.

The use of pedestal dishes by the people of both cultures implies some form of contact, for this type of vessel, though very common in the Harappā Period, is not known in the previous Amri Period. Here again, the Jhukar examples resemble their predecessors in general form, although the manner in which they are decorated is entirely different.

A certain type of bowl-shaped jar-cover with a knob handle inside (Pl. XXVI, 12-34) was in common use during the Harappā Period, and a similar specimen illustrated in Pl. XL, 17 is of Jhukar work. When it was first unearthed, it was thought to be of earlier date, but subsequent cleaning revealed incised patterns of a type never found on vessels of the Harappā Culture.

The use of red polished slips is another link between the two periods, though the patterns employed are entirely different.

Resemblances between the Jhukar and Amri Wares. In the use of red bands and geometric style of decoration the Amri pottery has much more in common with the Jhukar wares than with those of the Harappā Culture which succeeded it. Other points of resemblance are to be found in the popularity of the rhomb, four-petalled rosette, and loop as motifs. As regards choice of colours, apart from the red or brown bands decorating the Amri pottery, the motifs and patterns upon it are always painted in monochrome on a cream or pink-coloured slip,[114] whereas the designs on the Jhukar vessels are most frequently in polychrome. The use of pink slips and brown paints is, however, common to both periods, but the Jhukar forms are quite different from those of the older culture.

Evidences of the Amri Culture first came to light at the site from which it takes its name and Mr. Majumdar, who was the first to identify it, claimed that it must antedate the Harappā civilization as all his finds of this new culture lay below Harappā material.[115] Other material of the Amri Culture has been found at Tando Rahim Khan and Chauro Landi, but the absence of remains of any later culture on these two Sindhi sites render any exact correlation impossible.[116]

At the site of Ghazi Shah in Sindh, Amri pottery overlapped Harappā wares at certain levels,[117] and even came to light in places high up on that mound, its presence being attributed by Mr. Majumdar to building activity in Islamic times.[118] In any case, the fact that specimens of Amri and Harappā wares were found intermingled at Ghazi Shah is

[114] Majumdar, *Explorations in Sind*, p. 26.
[115] *Ibid.*
[116] *Op. cit.*, pp. 86, 123.
[117] Majumdar, *Explorations in Sind*, p. 81.
[118] *Op. cit.*, p. 82.

particularly interesting. The Harappā people, as we know, were a trading rather than a war-like race and it seems to me not impossible that they allowed the Amri people to live unmolested in the same country with them, though borrowing nothing from their less important, and we can assume less civilized, neighbours.

The resemblances between the Jhukar and Harappā, and again between the Jhukar and Amri wares have already been noted. It is, however, significant that no relationship appears to exist between the Harappā and Amri wares. The ceramic art of the former is certainly intrusive and derives nothing from that of any earlier Indian culture.

Comparisons between the Jhukar and Tell Halaf Wares. Certain striking analogies between the Jhukar and some Tell Halaf pottery have already been mentioned in this chapter but they can usefully be recapitulated in this survey. They are as follows:

(a) The red bands dividing some vessels of both cultures into horizontal registers.
(b) Chequer patterns with crossed lines used to fill in otherwise blank squares.[119]
(c) Zig-zag pattern in two colours.[120]
(d) Rhomb motifs with incurved sides (also appearing on the Al-'Ubaid pottery).[121]
(e) The use of horizontal and vertical hatching as a border pattern.[122]
(f) Figure-of-eight or *bukranium* pattern on a hatched or stippled ground.[123]

In shape the vessels of the two periods are quite different, and the Jhukar decoration is much more advanced and sophisticated in style.

It is difficult to explain why two such widely separated cultures should have so many points in common as regards their pottery decoration, for to term these fortuitous appears to me to under-estimate the evidence. It is possible that the Tell Halaf people wandered far afield, taking their ceramic craft with them, and though the distance between Northern Assyria and the Indus valley is roughly fifteen hundred miles as the crow flies, it must be remembered that about two thousand years divided the two cultures, ample time for artistic conceptions to penetrate from one far country to another. Some authorities consider that the Tell Halaf civilization originated in Syria,[124] and resemblances between its pottery and that of Iran and Baluchistan have even been noted.[125] From the latter country favoured patterns could easily have spread to India. Sufficient evidence now exists to prove that the Jhukar people in later times also had associations with their neighbour on the west.

Relations between Jhukar Pottery and some Wares of Baluchistan. It has been known for some time that the people of the Harappā culture had trading relations with Baluchistan; indeed, they may have had settlements there, for their distinctive products have been found

[119] As Pls. XLVI, 1, 2, 6, XLV, 32.

[120] Frontispiece (b), 1, 3, 9, XLII, 11, 13, 15, 17, XLVII, 13, 17-19, 24, 27.

[121] Pl. XLVI, 12, 17.

[122] Pls. XLV, 39, XLVI, 6, 10, 28, XLVII, 28.

[123] Pl. XLV, 39. It would be more correct, perhaps, to term this ground "filling," as the motif was certainly painted first.

[124] With this Mr. Mallowan is inclined to agree, *Prehistoric Assyria*, p. 177.

[125] *Op. cit.*, p. 178.

in many parts of that province. The same trading, and perhaps also a cultural, connection existed in the Jhukar Period, for certain wares which are either of Jhukar manufacture or locally made copies, have come to light in several parts of Baluchistan. I have not had an opportunity of examining these painted wares closely, but they are said to be decorated in black and are sometimes without a slip, features which also appear in some of the Jhukar pottery.[126]

Several small vessels from the site of Periāno-ghuṇḍai in North Baluchistan [127] are very similar in form to some found in a burial chamber at Damb-Buthi in Sindh.[128] Mr. Majumdar has compared this burial-pottery with some Amri wares, but a large jar found with it singularly resembles a Jhukar type; moreover, it is decorated in much the same way as a Jhukar fragment from Chanhu-daro seen in Pl. XLV, 38.

But we are concerned not so much with the forms of these Baluchistan wares as with the designs they bear. Two mounds in the northern part of that province have yielded some small jars on which is depicted the same plant device that so commonly appears on the pottery from Chanhu-daro (Pl. XLIII, 3, 7, 10, etc.).[129] Again a sherd from Jāī-damb in Southern Baluchistan is decorated with a ball and stem motif like the Jhukar examples in Pl. XLV, 25, 28, 35, 37, etc.,[130] and another from Sar-Parōm, evidently part of the edge of a dish of a food-stand, bears a multiple loop pattern, often found on similar Jhukar dishes.[131] Furthermore, on a sherd from Periāno-ghuṇḍai there appears the figure of a running animal, which might, though with less certainty, be attributed to Jhukar work,[132] and should be compared with the animal illustrated in Pl. XLV, 21, which is also shown in motion.

Mr. Mallowan has pointed out that "certain of the polychrome sherds of Sūr Jangal and related wares, in feel, colour, and minuteness of design, bear an apparent kinship to that of Tell Halaf"—but bids the reader to beware of fortuitous resemblances.[133] Apart from its polychrome colouring the resemblance between the Sūr Jangal and Jhukar wares is slight. The wavy lines in two colours on the former [134] are not unlike the patterns illustrated in Pl. XLII, 8, 9 of this book and a cross-like marking on another Sūr Jangal sherd [135] has its counterpart on the Jhukar dish in Pl. XLVII, 31. In all probability this Sūr Jangal pottery is of considerably earlier date than the Jhukar material and its likeness in certain respects to the Tell Halaf wares is perhaps not surprising, for the two types were possibly separated by a shorter interval of time. I can see no connection between the Sūr Jangal wares and

[126] No slips are present on the sherds in Pls. XLIV, 6, XLVII, 24, 27, though they are painted in one or two colours.

[127] Stein, *Mem. Arch. Surv. Ind.*, No. 37, pl. VII.

[128] *Explorations in Sind*, pl. XXV, 26-43.

[129] Moghul-ghuṇḍai and Periāno-ghuṇḍai: Stein, *Mem. Arch. Surv. Ind.*, No. 37, pls. VII (P. C. 10), (P. SW. 4), VIII (P. SW. 4), (P. SW. c. 1), XI (MM. E. 13, 15).

[130] Stein, *Mem. Arch. Surv. Ind.*, No. 43, pl. III (J. D. 2).

[131] *Op. cit.* (S. P. 6).

[132] Stein, *Mem. Arch. Surv. Ind.*, No. 37, pl. X (P. 36).

[133] *Prehistoric Assyria*, p. 178; cf. Stein, *Mem. Arch. Surv. Ind.*, No. 37, pls. XX, XXI.

[134] *Op. cit.*, pls. XX (S. J. vi. 8); XXI (S. J. 16).

[135] *Op. cit.*, pl. XXI (S. J. 107).

those from Periāno-ghuṇḍai and Moghul-ghuṇḍai, although the latter, as already mentioned, appear to be closely related to the Jhukar pottery.

If the Jhukar people were actually in occupation of the parts of Baluchistan where their relics have been unearthed, their sphere of influence must have been considerable. The Periāno-ghuṇḍai and Moghul-ghuṇḍai sites, for instance, are some two hundred and seventy miles west of Chanhu-daro. Chanhu-daro is mentioned particularly because more material of the Jhukar Culture has been found there than anywhere else. But this settlement was, after all, a small and comparatively unimportant one and more relics of this people may eventually come to light in greater abundance elsewhere. It is, however, doubtful whether their culture extended much further to the east in Sindh, for the nature of the country in that quarter is extremely inhospitable.

CHAPTER VIII

LATER WARES, AND STONE AND FAIENCE VESSELS

This chapter deals with the later wares found at Chanhu-daro in their chronological order. Further particulars of this pottery will be found in the catalogue at the end of this book.

JHANGAR POTTERY

An appreciable quantity of the distinctive material belonging to this culture first appeared about two miles south of the village of Jhangar near Sehwān.[1] Here was unearthed a considerable amount of incised pottery, black or grey in colour, of a type not hitherto met with in Sindh.

During the preliminary work on the summit of Mound II at Chanhu-daro, similar pottery was found at levels ranging from 18.9 to 22.3 feet above datum level. The sherd illustrated in Pl. XXXIX, 7, a and the small bowls in Pl. XL, 6, 9, a came from much lower levels, but there is no doubt that these pieces had rolled down the mound in ancient times and had then become buried.

The fact that this pottery was found at such high levels at Chanhu-daro proves that the people who made it occupied Mound II after the Jhukar people had deserted it. In some cases the wares lay just above the Jhukar stratum, in others there was a little overlapping, probably the result of the soil being disturbed by later searchers for building material.[2] At Jhangar itself, however, this black pottery could not be correlated with either earlier or later wares; possibly the site itself had been occupied by the one culture.

At Chanhu-daro no painted wares were associated with this dark-coloured pottery. Jhangar, however, produced with it a few red sherds bearing designs in chocolate-coloured paint on a cream or light red slip[3]. The remarkable resemblance of the conjoined jars in XXXIX, 2 to a painted triad of red clay from Baluchistan, coupled with the Jhangar evidence, indicates that painted red wares were also in use by the people of this incised pottery.

With the exception of the roughly made kohl-jars illustrated in Pl. XXXIX, 4, 5, 7, this Jhangar pottery appears to have been raised on a slow wheel or *tournette*. It is true that the rims of some of the vessels show slight striations, but markings such as these are often present on other hand-made pottery. There are no indications that wheel-marks were removed with the aid of a paddle, that instrument always betrays itself by the slight faceting it leaves behind.

The Jhangar pottery from Chanhu-daro is exceptionally well made of a light or dark-

[1] Majumdar, *Explorations in Sind*, pp. 68-70, 78; pls. XXXI, 4-6, 11-13, 20-22, 27, 28, 32, 33; XXXV, 5, 10. Jhangar is situated about 43 miles North-west of Chanhu-daro.

[2] It should be remembered that Muhammadan graves of an early date were found on the summit and sides of this mound.

[3] *Explorations in Sind*, p. 79.

grey paste (sometimes almost black), very gritty to the touch. Lime and mica were used as dégraissants, the former being especially conspicuous in the dark-coloured clay. Most of the vessels bear polish markings caused by rubbing their surfaces horizontally with a pebble or piece of bone.

A black coating which adheres very closely to the surface of the pottery but has not quite the same appearance as a clay slip, is to be seen on the bowls in Pl. XL. 6, 7 and possibly once covered the rather weathered vessels in Pls. XXXIX, 2, XL, 7, a. This coating may have been caused by applying to the surface of the vessel a resin or the juice of a plant which burned black when the pot was fired.

The grey pastes used for this pottery were possibly produced by mixing with the clay some kind of organic matter. This would carbonize in the furnace and impart to the clay the grey colour and the gritty feel that is so characteristic of it.[4] Markings on some of the vessels indicate that they were baked in an open furnace heaped over with chopped straw or reeds.[5]

Most of this pottery is well made, with comparatively thin walls. The small kohl-jars illustrated in Pl. XXXIX, 4, 5, 7 are, however exceptions and are of the roughest workmanship; they do not seem to have been the work of an experienced potter. The restrained use of simple patterns, such as triangles, chevrons, and zig-zags, adds greatly to the beauty of this Jhangar ware, and the shapes of the bowls, especially those that are carinated, are without reproach.

Except for their pottery, the Jhangar people left nothing behind them at Chanhu-daro. Their settlement seems to have been a very small one, and it is possible that they never occupied Mound II permanently at all, but merely used it as a convenient camping site. There is no evidence that burials of this people ever took place there.

At Jhangar itself no traces were found of any buildings that could be ascribed to this grey ware folk and it must, therefore, be assumed that they lived in huts of some perishable material, such as grass or matting. The very appearance of their pottery suggests that they were a primitive people. They may have been, indeed, an aboriginal tribe, like the Bhils, who have now penetrated into Sindh and have formed little communities, which, in that province at least, keep strictly to themselves.

Plate XXXIX. No. 1 (see also Pl. XL, 11). Dark grey with polished surface. Three scored lines, partly smoothed over, round shoulder. Well made and regular in shape.

No. 2. Three small bowls, each 2.4 inches high, joined together. Irregular aperture, 0.4 inch in diameter, between the three was possibly for inserting a rod to support them on a stand. Dark grey, porous paste containing small particles of lime. Surface coloured black and shows horizontal polish markings. Each bowl was separately made and joined before the clay was dry. Found with the kohl-jar seen in No. 5.

A group almost identical with the above, except that it is painted, was unearthed at

[4] This method of producing black or grey wares is common to modern as well as ancient primitive wares.

[5] These markings are especially noticeable on the vessels in Pl. XXXIX, 3, 6, 8. It will be remembered that straw impressions have also been noted on the Jhukar pottery.

Shāhī-tump in Southern Baluchistan, where it lay about five feet below the surface surrounded by painted grey-coloured vessels.[6] It would thus appear that these two triads are products of the same culture, yet the pottery associated with Shāhī-tump specimen is entirely different from any of the vessels found either at Jhangar or Chanhu-daro.[7]

No. 3 (see also Pl. XL, 9). Dark grey ware, no slip. Straw markings on surface. Thin for its size and decorated with two shallow grooves round the shoulder, which have become partly obliterated by polishing.

No. 4. Dark grey paste. 2.36 inches high. Roughly incised triangles with single hatched interiors decorate the lower portion of this little kohl-jar. Thick for its size and with little interior capacity, the diameter of its mouth being only 0.24 inch.

No. 5. Dark grey, almost black paste. 3.77 inches high with an opening 0.32 inch in diameter. The greater part of this cosmetic jar is decorated with a deeply incised chevron pattern set between triple vertical partitions. Its flat rim is ornamented with roughly scratched transverse parallel lines arranged in three groups of five lines each.

No. 6 (see also Pl. XL, 10). Grey paste containing a little lime and mica. Horizontal polish markings and some straw impressions on face. Two incised lines, partly smoothed over, form a kind of moulding round the rim. A row of deeply incised triangles occurs a little lower down.

No. 7. Dark grey almost black paste. 3.4 inches high. Aperture 0.28 inch in diameter. Rim missing, but probably resembled that of No. 5, the decoration of the two specimens being very similar. Has little capacity and was found to contain traces of a black pigment which, on analysis, proved to be a simple soot.

No. 7, a. Grey-coloured sherd measuring 2.3 inches across and 0.21 inch thick. Bears slight polish and is ornamented with bands of incised oblique lines.

No. 8 (see also Pl. XL, 8). Light grey paste. The partly polished surface of this bowl is pitted here and there with straw marks. Incised line at the rim and a triple row of zig-zags just above its carination.

Plate XL. Nos. 8-11 in this plate appear in photograph in Pl. XXXIX and have already been described.

No. 5. Dark grey paste. Semi-polished surface showing horizontal rub-marks. Incised lines round rim and shoulder.

No. 6. Grey paste, rather lightly baked. Traces of a black coating which does not appear to be that of a true slip. Band of incised hatched triangles above its carination.

No. 7. Grey paste containing lime and mica. Evidences of a black coating. Thick for size and has a scored line just below the rim.

No. 7, a. Dirty-looking grey paste containing lime and mica. Originally coated black.

No. 9, a. Dirty grey paste. No signs of polish. Rim missing. Decorated with an incised pattern of oblique lines in registers.

[6] Stein, *Mem. Arch. Surv. Ind.*, No. 43, pl. XIII, p. 93.

[7] I can find no evidence of incised grey pottery occurring in Baluchistan at all. The Shāhī-tump grey pottery is thought to have been expressly made for burial purposes, *op. cit.*, p. 99.

Some of the pottery described above was found in groups. The two pieces in Pl. XXXIX, 2, 5 were found in Square 8/D, locus 82 (see plan in Pl. I) at the level + 22.0 feet. Square 9/D, locus 95 contained the three vessels shown in Pls. XXXIX, 1, 4, XL, 5 at the level + 19.3 feet, while close by lay two other bowls (Pl. XXXIX, 6, 8) at the level + 22.2 feet. The remaining pieces came to light in various parts of Mound II.

Trihni Ware

In the preliminary trenching on the southern side of Mound II, a number of painted sherds were found at levels ranging from 1.6 to 6.8 feet below datum level (pl. XLV, 1-18). Other pottery of the same description, but in a badly weathered condition, was picked up from the surface of the plain,[8] some distance from the mound. All this material, some of which is painted in two colours in addition to the slip, is apparently the work of a people who occupied Sindh some considerable time after the close of the Jhukar Period.

Pottery of exactly the same type has appeared at two other sites in Sindh, namely at Trihni and at Shah Hasan, both being close to the shores of Lake Manchhar.[9] These two settlements may have been occupied in ancient times by fisher-folk who left behind them little beyond their pottery and some coarse flint flakes.[10] I cannot accept the view that the triangular pottery objects, perforated wares, toy cart-frames, and pieces of incised food-stands[11] found also in or on these two mounds were products of this Trihni people. The water stood at too high a level in both mounds for a proper examination of their lower contents to be made and their excavator himself, after noting that some of his finds closely resembled objects belonging to the Harappā Culture, concluded that they belonged to a later phase of that civilization.[12] That the mound Trihni, moreover, had some connection with the Jhukar people appears likely as evinced by the fragment of a dish bearing a typical pattern of that period that was found there.[13]

The Trihni ware is wheel-made, of a light red clay containing a small percentage of lime and sand, the latter charged with mica. It differs from the other pottery of Chanhu-daro in the fact that the back of every sherd—nothing like a complete vessel has been found—is thickly coated with micaceous sand. This was evidently applied to prevent the inside surface of a jar from sticking to a tool held against it, while its outer parts were tapped and consolidated with a paddle.[14] This particular technique produces a very thin pottery with a smooth but unpolished surface; the paddle, when properly used, leaves an almost imperceptible faceting.

The slips on this ware are never polished and vary greatly in colour and texture. Sometimes they are so thin that the colour of the pottery shows through; on some sherds the

[8] About 5 ft. below datum.

[9] Majumdar, *Explorations in Sind*, pp. 60-65; pl. XXIII.

[10] *Ibid.*

[11] *Op. cit.*, pp. 63, 72, 73.

[12] *Op. cit.*, p. 63.

[13] *Op. cit.*, pl. XXIII, 35.

[14] This use of a paddle upon pottery is known in modern Egypt, Malay States, Ceylon, and the Solomon Islands. For an account of its modern use in Sindh, see *Journ. Roy. Anthrop. Inst.*, vol. LX, p. 130. The Jhukar fragment of a large storage jar in Pl. XLV, 39 has also been treated in this way but is quite exceptional.

coating is so thick that it tends to scale. The fragments in Pl. XLV, 1-3, 5-7, 15, 18, bear a cream-coloured slip and Nos. 4, 10, 11, and 17 a pink coating. A very distinct yellow appears on Nos. 12, 14, and 16 and Nos. 8 and 9 have no slip at all.

Black and red are the two colours most used, the former being employed for the motifs and the latter for the horizontal bands, which are a feature of the scheme of decoration. These bands are often edged with a deeper shade of red or with black. The motifs in Pl. XLV, 1, 17 are outlined in brown paint and those in Nos. 2 and 13 with red, while this colour appears with black or brown to embellish the patterns on Nos. 1, 9, and 16.

This Trihni ware resembles the earlier Jhukar pottery as far as the use of red bands and the occasional employment of a pink slip or a brown paint are concerned, but the similarity ceases when a closer examination is made, for there is no resemblance whatever between the fabrics used in the two periods or between the decorative motifs employed.

The reasons for assuming that the Trihni pottery is of fairly late date are as follows: (a) its position at Chanhu-daro where it was found either on the surface of the plain or beneath late débris that had been washed down the sides of Mound II; (b) its resemblance to the modern wares of Sindh rather than to the earlier pottery on which the paddle was not employed; (c) the presence of the palmetto ornament on a sherd from Trihni,[15] which can hardly be dated prior to the VII Century B.C.; also, the very realistic figure of a duck or goose in Pl. XLV, 2 is not of early style.

Until we can correlate this pottery with later material we may provisionally assign it to the centuries immediately preceding the Christian era.

Plate XLV. No. 1. 4.04 inches long; 0.14 inch thick. Part of the shoulder of a large vessel. Cream slip. Decorated with seven red spots enclosed in a circle of brown paint and with a group of five wavy lines, also in brown. At the corners of the parallelogram formed by the lines are spots of red paint. Red bands, edged with brown paint, border the design above and below.

No. 2. 5.7 inches long; 0.19 inch thick. Portion of rim and shoulder of jar. The duck or goose is painted in a purplish-red on a cream slip. Light red bands above and below bordered by darker lines. The bird is shown preening its feathers and the ruffling of the breast provides a realistic touch.

No. 3. 1.72 inches long; 0.1 inch thick. Pattern in black on a cream-coloured slip.

No. 4. 3.82 inches long by 0.2 inch thick. Part of the rim and neck of a large jar. Black zig-zag pattern and spots on a pink slip, bordered by dark red bands.

No. 5. 2.9 inches long by 0.2 inch thick. Part of the rim and neck of a jar. Zig-zag lines and spots in black on a cream slip. Red band round top of rim with triangles in black.

No. 6. 5.4 inches long by 0.18 inch thick. Fragment of the neck and shoulder of a large jar. Purplish-black motifs on a cream ground. Light red bands, edged with a darker shade above and below.

No. 7. 5.26 inches long. Rim of large vessel. Pattern in purple-black on a cream slip. Light red band below.

[15] Majumdar, *Explorations in Sind*, pl. XXIII, 10, 41.

No. 8. 1.95 inches long by 0.16 inch thick. Purplish-black motif painted directly on the surface of the pottery.

No. 9. 4.2 inches long by 0.2 inch thick. Plant motif in light red and black on the natural surface of the pottery.

No. 10. 2.9 inches long by 0.22 inch thick. Part of neck and shoulder of medium-sized jar. Black motifs on a pink-coloured slip. Light red band above bordered by black.

No. 11. 2.75 inches long by 0.15 inch thick. Dark red motifs on a pink ground with black lines above and below.

No. 12. 3.3 inches long by 0.21 inch thick. Black loops on a light yellow slip, bordered by dark red bands edged with black.

No. 13. 2.15 inches long by 0.19 inch thick. Dark red, wavy zig-zag line and spots on a pink-coloured slip.

No. 14. 1.62 inches long by 0.13 inch thick. Purplish-black motifs on a yellow ochre slip.

No. 15. 2.77 inches long by 0.19 inch thick. Black loops on a cream ground, with a light red band edged with black below.

No. 16. 1.92 inches long by 0.13 inch thick. Red and black loops on a yellow slip.

No. 17. 6.0 inches long. Portion of rim of large vessel. Brown coloured motifs on a pink slip.

No. 18. 6.31 inches long and varying from 0.15 to 0.25 inches in thickness. Part of rim and shoulder of large vessel. Circles and groups of lines in purplish-black on a cream-coloured ground. Light red band edged with dark red appears between the motifs and rim. Inside the brim are dark red lines.

A favourite motif on this Trihni ware is a zig-zag line with the intervals filled in with spots (Pl. XLV, 4, 5, 13). This form of decoration, simple as it is, does not appear on the Jhukar and Harappā pottery, though it is common, but without the spots, on wares from other sites. The large roundel with spots inside, shewn in Pl. XLV, 1, may be compared with one on a sherd unearthed at Trihni.[16] Another fragment of pottery from Shah Hasan [17] bears a pattern identical with the one appearing in Pl. XLV, 7, 17.

This kind of pottery does not appear to have been made anywhere in Baluchistan, but only personal handling of material from that country would settle the point. In any case the people who made it do not seem to have belonged to an important culture and it is, therefore, unlikely that articles made by them would travel far beyond the places where they were produced.

Muhammadan Pottery

Before concluding this survey of the various wares unearthed at Chanhu-daro mention must be made of some large pottery vessels that were used to roof the brick-lined graves found on the summit and slopes of Mound II and described in Chapter III.

The three large jars shown in Pl. XL, 1-3 formed part of a group of seven used to cover

[16] Majumdar, *Explorations in Sind*, pl. XXIII, 36.

[17] *Op. cit.*, pl. XXIII, 45.

a Muhammadan tomb. The photograph of an adjacent tomb in Pl. XVII(d) shows how these were arranged: their original position on the mound will be seen in Pl. III, Square 7/E, locus 88, where six of these tombs were discovered in two groups of three. They, and, of course, the pottery covering them, date from about the XVII Century A. D. Certain bricks used to line them are of the same type as those used in a Muhammadan cemetery, now deserted, about half-a-mile to the south of Chanhu-daro.[18]

The three jars that we illustrate are exceedingly well made. Their thin walls, dressed as in the case of the Trihni pottery by a paddle, are as perfect as when they left the potter. They are made of the same clay as that employed for the more ancient wares and both lime and sand were used as tempering materials. An interesting feature of this pottery is the thick coating of sand that covers their lower portions on the outside. It has already been mentioned that some of the storage jars made by the people of the Harappā Culture were also treated in this manner, a process still carried out in Sindh to-day. It is said that the extra thickness helps to keep the contents of a jar cool.[19]

Nos. 1 and 2 in Pl. XL have a cream-coloured slip. The neck and rim of the latter is coated inside and out with a thick polished red slip. No. 1 is decorated with purplish-black lines enclosing broad bands of a light red colour and No. 2 has bands, spots, and lattice pattern, all painted in a light red colour. A prominent rib encircles this last jar, incised with oblique markings that are cross-hatched at intervals. No. 3 in the same plate has no slip. Its upper portion is very smoothly finished but not polished and its lower portion as far up as to the line has an exceptionally thick coating of sand.

This use of spot motifs and of red bands on these late Sindhi vessels is of considerable interest, for they are direct survivals of some of the Jhukar forms of decoration, carried through, as we have seen, by the Trihni people. Red bands, indeed, remain a favourite form of pottery ornamentation in the remoter parts of Sindh to-day.

Stone Vessels

Few recognizable fragments of stone vessels have been recovered at Chanhu-daro, and of these we have been able to ascertain the original forms of only three examples.

No. 47 in Pl. XXIX (2984). In three fragments. Light grey sandstone.

No. 48 (2245). Dark grey sandstone fragment. Smoothly finished inside and out but unpolished.

No. 30 in Pl. XCIII (2178). 2.55 inches long; 0.23 inch thick. Dark grey steatite. Fragment of dish broken anciently and repaired. Seven small rivet holes, averaging 0.02 inch in diameter along is broken edge. Well made but surface finish not particularly good.

The above three dishes belong to the Harappā Period; the first two are of poor quality stone.

[18] A gravestone in this cemetery is dated to 1031 of the Hegira.

[19] This is peculiar to the Sindh wares, whether ancient or modern.

Faience Vessels

These also are rare, possibly for the reason that the inhabitants of Chanhu-daro were, in the main, too poor to use such expensive luxuries. That glazing, however, was extensively practised at this site is proved by the many materials found that were employed in this process. Three of the four specimens that we are able to illustrate (Pls. XXIX, 54, 56, LXXXIX, 2) can be assigned to the Harappā Period, two of these being found on Mound I. One (Pl. XXIX, 55) was taken from a high level on Mound II and may be either of Jhukar work or re-used in that period. The cores of all three are white or light grey in colour.

No. 54 in Pl. XXIX (4720). 2.09 inches high. Neck and rim of tall vessel. Light green glaze. Incised with chevron pattern. Hole through neck is 0.25 inch in diameter. Small hole on each side of rim, possibly to secure a cover. Evidently a portion of a kohl-jar of a type perhaps once resembling the bronze jar in Pl. LXXIII, 39.

No. 55 (1487). 1.3 inches high. Light green glaze. Small hole on each side and incised line just below rim. Inside this little cosmetic vessel are brown stains suggesting that it had once held a scented fat or ointment.

No. 56 (4743). 1.42 inches high. Glaze now light grey in colour. Two small holes through neck not exactly opposite to one another.

No. 2 in Pl. LXXXIX (2936). 1.5 inches high. Traces of glaze of a light green colour. Scoring on the base of this little cosmetic jar proves that it was made or finished on a wheel.

Chapter IX

SEALS, SEAL-AMULETS, AND SEAL IMPRESSIONS

The seals, seal-amulets and seal impressions described in this Chapter fall naturally into two groups: (a) Those of the Jhukar Culture, and (b) those which belong to the earlier Harappā Culture. I have mentioned in Chapter III the presence at some later date on the summit of Mound II of an apparently primitive people, much of whose dark grey, polished ware was decorated with simple geometric patterns. These people, however, as far as we are at present aware, neither made nor used seals or seal-amulets. It is convenient to describe the Jhukar group first, as they are types which are quite new to us. They were made and used by a people whose pottery also has shown them to have been of another family than the people of the Harappā Culture, with whose products we are so well acquainted at Mohenjo-daro and Harappā.

Seal-Amulets and Impressions of the Jhukar Period

These Jhukar seals and amulets are illustrated in Pls. XLIX, L, LXXXVII, and it will be seen how radically different they are both in shape and in the designs they bear from those of the Harappā Culture (Pls. LI, LII). They can be divided into four types, though it is not yet quite certain that the last type actually belongs to the Jhukar Period. I prefer the term "seal-amulets" to "seals," for many of these objects could not have been used to make impressions; in fact, some of them had been impressed by seals or stamps and were presumably carried merely for their amuletic properties. Indeed, it is far from certain that the so-called "seals" of the Harappā Culture (Pls. LI and LII) were really seals, and I have always termed them seal-amulets as they would have served either purpose.

(I). Bead-amulets, lenticular or round, with more or less convex faces, a curved edge, and perforated transversely. This type of amulet was made of pottery (Pls. XLIX, 7, 9, 11-13, L, 2, 9, 11, 12, 14, 15) or stone (Pls. L, 4, 16; LXXXVII, 1). One or both faces bear incised designs.

(II). Bead-amulets, round, with flat faces and edge, the latter sometimes with two or three grooved lines as decoration. This type was apparently not made of pottery. One stone (Pls. L, 1, LXXXVII, 20) and five faience specimens were found (Pls. L, 5, 7, 8, 10, LXXXVII, 23, 24).

(III). Handled amulets, round, with only one inscribed face and roughly made perforated handle at the back, as seen in Pl. XLIX, 1, 3, 14, 15. The majority were made of pottery (Pls. XLIX, 1, 3, 10, 14, 15, L, 13), others are in faience (Pl. XLIX, 2, 4, 5), but several of superior make are stone (Pl. XLIX, 6 or metal (Pl. XLIX, 8). Like the handleless types, they bear varied devices.

The handles of the amulets of this type vary somewhat in shape. The most common form is seen in Pl. XLIX, 1, 3, 6, 14. No. 8 in Pl. XLIX is ledge-like in form, and to judge from a fracture on its back No. 10 in the same plate had once a handle of similar shape. The square amulet, Pl. L, 6, has a pierced rectangular lug at the back which is obviously unfinished; it may have been intended to take the round boss-like shape that is so common in the seals of the Harappā Culture, but some uncertainty about this last specimen makes it possible that it belongs to the earlier period.

The faience amulets (Pl. XLIX, 4, 5) also have perforated handles at the back, and the very rough handle of No. 15 in Pl. XLIX was more useful than any of the better finished examples.

(IV). A fourth type, akin to Type I, is elliptical, with slightly rounded faces, and is perforated longitudinally (Pl. L, 3). It is made of glazed paste and is the only one of its shape to be found.

With the exception of Nos. 2, 5, 6, 10 in Pl. XLIX and Nos. 1 and 4 in Pl. L, these amulets were coarsely and roughly made. Nor is it likely, as already stated, that many of them were used as seals. No. 15 in Pl. XLIX is so undercut that it was difficult to obtain an impression from it. Here it should be noted that where impressions could be made they are illustrated; No. 6, a in Pl. XLIX and No. 9 in Pl. L are photographs of the actual faces.

The designs on these amulets, though mostly very simple, vary considerably. No. 15, a in Pl. XLIX resembles No. 12 with the addition of a ring to frame it, and there is some similarity between Pl. XLIX, 4 and that on Pl. L, 5. Some of the designs suggest home manufacture, as, for instance, Nos. 7, 12, and 15, a in Pl. XLIX.

The amulets in faience are greatly superior in finish to those made of pottery; they could hardly have been made by any but a skilled craftsman. And the stone amulets (Pls. XLIX, 6, L, 1, 4, 16) are so advanced in technique and finish that very considerable time and trouble must have been taken over their manufacture.

All except one of the amulets of this group were found on Mound II at varying levels. Nos. 1, 3-5, 9-11, 13, 15 in Pl. XLIX, Nos. 3, 5, 7-9, 12, 13, 16 in Pl. L, and No. 24 in Pl. LXXXVII were found close to the summit of the mound at levels ranging from 11.5 to 20.2 feet above datum, i. e., at an average of + 15.7 feet. No. 6 in Pl. XLIX came from the summit of Mound I at the level + 13.6 feet. The remaining specimens, namely, thirteen out of a total of thirty-one, were unearthed on the sides of Mound II at levels ranging from + 0.8 to + 11.5 feet—the important amulet, No. 1 in Pl. L, from the low level − 0.1 foot—whither they had rolled or been swept down from their original level by the rain-storms which have left their mark on the sides of the mound as deep gulleys and water-courses.

Here it should be mentioned that none of the typical Harappā seal-amulets were found at a higher level than + 15.4 feet (Pl. LII, 16). The amulet (Pl. L, 9) found at + 17.7 feet seems to have been impressed by a square seal of a type well known at both Mohenjo-daro and Harappā, which has not yet appeared at Chanhu-daro.[1] Possibly the seal itself was picked up at a lower level and used by one of the Jhukar people to impress

[1] *Further Excavations at Mohenjo-daro* (F. E. M.), pl. XCI, 1.

this amulet. One or two other amulets in the Jhukar level show definite indications of the influence of the Harappā Culture, notably Nos. 7 and 8 in Pl. L, the pattern on which is obviously derived from the intersecting-circle design of former days. Despite this resemblance, however, neither of these two amulets is in make and shape really like any from Mohenjo-daro and Harappā. I am doubtful about No. 6 in Pl. L, which was found at a level which would lead one to date it to the Harappā Period. It is made of dark brown steatite, and on it is engraved an antelope standing in a thicket, a somewhat unconventional device for a seal of the Harappa Culture. Save for these few examples, the Jhukar amulets are quite unlike those used by the people of the earlier period.

The designs in Pls. XLIX, 5, L, 8, a, 13 are undoubtedly solar motifs; the radial markings in the first are very pronounced. A human figure is certainly portrayed in Pl. L, 3, very stiffly executed and not unlike some of the figures common in the Harappā script. Animals are somewhat rare. The two couchant antelopes, one above the other, on the pottery seal in Pl. XLIX, 10, certainly show an Elamite touch in their arrangement. Couchant animals very rarely appear in prehistoric Indian glyptic art. I know of only one example from Mohenjo-daro, which, for this and other reasons, I regard as an importation.[2] Both sides of the white steatite bead-amulet in Pl. L, 1 show scenes that are unusual on Indian seals. The standing ibex with massive horns and the conventional leaf motifs used to fill in the bare spaces around it are unknown on the seal-amulets of the Harappā Culture; so also is the couchant antelope on the reverse, with the secondary flower motif (pomegranate?) and other devices. Both the shape and the animals engraved upon this seal are quite foreign to anything found in the Harappā Culture.

Particularly interesting is the seal pictured in Pl. L, 4, 4, a. It is fashioned from a very hard, cream-coloured stone, its faces are rounded, and its motifs most unusual.[3] The endless coil pattern on one side is quite unlike the rare coil patterns of Mohenjo-daro.[4] On the other side there is an apparently composite animal, a combination of a humped bull and a rhinoceros, with a tail bent over its back that does not properly belong to either of these animals. This seal, for as such it was probably used, was very carefully cut and has a milled edge shown in Pl. LXXXVII, 1, through which it is pierced for suspension.

In Pl. XLIX, 1, a two oxen, one above the other, face to the right, and on the much defaced amulet, No. 9 in the same plate, there seems to be an antelope, facing to the left. There are also two animals on each side of the pottery amulet in Pl. L, 14, 14, a. Very conventional trees are seen on the copper or bronze seal (Pl. XLIX, 8, a) and the clay amulet (Pl. L, 11). The coiled pattern on the reverse of this last amulet is similar to the pattern incised on the handle of a jar-cover of Jhukar date, seen in Pl. XLVIII, 11. No. 15, a in Pl. L is rather a puzzle. Though there appear to be three serpents on the upper part of this pottery amulet, erect and ready to strike, the markings below are not correctly placed if they are indeed intended to represent the tails of the supposed reptiles.

[2] *F. E. M.*, pl. C(b).

[3] The stone from which this seal was cut appears to be identical with that of the seal mentioned in note 1 above.

[4] *M. I. C.*, pl. CXVIII, 5; *F. E. M.*, pls. LXXXII, 3, XC, 23.

In some respects the design in Pl. L, 7 resembles those on certain copper seals found by Sir Aurel Stein at Shāhī-tump in Southern Baluchistan.[5] The latter seals were all associated with burials in the upper levels of that mound; they are therefore late in date, for the burials took place when the mound was already of considerable age and had been badly denuded.[6] But the pottery found with these Shāhī-tump seals in no way resembles that of the Jhukar Culture at Chanhu-daro; indeed, it differs from it as much as does the latter ware from that of the Harappā Culture. The Shāhī-tump copper seals, however, may be allied to the group of three small bowls[7] joined together, which was also found on this mound and is identical in shape with a similar vessel of the Jhangar Period unearthed at Chanhu-daro (Pl. XXXIX, 2), particulars of which are given in Chapter VIII. Apart from these copper seals, therefore, and the triplet bowls already noted and some few sherds and vessels, the latter undoubtedly of Jhukar work,[8] we can trace few definite connections between the ancient Balūchī and the Jhukar Cultures.

There are no characters or pictographs on any of the amulets of this period, unless the marks in the upper parts of Nos. 1, a and 9 in Pl. XLIX were intended to be signs; but the majority of the amulets are so roughly executed that it seems probable that they were made by illiterate craftsmen and for uneducated people. It is unsafe, however, to assume that writing was unknown in the Jhukar Period by reason of the absence of any script on these amulets, even though practically every amulet and seal-amulet from Mohenjo-daro and Harappā bore an inscription of some kind.

Round seals or amulets are exceedingly rare in the Harappā Culture, but all the Jhukar amulets are of that shape except No. 6 in Pl. XLIX and Nos. 3 and 6 in Pl. L. A great many are lentoid with rounded edges and faces that range from being flat to having a pronounced convexity. Four of them, Nos. 1, 5, 8 in Pl. L and No. 24 in Pl. LXXXVII, of which the first is stone and the others faience, have edges square cut and flat, and ornamented with two or three grooves running round them, giving them a fluted appearance.

There is a curious ornamentation on the bevelled edge of the square seal in Pl. XLIX, 6, which has been carefully notched all round. The edge of the fine stone seal Pl. L, 4 had been milled to enhance its appearance, as will be seen in Pl. LXXXVII, 1. The shape of No. 9 in Pl. L, which is so round that it might almost be termed a bead, prevented a satisfactory impression being taken; it was therefore photographed direct.

The larger number of amulets have no handles, but that they were all worn on a cord or wire is shown by the holes that perforate them. Some of these holes, as for example in Pl. XLIX, 13, are badly worn; obviously many of these amulets were continually carried about. In the hole of the glazed amulet Pl. L, 7 a fragment of the copper wire still remained. That some difficulty was experienced in boring the stone amulet Pl. L, 16 is proved by its sharply biconical hole.

The majority of these objects were made of ordinary clay, of a light red colour and

[5] *Mem. Arch. Surv. Ind.*, No. 43, pl. XIV.
[6] *Op. cit.*, p. 98.
[7] *Op. cit.*, p. 93; pl. XIII, vi. 3.
[8] Stein, *Mem. Arch. Surv. Ind.*, No. 37, pls. VI, VII, XI.

frequently containing mica. Nos. 10 in Pl. XLIX and 11 in Pl. L were made of drab-coloured clay, and No. 1 in Pl. XLIX and No. 12 in Pl. L of grey clay. Not one of the amulets had either slip or wash to improve its appearance, as was almost invariably the rule with the pottery amulets of the Harappā Period.[9]

On those amulets which had handles the latter were rarely sufficiently large or suitably shaped for them to be held easily between the fingers. Like those on the seal-amulets of the Harappā Culture, they could only have been held firmly with the assistance of the cord which passed through them, and it is not surprising to find that the handle was dispensed with on many of the amulets and a hole through the article itself substituted.

In most cases the designs on the amulets, whether of pottery or faience, were cut with a knife or some other sharp tool, though possibly not always so, for the glaze is apt to obscure such details. There is no doubt, however, that a chisel or gouge was used on the amulets in Pls. XLIX, 15, L, 3. The roughness of the former suggests that it was left unfinished.

A certain resemblance can be traced between these amulets and those of the archaic period of Elam, the chief difference being that the latter objects were mostly made of stone and the majority of those from Chanhu-daro of pottery.[10] Even the very curious amulet in Pl. XLIX, 7, is comparable with a limestone seal from Persia both in shape and in the pitted design it bears.[11] No. 13 in Pl. L also has the same motif as on a stone amulet unearthed in Persia.[12]

But the amulets from Chanhu-daro are of later date than the archaic objects from Elam—probably a thousand years later—and we must look further afield for resemblances of contemporary date. The coil pattern on the fine stone seal Pl. L, 4 is practically identical with that on a round haematite seal said to be Hittite;[13] and, indeed, many of the other amulets in Pls. XLIX, L resemble in designs and shape certain Syro-Cappadocian seal-amulets. It would seem that in Elamite art there was a resuscitation of old forms of seals and their primitive designs, which doubtless arrived from the west, and it is to the same source that we may perhaps also trace the new form of seal-amulet that quite suddenly appeared in India after the long vogue of the square and rectangular Harappā seals with their animal devices.

It is even possible that the stone seal pictured in Pl. L, 4, 4a came from Elam or Cappadocia despite the fact that the rhinoceros that is engraved on one side suggests Indian work.[14] The shape of this seal-amulet and, in particular, its rope design, together with the unusual stone of which it is made,[15] appear to me to point to western workmanship. About

[9] Generally this was red.

[10] Delaporte, *Cat. des Cyli.*, t. I, pl. 14, nos. 4a, 4b, 5, 6a, 6b. Stones suitable for seals and amulets were more plentiful in Elam than in the Indus valley.

[11] *Op. cit.*, pl. 16, no. 17.

[12] *Ibid.*, no. 17.

[13] Ward, *Seal Cylinders of Western Asia*, p. 269, no. 802.

[14] The rhinoceros here appears to have been carved by someone who had never actually seen this animal.

[15] A cream-coloured hard stone which cannot be scratched with a knife. It is possibly a quartz of some kind.

1750 B.C., there was an influx of peoples from the west into Mesopotamia, and it was perhaps about this time that an Indian merchant had this seal made in its foreign pattern. The fact, also, as I have already shown, in Chapter VII, that the polychrome pottery found with these new types of Indian seals and amulets has many points in common with certain North Syrian pottery,[16] despite the much earlier date of the latter, might ultimately assist us in the elucidation of the dark period that followed the disappearance of the Harappā Culture.

Seal-amulets and Impressions of the Harappā Period

That seal-amulets were manufactured as well as used at Chanhu-daro is evident from the number of unfinished specimens found at that site. Unfortunately, owing to the use of a substance that appears to have been powdered steatite compressed into block form, a few of the seals were in very bad condition; salt attacks this composition more readily than the natural stone. Their fragility made it unsafe to take impressions of some of them and they were accordingly photographed direct (Pl. LII, 1-6, 11). The remainder of the seal-amulets in Pls. LI, LII are full-sized photographs of impressions in plasticine.

The unfinished specimens (Pl. LI, 1-10) are of particular interest, but whether seal-amulets were made only for local use or to be traded over an extended area it is impossible as yet to say. Examination shows that the engraving of the animals and signs was commenced before the backs were completed, as is seen in Pl. LI, 2, 5, 8 and other specimens whose reverses are not illustrated. The engraving, of course, was the most difficult part of making the amulet; its shaping and the perforation of the boss-like handle were comparatively easy. Yet accidents frequently occurred, particularly in the preliminary rough shaping of the handles, and several seal-amulets had to be discarded for the reason that the handle split away from the body of the seal while being shaped. As a saw was invariably used for this purpose (Pl. LI, 1, 2, 5, 8), with teeth of a rudimentary type,[17] it is not at all surprising that these accidents were frequent, even in working a homogeneous stone like steatite. On two of the unfinished amulets (Pl. LI, 4, 5) the handles were perforated before being finally shaped; in others, such as No. 2 in the same plate, the making of the hole was left until the engraving was done. In Nos. 2, 6, 8, 10 in Pl. LI work on the face of the seal-amulet was well under way before the reverse was done, and in No. 9 in the same plate, the inscription had apparently been finished before the animal was completed. The obverse had already been finished in Nos. 12, 18, 21, in Pl. LI; whereas the handle of No. 12 is only a roughly square, unperforated projection like that of No. 2 in the same plate. No. 18 was very nearly finished except that there were saw marks at the back to be removed, and in No. 21, though the handle was perforated, the back was unfinished and there was still much to be done.

As all these seal-amulets were made to be carried on a cord at either neck or wrist,

[16] The later Tell Halaf ware.

[17] Several saws have been found at Mohenjo-daro and one at Chanhu-daro, for which latter see Pls. LXIII, 1, LXXIV, 4.

their perforated handles often subsequently came away, wholly or in part. Because of an accident of this kind, a second hole was made in No. 16 in Pl. LII—very carelessly and apparently by the owner. No. 8 in Pl. LII was once the inscribed part of a square seal from which it had been carefully cut off, and with the back rounded it had been put into use again; further damage, however, led to its being thrown away. In its new shape this cut-down seal resembled certain oblong seals with rounded backs that were common at Mohenjo-daro but have not yet been found at Chanhu-daro. I should mention here that the square or rectangular copper tablets with an animal incised on one side and an inscription on the other, which are so plentiful at Mohenjo-daro[18] and so rare at Harappā, have also not yet appeared at Chanhu-daro; they may have been a purely local product of the former city.

Before the engraving of these seal-amulets was commenced it is clear from Nos. 3, 5, 8 in Pl. LI that the subject was first roughly outlined with a sharp point; but I confess I can see no sense in the rough scratches on No. 5, whichever way it is looked at, though they must have been of some significance to the engraver. The cross on No. 3 is a rough guide rather than a drawing, though the engraver had used his drill with some courage before commencing the cutting of his design. Possibly this unfinished amulet was a beginner's trial piece. The obverse of No. 8, a was nearly finished, and it shows that even the inscriptions were planned out before being engraved in order that the characters might be properly spaced.

The faces of the unfinished seal-amulets Nos. 2 and 8 in Pl. LI were thickly coated with dark red ochre, and as this colour appears on no other part of these two seals its presence on the obverse of each can hardly be accidental. Possibly it was used for making a trial impression to see how the work was progressing, though the use of colour for this purpose would imply that a smooth, hard surface instead of some plastic material was used to receive the impression, which would merely have shown the outline of the body and none of the modelling of the animal.

No. 4 in Pl. LI is an irregular piece of dark grey steatite, on a flat side of which are five roughly cut characters; it looks to be a trial piece of an engraver's pupil. Most of the amulets in Pls. LI, LII are the work of experienced craftsmen, but it is obvious that the man or boy who engraved the unusually large seal-amulet No. 25 in Pl. LI was far from being proficient at his work. The long line of characters above the animal is very roughly cut, and even more does the animal itself reveal an inexperienced hand.

The one-horned animal, or urus ox with which it has been identified[19] by some, was by far the most favoured device on the seal-amulets of Chanhu-daro. Out of a total number of 55 on which animals appear, no less than 44 picture this beast. It therefore occupied as important a place in the mythology of the people of Chanhu-daro as it did at Mohenjo-daro and Harappā. The cult-object or stand beneath the head of the animal is the same, and it varies slightly in form as it does on the seals of these two cities. In the particularly

[18] *M. I. C.*, pls. CXVII, CXVIII: *F. E. M.*, pl. XCIII.

[19] Friederichs, *Der Alte Orient*, B, 32, H. 3/4, 1933.

clear example in Pl. LI, 33 its upper portion suggests an inverted round-based basket. Other representations show a flat or concave top. No really satisfactory explanation of the meaning or purpose of these cult-objects has yet been recorded; they have been termed cages, racks for fodder, and stands on which incense was burned. Always associated with the one particular animal, this cult-stand presents a problem which one day, no doubt, will be satisfactorily solved; on most of the seals it looks to have been made of wicker- or basket-work.

The trappings of this ox are exactly the same as those of the animal on the seals from Mohenjo-daro. What appears to be a saddle-cloth thrown across the back of the animal in Pl. LII, 26 is a very unusual feature; as a rule the cloth, if it be a cloth, was placed across the withers. That its unusual position on this seal-amulet is not an engraver's error is proved by its similar position on a seal from Mohenjo-daro.[20] Many of the urus oxen also have an ornamented collar round the neck (Pl. LII, 28, 30, etc.).

Representations of other animals on the seal-amulets are comparatively rare. On four the tiger is shown, but three of these seals are, unfortunately, badly mutilated. On a fragment of a seal (Pl. LI, 7) three of these animals are joined together by their middles, a motif which is more clearly illustrated on a seal from Mohenjo-daro,[21] where it forms a somewhat confused but nevertheless very decorative pattern. The tiger on the broken seal Pl. LI, 16 may have been the sole motif or may have formed part of a well known scene, of which we have a fragment (Pl. LI, 19), which depicts a man seated in a tree with a tiger below looking up at him. Part of a tree is clearly indicated on this seal.[22] On the fourth of these seal-amulets, which is intact (Pl. LI, 18), we see a man on one knee, apparently invoking a male tiger who would seem to be licking his face, perhaps in anticipation of the feast. Above is a tree—most likely placed here to show that the man had descended from it. The figure carrying water-jars suspended from a yoke on his shoulders is a sign that is well known in the Harappā script; it probably has no bearing on the scene below.

Three short-horned bulls or bisons appear severally on seals 13-15, 17 in Pl. LI, associated with the manger-like object that with only one or two exceptions always appears with this animal and which, as No. 15 shows, was made of some kind of wickerwork. The trappings on the bull in Pl. LI, 15 should not properly appear on this kind of animal; in all the known seals from other sites they appear to belong strictly to the urus ox and no other beast.[23] The bison on No. 13 is trampling a human figure lying prostrate on the ground. This figure wears a very peculiar form of head-dress, which can just be made out at the right; one arm and one leg are raised as if to fend the animal off.

The elephant in Pl. LI, 20 was very carefully engraved, and the row of bristles along the back, indicating a young animal, mark great attention to realism. A manger beneath the head of the animal on some of the seals from Mohenjo-daro suggests that this animal was kept in captivity.

[20] *F. E. M.*, pl. LXXXII, 691.
[21] *M. I. C.*, pl. CXII, 386.
[22] *Op. cit.*, pl. XCVI, 522.
[23] The seals from the site of Harappā have not yet been published.

From the set of its horns the animal on the seal-amulet Pl. LI, 21 is, I think, a fabulous animal. It has the same shaggy neck as many of the better finished urus oxen, and apparently it is also provided with a saddle-cloth. Exactly the same beast forms part of a composite animal with three heads on several seals from Mohenjo-daro.[24] The object below the head of this animal is quite new to us, yet bears a remote resemblance to the stands associated with the urus bull, and like them appears to be made of basket work. Another seal of interest is No. 22 in Pl. LI. Here again is the urus, with a human being standing beneath its head. The nearest approach to this scene appears on a seal-amulet from Mohenjo-daro, where a tailed monkey-like figure stands before the animal.[25]

Seal-amulet No. 23 in Pl. LI is of interest on account of its shape. Round seals are especially noticeable among the square and rectangular seals that were so popular in the ancient Indus valley. Of hundreds of seal-amulets of the Harappā Culture, a very small proportion indeed are round, and the greater number of these have come from Sumerian sites, principally from Ur.[26] Not one of the latter has an urus bull engraved on it, as on this seal-amulet.

The unfinished object Pl. LI, 6 appears to represent a figure riding an animal; the apparent rider is, however, a flaw in the stone and the animal itself is incomplete. The back of this object is badly fractured. It is perforated by a transverse hole from edge to edge.

With one exception, all the seal-amulets from Chanhu-daro were cut from steatite or from the artificial substance made from it which has already been mentioned. Three seals which are black were once covered with a glossy-white coating like that often present on the seals from Mohenjo-daro and Harappā. The substance of eleven seals was dark or light grey, though they had been whitened outside by the same process as that used with the black seals. Of two yellow seals, one had remains of this same white coating, whereas the other, being unfinished, was in its natural state. Two out of three brown steatite seals also had a white slip, the third being left untreated. One seal (Pl. LI, 9) was made of dark grey stone with a gritty feel, a most unusual material. The white slip on similar seal-amulets has been examined by Mr. Horace Beck and is stated by him to be an alkali fused by heat.[27] It gave a smooth glossy finish to the seals which greatly enhances their appearance, and it has withstood the ravages of time excellently. Some of the steatite beads were treated in the same manner.

It is rare to find a single sign as the whole of the inscription above an animal, as in Pl. LI, 31. I know of only two examples among several hundreds of seals.[28] The sign so employed appears on eight other published seals—both as a prefix and as a suffix. An inscription of two characters is fairly common, but three or more is the rule. The diversity of the characters on the seal-amulets of Chanhu-daro and elsewhere implies that they do

[24] *M. I. C.*, pl. CXII, 382; *F. E. M.*, pl. XCVI, 494.

[25] *F. E. M.*, pl. LXXXVIII, 316.

[26] C. J. Gadd, "Seals of Ancient Indian Style found at Ur," *Proc. Brit. Acad.*, vol. XVIII, pp. 3-22.

[27] *Ancient Egypt and the East*, II, 1934, pp. 69-83.

[28] *F. E. M.*, pls. LXXXII, 704, XCVII, 554. I exclude the seals from Harappā which I have not yet seen.

not refer to the animal or scene beneath; it is generally thought that they are personal names, perhaps with titles appended. One new sign at least occurs on the seals from Chanhu-daro; namely, the first from the right in Pl. LI, 30, which appears to be a combination of several characters.

The majority of these seal-amulets were found in Mound II at levels ranging from −5.7 feet (Pl. LI, 3) to as high as +15.4 feet (Pl. LII, 16). Only three, however, lay at a high elevation, namely, No. 16 in Pl. LII, that of Pl. LI, 31, from +14.9 feet, and the unfinished seal Pl. LI, 9, which came from +12.2 feet. Above these levels are found most of the pottery and amulets of the Jhukar Culture. Only six seal-amulets come from the lower levels of Mound II, namely, Pls. LI, 3-5, LII, 5, 9, 29, found at levels ranging from −5.7 to +3.8 feet. But as these low levels were only reached in the trial trenches on the northern side of the mound and in the Great Cutting on the South-western side, further deep digging will doubtless produce more. A few seal-amulets were found in the upper levels +13.1 to +16.8 feet of Mound I (Pls. LI, 10, 25, LII, 7, 8, 17, 25). As yet only part of the summit of this mound has been examined, and it does not appear to have been occupied by the people of the Jhukar Culture—though it is evident that they visited it, for they left several objects behind, including the seal illustrated in Pl. XLIX, 6.

Clay and Faience Amulets and Impressions

Clay or faience amulets or impressions of the Harappā Culture were distinctly rare at Chanhu-daro: only six specimens have been found, one of which we are not able to illustrate (Pl. LII, 33-36). No. 33 is a direct photograph and slightly enlarged; the actual amulet measures 1.8 x 0.41 x 0.3 inches and is light red pottery with no trace of a slip. Both faces are very much rubbed, as are many of the pottery amulets from Mohenjo-daro, and from certain marks on the sides it would seem that this article had been made from two impressed strips of clay joined back to back. On one side there are in relief three gharials, or fish-eating crocodiles, and two fishes, and on the other a row of pictographs, of which some are nearly illegible. Cutting, locus 469. Level: −1.12 feet.

No. 34 is one of two faience amulets that had been made in the same mould. It is of cream-coloured paste with light yellow patches on the surface, which are probably the remains of glaze. The back of each one is plain and neither had been perforated. The one illustrated measures 0.75 x 0.47 x 0.25 inches. Square 8/F, locus 182. Level: +10.8 feet.

No. 35 is a definite sealing made of drab-coloured clay which owes its preservation to having been partly burnt. Part of the back is missing and it is possible that this is due to its having been attached to a bale or document. It measures roughly 0.8 inch in diameter and 0.31 inch thick. The inscription upon it was impressed by a square seal. Square 9/D, locus 215. Level: +9.5 feet.

Another seal-impression, Pl. LII, 36 (see also Pl. LXXVII, 1). averages 1.45 inches in diameter by 0.61 inch thick. The rounded back shows no trace of ever having been attached to anything. The scene on its face was impressed by a square seal measuring 0.71 x 0.71 inches, and through much use the details are far from sharp; two nude female figures are seen, each holding with one hand a standard, from which spring on either side two conventional branches terminating in pipal leaves. The free hand of each figure rests on the hip, and the general attitude somewhat resembles that of the bronze dancing-girl found some years ago at Mohenjo-daro.[29] Those who have argued from its style that this bronze figure was of later date than the stratum in which it was found should be convinced by the style of this sealing that it is in actual fact contemporary. Cutting, locus 465. Level: + 1.1 feet.

A clay sealing (No. 4170) which we are not able to illustrate measured 1.08 inches in diameter and had a slightly rounded face and back. On the face was impressed a motif of three animals tied together at their middles. One of the animals was a tiger; the others could not be recognized. This three-animal motif has been found on a seal from Mohenjo-daro,[30] and something not unlike it occurs on the fragment illustrated in Pl. LI, 7. Being imperfectly fired, this sealing dissolved in the water in which it was being cleaned. Cutting, locus 481. Level: + 0.4 feet.

[29] *M. I. C.*, pl. XCIV, 6.
[30] *M. I. C.*, pl. CXII, 386.

Chapter X

FIGURINES AND MODEL ANIMALS

Human Figurines

With the possible exception of the head in Pl. LIII, 11, 11, a, all the human figurines pictured in Pls. LIII and LIV belong to the Harappā Period; and they were not found at a higher level in Mound II than + 13.5 feet (Pl. LIII, 3). The possible exception came from the comparatively low level of + 10.4 feet, and owing to its technique and complete dissimilarity to the other figurines I was inclined at first to assign it to the Jhukar Period, but at present I am not so sure. I have already pointed out in various places that objects of the last culture were quite often found in the lower levels on the sides of the mound, where they had rolled down in the denudation of the site.[1]

The figurines of Chanhu-daro are of four types:

(I). Hollow female figures with swollen bodies (Pl. LIII, 1-4, 7), each with a flat open base upon which it stands quite firmly.

(II). Solid seated figures with very rudimentary legs (Pls. LIII, 5, 10, LIV, 1, 3, 5, 8-12), nearly all of them males. The lower parts of Nos. 6, 9 in Pl. LIII are missing, but I have no doubt that they also belong to this type of figurine.

(III). Solid female figurine with a pan before her containing a quern (Pl. LIII, 13). This little model was probably a plaything rather than a religious or votive object.[2] Nos. 8, 12 in Pl. LIII and Nos. 2, 6, 7 in Pl. LIV are fragments, I think, of similar figures.

(IV). Pottery head (Pl. LIII, 11, 11, a) with a long neck which evidently once fitted into a separate body, or possibly the top of a support.

The figurines of Type I were fairly numerous, though, being hollow, some of them had been smashed too badly to be illustrated. With their squat, swollen bodies they recall similar figurines unearthed at Mohenjo-daro and Harappā,[3] though they differ from them in standing upon flat, more or less open bases. There is no doubt, I think, that the figurines of this type represent a deity, possibly the Mother-goddess of the Harappā Culture and other parts of the ancient world, whose emblem the dove (Pl. LVII, 6, 12, 15, etc.) we have found so frequently in the Indus valley cities. The legless figurines of Chanhu-daro are

[1] This particular head was unearthed in Sq. 7/C, loc. 238, and reference to the plan in Pl. III will show its exact position. I base this doubt on the resemblance between this head and one from Mohenjo-daro; see *F. E. M.*, pl. LXXVI, 9.

[2] A very similar figure to this one has been found at Harappā: *Ann. Rep. Arch. Surv. Ind.* (1926-7), pl. XXIII, c.

[3] *M. I. C.*, pl. XCV, 29, 30; *F. E. M.*, pl. LXXV, 7, 12, 19.

comparable with certain truncated female figurines from various prehistoric sites in Northern and Southern Baluchistan,[4] which Sir Aurel Stein has tentatively suggested, on the basis of Buddhist and Hellenistic iconography,[5] may represent an earth-goddess, but personally I would regard the truncation as serving a utilitarian purpose—figures so made stand more securely than those with feet, a most useful feature if these figures were household deities kept on a shelf or in a little recess in the wall. A curious feature of some of the Mother-goddess figurines from Mohenjo-daro is that the backs were left unfinished, and particularly their jewellery, which was shown only in front, suggesting that the back of the figure was not intended to be seen. Some of the figurines from Chanhu-daro, however, were as well finished behind as in front; for instance, the necklaces of Nos. 2, 13 in Pl. LIII were very carefully made at the back, which fact would suggest that they were taken down on certain occasions and placed in a position where they could be viewed all round.

Whether these figurines were made by a professional idol-maker or were of home manufacture, it is difficult to say. The making of images is a common profession in India today, but the figures are not regarded as consecrated until they have undergone special rites in the house or shrine of their purchaser.

Truncated figurines have been found in Elam, Cyprus, Crete, and elsewhere; but it is not always certain that their lower parts do not represent long skirts covering the feet. Some of the figurines of the Mother-goddess from Mohenjo-daro and Harappā, though of a different type from those now under review, wear short skirts; the latter are, however, lacking in the squat, large-bodied type of figurine from Chanhu-daro.

The figures of Type II are in every case solid, and with few exceptions (Pls. LIII, 8, 12, LIV, 6, 7) are male. Some are so coarsely modelled that they may well be the work of children, and many have a peg-hole in the base suggesting that they were fastened to something. At first it seemed possible that these little figures served as drivers for the little toy carts that were so popular at Chanhu-daro (Pl. LVIII), but neither pin nor hole to accommodate such figures has as yet been found in the sled-like frames of these carts. Certain of these seated or kneeling figures, noticeably Pl. LIII, 5, 10, are better made than the others: the attitude of No. 10 in Pl. LIII even appears to be one of respect or devotion. The legs of the very quaint figure No. 5 in Pl. LIV are intact, and from its make this figure looks to me to have been modelled by a child.

I have included the figurines of Pls. LIII, 8, 12, LIV, 2, 6, 7 in Type III, though the legs are missing, for they were undoubtedly once seated figures, and the fact that they are all female bears out this assumption. Though coarsely made they all show a certain amount of childish attention to detail. Figures of this type were also fairly common. The most perfect is Pl. LIII, 13, a woman seated before a pottery pan in which is a quern. The arms are missing, but the perfect example that I have quoted as coming from the site of Harappā shows them resting on the upper stone of the quern. So rough is the modelling of this figure that the legs have been entirely omitted, as they are also in the Harappā specimen. The women of the household grinding grain must have been a familiar sight

[4] *Mem. Arch. Surv. Ind.*, No. 43, pp. 126, 162, pl. XXII.
[5] *Ibid.*

at Chanhu-daro, and it is not surprising that the children copied them in the little models that they made.

The curious long-necked figure (Pl. LIII, 11, 11, a), which alone constitutes Type IV, was once fitted to a body, but whether this was of pottery or of some other material is not known. The shaven head, the prominent supra-orbital ridges, and the large eyes and small mouth, all suggest a Sumerian origin rather than a product of the Harappā Culture. The nose, unfortunately, is missing and there is no means of ascertaining whether like those of Sumerian figures of this date it was represented as unduly large; from the extent of the broken surface I should say it was. That a short beard is worn is indicated in a manner which recalls the modern Sikh mode of wearing the beard. This head, which together with its neck is 1.75 inches high, has been carved (though it is possible that it was roughly modelled first) with a fairly broad-edged tool. The neck, 0.45 inch in diameter, has a small vertical hole in it, 0.14 inch in diameter and 0.53 inch deep, which doubtless accommodated a peg to fasten it to the body. The shape of the head is brachycephalic, but we cannot accept this as any indication of race, for it is doubtful whether its carver purposely observed any such distinction; that he purposely accentuated the long face and prognathous jaw seems evident. Though broadly executed this head has plenty of characterization and is a valuable addition to what we know of the racial types of the ancient Indus valley. It is impossible to say with certainty to what period this head belonged. Found, as I have said, at the level of + 10.4 feet in a stratum of the Harappā Culture, it lay fairly close to the edge of the mound and might have rolled there from a higher level. I am doubtful if it belongs to the Jhukar Period, but, unfortunately, we have as yet no other figures of that culture with which to compare it.

It will be noticed that the head-dress of the female figurines is the high fan-shaped affair so common at Mohenjo-daro and Harappā, but without the curious pannier-like appendages that were so fashionable. This cannot, however, be explained as due to local custom, for a mutilated figure found at Chanhu-daro in a preliminary investigation had worn this characteristic head-dress of the Harappā Culture.[6]

These fan-shaped head-dresses at Chanhu-daro were ornamented in various ways. In Pl. LIII, 1 is represented a band of material or embroidery which was perhaps studded with sequins or other ornaments. No. 8 in Pl. LIII had three bands on the left side and four on the right, one of which alone was decorated. No. 2 in Pl. LIII has six simple bands on either side, which it is possible, may have represented long ropes of hair brought from the back of the head to the front over a framework of some kind. In Pl. LIV, 4, 4, a a thick strand of hair starting from the top was taken round the back of the head to the right-hand side, being apparently held in place by strips of material passed round it with the ends secured by a medallion well above the forehead. One end hangs as a loop over the left temple; another which is prick-marked dips as far as the neck. In Pl. LIII, 12, also, a thick strand, starting from the left side of the head, is brought round at the back to the right.

Tight collars, worn by men and women alike (Pls. LIII, 2, 13, LIV, 10) appear to have

[6] Majumdar, *Explorations in Sind*, pl. XXI, 1. For a perfect figure see *F. E. M.*, pl. LXXV, 21-23.

been made of large beads strung closely together; but the choker of the last-mentioned figure is more solid than the others and suggests a metal original. Another figure, not illustrated (No. 3366), wears a similar collar. Longer necklaces, each with a large pendant, are seen in Pl. LIII, 7, 8. As is evident from Pl. LIII, 1, 3, 7, bangles were worn on the upper arms as well as the wrists; from their great size they were doubtless made of pottery like the single and multiple pottery bangles that were found in such numbers at Chanhu-daro (Pl. XC, 26-29, 34).

These pottery bangles were far from beautiful and must, I imagine, have been worn for other reasons than mere decoration. With the exception of Pl. LIII, 10, the male figurines wear a simple string or band round the neck, fastened in front with the ends hanging loosely over the chest (Pl. LIV, 5, 11, 12). This same band is worn by many of the male figures from Mohenjo-daro, and it may have been a sacred cord or a badge of office.[7]

No clothing is worn by any of the male figurines; this lack can hardly be due to the difficulty of representing a fabric in pottery, for the navels are always represented with care, though even light clothing would have hidden them. But whereas the male figures of Mohenjo-daro were always represented as unclothed, the women are shown wearing short skirts, except those certain corpulent figures already stated to be very like those in Pl. LIII, but with legs. It is still a moot point whether these stout figures are intended to suggest pregnancy; if so, they may have been especially made as votive offerings and deposited in a shrine for the purpose of securing children or ensuring safe child-birth.

In the female figures in which the arms are preserved, the left arm is held across the lower part of the body while the right is brought up between the breasts or almost touches the mouth (Pl. LIII, 1, 4, 7). A variant position is shown in Pl. LIII, 3, where the left arm is held in almost the same position as the right, the latter touching the mouth. The posture of Pl. LIII, 4 was perhaps the same, for though the left arm is missing, it has left its impression behind. The same position of the arms as in Pl. LIII, 4 has been observed in the stout figurines from Mohenjo-daro.[8]

Except in the unusual head (Pl. LIII, 11, 11, a) and one other figure (Pl. LIV, 9), the eyes of both male and female figurines are represented by simple flat pellets of clay, more frequently than not indented in the centre to indicate the pupil. In Pl. LIII, 11 the sockets were deeply carved with a tool; in Pl. LIV, 9 they were merely deep incisions. The nose was formed by pinching up the clay with the finger and thumb, leaving two deep hollows in which the eye discs were placed.[9]

Two holes indicate the nostrils in Pl. LIII, 8. When it is represented, the mouth is a simple cut in the clay, and we have yet to find the lips depicted in the strikingly realistic manner of certain figurines of Mohenjo-daro.[10] Some approach to this latter technique is to be seen in Pl. LIV, 9, where the mouth is an oval strip of clay, but unindented.

[7] *F. E. M.*, p. 262; pls. LXXII, 7, LXXV, 13, LXXVI, 15, 22.

[8] *F. E. M.*, pl. LXXV, 7, 12.

[9] The heads of human figures were modelled in exactly the same way by some children in our camp who were given plasticine to play with.

[10] *M. I. C.*, pls. XCIV, XCV; *F. E. M.*, pls. LXXII, LXXV, LXXVI.

It is very unusual to find the ears represented, as the head-dress generally covers these features. Yet three of the figurines (Pls. LIII, 12, LIV, 6, 7) show ears, bored for earrings.[11] Most of the figurines, it is noteworthy, appear to depict a young goddess, and we do not see the generous breasts that are such a feature of the mature deities of Sumer and further west; but the pendant breasts of Pls. LIII, 12, LIV, 6 are those of aged people. The navel was indicated in most of the figurines, but the careful representation of the fingers in Pl. LIII, 10 is most unusual at Chanhu-daro or elsewhere. The figure in Pl. LIV, 6 never had arms, but in other figurines where these members are missing, breaks show that they once existed.

The clay used for making these figurines was the same as that used for the pottery, and in some cases had a large proportion of lime and mica added. The figures are light red in colour and save for the occasional use of a cream slip are undecorated in any way. Nos. 5, 6, 9, 10 in Pl. LIII were coated with a light or dark red wash or slip, as are so many of the figurines of Mohenjo-daro; but possibly more were treated in this way and have lost their colour in the damp and salty soil of Chanhu-daro.

Model Animals

The very varied collections of model animals in Pls. LV, LVI, LVII are with two exceptions (Pl. LVII, 1, 4) in pottery, left either a natural light red colour or coated with a cream or red-coloured slip. A few of these animals are ornamented with red lines to represent hair or feathers. Those illustrated, with the exception of Pl. LVII, 13, all come from Mound II between the levels — 12.5 feet (Pl. LVII, 15) and + 14.6 feet (Pl. LVII, 10, 14). They therefore belong to the Harappā Culture. But in the Great Cutting, in the South-western side of Mound II, were unearthed four little pottery bulls, whose curious attitude and make differentiate them from the other model bulls unearthed either at Chanhu-daro or at other Indian cities of contemporary date. These four little models appear to have been made by another people who may well have been the people of the Jhukar Culture, for comparatively close by them lay a finely painted headrest (Pl. XCII, 38), which, by its decoration, is safely assigned to this latter period together with the stone seal (Pl. L, 4, 4, a).

The most common model animal at Chanhu-daro was the humped bull (Pl. LV, 2). As a rule these bulls were coarsely made, with simple round clay pellets for eyes, a pronounced hump, long, rather thick, horns projecting forwards, and fore-legs and hind-legs joined together. This union of the legs in pairs has been noticed in the model bulls from the lower levels of Mohenjo-daro, whereas the animals from the upper levels invariably have the legs separate.[12] Indeed at Mohenjo-daro this difference served approximately to date the levels, and as we suspect that Mound II of Chanhu-daro was deserted at an earlier period than Mohenjo-daro, it is possible that the upper levels of the former site are contemporary with the lower levels of the latter city. These model bulls with joined legs lend some support to this hypothesis.

[11] Ears are rarely represented on the clay figures of Mohenjo-daro.

[12] *F. E. M.*, p. 288, pl. LXXIX, 16, 17, 26.

Sometimes the eyes of the model bulls, like those of the figurines, are indented in the middle to represent the pupils; indeed, one bull (No. 902), which is not illustrated, has its eyes represented by two strips of clay deeply enough indented to have taken ball-like pellets of clay. So realistic an eye was, however, as rare at Chanhu-daro as it was common at Mohenjo-daro.[13] These model bulls—we have not found any recognisable cows—average 3.5 inches long, and few are coloured red, as was so often the case at Mohenjo-daro. Nostrils were commonly indicated by holes and the mouth by a shallow cut.

Whether these bulls are all to be regarded as toys it is difficult to say. That a great number were is certain, for their shoulders are perforated laterally, as is seen in Pl. LVIII, 7, 8, so that they could be fitted as draught cattle to the toy carts that were so plentiful (Pl. LVIII, 21, 22, 23, 26). This again marks a difference between the model bulls of Chanhu-daro and those from Mohenjo-daro. Though there is no doubt that many of the model cattle from the latter city belonged to toy-carts, their shoulders never had holes to take the beam of a yoke, as is so often the case at Chanhu-daro, where a much less realistic yoke was required.

The model bulls are commonly not of the Brahmani type; they can best be compared with the little grey cattle that trundle round in pairs in the present-day Sindh drawing after them small carts with two wheels of a pattern that closely approximates to the model carts illustrated in Pl. LVIII. These modern Sindhi cattle have their horns set exactly like those in Pl. LV, 2, a small compact hump and a more or less pronounced dew-lap, which in many of the model animals from Chanhu-daro is either merely indicated by roughly pinching together the clay in front of the shoulders (Pl. LVIII, 8) or is absent.

Quite possibly the head in Pl. LV, 1 was intended to represent a Brahmani bull, which, though fairly common on the seals of the Harappā Culture, was very rarely modelled in clay.[14] The head illustrated is that of a humped bull with long crescentic horns which stand upright instead of projecting forward. This breed no longer exists in Sindh, though it evidently did in ancient times.

The horn seen in Pl. LV, 6 may also have belonged to a model of a Brahmani bull. It measures 2.2 inches long by 0.63 inch in diameter at its widest end, and is ornamented at intervals with bands of dark red paint. A hole, 0.08 inch in diameter, near the tip suggests that a ring or similar ornament was once attached to this horn—a feature as yet unknown in the very fine models of bulls from Mohenjo-daro; nor have I seen it in modern India. Possibly, the bull to which this horn once belonged was a cult image, of which many examples have been found at Mohenjo-daro and Harappā, made of stone as well as pottery.[15] The bull's head in Pl. LV, 7, of which only the horns are missing, is certainly a cult-object, whose exact treatment is as yet unknown. Certain bulls' heads from Mohenjo-daro have a large hole in the base of the neck which it is thought may have been for fixing on a

[13] *M. I. C.*, pls. XCVI, 22, 23, XCVII, 23, 24, 26; *F. E. M.*, pls. LXXVIII, 1, LXXIX, 33, LXXXI, 1, 1, a.

[14] *F. E. M.*, pls. LXXXIII, 9, LXXXVIII, 306, XCIX (C).

[15] These cult-figures are always of the short-horned bull and not the Brahmani, *F. E. M.*, pl. LXXIX, 24, 30.

ceremonial staff.[16] The head from Chanhu-daro has a similar hole but it is very small, only 0.1 inch in diameter by 0.72 inch deep. Very possibly these pottery bull's heads were carried in sacred procession; alternately they may have served as an ornament of some kind, or as an amulet fixed on the wall of the house. In the specimen under discussion the hole is much too small to take a rod of any size, but it would have sufficed to fasten the head on a nail. The eyes are thick round discs which are deeply incised in the centre. The broad muzzle has two deep holes to indicate the nostrils and a shallow incision beneath for the mouth. Shallow marks above the eyes denote either wrinkles or hair.

The four bulls in Pl. LV, 4, 5, 9, 12 are especially interesting; it will be seen at once that they are different from the placid animal, No. 2 on the same plate. Their very short, sturdy bodies, their high rumps, and their short projecting horns, brought together at the tips in the case of No. 9, mark them as an entirely different breed from any other bull of which we have found models on any Indus valley site. No. 5 is exceptionally interesting in that its hump is partly sub-divided into two portions. Two of these models have a thick, light red burnished slip (Pl. LV, 9, 12), but whether or not to show that the real animal was red in colour it is difficult to say. A red wash or slip is quite frequently seen on model animals and figurines of the Harappā Culture, but it was rare at Chanhu-daro. Two of these beasts have their legs joined in pairs, but Nos. 9 and 12 have only the front pair so arranged; the hind-legs are separate though not well formed. Unlike the other model bulls which, however roughly made, always have eyes, these four have none. They were all found fairly close together in the Great Cutting, at not greatly different levels, and it is possible that they were made by the same man. Such spirited models were possibly intended to represent fighting animals, and it may be that bull-fighting was one of the sports of Chanhu-daro. On a seal from Mohenjo-daro[17] a man appears to be vaulting over a bull, as in the bull sports of Crete, and on a seal (Pl. LI, 13) of this book, an animal, which appears to be a bison, is trampling on a man, who may be a competitor. I have suggested that these four bulls, all obviously of the same date, should be assigned to the Jhukar Culture—the Harappā Culture had no model animals exactly like them. If bull-fighting and vaulting were actually popular sports in the Harappā Culture, they may have been acquired from it by its Jhukar successor.

In the very interesting one-horned animal (Pls. LV, 10, 11, 13-15, LVI, 2) the single horn is quite definite, and though in general appearance the animal is not unlike the so-called "one-horned animal" on the seals (Pl. LI, 26-33), the horn, which in only one figure projects forward (Pl. LV, 11), has not the usual double curve. Mr. Majumdar, who also found a similar model in one of his trial trenches at Chanhu-daro,[18] suggested that this animal may be the same as that represented on the seals, but further evidence makes this unlikely. These six figures give me the impression of being intended to represent donkeys. The large ears of a donkey, especially a young one, would have very much the same appearance as the apparent horns of these animals, and if, as is now the Arab custom, the tips of the ears were sewn together, the resemblance would be still closer.

[16] *F. E. M.*, pp. 288, 289; pls. LXXVIII, 6, LXXIX, 22, 23.

[17] *F. E. M.*, p. 337; pls. CII, 5, CIII, 8.

[18] *Explorations in Sind*, p. 38; pl. XXI, 4.

Similar model animals were found at Mohenjo-daro, and from the roughness of their make they all appear to be the work of children; the limitations of their material perhaps made it difficult to represent closely set horns or ears separately. No. 10 in Pl. LV has a cream-coloured slip and No. 14 red. All these models have the fore-legs and hind-legs joined together in pairs; in Nos. 10, 11, 13, 14 of Pl. LV there is a vertical hole, averaging 0.1 inch in diameter, between the two pairs of legs, for what reason it is difficult to say. All have the usual pellets for eyes, much exaggerated in size in No. 11 of Pl. LV.

The stripes of black paint on the body of No. 3 in Pl. LV, together with the exposed teeth, suggest that this animal is a very rough model of a tiger. It is coated with a thick red slip, two holes served for nostrils, and three round pellets inserted in a slit in the clay represented the teeth. The oval eyes are pitted in the centre, with incised eye-lashes above and below. Hair is represented by incisions between the now partly missing ears, and the wrinkles above the muzzle are shown by rough scratches. There is a vertical hole, 0.11 inch in diameter, just behind the fore-legs which are separate. The tiger, as we know, was familiar to the people of the Harappā Culture and it is represented on four of the Chanhu-daro seals (Pl. LI, 7, 16, 18, 19). But it was very rarely portrayed in clay and never with the same skill as on the seals.

It is difficult to identify the strange beast in Pl. LV, 8. Roughly made of pottery and uncoloured, it has a hollow body, from which the hind-quarters, legs, and tail are now missing. The head was modelled separately and then attached to the body by inserting a long backward projection into the open tubular trunk; apparently the legs were attached in much the same way. The badly mutilated face is human and wears a long, thin beard. On the seals from Mohenjo-daro there are representations of human-headed rams,[19] and it is possible that here we have exactly the same fabulous beast. This figure could hardly have been used as a toy and was probably a cult figure.

What No. 1 in Pl. LVI was intended to represent is uncertain—possibly a dog, for ears were once present, and no horns. Made of drab-coloured pottery, it has divided legs and uses round discs for eyes. Nor can No. 3 in the same plate be satisfactorily identified, for it is not known whether it formerly had horns or ears. Its very rotund and roughly made body, which seems to be hollow, is covered with a cream-coloured slip.

No. 4 in Pl. LVI, is undoubtedly a boar; the prominent ridge along the back is a characteristic feature of this animal. It has been badly knocked about and part of the muzzle is missing. Round pellets comprise the eyes, and the legs are joined in pairs. Indifferently made, it was covered with a thin cream slip.

We are also on sure ground with Nos. 5 and 6. Both are dogs as shown by the tall prick ears, the tail tightly curled over the back, while light red spots are painted on them both. No. 5 has the fore-legs separate; the hind-legs are, unfortunately, missing. A short cut indicates the mouth; the eyes are the usual pellets of clay; and a small hole marks the anus. The irregular spots of light red paint on the body cannot be seen in the photograph. No. 6 is much the better made of the two. The eyes are more natural; two holes represent the nostrils; and the spots, being in dark red, are very distinct.

[19] *M. I. C.*, pl. XII, 18; *F. E. M.*, pls. XCIV, 411, XCV, 450, XCVI, 493.

Several breeds of dogs have been identified among the models from Mohenjo-daro. From the way they carry their tails, the two illustrated here are of the pariah breed common all over India.

No. 7 in Pl. LVI is a ram's head of pottery, which was once inserted in a hollow body mounted on two wheels to be drawn along as a plaything. as in Pl. LVIII, nos. 11, 12, 15.

The horn of the strange-looking animal in Pl. LVI, 8 identifies it as a rhinoceros, though this animal is nothing like so realistic when modelled as when carved on the seals. The body is too short and the muzzle too attenuated. This figure was evidently modelled by somebody who was not well acquainted with the real animal; even the horn is curved the wrong way. A deep groove at the end of the snout indicates the mouth, above which are two deep holes for the nostrils. Despite its inaccuracy, some care was evidently taken with the modelling, though but for the horn it would be difficult to recognize it. It is covered with a cream-coloured slip.

Models of elephants are rarely found in the Indus valley sites, though this animal frequently appears on the Mohenjo-daro seals (see also Pl. LI, 20). The figure that we illustrate in Pl. LVI, 9 was a very welcome find. The short legs, spinal ridge, and sloping hind-quarters are carefully portrayed, but the trunk is much too short. The vertical and horizontal red lines all over the body of this animal may represent trappings (or perhaps a net). A ring of red round the end of the trunk and the painted line down its front doubtless represent those that are frequently seen on elephants when dressed for state and festive occasions; great ingenuity is shown in decorating the heads and trunks of the real animals with various patterns in coloured paints.

No. 3 above in the same plate may also have been intended for the figure of an elephant. It has no eyes and the ears must have been unduly small.

No. 10 in Pl. LVI, like No. 7 above it, is a ram's head, formerly part of a toy like those in Pl. LVIII. Red lines, now far from clear, indicate the rough fleece of the animal.

The alert-looking beast, No. 11 in Pl. LVI, is undoubtedly an antelope. The large ears, one of which is missing, are a feature rarely found on any model of a horned animal. Both pairs of legs are joined, and the body shows some traces of red slip.

Representations of ducks, in whatever medium, are very scarce. This bird appears once among the pictographs on a seal from Mohenjo-daro,[20] and a fragment from a model also comes from that site.[21] From its weight the model bird shown in Pl. LVI, 12 has a solid body, and it is complete save for a small portion of the bill. Another duck (Pl. LVII, 2) is more realistic, though more roughly modelled; unfortunately, the tail and part of the body are missing. No. 3 in the same plate has lost part of the tail; it has round pellets for eyes, and broad vertical red lines across the back and tail represent the plumage. All these model ducks are legless; nor have they any holes to attach them to anything. They were probably toys, though none of them will float.

Several other model birds, too mutilated to photograph, are shown by their broad bills to be ducks. Two of them were roughly ornamented with light red lines to represent the

[20] *M. I. C.*, pl. CVI, 93.

[21] *F. E. M.*, pl. LXXX, 16.

plumage. Another, headless but with a stout body like that of the bird in Pl. LVI, 12, was decorated in much the same way.

The species of bird in Pl. LVII, 4 is doubtful; its beak and the hinder part of the body are missing. The eyes are mere shallow depressions, and incised lines roughly suggest the longer feathers of the wings. It is an unfinished paste figure.

No. 8 in Pl. LVII is a very strange-looking bird, made of pottery coated with a pink-coloured slip. One of its legs, which were separate, is missing, and between them is a hole, 0.1 inch in diameter and 0.49 inch deep. The eyes, one of which has disappeared, were plain flat pellets of clay and the nostrils are marked by two depressions, below which a slight cut appears where should have been the beak. On the back of this bird shallow incised lines represent the folds of the wings across the back.

The bird seen in Pl. LVII, 13 has the eyes indicated by circular indentations, made with a tubular instrument so that the cores represent the pupils. The badly broken wings appear to have been open and the head was once fastened to a body mounted on wheels. A portion of the beak is missing, but there is no doubt that this is a small model of a pigeon.

In Pl. LVII, 10, 14 is a bird's head, very roughly made of pottery, with a light yellow slip roughly ornamented with dark red lines; even the eye is painted in with this colour. It doubtless once formed part of a chariot, as did also No. 13 in the same plate and the ram's heads in Pl. LVI, 7, 10.

These bird-chariots had a very wide geographical range. Specimens have been found at Mohenjo-daro and Harappā; they occur in historic times in India, in China just after 200 B.C., and are known from the Bronze Age of Europe.[22] Sometimes they have a ram's head, like Nos. 7 and 10 in Pl. LVI, fitted to a bird's body, and they seem to have been used as toys, though why they are sometimes of a composite nature is difficult to explain. No complete specimen with a bird's head and body has as yet been found at Chanhu-daro, though the mutilated specimens here described show that they once were made there.

The unfinished animal in Pl. LVII, 1 is made of a white paste which was never glazed. It was intended, I think, to represent a ram. The legs are united in pairs, but it may have been intended to separate them later, as the figure is obviously in its first stage.

Many roughly modelled pottery figures were unearthed, too badly broken to make satisfactory illustrations. One of these, a ram (2062), found at the level −3.8 feet, came from Trench G(1), locus 67. Another, also a ram (523), had its fore-legs joined together, but the hind-legs were missing. It was very roughly made, and was taken from Trench A(3), locus 40, at the level −2.7 feet.

Nos. 5-7, 9, 11, 12, 15 in Pl. LVII are representations of doves with outstretched wings, all of which have a vertical hole in the base for fastening to something by wooden pins. Many have unformed legs, as No. 11 in Pl. LVII, which shows the appearance of the reverse side of some of these model birds. Sometimes these legs take the form of flanges that ran axially with the bodies of the birds, a feature which with the hole between suggests that they served in some way, not at all clear, to prevent these models from twisting on the stands to which they appear to have been attached. Practically all the specimens found

[22] *M. I. C.*, pp. 560, 561.

have or have had eyes made of round discs of clay. These birds are frequently plain; two, not illustrated, were coloured red. A few, like Nos. 6, 7, 9, 11 in Pl. LVII, were decorated roughly with red lines to denote the plumage, often with a red ring round the neck to show, perhaps, that they were ring-doves. No. 6 is unusual on account of its slight crest; it also has two incised lines round the neck and crossed lines incised upon the back to show the position of the wings.

Practically all these little model doves are broken; they had evidently undergone hard usage, whether as toys or, more probably, as cult objects. We know that in Sumer, Crete, Sardinia, and elsewhere the dove was regarded as sacred and was dedicated to the Mother-goddess, for whose worship in the Indus valley cities also we have strong evidence. Possibly these little models were votive objects set in shrines of the Indian Mother-goddess, either on a little stick stuck in the ground or perhaps on a special stand like the ritual candles of today, and like most votive offerings were thrown out to make place for new ones. Very similar doves with outstretched wings, which stood on little pedestals attached to them, are well known from the excavations at Mohenjo-daro and Harappā,[23] and birds of exactly the same pattern have been unearthed at Kish, Ur, and other Sumerian sites, where we know a Mother-goddess was worshipped. The pedestal type of figure was as rare, however, at Chanhu-daro as it was common at Mohenjo-daro. On a figurine of the Mother-goddess from Mohenjo-daro there appear to be dove-like birds seated on her head-dress,[24] as in certain Minoan representations of this goddess. At the present day in India, a certain amount of reverence is paid to the dove, especially among the Muhammadans, but this may be a survival of pre-Islamic times when the bird was the symbol of a Semitic deity.

A dove in cast bronze, which could not be photographed before our expedition left India, is very like in appearance to No. 15 in Pl. LVII. It measures 1.4 inches long and was found in Square 9/G, locus 439, at the level + 7.5 feet.

[23] *M. I. C.*, pl. XCVI, 1; *F. E. M.*, pl. LXXX, 25.
[24] *F. E. M.*, p. 280, pl. LXXVI, 5.

Chapter XI

TOYS AND PLAYTHINGS

Like the cities of Mohenjo-daro and Harappā, Chanhu-daro has produced a great variety of toys and playthings. Evidently the people of the Harappā Period, like the Indians of today, paid great attention to the enjoyment of the younger population; and, though the children of the ancient Indus valley often amused themselves by making their own simple toys in clay, they had many playthings that could have been made only by skilled craftsmen.

Toy Carts

To judge from the number of wheels and broken frames that have been found, toy carts were extremely popular playthings at Chanhu-daro. They seem to have been made as easily as they were broken, and fragments were brought in on most days by our workmen, though few of the frames could be put together or even satisfactorily restored; only two were found unbroken (Pl. LVIII, 19, 21, 22). Indeed, the pieces were mostly so small that one can only suppose that when the toys were broken they were used for other games until they became so fragmentary that all interest in them was lost. Owing to their solid construction the wheels had rarely suffered much damage.

The most usual cart-frame was the type illustrated in Pl. LVIII, 21. It was strongly made of pottery with four vertically pierced holes on each side to take stakes of wood, exactly as in the little farm carts used at the present day in Middle and Upper Sindh. The four holes at the middle took longer stakes projecting from the underside of the frame in pairs, between which the easily removable axle of the wheels was held. There were also horizontal holes for the shaft through one end of the frame and the middle cross-piece. A reconstructed cart of this type is seen in Pl. LVIII, 25, though the wheels with it were not found with this actual frame. With a floor of matting or a ropework net, the open frames of these carts were well adapted for carrying agricultural produce, such as straw, hay, and the like, which the uprights would have kept in place. On No. 18 in Pl. LVIII a mesh-work of lines of red paint indicates a net in position.

We now have definite evidence in a painted model wheel from Chanhu-daro (Pl. LVIII, 20) that the wheels used there were even simpler in construction than those used in Sumer at the same period. They were made of three solid pieces of wood securely fastened together, the projecting hub probably being one with the middle plank of the wheel. This three-piece construction was doubtless necessitated by the impossibility of procuring planks of sufficient width for the whole diameter of the wheel. But how the three portions were joined together our model wheel, being made of pottery, does not show us. Doubtless, tenons were used, but alone these would not have sufficed to hold the wheel together, and lashings or battens of some kind must also have been employed. It should be mentioned that the reverse of the painted wheel in Pl. LVIII, 20 is flat and painted in the same manner, with the bands of paint on the two sides coinciding. Three pieces of wood are to this day used in making the cart-wheels of Sindh, but the wheels are perforated (the prototype of spokes) to make them less heavy and iron bands reinforce the tenons.

A second type of cart is illustrated in Pl. LVIII, 19. This is box-like in shape with a partition across the middle. At first it was thought that these miniature carts were dishes of some kind which were later converted to use as toys, especially as the holes for shaft and axles were drilled after firing and not pushed through the clay while still wet.[1] Later, however, it became clear that these were carts of another variety with horizontal and vertical red lines painted on the sides to represent either wickerwork or netting; if the latter, we shall have to assume that the sides of this type of cart also were not solid, and that uprights supported netting as in the already described models, e. g., Pl. LVIII, 25.[2]

A second cart of this type (No. 4071), which is not illustrated, has almost the same size and shape and is similiarly decorated, except that the painted lines are horizontal and oblique. The holes to take the axle-pegs are 0.15 inch in diameter; and the shaft-hole, which is very irregular and 0.31 by 0.2 inches in size, appears to have been altered after the first boring so as to make the shaft more horizontal. In this second model, too, the base is flat and a thick deposit of sand and mica shows that it had been laid to dry on a sand bed. It comes from Sq. 7/F, locus 298, level + 6.7 feet.

A little cart body of much the same type (Pl. LVIII, 14) also had a hole for a shaft and four pins to hold the axle in place. It is, however, unpainted, and had evidently been discarded because badly over-fired in the kiln.

A third type of frame (Pl. LVIII, 22, 26) was even more like the modern carts of Sindh. A hole for the shaft pierced the frame longitudinally and in the better-made examples there were holes for uprights along both the longer sides. No. 4 in Pl. LVIII has slightly raised sides, approximating to the box pattern, and for this reason perhaps there are no holes for uprights, but only four for the axle ties.

Nos. 5, 6, 10 in the same plate are probably some form of bird or animal chariot. A considerable number were found, but in every case they were badly broken. The turned-up end is complete in No. 5 only, and probably represents the tail of a bird or other animal. That there was a head on this type of chariot is indicated by the fracture that is always present at the forward end, but up to the present, curiously enough, we have found no heads that could have belonged to these particular chariots. But a number of heads have been found, e. g., No. 16 in Pl. LVIII, that without doubt came from the animal bodies on wheels, Nos. 11, 12, 15 in the same plate.

Yet a fourth type of toy cart or chariot frame is shown in Pl. LVIII, 9, 13. Unlike those already described, these carts had four wheels, and the canopy-like arrangement in front was in the real cart obviously intended to shield the driver. No four-wheeled carts or chariots have yet appeared at Mohenjo-daro or Harappā, but they are well known at some of the Sumerian sites contemporary with the Harappā Culture.[3]

[1] The two wheels with this particular cart were found with it.

[2] The sides of certain model vehicles from Northern Mesopotamia are painted in the same way: Speiser, *Excavations at Tepe Gawra*, p. 75, pl. XXXV, a.

[3] Mackay, *Anthropology Memoirs*, Field Museum, Chicago, vol. I, p. 211, pl. XLVI.

A specimen, also in pottery, is also known from Anau.[4] Another four-wheeled cart (No. 4686), with the same shield-like canopy, unearthed at Chanhu-daro, seems like No. 9 in Pl. LVIII to have had wheels of larger diameter in front than behind, a very unusual feature in the ancient toy vehicles of any country.

As we know that the people of the Harappā Culture were well acquainted with the Sumerians, it is not surprising that both two-wheeled and four-wheeled vehicles were in use in both countries, but where the wheeled cart was originally invented it is not so easy to say. From the model carts and chariots found at Sumerian sites and their representations in relief and mosaic, we can say that the type of chariot used in Sumer was definitely less primitive than anything yet found in ancient India.

The dearth of war-like weapons in the cities of the Harappā Culture has led to the belief by many that the Indus valley in ancient days was not troubled as was Sumer by inter-racial feuds, and that the inhabitants had no enemies of importance to fear. But the shield-like fronts of the chariots shown in Pl. LVIII, 9, 13—obviously intended to protect the driver—do certainly suggest something in the nature of a vehicle used in warfare, unless as seems a reasonable explanation, they were simply for protection against mud or dust thrown up by the animals that drew them. Before any decision can be reached in this matter, we must find specimens that are better finished and unbroken.

We were fortunate in finding two toy carts made of metal, presumably bronze, not copper, in place of the usual pottery. The first (Pl. LVIII, 1, 2) is only 2.93 inches long, 1.2 inches wide, and 1.75 inches high, and is nearly perfect, save that the front of the cart (facing right in No. 1), which was originally in the same line as the rest, had been bent upwards. There are also fragments missing from the rear of the cart. Its frame resembles No. 21 in Pl. LVIII, save for having six cross-bars instead of three. The man seated in front holds a stick in his right hand, and before the frame was bent did not occupy the restful position in which he now appears to recline. The sides of this cart consist of an upper and lower bar connected by uprights at each end, and differ in this respect from the more usual type. The wheels, 0.93 inch in diameter and 0.09 inch thick, are solid and lack the projecting hub of some of the pottery wheels (Pl. LVIII, 3, 20). The shaft, unfortunately broken in the model, ran under the cross-bars instead of through them, as was probably the case in the actual carts of the period; this arrangement with the necessary fixtures could not be copied conveniently in making the pottery toys. The wheels are now immovable, but they must originally have revolved in two axle-brackets cast in one with the frame. When the metal of which this model is made can be analyzed, it will, no doubt, be found to be an alloy.

The figure of the driver is too corroded to show what garments he is wearing. He sits on one of the cross members of the frame with his feet on what is left of the shaft.

The other metal vehicle found (Pl. LVIII, 2) is of quite a different pattern; in some respects it resembles the " ekka " of modern India. Its present height is 2.4 inches, its

[4] Pumpelly, *Explorations in Turkestan*, pl. 47, fig. 11. See also the representations of the four-wheeled wagons of Ur in Woolley, *Royal Cemetery*, pl. 92.

length 1.71 inches, and width 1.1 inches. The under-frame was originally 2.13 inches long by 0.9 inch wide, and was curved and had four cross-bars instead of the three that appear in the pottery frames (Pl. LVIII, 21). Each side has crossed struts between supports at each end for a pent-roof. From the way in which it was strengthened by cross-pieces, the latter appears to have been a wooden frame covered over with a lighter material, such as matting or cloth. A transverse cross-bar at each end of the cart kept the canopy supports upright. This little model also is slightly bent, probably by earth pressure. It now has no shaft, and the eyelets, with holes 0.14 inch in diameter, through which the axle passed, are bent towards one another so that they touch.

An almost similar toy was found by Mr. M. S. Vats at Harappā some years ago.[5] It also has a canopy and sides strengthened by cross-members set on an open frame; indeed, it differs from the Chanhu-daro vehicle only in having a driver, very like the little figure seen in Pl. LVIII, 1. The distance of Harappā from Chanhu-daro is well over 400 miles, and the close resemblance between model carts found in these two cities so widely separated argues a wide-spread and homogeneous culture in those days.

From these little model carts we can visualize the actual vehicles that took people to and fro between the cities and the various ferries across the river, and most likely in the evenings carried people to pleasure resorts outside their cities; in fact, which served all the purposes of the " tonga " and the " ekka " of the present day.

Wheels

The pottery wheels of the toy carts were of three main types. Nos. 3, 20 in Pl. LVIII show the most common form, with a pronounced hub on one side, which was either roughly moulded with the fingers or finished off with a sharp instrument to obtain a better shape. In another type (Pl. LVIII, 23) the hub is not emphasized, both sides of the wheel being markedly convex. In the third type (Pl. LVIII, 24, 25), the wheel is plane on both sides and frequently covered with a thick deposit of sand and mica, showing that these objects had been shaped or laid to dry on a sand bed. These pottery wheels vary greatly in size, ranging from just over an inch to as much as 4.5 inches in diameter and averaging 0.5 inch in thickness, including the hub. They are frequently very much out of shape and the holes in many are acentric.

That the animals drawing these model carts were humped oxen is suggested by the large number of model oxen that were found, each with a hole through the shoulders (Pl. LVIII, 7, 8) to take one end of a yoke (Pl. LVIII, 22). Possibly the ass also was used for this purpose, as we know was the case in Sumer.[6] The ox, however, makes a very good draught animal; it can travel a considerable distance at a quick trot.

Animal Figures on Wheels

The three ram chariots (Pl. LVIII, 11, 12, 15) are typical of many that have been found at Chanhu-daro, but nearly always badly mutilated. Their hollow bodies were very

[5] *Ann. Rep. Arch. Surv. Ind.*, 1926-27, pl. XXIII, fig. d., p. 105.

[6] M. Hilzheimer, "The Evolution of the Domestic Horse," *Antiquity*, vol. IX, p. 133.

liable to break, and the heads which were added to the bodies by the insertion of a long prolongation of the neck (Pl. LVIII, 16) frequently came away at the joint. The heads which are undamaged all have the tightly curled horns of a ram, and the bodies are invariably decorated with crossed red lines which presumably represent the fleece. These not very realistic bodies are nearly always triangular in cross section, with the base, front, and back quite flat; and there is rarely a tail. That these objects were toys is shown by the fact that most of them have a hole through the neck to take a cord for pulling. Though there were also chariots with bird's heads, none were found unbroken; two such heads are seen in Pl. LVII, 10, 13, 14.

A few of the model rams have a normal ram's body, but the legs are joined together in pairs, like those of the model oxen. Lateral holes through the joined legs show these toys to have been mounted on four wheels. Unfortunately, all the toy rams of this group were too mutilated to be photographed.

The long-necked creature, No. 17 in Pl. LVIII, was also once mounted on four wheels, but what animal it represents it is difficult to say. It has minute, round discs for eyes, and a fracture on the forehead suggests that it had once a single horn here. In the narrow vertical slits on either side of this fracture, ears of some other material may have been inserted. The long neck is encircled with bands of dark red paint, and there are two red bands across the withers, others round the middle, and six across the hind-quarters. The very short legs are joined in pairs, pierced laterally by holes, 0.17 inch in diameter, for the axles of the wheels. A small lateral hole through the neck just below the muzzle evidently took a draw-string.

Bull with Moveable Head

The bull with moveable head in Pl. LIX, 1 was not found complete as photographed. It is a somewhat rare toy and only a few were found at Mohenjo-daro.[7] The head, hinged on a wooden pin which passed through projections on either side of the neck, was moved by a cord or piece of fibre threaded through holes in the shoulders, hump, and hind-quarters. Experiment has shown that a piece of stiff fibre works the head better than a loose cord, which is apt to stick in the three holes.

Figure with Moveable Arms

The pottery figure in No. 2 of Pl. LIX once had moveable arms suspended on a wooden pin passed through a hole, 0.11 inch in diameter, in the shoulders. The head and lower part of the legs are missing, but a similar figure, almost perfect, found at Mohenjo-daro has a monkey's head from which the ears are missing.[8] The head of a third such figure found in a later season has two long upright ears, which belong to a quite different animal.[9] No. 2 in Pl. LIX, like most such figures, has a very prominent abdomen, but that this was not meant to suggest pregnancy is proved by the male organs on our Chanhu-

[7] *M. I. C.*, pl. CLIII, 39; *F. E. M.*, pl. LXXXI, 10.
[8] *M. I. C.*, pl. CLIII, 38.
[9] *F. E. M.*, pl. LXXXI, 8.

daro figure. An irregular dark red band round the broken neck of this figure represents a necklace or collar.

Whistles

A very favourite toy at Chanhu-daro was a pottery whistle in the shape of a hen, invariably set on a little pedestal with a hollow base. These whistles have been found in large numbers at the other Indus valley sites. Though sometimes left unornamented, they are more frequently decorated with coarse red lines to represent the feathers (No. 6 in Pl. LIX). There is always a hole, averaging 0.2 inch in diameter, in the back just in front of the tail, and by blowing into this a shrill sound can be produced. These bird-shaped whistles average 2.29 inches high. Some have a red line round the neck suggesting a collar, and one imperfect specimen (No. 1623) has a collar made of a strip of clay.

Another form of whistle (Pl. LIX, 18-20) is a little hollow pottery vessel with a rounded or slightly pointed base, and a circular or irregularly-shaped aperture at the top, varying from 0.19 to 0.46 inch in diameter; there is also a smaller hole in the middle of the side (No. 18) or close to the top (No. 19). Experiment has shown that various modulations of sound can be produced by using the finger on the smaller hole when blowing flute-fashion into the large one at the top. These objects do not vary much in size; they average 1.7 inches high. Only two were decorated; one with a red band painted round the upper hole (No. 3879), and on the second (No. 910) were traces of red lines round the body. These whistles must definitely be assigned to the Harappā Culture.

Rattles

Nos. 7-10 in Pl. LIX and 1-7 in Pl. LXI are rattles, made of pottery and ornamented with lines of red paint. A very large number were found, especially in the lower levels of Mound II, where they had rolled down from above. Though hollow, they are very rarely found broken. Similar toys from Mohenjo-daro and Harappā are not so carefully decorated as those from Chanhu-daro; broken specimens from the former site show that they were made by wrapping the clay round a combustible core of some kind, which disappeared except for a small amount of ash when the rattle was baked. Two or three irregular pellets of clay were found in some of the rattles at Mohenjo-daro and doubtless they exist in those from Chanhu-daro also. A great deal of attention was paid to the decoration of these playthings, though in some cases the paint was applied directly to the pottery surface without an intervening slip. These rattles range in size from an exceptionally small specimen, 0.7 inch in diameter, to 2.5 inches in diameter, with an average of 1.8 inches. As the illustrations in Pl. LXI show, the patterns on them are very diverse, the most frequent ornamentation being three or four, or even five circles (Nos. 7, 9) around a large spot with the intervening intervals filled in with parallel curved lines (Pls. LIX, 7-9, LXI, 1-4, 6, 7). The surface of one rattle was quartered by two lines at right angles to one another (Pl. LXI, 5). A few of these toys were undecorated, but possibly the paint had disappeared. Nos. 9 and 10 in Pl. LIX were found together.

Marbles

A considerable number of pottery marbles, like those illustrated in the upper register of No. 11, and No. 12, Pl. LIX, were found in the lower levels of Chanhu-daro, whither many of them had rolled down from higher up the mound. Most are made of pottery, some beautifully rounded, but others far from accurate; and they range in size from 0.8 to 1.9 inches in diameter. It is not absolutely certain that all these little balls were playthings. Some could have been used as missiles with a sling or a sling-bow, a weapon that is commonly used in Sindh at the present day. Others, however, are roughly decorated with red spots (Pl. LIX, No. 11, upper register), and it is clear that this trouble would not have been taken with them unless they had been used in a game.

A certain number of balls of flinty limestone (Pl. LIX, 3) are white, cream, or light grey in colour, some beautifully made and others far from round. It would seem that the natural nodules commonly found in limestone formations were used for making them, being rubbed down to the requisite size and shape. These stone balls have a greater range of size than the pottery ones. The largest was 2.4 inches in diameter and the smallest 1.1 inches. More rarely, marbles were made of a softer limestone, light yellow in colour; others were of harder stones, but many of these were not particularly well finished and do not come up to the standard of the finely made articles found at Mohenjo-daro, of which some of those made of the rarer stones are beautifully finished and polished. A shell marble (No. 3823), 0.89 inch in diameter, is not well finished.

Five balls, made of a white paste bearing traces of glaze whose colour had disappeared except on one which is light green, were found in the higher levels of Mounds I and II and may have been products of the Jhukar Culture. The smallest was only 0.4 inch in diameter and the largest 0.89 inch, and none was perfectly round.

A faience marble, No. 13 in Pl. LIX, is pitted all over with little incised circles 0.12 inch in diameter; and another, Pl. LIX, 4, made of pottery is similarly decorated.

The rather larger pottery balls in Pl. LIX, 16, 17, 23, 24 were perhaps used for throwing. The first and last were found together, and bear all over the imprints of a finger- or thumb-nail. No. 23, which is fragmentary, has a number of carefully impressed circles upon it, and No. 17 has been incised with a semi-circular edge.

The two large balls in Pl. LIX, 14, 15 are of shell, having concentric circles incised on six sides with their edges nearly meeting. This type of ball is already well known from Mohenjo-daro, where specimens were also made of shell and, more rarely, of faience. It is thought that the circles were once filled in flush with the face with a coloured paste. The sizes of these marbles, for such they seem to be, were limited by the size of the columella of the shell from which they were cut, and the larger of the two illustrated—the only two yet found at Chanhu-daro—is 1.3 inches in diameter.

Three pellets (Pl. LIX, 11, lower register), each with a groove incised round the equator, are difficult to explain. Quite a few have been found, all treated in the same way. The groove suggests that a cord was tied round them, and I can only suggest that they were net-sinkers of some kind or else were used as bolas balls against very small game. They could also, I imagine, have been employed with a bow, the string fitting into the groove round the pellet, but the balls used in Sindh today are held in place by a pocket of leather or cloth.

Gamesmen

Gaming pieces, particularly of the type seen in Pl. LIX, 25-27, 28-30, and Pl. LX, 6, were fairly common. Mostly made of pottery but very rarely coated with a slip, they are four-sided, pyramidal in shape, with rounded angles and points. I do not think they were used on a board. They might have been tossed up and received on the back of the hand, as in the game similar to " jackstones " that is played in most parts of the world and is especially popular in India. In fact, these little pieces, are not unlike certain seeds that are used in play at the present day. They average in size 0.55 inch across each of the four sides. Three of these objects were found together with a fourth piece of irregular shape (No. 4208), the four seeming to form a set; two of these were light red and the third and fourth made of a greyish clay. All these gamesmen belong to the Harappā Culture.

Sir Leonard Woolley has found gaming pieces of exactly similar shape in the Royal Cemetery at Ur, but made of lapis-lazuli or shell, and decorated at the points with inlay. Four were found together and it was assumed that two of the set had been lost. In view, however, of the group of four just mentioned from Chanhu-daro, this may have been the accustomed number for a set.[10]

Other, and some of them more usual, types of gamesmen are illustrated in Pl. LX, 1-5, 7-11. Of especial interest is No. 7, which is most beautifully and regularly made of faience and is now light blue. The corners of this piece are very slightly rounded but the edges are sharp. Evidently nearly new, this piece is little worn. This tetrahedral gamesman is of a shape known, though it is comparatively rare, at Mohenjo-daro, where also it was most commonly made of faience.[11] One made in bronze has also been found in the latter site.[12] The type is also well known at some of the Sumerian sites, though made of stone. Gamesmen of exactly similar shape have been found in Palestine, but dated there to a much later period (c. 1500-1230 B.C.).[13]

No. 4 in Pl. LX is a curiously shaped object which was made from a part of one of the excrescences on the outside of a *śaṅkha* shell. It was very carefully cut and polished, and is more likely to have been a gaming-piece than anything else. Perhaps the faience object of similar shape in Pl. LXXXIX, 1 was also a gamesman.

A well-made piece, No. 8 in Pl. LX, 1.5 inches high and of faience, now cream-coloured, is of a type well known in other parts of the ancient world. Similar pieces to No. 9 in the same plate, which is made of a hard black stone, also occur at Mohenjo-daro and Harappā. This last was found together with a roughly made pottery piece (No. 4431),

[10] *The Royal Cemetery*, p. 279, pl. 95.

[11] *M. I. C.*, pl. CLIII, 40, 41; *F. E. M.*, pl. CXLII, 64, 73, 74.

[12] *F. E. M.*, p. 572; pls. CXXXIX, 11, CXLII, 63.

[13] Hamilton, *Quarterly of the Department of Antiquities in Palestine*, vol. IV, pl. XXXV. And see also W. F. Albright, " A Set of Egyptian Playing Pieces and Dice from Palestine," *Mizraim*, vol. I, pp. 130-134, pl. XIV.

which is a roundel with a fairly flat top and base. No. 10 is a simple faience piece, now cream-coloured, which still bears traces of glaze; and No. 11, made of the same material, now light grey, has a depression in its top, in which there was formerly set a piece of inlay, but of what material we do not know, though it was probably a paste of a different colour.

Nos. 21, 22, 31, 32, 38, 39 in Pl. LIX are either counters or draughtsmen. All except two are pottery sherds which have been roughly rounded by chipping. No. 32 is square and plaque-like, and is made of a drab-coloured clay that was insufficiently burnt. At one time it was thought to be a weight (15.070 grammes), but its material makes it more likely to have been a draughtsman. No. 39, which is 1.83 inches in diameter, is also of pottery; its smooth surface and edges suggest that it was used in a board-game.

Except for the pyramidal gamesman which were found in plenty and were, as we think, used without a board, and certain bobbin-like pieces to be referred to later, the number of gamesmen found at Chanhu-daro was small. Possibly the inhabitants of that city had little time for board-games and similar diversions as compared with the wealthier and probably more leisured inhabitants of the larger cities of the Indus valley.

Knuckle-bones

On Pl. LIX, 37, 43 are two knuckle-bones which were probably used in the same way as the little pottery pyramids already described. The larger bone, which is 1.28 inches long, was found in one of the Harappā levels and is polished by much use. The smaller is very badly weathered and was unearthed at a high level. It may belong to the Jhukar Period or to even later times.

Bobbin-like Objects

Nos. 33-36, 40-42 in Pl. LIX and Nos. 13-15, 17-20 in Pl. LX are very puzzling. Large numbers of them have been found at Chanhu-daro, both in the upper levels and in the lower, whither they had rolled. They are of three types:

(a) Almost cylindrical, with flat or rounded ends (Pl. LX, 15).
(b) Hour-glass shape with rounded ends (Pl. LX, 17, 19).
(c) Hour-glass shape, one or both ends flattened (Pl. LX, 13, 14, 18, 20).

They vary much in size as well as shape. The largest found is 1.8 inches long and the smallest 0.38 inch.

These objects are generally roughly made of either drab-coloured or grey clay. Few of them will stand upright, and most are perforated longitudinally by a small hole that may have been made with a thorn; but this hole is sometimes very oblique or penetrates a very short distance.

I have provisionally identified these objects as used in a game, though how they were used is a matter of surmise. Certainly not on a board, as few will stand, but perhaps in holes scooped in the ground. Another possible explanation is that they were bobbins used in some way in weaving and that something was fixed in the holes by which to suspend them. Nos. 40-42 in Pl. LIX could have held a fair quantity of thread, but not so with Nos. 33-36. The ends of No. 42 in Pl. LIX are concave.

Nothing resembling these objects has turned up at Mohenjo-daro. At Chanhu-daro they were first unearthed in the upper levels of Mound II in considerable numbers. Lower down they became fewer and fewer as the buildings of the Harappā Period were cleared, and such specimens as were found came from the edges of the mound. I am, therefore, quite confident that these bobbins or playthings were products of the Jhukar Culture.

Dice

Many little slips of ivory found at Mohenjo-daro appear from the marks upon them to have been used as dice,[14] whereas others were gaming pieces. At Chanhu-daro only two dice have as yet been found, and both were too badly broken to be photographed. The first (Pl. LX, 12) is estimated to have been 1.8 inches long, with a rectangular section measuring 0.27 × 0.32 inches. Made of ivory, now deep brown in colour, it shows the polish of much use. On one side are two longitudinal grooves, on two sides circles, each with a central dot, at each end, and the remaining side plain. As one end of this die is missing, it is uncertain whether the blank side had a circle on it or not.

On the two opposite sides of the second die (Pl. LX, 16) two grooves ran along its length. On one end of each of the other two sides two concentric circles were incised. This die also had a portion missing from one end, and there may originally have been other circles now missing. It has been badly damaged by fire.

Cones

The cones illustrated in Pls. LX, 21-39 and LXXXVIII, 4 are included in this chapter as there is a possibility that they were used in a game or amusement of some kind, despite the fact that in Sumer cones similar in shape to Nos. 35-39 were used in large numbers to decorate walls. Pottery cones were inserted in mud-brick walls as far as their broader ends, which were painted in various colours. This mode of decoration was particularly well developed at Uruk, where columned walls are covered with a mosaic of pottery cones in black, white, and red.[15] In the Indus valley, however, they could not have been used for this purpose: for one thing, the sides of the cones are frequently decorated, either with paint or incised markings, which would have been hidden by insertion in a wall. Moreover, both at Mohenjo-daro and Chanhu-daro they have been found in comparatively small numbers, and made of shell as well as pottery. It has been suggested that these cones, or at least some of them, were *lingams*; but personally I do not think this was so, even though *lingam* worship appears to have been practised in the Indus cities, as at the present day in India.

The cones from Chanhu-daro fall into the following groups:

[14] *M. I. C.*, pl. CXXXII; *F. E. M.*, pl. CXLIII, 18-54.

[15] Jordan, *Abhandlungen der Preussichen Akademie der Wissenschaften. Phil.-Hist. Klasse (Ausgrabungen in Uruk-Warka)*, 1929, 7; 1930, 4; 1932, 6. Also see Woolley, *The Development of Sumerian Art*, Chap. I.

(a) Squat type, with flat base (Pls. LX, 21-23, LXXXVIII, 4).
(b) Long conical type with flat base (Pls. LX, 24-26, 29-31, 34-37, 39).
(c) Long conical type with projection in the centre of the flat base (Pl. LX, 27, 32, 33, 38).
(d) Long conical type with rounded base (Pl. LX, 28).

Only four of Type (a) have yet appeared at Chanhu-daro, though they were common at Mohenjo-daro. They are solidly made, with broad bases on which they can stand without rocking. No. 21, of pottery coated with a dark brown slip, is now 1.62 inches high. Two deep grooves ornament its base. No. 22, also of pottery, has a purplish-black slip applied over a red slip.[16] To a height of 1.02 inches, the lower part of this cone is ornamented with a scored spiral line, a very usual feature in this type of cone. There is also a conical hole, 0.2 inch in diameter and 0.45 inch deep, in the centre of the otherwise flat base. No. 23 has a dark red slip, but is otherwise unornamented, and it stands well on its substantial base. The points of all these three cones were broken off or otherwise damaged, as is the case with nearly all the similar cones at Mohenjo-daro, a condition that has never been satisfactorily explained. If they had been *lingams*, one would expect more care to have been taken of them, with more surviving unbroken. If, however, they were used in some kind of game, damage of this kind would have to be expected.

No. 4 in Pl. LXXXVIII is 1.2 inches high. It is of plain pottery and may be a large gamesman. The small truncated cone in Pl. XXIX, 63 measures 1.02 inches high and 1.0 inch in diameter. In the top of this object is a hole, not central, 0.09 inch in diameter and 0.12 inch deep. Two vertical holes opposite one another in the sides of this cone look as if they had been pierced with a thorn. Square 9/C, locus 208, level: + 6.9 feet.

The long conical Type (b) is that most frequently found. The flat bases of these specimens (Pl. LX, 24-26, etc.), however, do not always enable them to stand securely, for often the base is far from regular and the cone is inclined to wobble. No. 24 in Pl. LX is made of shell, and was found with the very elaborate cone No. 30. It was cut from the columella of a large shell, and the spiral line round it was not artifically incised but is part of the natural twist of the shell. The pottery cone, No. 25, once had a red slip, and is exceptionally well made, with a smooth and almost polished surface. Its uneven base barely allows it to stand alone. No. 26, which cannot stand at all, is made of pottery coated with a cream-coloured wash. No. 29, also made of pottery but without a slip, once had a sharper point than it now possesses; the present one shows signs of having been rubbed down. Nos. 30 and 31 are exceptionally fine cones, both made of shell; and each has a pattern incised immediately above the base, which was once filled in with a black pigment. No. 30 stands well, No. 31 with difficulty. The tip of the latter is chipped and had apparently been rubbed into shape again. No cones like these two last are known from Mohenjo-daro. No. 34 is of pottery, with five broad red bands roughly painted on its natural surface. It stands very unsteadily.

Both No. 35, which is a well made pottery cone, and No. 36 rest with ease on their

[16] These two slips are frequently found together on the pottery of the Harappā Culture.

flat bases. The latter, which is made of shell, had been accidentally burnt and blackened No. 37, also made of shell, has lost its point, but stands well. The tip of the pottery cone No. 39 is missing. This was very carefully made and decorated with narrow lines of red paint on a semi-polished surface.

Type (c) (Pl. LX, Nos. 27, 32, 33, 38) was nicknamed "carrot" by the diggers. They are all pottery and carefully made; only Nos. 27 and 33 will stand, and that with difficulty. Each has a more or less roughly finished projection at the base. No. 27 is pottery with no slip, No. 32 also. The latter, however, shows signs of accidental burning, and a white substance which superficially resembles gypsum and needs further examination had been inset in its base. No. 33 is drab-coloured pottery, very hard baked, its tip is missing. This cone, which will only just stand upright, is ornamented with four lines of pricking, a form of decoration which also occurs on similar cones from Mohenjo-daro. It also has a shallow hole in the base. No. 38, of pottery, is covered with a dark-grey slip. Its point is missing, and it has a very slight projection at the base.

Type (d) is illustrated by only one cone, No. 28 in Pl. LX; it has a rounded base; is unbroken, and was either made of grey-coloured clay or is coated with a grey slip.

From these brief observations it will be noted how few of the points of these cones are unbroken, and how few of them will stand securely on their bases. If they were used in some form of game—perhaps to be knocked down by the little pottery balls frequently found at Chanhu-daro—their unsteady stance would have added to their value. But if they were so used, they would, more likely than not, have been set on dusty ground, in which case they would readily stand whether their bases were even or not. That they experienced rough treatment is obvious. I see no reason to believe that they were votive offerings.

Chapter XII

COPPER AND BRONZE OBJECTS AND UTENSILS

OBJECTS OF THE HARAPPĀ CULTURE

Mound II at Chanhu-daro yielded a large quantity of tools and implements, both of copper and bronze. Altogether four large hoards, containing from sixteen to twenty-eight objects each, were unearthed and, in addition to these, a number of smaller deposits of over six objects each were also discovered. All these groups save one came from levels ranging from 9.1 to 10.4 feet above datum, and must, therefore, be assigned to the Harappā II Period. The exception was the large hoard No. 2199, which was found at the level + 11.3 feet, and so belongs to the Harappā I occupation above.

It is not possible to say at present how many of these objects are of bronze and how many of copper, for no analyses of them have yet been made, although a quantitative spectographic analysis of those received by the Museum of Fine Arts is to be made by Mr. William J. Young of the Museum staff for future publication. Bronze was, however, almost as common as copper in the lowest levels of Mohenjo-daro, and there is every reason to believe that at Chanhu-daro the same proportions will hold good.

The people of the Harappā Culture may have obtained their copper either in India itself but more likely from sources outside that country. Baluchistan, Afghanistan, and Persia have all been mentioned as possible fields of supply.[1] The writer for several reasons would favour Persia, for both tin and copper ores occur plentifully in that country. Tin is rare in India; nowhere has it been found in workable and commercial quantities.[2] There is a large source of supply in Burma and the Malay Peninsula, but these must be ruled out as far as the Harappā Civilization is concerned. Tin is, however, known in North-eastern Persia and, as Dr. Lucas has shown, that country is also rich in copper ores.[3]

It may have been the occurrence of tin and copper in close proximity, as for instance, in Persia, that led to the discovery of bronze by the accidental mixing of the two metals.[4] Alloys from Mohenjo-daro have been found to contain as much as 26.9% of tin and, when thirty-one fragments of bronze from that site yielding 2% and upwards of the metal were examined, the average proportions of tin to copper was found to be as high as 11.91%.[5] The percentage, however, varied so much for individual specimens that it was obvious that the mixing of the two metals was performed in a most perfunctory manner.[6] A greater proportion of tin would naturally be required in tools used for heavy work and for intricate castings,

[1] See Sir Edwin Pascoe in *M. I. C.*, p. 676.

[2] *Op. cit.*, p. 682.

[3] *Journ. Eg. Arch.*, May 1928, pp. 97-108.

[4] Lucas concludes that this was so; *ibid.*, p. 108.

[5] From analyses made by Dr. C. H. Desch and Khan Bahadur Mohammed Sana Ullah; *M. I. C.*, pp. 484, 486, 487; *F. E. M.*, pp. 479-482.

[6] This variation also occurs in Egyptian bronzes. See Lucas, *Ancient Egyptian Materials*, p. 235.

though bronze containing a high percentage of tin is hardly suited to the making of wrought utensils owing to its brittleness.[7]

The same high tin value has also been noticed in bronzes unearthed by Sir Aurel Stein in Southern Baluchistan. A sample from Zangiān-damb contained 23.1% of tin, and a vessel from Gatti no less than 27% of tin.[8] Both sites appear to be of later date than the Harappā Culture.

Up to the present time only negligible quantities of copper ore have been found in the excavations at Mohenjo-daro[9] and none at all at Chanhu-daro. Samples of tin ore of any kind that could have been used in the local preparation of bronze were absent on both these sites. It appears likely, therefore, that the people of the Harappā Culture had to use their bronze in the state in which it was brought to them and that they had no sure means of ascertaining, except in the roughest manner, its tin content. In any case it would have been impossible for them to regulate the proportions of tin and copper unless they obtained the two metals separately. It would seem that the bronze was not prepared in India but brought in from outside in the form of ingots and the smelters, whoever they were, were in the habit of mixing the two metals somewhat indiscriminately. These smelters had probably no experience in working up the bronzes to their final forms and, in turn, the coppersmiths who converted this material into useful forms in all probability knew nothing about smelting.[10]

If the people of the Harappā Civilization originally came from the west, as many people now think, they may quite possibly have continued to obtain their supplies of copper and bronze from the place where they originally procured it and thus maintained trade connections by land or by sea with their old home.

Most of the copper and bronze unearthed at Chanhu-daro came from Squares 8/B, 8/C, and 9/C (see Pl. IV). These areas probably represented the quarter of the city inhabited by the metal workers, for unfinished castings as well as an ingot were discovered in several of the hoards (Pls. LXV, 9, LXVIII, 4, 5, LXXIV, 2, 16, LXXV, 4). The contents of every collection, large and small, were all carefully cleaned under the supervision of the Archaeological Chemist in India.

The largest deposit (No. 2529) contained thirty-seven pieces in all and came from Square 8/C, locus 297, at the level + 10.4 feet. The action of the salt in the soil had cemented together all the objects it contained and some of the objects in this group were in too bad a state of preservation to be illustrated. Pls. LXII, 1-23, LXIII, 1-5, and LXXIV, 2-9, however, all show specimens from this most instructive hoard.

No. 2593, whose condition when unearthed is shown in Pl. LXXIV, 15, comes next in importance and was found in Square 9/C, locus 212, at the level + 9.1 feet. After it had been cleaned it was possible to pick out the fine objects illustrated in Pls. LXIV, 1-11, LXV, 1-9, LXVI, 1-5, LXXIV, 10-17.

[7] What is known as a full bronze mixture contains 10% of tin.

[8] From analyses made by Dr. Desch.

[9] *F. E. M.*, p. 41.

[10] It was perhaps more economical to smelt the ores at their sources of supply, as was done in Sinai and Eastern Palestine.

If the number of objects contained in each hoard be taken into account, No. 2199 must be mentioned next. The specimens shown in Pls. LXVI, 6-21 and LXXV, 11-13 came from this collection, which was discovered in Square 9/C, locus 227. The high level (+ 11.3 feet) at which they were found makes it impossible to date them earlier than the Harappa I occupation.

The fourth large hoard (No. 2365) found in Square 8/B, locus 284, at the level + 9.5 feet, is shown in Pl. LXXV, 1, exactly as it was when first uncovered. Its contents, after cleaning, are illustrated in Pls. LXVIII, 1-16 and LXXV, 1-9.

Other and smaller groups were discovered at varying levels all over Mound II, and some of these were undoubtedly the private property of the occupants of the various houses and rooms that were cleared. These collections, which usually consisted of small objects, such as razors, pins, small knives, and the ubiquitous chisel, were sometimes found stored in pottery vessels. The bangle, chisel, and axes in Pls. LXIX, 11-15 and LXXVI, 5, 6, were preserved in this way, together with a skull and a large shell.[11] The large pan in Pl. XXIX, 37 contained quite a collection of copper and bronze objects, most of which are to be seen in Pls. LXVII, 1-12 and LXXIV, 1, 1a. All these objects are naturally in a far better state than those which were found embedded in the soil.

It is not proposed, however, to describe the contents of these hoards of metal piece by piece, as objects similar in type to them have, in many cases, been found at Mohenjo-daro.[12] Only specimens which are new to us or present features of especial interest will, therefore, be mentioned here, but all the objects illustrated are tabulated in the Catalogue preceding the plates, where particulars are given of their position at the site and the levels where they were found.

Copper and Bronze Utensils (Pls. LXII, 1-4, 8, 10, LXIV, 9, LXVI, 1, 7, 12, LXVII, 2, LXVIII, 1-3, LXIX, 3, LXXIII, 34, 35, 37-39, LXXIV, 7, 10, LXXV, 1-3, 7, 10, 14-16, LXXVI, 2, 32)

Although so simple in form, No. 1 in Pl. LXVIII (see also Pl. LXXV, 2) is a type of jar that has not yet appeared at Mohenjo-daro. Its surface is too encrusted, however, for us to tell whether it is of beaten work or was cast. The dish in Pl. LXXIII, 35 was certainly cast in bronze and is of unusual weight for its size.

No. 37 in the same plate (see also Pl. LXXV, 15) was found in a sadly battered state. This copper canister is fitted with wire loop handles, the ends of which have been passed through two holes on either side and then bent up against the inner walls. The wire used for this purpose is also of copper and measures 0.12 inch in diameter. Apart from the pans described below, this is the only example of a handled metal vessel belonging to the Harappā Culture which has so far come to light.

The handled pans in Pls. LXVI, 1, LXVIII, 2, LXIX, 3, LXXV, 7, LXXVI, 2 are types of vessels well known at Mohenjo-daro. They are simply constructed of one piece, the

[11] For the pottery vessel see Pl. XXIV, 4. The skull is fully described in Chapter XVI.

[12] These are dealt with fully in the reports on Mohenjo-daro.

handle being formed by bending the metal over or under in tubular fashion, with the edges meeting closely.[13] No. 1 in Pl. LXVI has a slightly oval dish, measuring 4.02 by 3.8 inches inside. No. 3 in Pl. LXIX is shown again in photograph in Pl. LXXVI, 2. These pans were certainly used for frying and resemble our modern utensils to a remarkable degree.

The fine bowl, No. 38 in Pl. LXXIII (see again Pl. LXXV, 16), was raised from a piece of sheet copper and is of entirely new shape, although slightly distorted by earth pressure.

The fluted cosmetic jar in Pl. LXXIII, 39 and LXXVI, 32 is, of course, a casting and is perfect except for a small portion missing from the base. The latter is slightly convex so that the vessel does not stand properly, and proves that it is unfinished. The narrow mouth (0.22 inch) and the long neck of this piece suggest that it was made to hold a fine powder such as kohl, while the fluting ornamentation is unique as far as the Harappā Culture is concerned; the nearest approach to this kind of decoration is the horizontal fluting on the stem of a copper food-stand from Mohenjo-daro.[14] Fluting is, however, often found on Sumerian vessels contemporary with, and earlier than, this specimen.[15] The process was at first intended to stiffen the sides of metal vessels, but later on, as so often happens, it was adopted as a mode of decoration.

The large shallow platters seen in Pls. LXXIV, 10 and LXXV, 10, 14 were well known at Mohenjo-daro, although it is not certain how they were used. They are frequently found nested together in hoards (see Pl. LXXV, 10) and are sometimes impossible to separate without breaking. Specimens from Chanhu-daro vary but little in size, the smallest being 9.7 and the largest 10.21 inches in diameter. Their substantial make indicates that they are all castings.

The unfinished casting in Pl. LXX, 27 so closely resembles the moulded upper portions of certain food-stands (Pl. XXV, 21) that it is possible that miniature vessels of this type were also made in copper and bronze as well as in faience.[16]

Jar-covers (Pls. LXVI, 6, LXXIII, 36, LXXV, 11)

These are made of beaten copper and are similar in type to specimens found at Mohenjo-daro. The form is also known in pottery (Pl. XXVI, 45). In Pl. LXXV, 11 one of these covers is seen adhering to two tools, its underside only appearing in the photograph. A better idea of what it originally looked like may be gained from the restoration illustrated in Pl. LXVI, 6. The boss surmounting the cover is secured by a strip of metal, 0.3 inch wide, whose ends pass through the top of the cover and are then bent back inside the boss.

No. 36 in Pl. LXXIII has its edge stiffened by being slightly turned up all round, while the punch markings round it, which have been made from the under side, are probably intended to serve the same purpose. These marks form three lines of pimples round the cover and the boss on the top has been perforated to take a metal ring-handle. This handle

[13] *F. E. M.*, pls. CXXII, 10, CXXVIII, 15.
[14] *M. I. C.*, pl. CXLI, 5.
[15] Woolley, *Antiquaries Journal*, vols. II, pl. VI, VIII, p. 24.
[16] For a model dish of this type of vessel in faience, see *F. E. M.*, pl. CVI, 10.

must have been anciently lost for a transverse hole has been bored through this part of the cover to take a string.

Scale-pans and Beams (Pls. LXII, 2-4, 8, 10, LXIII, 9, 13, LXVI, 12, LXVII, 2, LXXIV, 5)

Quite a number of scale-pans were unearthed at Chanhu-daro. They are all simple dishes of beaten work and in some cases have become considerably thickened by metallic deposits. Occasionally the three holes by which these pans were suspended are still to be seen, but often they have become blocked up and cannot now be traced.

Beams that belonged to various balances are illustrated in Pls. LXIII, 11, LXXI, 1-3, LXXVI, 18, but curiously enough none have been found with a hole in the centre to take a suspension cord or chain. All these beams have slightly thickened ends to prevent the strings which held the pans from slipping off. A very corroded object unearthed at Mohenjo-daro was also identified as a scale-beam; [17] this too had no central hole. It was found near two small pans and bore string-markings at one end.

Two pans, one very badly preserved, were found in the group that contained the beam illustrated in Pl. LXIII, 11.

Blade-axes (Pls. LXII, 20, 22, LXIII, 3, LXVI, 3-5, 15, LXVII, 21, LXIX, 13-15, LXX, 29, 30, LXXI, 4-6, 11, LXXIV, 1, 8, 11, 14, LXXVI, 4-6)

As at Mohenjo-daro these blade-axes are of two main types, long and short. They all appear from their colour to have been made of hard bronze; some are mere fragments that have obviously been preserved in order to be melted down.

Nos. 1 and 1a in Pl. LXXIV are line drawings of the incised inscriptions found on the sides of a broken axe. Some of the signs in No. 1 appear to represent numerical characters and are similar to those incised on an axe of the same shape discovered at Mohenjo-daro.[18] Possibly these numbers are meant to be read as thirty-five (or thirty-six if the last digit is not meant for a stick in the hand of the man alongside). On the Mohenjo-daro blade the numbers apparently denote seventy-six. If this interpretation of the characters is correct, they are more likely to refer to the number of implements in the owner's possession rather than to the weight of the object on which they are placed. This most interesting fragment was found, together with various other metal objects, in the large pottery pan shown in Pl. XXIX, 37.

Another inscription was cut on the complete axe seen in Pl. LXIII, 3 (see also Pl. LXXIV, 8). There would seem to have been five characters on one side of this blade; of these only the first three are decipherable. Reading from the left these appear under numbers ccxxxviii, clvii, cliv in Smith and Gadd's sign list.[19]

At Mohenjo-daro inscribed implements were rare and were found only in the lower levels of that city, so that the finding of these two axes at Chanhu-daro at levels + 10.4

[17] *F. E. M.*, p. 477, pl. CXXXII, 7.
[18] *F. E. M.*, p. 454; pl. CXXVI, 5.
[19] *M. I. C.*, pls. CXIX-CXXIX.

and + 9.3 feet respectively adds another link to the chain of evidence that the Harappā II level at the latter is equivalent in date to the Intermediate Period at the former site.

No. 20 in Pl. LXII is shaped like an axe but is too thin to have been anything but a model. The same applies to No. 29 in Pl. LXX, which is of the colour of bronze and is fashioned out of sheet metal 0.03 inch thick.

The broken fragment shown in Pl. LXII, 22 must have been part of an axe of exceptional size and weight, and the absence of its lower portion is, therefore, all the more regrettable.

The little axe seen in Pl. LXX, 30 and again in Pl. LXXVI, 4 has a very narrow butt and differs in this respect from the usual type. From its colour it would seem to be in hard bronze.

It is interesting to note that fragments of the butt ends of axes are more often found than pieces from the edge ends. Possibly the latter flew off and became lost in the undergrowth when these tools became broken, whereas the former remained in their lashings on the handles. The broken edges, both of fractured axes and other tools, often show a certain amount of crystallization. Doubtless this commenced when the implements were being hammered into shape and was intensified during use.

Adzes (Pls. LXII, 21, 23, LXIV, 8, 10, 11, LXVIII, 11, 12, LXXI, 9, 10, LXXIV, 3, 9, LXXV, 5, 8)

These differ from the blade-axes in that they are longer and slenderer. There is no marked dissimilarity between the Chanhu-daro and Mohenjo-daro specimens. No. 11 in Pl. LXVIII (see also Pl. LXXV, 5) is unusually long and may have been made for some special purpose.

Saw (Pls. LXIII, 1, LXXIV, 4)

This interesting tool is without teeth, handle, or even rivet holes for a handle to be attached. In general shape it is not unlike a saw discovered in our early work at Mohenjo-daro.[20] The absence of a toothed edge suggests that it was used exclusively for stone working, possibly to slice nodules of agate or carnelian; some agate bars which were to be converted into beads actually bear saw-marks (Pl. LXXXVI, b, 9). The saw for this kind of work would preferably be of copper rather than of bronze, with possibly a stiffening bar of wood or metal along the upper edge, like that on a modern tenon saw. To assist its action an abrasive of some kind, such as powdered quartz or emery, would also be necessary. Fragments of soft stone, such as alabaster, limestone, and steatite, found in the Indus cities show that a workman was rarely able to cut straight through even a soft piece of stone but attacked it from various angles until he was able to break it in the centre of the cuts. This is just what one would expect to happen if a saw of the kind we illustrate was used on stone, especially if, as seems likely, its range was limited by a support along the top.

[20] *M. I. C.*, pls. CXXXVII, 7, CXXXVIII, 8.

Spear-heads (Pls. LXIII, 2, 4, 5, LXV, 1, 9, LXXI, 12, LXXVI, 17)

These large blades are presumed to be spear-heads, although they resemble some of the larger knives in shape.

No. 12 in Pl. LXXI (see also Pl. LXXVI, 17) is nearly thirteen inches long, but its blade is only 0.12 inch thick. A wooden mid-rib, probably formed by the split and tapered end of the shaft to which this head was once affixed originally supported the blade and was secured in place by thongs passed through the two large holes near the base of the head. A rivet hole at the end of the tang also helped to hold the blade firm. A specimen very similar to this but about two inches longer was found in the excavations at Mohenjo-daro.[21]

Certain spear-heads from Cyprus and the Cyclades have holes or, more often, slits by which they could be lashed to split shafts,[22] and the same feature appears in certain spear-heads of the Late Bronze Age from England and France, although by this time the mid-rib had become bronze and was cast as an integral part of the blade.[23]

The remaining specimens do not merit much description. They average 0.11 inch in thickness, which is certainly on the thin side for this type of weapon, though they would, of course, have been strengthened to a great extent by the addition of the wooden mid-rib explained above.

From its shape the rough casting seen in Pl. LXV, 9 and again in Pl. LXXIV, 16 was probably intended for one of these flat blades. It has slightly bevelled edges and the metal, presumably bronze, had been poured into a simple open mould.

Lance-head (Pl. LXX, 31)

This little blade with its two tie- and rivet-holes may conceivably have been used as a lance-head.

Daggers (Pls. LXVIII, 13, 15, LXXV, 9, LXXVI, 30)

Only three of the various blades found are likely to have been used as daggers. The first, No. 13 in Pl. LXVIII (see also Pl. LXXV, 9), is without mid-rib or even any thickening down its axis and has a slightly rounded point. The second, No. 15 in the same plate, has straight shoulders and edges that show repeated sharpening. No. 30 in Pl. LXXVI is in a very corroded state; it measures 12.12 inches in length.

Daggers belonging to an advanced civilization are frequently difficult to distinguish from knives, and this is especially true of implements found in the cities of the Indus Valley.

Large knives (Pls. LXII, 16, 17, LXIV, 1-7, LXV, 2-8, LXVII, 12, 14-16, 20, LXVIII, 10, 16, LXIX, 1, 2, 4, LXXII, 1-5, LXXIV, 17)

The above knives, which were also very common at Mohenjo-daro, are, with one exception, simple in shape. Their tangs are seldom pierced by rivet-holes and their double

[21] *F. E. M.*, pp. 459, 460; pl. LXXI, 33.

[22] Hall, *Bronze Age of Greece*, p. 87.

[23] *Guide to the Antiquities of the Bronze Age*, Brit. Mus. (1920), p. 129, fig. 136; *Antiquaries Journal*, vol. VIII, p. 32, pl. XII.

edges are sometimes markedly concave through constant sharpening. All originally had wooden handles which were probably secured in place by lashings, aided, perhaps, by some kind of cement. A knife (No. 2594, e) which is not illustrated here has a large hole in its tang through which a round, slightly tapered piece of wire has been passed to serve as a rivet, and the ends of this have been bent at right angles to keep the handle (now, of course, non-existent) in place. Judging by the distance between the bends, the handle must have been 0.99 inch thick, or possibly even a little more if the ends of the rivet were embedded in the wood. A second rivet-hole in this same knife, well below the tang, shows that the handle must have extended some way along the blade itself.[24] The high position of the rivet-hole in No. 1 of Pl. LXIX indicates that its handle must also have enclosed a considerable portion of its blade.

The knife with a curved point seen in Pls. LXIV, 5 and LXXIV, 17 is of a type well known at both Harappā and Mohenjo-daro[25] and is thought to have been used in preparing leather. In shape it closely resembles a gold blade found in one of the Royal Tombs at Ur,[26] except for the fact that the latter has a toothed edge. More often than not this type of Indian knife is found with a missing point.

The fragment shown in Pl. LXIV, 7, once part of an unusually large blade, has an exceptionally long tang.

It will have been noticed that the daggers and knives illustrated here are all without mid-ribs. Their blades are in every case very thin and only No. 20 in Pl. LXVII has any perceptible thickening down its centre. This method of stiffening blades was, however, rarely carried out; it is found on only two daggers and two swords from Mohenjo-daro.[27] The comparative rarity of the device in implements of the Harappā Culture may be attributed to the fact that most of them were made of sheet metal and not cast.

Small knives (Pls. LXII, 11, LXIII, 10, 14, LXVI, 16, LXVIII, 8, LXX, 21-25, LXXI, 7, 8, LXXV, 11, LXXVI, 8, 25-27)

These are more varied in shape than the larger knives. No. 11 in Pl. LXII has a short, wide tang and has been honed so often that it is no longer symetrical. Both ends of No. 10 in Pl. LXIII are missing; its cutting edge is on the curved side and the top edge is slightly thickened. The crescent-shaped object No. 14 in the same plate may have been used for flaying. It now measures 3.83 inches long and both ends are missing. The inner side or back is 0.2 inch thick and slopes gradually to an edge along the outer curve. No. 16 in Pl. LXVI (see also Pl. LXXV, 11) has a rivet that originally secured a wooden handle. The little blade without a tang in Pl. LXVIII, 8, which is shown again in Pl. LXXVI, 25, is new to us in its present form; it may have been kept in use after the tang was broken off.

[24] This knife was associated with the tools appearing in Pl. LXXVI, 29-30.

[25] *Ann. Rep. Arch. Surv. Ind.*, 1926-27, pl. XXII, 4, 5; *M. I. C.*, pl. CXXXV, 6; *F. E. M.*, pl. CXXXIII, 28, 31.

[26] Woolley, *Royal Cemetery*, p. 309, pl. 229.

[27] *F. E. M.*, pp. 466-7; pls. CXX, 17-19, CXVIII, 9.

The two blades in Pl. LXX, 21, 22 are both in a bad state of preservation; indeed the last is so worn that it is almost shapeless. Three knives, Nos. 23, 24, 25 in this same plate, are all types that are well known at Mohenjo-daro. Nos. 23 and 25 of these appear again in photograph in Pl. LXXVI, 26, 27; their cutting edges are on the lower portions only.

No. 7 in Pl. LXXI (see again Pl. LXXVI, 8) is a thin blade with a rivet hole in the handle and another well up the body. No. 8 in the same plate has been badly damaged by salt and is greatly swollen in consequence; originally it seems to have been quite a thin blade.

Knives of so small a size as these can hardly have been used for ordinary household purposes; probably they were needed for some particular craft or trade.

Razors

Razors, as at Mohenjo-daro, came to light in a surprising variety of types, which may be catalogued as follows:

(a). Double-bladed (Pls. LXVII, 1, LXXIII, 25-27, LXXVI, 34-36).
(b). L-shaped (Pls. LXXIII, 33, LXXVI, 33).
(c). Hook-shaped (Pl. LXXIII, 22, 28).
(d). Simple blades (Pls. LXVII, 7, LXX, 28).

To these must be added two new types which, so far, have been found only at Chanhu-daro:

(e). U-shaped (Pls. LXXIII, 32, LXXVI, 28).
(f). Crescent-shape (Pl. LXXIII, 31).

The double-bladed razors of Type (a), of a shape peculiar to the Harappā Culture, are by far the most common. It is a moot point whether their long tangs were encased with wood, but the exceptional length of the tang of the instrument in Pl. LXXIII, 25 (see again Pl. LXXVI, 35) indicates that here, at any rate, wood cannot have been used, although a cord may have been wound around to ensure a firmer grip. The nearest approach to this type that I have seen comes from Rollestone in England.[28]

Two examples of Type (b) were unearthed at Mohenjo-daro[29] and two more have appeared at Chanhu-daro. One of these is shown in Pl. LXXIII, 33 and again in Pl. LXXVI, 33. The other (No. 2594, M) measures 2.8 inches in length and 2.7 inches in width and was found with the three objects depicted in Pl. LXXVI, 29-31.

The hook-shaped Type (c) shown in Pl. LXXIII, 22, 28 has the cutting edge on the straight end only, while a curved handle, usually terminating in the head of a duck or goose, enables the instrument to be manipulated easily. This last feature, however, does not appear to advantage in the Chanhu-daro examples and the reader is referred to a better finished specimen from Mohenjo-daro.[30] Most of these razors, irrespective of type, were cut out of

[28] *Catalogue*, Devizes Museum, No. 18a.
[29] *F. E. M.*, pls. CXVIII, 7, CXXV, 41, CXXI, 26.
[30] *F. E. M.*, pls. CXXI, 41, CXXV, 39.

thick sheet metal and finished on the anvil, but in the case of Type (c) a certain amount of cutting or filing would have been necessary to round off the edges of the handle and shape the bird's head. Razors rather similar to this last type have been found in Denmark,[31] but an even closer comparison may be drawn between the Chanhu-daro examples and razors found in the Bord-ed-Djedid graves of Carthage,[32] especially with regard to the bird's head on the handle.

The very thin rectangular piece of copper in Pl. LXX, 28 has an edge at either end and, although it is really a new type, it may for the present be included with Type (d). A second blade of the same kind, but considerably narrower, may be seen in Pl. LXVII, 7. These two razors were probably held by a split wooden handle set at right angles to the blades.

Two examples of the new Type (e) are shown in Pls. LXXIII, 32 and LXXVI, 28; unfortunately they have suffered from corrosion and it is now difficult to say which was originally the cutting edge. It seems likely, however, that it was on the rounded outer margins of the instrument and, if this was so, a straight wooden handle may have been fitted between and enclosing the two ends, making the razor resemble a type known in the British Isles.[33]

The crescent-shaped example of Type (f) in Pl. LXXIII, 31 has a definite edge round the outer margin, and the ends, one of which is now missing, may have been inserted in a bar handle like that described in connection with Type (e) above.

Of the above-mentioned six types, razors conforming to Type (d) only have been found in Sumer or adjoining countries, and it must be assumed that, so far as the Middle East is concerned, the other five are peculiar to India.

Arrow-heads (Pls. LXVIII, 6, LXXIII, 1-4, 13-16)

With two exceptions these arrow-heads are of the Mohenjo-daro type, being without tangs and having such long fragile barbs that very few of them have survived intact. They have all been cut from thin pieces of sheet copper, varying from 0.02 to 0.05 inches in thickness, and must have been set in the tapered and slit ends of their shafts, so that the latter formed a stiff wooden mid-rib. A cement of some kind must have been used to fix these heads in place, for no tie-holes in them occur.

Strangely enough, metal arrow-heads of this type apparently do not occur in either Mesopotamia or Persia and but rarely in other countries. Stone specimens of which the Indian examples are copies are well known, however, in these two countries. The flint form, as a matter of fact, has been found in Northern Europe, the Danube Corridor, Spain, and Portugal, and it was also used in Egypt in Badarian times.

No. 1 in Pl. LXXIII is a new type, being without barbs; what is left of its broken tang is 0.19 inch wide and 0.08 inch thick. It may once have resembled an arrowhead found

[31] *Guide to the Antiquities of the Bronze Age*, Brit. Mus., 1920, p. 135, fig. 144.
[32] Moore, *Carthage of the Phoenicians*, pp. 92, 98.
[33] *Guide to Antiquities of the Bronze Age*, Brit. Mus., 1920, p. 56, fig. 46.

at Ghazi Shah.[34] No. 13 in the same plate is unique as far as the Harappā Culture is concerned. As it was found high up in Trench B(5) it may have been washed down from above. It could well be of the Jhukar Period but we have no other specimen of that period with which to compare it. Apart from its excessively long tang, however, it does not materially differ from the earlier examples.

Fish-hooks (Pls. LXXIII, 5-8, 17, 18, LXXVI, 15)

These again are of the same type as those found at Mohenjo-daro, but Nos. 6 and 8 in Pl. LXXIII are unusual in possessing no barbed points. All these hooks are made from stout bronze wire and were sometimes liable to become bent out of shape, as No. 7 shows. None of the points are off-set in any way. Barbed fish-hooks of such an early date are unknown outside India.

Chisels

Chisels were by far the most common tool found at Chanhu-daro. As was the case at Mohenjo-daro, they fall into five main categories:

(a). Long, rectangular or square in section, generally of uniform thickness throughout their length (Pls. LXII, 18, 19, LXIII, 6-8, LXVI, 13, 17-20, LXIX, 12, LXX, 8-12, 17, 19, 20, LXXVI, 3, 10, 11).

(b). Rectangular or square in section with a long flattened tang (Pls. LXII, 12, 13, LXIII, 12, LXVII, 11, 18, 19, LXX, 13-15, LXXVI, 9, 14).

(c). Round in section. The two chisels (Nos. 3325, 4830) of this type are not illustrated.[35]

(d). Short, round, or rectangular or square in section (Pls. LXII, 15, LXVII, 9, 10, LXX, 1-5, 7, LXXIV, 6, LXXVI, 12).

(e). Short and pointed (Pls. LXX, 6, LXXVI, 13).

Chisels belonging to Type (a) are the most common. Their angular bodies made them easy to manipulate with the fingers. They must have been used on various kinds of work, and gravers such as could have been used to carve the seals were included amongst them. Type (b) is peculiar to the Harappā Culture and was probably used only in wood-working. Their long flat tangs were undoubtedly encased in wooden handles and their butt ends in consequence are rarely found burred by the hammer.[36] Type (c) is definitely rare, although simply made out of a round rod of copper or bronze flattened at one end to form an edge.

The short chisels coming under Types (d) and (e) appear to have been used exclusively on metal; their heads frequently show heavy burring. It is possible that some of them

[34] Majumdar, *Explorations in Sind*, p. 103, pl. XLI, 24.

[35] The first was found in Square 8/B, locus 449. Level: + 7.8 ft. The second comes from Mound I, Square 13/J, locus 5. Level: + 13.5 ft.

[36] Remains of a wooden handle were seen on each side of the tang of No. 2529 (E. E.).

were originally clasped in a handle set at right angles to the tool. No. 7 in Pl. LXX is unusual because its head has become pent-shaped from being used at an angle. The pointed examples coming under Type (e) are distinctly rare.

The curious longitudinal groove down the centre of both sides of the chisel in Pl. LXVII, 10 suggests that an attempt had been made to divide it into two equal parts. The long, flat tool in Pl. LXVI, 17 was found closely folded over twice and was evidently awaiting consignment to the melting pot. One unfinished chisel (No. 2594, D), belonging to Type (b) was unearthed together with the other tools illustrated in Pl. LXXVI, 29-31.

All the examples that we illustrate, except the pointed ones, have double-sloped edges and in this respect are quite unlike their modern counterparts.

Awls

These are of two types:

(a). Rectangular or round in section, rounded at one or both ends (Pls. LXII, 14, LXXII, 6-10, 12-15).

(b). Round in section (Pls. LXII, 9, LXVI, 14, 21, LXX, 18, LXXII, 16, 17, LXXV, 13).

Type (a), which is made from a square or rectangular rod of copper or bronze, is frequently pointed at both ends. Sometimes these points are abrupt but more often they are attenuated like those in Pl. LXXII, 7, 9. The point of No. 9 now takes a hook-like form; it is uncertain whether this is by accident or design. No. 13 in the plate has a broad edge at one end and may have been used as a scraper as well as an awl. Awls of this type have, or had, points at both ends.

Type (b) is as common as Type (a). Some of these might have served equally well as pins, either for the hair or for fastening a cloak.

An interesting group of eight awls (No. 4712) was found in our Great Cutting.[37] These were all firmly cemented together by corrosion and could not, therefore, be properly inspected. Each awl had a rounded point at both ends and the largest of them is 4.05 inches long and 0.2 by 0.2 inch square in section in the middle.

Rods (Pls. LXX, 16, LXXII, 11)

No. 16 in Pl. LXX is a long rod, round in section, with a portion missing from one end. It may have been originally a chisel or an awl.

The object of bronze (from its colour) in Pl. LXXII, 11 is rectangular in the middle and rounds off towards the two ends, which average 0.17 inch in diameter. This object may have been the beam of a balance, although it differs slightly from the other examples in Pl. LXXI, 1-3. Before it was cleaned its surface showed in places the imprint of a woven fabric which, to judge from our experience at Mohenjo-daro, was made by a cotton cloth.[38]

[37] Square 9/F, locus 469. Level: + 0.05 ft.

[38] *F. E. M.*, pp. 591-3.

Spatula(?) (Pl. LXVII, 8)

This specimen has one end missing; from its shape and thinness, it would seem to have served the purpose of a spatula. It would have been useful in preparing fatty cosmetics or colours.

Tubular Drills (Pls. LXII, 7, LXXX, 9, LXXXI, 15)

Actual examples of these drills are rare, and in any case they do not appear to have been employed to any great extent at Chanhu-daro. Mohenjo-daro, however, has provided plenty of evidence that they were largely used there, principally on soft stones like limestone and alabaster.[39] These drills take the form of tapered tubes of thin copper or bronze and are so carefully made and perfectly rounded that it seems likely that they were shaped on a mandrel. Their edges meet exactly and do not overlap in any way. No. 15 in Pl. LXXXI is 1.62 inches long and has been so thickened by incrustation that it was for some time mistaken for a bead. Another drill of the same type, which is not illustrated, is 1.6 inches long and 0.4 inch in diameter at one end and 0.22 inch at the other.[40] This last specimen was discovered with a number of steatite beads of the wafer type (Pl. LXXXIII, 35-44) and could well have been used to form this type of bead.

Bead-tools (Pls. LXXX, 1-8, XCIII, 12, 13)

Six examples of this new type of tool were found in a room with a number of beads of minute size and it appears likely that they were used in their manufacture. No. 1, measuring 1.9 inches in length, appears to be a bronze casting. A point protrudes from its lower end and this is partly shielded by a flange that encircles it. No. 2, which was associated with No. 1, is 1.65 inches long. It has much the same shape but is without the flange and has a deep depression in its upper end. These two objects are badly preserved, as Pl. XCIII, 12, 13 show, and further cleaning, if this be possible, may reveal that they are really of tubular construction and resemble, therefore, the remaining tools to be described.

No. 3 is a copper or bronze tube, 0.95 inch long, with a fine tube of the same metal, whose point is missing, inserted in the lower end. No. 4, 1.05 inches long, has a strip of metal 0.28 inch in diameter and 0.12 inch wide wrapped round its bottom edge. The point or tube of this instrument, however, is missing. Nos. 5-8 are all of similar shape and construction. No. 6 has the best-preserved tubular point, which measures 0.25 inch long and 0.08 inch in diameter, while the overall length of the tool is 0.93 inch. No. 8 has its hollow point inserted in a copper ring 0.26 inch in diameter; whether by accident or design it is difficult to say.

When these strange tools first came to light it was decided that they had been used in the manufacture of the minute beads which appear *en masse* in Pl. XCIII, 5 and will be described in the following chapter. And Mr. William J. Young of the Museum of Fine

[39] *F. E. M.*, pp. 320, 597, 598; pl. CXLIV, 5.
[40] No. 2394. From Square 9/D, locus 215. Level: + 9.7 ft.

Arts, Boston, after examining specimens Nos. 6 and 7 has come, quite independently, to the same conclusion. He suggests that the bead-makers forced a powdered steatite mixed to a thick paste through the fine tubular points of these instruments in much the same way that confectioners to-day force frosting through tubes to ornament cakes. The necessary pressure could easily have been supplied by means of a metal or wooden rod sliding inside the upper tube of the tool, which, as already stated, was very carefully made with strictly parallel sides. A bag does not appear to have been used, for there is no attachment on the top of any of the instruments to which it could have been fastened.

Six of these tools, together with four others not illustrated, came from Square 9/D, room 215, which from the objects found in it was evidently a bead factory.

Shovel (Pl. LXXIV, 13)

This very modern-looking implement may have been used in lifting charcoal or grain. It measures 16.3 inches in length with its handle, and is the first specimen of its kind that has appeared in any of the Harappā cities. The sides and base of this tool are 0.2 inch thick and it now weighs 3 lbs. 10½ ounces. The plain flat handle which is of one piece of metal with the pan is 4.87 inches long by an average of 1.5 inches wide and 0.21 inch thick. This last has no rivet holes, but is obviously too short to have been used without a longer attachment, probably of wood.

Stave-heads (Pls. LXVIII, 4, 5, 7, LXXV, 4)

The two objects seen in Pl. LXVIII, 4, 5 (see also Pl. LXXV, 4) may have served to surmount ceremonial staffs. Both are bronze castings of the same height and breadth but slight differences between them prove that they were not made in the same mould. They are of exceptionally clean workmanship and little was required to be done to them beyond smoothing their surfaces.

The cap in Pl. LXVIII, 7 is also well made and like the stave-heads described above was obviously intended to be riveted to something of a rod-like nature.

Plumb-bob(?) (Pl. LXX, 26)

This object appears, from its shape, to have been a plumb-bob; something missing from its upper end was perhaps a perforated lug by which it was suspended. The surface of this article has been either exceptionally well finished or else polished by much use.

Ingots (Pl. LXXIV, 2)

Up to the present only two ingots have come to light in our excavations at Chanhu-daro. The first, which appears in Pl. LXXIV, 2, is a long round bar, 13.75 inches in length and varying somewhat in diameter. The metal is bronze, judging from its colour, and it was formed by pouring the molten metal into a vertical hole in the ground. The numerous objects illustrated in Pls. LXII, 1-23, LXIII, 1-5, LXXIV, 2-9 were associated with this ingot.

The second example is not illustrated,[41] but in shape it resembles closely certain ingots from Mohenjo-daro.[42] It has a flat top and a rounded base, and its diameter measurement is 1.67 inches.

Lead Fragments

Small masses of lead of irregular shape were found in various parts of Mound II. It is not yet known for what purpose this metal was used.

OBJECTS OF THE JHUKAR PERIOD (?)

Socketed Axe (Pls. LXXII, 25, LXXVI, 37)

This most interesting tool was found at the high level of + 17.6 feet on Mound II, and there are strong reasons for ascribing it to the Jhukar Period. It is much too well made to have been the work of the Jhukar people, if the style and workmanship of their pottery is any criterion, nor can it belong to the Harappā Period, for we know that no such tools were manufactured or used by the people of that culture.

The implement is made of bronze, is 3.95 inches long, and its lunate edge is 1.94 inches wide. The interior dimensions of its slightly oval socket are 0.82 by 0.71 inches. It appears to have been cast edge down, for there is a slight projection at the back of the socket where the metal was run in. It has a smooth, even surface and great care was evidently exercised in its finish.

The socketed adze-axes unearthed at Tepe Hissar[43] so closely resemble the Mohenjo-daro specimen found some time ago,[44] as to make it likely that they are all products of the same period. With them must now be included the present Chanhu-daro implement, which, though of a less complex pattern, is nevertheless allied in conception and technique. A date which covers the period 2000-1500 B. C. has been put forward for stratum III in which the Hissar axes appeared. Heine-Geldern, however, takes the view that the Mohenjo-daro axe cannot be earlier than about 1200 B. C.,[45] a dating considerably later than that allowed for its Tepe Hissar counterpart, and also at variance with that allowed for the Astrabad Treasure, which contained several adze-axes of a similar type.[46] On the strength of the Chanhu-daro tool I do not think we shall be very far out if we place the Jhukar Period as coeval with the middle of the Hissar III Period and with the First Dynasty of Babylon.[47]

[41] No. 1113, found in Trench H(1). Level: — 7.9 ft.

[42] *F. E. M.*, pl. CXXXII, 37, 38.

[43] E. F. Schmidt, "Tepe Hissar Excavations, 1931," *Mus. Journ.*, Univ. Mus., Philadelphia, p. 400, pl. CXVIII (H. 168).

[44] *F. E. M.*, pp. 457, 458; pls. CXX, 27, CXXII, 12.

[45] *Journ. Ind. Soc. Orient. Art*, vol. IV, 1936, p. 103.

[46] Ascribed to the first half of the second millennium B. C.

[47] The middle or Hammurabi Period of the First Dynasty of Babylon is now closely dated by Sidney Smith to 1792-1750 B. C. (*Alalakh and Chronology*, p. 29).

Whatever way one looks at the problem we cannot exclude the possibility that the socket invention, or perhaps the actual tools themselves, must have taken some time to reach India from the original source. Possibly an innate conservatism prevented the Harappā People from adopting this form of axe, though it is more than likely that some of them must have become acquainted with it in the course of their trading relations with Sumer. The original Sumerian holed axe is, however, of quite a different form to that of the perforated Indian examples, which last seem to have reached India from Persia via Baluchistan, where, as we have already seen, Jhukar pottery has been found.[48]

Chisel (Pl. LXXII, 23)

To judge from the high level at which it was found, the chisel shown in Pl. LXXII, 23 may also be attributed to the Jhukar Culture, but unfortunately it is impossible to be certain on this point, as we do not yet know of a single metal tool or copper object which definitely belongs to that time. The pins numbered 18-20 in the same plate, which will be described in the next chapter, may be an exception but only because they differ so much from the pins used by the Harappā people. The upper levels of Mound II were very much disturbed, because the Jhukar people used earlier material. Muhammadan graves were there, and brick robbing took place at all times. It was, therefore, difficult in some cases to ascertain what the people of the various cultures had made themselves and what they had borrowed from the lower levels. The pottery, the seals and a few other objects of this period are nevertheless quite distinctive.

LATER PERIODS

Iron Arrow-head (Pl. LXXII, 24)

This is the only iron object found at Chanhu-daro. It came from Trench B(1) at the level −2.7 feet and close to the surface of the ground. It is tolerably well preserved, has no sign of a mid-rib, and has lost a part of its tang, which appears originally to have been a long one. I would, for the present, attribute it to the Jhangar Period, on the ground that some of the pottery of that culture resembles certain Iron Age wares from southern India.

The remaining copper and bronze objects, such as bangles, rings, pins, and so forth, are more appropriately dealt with in the following chapter on "Personal Ornaments."

[48] Chap. VII.

CHAPTER XIII

PERSONAL ORNAMENTS

Although the ornaments unearthed at Chanhu-daro are comparatively few in number and consist of bracelets, pendants, rings, and pins in copper and bronze only, they form nevertheless an interesting collection. Gold and silver jewellery, even of the simplest description was, however, entirely absent, although occasional fragments of thin gold foil were found adhering to copper beads and bangles. One must not infer that these metals were not worn by the Chanhu-daro people at all; indeed, it is likely that the women of that city carried their wealth on their persons in the form of ornaments, as do many of the poorer people of India to-day, and that they took these away with them when they deserted the city. The above remarks apply only to the excavation of Mound II, for the greater part of Mound I still remains to be cleared. Judging from the poorly built structures—probably the dwellings of working-class people—on the summit of the latter mound, there is, however, little reason to expect that this part of the city will prove any richer than the rest.

The exceptionally fine jewellery found both at Mohenjo-daro and at Harappā has, therefore, no counterpart at Chanhu-daro, but from the way the people lived and the fact that they were chiefly engaged in crafts of various kinds one can hardly expect them to have worn anything that was exceptionally rich or precious. As a matter of fact, they were quite capable of fine work, even in copper or bronze, as the two ornaments illustrated in Pl. LXXVIII, 1, 2 show.

Beads, it is true, were discovered in large quantities, but these came from the quarters of the craftsmen who made them and were not necessarily intended for people of substance in the city itself. Chanhu-daro was undoubtedly a great bead-making centre, which supplied many more prosperous communities, perhaps in Sumer itself, and the best examples of the craft were obviously reserved for export.

Copper or Bronze Bracelets

These are quite common and are of three distinct types:

(a) Those made from stout rods or wire, round in section (Pls. LXII, 5, LXVI, 2, 8-11, LXIX, 11, LXXIII, 19, 23, 24, 29, LXXV, 11, 12, LXXVI, 19, 20).

(b) Those made from half-round rods or wire (Pls. LXII, 6, LXVII, 4, 5).

(c) Those made from thin sheeting and U-shaped in section (Pls. LXXIII, 30, LXXVI, 21).

Bracelets of Type (a) are by far the most common, the round copper or bronze rods out of which they are made ranging from 0.13 to 0.27 inches in diameter.

Type (b), however, is distinctly rare and only three examples, two of which are illustrated, have been found. It is difficult to say whether the rods from which these bangles were made were half-round in the first place, or the flattening, always to be seen on the inside of the bracelet, came from being shaped on a mandrel.

Type (c) is complex in workmanship compared with the other two. Specimens belonging to it seem to have been constructed out of circular pieces of flat sheeting, about 0.02 inch thick, which was worked into a U form, the open end of the section being always on the inside. This type of bangle was probably shaped by hammer and chisel on a bitumen support, and when it was finished its hollow interior was probably filled with a resinous substance to prevent buckling. Owing to the thinness of the metal employed, articles of this type are generally badly preserved. Fragments of two, if not three, of these were found adhering to the dish in Pl. LXVII, 2 and averaged 0.19 by 0.13 inches in section. Another bangle made in the same way (No. 2529, T, a) was of very much the same size in section; this last came to light with the examples of Types (a) and (b) shown in Pl. LXII, 5, 6. Bracelets belonging to these three categories have diameter measurements varying from 1.7 to 2.8 inches, but the specimen illustrated in Pl. LXXIII, 30 and again in Pl. LXXVI, 21 is of exceptional size (2.9 ins.). This last belongs to Type (c) and must either have been made for a man or worn as an armlet.

The ends of most of the bracelets were found open and appear to have been worn in this condition. The bangles shown in Pls. LXVI, 2, 11 and LXIX, 11 are so small, however, that they were probably made for children. No joint can be seen in the Type (a) bangle in Pl. LXVI, 9 (see also Pl. LXXV, 11) nor in that shown in Pl. LXXIII, 30 and again in Pl. LXXVI, 21. An opening in this last Type (c) example cannot be expected, seeing that it was made in a different way to the others.

Type (c) is unknown at Mohenjo-daro, but the other two kinds were quite common. There, however, it was Type (b) not Type (a) that was the most well favoured.

Faience Bracelets (Pls. LXXVII, 2-5, 8, 10, XC, 35-38)

Owing to their fragile nature, bracelets of this description are never found intact. Their pieces have been discovered over various parts of Mound II and they are just as common in the upper as in the lower levels. Exactly similar fragments, both in make and in the patterns incised upon them, are known at Mohenjo-daro and also at Lohumjo-daro, another site in Sindh.[1]

These faience bangles were made in moulds and formed of a soft, light grey paste coated with a thick glaze, which in most cases has lost its colour. Nos. 37 and 38 in Pl. XC (the latter being shown in line in Pl. LXXVII, 10) are now pale blue. Nos. 2, 3, 5, 8 in Pl. LXXVII and No. 36 in Pl. XC are light green, while the remaining specimens are now cream colour. No. 4 in Pl. LXXVII, the only example with a hard core, is made of a paste which has an addition of a certain amount of glaze and was converted by firing into a hard vitreous substance not unlike glass in appearance and of a uniform tint throughout. This particular specimen is of an apple-green colour inside, though its surface has faded to a dull white. Both methods of making these bangles were also practised at Mohenjo-daro and the same technique was also adopted in bead-making.

[1] Majumdar, *Explorations in Sind*, pl. XXXIII, 6, 6a.

Although No. 10 in Pl. LXXVII (see also Pl. XC, 38) is distinctly oval in section, most of these bangles are semi-circular in this respect and average 0.15 in. wide and 0.18 in. thick. All are decorated in some way, the most common device being two parallel lines of notching round the circumference (Pl. LXXVII, 2, 3, 5, 8). The chevron pattern seen in Pl. LXXVII, 10 (see also Pl. XC, 38) is also known on similar bracelets from Mohenjo-daro.[2]

Shell Bracelets (Pls. LXXVII, 6, 7, XC, 15)

These are rather uncommon, for shell-working was not a craft that was extensively practised at Chanhu-daro. The material used was the univalve shown in Pl. XC, 1.[3]

The four bracelets illustrated in Pl. XC, 15 are unfinished. They have all been sawn from the same part of the shell, but because the shell tapered a little and a coarse saw was used, the diameter measurement, which averages 2.2 to 2.65 inches inside, varies slightly in each specimen. The bangles, which are oval in shape, are also irregular in section, but this last unavoidable defect would have been remedied to some extent if they had been smoothed over and polished.

The small fragment, No. 6 in Pl. LXXVII, is decorated with two deep grooves round the circumference. A small hole at one end has obviously been made in an attempt to repair the bracelet to which this piece once belonged. No. 7 in the same plate is also ornamented in this way but with the addition of incised markings at the base of the grooves.

Pottery Bracelets (Pls. LXXVII, 9, 11-13, XC, 26-29, 34, 39, 40)

In spite of their crudeness, some of these bangles are of considerable interest. The plain varieties, four of which are illustrated in Pl. XC, 26-29, are made from rounded strips of clay with the ends roughly joined together, little or no attempt having been made to conceal the unions. Very few of these bracelets are symmetrical and none of them bears a slip or wash of any kind. They average 2.4 inches in diameter outside and are just large enough to slip over a woman's hand. Ornaments, if one may so call them, of this kind were also worn at Mohenjo-daro,[4] but at Chanhu-daro they were far more common.

A singular specimen, hitherto quite unknown to us, appears in Pl. XC, 34. This measures 2.26 inches wide, 2.7 inches in diameter, and is made up of seven bracelets of the type described above, arranged so that their joints are in line. On the inside this bracelet is slightly oval and measures 1.93 by 1.8 inches each way, while the segments composing it are round in section, averaging 0.31 inches in diameter. When a bracelet of this type first came to light it was thought that some bangles had become accidentally united in the kiln, but this supposition proved false when other examples turned up in various parts of the site, all made in the same way, although the number of rings varied in each case.[5]

[2] *F. E. M.*, pl. CXL, 58.

[3] *Murex (Chicoreus) ramosus*, Linn.

[4] *M. I. C.*, p. 530, pl. CLII, 11.

[5] For another bracelet of this type from Chanhu-daro, see Majumdar, *Explorations in Sind*, pl. XVII, 40.

Two examples of another new and very curious bracelet are shown in Pls. LXXVII, 9, XC, 39, 40. These are almost round in section, have no slip or paint, and are crudely ornamented with deep finger impressions round their circumferences. Nothing like them has been found elsewhere; they appear to be a local product. No. 39 measures 0.25 inch wide by 0.28 inch thick, and No. 40 (which appears again in line in Pl. LXXVII, 9) is 0.43 inch wide by 0.44 inch thick.

Specimens of a third type are illustrated in Pl. LXXVII, 11-13. These, however, are far more carefully finished than the bracelets described above, and all of them are decorated with transverse markings in dark or light red paint that has not always been carefully applied. No. 11 is flat in section, measuring 0.35 inch wide, 0.12 inch thick on the outer side and 0.26 inch thick on the inner. It is coated with a pink slip and is decorated on both sides, as the illustration shows, with a pattern in dark-red paint. No. 12 has no slip, but is irregularly ornamented on both sides with red lines. This specimen resembles No. 11 in section, its inside measurement is 0.18 inch in thickness, graduating down to 0.12 inch on the outside. No. 13 is round in section (0.32 inch in diameter), and is carefully made and finished, the outside edge being adorned with dark red stripes applied on a slip of yellowish-pink.

All these bracelets appear to have been made of ordinary clay, identical with that used for the pottery, but it is difficult to explain why so many of them are of such bad workmanship. Poverty cannot be pleaded as an excuse, for the material was there for the asking and ornaments of this kind could have been made just as well at home as in a potter's workshop. A theory that has been put forward is that the coarser type of bangle was venerated in some way and perhaps issued to pilgrims after a visit to some sacred shrine or temple.

Rings (Pls. LXXIII, 9-12, 20, 21, LXXXIX, 8)

The copper or bronze rings in Pl. LXXIII may have served as earrings, finger-rings, or toe-rings, and fall into two main categories, "plain" and "coiled." The former is the more common of the two, but both types occur comparatively rarely at Indus Valley sites, because metal rings are not objects that are easily lost or broken.

No gold or silver rings were unearthed at Chanhu-daro, not because such objects were not made, but because they probably represented the portable capital of their owners and, as mentioned earlier in this chapter, were removed when the city was deserted.

Two examples of the "plain" rings are shown in Pl. LXXIII, 20, 21. Both have slightly tapered ends like those of the bangles, and are fashioned out of round wire, 0.12 inch in diameter. Another ring, which is not illustrated, is made of a piece of wire 0.11 inch square in section.[6] These plain rings occasionally have ends that overlap a little, but generally they merely touch.

Rings of the coiled type (Pl. LXXIII, 9-12) are by far the most ornamental. Nos. 9 and 11 are made of round wire, 0.1 and 0.07 inches in diameter respectively. No. 10 is fashioned out of half-round wire measuring 0.1 inch wide and 0.05 inch thick, while that

[6] No. 3158, from Sq. 9/D, loc. 175, lev. + 7.9 ft.

composing No. 12 is slightly oval in section. All these specimens are undoubtedly finger-rings, for they are too wide to have been carried in the ears. Similar rings to these, made in gold, silver and copper, were very popular in Sumer at a time contemporary with the Harappā Culture.[7] They have also been found on Persian sites of about the same period as well as on those of earlier date.[8]

A ring in pottery is shown in Pl. LXXXIX, 8. This bears traces of a polished red surface. It is 0.91 inch in diameter and its joint is rather rough. Rings in this easily broken material are decidedly rare.

Fillet (Pl. LXVIII, 14)[8a]

The sole example of a fillet so far discovered consists of a thin band of copper, now only 3.45 inches long, the greater part of it being missing. Originally it must have been worn round the fore-head and secured by strings tied at the back of the head. Very similar ornaments made in silver and gold have come to light at Mohenjo-daro.[9] Fillets of the same form are well known at Kish and Ur in Mesopotamia as well as at Tepe Hissar in Persia.[10] The Indian examples as well as those from the countries I have named are frequently stiffened with punch markings or devices embossed on the thin metal.

Pins (Pls. LXVII, 13, LXVIII, 9, LXIX, 5-10, LXXII, 21, 22, LXXV, 6, LXXVI, 22-24, LXXXIX, 5)

The pins recovered from Chanhu-daro are made in copper or bronze with the exception of one in ivory shown in Pl. LXXXIX, 5. This last has lost its point and is now 1.7 inches long.

The simplest type of pin appears in Pls. LXVII, 13 and LXIX, 6. The first was found with a number of copper and bronze objects and its finish, to say nothing of its very definite head, prevent it from being classed as an awl. No. 6 in Pl. LXIX, which has lost its point, is a plain round rod of copper.

The type most commonly found at Chanhu-daro is illustrated in Pls. LXIX, 5, 7-10, LXXII, 21, 22, LXXVI, 22-24, and was made by thinning out one end of a copper rod and then coiling it downwards to form a head. Curiously enough, only one specimen of this type of pin has turned up at Mohenjo-daro and that in a very low level,[11] while, so far as the writer is aware, nothing like it has ever been unearthed in other settlements of the Harappā Culture.

This type of pin, together with one very similar, whose coiled head is made of flattened,

[7] Woolley, *Antiquaries Journal,* vol. XII, p. 368.

[8] E. F. Schmidt, "Tepe Hissar Excavations, 1931," *The Museum Journal,* Univ. Mus., p. 381, pls. CV (a), CXXI (b, d).

[8a] This object was inadvertently omitted from the drawing for this plate.

[9] *M. I. C.,* p. 527, pl. CLI, a, 4, 5; *F. E. M.,* pp. 526, 529; pl. CXXXV, 4.

[10] E. F. Schmidt, "Tepe Hissar Excavations, 1931," pl. CXXII (a, d).

[11] *F. E. M.,* p. 539, pl. C, 4. This pin provides further evidence that the lower levels of the city are contemporary with the upper levels of Chanhu-daro.

not round wire, has a tremendous geographical range. It has come to light in Bronze Age Germany and Bulgaria;[12] at Troy (first and second cities);[13] in Predynastic Egypt;[14] and in Mesopotamia[15] and Persia,[16] including the Caucasus. Why the type should be so common at Chanhu-daro and so rare at Mohenjo-daro cannot at present be explained. At the former site it occurs at levels ranging from +0.05 to +21.5 feet, the latter figure, of course, being well in the Jhukar Period.

Altogether four of these pins were found in the Jhukar levels of Mound II (Pls. LXIX, 5, LXXII, 21, 22,[17] and the supposition is that they were made in that period as well as in the one before. In all probability this type of pin was introduced into India from either Mesopotamia or Persia at about 3000-2500 B.C.

Only one example was found of the double-coiled pin shown in Pls. LXVIII, 9 and LXXV, 6. It has no counterpart yet at Mohenjo-daro or in any other city inhabited by the Harappā people, and is made of one piece of metal, the split ends of which were carefully fined down and then twisted into two opposite coils, 1.15 inches in total width. Specimens of this type have been discovered in ancient settlements as remote as Germany and other parts of Europe.[18] One pin of this type has turned up at Anau,[19] quite a number at Tepe Hissar in Western Persia, all dated to the Hissar II Period[20] and Troy has produced a number of specimens. Two have come to light at Sialk in Kashan.[21]

Heine-Geldern inclines to the view that the beginnings of the Hissar II Period reach back at least to the beginning of the second millennium, if not to the late centuries of the third millennium B.C.[22] If the last be correct, our Chanhu-daro specimen, which certainly belongs to the Harappā Period, can be linked with the Hissar II pins. As the type is unknown in Mesopotamia it presumably reached India by the overland route through Baluchistan, although no examples of it have, up to the present, been reported as coming from that country.

Jhukar Pins (Pl. LXXII, 18-22)

The first three copper or bronze pins are interesting, as nothing like them has as yet appeared in any other Indian site. For this reason and also because the chevron pattern, a decorative feature of much of the Jhukar pottery (Pl. XLII, 11-13, 15-18), occurs on two

[12] Ebert, *Reallexikon Der Vorgeschichte*, vol. 8, pls. 75, 93.

[13] Schliemann, *Troja*, p. 139, nos. 62, 63.

[14] Petrie and Quibell, *Nagada and Ballas*, pl. LXV, 15; Brunton, *Mostagedda*, pls. XL, 42, 43, XLIII, 25-27; Childe, *Most Ancient East* (2nd Edition), p. 72, fig. 22.

[15] Woolley, *Royal Cemetery*, p. 310, pl. 231; Preusser, *Tell Asmar and Khafaje*, fig. 52.

[16] Speiser, *Excavations at Tepe Gawra*, p. 110, pl. LXXXII, 14, 16.

[17] The fourth (No. 1349) was found in Sq. 8/D, loc. 84, lev. +21.5 ft. It measures 3.3 inches in length and 0.18 in. in diameter.

[18] Ebert, *Reallexikon Der Vorgeschichte*, vol. 8, pls. 131, 132, 140; Peet, *Stone and Bronze Ages in Italy*, p. 351, fig. 184.

[19] Pumpelly, *Excavations in Turkestan*, I, p. 152.

[20] E. F. Schmidt, "Tepe Hissar Excavations, 1931, pl. CIV (c).

[21] R. Ghirshman, *Fouilles de Sialk*, vol. I, pls. XXIX, b, XCV, a, e.

[22] "Archaeological Traces of the Vedic Aryans"; *Journ. Ind. Soc. Orient Art.*, vol. IV, no. 2, p. 94.

of them, it seems probable that they are products of that period. Nos. 18 and 19 came from levels where Jhukar material was beginning to appear in abundance, while No. 20 was found high up in the "Cutting," having no doubt been washed down from above.

No. 18 is 6.38 inches long and has a square shoulder measuring 0.3 × 0.27 inch. The rounded head is 0.29 inch in diameter and on two sides of the shoulder traces of an incised decoration can just be made out. The other two sides were probably ornamented in the same manner, but no markings can now be seen.

No. 19 is a similar but better finished object. It is 4.3 inches long and bears an incised chevron pattern on one side of its shoulder, which measures 0.23 inches square.

The nearest approach to this type of pin is a specimen from Tepe Sialk assigned to Period IV of that site.[23]

No. 20, which has unfortunately lost its point, is now 4.97 inches long and has an elaborately decorated flat head measuring 0.6 inches square. Incised on this is a four-petalled design following the outline of the head, with circle and dot motifs, apparently cut with a drill, ornamenting the angles and centre of the pattern. The lower rounded part of this specimen is 0.1 inches in diameter.

It is still a matter of conjecture whether these pins were worn in the hair or used to fasten garments, nor can any information on this point be gained from the figurines. A hair pin is, however, certainly indicated on a statue head of a man in limestone found at Mohenjo-daro.[24]

Comb (Pls. LXXXIX, 12, XCI, 4)

This fine ivory comb, which was found in pieces, now measures 1.79 inches long by 0.2 inch thick. It is decorated on both sides with an identical pattern of roundels and has been very carefully made, though the teeth are rather roughly cut.[25] This object is not unlike one unearthed at Mohenjo-daro.[26] The fact that a comb came to light near the head of a female body at Mohenjo-daro would indicate that these articles were actually worn in the hair.

Bullae (Pl. LXXXVIII, 1-3)

These strange objects were quite common at Mohenjo-daro.[27] They appear to be copies of stitched leather amulet cases and were probably valued as amulets as well as ornaments. Bullae of this description are invariably made of pottery and decorated on one side only. Of the specimens illustrated only No. 1 is coated with a slip, in this case red. All are perforated with two holes by which they could be hung from the neck or attached to the clothing.

[23] R. Ghirshman, *Fouilles de Sialk*, Vol. I, pl. XCV, c.
[24] *M. I. C.*, pl. XCIX, 5, 6.
[25] These were made with a saw.
[26] *F. E. M.*, p. 542, pls. XCI, 26, CXXV, 24.
[27] *Op. cit.*, p. 524, pls. LXXI, 14, CXXXVI, 80, CXL, 34, CXLII, 1, 2, 4.

No. 1 is 1.5 inches in diameter, 0.22 inch thick, and has a flat, oval slip of clay just below its two holes, though why this was added here is difficult to say. It is ornamented with a double row of pittings round its margin which, however, do not perforate it. No. 2 is of the same thickness and averages 1.36 inches in diameter; its stitch markings are very irregular. The two holes by which it was suspended have been strengthened by a thin strip of clay. No. 3 has only a single row of stitching.

Button-ornaments (Pls. LXXVIII, 3-7, 9, 12-15, LXXXVIII, 5)

The most popular type of button, one that was equally common at Mohenjo-daro, is that shown in Pl. LXXVIII, 14. This specimen is 1.0 inch in diameter and 0.2 inch thick and is made of steatite, the usual material. In its base are two converging holes by which it could be secured to a garment. Buttons of exactly the same pattern have been found on many ancient sites from Persia to places as far afield as Western Europe.

Another type of button, much favoured at Chanhu-daro but somewhat rare at Mohenjo-daro,[28] is shown in Pl. LXXVIII, 3-7, and occurs in two varieties, " plain " and " knobbed." These were shaped in a mould, but before they were glazed, their flat bases were roughly scooped out, leaving behind a bar of the material to bridge the hollow thus formed. Lastly this bridge was perforated laterally to take a fastening or thread. Nos. 5-7 clearly show in what a perfunctory manner this hollowing was done; the reverse side of these ornaments was evidently not intended to be seen. Nos. 3, 5-7 are of an apple-green shade, and though No. 4 has lost its colour and is now white it still retains its glaze.

No. 9 in Pl. LXXVIII is a small button of steatite with a perforated projection at the base to secure it to clothing. In colour it is now white, but yellow patches here and there are remains of a decomposed glaze. A second specimen of much the same type appears in Pl. LXXXVIII, 5. This is made of pottery and is 1.8 inches in diameter and 0.7 inch in thickness. Round its margin is a single row of indentations which, as in the case of the bullae already described, may be intended to represent stitching. No. 13 in Pl. LXXVIII is a simple button made in shell and measuring 1.2 inches in diameter and 0.25 inch thick. Originally it had only two holes in the middle, in the modern manner, but subsequently others were bored, two of which are broken.

Nos. 12 and 15 in Pl. LXXVIII represent a new type. The first is in faience and bears a glaze that has now faded to cream. It measures 0.60 inch long and the edge of its slightly concave base is bored with two holes as shown in the line drawing. No. 15, also in faience, is better finished and is decorated with an incised chevron design similar to that on the metal pins in Pl. LXXII, 18, 19. This chevron motif was, as we have seen, a favourite pottery motif in the Jhukar Period and this, taken with the fact that both these specimens come from high levels, makes it probable that these two buttons are of Jhukar workmanship.

Nose or Ear Ornaments (Pl. LXXVIII, 8, 10, 11, 16)

Except for the absence of a small head at the end of the shank, No. 8 resembles a

[28] *M. I. C.*, pl. CLV, 5; *F. E. M.*, p. 542; pls. XCI, 29, 30, CXXV, 23.

type of faience plug that was common at Mohenjo-daro.[29] Light green in colour and 0.8 inch in diameter, the moulded face of this object bears the divided circle design, which almost invariably appears on ornaments of this sort as well as on the painted pottery.

Nos. 10, 11, and 16 are also in faience; the glaze of the first has turned to a cream colour. None of these plugs has a head at the end of its stem but the slightly concave sides were probably sufficient to keep it in position in the nose or ear. No. 16, which measures 0.84 inch in diameter, has a curious serrated edge, which possibly prevented it from turning round when set in place.

Head-cones (Pls. XXIX, 67, 68 [Jhukar]; XC, 5, 11, 12 [Harappā Period])

No. 67 is in perfect condition and is in faience coated with a thick light green glaze. It measures 2.3 inches high and 1.3 inches in diameter and the depth of its interior is 0.98 inch. Six holes, more or less regularly spaced and averaging 0.12 inch in diameter, pierce the lower edge of this rather roughly made object. The second cone, No. 68, was found with a small collection of glazed beads of indifferent workmanship, one of which is illustrated in Pl. LXXXVII, 7, a. The upper part of this object is missing and it now measures 2.8 inches in height; its hollow interior is 1.48 inches deep. Like No. 67 it has six small holes round its lower edge.

The above two cones, both of which are roughly made and glazed, are undoubtedly of Jhukar manufacture. They were probably sewn to a head-dress and are not unlike certain copper, silver and gold head-ornaments that have been found at Mohenjo-daro.[30]

The three shell segments, Nos. 5, 11, 12 in Pl. XC, come from a type of cone of which numerous, but rarely perfect, examples have been found in the cities of the Harappā people.[31] Two of these segments (Nos. 5 and 11) fit together to form part of a cone 1.2 inches in height and 3 inches in diameter; a third piece which would complete this cone is missing. No. 12 comes from another cone which is estimated to have been 1.0 inch high and 2.78 inches in diameter.

It is not yet known how these segments were joined together. They have no holes, and metal fastenings would therefore appear unlikely. Possibly a cement, such as shellac, was used. The marginal incised lines round these pieces were filled in with a red-coloured pigment, a usual procedure with objects of this kind.

Metal Ornaments (Pl. LXXVIII, 1, 2)

No. 1 is a very unusual ornament and may have been a pendant. Its overall measurements are 1.61 inches high, 1.31 inches wide, and 0.62 inches thick. The copper cone-shaped portions are separated from one another by copper and white steatite disc-shaped beads. A similar arrangement of larger beads projects from the top of the ornament. Each set of cones and beads is kept in place by a copper wire, the two ends of which pass through

[29] *F. E. M.*, p. 532, pls. C, 12, CXXXVI, 90, 91.
[30] *M. I. C.*, p. 519, pl. CXLVIII, A(2); *F. E. M.*, p. 529, pls. CV, 22, CXXIV, 30, CXXXV, 7.
[31] *M. I. C.*, pl. CLVI, 13, 16, 17; *F. E. M.*, pls. CV, 42, CXXV, 28.

two thin copper plates at the base, are then brought upwards through the cones, next through an upper plate, which is eight-shaped, and finally end somewhere in the beads on the top. The whole affair is very carefully made and quite probably the copper parts were once gilt.

No. 2 in Pl. LXXVIII is made up of two bell-shaped pieces of thin beaten copper, 0.39 inches in length and 0.65 inches in diameter, joined together by a thin copper rod, 0.06 inch thick. Strung on this connecting piece is a cylindrical copper bead, which may once have had beads of a contrasting colour on either side of it. A fragment of a second ornament of the same kind adheres to the lower bell.

This ornament, which possibly represents two flowers of the convolvulus type, may have been suspended from its central bar, now slightly out of shape. It is a beautiful example of fine metal-work and bears no resemblance to anything found at Mohenjo-daro. Flower-shaped ornaments are characteristic of much of the material discovered in the Royal Tombs at Ur, so it is possible that this Chanhu-daro ornament is a copy of the work of some Sumerian jeweller. As already mentioned, there were originally two of these articles, only one of which has survived intact; it is likely they were intended to be worn as earrings.

BEADS

A description of the materials from which the beads shown in Pls. LXXX-LXXXV and LXXXVII are made will be found at the end of this book. All the beads, except when otherwise shown or stated, are round in section and excepting those in Pl. LXXIX are drawn to full scale. As many of them represent types well known at Mohenjo-daro, it has been thought necessary only to describe the rare examples, especially those which are peculiar to Chanhu-daro. Some of the most popular northern varieties, curiously enough, have never come to light on this site. For example, the favourite Mohenjo-daro bead-types—"cog-wheel," "tubular denticulate," and "fluted tapered"[32]—do not seem to have been made or worn at Chanhu-daro at all; on the other hand, some beads from that city apparently occur nowhere else. All these localized products are in the softer materials, such as faience and steatite, and were evidently made to oblige the prevailing fashion in each particular settlement.

Decorated Carnelian Beads (Pl. LXXIX, 1-16)

Among the numerous specimens of this type of bead many were found unfinished, broken in boring, or rejected on account of bad colour and the like, thus proving that they were actually made at Chanhu-daro and not imported.

Mr. Horace Beck in a most interesting article on the subject of these beads,[33] places them under the following three headings:

[32] *F. E. M.*, pp. 509, 511, 515.
[33] *Antiquaries Journal*, vol. XIII, pp. 384-398.

(I) White on red. The most common type.

(II) Black on a white coloured base (found at Mohenjo-daro, Taxila, Baluchistan, Tell Asmar, and Ur).

(III) Black on a red ground (found at Taxila and Harappā).

Only specimens of the first two types have come to light at Chanhu-daro, Nos. 1-5, 7-9, 11, 13, 15, 16 in Pl. LXXIX coming under Type I, and Nos. 6, 10, 12, 14 under Type II. Examples of the more common Type I (i. e., white on red variety) have been unearthed at various sites in India as well as in Mesopotamia at Tell Asmar [34] and Ur.[35] Other examples come from Nineveh,[36] while Tepe Hissar in Western Persia has also provided several.[37] All these foreign examples bear the same devices as those appearing on the early Indian beads, and all are approximately of the same date.

Only one specimen belonging to Type II has appeared at Mohenjo-daro [38] and it is equally rare at Harappā. Four beads, three of them broken, have turned up at Chanhu-daro (Nos. 6, 10, 12, 14), all of which were evidently throw-outs.

Neither Chanhu-daro nor Mohenjo-daro has, as yet, produced the very rare Type III, with its pattern painted in black directly on the natural red surface of the carnelian. A specimen, as yet unpublished, is reported by Beck as coming from Harappā and a second has been found at Taxila. The latter is dated to the First Century A. D., some 2500 years later than the former, but there remains the possibility that it is a more ancient bead that had been picked up and worn again.

The patterns on the Type I beads were made by using for paint an alkali, such as carbonate of soda, and then fixing it by heat. The paint is left with a glossy white surface and adheres to the stone so firmly that it is almost impossible to remove it by fair means. This technique is still carried on in Persia, on the borders of China and Tibet, and sporadically in Sindh.[39] In the last province the juice of a plant is mixed with the alkali, presumably to keep it from flaking off the stone before it has been made fast by heat.

It is uncertain what medium was used to produce the black coloured patterns on the Type II beads. The white background was formed by flooding the red carnelian with the alkali, thus creating a white, opaque surface. Mr. Beck, in a personal communication states: "I have succeeded in making the black lines on whitened carnelians and agates. I have used copper, cobalt, and manganese, but have failed with lead and only got a very pale effect with iron. The cobalt is the easiest, but I think that the copper gives the closest resemblance. Manganese, unless very thickly done, has a rather purple appearance."

It is therefore possible that a copper solution was the paint used, but as the black

[34] Frankfort in *Illust. Lon. News*, Nov. 1, 1932, p. 504, fig. 7: and in "The Indus Civilization and the Near East," *Ann. Bib. Ind. Arch.*, 1932, pl. I (d, m).

[35] Woolley, *Royal Cemetery*, pl. 133.

[36] Thompson, *Archaeologia*, Vol. LXXIX, p. 143. These, however, may be late.

[37] E. F. Schmidt, "Tepe Hissar Excavations, 1931," p. 438, pl. CXLIV.

[38] *F. E. M.*, p. 505, pl. CXI, 4.

[39] Mackay, "Decorated Carnelian Beads," *Man*, Vol. XXXIII, sect. 150.

pattern on Bead No. 12 has a decided purplish tinge, a manganese paint may well have been employed in this particular case.

The greatest skill must have been required in the working of two out of these three types of beads. To apply fine, even lines, such as appear on the specimens in Pl. LXXIX, 13, 14, 16, on a hard, polished surface needed a sure hand and a well made brush or pen. The most difficult process of all, however, was the firing; personal experiment has proved how difficult this was; too much heat destroys the colour as well as the translucency of the stone, too little fails to fuse the alkali sufficiently.

Beads of Type II were by far the easier to decorate. There was no red colour to be anxious about and the white surface was comparatively easy to obtain. Even beads that had failed to survive the other two processes could have been altered to that used for Type II.

Few of the beads shown are in perfect condition. Some of them, for instance, Nos. 2, 5-7, 12, 15, have been broken in boring, a process which seems invariably to have been carried out after the beads were painted and fired.

The most popular pattern was the figure-of-eight appearing on Nos. 4-7. Four other beads, that are not illustrated here, bear the same motif;[40] another example was found by Mr. Majumdar in his early work at Chanhu-daro;[41] it also occurs on beads from Tell Asmar, Kish, and Ur. It is present, in combination with the trefoil motif, on the robe worn by the steatite figure of a priest or deity found some years ago at Mohenjo-daro.[42] The two joined circles composing it are generally empty, but occasionally their interiors are filled with small circles as in Nos. 9-11. No. 14 is a variation of the same pattern carried out in very fine lines. This figure-of-eight device is still in use in parts of India at the present day. It is said to be a protection against the Evil Eye and on this account is sometimes employed as a brand for cattle.[43] It occasionally appears on the early punch-marked coins.[44]

No. 8 in Pl. LXXIX has a guilloche pattern that is not found on carnelian beads outside India, although it often appears on Sumerian seals dating from Early Dynastic times and onwards.[45] The markings on beads Nos. 12, 13, 15 are identical with some on beads from the Royal Tombs at Ur.[46]

The chevron motif on No. 16 is again known on beads from Tell Asmar[47] and Ur.[48] This particular bead is of a most unusual dark red colour, but this in no way impairs the beauty and translucency of the stone. The white lines forming the pattern are extremely fine and regular.

[40] No. 940, Trench D(1), loc. 41, lev. − 4.4 ft.; No. 1120, Trench I(1), loc. 73, lev. − 3.2 ft.; No. 2669, Sq. 9/D, loc. 211, lev. + 9.5 ft.; No. 4221, Sq. 9/F, loc. 474, lev. + 10.8 ft.

[41] *Explorations in Sind*, pl. XVII, 25.

[42] *M. I. C.*, pl. XCVIII, 1, 2.

[43] "Evil Eye Brands," *Illust. Weekly, Times of India*, 26/4/31.

[44] J. Allen, "Ancient Indian Coins," *Cat. Brit. Mus.*, 1936. Index, IV, p. 7.

[45] For the use of this motif as a pictographic character on the Mohenjo-daro seals, see Smith and Gadd in *M. I. C.*, pl. CXXIV (clxxxii).

[46] Woolley, *Royal Cemetery*, pls. 133, 220.

[47] Frankfort, *Ann. Bib. Ind. Arch.*, 1932, pl. I(d).

[48] Woolley, *Royal Cemetery*, pl. 133.

The pattern painted on beads Nos. 12, 13, also popular at Mohenjo-daro[49] and on similar beads from the Royal Cemetery at Ur, is curiously enough not found on any other kind of objects. The motif on No. 15 is undoubtedly derived from the well-known divided circle design which, as we have already seen, appears on many objects of the Harappā Culture and was also popular in Sumer and far-away Crete.

It will have been noticed that these carnelian beads have been shaped to lie as flat as possible. The motif is always repeated on the reverse side of each bead.

Spacers (Pl. LXXX, 10-20)

The types shown in the above plate are well known in other centres of the Harappā Culture and therefore do not merit further description here. The materials of which they are made and other information concerning them will be found in the catalogue at the end of this report.

Terminals (Pls. LXXX, 21-25, LXXXV, 32)

No. 22 in Pl. LXXX measures 0.79 inch wide and is made in faience which has a greenish glaze. The separate ends of the strings of beads were first attached to a short bar of some kind, which was then inserted in the slot carved in the straight or inner side of this terminal; after this they were gathered together and passed through the hole to the opposite side where they were twisted into a cord by which the necklace could be tied.

No. 23 is roughly made of pottery and has no slip or ornamentation. Like the previous example it has a slot[50] to receive a tying-bar, which was probably fastened in with cement. The large size of this terminal (2.6 inches wide) suggests that it once formed part of a girdle composed of long, barrel-cylinder pottery beads similar to those shown in Pl. LXXXI, 25-30. Such a girdle must have been a fairly close copy of the magnificent carnelian and bronze specimen discovered some years ago at Mohenjo-daro,[51] where terminals very similar to this one but made in faience and of better workmanship, have also came to light.[52]

No. 24 is in faience, bearing traces of a green glaze. In this case each of the four strings of the necklace was passed through a separate hole. A fifth hole at the apex of the terminal took the cord by which the necklace was tied. This again is a variety known at Mohenjo-daro.[53]

No. 32 in Pl. LXXXV is roughly made in Amazon stone, a material which appears to have been liked but rarely used by the Harappā people.

Pendants (Pls. LXXX, 26-34, LXXXV, 27, 29, LXXXIX, 6, 18)

The pendants shown in Pl. LXXX are black or dark brown in colour and, with the exception of the first, are carved from a variety of hornblende. No. 26 is of dark grey steatite,

[49] *M. I. C.*, pl. CXLVI, 43; *F. E. M.*, pls. CXXV, 5; CXXXV, 3, 19(g).
[50] This slot measures 0.12 inch in width and depth.
[51] *M. I. C.*, pl. CLI, b(10).
[52] *F. E. M.*, pp. 520, 521; pls. CXXXIV, 24, CXXXVI, 47, etc.
[53] *M. I. C.*, pl. CXLVII, 27.

a most unusual material for an ornament of this kind. This type of pendant has been found in considerable numbers at Mohenjo-daro, in some cases in collections of jewellery. They would seem to have been attached to necklaces by means of threads or wires tied round the grooves which are always found in their upper portions. Nos. 32 and 34 are forms which, at present, are unknown elsewhere. The first is perforated with a hole and may originally have been one of several ornaments threaded side by side on a cord.

The pottery object, No. 27 in Pl. LXXXV, is probably an amulet of some kind. It is composed of three separate strips of clay and has a plain, flat back. No. 29 is in shell; its lower part is missing.

No. 6 in Pl. LXXXIX is made of steatite, dark grey in colour and 1.14 inches long. It is rectangular in section, measuring 0.5 by 0.3 inches at the base and tapering to 0.39 by 0.25 inches at the top. A roughly cut groove encircles its upper portion. No. 18 in the same plate is a pendant of shell, 2.45 inches long bored with a hole 0.11 inch in diameter.

Plate LXXXI. The parallel-sided beads seen in this plate (Nos. 1-24) are round, square, or elliptical in section and made of various materials such as vitreous paste, pottery, steatite, copper or bronze, Amazon stone, and lapis-lazuli. The last named examples (Nos. 5, 14, 20, 23) may be importations from Sumer, where this stone was much more abundantly used than in India. On the other hand two unfinished beads of it found at Chanhu-daro show that it was occasionally worked there.

No. 2 is cylindrical in form and made of coiled copper wire. Several of these wire beads were found in the "Great Cutting" at the depth of −20.5 feet.[54] No. 33 in Pl. LXXXV is a wire bead of a simpler kind, and Nos. 30 and 31 in the same plate may also have been beads. Only one bead like No. 2 has turned up at Mohenjo-daro; like it it is cylindrical in form.[55]

Nos. 17-19, 21 in Pl. LXXXI are made of either copper or bronze. The first two and last were found adhering together and must have belonged to the same necklace. Group No. 17 is composed of a brown and white barrel-shaped jasper bead with a cylindrical metal one on each side. No. 18 has lost one of its companion beads. The central bead of No. 21 is oval in section and made of variegated jaspar; the bronze ones flanking it are of similar shape. No. 19 is a plain bronze tubular bead which must have been worn on a very thick cord. Its present oval shape in section is perhaps due to earth pressure. A copper wire fills the interior of No. 22, which is of faience coated with a glaze that has now faded to a cream colour.

Cylindrical beads even smaller than those shown in Pl. LXXXI, 1 were made at Chanhu-daro. A mass of these appear in Pl. XCIII, 5 and will be mentioned again later on in this chapter.

The long, barrel-cylinder pottery beads, Nos. 25-30, in Pl. LXXXI were popular among the poorer people of the Harappā Culture. They are copies of carnelian beads and nearly all of them have, or had, burnished red slips to imitate the colour of the natural stone. One

[54] No. 5351. From Sq. 10/G, loc. 481.

[55] F. E. M., pl. CXXXVII, 96.

specimen, not illustrated, is made of grey coloured pottery.[56] These barrel-cylinder beads, which are often roughly made, were moulded with the fingers round a straw or stalk which burned away when the beads were fired, leaving behind a smooth and straight aperture. Many stone beads were made in this shape; some appear under numbers 31-36 in this plate and others in various stages of finish are illustrated in Pl. XCIII, 14.

Plate LXXXII. The long barrel-shaped beads shown in this plate are either round or elliptical in section and mostly made of faience or a vitreous paste, the latter being blue in colour. Many of the faience specimens have retained in a measure their original blue or green colour; in others this has entirely faded away although their glazes are still perfect. No. 13 in this material is particularly interesting on account of the longitudinal ridges on either side that show it was made in a closed mould. The hole inside this bead has corresponding ridges. No. 5 is of banded jasper, dark brown in the centre with a dark red band on either side and dark green ends. Jaspers of various kinds and tints, agate, breccia, steatite, and even dull coloured limestone were all used in the manufacture of this type of bead.

Nos. 14-22 are peculiar to Chanhu-daro and have appeared at levels ranging from −7.8 to +11.3 feet. All are made in faience with a white or cream-coloured surface, but patches of yellow pigment upon some of them are the remains of a decomposed glaze. A characteristic feature is the purple or brownish-black central band, which has been applied thickly and often very carelessly, the colouring being due to manganese. This make of bead may have suited a local demand; they are not found elsewhere and are unknown at Mohenjo-daro.

The stone of which No. 32 is made is a fossil, the scaly carapace and sternum of some creature being clearly distinguishable. The interest taken at Chanhu-daro in fossils is indicated by the three illustrated in Pl. XCIII, 21-23, while some of the patterns incised on dishes of food-stands (Pl. XXXVIII, 14, 16, 17, 19, 21) are, as already pointed out, derived from fossil ammonite shells. No. 38, of grey limestone, is unfinished; it was evidently waiting to have its angles rounded off.

Plate LXXXIII. The short-barrelled, globular, and disc-shaped beads in this plate (Nos. 1-42) are types well known at Mohenjo-daro. The materials of which they are made include pottery, faience, carnelian, onyx, quartz, hornblende, and shell.

The majority of the small disc-beads (Nos. 27-34), each with a well-defined median ridge, are in pottery or faience. The pottery examples (Nos. 30-33) are very carefully made and coated with a burnished red slip. Here again the intention was obviously to imitate carnelian, though surprisingly few beads of this exact type have been found made of that stone. Unfinished specimens in various stages of completion (Pl. LXXXVI, a, 1-3) and also an allied type without a ridge are, however, quite common.

Spherical beads in stone are very uncommon and no examples are known at Mohenjo-daro. In any case beads of this shape, even those in faience, were not much worn by the

[56] No. 1881, 2.12 inches long, from Trench G(1), lev. −8.7 ft.

Harappā people. No. 42, which is of pottery, is quite a new type and is hand-made without a slip.

The wafer beads, Nos. 35-41, 43, 44, are almost invariably made of glazed steatite or a steatite paste.[57] The type was an extremely popular one and large numbers are found on most Indus Valley sites. They vary considerably in size and thickness, are often of a black or light yellow colour, and occur more frequently in the lower than in the upper levels of a city. It is still uncertain how they were made; possibly the larger ones were punched out of thin sheets of stone or paste, the hole being formed at the same time. Quantities of very minute wafer beads in an unfinished condition were recovered from a bead-maker's shop; an enlarged view of one is shown in Pl. LXXXVI, a, 6. All of them had been bored, though obviously not completed.

Nos. 45-48 are a favourite variety of wafer bead, which was always made in faience, and bear a grooved pattern on both faces.

The carved steatite beads, Nos. 49-51, were also popular at Mohenjo-daro.[58] These take several forms and in most cases the pattern upon them is the trefoil, a motif that had a special significance for the people of the Harappā Culture. The cloisonnés formed by the trefoils were once filled in flush with the surface with a red paste or inlay.

Nos. 52 and 53 are segmented beads in faience, and numbers of these in various lengths have been found at Mohenjo-daro. Beads of this type and material are well known in Sumer; at Ur copies of them have been found in gold.[59] In Assyria they appeared in the "G" stratum at Ashur.[60] Examples in stone have been unearthed in Badarian settlements in Egypt,[61] and the type, in faience, was in use again in that country at the close of the Middle Kingdom. At Tepe Hissar in Western Persia a number of segmented beads in faience were found in a grave dated to Period III of that site,[62] while in Crete they were common, both in steatite and faience, the former belonging to the M. M. I Period and the latter to the M. M. III Period.[63] Finally faience examples have been recovered from Early Bronze Age burials in England,[64] which have now been proved to be importations from Egypt.

As these segmented beads have appeared over such a wide area, it is quite impossible to say where the type originated. Indeed such a simple form of bead need not have had a particular country of origin at all. At Chanhu-daro as well as at Mohenjo-daro such beads were produced by a kind of mass production. They were made in long rods which after glazing were to be divided into segments of uniform length.[65] The rods found at Chanhu-daro were too long and too delicate to have been used for any other purpose than to be broken into convenient lengths.

[57] Four examples of this type of bead have been found made of mother-of-pearl.

[58] *M. I. C.*, pl. CXLVI, 49, 55; *F. E. M.*, pls. CXXXVI, 57, 66, CXXXVII, 97, 98.

[59] Woolley, *Royal Cemetery*.

[60] A. W. Andrae, *Die Archaischen Ishtar-Tempel in Assur*, p. 82, fig. 61(c).

[61] Brunton and Caton-Thompson, *Badarian Civilization*, pl. XLIX.

[62] Schmidt, "Tepe Hissar Excavations, 1931," pl. CXLV (H. 490, a).

[63] Evans, *Palace of Minos*, Vol. II, p. 179.

[64] *Antiquity*, Vol. I, p. 427.

[65] *F. E. M.*, pl. CXXXVI, 6.

Nos. 54-56 are roughly made pottery beads coated with a red slip. This is a very rare type; two are reported from Mohenjo-daro and only three have been found at Chanhu-daro.

Of yellow agate, veined with white, No. 57 is an unfinished bead measuring 1.61 inches long and but 0.35 inch thick. It is unbored, and grinding has failed to remove many of the facets of its preliminary flaking. Beads of this particular shape and size are well known objects in Mesopotamia[66] and in Persia.[67]

Plate LXXXIV. Beads 1-3 in this plate are of a type that was particularly favoured by the people of the Harappā Culture; they are usually made in faience or the more enduring vitreous paste. No. 4 is an elbow-shaped bead of brown translucent agate with a high polish and veined with the same, but deeper, shade. It is elliptical in section and 0.15 inch thick. At Mohenjo-daro the nearest approach in shape to this bead is one composed of steatite paste and coloured to imitate decorated carnelian.[68] Other examples made in hard stones are known at Ur,[69] Merkes,[70] and Egypt.[71] None of these, however, has anything like the right-angled bend of our Chanhu-daro specimen.

No. 5, which is also of agate, is a most unusual shape for a bead in this hard material.

The tapered beads, Nos. 6 and 7, are in shell and probably alternated with beads of a similar shape but in a darker, contrasting colour. Their very large apertures show that they had been strung on a very thick cord. No. 8, which is also tapered, is made of a dark grey stone.

A grooved bead resembling Nos. 10 and 11 was unearthed at Mohenjo-daro,[72] but was round in section and carved in steatite, whereas the two we show are of pottery. This type of bead, it would appear, is peculiar to the Harappā civilization.

No. 12 is a carnelian bead with a *natural* white line round its margin. No. 13 is of yellow agate veined with red and although well shaped had been discarded unfinished owing to a serious flaw on one side.

Of the collection of pottery beads (Nos. 14-30) all but No. 20 are decorated in various ways with incised markings; the exception bears dark red patches applied on the natural surface of the pottery. Made of the same clay as that used for the pottery, they vary considerably in finish. Some of the better made have had their ends rubbed down so that they might fit closer together.[73] Nos. 25, 27, and 29 show traces of a bright red slip, the remainder possesses no slip at all. The levels at which they lay were widely divergent; No. 30 was uncovered as low as −18.2 and No. 19 as high as +15.6 feet. Beads of

[66] Mackay, *Anthropology Memoirs*, Field Museum, Chicago, Vol. I, pl. LX, 1, 2.

[67] Schmidt, "Tepe Hissar Excavations, 1931," pls. CXLIV, CXLVI.

[68] *F. E. M.*, p. 517; pls. CXI, 8, CXXXIX, 99.

[69] Woolley, *Royal Cemetery*, p. 372, fig. 79.

[70] Koldewey, *Excavations at Babylon*, p. 263, fig. 185.

[71] Edwards Collection, University College, London. This is made in onyx and dated to the Twelfth Dynasty.

[72] *F. E. M.*, pl. CXXXIV, 1.

[73] This treatment of the ends was a definite refinement and not caused by one bead rubbing against another.

exactly the same type have appeared on many sites in Sindh,[74] including Mohenjo-daro where they were very common.[75]

Plate LXXXV. Nos. 1-10, 19, 21, 28 in this plate are faience beads of a type that up to the present have been found on only two sites in India, namely Chanhu-daro and Lohumjo-daro, which are some sixty miles apart.[76] For this reason they were first assigned to the Jhukar Period, but eventually too many of them came to light at levels ranging from + 3.0 to + 13.2 feet for this to be likely. One bead (No. 5) was found on the summit of Mound I.

These very ornamental beads are made of a light grey paste, gritty to the feel, except two (Nos. 19, 21) which are composed of a yellow substance not unlike in appearance and feel that used for certain amulets from Mohenjo-daro.[77] Many of the examples shown have lost their colour but not their glaze. Nos. 5, 7, 10, 28 show a slight tinge of green. The glaze covering No. 20 is of a definite purple colour, manganese having been used instead of copper as the colouring agent. The bobbin-shaped bead No. 28 is different from the others but it, too, has been made in a mould; its glaze, which is well preserved in places, is apple-green in colour. The patterns on these beads vary somewhat; all were carved with a sharp instrument previous to glazing.

Nos. 11-18, 24-26 are undoubtedly allied to the beads described above. They are made in exactly the same way and like them are beaded at both ends. Three are incised with markings also of very much the same nature as on the beads above. The cores of Nos. 15, 17, 26 are light yellow in colour, and No. 17 shows evidence of a red-coloured glaze.[78] Beads of this sub-type are foreign also to Mohenjo-daro.

No. 22, which is made of lapis-lazuli, has already been included among the terminals. No. 23 is made of the same stone, which in this case is of poor quality. This last bead is rectangular in section and 0.47 inch thick; for some reason a part of its lower end has been cut away.

The shell ornament No. 34 has been accidentally burned and is now much warped. It averages 0.75 inch high and is possibly a fitting of some kind rather than a bead.

Plate LXXXVI, b. Nos. 1-6 in this plate are small shells, four of them being cowries. The spires of Nos. 1 and 6 have been removed to convert them into beads; the cowry No. 2 has been bored for the same reason. The remaining shells have no holes at all or other means of attachment and may, therefore, have been preserved as curios by their former owners. No. 3 is the largest of the six and measures 1.9 inches in length.

Shells actually used as beads, as distinct from beads made of shell, were not very popular with the people of the Harappā Culture; cowries are particulary rare, Mohenjo-

[74] Majumdar, *Explorations in Sind*, pl. XXXIII, 35, 36, 70, 71, 82.
[75] *F. E. M.*, pp. 514, 515; pls. CXXXVI, 11, CXXXIX, 48, 49.
[76] Majumdar, *Explorations in Sind*, p. 52, pl. XXXIII, 10.
[77] *F. E. M.*, p. 350; pls. XCI, 1, XCII, 2, 3, 10, CII, 3, 9.
[78] Red glazes are also known at Mohenjo-daro. *M. I. C.*, p. 686; *F. E. M.*, p. 417.

daro having produced only one specimen.[79] The remaining objects in this plate will be explained later.

Plate LXXXVII (Jhukar Beads). No. 1 is a section of the Jhukar bead-seal illustrated in Pl. L, 4, 4a and described in Chapter IX.

The long-barrel faience beads Nos. 2-7 are round in section, rather carelessly fashioned, and bear roughly incised markings. Their cores consist of a gritty paste, light grey in colour and thickly coated with a glaze that is now light green. No. 7a, although undecorated, certainly belongs to this series and was found, with other beads of the same type, with the head-cone shown in Pl. XXIX, 68. These beads are undoubtedly of Jhukar workmanship. Most of them were found at levels ranging from 16.7 to as much as 22.7 feet above datum level. Though the form is common, the very distinct and unusual markings show them to be foreign to anything made by the people of the earlier culture.

The strange-looking beads Nos. 8-10 are also made in faience. Two of these were found at high levels and a third (No. 9) was taken from the foot of Mound II. All three are round in section and shaped entirely by hand; only one has retained its original green colour.

The bi-cones, Nos. 11-19, 21, are all round in section and made of pottery. Beads of this type were found in large numbers at Chanhu-daro at the average level of + 16.6 feet, and many also were uncovered on the outskirts of Mound II where they had been carried by erosion. The great majority are made of a grey clay; a few are pink or drab in colour, No. 19 being of the last. The surfaces of some of these beads show a certain amount of faceting due to careful paring after they had been first moulded into shape by hand, which treatment also accentuated their pronounced median ridges. Some of these beads show distinct traces of polish, others such as Nos. 11 and 14, are coated with a black slip. No beads of this particular make were worn at Mohenjo-daro.

Nos. 20, 23 and 24 are faience seal-amulets of Jhukar workmanship and described in Chapter IX.

Jhangar Bead

The large bead No. 22 in Pl. LXXXVII (see also Pl. LXXXVI, b, 7) is made of a dark grey clay that contains much carbonized matter. It is roughly made and the incised triangular pattern it bears correlates it with the incised pottery of the Jhangar Period illustrated in Pl. XXXIX, 1-8. A bead, not unlike this one, but described as unburnt, was unearthed at the site of Jhangar itself.[80]

Materials Used in Bead-making

Agate and carnelian were the materials most generally used in the manufacture of beads during the Harappā Period, carnelian being decidedly the rarer. Next follow faience and vitreous paste, while steatite, or a substance formed from it, comes a bad fifth. Pottery was also quite common and is next on the list. Beads made of other materials were dis-

[79] *F. E. M.*, p. 582.

[80] Majumdar, *Explorations in Sind*, pl. XXXIII, 64.

covered in the following quantities: copper or bronze (16 beads); shell (16 beads); lapis-lazuli (15 beads); jasper (14 beads); a variety of hornblende (13 pendants and beads); crystal (10 beads and lumps); quartz (8 beads); Amazon stone (8 beads); chalcedony (7 beads); limestone (5 beads); onyx (4 beads); fuchsite-quartzite (2 beads); haematite (1 bead); breccia (1 bead); plasma (1 bead). No amethyst beads were found, but two masses of this stone came to light, one of these being illustrated in Pl. XCIII, 2.[81]

Two unfinished beads of lapis-lazuli prove that this stone was actually worked at Chanhu-daro; the finished specimens are not, therefore, likely to be importations. The source of this mineral is thought to be Badakshān,[82] while new provenances for Amazonite (eight beads of which have been found, as against only three at Mohenjo-daro) is, according to Mr. D. H. Gordon, to be found in the pegmatites near Jhajha (Monghyr District, Bihar), the Nellore District of Madras,[83] and near the village of Derol, just north of Ahmadabād.[84]

The two beads of fuchsite-quartzite are particularly interesting, for, although this rare mineral was never used for beads at Mohenjo-daro, a large cup carved in almost pure fuchsite was found there, together with a collection of copper and bronze tools and other objects.[85] The colour of this stone is light green and its source, according to the Geological Survey of India, is most probably Mysore.[86]

Four wafer-shaped mother-of-pearl beads were unearthed together in Square 9/C, locus 206 at the level + 9.7 feet. Beads of this particular substance are very rare, Mohenjo-daro having produced only one example.[87] Jade seems never to have been worked at Chanhu-daro at all, and this statement also applies to various other stones that were used for beads at Mohenjo-daro.

A large number of nodules of carnelian and agate were discovered in Squares 7/C, 7/F, 9/C, and 9/D (see Pls. IV, XCIII, 17-20), the former being as a rule easily distinguishable from the latter by the darkness of its skin. Some of these nodules have been slightly chipped, as if an attempt had been made to see the colour within, and a considerable quantity was found in a bead-maker's workshop in Square 9/D, room 215 at the level + 10.4 feet. It is, of course, impossible to say whether these nodules had been burnt to improve their colour before or after their arrival at Chanhu-daro.[88]

Small blocks of steatite in light yellow, dark grey, and black were not uncommon in various parts of Mound II. Many of them bear the marks of the saw which had cut them up into shapes suitable for both beads and seals. Pieces that could not be used for any other purpose were ground into powder and then compressed into blocks, from which

[81] The second lump (No. 3417) was found in Sq. 7/E, loc. 306, lev. + 6.6 ft.

[82] *M. I. C.*, pp. 542, 543.

[83] *Man*, 1925, sect. 49.

[84] *Iraq*, vol. VII, 1940, p. 9. This last source is roughly 350 miles distant from Chanhu-daro.

[85] *F. E. M.*, pls. CXVI, 2, CXVIII, 9.

[86] *Op. cit.*, pp. 320, 321. I have to thank Dr. A. M. Heron for the identification of the two Chanhu-daro beads.

[87] *Op. cit.*, p. 497, pl. CXXXVII, 43.

[88] Possible sources for the raw material are given by Sir Edwin Pascoe in *M. I. C.*, p. 681. See also A. J. Arkell, "Cambay and the Bead Trade," *Antiquity*, Vol. X, pp. 292-305.

beads and even occasionally seals were made. This made-up steatite is always white in colour and was probably calcined before compression. It is often very difficult to detect, especially as objects composed of it are more often than not coated with a glaze. The composition is apt to crumble after long sojourn in a salty soil, whereas the natural stone remains unaffected.

Mr. Horace Beck, however, is not disposed to agree that reformed steatite was used by the people of the Harappā Culture.[89] Dr. F. A. Bannister, of the Mineral Department of the British Museum, informs me that steatite paste would become indistinguishable from the natural material after being subjected to a very high temperature. Steatite beads were sometimes heated to a temperature exceeding 1200° C. in ancient India and it has been proved that the heap of minute beads in Pl. XCIII, 5, which will be described later, was treated to this degree of heat.[90] These beads must have been composed of a paste which could be forced through fine tubular instruments similar to those appearing in Pl. LXXX, 1-8.

As already pointed out, faience beads were sometimes shaped in a mould, the holes being made at the same time. One unglazed cylindrical bead, which had undergone this moulding process, has been left unbored, and though the operation could easily have been done afterwards in such soft material, it would have been simpler to do the two together.[91]

Traces of gold foil of appreciable thickness were found adhering to one of the copper beads, and it is, indeed, quite possible that many of the beads and bangles in this metal were originally thus covered. A bronze bead coated with thin gold is reported also from Mohenjo-daro.[92]

Bead-making

The majority of the beads found at Chanhu-daro were unfinished, and a certain amount of information concerning the various technical processes used in the making of them has already been published.[93] It seems unnecessary, therefore, to recapitulate what has already been said on this subject.

Nos. 1-3 in Pl. LXXXVI, a, are disc-shaped carnelian beads that are made as shown in No. 2 from roughly flaked stone blanks averaging 0.58 inch in diameter and 0.21 inch thick. Each of these beads has been bored with a chert drill of the type that appears in Pl. XCIII, 6-8. All the holes are splintered rather than cut and would have to be smoothed down and polished later. Before this was done, however, the beads were shaped by grinding, as No. 1 shows. A number of these were probably strung on a thread, or, more likely still, a piece of copper wire, and then rolled to and fro on grit-stones of various grades, each bead allowed sufficient play for its rounded edge to be properly formed. Those illustrated in No. 1 are well on the way to completion and average 0.33 inch in diameter. They were found associated with the bored blanks in No. 2, in a building which had been given over to the craft of bead-making for several generations. Nos. 3a, 3b are micro-

[89] "Notes on Glazed Stones (Glazed Steatite)," *Ancient Egypt and the East*, 1934, pp. 1-15.

[90] Mackay, "Bead Making in Ancient Sind," *Journ. Amer. Orient. Soc.*, Vol. 57, pp. 11, 12.

[91] No. 2560; from Sq. 9/C, loc. 244, lev. + 9.3 ft.

[92] *F. E. M.*, p. 501.

[93] Mackay, "Bead Making in Ancient Sind," *Journ. Amer. Orien. Soc.*, Vol. 57, pp. 1-15.

photographs, enlarged three times, of one of the unfinished beads in No. 2. The first is a sectional view and shows how these beads were bored from both sides, the borings meeting in a hole in the middle; it depicts clearly the rough surface left by the drill which had to be smoothed down later.

No. 9 in Pl. LXXXVI, b is a slip or bar of agate, 3.30 inches in length and roughly rectangular in section. It had first been severed from the parent nodule by sawing and then by splitting. The saw used may well have been of the type shown in Pl. LXIII, 1, and the kerf it left can be clearly seen in the longitudinal line bisecting the photograph. A saw made of so soft a metal as copper or bronze would, however, have been useless without the aid of an abrasive such as emery or powdered quartz, but given these, a copper saw would be more effective than one in a harder metal.

The group in Pl. XCIII, 14, a-e illustrates the various stages through which a bead of the long barrel-cylinder type had to pass before it was completed. The shaping was carried out entirely by careful flaking (beads d and e), and when this was over the beads were ground on hones of varying grades, similar to those appearing in Nos. 9, 10, 15 on the same plate. When all depressions and irregularities had been smoothed away by grinding (partly performed in beads b and c), the object was then polished (bead a). It is not yet known how this last process was carried out. A finely divided iron oxide used in conjunction with a leather-covered board would have been admirable for this purpose.

Before this final finish took place, however, the bead, as already mentioned, had to be bored, a process that was carried out from both ends by means of a drill similar to one of those in Pl. LXXXVI, b, 8. The working end of these drills (shown point downwards in the photograph) was provided with a small depression to hold the fine abrasive and water that gave the drill the necessary bite. This depression can be seen very clearly in the micro-photograph (× 12 times) in Pl. LXXXVI, a, 5, while No. 4 in the same plate, which depicts the end of a bead broken in drilling (× 9), distinctly shows the small pimple formed by the cavity in the drill. In the case of hard stone beads such as these it was impossible to

PERSONAL ORNAMENTS 211

photographs, enlarged three times, of one of the unfinished beads in No. 2. The first is a

In spite of the care that must have been exercised in using such brittle instruments, the number of breakages must have been immense. Broken drills were found everywhere in Mound II and though these might have served again in the boring of the shorter hard-stone beads, it is obvious that the drill-makers, if, indeed, the bead-makers did not manufacture their own tools, must have been hard put to it to supply the demand.

Though unfinished beads of hard stones have been found on many Sumerian sites, only one stone drill, of the type just described, has been found in that country. This was identified by Mr. Beck among some objects from Ur, who first of all classed it, on account of the cavity in its point, as an unfinished bead.[96] Indeed, it is not at all unlikely that bead-making in Sumer was carried on by Indian craftsmen.

No. 6 in Pl. LXXXVI, a, is a micro-photograph (× 25) of one of a large collection of unfinished wafer-shaped beads in a dark-brown steatite. The specimen illustrated actually measures 0.15 inch across its widest part. Mr. Beck, who has examined some of these beads, writes to me as follows: "This find is of great interest. It consists of a great number of small flat plates of steatite which have been perforated, and is evidently a collection of partly made beads. Marks made by files or abrasive on the flat surfaces of the plates show that they have been worked down to the length of the bead. These plates are either unfinished beads in the process of manufacture, or beads that have for some reason been discarded when only half made. The thickness of the plates varies from 0.12 to 0.02 inch in the specimens measured. It is interesting that they are made of steatite that does not appear to have been treated by burning."

How these very minute plates were bored remains an unsolved problem, for the holes in them average 0.369 mm. in diameter and are sometimes far from round. The polish caused by the boring tool is well seen in Pl. LXXXVI, a, 6. Possibly they were held by moisture on the tip of the finger and a fine metal point used, a task that could be easily performed by a person with good sight; the stone, moreover, is extremely soft. The beads may well have been rounded off after they had been tightly strung together on a wire or thread.

Plate XCIII. Nos. 1-4 are masses of stone ready to be cut up for beads. The first is a lump of crystal, 2.0 inches in length, the second is of amethyst, of a pale violet colour, and the third and fourth of carnelian, both of a light pink colour.

The pile of minute steatite beads, No. 5, was an exceptional find. They were treated with a preservative directly they were uncovered and photographed at once. The manner in which these beads lie in lines on the pile proves that they were originally strung together, indeed, the microscope has revealed traces of thread inside some of them. They are not glazed, and the stringing may have been done as a preliminary to this process. Under them is a little copper pan that possibly belonged to a pair of scales and suggests that they were sold by weight. A small pottery jar (No. 4014), standing 1.8 inches high and containing a large number of these beads, was found in the "Cutting."[97]

of these drills has a roughly faceted end so that it could be fixed without risk of turning in a chuck or apparatus worked with a bow.

[96] The writer made the same mistake when the first of these drills appeared at Chanhu-daro.

[97] Sq. 9/F, loc. 404, lev. + 2.94 ft.

Drs. F. A. Bannister and G. F. Claringbull, of the Mineral Department of the British Museum (Natural History), who have examined some of these beads, report on them as follows: "The beads submitted to us are small hollow cylinders which vary in external diameter from ½ (.019 inch) to 1 mm., and in length from ½ to 1½ mm. When freed from loosely adherent soil they are pure white and very hard. Nearly every bead is furrowed along its length spirally, always in a clockwise direction. It is not uncommon to find two beads joined together with the spiral furrowing running continuously and in perfect alignment from one to the other. We have carefully examined alternative views of how these tiny beads were made, but so far have been unable to reconcile all our observations with any one theory. The physical and chemical data are conclusive, however, as to the material from which these beads were made. Their specific gravity is 2.85 and the refractive index of crushed fragments is 1.60. The beads can only be fused in the electric arc, and then yield glassy spheres with a lower specific gravity 2.72. Magnesium and silicon but no other elements could be detected with the quartz spectograph and X-ray powder photographs show that the beads are steatite that has been completely dehydrated and heated to a temperature exceeding 1200° C."[98]

The furrowing that Drs. Bannister and Claringbull speak of strongly supports the theory that these beads were made from a steatite paste with the aid of the instruments shown in Pl. LXXX, 1-8 and described in Chapter XII. A thick, wet substance forced through a minute copper tube would necessarily show on its outer surface any imperfections present on the interior surface of the tube, as, for instance, the seam. The fact that this grooving is continuous and in alignment on two beads adhering together, further increases the probability that these minute cylindrical specimens were shaped by mechanical means.

Mr. Beck informs me that similar beads have been found at Harappā,[99] but that the Chanhu-daro examples are more uniform in size and rather smaller. At Ur great numbers were discovered, but they varied considerably in size, and, being associated with small beads of carnelian and lapis-lazuli, are thought to have formed part of a girdle. The smallest of the specimens from Ur measured 0.04 inch in diameter.

Some minute faience beads found in Egypt many years ago and thought extraordinary because they numbered 93 to a grain weight[100] no longer hold the record in this respect, for the Chanhu-daro beads number 150 to the grain.

Nos. 6-8 in Pl. XCIII are three drills of light grey or brown chert, the first of which measures 2.43 inches long, and came, with another similar drill, from the workshop that contained the unfinished beads shown in Pl. LXXXVI, a, 1, 2.

The irregular sandstone block, No. 10, is dark grey in colour and measures 12.25 inches long. The deep lateral grooves were formed by beads being rubbed into shape upon it. Both the stones Nos. 9 and 15 are of grey sandstone. The first measures 9.01 inches long; its top and base are nearly flat. The carnelian bead that rests upon it was

[98] The above observations are taken from the article by Mackay in *Journ. Amer. Orien. Soc.*, Vol. 57, No. 1, pp. 11, 12.

[99] These have not yet been published.

[100] Petrie, *Illahun, Kahun and Gurob*, p. 23. These were found in a small wooden box in the tomb of Maket at Kahun and are dated to the Twelfth Dynasty.

not found with this stone, but has been put there to indicate the way the stone was used.[101] Each end of these long beads was rubbed down separately in order to preserve the barrel-shape formed in the preliminary flaking. The second stone No. 15, is 3.2 inches long. It has three grooves, slightly polished by wear, on one side and a fourth on the reverse. Whether an abrasive was employed with these stones to assist the grinding or only water was used is uncertain. Numbers of these stones in various shapes and sizes were taken from Mound II.

Nos. 11 and 16 are dark grey sandstone hones in the form of animals. The first is 9.45 inches long and has four separate feet. The eyes are in relief and the figure once possessed, as we learn from Mohenjo-daro, a thick, short tail held horizontally. The lateral grooves on the back prove this object to have been a hone. No. 16 is 9.6 inches long and of rougher workmanship. Exactly similar and, in one case, better preserved animal figures have come from Mohenjo-daro; there, too, they were used as hones.[102] These figures resemble a mongoose rather than any other animal.

Nos. 12 and 13 are bead-making implements either of copper or bronze. They appear in outline in Pl. LXXX, 1, 2, and a detailed description of them will be found in Chapter XII.

The separate beads shown in No. 14 come from different parts and levels of Mound II. The longest specimen (c), of yellow agate, measures 3.63 inches in length and is slightly rectangular in section. Its flaking had been completed and it was ready for its final shaping on a stone. No. 14(b), of yellow agate, is 3.0 inches long, and though it is yet far from round much has been done in removing its angles. No. 14(a) is a finished carnelian bead of a clear red colour, skilfully polished and bored; it measures 2.27 inches long.

The four objects, Nos. 17-20, are carnelian nodules with red-brown surfaces, which were found with many others, including agate, with a number of unfinished beads, in a bead-maker's workshop. Some of these nodules are so translucent that it is possible, despite their rough cortical surfaces, to inspect their interiors in a strong light. Several of them that were broken show that the colour inside is rarely uniform; yellow and brown areas occur mixed with the red.

There is some reason for believing that the beads made from this raw material underwent a further treatment to redden them. Practically all the unfinished beads show mixed colouring, whereas the finished ones are usually of a flawless uniform red. Various methods are used in Europe as well as in India at the present day to convert agates into carnelians and it would seem that the lapidaries of Chanhu-daro were conversant with at least one of them. For instance, agates or defective carnelians can be turned a uniform red by heating them in a crucible with either unslaked lime or iron filings.[103] The latter, of course, were not procurable in ancient India, but a natural oxide of iron would, no doubt, have been made to serve the same purpose.

[101] This bead measures 2.48 ins. long and 0.39 in. in diameter in its middle.

[102] *M. I. C.*, p. 465, pl. CXXX, 24; *F. E. M.*, p. 406, pl. LXXI, 24.

[103] Streeter, *Precious Stones and Gems*, p. 47.

Chapter XIV

MISCELLANEOUS OBJECTS

The main measurements of each specimen mentioned in this Chapter, together with many other particulars, will be found in the Catalogue of Objects at the end of this book.

OBJECTS OF CLAY

Drain-pipes (Pls. LXXXVIII, 14-18, XC, 30-33)

Pottery drain pipes were evidently much used at Chanhu-daro, but only in one place have they been found undisturbed.[1] Although the two pipes discovered in Square 9/C, locus 212 were lying close together when unearthed, they had, as a matter of fact, been removed from their original position and probably belonged originally to a little privy close by, of which only the pavement remained.[2] The other specimens illustrated come from various parts of Mound II. These had evidently been torn up and discarded as not worth using again.[3]

All these drain-pipes are the work of the people of the Harappā Culture and they fall into three distinct categories:

(a) Simple tapered pipes (Pls. LXXXVIII, 17, 18, XC, 30, 31).
(b) Pipes with spigoted ends (Pls. LXXXVIII, 14-16, XC, 32, 33).
(c) Spigoted pipes with projecting flanges.

Type (a) is the simplest of the three; examples were found at levels ranging from − 10.8 to + 8.5 feet. No. 17 in Pl. LXXXVIII has almost parallel sides, and the taper in No. 18 really commences about three-quarters of the way up.

Type (b) has more or less well-defined spigoted ends, this feature being less noticeable in the case of No. 16 in Pl. LXXXVIII than in the other examples. The type has been found at levels varying from + 9.3 to + 11.7 and is undoubtedly an improvement on Type (a).

Type (c) has not yet appeared at Chanhu-daro, although it was fairly common at Mohenjo-daro.[4] It differs from (b) in having a stout projecting flange round the base of the spigot, an attachment which doubtless helped to anchor the pipe itself, as well as provide a butt to the one that fitted it.

All these pipes are wheel-made; markings that occur on the outside of some prove that

[1] Trench H(1); Pls. III, X(b), LXXXVIII, 18, XC, 30.

[2] See Pls. IV, XVI(e), LXXXVIII, 14, 15.

[3] Doubtless these objects were handled with some reluctance, as was certainly the case with the paving bricks of privies.

[4] *M. I. C.*, pl. LXXXIII, 5; *F. E. M.*, pls. CVIII, 30, CX, 35.

they were tied round with cords to prevent warping or cracking while being dried before baking. They are made of ordinary clay plentifully tempered with sand and lime.

The inside of a pipe is, as a rule, better finished than the outside, except for unavoidable wheel striations. It would seem that the potter appreciated the importance of a smooth interior; a roughly finished exterior would, of course, be an advantage in an object of this kind. The concave sides of No. 15 are possibly intentional, for a pipe of this form was less likely to slide from its position and become disconnected.

A drain-pipe closely resembling the simple and older Type (a) came to light some years ago at Al-'Ubaid in Sumer and belongs to a very early period.[5] Type (b) is represented in Crete where it takes a form very much like No. 16 in Pl. LXXXVIII.[6] A similar variety was in use at late as Byzantine times at Jerash in Transjordan.

Pipes very similar to Type (c) have been found at Tell Asmar in Sumer and dated there to the Third Dynasty of Ur,[7] and examples unearthed at Knossos have been assigned to the Middle Minoan Period.[8] The Minoan pipes, however, differ from the Indian examples in having perforated lugs on their outside. These were probably intended to take lashings to bind the various sections together or, alternatively, to prevent these sections from moving when once placed in position; in any case, attachments of this kind would not have been required for lifting such light pipes. The earliest flanged specimen extant comes from Ur, and was found by Sir Leonard Woolley in the pre-Flood town which he dates to 3,500 B. C.

Drain-pipes were occasionally placed in vertical positions at Mohenjo-daro and embedded in brickwork.[9] At that site gypsum was sometimes used for the joints, whereas at Chanhu-daro mud was the only material employed to lute the various segments together.

Gutters (Pl. XCI, 17-19)

Gutters were sometimes formed by scooping out the face of a brick, as Nos. 17 and 18 show. This type of channel was frequently used to carry water away from bathrooms and privies and specimens sometimes appear in their walls at pavement level. At Mohenjo-daro, where they have often come to light in their original position, they took the water through or from a wall to a cess pit or jar in the street outside.[10]

No. 17 is an ordinary brick in which has been cut a longitudinal channel, 3.5 inches wide and 1.5 inches deep. A similar channel in No. 18 measures 4.2 inches wide and 1.0 inch deep, the bases of both these hollows being curved. The end of the brick in No. 18 has been cut away slantwise at an angle of about 45°, either to fit it more closely to another brick cut in reverse manner or to hasten the flow of water down it; the floor of the channel itself slopes gradually towards this cut.

[5] H. R. Hall, *A Season's Work at Ur*, p. 272, fig. 253.
[6] H. B. Hawes, *Gournia*, pl. I, fig. 22.
[7] Frankfort, *Tell Asmar, Khafaje and Khorsabad*, II, p. 21, fig. 14.
[8] Evans, *Palace of Minos*, I, pp. 141-3, figs. 103, 104; III, pp. 252-3.
[9] *M. I. C.*, pl. XLIV (a); *F. E. M.*, pl. XXXIX (d).
[10] *F. E. M.*, pl. XXXVIII (d).

No. 19 has been moulded entirely by hand and its measurements are somewhat irregular in consequence, the width inside varying from 4.2 to 3.1 inches and the inside height from 3.4 inches in the centre to 2.4 and 2.7 at either end. This runnel was found inserted in the end of the long pipe drain shown in Pl. X (b), but it is doubtful whether it was made originally for that purpose. Mohenjo-daro has produced several gutters of this kind which appear to have been expressly made to carry water from the roofs of houses.[11]

Pottery Tubes (Pls. LXXXVIII, 7-10, 12, 13, XC, 24, 25)

It is impossible to say definitely how these curious objects were used. They always have one end, generally the wider one, missing. At first it was thought that they might have belonged to jars, but spouted pottery, with the exception of the feeding-cup type shown in Pl. XXV, 56, 60, appears never to have been in use by the people of the Harappā Culture.[12] Again the appearance of the wider ends of these tubes, when intact as in Pl. LXXXVIII, 7, 8, proves that they could never have been attached to any vessel. The definite flange on No. 8 indicates that this tube was made to be inserted *in* something. It is not impossible that these peculiar objects were originally the nozzles of water-skins which are much used in eastern countries at the present day.

About a dozen of these tubes were discovered at Chanhu-daro at levels ranging from − 16.2 to + 14.3 feet, hence they do not belong to any one occupation. Two were unearthed at Mohenjo-daro at low levels.[13] All are fashioned of ordinary clay plentifully mixed with sand and mica and are ornamented with broad bands of red paint applied directly on the natural surface of the pottery. No. 8, which is 6 inches in length, has a flanged end projecting 0.24 inch above the surface of the tube, a feature to which reference has already been made. The mouths of Nos. 10 and 12 in the same plate and of Nos. 24 and 25 in Pl. XC are smoothly finished. The hole through No. 25 grades from 0.32 to 0.45 inches and that of No. 24, which is shown in line in Pl. LXXXVIII, 12 measures 0.71 inch at its wider end.

Another suggestion made is that these objects were used as flue apertures, but their very clean appearance, coupled with the fact that they show no trace of heat beyond that of ordinary firing, does not support this theory. Again, to decorate an object destined for such an ordinary purpose would surely have been quite unnecessary.

Bricks Adapted to Special Purposes (Pls. XCI, 14, 15, XCII, 1, 8, 34)

No. 14 in Pl. XCI is one of the many fragments which, as well as whole bricks, were used as door-sockets. The pivot hole in this particular specimen measures 1.92 inches in diameter and 0.7 inches deep, and curious dark red stains in the smoothly worn cavity suggest that the door itself was either painted red or that an oil of this colour was poured in the socket to stop a squeak.

[11] *F. E. M.*, pls. CIV, 19, CVII, 18.
[12] *M. I. C.*, p. 228.
[13] *F. E. M.*, p. 435, pl. CIX, 47, 53.

No. 15 has been made from a larger piece of brick, first, by cutting with a saw and then by rubbing on a flat stone. It was probably employed to fill an awkwardly-shaped place in the well-laid masonry of some bathroom pavement.

No. 1 in Pl. XCII shows two ordinary bricks that once formed part of a water-chute. They have identical slant cuts each being 7.5 inches wide and running at an angle of about 45°. The chute was probably composed of more than these two bricks; the others were possibly thrown aside when quarriers pulled down the wall in which it was set. No perfect chutes of this kind have as yet been found at Chanhu-daro due to the fact that the upper walls of most of the houses there were in a ruinous condition. At Mohenjo-daro, however, many perfect examples can still be seen.[14]

No. 8 in Pl. XCII is a brick that was made in a right-angled frame and was intended either for a corner of a wall or, more probably, to fill in an angle in a pavement.[15] No. 34 in the same plate has been carefully hollowed out along one of its longer sides, the curved cut being 8 inches across and 1.85 inches deep. This was perhaps one of a number of similar bricks arranged side by side to form a water-channel.

Grating (Pl. XCII, 20)

This object is estimated to have been 6.86 inches long and 6.0 inches wide when perfect. It is undecorated and is without a slip. The slits, which were roughly cut out when the clay was damp, average 2.23 by 0.61 inches. Articles of this kind, used to cover ventilation holes, are well known at Mohenjo-daro and were made in stone as well as pottery.

Pedestal (Pls. LXXXIX, 4, XCII, 36)

No. 4 in Pl. LXXXIX, which appears again in photograph in Pl. XCII, 36, is a copy in pottery of a type of stone stand represented at Mohenjo-daro by several examples.[16] Our particular example was made on a wheel, is well finished on the outside, and has no slip or decoration of any kind. Its hollow base, which as Pl. LXXXIX shows, is very uneven inside, suggests that this stand had a fixed position. The shallow flat recess in its top measures 2.4 inches across and 0.33 inch deep.

Such stands are invariably well made and in some cases decorated. They may have been intended to support a cult object, though nothing has as yet been found that could have fitted them. Several of these stands from Mohenjo-daro are provided with dowel-holes in their recessed tops proving that something had been permanently fixed upon them.[17]

Pottery Tables (Pl. XCI, 1, 2, 6-8)

With the exception of No. 1, whose top is too curved for anything to have stood safely upon it, all these small tables may have been used as toilet stands.

[14] *M. I. C.*, pls. LXXIII (c), LXXV (a); *F. E. M.*, pls. XXXVIII (b), XXIX (d).
[15] For a brick of similar shape see *M. I. C.*, pl. CXXX, 14.
[16] *M. I. C.*, pl. CXXXIII, 18; *F. E. M.*, pls. LXXI, 21, CIV, 22, 23, 26; CVI, 48, CVII, 35, 36.
[17] *F. E. M.*, pls. CIV, 26; CVII, 35.

No. 1 is decorated on all four sides with two lightly incised lines and is so carefully and solidly made that it still remains in perfect condition. It is composed of a clay that was mixed with an unusual amount of either coarse black sand or ground basalt. Its legs show evident signs of wear, indicating that this table had been much moved about. Judging from its curved top and the peculiar grittiness of the paste of which it is made, this object was probably a tool of some kind. It may have been used for dressing fine leathers by pulling them to and fro across its rough surface to remove hair or tissues. Nothing exactly resembling it is known at Mohenjo-daro.

No. 2 depicts the upper part of a table whose slightly convex top is covered with a cream slip and ornamented with red marginal bands and a spot of the same colour in the middle. It is without feet and stands rather unsteadily on the edges of its two longer sides. The same slip and decorative scheme appear on table No. 6; this last is of very rough workmanship, the underside and legs, which are 0.83 inch square, being carelessly finished.

No. 7 has lost its legs as well as both ends. It has a red band round the sides and is cross-hatched in the same colour on top. The upper surface of No. 8 is smooth and slightly concave, and is ornamented, as illustrated, with dark red paint applied on a cream-coloured wash; its underside and the little that remain of the legs show no attention to finish.

Three other tables which are not illustrated average 5.49 inches in length. The first (No. 1057) is unpainted except for a cream-coloured slip; the second (No. 2150) is ornamented at each corner with a pattern in red paint resembling that on No. 8, while the third (No. 2719) has a red marginal band round all four sides, like that on No. 2, and an additional band across the centre, which divides the top into two compartments.[18]

Two small stands much like the objects just described have appeared at Mohenjo-daro; one of these is in stone, the other in pottery.[19]

Portion of Mould(?) or Muffle(?) (Pls. LXXXVIII, 11, XCI, 35)

This mould, if mould it be, is the only one of its kind that has been found in any Indus city. Its flat surface is filled with depressions of various shapes and depths, the one marked "D" being the largest. The two holes "F" and "K," though not deep, may originally have held a peg by which the missing upper half was kept in place. With regard to the other cavities, "A" is 0.22 inch deep at one end and 0.12 inch deep at the other. The depths of the remaining holes are as follows: "B" 0.51 inch; "C," 0.42 inch; "D," 0.9 inch; "E," 0.57 inch; "F," 0.12 inch; "G," 0.35 inch; "H," 0.3 inch; "I," 0.24 inch; "J," 0.15 inch; and "K," 0.1 inch. Holes "H" and "K" have rounded bases.

The interiors of these cavities are far from smooth and in some cases even slightly undercut. It is evident, therefore, that articles cast in this mould must have been made of a substance that would shrink considerably in drying; otherwise they could not have been extracted at all. Alternatively, we may not have a mould here at all, but something intended

[18] No. 1057: Trench A(3), loc. 35, lev. −6.2 ft. No. 2150: Sq. 7/E, loc. 121, lev. + 13.3 ft. No. 2719: Sq. 9/E, loc. 200, lev. + 8.2 ft.

[19] *F. E. M.*, p. 395, pls. CVIII, 28, CIX, 23.

to hold small beads and the like while they were undergoing a firing process. In the latter event the depressions may have served as cradles and a hollow cover may have enclosed the whole. In other words, it may be more correct to describe this object as the base of a muffle.

Head-rests (Pls. LXXXIX, 3, XCII, 38)

The head-rest shown in Pl. LXXXIX, 3 is a small model measuring only 1.3 inches long. It is made of grey-coloured pottery and coated with a semi-polished black slip. Taking into account the fact that this object was found at the high level of + 16.1 feet and that head-rests were used only rarely, if at all, by the people of the Harappā Culture,[20] it appears likely that this little model was produced by one of the Jhukar or Jhangar people, most probably by one of the latter if the colour of its clay and the nature of its slip is any criterion.

The very fine head-rest illustrated in Pl. XCII, 38 is 12.3 inches in length, 2.4 inches thick at the base, and tapers to 1.6 inches at the top. It is coated with a cherry-coloured slip and adorned with various devices in a purplish-black paint. A portion has been hollowed out of each side to reduce the total weight; leaving a vertical pillar in the centre where the head would press most heavily. Perhaps to reduce its weight still further, triangular cuttings have been made in the walls on each side. This head-rest is in perfect condition except for a small piece missing from its left top end. It came to light at a high level in the "Great Cutting" where it lay in débris that had obviously been washed down from the top of Mound II. That it can be assigned to the Jhukar Period is certain from the nature and colouring of its decoration.

Ink-pot(?) (Pl. XCI, 3)

This little object, which has been badly knocked about, measures 1.89 inches in height and, although no stains or marks of its former contents appear inside, could have been used as an ink-pot. It is hand-made, without a slip, and of very careful workmanship, a roll down each of its four corners giving it distinction. The well inside, which is not perfectly round, averages 1.0 inches in diameter and 1.52 inches deep.

Rolling-pins(?) (Pl. XCI, 47-49)

Pottery cylinders of this type are also well known at Mohenjo-daro[21] and are thought to have been used to roll out the thin bread or *chapātis* that are so much used in India. With the exception of two stone specimens, one from Mohenjo-daro and the other from Chanhu-daro,[22] these objects are always in pottery, generally without a slip or wash. The length of Nos. 47-49 is 4.29, 3.3, and 3.18 inches respectively. The first two are fairly

[20] A very doubtful head-rest from Mohenjo-daro is made from an ordinary brick: *F. E. M.*, p. 428, pl. CVIII, 16.

[21] *F. E. M.*, p. 434, pl. CVIII, 22, 23.

[22] No. 2831 (not illustrated). Of cherty limestone and measuring 6.01 ins. long and 2.0 ins. in diameter. From Sq. 9/D, loc. 139, lev. + 8.4 ft.

well made, the last is not quite cylindrical and differs from the others in having rounded ends; its surface shows a considerable amount of weathering.

Whorls (Pl. XCII, 4-6)

These objects have also appeared at Mohenjo-daro[23] but we have yet to understand how they were used. No. 4, which is 1.5 inches in diameter, is roughly made and not quite round. A bi-conical hole, 0.09 inch in diameter in the centre and 0.29 inch on the outside, perforates this whorl vertically and round its circumference is a shallow groove measuring 0.11 inch wide and 0.05 inch deep. No. 5 is also not exact in shape. It is of much the same size as No. 4 and has a similar groove round the edge. The hole that perforates it is 0.15 inch in diameter. No. 6 is of better finish. It measures 1.9 inches in diameter and the hole through the centre is 0.3 inch wide. The deep slot encircling it averages 0.22 inch wide and 0.33 inch deep.

The generally accepted view is that these objects are spindle-whorls. They are seldom carefully made and in some cases (e.g. No. 4) the holes that pierce them are too small to have accommodated anything but a metal spindle. The grooves round their edges show no signs of wear and this feature still remains unexplained.

No. 7 in Pl. XCII is a different type. It measures 2.01 inches in diameter and has a domed top. A blind hole in the centre of the base is 0.14 inch in diameter and 0.39 inch in depth and is by no means sufficient to hold a spindle securely. Like the three whorls just described, this one is also grooved round the edge to a depth of 0.1 inch, but it differs from the others in having two small blind holes in the middle of its rounded top, together with horizontal holes on either side that meet in the middle of the object.

Net-sinkers (Pl. XCII, 9, 14)

These two objects, both of rectangular shape with grooves down their opposite sides, could have been employed usefully as net-sinkers. No. 9, which measures 3.1 inches in length, is pierced by an axial hole 0.15 inch in diameter. No. 14 is 2.6 inches long, but here the grooves, which average 0.16 inch in width and depth, do not coincide properly at the ends.

Pottery spoon (Pl. XCII, 25)

A portion of the handle, oval in section, of this spoon is missing, it now measures 4.6 inches in length. Roughly made of ordinary pink coloured clay, its bowl is so shallow that it could not have been of much use for anything except stirring, unless it was employed as a censer. Objects of this kind are unknown at Mohenjo-daro.

Model Tools (Pl. LXXXIX, 24, 30)

From their shape both these objects appear to be copies of the well known type of blade axe shown in Pl. LXVI, 3, 5, 15. They are carefully made and have double-sloped edges.

[23] *F. E. M.*, p. 419; pls. CV, 47, CIX, 51, 59.

No. 24 is 2.21 inches long and its edges have been rubbed down square upon a flat abrasive surface. Its mimic cutting edge was also formed in the same way. No. 30, which is 2.68 inches long, has slightly bevelled edges. Both these models were, as their slight curvature shows, formed from thick sherds; they may, therefore, have been the work of children. A considerable amount of skill and patience was exercised in making them.

Stopper(?) (Pls. XXIX, 69, XCI, 9)

An article such as this could have had various uses. It measures 1.56 inches long and a hole, 0.1 inch in diameter, perforates its shank. A string, or more probably a rivet, was probably passed through the hole to secure this object to something.

Pottery Handle (Pls. LXXXVIII, 6, XCI, 10)

This is undoubtedly a handle, but it appears to be unfinished; except for a shallow groove in the lower end, there is at present no way of attaching it to a blade. A hole to take the tang of a knife or dagger was probably to be drilled later. This interesting object—for handles of any kind are exceedingly scarce—measures 3.68 inches in length. A hole through its upper portion communicates with a vertical groove on either side so that a wrist cord passed through it might lie flush with the surface. Though a trifle out of shape the handle is well made but is without a slip or wash of any kind. The fact that it was found as deep as −20.5 feet in the "Great Cutting" is particularly interesting.

Brick With Imprint of Animal's Feet (Pl. LXXXVI, b, 11)

Bricks bearing the foot-prints of animals that have walked over them while drying in some brick-maker's yard are common objects in many ancient settlements. The example we illustrate, however, is unusual because it has been marked both by a cat and a dog. Dr. Glover M. Allen, who has examined this brick, states: "The two tracks on the brick must have been impressed when it was freshly laid out to dry in the sun. The one with the mark of the posterior lobe tripartite on the hind margin of the main lobe is that of a cat while the other with the hind margin of the main lobe evenly outlined is that of a dog. Claw marks seem to be indicated on that of the dog but not in the case of the cat's. The deep impress of the pads and their spread indicate the speed of both animals. Here then is a record of a prehistoric dog chasing a large prehistoric cat, the dog's imprint slightly overlapping the cat's shows that he came second."[24] This brick has one end missing and measures 5.2 inches wide and 2.32 inches thick.

Pottery Objects Still Unclassified (Pls. XCI, 16, XCII, 17, 18, 21, 23, 24, 26, 35, 37)

No. 16 in Pl. XCI is 2.5 inches long. Two holes, each 0.23 inch in diameter, have been bored through it, and it also has a deep groove at each end. Of very rough workmanship and may have been employed in some way in weaving.

[24] Two species of cat may be mentioned in this connection: *Felis bengalensis*, which is the size of a domestic cat but with longer legs, and *Felis viverrina*, the Fishing Cat of India. The latter is somewhat larger than the domestic cat, and, as the print on the brick is that of a *large* paw, it is possible that an animal of this type made the mark. (G. M. A.)

No. 17 in Pl. XCII is a coil of pottery that measures 1.4 inches across and is flat on the underside. It is perhaps an attempt to imitate an ammonite shell. As already pointed out, ammonite shells were reverenced by the people of the Harappā Culture, a practice continued by certain sects in India to the present day.

Numbers of round or triangular pottery plaques, resembling those illustrated in Nos. 18, 21, 23 and 26, have been unearthed at Mohenjo-daro and other kindred settlements of the Harappā Culture. One triangular specimen was found in the "Great Cutting" at Chanhu-daro at the level — 15.1 feet and many others were found below the level + 11.4 feet at which stratum they disappear. At Mohenjo-daro they occur as low down as — 42.0 ft.[25]

It is still uncertain how these objects were used; they may be model cakes intended for votive offerings. Some of them are carefully shaped, but all the pottery examples are made of a very inferior drab or straw-coloured clay, and they are always badly fired. No. 15 is a copy in sandstone of one of these plaques and a very similar one also came to light in one of our trenches.[26]

No. 24 in Pl. XCII, which resembles a jar-cover in shape, is 1.72 inches high. A blind hole in the centre of its flat top (or base) measures 0.41 inch in diameter and 1.55 inches deep. A number of very minute holes round the edge communicate with others irregularly spaced on top. A beaded edge round the lower part, or perhaps handle, of this object is broken in places. This very curious piece, which has been much over-baked, is now of a light grey colour. It is not impossible that we have here the body of a brush, in which case the hairs would have projected from the edge like those in a modern flue-brush. Examples unearthed at Troy show that some of the brushes used there had pottery bodies; in shape, however, they do not resemble in any way the object before us.[27] The hairs or fibres in this object must, of course, have been inserted after the body part had been baked. The holes may have been formed in the first place by a thin wire.

It is impossible to provide any indication of the real nature of Nos. 35 and 37. Both are exceptionally well made of a pinkish coloured paste coated with a thick, unpolished, cream-coloured slip, whose surface bears numerous straw markings that show the nature of the fuel used to bake them and recall the similar markings on much of the Jhukar pottery. Taking this latter fact into account and also remembering that these two objects came from the levels + 15.1 and + 16.1 respectively, it is reasonably safe to assign them to the Jhukar Period.

No. 35 measures 2.4 inches long, 1.03 inches wide, and 2.2 inches high, and is most carefully finished. It was obviously not made to stand in any particular position. No. 37 is 4.05 inches long and is oval in section, averaging 1.4 inches wide and 0.73 inch thick. Both ends are slightly flat and all angles have been neatly rounded off. These objects may enclose something of interest; it may be desirable at some future date to open them and find out.

[25] *F. E. M.*, p. 429, pl. CXII, 4.
[26] No. 2159, 4.12 ins. long. Trench J(1), loc. 73, lev. — 7.9 ft.
[27] Schliemann, *Ilios*, p. 414, nos. 488, 489; *Troy and its Remains*, p. 297, no. 217.

STONE OBJECTS

Mace-heads (Pls. LXXXIX, 16, 17, 19, 20, 22, 23, 25, 26, 29, XCII, 11, XCIII, 32-36)

Many examples of two different types of mace-heads were unearthed at Chanhu-daro, Mound I furnishing no less than six specimens. The material most commonly used is a hard, cherty limestone, which is grey, light yellow, or cream in colour. A purplish-grey sandstone was employed for No. 16 in Pl. LXXXIX and a hard, greenish-black stone for two others; one appearing in Pl. XCIII, 34.[28] A globular mace-head made in pottery was found on the summit of Mound II and may be of Jhukar manufacture. This was a badly made object measuring 2.15 inches in diameter and 1.3 inches in height, pierced by a straight hole, 0.45 inch in diameter.[29]

The maces of the Harappā Culture fall into three types:

(a) Lentoid (Pls. LXXXIX, 16, 17, XCIII, 32-34, 36).
(b) Spheroid (Pls. LXXXIX, 19-23, 25, 26, 29, XCII, 11, XCIII, 35).
(c) Pear-shaped. Not represented at Chanhu-daro.

Type (a) is very common and was equally well known at Mohenjo-daro and Harappā. The holes that pierce the heads of this type are almost always conical, showing that they were worked from either side. Their circumferential edges are either blunt as in Pl. LXXXIX, 16, or acute as in No. 17. This lentoid form is probably derived from a round, flat pebble, whose edges were sharpened. I have already compared this type with many European examples,[30] but a mace-head that I have seen in a private collection, made of a highly polished yellow stone and said to come from Shuruppak in Sumer, exactly resembles in shape the Indian Type (a). Lentoid maces are also well known at Susa and are found there at levels contemporary with those of the Indian sites.[31]

Type (b), of which a considerable number was found, are all, with the exception of the unfinished specimen in Pl. LXXXIX, 29, provided with blind holes in which their handles were originally set. In some cases, for instance Nos. 19, 25, 26 in Pl. LXXXIX and No. 11 in Pl. XCII, these holes are barely deep enough to hold a handle securely and they must therefore have been kept in place by some other means, as, for instance, lashings or a leather covering. A mace-head of this type found by the late Mr. Majumdar in his preliminary investigations at Chanhu-daro substantiates this notion.[32] The head in question, which is of alabaster, has a short, blind hole and is incised with criss-cross markings that are obviously intended to represent cord fastenings.

The hole in No. 25 in Pl. LXXXIX is much undercut, and this feature would have been of great advantage if its handle had been kept in place with a cement. No. 29

[28] The second (No. 4103) was found in Sq. 8/B, loc. 91, lev. + 8.7 ft.

[29] No. 1492. From Sq. 8/D, loc. 108, lev. + 17.4 ft.

[30] F. E. M., p. 398. See Childe, *Danube in Prehistory*, pp. 29, 65; *The Aryans*, p. 128.

[31] *Mém. Dél. en Perse*, t. I., p. 194, fig. 420; De Morgan, *La Préhistoire Orientale*, t. III, p. 101, fig. 1, a.

[32] *Explorations in Sind*, p. 44, pl. XII, 36.

in the same plate is unfinished, the work on its hole being not even begun. The deep groove round its lower portion would have been of some assistance in keeping thongs in place. No. 19, together with Nos. 23 and 29, already described, is distinguished by a beading round its base, a feature present also on a mace-head from Mohenjo-daro,[33] and another from Tepe Gawra in Iraq.[34]

No. 11 in Pl. XCII, which measures 1.95 inches high, is also unfinished. In this case the hole in its base, 0.9 inch in diameter and 0.7 inch deep, was bored with some kind of centre-bit and not with a tubular drill. The outside of this head, as the photograph shows, is far from finished.

Mace-heads of this spheroid form, bored with blind, and frequently very shallow, holes have been discovered in Sumer[35] and at various Persian sites.[36] A very similar type, but with a flattened base common to these two last countries, is unknown in India.

Of Types (a) and (b), the latter is the earlier; it occurs at Chanhu-daro as low as − 3.8 feet. The former first begins to appear at about datum level. Both types then continue in use together up to about + 13.3 feet.

The pear-shaped Type (c) has not yet appeared at Chanhu-daro, and was very rare at Mohenjo-daro.[37] It was evidently not a favoured form with the people of the Harappā Culture, though popular in Egypt, Sumer, Persia, and elsewhere.

Drill-heads (Pls. LXXXIX, 28, XCII, 2, 3, 10)

The roughly cut, shallow hole in the base of No. 28 in Pl. LXXXIX measures only 0.6 inch in diameter and 0.35 inch deep, but there seems to have been no intention to carry it any further. This one, which measures 1.9 inches high, should be regarded as an unused drill-head rather than an unfinished mace-head.

No. 2 in Pl. XCII is 1.5 inches high and made of a white limestone. Signs of definite wear inside its blind hole, which is 0.57 inch wide and 0.29 inch deep, show that it once formed part of a lathe or drill. No. 3 in the same plate measures 2.13 inches in diameter and has been cut from a hard black and white coloured stone; its cavity is 0.88 inch wide and 0.45 inch deep.

The cone-shaped object in Pl. XCII, 10, made from a hard stone of a cream colour mottled with red, was also a drill-head. Judging from its shape it was probably a fixture in a wooden socket. It measures 0.93 inches high and its conical hole, much polished through wear, is 1.3 inches across at its wider end.

Weights (Pls. LXXXIX, 9-11, XCI, 23-32)

The very interesting series of weights unearthed at Chanhu-daro is dealt with by

[33] *F. E. M.*, pls. CIX, 35, CX, 28.

[34] Speiser, *Excavations at Tepe Gawra*, vol. I, p. 87, pl. XLII, 2.

[35] Mackay, *Sumerian Palace and "A" Cemetery at Kish*, Field Museum, Chicago, p. 125, pl. XXXVII, 2.

[36] *Mém. Dél. en Perse*, t. XIII, p. 19, figs. 92, 93; Speiser, *Excavations at Tepe Gawra*, I, pp. 86, 87, pls. XL, a, 2; XLII, 1.

[37] *F. E. M.*, pl. CX, 22, 36.

Dr. A. S. Hemmy and Miss A. R. Hall in Chapter XV. There appears no doubt that these objects were actually manufactured on the site, or that weight-making was one of the crafts practised there in conjunction with bead-making. Many unfinished examples have been found in bead factories along with some exceptionally well made specimens, the latter apparently being used for testing purposes. No. 30 in Pl. XCI is an example of one of these master-weights.

These very distinctive products of the Harappā Culture are grouped in six main types, according to their shape: [38]

(a) Cube-shaped (Pl. XCI, 29-32).
(b) Spherical with flattened top and base (Pls. LXXXIX, 10, 11, XCI, 27, 28).
(c) Cylindrical with flat top and base (Pl. LXXXIX, 9).
(d) Conical with hole for rope or wire handle.
(e) Barrel-shaped.
(f) Pebble-weights (Pl. XCI, 23-26).

Types (d) and (e) have not come to light at Chanhu-daro.

Type (a) is by far the most common and is followed in order of popularity by Types (b) and (f). Only one example was found of Type (c), but this variety was also rare at Mohenjo-daro. The large weights that come under Type (d) and those of barrel-form (e) only occur in the upper levels of Mohenjo-daro; their absence, therefore, at Chanhu-daro is not surprising, seeing that, as already mentioned, the upper levels of the latter site are equivalent in date to the Intermediate levels of the former.

The pebble-weights belonging to Type (f) were not uncommon and were in all probability used by itinerant traders who had to carry about weights that could not easily be chipped or become defective. All these pebble weights have been rubbed down here and there to make them as accurate as possible, but even so they do not conform to the high standard of the well-shaped weights.

Plate LXXXIX. No. 9 of Type (c) is unfinished and was therefore not weighed. It is made from a brown and yellow agate and stands 0.11 inches high. No. 10 of Type (b) is also made of agate and is slightly chipped. It weighs 27.36 grammes and is 0.75 inch high. No. 11 of Type (b) is unfinished. It is 0.52 inch high and of agate.

Plate XCI. No. 23, of Type (f), measures 1.37 inches long and made of a dark grey pebble flecked with white. It weighs 27.19 grammes and is fairly regular in shape; both faces are slightly flattened by rubbing. No. 24, Type (f), is 1.74 inches long. It is made of an amphibole-schist, white in colour and speckled with black. In form it is an elongated egg and its weight is 30.28 grammes. No. 25, of Type (f), weighs 27.68 grammes and is a dark grey-green pebble with lighter bands of the same colour. Measuring 1.4 inches in length it is irregular in shape with a base that has been rubbed flat. No. 26, of Type (f), is of the same stone as No. 24. It is fairly regular in shape with a slightly flattened base, weighs 21.39 grammes and is 1.3 inches long. No. 27, of Type (b), is of light red quartzite,

[38] For a fuller description of these types see *F. E. M.*, pp. 400-404.

measures 2.11 inches high, and weighs 273.59 grammes. No. 28, Type (b), is made in a quartzite of a dark grey colour. It is well made with a smooth but unpolished surface. Its weight is 544.77 grammes, and it stands 2.4 inches high. No. 29, of Type (a), weighs 27.53 grammes. It is cut from a mottled dark and light grey chert, measures 1.0 inch long, 0.98 inch wide and 0.76 inch high. It has a semi-polished surface, and its angles are slightly bevelled. No. 30, of Type (a), is made of agate of a light brown colour veined with white. This weight, with its slightly bevelled edges, is so well finished and so highly polished that it is possible that it was used as a test piece. Weighing 27.66 grammes, it measures 1.0 inch long and wide and 0.77 inch high. No. 31, of Type (a), is made of yellow-grey chert veined with dark brown. It is well made with carefully rounded angles, and is unusually flat. Weight 27.14 grammes and dimensions 1.11 × 1.11 × 0.6 inches. No. 32, of Type (a), is of brown agate with yellow and grey markings. Although the sides of this weight are not perfectly plane it is highly polished and has carefully bevelled angles. Dimensions 0.9 × 0.9 × 0.9 inches; weight 27.34 grammes.

Whetstones (Pls. LXXXIX, 21, XCI, 36-39, XCIII, 9-11, 15, 16)

The stone in Pl. LXXXIX, 21 is an exceptionally well finished hone, 7.37 inches in length, made of a fine grained slate, grey-green in colour. The sides and base of this stone are remarkedly plane.

The other stones illustrated are of various shapes and sizes, and were probably used in bead-making. Those shown in Pl. XCIII, 9-11, 15, 16 have been described in the previous chapter on "Personal Ornaments." All are in sandstone of a dark grey or purple colour, excepting No. 37 in Pl. XCI, which is cream-coloured and of a finer grade than the others. The irregular slabs in Pl. XCI, 36, 39 have obviously seen much service. Blocks of this kind were frequently worn by use to an hour-glass form, like that of No. 36. No. 38, which is 4.4 inches long, is a hard, fine-grained stone that appears once to have been a pebble taken from a river-bed. The well formed stone No. 44, which measures 9.28 inches long, is provided with a hand-hold at one end; its grain is of medium fineness.

Saddle-querns (Pl. XCI, 33, 40)

These stones were very plentiful and all take more or less the shape of the two illustrated. No. 40 is a top view of one. They are made of a hard, grey-brown porous rock of igneous origin, and their undersides are invariably rounded and roughly trimmed, as is seen in No. 33. To prevent them from rocking while in use they must have been set in a wooden support or in well packed earth.

"Curry stones" was the name given to these objects by our Sindhi labourers, but it is unlikely that they were used exclusively for grinding herbs. It would, however, have been difficult to grind loose grain on their curved and narrow surfaces. The practice in some parts of India today is to soak the grain overnight and after removing the husks to grind the wet mass on a stone to a kind of dough; possibly this method was in use at Chanhu-daro and other kindred cities. The preliminary wetting process assists the grinding very considerably. The long upper stone used on these querns was held in both hands at right angles to the lower and in time wear reduced the upper stone to much the same shape as the nether one. These stones average 15 inches in length and are found at all levels; their kind is well known on most ancient sites of the Near and Middle East.

Leather-block(?) (Pl. XCI, 41)

Made from a cherty limestone of a light brown colour, this object measures 3.61 inches long and possibly belonged to a leather worker. Its smooth and markedly convex face shows signs of much polish through wear. It would seem once to have been a large pebble and its lower rounded part was probably fixed to a bench or upon a post. Stones similar to this one in shape and material have been unearthed at Mohenjo-daro.

Palettes (Pl. XCI, 34, 42, 43)

At least twelve of these objects were found, but few were in perfect condition. With one exception they are made of a yellow or light brown coloured stone possessing a fine, close grain, with the hardness of 4-5 (Moh's scale). They vary from 3.02 to 4.91 inches in length, and from 0.2 to 0.7 inches in thickness, and all are, or were, of much the same shape as that of the three illustrated. Their upper surfaces, and occasionally their lower, bear grooves caused by something that had been used upon them, as for instance in No. 43. The reverse sides of these slabs are often rounded and uneven, presenting quite a different appearance to their upper surfaces, which were remarkably plane before work had been started upon them. One of these stones (not illustrated) is coated underneath with a yellow deposit that looks very much like the remains of a cement used to fasten it down.[39]

No. 34 is 4.91 inches in length. Its once flat upper surface has become concave through wear and a shallow groove runs down its axis. Its reverse side is roughly finished and slightly convex. Use has been made of both sides of No. 42, which is 4.08 inches in length. No. 43, which is 4.21 inches long, has a polished upper surface bearing a shallow longitudinal depression; it is irregular in thickness and has a roughly finished underside.

What was used upon these fine grained stones can only be conjectured. Beads would have made longer and narrower grooving. That these stones had been subjected to considerable pressure is shown by the number of broken specimens found. They are unknown at Mohenjo-daro, and at Chanhu-daro have been found only between the levels − 5.6 and + 7.5 feet.

Cylindrical Stones (Pls. XCI, 45, 46, XCII, 22)

No less than fifteen large stones of this form were brought to light, all of them cut from a cherty, sometimes fossiliferous limestone, cream or light grey in colour. They average 5.04 inches in height and 12.78 inches in diameter. Some of them were unfinished and

[39] No. 1038. From Trench D(1), lev. − 5.6 ft. This particular stone is black in colour and resembles a slate.

the marks of the tool employed in dressing them down still disfigured their sides. Both pointed as well as flat edged chisels were used to shape them.

These blocks may either have served some household purpose or have been used as benches by craftsmen. Their tops, usually slightly convex, often show the polish of much use, and abrasions on their flat bases indicate that they had been moved about. They have been uncovered at all levels and occur as high as + 16.7 feet on Mound II.

The dimensions of No. 45 in Pl. XCI are 5.22 inches high and 15.4 inches in diameter. The smooth top is slightly convex; its vertical sides show traces of having been rubbed down with a piece of coarse sandstone. Patches of polish are also seen on its practically flat base. The sides of No. 46 have been trimmed with a pointed tool; its upper and lower faces are smooth and slightly convex. This block has a perceptible taper, the diameter of its base (12.62 inches) being one inch larger than that of the top.

No. 22 in Pl. XCII is a top view of a cylindrical stone measuring 4.5 inches high and 11.85 inches in diameter. It is uncertain whether this particular block had been used as a door-socket or for some other purpose. A cavity in the centre of its top measures 3.25 inches across by 1.25 inches deep; two depressions, one on each side of the cavity, are slightly smaller. All three holes show marked striations such as could have been caused by the pivot of a door or perhaps by a revolving stone. An article very similar to this one is in the museum at Mohenjo-daro.[40]

Rubbers and Pounders (Pls. LXXXIX, 27, XCII, 12, 16, 19)

The curiously formed object in Pl. LXXXIX, 27 is probably a rubber. It stands 3.97 inches high. The material is a fine-grained stone, dark-grey in colour, resembling limestone. Its polished flat base is oval in shape. This was first regarded as a weight, but Miss A. R. Hall of the Museum of Fine Arts, Boston, after testing it, reports that it weighs 1647.81 grammes and says " as the value of ratio 1600 on the calculated unit of .856 is 1396.60 the difference of 278.21 appears well beyond the average difference."

No. 12 in Pl. XCII stands 3.7 inches high and is a natural nodule of cherty limestone that has been trimmed to suit some special purpose. It is quite regular in shape, though not in finish, and its flat base bears a slight polish.

No. 16 in the same plate is a dark brown sandstone cylinder, 2.07 inches high, with rounded top and base. Pounders or rubbers of this type are common objects in all the Indus cities.

The pestle, No. 19, has been shaped from a piece of dark grey basalt. A portion is missing from its upper end, and it now measures 4.72 inches high. Pounders so regular in shape as this are far from common.

Plumb-bob(?) (Pl. XCI, 11)

This irregular mass of yellow-coloured limestone stands 2.0 inches high; the groove round its upper portion suggests that it was used as a plumb-bob. It was found to be 57.17 grammes when weighed and is obviously not a weight.

[40] *F. E. M.*, p. 393, pls. CIV, 24; CVII, 31.

Pedestal (Pl. XCII, 13)

Fashioned out of fine grained sandstone of a dark red colour, this little object was intended to support something that was fixed in the recess on its top. It is 2.03 inches high, and each of its four sides is divided into three registers by grooves averaging 0.08 inch wide and 0.04 inch deep. These were once filled with slips of shell inlay, as is proved by a short length that was still in position when the pedestal was found. Some of these grooves are provided with key-holes to improve the hold of the cement that was employed to keep the inlay in place. The object is well made on the whole, but is not quite regular in shape. It is akin to the round stand (No. 36) in the same plate.

Chert Ribbon-flakes (Pl. XCIII, 6-8, 24-26)

Flakes of this description were struck from cores similar to that illustrated in Pl. XCIII, 28. They must have had many uses, were easily and quickly made, and were utilized in most households.

Nos. 6-8 are flakes of trapezoidal section whose ends have been retouched to convert them into drills. These somewhat primitive tools were used to bore holes in a certain type of bead (Pl. LXXXVI, a, 1, 2, 3a, 3b), as is explained in the previous chapter. No. 8 measures 1.5 inches long.

No. 24 in the group of flakes below is 4.6 inches long. It was perhaps intended to make this into a saw, for part of one of its edges is serrated.

Chert Saw (Pl. XCIII, 27)

This well made tool was found with two other similar instruments. It measures 4.07 inches long and is of a light grey colour. Both its edges have been carefully notched, but no wear or polish is visible on the teeth.

Chert Cores (Pl. XCIII, 28, 29)

The first object is a grey coloured core, 3.68 inches in length, from which flakes, similar to those described above, have been struck. Later on this core was used as a polisher, as the partial smoothing out of its faceting shows. Cores that have been used in this way as burnishers are well known at Mohenjo-daro.[41] No. 29, which is 3.27 inches long, is a rough core, light brown in colour, that has been indifferently flaked.

Fossils (Pl. XCIII, 21-23)

These three fossil shells may have been kept as curios. Nos. 21 and 22, which are 2.71 and 1.63 inches long respectively, come from high levels, and No. 23 from the "Cutting." As there are no limestone outcrops in the vicinity of Chanhu-daro, these objects must have been brought from a distance, possibly from the borders of Baluchistan. No. 22

[41] *F. E. M.*, p. 396, pl. CVIII, 20.

was found in the same mound as a piece of fossil wood.[42] A small fossil of a crustacean, found also at a high level, was actually converted into a bead (Pl. LXXXII, 32). The Jhukar as well as the Harappā people would appear to have taken great interests in these relics of a remote past.

Fragment of Stone Dish (Pl. XCIII, 30)

Of dark grey steatite and measuring 2.55 inches long, this fragment was once part of a dish whose external diameter was 3.8 inches. That it had been broken anciently and repaired with rivets or lashings is proved from the seven small holes along two of its broken edges.

OBJECTS IN SHELL

Jar-stopper(?) (Pl. LXXXIX, 13)

This simple object might have been used to stop the mouth of a cosmetic jar or to close the leg of a water-skin. It is not perfectly round, owing to the shape of the columella of the shell from which it was cut. A stopper not unlike it has been found at Mohenjo-daro.[43] It measures 0.63 inch long.

Plumb-bob(?) (Pl. LXXXIX, 18)

It is uncertain whether this object, which is fashioned from the columella of a shell, was used as a plumb-bob or worn as a pendant; its lack of finish supports the first theory. It is 2.45 inches long and the hole that perforates it is 0.11 inch in diameter.

Large Shell (Pl. XC, 1)

One of a considerable number of shells found in various parts of Mound II, this fine specimen (*Murex Chicoreus ramosus*, Linn.), was found with two others of the same species in a bead-maker's work-shop. Shells of this kind, as well as other varieties, were largely used in the manufacture of bangles (Pls. LXXVII, 6, 7, XC, 15), ladles, feeding-cups, beads (Pl. LXXVIII, 13, LXXXIII, 9, LXXXIV, 6, 7), and other articles. They average in size 6.26 inches long.

Many of these shells, including the one illustrated, are pierced with irregular holes. This may have been done either to kill quickly the animal inside or to allow ants or sea-lice to enter readily and clean out their insides. The hole is rarely large enough to allow the contents of the shells to be extracted through it.

Feeding-cup (Pl. XC, 2)

Made from a shell similar to the one described above, this interesting object, which measures 4.82 inches long, has been embellished by two incised lines carried round its

[42] No. 4744. Light brown in colour, irregular in shape, and 3.3 ins. long, from Mound I, sq. 12/J, loc. 19, lev. + 16.0 ft.

[43] *M. I. C.*, pl. CLVI, 6.

open edge. Sumer has also produced vessels of much the same type, and these have long been regarded as lamps.[44] An objection to this identification is that a flame would have blackened and also calcined the spouts of these vessels, as has, in fact, happened to the edge of the ladle shown in No. 17 in the same plate. Feeding-cups similar have been found at Mohenjo-daro,[45] and they show signs neither of charring nor of blackening. Cups, of this type, I am informed, are commonly in use in Madras to-day to feed young children.

Dishes (Pl. XC, 3, 4, 9, 10, 22)

The walls of the larger shells were readily converted into simple dishes, some of which are shown in various stages of completion. Nos. 3, 4, 9, 10, the largest of which measures 3.01 inches in length, have irregularly curved bases and consequently do not stand very well. No. 22, 5.71 inches long, is extremely well finished. A depression on its further edge looks as if it had been expressly formed to provide a thumb-hold, and it is possible that this dish as well as some of the others was used as a dipper or spoon.

Segments of Cones (Pl. XC, 5, 11, 12)

The head-ornaments of which these three objects once formed part are described in the previous chapter.

Ladles (Pl. XC, 6, 13, 14, 17)

No. 6, which measures 9.61 inches long, is unfinished. After the removal of its excrescences it would have resembled No. 14 in appearance. No. 13 is only 1.23 inches long and may be a cosmetic spoon; an even smaller one of the same type has appeared at Mohenjo-daro.[46] No. 17 may have been used temporarily as a lamp, for smoke stains as well as calcination have disfigured its farther edge.

Bangles (Pls. LXXVII, 6, 7, XC, 15)

These are described in Chapter XIII. The segments in Pl. XC, 15 are all cut from one piece of shell.

Inlays (Pl. XC, 7, 8)

Inlays of any kind are rare at Chanhu-daro, perhaps for the reason that the inhabitants of that city were in the main too poor to have used articles decorated in this manner. The two pieces illustrated, which evidently come from the same article or box, are marked with deeply incised lines on one side and measure 1.5 and 1.36 inches long respectively. Though not actually found together, they come from the same square on Mound I.

[44] Woolley, *Royal Cemetery*, p. 101(a).
[45] *F. E. M.*, p. 423, pl. CVI, 36.
[46] *F. E. M.*, p. 422, pl. CVI, 33.

Carved Shell Objects (Pl. XC, 16, 19-21)

Two sides of No. 16 are illustrated. It measures 3.41 inches long across its chord and varies in width from 0.3 to 0.19 inches at its perfect end; its wider end has been torn away from something and also has marks of burning. The greater part of this very curious object is triangular in section, and one angle is deeply serrated. It is suggested that this object was originally one of a pair set in the mouth of an image of a deity. If this was the case, the figure must have presented an exceptionally malignant appearance, though perhaps not more so than some goddess figures in India to-day.

Nos. 19-21 are three different views of a very unusual object taken from the "Great Cutting" at the low depth of −25.1 feet. When it first appeared, it was so concreted and covered with mud that it was mistaken for the hoof of an ass and after hurried drying and treatment sent to Boston with other bones for identification. Miss A. R. Hall and Mr. W. J. Young, to whom it was entrusted, eventually discovered that it was the end of a large shell with the figure of a gharial, or fish-eating crocodile, carved upon it.[47] The bulbous end of the snout and the nostrils of this animal can be clearly seen on the left and right of the photographs Nos. 19 and 20 respectively, while some of its legs, somewhat out of proportion, appear in No. 21. This curious piece of work has been accidentally burnt and is now black in colour; its present polish is partly due to the wax with which it has been impregnated. It measures 2.37 inches high[48] and 3.2 inches across. It is difficult to pronounce the use of this object. It may have been a cult symbol illustrating the relation between the sacred river Indus, represented by the crocodile, and the sea, whose emblem was perhaps the shell.

OBJECTS IN BONE AND IVORY

Various Fittings (Pls. LXXXIX, 7, 15, XC, 18)

The ivory peg, 1.72 inches long, shown in Pl. LXXXIX, 7, is pierced with a hole 0.17 inches in diameter. Though regular in shape and showing the polish of much wear, it appears to have been carved by hand and not turned on a lathe. There is reason to think that this object once belonged to a chest; an almost similar article was found at Mohenjo-daro.[49]

No. 15, also of ivory, is 1.59 inches long. This appears to have been the cross-bar of some object, on account of the tenon at either end. Three of its sides are flat; the fourth is slightly rounded and has in its centre a blind hole measuring 0.14 inches in width and depth.

No. 18 in Pl. XC, which measures 2.51 inches long, has a tenon projecting from its perfect end. It is of ivory and is triangular in section. One face bears incised hatching, the

[47] This species of crocodile, common in the river Indus, frequently appears on the amulets of the Harappā Culture and was evidently a sacred animal; see pl. LII, 33.

[48] This measurement was taken when the object was in the position shown in No. 20.

[49] *F. E. M.*, pls. CIX, 3, CX, 14.

other two are curiously ornamented with a series of transverse parallel markings, originally filled in with a red pigment, some traces of which remain. The markings and the shape of this object suggest the horns of a ram and the piece may have come from a figure of that animal.

Bone Implement (Pl. XC, 23)

This tool, made from the rib of a large ruminant, was found inside the painted jar shown in Pl. XXXV, 2. It now measures 14.23 inches in length but was once longer, for a portion is missing from the smaller end. In shape the object resembles a paddle and has a slight natural curvature. It bears no signs of wear which could help to provide a clue to its use; it may have been employed to stir liquids or to beat linen.

Roller (Pl. XCI, 5)

Made of bone and badly warped and weathered, this roller-shaped object is 3.5 inches long. A hole, 0.21 inch in diameter, pierces it from end to end and this also shows signs of wear. It is apparent that we have here a roller of some kind which may once have formed part of the mechanism of a loom.

Bone Awls (Pl. XCII, 28-33)

The largest of these six awls measures 4.37 inches long. Four of them (Nos. 28, 30, 31, and 33) are irregular in shape and appear to be the bones of birds. From the levels at which they were found, they should be of Jhukar fabrication. No. 31 has a point at one end and a flat edge at the other. The remaining two (Nos. 29 and 32) are of better finish and are assigned to the Harappā Period. Awls of the rougher type were rare at Mohenjo-daro.

OBJECTS IN OTHER MATERIALS

Paste Plaques and Cylinders (Pl. XCI, 12, 13, 20-22)

A considerable number of these interesting objects were found in various parts of Mound II at levels ranging from -8.1 to $+6.9$ feet. They take two forms, either flat and rectangular (Nos. 21, 22) or cylindrical with a slight taper (Nos. 12 and 13). They are composed of a white, porous paste with a texture like a fine pumice but sufficiently friable to be scraped away easily with the finger-nail. Though these articles were soaked for a considerable time in water to remove salt deposits, they were not found to be soluble in this liquid to any extent and the paste holds together extremely well.[50] Dr. A. Lucas, who has examined one of these paste objects, states that they are made of finely divided silica and

[50] Some of these plaques have unfortunately become stained by rust, owing to being placed in an iron pan.

possibly constitute the body material of faience, an opinion with which the present writer is in agreement.

It would appear that these slabs and cylinders were kept in readiness to be converted later into a paste from which various faience articles could be made. What flux or cement, if it was not a glaze, was mixed with the final preparation remains a problem. A mild and colourless adhesive must certainly have been mixed with the silica particles that form these plaques; none of them, as far as can be seen, shows signs of any incipient fusing.

Nos. 12 and 20 in Pl. XCI measure 3.55 and 3.9 inches in length respectively. The second specimen has burnt patches of glaze adhering to one of its sides. A number of these objects were found together in Square 9/E, locus 171, in a deposit of ashes, and many others were found in the trenches cut on the northern side of Mound II. These last may have been washed down from a higher position.

Stick of Red Ochre (Pl. XCII, 27)

Lumps of red ochre of irregular forms were common objects at Chanhu-daro. No. 27, however, has been very carefully shaped and would seem to have been a toilet article. It has lost its upper end and is now 1.75 inches long. In colour it is bright red with a trace of orange, and its double-sloped edge was probably formed by rubbing upon a palette or perhaps upon the face itself.

Chapter XV

OBJECTS OF SCIENTIFIC INTEREST

Weights at Chanhu-daro. (By A. S. Hemmy)

Some 132 stone objects have been found which are noted as probably or possibly weights. These have been tabulated and the results (Col. III) tabulated in descending order in Table I of this Chapter.

The nearest ratio to the Harappā standard of 13.625 gms. has been assigned (Col. IV) and in Col. V the corresponding value of the unit has been given.

Many of the specimens are chipped or broken, others appear to be unfinished, some appear to have been damaged by fire. Their condition is noted in Col. II. A number are noted as doubtfully weights. In the cases where the calculated values of the unit diverge markedly from the Harappā standard, it is unlikely that they were used for weighing. Such are marked in Col. II with a question mark. The remainder, of which the field numbers are underlined in Table I, have been used in the calculation of the distribution curve. The great majority have units which lie between 12.6 gm. and 14.6 gm. The few divergent cases form no grouping and can be left out of account.

The calculation is performed as follows. Dividing the whole range into steps of a tenth of a gramme range, the numbers of specimens differing from the mid-point value of a step by not more than a twentieth of a gramme are counted and the result is tabulated in Col. II, Table II. These numbers are now smoothed (Col. III) by substituting the value of $(a + 2b + c)/4$ for b, where a, b, and c are the numbers of specimens for three successive steps.

In Fig. 1 a distribution curve is plotted in which the abscissa x is the weight of the mid-point of the step and + coordinate y is the smoothed value of the number of specimens with weights within the range of the step.

There is a single maximum, so only one standard is involved.

The Mode, or value of maximum frequency, has a value of 13.64 gm. This is the most probable value of the unit from the data. From the much larger number of specimens collected at Mohenjo-daro and Harappā the value of the standard has been calculated as 13.625 gm.[1]

The standard at Chanhu-daro is evidently the same. The difference can readily be accounted for from the paucity of numbers at Chanhu-daro as well as from the fact that it was a place of manufacture of weights so that many of the accepted weights have not been finally adjusted to their correct values, thus making the Mode a little high.

The weights have much the same characteristics as shown by those found at Mohenjo-daro. The majority are of chert and more or less cubical in shape (Pl. XCI, 29-32). There seem to be a larger proportion of misshapen weights, a condition to be expected at the place of manufacture. They may be rejects.

[1] Hemmy, "Statistical Treatment of Ancient Weights," *Ancient Egypt*, Dec., 1935, p. 88.

In the list in Table I, in order to obtain a unit approximating to the Harappā standard. such ratios as 30, 15, 3, 1/24, etc. have been used. As ratios involving the factor 3 are foreign to the system, the specimens are probably aberrant; even with the ratios assigned, only rarely is the unit found a good approximation.

The ratio 5/2 shown by one cube weight and one doubtful specimen, is a possibility, as it would be ten times the quarter standard, but as only three weights of about that standard have been found elsewhere, the possibility is dubious.

The data herein discussed were now combined with those of the previous finds at

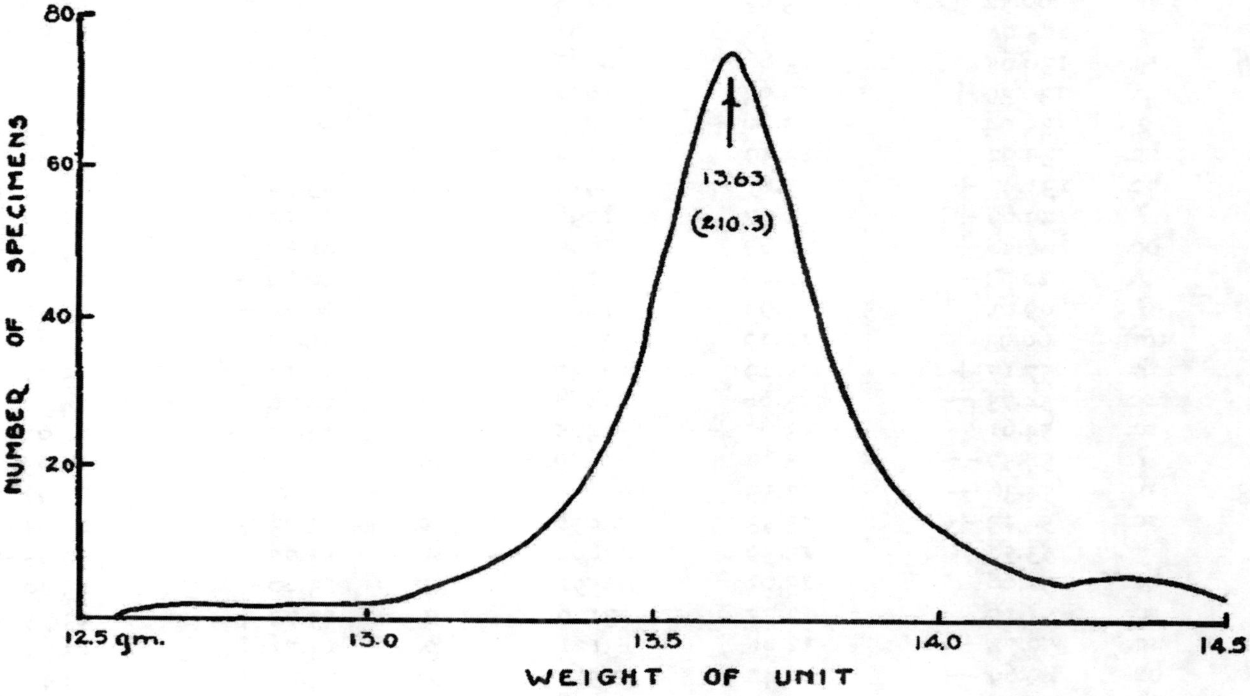

Fig. 1. DISTRIBUTION CURVE: Harappā, Mohenjo-Daro, and Chanhu-Daro combined, omitting all doubtful ratios and weights below six grammes.

Harappā and Mohenjo-daro. All doubtful specimens were rejected, including those with unlikely ratios, as well as all with weights below 6 gms. The smaller weights were definitely less accurate than those weighing between 6 gms. and 150 gms. After this revision the number of specimens within the range of each step is given in Col. IV, Table II, and the smoothed values in Col. V. The results are plotted in Fig. 1.

The value of the Mode is 13.63 gm. (210.3 gm.). This must be a close approximation to the true value and must express the Harappā standard to the nearest centigramme. This result was checked and confirmed by repeating the process with the difference that, instead of taking the mid-points of the steps as 12.6, 12.7, etc., the mid-points were placed at 12.65 gms., 12.75 gms., etc. This change should show if any bias in favour of round numbers existed.

TABLE I

List of Weights

I Field No.	II Condition	III Weight	IV Ratio	V Unit	I Field No.	II Condition	III Weight	IV Ratio	V Unit
5056	bc.	1330.68 +	100	13.31 gm.	2303	g.	27.41 —		13.70 +
2075	g.	544.77 +	40	13.62	3822	sc.	27.36 —		13.68
3482	unf.	392.76 +	30	13.09	3164	sc.	27.34 —		13.67
2016	unf.	273.59	20	13.68	2904	sc.	27.30 +		13.65 +
1287	?	260.52		13.03	2264	g.	27.26 +		13.63
5234	?	185.04	15	12.34	881	?	27.19 +		13.60 —
2529, ff	sc.	136.65	10	13.66	2867	g.	27.14 —		13.57
3025	p.	136.39 +		13.64	1814	g.	27.10 +		13.55 +
2650	g.	136.04		13.60 +	1737	g.	26.98 —		13.49 +
4669	bc.	133.92		13.39	4598	sc.	26.68 +		13.34
2474	bc.	131.47 +		13.15 —	2415	unf.	23.70 +		11.85 +
3593	?	129.69 +		12.97	1096	?	23.12		11.56
1590	bc.	126.58 +		12.65	1095	?	21.39	3/2	14.26
2029	g.	120.88 —		12.09	1750		20.89 +		13.93
1488	?	69.61	5	13.92	1482		20.24 —		13.49
1412	unf.	60.93		12.19	1265	?	19.33		12.89
157	?	57.17 +	4	14.29	3837	?	18.10 +		12.07
2423	sc.	54.73 —		13.68	1888	?	14.90 +	1	14.90 +
4756	sc.	54.61		13.65 +	2475	?	14.61 +		14.61
5074	?	54.50 —		13.62	2659, a	bt.	14.03 +		14.03
2326, g	p.	54.36 —		13.59	" , b	bt.	13.97 +		13.97
1951	sc.	54.13 +		13.53	4058	sc.	13.93 +		13.93
1298	?	53.58		13.39	3692	sc.	13.85 +		13.85 +
3881	bc.	52.08		13.02	2592	g.	13.80 +		13.80 +
4716	sc.	51.10		12.77	3116	g.	13.75 +		13.75 +
4774	sc.	50.72 —		12.68	3121	p.	13.71 +		13.71
2388, b	bc.	49.69 —		12.42	2569	sc.	13.68 +		13.68
1927	?	45.55 +		11.39	3078	sc.	13.64 +	1	13.64
765	?	42.88 —	3	14.29	2320	p.	13.51 —		13.51
2413	sc.	33.10 +	5/2	13.24	1404	sc.	13.45 +		13.45
1389	?	32.38 +		12.95	3236	?	13.42 +		13.42
2545	?	30.39 —	2	15.19	3504	sc.	13.41 —		13.41
1072	?	30.28 —		15.14	884	?	12.40 +		12.40
1055	?	29.15		14.67	3523	?	10.65		10.65
3629	sc.	28.87 +		14.44	1260	?	9.13 +	2/3	13.69
1461	?	28.36 —	2	14.18	2472	?	8.906		13.36
1631	?	28.27 +		14.14	2451	sc.	8.520		12.88
2388	bt.	28.14 +		14.07	921	p.	7.457	½	14.91
1787	sc.	28.05 +		14.03	2326, b	p.	7.345		14.69
4897	sc.	27.95+		13.98	2374	g.	7.147		14.29
2760	p.	27.66 +		13.83	3626	sc.	6.985		13.97
3189	sc.	27.53 —		13.76	557	g.	6.9435		13.89

Abbreviations: Column II. p. = perfect; g. = good; sc. = slightly chipped; bc. = badly chipped or fractured; unf. = unfinished; bt. = damaged by fire. The question mark denotes doubtfully a weight.

I Field No.	II Condition	III Weight	IV Ratio	V Unit
4843, *a*	g.	6.8595		13.72
2461	p.	6.845		13.69
2326, *h*	g.	6.836		13.67
" , *d*	unf.	6.8255		13.63
4760	?	6.808		13.62
2306	g.	6.783		13.57
2040	g.	6.649		13.30—
2933	sc.	6.641		13.28
3416	?	6.634		13.27
3699	?	6.149		12.30—
1137	?	5.956		11.91
4900	?	5.471—		10.94
1475	?	4.844	1/3	13.43
1252	?	4.520	1/3	13.56
4833	p.	4.227		12.68
2494	g.	4.040		12.12
2418	g.	3.865	¼	15.46
2326	g.	3.800		15.20—
3203	sc.	3.644		14.58
2214	sc.	3.543		14.17
4426	g.	3.517		14.07
2543	p.	3.4685	¼	13.87
1925	sc.	3.4055		13.62
3883	sc.	3.405—		13.62
3548	sc.	3.3285		13.31
4702	?	2.961		11.84
4843	g.	2.365	1/6	14.19
3913	p.	2.063—	1/8	16.50
2326, *n*	p.	1.9395	1/8	15.52
2317	sc.	1.891		15.13
1581	?	1.630		13.04
178	bc.	0.886	1/16	14.18
2317	g.	0.5985	1/24	13.36
2326	g.	0.5695	1/24	13.67

TABLE II

Distribution of Unit

I	II	III	IV	V
	Chanhu-daro		Combined	
Mid.-pt. of Step.	No. of Spec.	Smoothed	No. of Spec.	Smoothed
12.6 gm.	0	0.2	2	1.7
.7	1	0.7	2	1.7
.8	1	1.0	1	1.5
.9	1	1.0	2	1.5
13.0	1	0.7	1	1.5
.1	0	0.5	3	3.5
.2	1	1.7	7	6.5
.3	5	4.0	9	10.2
.4	5	5.0	16	19.7
.5	5	7.7	38	44.7
.6	16	13.0	87	70.0
.7	15	12.5	68	62.7
.8	4	7.0	28	35.2
.9	5	4.2	17	19.5
14.0	3	3.0	16	12.7
.1	1	1.7	2	6.7
.2	2	1.5	7	5.7
.3	1	1.2	7	6.2
.4	1	0.7	4	4.7
.5	0	0.2	4	4.0
.6	0	0.0	4	3.0

The Cube Weights in Boston. (By Ardelia Ripley Hall, Department of Asiatic Arts, Museum of Fine Arts, Boston).

Of 118 weights found at Chanhu-daro, 58 were sent to the Museum of Fine Arts[1] in the division of the finds. Of these 58, there were 36 cube weights, 5 spherical weights with flat base and top, and 17 pebble weights. Only a few of the important weights were weighed by the Expedition. Those which remained in India were weighed by Dr. Sd.

[1] A preliminary discussion of the weights in the Museum of Fine Arts was presented at the meetings of the Archaeological Institute of America, in December, 1937.

M. A. Hamid, Curator of the Central Asian Antiquities Museum in New Delhi. While the weights which came to the Museum of Fine Arts were first weighed there, later, through the kind cooperation of Professor F. G. Keyes and Professor L. F. Hamilton of the Massachusetts Institute of Technology, arrangements were made for them to be weighed by John E. Tyler, of their staff, to four points beyond the decimal on precise and delicate scales. This verification by the Massachusetts Institute of Technology has proven most valuable, especially in consideration of the smaller cube weights. The results obtained are given in Mr. Hemmy's Table I.

In Mr. Hemmy's report and accompanying list of all weights found, he has made a special and valued study of the frequency of distribution, showing that the "mode or value of maximum frequency" has a value of 13.64 grams. In connection with Mr. Hemmy's determination of the standard unit of weight for the Indus civilization as the Ratio 16 (13.63 grams), which he has so graphically illustrated in his "Distribution curve for Chanhu-daro" and for the three sites of "Mohenjo-daro, Harappā, and Chanhu-daro combined," there is a vast amount of material on the dominance of 16 in Indian culture.

John Allan,[2] with reference to Mr. Hemmy's report[3] that the ratio 16 was most frequently found at Mohenjo-daro, has stated with regard to coinage that, "Very little is known concerning the denominations and standards of ancient India," and added, ". . . We shall be content to point out that the ratio of 16 annas = 1 rupee goes back at least 2,000 years to the 16 *māṣakas* = 1 *kārṣāpaṇa* of the law-books."

Among the numerous literary references which Dr. A. K. Coomaraswamy has been so kind as to bring to my attention are those included in an "Appendix on So *Soḷasī*"[4] (*soḷasī* meaning sixteen). The author, in discussing the phrase "not a sixteenth part of" (which is comparable to our own use of "not an ounce of") has asked, "Why was this particular fraction used to express a minute value? It is common in Skt. works . . ., early and late, . . . and it became a conventional number, perhaps owing to the Sānkhyan system of subdividing. I have found a number of passages which I give here (a) to show a similar use and (b) the ideas from which this use arose." In the passages which he quotes the old formula is given in which the "metaphysical whole" is thought of as having sixteen parts.

Again, regarding the chapter of the Praśna Upanishad,[5] "Concerning the Person with sixteen parts," Professor Hume states, "These old conceptions, namely that the 'Lord of Creation' is sixteenfold and that a human person also is sixteenfold, are here philosophically interpreted . . ."

One other quotation, from the Jātakas,[6] is especially interesting because it reveals the

[2] John Allan, *Catalogue of the Coins of Ancient India.* (*A catalogue of the Indian coins in the British Museum*, vol. 7, 1936), Introd. p. clix.

[3] John Marshall, *Mohenjo-daro and the Indus Civilization*, vol. II, p. 596.

[4] F. L. Woodward, *The Book of Gradual Sayings* (*Anguttara-Nikaya*), vol. V, p. 240.

[5] Robert Ernest Hume, *The Thirteen Principal Upanishads*, p. 389.

[6] E. B. Cowell, *The Jātaka or stories of the Buddha's former births*, vol. I, p. 246 ("Mittavinda-Jātaka," 414).

persistence of the progression found in the Indus weights. "Now at that time one of the damned who had put on the circlet and was suffering the tortures of hell, asked the Bodhisattva—'Lord, what sin have I committed?' The Bodhisattva detailed the man's evil deeds to him and uttered this stanza:

'From four to eight, to sixteen thence, and so
To thirty-two, insatiate greed doth go
—Still pressing on till insatiety
Doth win the circlet's grinding misery.'"

It is, of course, well-known today that the conventional use of these numbers was dependent upon an ancient usage hitherto unsuspected; namely, that the traditional importance of 16 and the sequence of 4, 8, 16, 32 may be traced to the prehistoric civilization of the Indus Valley. This is a striking example of the imprint which these prehistoric people have left on the culture of India.

Mr. Hemmy has listed the Chanhu-daro weights under ratios from the fraction 1/24th to 100. He has taken the "value of maximum frequency" 13.64 grams as the standard unit of 1, and the value .856 grams as 1/16th. In the first report on Indus weights,[7] made by Mr. Hemmy,[8] this same unit of 13.6 grams was used as the standard unit "A" with the sequence represented as 1/4 A, A, 2A, 4A, etc. Later, in his report on the weights found at Mohenjo-daro,[9] the smallest weight then known of .856 grams was only "arbitrarily" taken as the unit. And it is now clear that it should be accepted as a 16th part of the standard unit. However, the fractional weights have multiplied, Chanhu-daro has notably contributed to the greater differentiation of small weights than has previously been recognized, and there are 39 weights in Table I below ratio 1. In this discussion of the cube weights in the Museum of Fine Arts, as a matter of convenience, we have followed the old ratios of 1 to 1600. By avoiding fractions, we believe the relation of one weight to another in the series is more readily discernable. And there is no mathematical difference between the two ratios, whether one rises from 1/16 to 100, or from 1 to 1600.

By transposing the ratios in Table I from 1/16th to 1, it may be found that most of the weights from Chanhu-daro fall in the simple ratios 1, 2, 4, 8, 16, 32, 64, 160, 320, 640, and 1600, with the possible intrusion of doubtful weights in the ratios 24, 48, 240, and 480, as well as ratios 40 and 80. The notable exceptions are fractional ratios of the usual series. The discovery of two weights (listed as ratio 1/24th) in the ratio of 2/3 of 1, or 2/3 of the smallest degree thus far recognized lend to Chanhu-daro the distinction of further extending the system by one degree. The excavations of Mohenjo-daro by Dr. Mackay have recently added to the upward extension by weights of the ratios 3200 and 12800.

All of the 35 cube weights in Boston, which are listed in Table IV, like the block weights found at other sites, were made of chert. Through the good offices of Mr. William

[7] *A. S. I., A. R.*, 1925-1926, p. 92.
[8] See footnote 1, Marshall, *Mohenjo-daro and the Indus Civilization*, vol. II, p. 589.
[9] *Ibid.*, p. 589.

J. Young of the Museum of Fine Arts, a group of ten have been further identified by Dr. Harry Berman of the Department of Mineralogy at Harvard University as agate, chalcedony, jasper, and calcite. The majority are beautifully veined and banded stones, opaque or semi-transparent. All were carefully squared and polished and occasionally the edges were bevelled. There is much of interest regarding these excellent examples. Of the 36 in the list 21 are undamaged and in good or perfect condition.

The five spherical weights with flat base and top now in Boston, were made of limestone, granite, and agate. As might be expected from previous reports, they fall into the simple ratios as the cube weights, with one exception which is unfinished (3482, see Table I) in the ratio 480.

Most of the pebble weights are granite, others are of limestone. This limited data bears out the observation already made by Mr. Hemmy[10] that "It is interesting to note that all weights which are not cubical are *not* made of chert . . . (and) on the whole not so accurate." All the pebble weights are only doubtfully regarded as weights. They are followed by a question mark in Table I. It is to these alone that Mr. Hemmy refers as "probably or possibly weights." It may be well to add a word as to why they have been included at all. Of the 17 in Boston, all are worn smooth like pebbles from the shore or a river bed, 9 are more or less worked stones with a flattened base. With but rare exceptions they weigh to the usual ratios and in the usual frequency, 11 are in the common ratios 8, 16, and 32. There is little doubt that pebbles were cheap and practical substitutes for the finer cube and spherical weights, just as the clay bangles were made to answer for the bracelets of faience and metal.

The cube weights, on the other hand, are without the slightest question weights. In fact Dr. Mackay regards them as master-weights. And for this reason we regard them as worthy of separate consideration. In omitting the other types and all substitute weights which are open to question we believe a fairer appraisal of the accuracy of weights from Chanhu-daro may be reached.

Following the method described by Mr. Hemmy[11] the calculated unit value of .865 grams was obtained for the 27 weights in Boston unmarred or only slightly chipped. This is slightly higher than the calculated unit weight from Harappā of .860 grams based on 34 examples, and that from Mohenjo-daro[12] of .865 grams based on 113 examples. If

[10] Mackay, *Further Excavations at Mohenjo-daro*, p. 605.

[11] Marshall, *Mohenjo-daro and the Indus Civilization*, vol. II, p. 589: "The method of arriving at the most probable value of the unit was as follows: a casual inspection of the weights showed that, with a few exceptions which were omitted, the weights fell into a series of groups which were in simple numerical ratios with one another. Giving the smallest the arbitrary value of unity, the others were in simple ratios, 2, 4, 8, etc. The mean weight of each group is divided by this ratio and multiplied by the number of specimens. The products for all the groups are added together and divided by the total number of specimens. This gives a mean value for the group of smallest weight in which every specimen weighed is allowed equal importance. The mean values of all groups are then obtained by multiplying this mean value by the ratio already found. In this way we arrive at the calculated values . . . ."

[12] *Ibid.*, p. 590: "Table I. Weights from Mohenjo-daro." The number of specimens listed in this table is 113. A typographical error appears under group C, where 9 instead of 2 is given for the

weights were manufactured at Chanhu-daro, it is possible that they were less worn by use. Certainly, the limited number on which the calculation is based is a factor. The calculated unit value based on the 174 examples from Harappā, Mohenjo-daro, and Chanhu-daro is .857. This unit value[13] has been used in Table IV to obtain the calculated value of the ratios.

The usual weights are much the same as those found at Harappā and Mohenjo-daro. In the list of cube weights in Boston, the locus and level where each weight was found has been given. The find spots of the weights and their association with one another appear very suggestive of their use. Most of the cube weights came from the Harappā II level of Mound II at Chanhu-daro, and 22 came from one house and its immediate neighborhood. (These 22 do not all appear in Table IV, as 6 remained in India). This house is the bead-maker's shop that has a room with flues running under the brick floor. It is already distinguished for that unusual feature, and also for the abundance of interesting objects found in its rooms and court. Beside bronze beads and stone beads of etched carnelian, lapis lazuli, and steatite, there were quantities of unfinished beads of carnelian and steatite found there, as well as the raw materials for the stone cutter (nodules of carnelian and a rock of crystal), and also stone polishers and copper and bronze bead-maker's tools. This was the establishment of a maker of fine jewelry of stone and metal.

In the small outer room of this house (Sq. 9/D, loc. 215) 14 weights and scale-pans of copper were discovered and an additional weight was found in the furnace-room (Sq. 9/D, loc. 287). Of the 15 weights 2 were in the ratio of 2/3 of 1, 2 in the ratio 2, 2 in the ratio 4, 5 in the ratio 8, 2 in the ratio 32, 2 in the ratio 64.

Just across the street (Sq. 8/D, loc. 290) was 1 weight of the ratio 16, and at the next corner (Sq. 9/D, loc. 192)[14] 2 more weights of the ratio 16 were found. In the building on the north side of the bead-maker's shop (Sq. 8/D, loc. 178) was a weight in the ratio 4. In the adjoining house on the other side (Sq. 9/D, loc. 179) were 2 weights of the ratios 64 and 160, and in the next building (Sq. 9/C, loc. 208) was the fine weight in the ratio 2/3 of 8. It seems probable that these weights may have been scattered at the time the city in this occupation was deserted. And we have, then, substantial evidence that these smaller weights (only those up to ratio 160 were found) were used to weigh the precious metals and stones used in the jeweler's craft and trade. This theory was first proposed by Ridgeway.[15] It is not astonishing that the smallest weights known should have been found in the workshop of a lapidary. It is possible that the weights were made there also, but no unfinished weights were found. One unfinished seal was found in the corridor leading from the outer room.

number of specimens. It is plain that this figure should be 2, from Table III in which the weights found at both Mohenjo-daro and Harappā are listed, from the list with expedition numbers given in the Appendix I, p. 596, and from Mr. Hemmy's statement, just below Table I, that "Out of a total of 120 weights selected for their good condition, only seven do not fall into the above table . . . ."

[13] Mr. Hemmy obtained .857 in his combined tables for Mohenjo-daro and Harappā.

[14] The level of Sq. 9/D, loc. 192 was + 8.75 feet, somewhat lower than the level at which all the other weights were found. This was probably due to subsidence, as the drains under the street dropped from + 8.2 feet at 211 to + 6.7 feet at 218.

[15] Marshall, *Mohenjo-daro and the Indus Civilization*, vol. II, p. 589.

The appearance of 2 weights in the ratio of 2/3 of 1 and another in the ratio of 2/3 of 8 with all the others in the usual sequence shows that, in actual use, these fractional weights were supplementary to the simple ratios and did not form a separate light system.

The weight in Boston, in the ratio of 2/3 of 1 (Exp. No. 2326 D) is almost a perfect cube of brownish jasper, weighing .5695 grams, it varies from the calculated value .5712 by only one thousandth of a gram (.0017). This is an extraordinary degree of accuracy, but no less remarkable than the minute beads running 37 to an inch, found in the same room. The second weight, weighing .5985 grams, is in India. One other weight which might be included in this ratio is from Mohenjo-daro, weighing .550 grams. Recently published,[16] it was listed as of an undetermined ratio.

Of the other exceptional weights found at Chanhu-daro, two were in the ratio of 1/3 of 8; again one is in Boston and the other remained in India. This ratio has long been known and is designated by Mr. Hemmy [17] in his table of Mohenjo-daro weights as "." The mean weight of the two Mohenjo-daro examples is precisely the calculated value of the ratio. Only the weight which remained in India approaches them in accuracy.

The ratio of 2/3 of 8 is another new ratio of which the two perfect cube weights from Chanhu-daro are so far the only examples known.

A rectangular block of grey stone is in the ratio 2/3 of 32 and varies from the calculated value by only 18 grams. However, it has been described as a doubtful weight and it was found at another level. In addition to these weights, there are others from Chanhu-daro that have been included, but they are not as accurate. Comparable weights from Mohenjo-daro and Harappā have also been listed, notably the sole weight in the ratio 2/3 of 2, which Mr. Hemmy had especially noted, "B (g) 23 (from Harappā) weighing 1.255 made of chert, is in excellent condition. It cannot be placed with any group."

We have now assembled a new series of 15 weights from the three sites, forming a secondary sequence of fractional ratios. The ratios 2/3 of 1, 2/3 of 2, 2/3 of 4, etc. to 2/3 of 32, may also be read as 1/3 of 2, 1/3 of 4, 1/3 of 8, etc. to 1/3 of 64. (It is possible that the missing smallest weight of 1/3 of 1 may yet be discovered). Again the whole series, with the smallest weight as 1 may be resolved into the usual sequence of 2, 4, 8, 16, etc. The limited number of fractional weights leads one to suppose that they had only a special use, and that like our Troy Weight, they were used in weighing gold, silver, and precious stones.

The use of thirds in a binary system is also an interesting extension of the mathematical knowledge of the Indus people. And in contrast to the cube form of the weights, there have been found tetrahedrons or small triangular pyramids of perfect form. One was found at Chanhu-daro in the bead-maker's shop along with the 14 weights. Others have been found at Mohenjo-daro. All are most carefully made of faience, limestone, and cast bronze. In each case all the sides are equal, so that each face is the plane surface of an equilateral

[16] Mackay, *Further Excavations at Mohenjo-daro*, pp. 604 and 607.

[17] Marshall, *Mohenjo-daro and the Indus Civilization*, p. 590, Table I.

TABLE III

Fractional Weights in a Series of Thirds

Ratio	Number of Specimens	Expedition Number	Source	Present Location	Weight	Calculated Value	Difference between Weight and Calculated Value
2/3 of 1 or 1/3 of 2	3	DK 12774 [1]	Mohenjo-daro	India	0.550	0.5712	.021
		2326 d	Chanhu-daro	Boston	0.5695		.0017
		2317	"	India	0.5985		.0273
2/3 of 2 or 1/3 of 4	1	B(g) 23 [2]	Harappā	India	1.255	1.1424	.113
2/3 of 4 or 1/3 of 8	5	HR 4331 [3]	Mohenjo-daro	India	2.33	2.2848	.05
		HR 3079 [3]	"	"	2.24		.04
		DK 2106 [3]	"	"	2.07		.21
		3913	Chanhu-daro	Boston	2.0626		.22
		4843	"	India	2.365		.083
2/3 of 8 or 1/3 of 16	2	2494	"	Boston	4.0403	4.570	.53
		4833	"	India	4.227		.25
2/3 of 16 or 1/3 of 32	2	DK 6346 [4]	Mohenjo-daro	"	8.850	9.140	.29
		2451 (?)	Chanhu-daro	"	8.520		.62
2/3 of 32 or 1/3 of 64	2	3837	"	Boston	18.1028	18.280	.18
		DK 5679 (?) [5]	Mohenjo-daro	India	17.970		.31

[1] E. Mackay, *Further Excavations at Mohenjo-daro*, vol. I, pp. 604, 607.
[2] J. Marshall, *Mohenjo-daro and the Indus Civilization*, vol. II, p. 592.
[3] *Ibid.*
[4] E. Mackay, *loc. cit.*
[5] *Ibid.* A cylindrical weight with plane ends.

triangle. The weight of the faience tetrahedron from Chanhu-daro (now in Boston) offers no obvious connection with the weights, nor would it seem plausible that weight would be of any consequence in a faience object of such a special form, because it could not be controlled. Rather the choice of faience offers an excellent material for a clean-out measurement of length and sharp angles. The length of the sides of the tetrahedrons seems to bear some relation to the length of the cube weights in the ratios 8, 16, and 32. These speculations are very inconclusive, yet the possibility that these faience tetrahedrons were a solid geometric form by which some standard of measurement was established may be worthy of further consideration.

TETRAHEDRONS

Expedition Number	Source	Material	Length of All Sides in Inches	References
2326 i	Chanhu-daro	Faience	1.0	(4.7724 grams weight)
SD 2880	Mohenjo-daro	"	0.94	Marshall, *Mohenjo-daro and the Indus Civilization*, vol. II, p. 559, vol. III, pl. CLIII, 40.
C 46	"	White limestone	0.75	Marshall, *loc. cit.*, vol. II, p. 559, vol. III, pl. CLII, 41.
8027	"	Faience	0.61	Mackay, *Further Excavations at Mohenjo-daro*, vol. I, p. 572 and pp. 577, 8; vol. II, pl. CXXXVII, 7
8110	"	"	0.70	E. J. H. Mackay, vol. I, *ibid.*, vol. II pls. CXXXIX, 12 drawing), CXLII, 64 (photo).
6386	"	"	0.85	Mackay, vol. I, *ibid.*; vol. II, pl. CXLII, 73.
6642	"	Cast Bronze	0.9	Mackay, *ibid.*, vol. I; vol. II, pls. CXXXIX, 11 (drawing), CXLII, 63 (photo).

Animal Bones

The expedition is grateful to Dr. Glover M. Allen, of Harvard University, for his identifications of certain animal bones from our site, some in a bad state of preservation.

No. 1480. Sambar deer (*Rusa unicolor*). Tip of tine of antler. From Sq. 8/E, locus 103, level: + 14.4 feet. Nos. 1628, 1819, 4039, and 4471 were also tines and pieces of antler of the Sambar deer.[2]

No. 1654. Tines of the Hog deer (*Cervus porcinus*). From Sq. 9/D, locus 130, level: + 16.8 feet.

"No. 3031. *Bos. sp.* Bone implement from an anterior rib (see Pl. XC, 23). It quite matches that of a large domestic bull, but it is not possible to tell whether it is from a wild or domestic animal, or what breed of cattle. This tool was taken from the inside of the

[2] No. 1628, from Sq. 8/C, loc. 109, lev. + 12.2 ft. No. 1819, from Sq. 8/C, loc. 152, lev. + 11.7 ft. No. 4039, from Sq. 8/E, loc. 104, lev. + 9.3 ft. No. 4471, from Sq. 8/F, loc. 418, lev. + 8.7 ft.

TABLE IV

Cube Weights in the Museum of Fine Arts, Boston

Ratio	Calculated Value	Number of Specimens	Expedition Number	Locus	Level	Material	Condition	Size in inches	Weight in grams	Mean Weight	Difference between mean weight and calculated value
1600	1371.2	1	5056	Mound 1, Sq. 12/K, loc. 15	Plus 15.0 ft.	Chert	Badly chipped	3.4 lg.	1330.6845		40.5155
			1590	Sq. 8/C, loc. 109	" 16.25 "	Chert	" "	1.6 "	126.5835		
160	137.12	3	2474	Sq. 9/D, loc. 179	9.8 "	"	" "	1.61 "	131.4735	131.4830	5.637
			3025	Sq. 8/F, loc. 418	8.3 "	"	Undamaged	1.52 "	136.3930		
			2388b	Sq. 9/D, loc. 215	9.38 "	"	Badly chipped	1.1 "	49.6895		
64	54.848	4	1951	Sq. 9/E, loc. 125	" 14.40 "	"	Slightly chipped	1.2 "	54.1315	53.2266	1.6214
			2326g	Sq. 9/D, loc. 215	10.45 "	"	Undamaged	1.3 "	54.3558		
			2473	Sq. 9/D, loc. 179	9.8 "	"	"	1.22 "	54.7299		
			4598	Mound 1, Sq. 13/K, loc. 36	" 14.12 "	"	Slightly chipped	0.9 "	26.6846		
			2867	Sq. 9/E, loc. 124	9.9 "	"	Edges rounded	1.11 "	27.1391		
32	27.424	6	2904	Sq. 9/F, loc. 401	8.28 "	"	Worn	1.01 "	27.3039	27.4769	.0529
			3164	Sq. 6/E, loc. 431	" 10.17 "	Agate	Undamaged	0.9 "	27.3394		
			3189	Sq. 8/E, loc. 280	" 7.0 "	Chert	"	1.0 "	27.5255		
			3629				"	0.93 "	28.8724		
2/3 of 32	18.280	1	3837	Cut. Sq. 10/F, loc. 465	2.4 "	"	Worn rectangular	1.0 "	18.1028		.1772
			3504	Sq. 8/B, loc. 453	7.55 "	"	Slightly chipped	0.7 "	13.4074		
			2320	Sq. 8/E, loc. 114	10.07 "	"	Undamaged	0.71 "	13.5098		
			2569	Sq. 8/D, loc. 290	9.85 "	"	Slightly chipped	0.78 "	13.6830		
16	13.712	7	3121	Sq. 9/F, loc. 407	6.55 "	"	Undamaged	0.8 "	13.7130	13.7388	.0268
			3692	Sq. 8/B, loc. 233	7.6 "	"	Slightly chipped	0.81 "	13.8548		
			2659b	Sq. 9/D, loc. 192	8.75 "	"	" "	0.87 "	13.9731		
			2659a	Sq. 9/D, loc. 192	8.75 "	"	Undamaged	0.70 "	14.0306		
			2933	Sq. 10/E, loc. 218	6.9 "	White chalcedony	"	0.6 "	6.6412		
			2326h	Sq. 9/D, loc. 215	10.35 "	Chalcedony	"	0.68 "	6.8361		
8	6.856	5	2374	Sq. 9/D, loc. 215	10.40 "	Chert	"	0.62 "	7.1470	7.0830	.227
			2326b	Sq. 9/D, loc. 215	10.40 "	"	"	0.61 "	7.3345		
			921	Trench B(3)	− 5.6 "	"	"	0.63 "	7.4566		
2/3 of 8	4.570	1	2494	Sq. 9/C, loc. 208	9.9 "	Calcite	"	0.5 "	4.0403		.5297
			3883	Mound I, Sq. 13/J, loc. 3	15.6 "	White chalcedony	"	0.5 "	3.4046		
			4426	Mound I, Sq. 12/K, loc. 26	14.08 "	Calcite	"	0.49 "	3.5168		
4	3.428	5	3203	Sq. 8/D, loc. 178	7.6 "	Chalcedony	"	0.53 "	3.6437	3.6460	.218
			2418	Sq. 9/D, loc. 287	9.9 "	Colored jasper	"	0.5 "	3.8654		
			23260	Sq. 9/D, loc. 215	10.45 "	Chert	Worn	0.49 "	3.7996		
2/3 of 4	2.285	1	3913	Cut. Sq. 10/F, loc. 423	2.88 "	Calcite	Undamaged	0.39 "	2.0626		.222
1	.857	1	178	Trench D(1)	− 1.65 "	Chert	Slightly chipped	0.3 "	.8856		.286
2/3 of 1	.5712	1	2326d	Sq. 9/D, loc. 215	10.40 "	Colored jasper	Undamaged	0.25 "	.5695		.0017

large painted storage jar illustrated in Pl. XXXV, 2 and is described in Chapter XIV." From Sq. 7/F, locus 110, level + 8.7 feet.

"No. 3820. Antler of Hog deer (*Cervus porcinus*)." From Mound I, Sq. 13/J, locus 3, level: + 15.8 feet.

No. 5450. A number of bones found at a very low level in the "Cutting" included *Bos. sp.*; a fragment of the forehead of a pig, but whether of *Sus scrofa*, wild or domestic, or of the Indian pig, *Sus cristatus*, cannot be determined from the small piece found. Goat (*Capra hircus*), two lower molars; they match better in size those of the goat than those of sheep, although the two are so alike that they cannot always be certainly identified. Sambar deer (*Rusa unicolor*). Fragment of base of antler and a piece of rib. From, Sq. 10/G, locus 481, level: – 25.1 feet.

Shells

We are indebted to the Director of the Zoological Survey of India, for the following information concerning some shells from Chanhu-daro.

Gastropods

(1) (Nos. 67, 332). *Cypraea (Cypraea) arabica* (Linne.).
(2) No. 1375. *Thais (Stramonita) bufo* (Lamarck).
(3) (No. 1662). *Oliva (Oliva) maura* (Lamarck).
(4) (Nos. 2147, 2927). *Telescopium telescopium* (Linne.).
(5) (2624, B). *Erosaria (Erosaria) lamarckii* (Gray).
(6) (No. 2589). *Terebralia palustris* (Bruguiere).
(7) (No. 3591). *Melanoides tuberculatus* (Muller).
(8) (No. 4250). *Xancus rapa* (Lamarck).
(9) (No. 4392). *Tibia curta* (Sowerby).

Pelecypods

(1) (Nos. 10, 279, 865, 1154, 2056, 3591). *Potomida rajahensis* (Lea).
(2) (No. 164). *Potomida favidens* (Benson).
(3) (Nos. 751, 798, 1690, 3850). *Lamellidens (Lamellidens) marginalis* (Lamarck).
(4) (Nos. 2021, 3624, 3651, 4809). *Arca (Anadara) granosa* (Linne.).
(5) (Nos. 2399, 4337). *Arca (Anadara) inaequivalvis* (Bruguiere).
(6) (No. 2656). *Indonaia caeruleus* (Lea).

"The first nine species are all Gastropods and, with the exception of No. 7, are marine species which are fairly widely distributed in the Indo-Pacific waters. No. 7 is a freshwater Gastropod which is found in confined waters all over India."

"Of the six Pelecypods, Nos. 4 and 5 are marine forms with a distribution similar to those of the marine Gastropods mentioned above, while the rest are freshwater mussels, the source of which is probably some tributary of the Indus."

Identification of Mollusca has been furnished by Dr. W. J. Clench, of Harvard University, as follows:

3909	*Conus* species (MFA 36.1866)
332	*Turbo* "
332	Arca inaequivalis Brug. (MFA 36.2342)
332	" " " (MFA 36.2343)
3690	*Arca rhombea Born*
1341	" " "
5122	" " "
400	Parreysia species (fresh water)
865	" "
279	" "
1154	" "
350	" "
399	" "
165	" "
2056	" "
747	Cypraea turdus Linn (MFA 36.2365)
1185	Cypraea acellata Linn (MFA 36.2369)
3114	*Murex ramosus* Linn (MFA 36.2567)
4395	" " "
4629	" " "
3436	" " "
3324	" " "
2818	" " "
2991	" " "
1184	" " "
4366	" " " (MFA 36.2384)
4864	*Rostellaria curvirostris* Linn
276	*Cypraea moneta* Linn
2408	*Fasciolaria trapezium* Linn (MFA 36.2736)
	Melania species (MFA 36.2351)
374	*Cypraea* species (MFA 36.2370)
2399	*Conus hebraeus* Linn (MFA 36.2367)
4918	*Potamides telescopium* Linn (MFA 36.2372)
4179	" " " (MFA 36.2373)
4846	*Conus*—probably *textile* Linn
2398	*Oliva bulbosa* Bolt
325	All fresh water clams, Unio. (s. l.) species (MFA 36.2332)
12(a)	" " " " " " "
1152	" " " " " " " (MFA 36.2333)

219	"	"	"	"	"	"	"	(MFA 36.2341)
3589	"	"	"	"	"	"	"	(MFA 36.2331)
279	"	"	"	"	"	"	"	(MFA 36.2352)
2656	"	"	"	"	"	"	"	(MFA 36.2345)

All these marine forms could be obtained along the coast or from the river in the vicinity of the Indus. (As stated for M. specimens, M. I. C., p. 673, note.)

Vegetable Remains

The late Dr. F. J. F. Shaw, Director of the Imperial Institute of Agricultural Research in Delhi, has contributed the following note on some samples of seed that, it will be remembered, were found (see Chap. III) in the upper levels of Mound II.

"Sample No. 2348. This consists of grains of wheat of two kinds: 1. Rounded grains which, while unlike those of most wheat species, strongly resemble those of *Triticum Sphaerococcum* Percival. They differ from the latter slightly in that the furrow is usually extremely shallow and the grain size and shape slightly more variable than in the variety of *T. sphaerococcum* available at Pusa. *T. sphaerococcum* is believed to be cultivated only in India though specimens of it have also been recorded from Persia." From Square 9/E, locus 162, level: + 15.3 feet.

"2. Slightly larger grains of the ordinary *vulgare* type. In his note in *Current Science*,[3] Professor Luthra of Lyallpur states that in some samples of wheat excavated at Mohenjo-daro two types of grain were found, namely, *vulgare* type and *compactum* type.[4] I am inclined to think that these two kinds were similar to those found in the present sample, and that possibly Professor Luthra classed one type as *compactum*, as he may not have had any sample of *T. sphaerococcum* to look at. Last year we received some samples of seed excavated at Harappā and the wheat from there was also of *sphaerococcum* type."

"The grains are completely carbonised and it was not possible to detect any structural details."

"Sample No. 2343. This appears to be quite definitely seeds of the field-pea (*Pisum arvense*). Most of the seeds had lost their seed-coat. The sample contained a few seeds of wheat also." From Square 9/E, locus 162, level: + 15.4 feet.

"Field-peas were also included in the samples from Harappā sent to us last year."

"Sample No. 2344. The seed appears to belong to a species of *Brassica* and is perhaps that of rai (*B. juncea*)." This was found in Square 9/E, locus 124, level: + 15.3 feet.

Eye-powders

Dr. A. Lucas, Chemical Advisor to the Government of Egypt, has kindly supplied the following note on powders found in two cosmetic jars, Nos. 1023 and 1411. The

[3] Vol. IV, No. 7, pp. 489-90, 1936.
[4] *M. I. C.*, p. 586.

first of these containers appears in Pl. XXVII, 91, and the second in Pl. XXXIX, 7, is a Jhangar vessel.

> Dr. Lucas remarks: "These two powders are very similar in composition. They consist of rather coarse dark grey powders with whitish particles. They do not contain either lead or antimony compounds. I would suggest that they consist of (a) coarsely powdered and incompletely burnt wood ash, (b) coarsely powdered charcoal of very poor quality, or (c) soot scraped from chimneys."

With reference to a possibility that some of the storage jars from Chanhu-daro once contained wine or beer we submitted to Messrs Watney Combe Reid and Co. Ltd., Mortlake, London, a sample of a heavy deposit found in the base of one of these jars. Their Head Laboratory favours us with the following report:

> "Microscopic examination and chemical analysis showed this sample to consist mainly of calcite (crystalline calcium carbonate) with a small proportion of sharp angular sand composed of grains of quartz, hornblende, and haematite. The whole was stained brownish by iron oxide disseminated throughout the material. No organic matter was present and no indications were obtained of the petrified remains of vegetable material such as seed tissue, yeast, etc."

Chapter XVI

SKULL FOUND AT CHANHU-DARO

BY

Wilton Marion Krogman and William Henry Sassaman *

LIST OF TABLES

LIST OF FIGURES

The location of the site and the circumstances of the find

In 1935-36 the joint expedition of the American School of Indic and Iranian Studies and the Museum of Fine Arts of Boston, under the field directorship of Dr. Ernest Mackay, undertook a systematic examination of Mound II at Chanhu-daro, located " some twelve miles east of the present bed of the Indus, about eighty miles S.S.E. of Mohenjo-daro" (*12*, p. 83).[1] There are three mounds at Chanhu-daro, comprising an area of nine acres, but the site was probably originally more extensive. The alluvium deposited over a long period of time now covers the lower parts of the mounds.

According to Dr. Mackay (*op. cit.*, pp. 83-6) there are represented at Chanhu-daro at least three cultural horizons: Harappā, Jhukar, and Jhangar. The first period falls into the middle of the third millennium B. C., while the second period may go back to the opening of the second millennium B. C.

In his preliminary report Dr. Mackay (*op. cit.*, p. 87) stated that " no skeletal remains of either the Jhukar people or Harappā people were found, save a skull that had been placed in a large storage jar together with a small collection of metal objects and a conch shell." No other human bones were found, either associated with the skull or representative of another individual.

* Study made at the Laboratory of Anatomy and Physical Anthropology, Western Reserve University, Cleveland. Dr. Krogman is now at the University of Chicago.

[1] References to the works quoted will be found at the end of this chapter.

Under date of October 20, 1936, Dr. Mackay wrote (personal correspondence) as follows:

" This skull (No. 3324, k) was found in a large storage jar (No. 3324, a) at the level of 9.2 feet above datum level, at Locus 324, Mound II.[2] I enclose a photograph of the jar taken as it was found. In order to remove the jar we had to take away some of the brick-work resting on it and around it, and when this had been done we removed the jar (which was badly cracked by earth pressure) from the top downwards. In doing so we found the skull that you are examining. On the same level as the skull a large conch shell was found and beneath a small hoard of copper and bronze implements.[3] The shape of the jar,[4] its surroundings, and the implements found in it, definitely fix it as belonging to the Harappā Culture (3000 to 2600 B. C.)."

In Figures 1-3 in Pl. XCIV, the jar and skull and their relationships to one another and adjacent structures are clearly depicted.

The exhumation and preparation of the skull

Under Dr. Mackay's direction, as seen in the photographs in Pl. XCIV, only the top, sides, squamous portion of the occiput, and upper portion of the face were uncovered. Cranial base and lower face, including palate, were undisturbed and were permitted to remain in their matrix of earth. The entire skull and the undisturbed matrix of earth were covered with paraffin wax (see Pl. XCV, fig. 4). In this condition the entire mass reached the Laboratory.[5]

The earth covering the cranial base and the palate was removed literally particle by particle. No vertebrae were found and the mandible was not present. The conclusion is inevitable that mandible and vertebrae were separated from the skull *before* the skull was put in the jar and that a sufficient period of time between death and interment (of the skull) had elapsed to permit the complete disassociation of skull from vertebral column and upper jaw from lower jaw.

This conclusion is strengthened when it is noted that a number of maxillary teeth—right central and lateral incisors, canine, first and second premolars, and left canine and first premolar—are missing. Their alveoli are intact, pointing to post-mortem loss. Yet a careful search of the surrounding earth did not reveal them: they had fallen out *before* the skull was put in the jar. Further, several teeth, especially the left central incisor and the right second molar, are fragmentary. The fragments are not present: the teeth were broken and the fragments lost *before* the skull was put in the jar. Finally, in the right ear only the malleus and incus, both broken, and in the left ear only a broken malleus, were

[2] This will be found in Square 7/E in Pl. IV.

[3] These are illustrated in pls. LXIX, 11-15; LXXVI, 5, 6.

[4] Pl. XXIV, 4.

[5] The authors of this report wish to go on record as expressing their appreciation of the care with which the skull was exhumed and prepared in the field and shipped to this Laboratory for study. The excellent procedure throughout renders our interpretation much more valid.

recovered. Right stapes and left incus and stapes were lost, and the other ear ossicles broken, *before* the skull was put in the jar.

When the entire skull was freed from earth and paraffin it was found that the roof, floor, and medial wall of both orbits were incomplete, the tip of the nasal bones broken off, and the squamous portion of the left temporal bone incomplete. Several sutures were " sprung " but were easily restored to normal relationships. The entire skull was hardened and preserved with *Zapon*.

In his study of the site of Chanhu-daro Dr. Mackay (*op. cit.*, p. 92) [6] concluded that " at least three floods, the third of which was perhaps the great flood that led to the desertion of Mohenjo-daro, have left their traces at Chanhu-daro. Living on the banks of a great river running through an alluvial plain must have proved even more disconcerting in ancient times than it does today in many parts of the world." This observation finds interesting confirmation in the fact that when the earth (alluvial silt) was carefully removed from the nasal area and paranasal sinuses, especially the maxillary sinuses, there was found a well-marked lamination. The laminae were so numerous, however, that they suggested an almost seasonal or annual flooding of the portion of the mound in which the jar was found.[7]

Craniologic observations and craniometric measurements

The skull is that of a female. It is small and smooth, with small teeth and short, broad palate and small mastoid processes. The supraorbital ridges are very slightly developed, but glabella is relatively quite prominent. The occiput is smoothly rounded, with very slightly developed lineae transversae and a very small inion. The cranial capacity (average of 10 trials) is 1222 c.c.

The skull is that of a young adult. Basilar suture is united, but all other sutures of vault and face are patent. There is no evidence of beginning union. All muscular impressions are very faint. Endocranially the margins of the venous sinus grooves are rounded and the grooves are quite shallow. The meningeal sulci are also shallow and with rounded margins. These characters point to an age of between twenty-two and twenty-five years.

The posterior area of the right and left parietal shows ectocranially a vascular pitting, evidence of a slight nutritional disturbance in childhood, too slight, however, to result in any aberrancy in the cranio-facial growth pattern. The skull is that of an individual with a good health history.[8]

The teeth that are present—right, first and second molars, left central and lateral incisors, second premolar, and first molar—do not in their morphology present any unusual features. The left first molar has an extensive carious lesion located at the contact surface with second molar. The left second molar was lost shortly before death, since alveolar

[6] See also Chapter II of this book.

[7] This can be explained by surface water percolating slowly through the jar in which this skull was found (E. M.).

[8] We are indebted to the late Dr. T. Wingate Todd for the observations on age and on health history.

absorption is incomplete. Both third molars are missing, nor can any trace of them be discerned in the X-ray.[9] The palate is broad and horseshoe-shaped, with the molar rows converging posteriorly.

Viewed from norma facialis the face is seen to be unusually broad and flat. In keeping with this the forehead is broad. The nasal aperture is also broad, with a tendency to "troughing" or "guttering," i. e., lack of sharp differentiation between lower nasal margin and alveolar portion of the maxillae. The interorbital distance is, on the other hand, rather narrow, with the upper half of the nasal bones excessively narrow. The distance between nasal floor and level of the teeth is very short. The orbits are slightly angular and tend to be low. Viewed from norma lateralis sinistra the facial flatness is emphasized. The forehead slopes back moderately to a low vault with tendency to a sagittal plateau. The occipital region—upper half of the squamous portion of the occipital bone—is very prominently bulged (*occiput en chignon*). Viewed from norma verticalis the skull is an elongate oval, broad frontally, narrower occipitally, with an increased breadth across the parietal eminences. There is no postorbital constriction and the temporal areas are evenly developed. Viewed from norma occipitalis the skull is roughly pentagonoid, the expanded parietal eminences again standing out.

There is an *os epiptericum* on both sides. The pterion, right and left, is H-shaped.

Figures 5-9 in Pl. XCV are photographs of the skull in the following views: facial, left lateral, vertical, occpital, basilar. Figures 10-12 in Pl. XCVI are craniographic drawings of the skull in the following views: facial, left lateral, vertical.[10]

In Table 1 the essential cranial measurements and indices, and in Table 2 the essential facial measurements and indices are given.[11]

With a length-breadth ratio of 71.07 the skull is dolichocranic, long-headed. The height-length ratio of 69.10 is chamaecranic, low-headed. The height-breadth ratio of 97.23 is metriocranic, moderately broad-headed. The transverse fronto-parietal ratio of 76.68 is eurymetopic, typical of a broad forehead. The gnathic or alveolar index of 97.87 is barely orthognathous, or straight-faced, i. e., evidence of only a slight downward and forward slant.

With an upper face height—bizygomatic breadth ratio of 49.03 the face is euryenic, broad and low. The ratios of 60.39, upper mid-face breadth to upper face-height, and of 98.02, maximum cranial breadth to bizygomatic breadth, are confirmatory of a broad face. The height-breadth ratio of the nose is 51.55, chamaerrhinic, characteristic of a wide nose. The height-breadth ratio of the orbit is 75.58, chamaeconchic, pointing to a low orbit. The breadth-length ratio of the palate is 89.88, brachystaphylic, indicative of a broad palate.

In summary, the skull is long, low, and broad at the forehead; the face is broad, low, flat, and only slightly projecting; the nose and palate are broad; the orbits are low. The long skull and the broad face are contrasting—disharmonic-features.

[9] Taken in the Broadbent-Bolton Roentgenographic Cephalometer of the Bolton Fund through the courtesy of Dr. B. Holly Broadbent.

[10] It will be noted that in Fig. 7 the parietal eminences are emphasized to a greater extent than in Fig. 12. This is due to the fact that the contour in Fig. 12 is at glabellar level, *below* the eminences.

[11] The measurements are according to Martin (14, pp. 625-62) and Morant (15, pp. 196-200).

Comparison with contemporary and with geographically related cranial material

When the skull was being worked out of its matrix of earth and protective covering of paraffin wax it was provisionally decided that its length-breadth proportions—obviously dolichocranic—placed it with the Proto-Mediterranean physical type. We were prepared for this, for we have concluded elsewhere (*10, 11*) that the Proto-Mediterraneans are basic not only to the geographic area from which they take their name, but also throughout the Middle East and the Indo-Iranian Area.

Accordingly we shall compare the Chanhu-daro skull first with female Proto-Mediterranean crania from Siālkot, Mohenjo-daro, Tepe Hissar, Anau, Ur, Kish, Alishar, and Hanai Tepe. Siālkot is stated by Sewell and Guha (*21*, p. 56, *6*, p. lxviii) to be " more or less contemporaneous with the Chalcolithic Age in India." Mohenjo-daro is dated at *ca.* 3250-2750 B. C. by Marshall (*13*, pp. 103-4), while Stein (*23*, p. 184) dates it during " the first quarter of the third millennium B. C." Tepe Hissar is divided into three periods by Schmidt, as follows: Period I, before 4000 B. C. to *ca.* 3500 B. C.; Period II, *ca.* 3500 B. C. to *ca.* 3000 B. C.; Period III, *ca.* 3000 B. C. to *ca.* 2000 B. C. (?) (see *10*, p. 227 and Table VI). Ur is dated as *ca.* 1900-1700 B. C. (*10*, Table VI). Kish " A " dates to *ca.* 2900-2800 B. C. (*10*, Table VI). Alishar Chalcolithic is dated as *ca.* 3500-3000 B. C., and Alishar Copper Age is dated as *ca.* 3000-2500 B. C. (*10*, Table VI). Hanai Tepe " B " dates to *ca.* 2000 B. C. (*10*, Table VI). The chronological range covered by these comparative data is approximately 500 years earlier and later than the accepted age of the Chanhu-daro skull.

In Table 3 are given selected cranio-facial measurements and indices of the several female Mediterranean skulls from the foregoing sites.[12] All of the skulls, including Chanhu-daro, are dolichocranic except the mesocranic Alishar Copper Age and Anau. With respect to skull height Chanhu-daro is chamaecranic, Hissar II and III are orthocranic, while Siālkot, Mohenjo-daro and Kish " A " are weakly hypsicranic. The facial breadth is euryen in Chanhu-daro, mesen in Alishar Chalcolithic, and lepten in Hissar II and III and Kish " A." The orbital shape is chamaeconch in Chanhu-daro, mesoconch in Hissar II and III, Alishar Copper Age, and Anau, and hypsiconch in Mohenjo-daro, Alishar Chalcolithic, and Kish " A." The nasal aperture is chamaerrhine in Chanhu-daro and Kish " A " and mesorrhine in the other groups.

If we summarize the general Proto-Mediterranean type it becomes dolichocranic, long-headed; orthocranic, vault of moderate height; lepten, narrow-faced; mesoconchic, orbit of moderate height; mesorrhinic, nasal aperture of moderate breadth. In comparison the Chanhu-daro skull is long-headed, low vaulted, broad-faced, and has a low orbit and a broad

[12] For Siālkot see Sewell and Guha, 22, Table 2, pp. 69-70 and Guha, 6, p. lxviii; for Mohenjo-daro see Sewell and Guha, *21*, pp. 645-6; for Tepe Hissar see Krogman, *11*, Table XXXVI; for Anau see Sergi, *19*, p. 446; for Ur see Kappers, 8, p. 108, p. 112; for Kish " A " see Buxton, *1*, p. 110; for Alishar Chalcolithic and Alishar Copper Age see Krogman, *10*, Tables IV-V; for Hanai Tepe " B " see Kappers, 8, p. 104. It is to be noted that a second lot of cranial material from Mohenjo-daro is being studied by Guha and Basu, while a series from Harappā is being studied by Basu (Guha, 6, p. lxviii).

nasal aperture. In only one character—the length-breadth ratio of the vault—does the Chanhu-daro skull conform with the ideal Proto-Mediterranean type.

Long-headedness is not confined to the Proto-Mediterraneans, nor, indeed, is it solely an attribute of White (Caucasic) groups; it is characteristic of the great majority of Negroid types. The presence of such a type in early Indian history is quite generally accepted. Hutton (7, p. 27) states that the "earliest element (in India) was probably Negroid." Dixon (2, p. 243) states that the earliest ethnic type in India was a "dolichocephalic, dark-skinned Negroid population." Sewell and Guha (5, pp. 194-5; 22, p. 80) state that the basic races of India show a "definite Negrito Type in Southern India, and form an undoubted constituent of the lower stratum of the Indian population." In the Iron Age of India Taylor found, in cairns at Jewurgi, crania which showed Negroid characteristics (6, pp. lxxix-lxx). Friederichs and Müller conclude that a Hamitic type was represented at Mohenjo-daro, especially in crania Nos. 6, 7, 19 (3, Table III, p. 392), which were classified as Mediterranean by Sewell and Guha. The Hamitic type was defined by Friederichs and Müller as long-headed, with moderate to high vault, with moderate to narrow face, and with high orbit and moderate to narrow nose. These characters, very obviously, do not depart in any significant detail from those defined for the Proto-Mediterraneans.

At Tepe Hissar (*11*, Tables XXI-XXII) there were eleven male crania classified as Negroid. In Table 4 these are compared with the Chanhu-daro skull. There is an expected sex difference in the obviously greater dimensions of the male crania. The Tepe Hissar Negroids are dolichocranic, long-headed; chamaecranic, low vaulted; mesen, face of moderate breadth; mesoconchic, orbit of moderate height; chamaerrhine, broad-nosed. The Chanhu-daro skull agrees in being dolichocranic, chamaecranic, and chamaerrhinic. The length and height proportions of the vault and the nasal aperture appear to fall into the Negroid category, as exemplified by the Hissar material. The broad face is still unplaced.

It is this puzzling facial breadth—a broad, flat face which becomes disharmonic when it is compared with the long, low skull—which leads to a comparison with "Mongoloid" or Eastern Asiatic types.[18] In Table 5 the Chanhu-daro skull is compared with female crania from Tepe Hissar (*11*, Tables XXIII-XXIV) and with female Nāga crania measured by Kitson and Morant (9, Table IV, p. 11) and female Burmese crania measured by Tildesley (24, Table VIII, p. 240). The Tepe Hissar crania and Burmese A and B are brachycranic, round-headed; the Nāga and Burmese C are mesocranic, middle-headed. The Tepe Hissar crania are orthocranic, vault of moderate height ;all the others are hypsicranic, high-vaulted. The Tepe Hissar crania are euryen, broad-faced; all the others are mesen, face of moderate breadth (Burmese B is nearly lepten, narrow-faced). All crania are mesoconchic, orbit of moderate height (Burmese B is nearly hypsiconch, high orbit). The Tepe Hissar crania and the Nāga and Burmese A are chamaerrhine, broad-nosed; Burmese

[18] We shall use the term Eastern Asiatic in preference to Mongoloid. The former refers to the typical Far Eastern broad-faced brachycephali, while the latter should be restricted to the inhabitants of Mongolia, the true Mongols, who in their cranio-facial dimensions and proportions may approximate certain Caucasic groups.

B and C are mesorrhine, nose of moderate breadth (though both are nearly chamaerrhine). The Chanhu-daro skull verges upon these Eastern Asiatic types only in general increase of facial breadth and in the marked increase in nasal breadth. These two facial features may, in this instance, be linked, i. e., the chamaerrhinity may be a reflection of a general tendency to an individual facial breadth expansion, possibly during early facial growth.

It appears, therefore, that the Chanhu-daro skull in its cranial and facial measurements, indices, and morphological features reflects characteristics which in their entirety may be attributed to no one single type. Rather does there seem to be a blend, a composite, of diverse ethnic strains.

Conclusions

The Chanhu-daro skull is that of an adult female approximately twenty-two to twenty-five years of age. It was placed in the jar in which it was found some time after death.[14] With Mackay (12, p. 87) we conjecture " why the skull only was thus preserved and not the other bones." Was this the skull of a royal personage? A priestess? A sorceress? A captive of high rank? or possibly merely the possession of an individual who interred it in a jar in whimsical jest? Does the presence of the lone skull hint at ceremonial decapitation? or magical rites associated with the head (brain) as the center of being? These and similar questions arise—they cannot be answered. The presence of the skull, without lower jaw, without vertebrae, without any other skeletal parts, is the one objective fact. Subjective interpretations have no place here.

When we come to the problem of physical type we are almost forced into the realm of the subjective. If this skull had been assembled from odd parts it could not present a more conflicting picture. It is Proto-Mediterranean in its length, in its moderate interorbital distance, in its narrow nasal bones, in its high nasal bridge, in its short semi-parabolic palate and small teeth, and possibly in its occipital development. It is Negroid in its low flattened vault, in its broad nose with its " troughing " or slight sulcus prae-nasalis, in its diminished subnasal height, in its low orbits, and possibly in its length and occpital fullness. It appears to be Eastern Asiatic in its broad, flat face, in its broad forehead, and possibly in its broad nose.

We are fortunate, indeed, that the skull was preserved in almost perfect condition. Had it been fragmentary, necessitating a more or less complete restoration, then the conflicting features might be traced to partial or faulty reconstruction. But we are not dealing with missing pieces, with fragments of doubtful contact margin, or with regional areas which may represent different rates of progressive development. The Chanhu-daro skull is an entity presenting in undisturbed relationship the several apparently contradictory features already outlined.

The basis of the definition of characters diagnostic of ethnic types is a problem to be considered, especially with reference to the range of variation. There are certain cranial

[14] Petrie traces the origin of the Egyptian *shawabti*-figures to " the primitive custom of dismemberment," when " the skull was kept apart and later added to the body." The Chanhu-daro skull may reflect this " primitive custom of dismemberment."

and facial measurements and indices that overlap, as, for example, the length-breadth ratio in Proto-Mediterranean and Negroid. There are also certain morphological features which overlap—the filled-out occiput of the Proto-Mediterranean and the bulging occiput of the Negroid. Again, it is possible that general increase in facial breadth may result in an increased breadth in component parts. If this be true, then the chamaerrhinity at first considered Negroid may here merely accompany a broadened face which is representative of either a possible intermixture [15] with an Eastern Asiatic type or an individual cranio-facial pattern.

The early history of the Mediterranean type (the Proto-Mediterranean) is somehow linked with the emergence of the Negroid type. Whether it is traceable to common origin or early intermixture we cannot say. The fact remains that in Neolithic Spain, Portugal, Italy— the northern fringe of African influence—there are cranial types that combine in almost equal degree Caucasic and Negroid features. With time, apparently, the latter features were bred out to leave a purely Caucasic Mediterranean type.

It is theoretically possible, assuming Negroid and Caucasic traits to be components of the emerging Mediterranean type, that re-combinations occur at a later date to simulate an earlier form. The identification of a " Hamitic type " at Mohenjo-daro may be additional evidence of this possibility.

We venture to conclude, therefore, that the Chanhu-daro skill represents a Proto-Mediterranean type in which ancestral Negroid traits have manifested themselves. Such a view would explain all craniofacial characters except the disharmonic face breadth. Does this represent mixture with an Eastern Asiatic type? We think not, preferring to regard it as an individual variation quite apart. We prefer also to regard the broad nose as somehow related to the bizygomatic expansion. In its composite character the Chanhu-daro skull is a most instructive instance of the combination of basic or primitive features associated with purely individual characters.

Since this report was written (1937) Vallois has published on Sialk and Fürst on Shah Tepe. I have considered all the recent relevant material in a forthcoming report for the Oriental Institute on crania from Tell al-Judaidah and Chatal Hüyük. Everything tends to confirm the ideas herein presented. (W. M. K., Feb. 9, 1941).

References

JRAI = Journal of the Royal Anthropological Institute.

OIP = Oriental Institute Publications, Chicago.

1. Buxton, L. H. D. and Rice, D. T. 1931. " Report on the Human Remains Found at Kish " (with Preface by S. Langdon), *JRAI*, 61: 57-119.
2. Dixon, R. B. 1923. " The Racial History of Man," *Scribners*, New York.

[15] It would be difficult to explain the long-headedness of the Chanhu-daro skull in the presence of intermixture with a round-headed type. According to our best knowledge brachycephaly is dominant in a cross. Nor does the evidence at our disposal warrant the unquestioned acceptance of chamaerrhinity as a concomitant of an increased bizygomatic breadth. Among euryprosopic types the nasal index varies from mesorrhine to chamaerrhine.

3. Friederichs, H. F. and Muller, H. W. 1933. "Die Rassenelemente im Indus-Tal während des 4 und 3 vorchristlichen Jahrtausends und ihre Verbreitung," *Anthropos.* 28: 383-406.

4. Hargreaves, H. 1929. *Excavations in Balūchistān,* 1925. *Sampur Mound, Mastung, and Sohr Damb, Nāl.* (*Mem. Arch. Surv. Ind.* No. 35), Calcutta.

5. Guha, B. S. 1934. "Racial affinities of the people of India" (Abst.). C. R. *Congrès Internat. des Sciences Anthrop. et Ethnol.,* pp. 194-5. London.

6. ——. 1935. *Census of India, 1931.* Vol. I, *India.* Part III, *Ethnographical.* A. *Racial Affinities of the Peoples of India,* pp. i-lxxi and 1-116. Simla, Govt. India Press.

7. Hutton, J. H. 1934. "Racial and cultural history of India" (*Abst.*). C. R. *Congrès Internat. des Sciences Anthrop. et Ethnol.,* pp. 27-39. London.

8. Kappers, C. U. A. 1934. *The Anthropology of the Near East* (with Chapter X by L. W. Parr). Amsterdam.

9. Kitson, E. and Morant, G. M. 1933. "A Study of the Nāga Skull," *Biometrika,* 25: 1-20.

10. Krogman, W. M. 1938. "Cranial Types from Alişar Hüyük and Their Relations to Other Racial Types, Ancient and Modern of Europe and Western Asia. (In "The Alishar Hüyük, Seasons of 1930-32," Part III, *OIP,* Vol. XXX, Chicago, by H. H. von der Osten, 1938.)

11. Krogman, W. M. 1940. "Racial Types from Tepe Hissar, Iran, from the Late Fifth to the Early Second Millennium, B. C., *Verhand. der Konink Nederl. Akad. Weten.* Tweedie Sectie, Vol. XXXIX, No. 2, pp. 1-87.

12. Mackay, E. 1936. "Excavations at Chanhu-daro by the American School of Indic and Iranian Studies and the Museum of Fine Arts, Boston: Season 1935-36," *Bull. Mus. Fine Arts,* Boston. 34: 83-92.

13. Marshall, Sir J. H. (ed.). 1931. *Mohenjo-daro and the Indus Civilization,* Vols. I-III, London.

14. Martin, R. 1928. *Lehrbuch der Anthropologie,* Second ed. Vol. II, pp. 625-62, Fischer, Jena.

15. Morant, G. M. 1922-23. "A First Study of the Tibetan Skull," *Biometrika,* 14: pp. 193-260.

16. ———. 1924. "A Study of Certain Oriental Crania Including the Nepalese and Tibetan Series in the British Museum (Natural History)," *Biometrika,* 16: pp. 1-105.

17. Petrie, Sir. F. Shabtis. *Brit. School Archeol. in Egypt.* London (see *Man* for April, 1937, No. 84, pp. 69-70).

18. Pumpelly, R. 1908. *Explorations in Turkestan, 1904. Prehistoric Civilizations of Anau* (2 vols.). Carnegie Inst. of Washington.

19. Sergi, G. 1908. "Description of Some Skulls from the North Kurgan, Anau," Vol. II, pp. 445-6 (in Pumpelly, *op. cit.*).

20. Schmidt, E. F. 1933. "Tepe Hissar Excavations, 1931," *Museum Journal,* Univ. Mus., 23: pp. 323-483.

21. Sewell, R. B. S. and Guha, B. S. 1931. "Human Remains Found at Mohenjo-daro," Vol. II, pp. 599-648 (in Marshall, *op. cit.*).

22. Sewell, R. B. S. and Guha, B. S. 1929. "Report on the Bones Excavated at Nāl," Appendix V, pp. 56-89 (in Hargreaves, *op. cit.*).

23. Stein, Sir A. 1934. "The Indo-Iranian Borderlands: their Prehistory in the Light of Geography and Recent Explorations," *JRAI,* 64: pp. 179-202.

24. Tildesley, M. L. 1920-21. "A First Study of the Burmese Skull," *Biometrika,* 13: pp. 176-262.

TABLE 1

Cranial Measurements and Indices of the Chanhu-daro Skull

Maximum length (l)	178.0 mm.
Minimum breadth (b)	126.5
Minimum forehead breadth (b′)	97.0
Basio-bregmatic height (h′)	123.0
Auriculo-vertical height (oh)	108.0
Basi-nasal length (lb)	94.0
Basi-prosthion length (gl)	92.0
Transverse arc (q′)	279.0
Sagittal arc (s)	353.0
Nasion-bregma arc (s_1)	126.0
Bregma-lambda arc (s_2)	116.0
Lambda-opisthion arc (s_3)	111.0
Horizontal circumference (u)	492.0
Bi-asterionic breadth	98.0
Cranial index (b × 100/l)	71.07
Height-length index (h′ × 100/l)	69.10
Height-breadth index (h′ × 100/b)	97.23
Transverse fronto-parietal index (b′ × 100/b)	76.68
Gnathic index (gl. × 100/lb)	97.87

TABLE 2

Facial Measurements and Indices of the Chanhu-daro Skull

Total face height, na-gn (gh)	——
Upper face height, na-pros (g′h)	61.0 mm.
Mid-face breadth (gb)	101.0
Bi-zygomatic breadth (j)	124.0
Nasal height (nhl)	48.5
Nasal breadth (nb)	25.0
Interorbital width (dc)	——
Orbital breadth (o_1 l)	——
Orbital breadth (o_1' l)	43.0
Orbital height (o_2 l)	32.5
Palatal length (gl′)	44.5
Palatal breadth (g_2)	39.0
Foramen magnum length (f m l)	37.0
Foramen magnum breadth (f m b)	30.0
Total facial index (gh × 100/j)	——
Upper facial index (g′h × 100/j)	49.03
Total mid-facial index (gh × 100/gb)	——
Upper mid-facial index (g′ h ×100/gb)	60.39
Nasal index (nb × 100/nhl)	51.55
Orbital index (o_2 l × 100/o_1' l)	75.58
Palatial index (g_2 × 100/gl′)	89.88
Foraminal index (fmb × 100/fml)	81.18
Transverse cranio-facial index (j × 100/b)	98.02

TABLE 3

Cranio-Facial Measurements and Indices of the Female Proto-Mediterranean Type

	Chanhu-daro	Mohenjo-daro Nos. 7, 10, 19, 26	Siālkot	Kish "A"	Ur	Anau	Hanai Tepe "B"	Alishar Chalco-lithic	Alishar Copper Age	Tepe Hissar I	Tepe Hissar II	Tepe Hissar III
	(1)	(4)	(1)	(1)	(4)	(1)	(1)	(1)	(1)	(1)	(7)	(32)
Maximum length	178.0	180.17	...	176.0	184.75	185.0	179.0	179.0	177.0	175.0	178.29	180.33 mm.
Maximum breadth	126.5	118.33	.	124.0	131.50	141.0	128.0	130.0	137.0	131.0	132.14	131.58
Basio-bregmatic height	123.0	136.00	. .	142.0	. .	. .	. . .				129.86	129.26
Cranial index	71.07	63.45	71.10	70.45	71.25	76.20	71.50	72.60	77.40	74.85	74.10	72.97
Height-length index	69.10	75.66	77.78	80.68	....	...	...	....	...	.	72.86	71.87
Total face height	.	...	....	....	....	....	....	...	....	. .	111.40	108.89
Upper face height	61.0	...	....	62.0	....	..	....	66.0	.	....	67.57	66.47
Bi-zygomatic breadth	124.0	94.00	....	110.0	....	....	....	124.0	113.0	....	116.20	120.56
Total facial index	....	. .	...	..	....	....	....	.	...	....	92.67	90.98
Upper facial index	49.03	...	....	56.36	....	....	....	53.20	....	....	56.38	55.31
Orbital breadth	43.0	38.25	....	37.0	....	36.0	....	38.0	37.0	..	38.71	39.94
Orbital height	32.5	32.94	....	34.4	..	30.0	..	35.0	31.0....	....	30.71	31.97
Orbital index	75.58	87.92	....	91.89	....	83.33	....	92.10	83.80	....	79.33	80.12
Nasal height	48.5	46.13	....	49.5	....	....	....	46.0	....	....	48.29	48.59
Nasal breadth	25.0	22.13	....	30.5	....	....	....	22.0	....	....	23.71	23.84
Nasal index	51.55	48.04	....	61.61	....	....	....	47.80	....	..	49.14	50.37

TABLE 4

Negroid Males at Tepe Hissar Compared with the Female Chanhu-daro Skull

	Chanhu-daro	Hissar III
	(1)	(2)
Maximum length	178.0	188.64
Maximum breadth	126.5	131.45
Basio-bregmatic height	123.0	129.90
Cranial index	71.07	69.66
Height-length index	69.10	69.41
Total face height		112.30
Upper face height	61.0	68.36
Bi-zygomatic breadth	124.0	125.30
Total facial index		89.57
Upper facial index	49.03	54.34
Orbital breadth	43.0	40.46
Orbital height	32.5	31.18
Orbital index	75.58	77.09
Nasal height	48.5	49.27
Nasal breadth	25.0	27.30
Nasal index	51.55	55.47

TABLE 5

The Chanhu-daro Skull Compared with Female Crania from Tepe Hissar and with Modern Female Naga and Burmese Types

	Chanhu-daro	Tepe Hissar	Nāga	Burmese A	Burmese B	Burmese C
	(1)	(2)	(8)	(38)	(17)	(18)
Maximum length	178.0	171.0	173.1	166.5	163.80	170.2
Maximum breadth	126.5	137.5	132.9	138.0	135.6	130.6
Basio-bregmatic height	123.0	125.0	127.6	130.4	130.8	129.4
Cranial index	71.07	80.45	76.70	83.10	82.90	76.90
Height-length index	69.10	73.19	76.60	78.30	79.80	76.00
Total face height	..	107.5				
Upper face height	61.0	68.0	63.9	66.0	66.1	63.9
Bi-zygomatic breadth	124.0	130.0	125.1	126.7	121.9	118.7
Total facial index		82.70				
Upper facial index	49.03	52.33	51.10	52.10	54.20	53.80
Orbital breadth	43.0	43.0	41.5	41.8	41.5	42.2
Orbital height	32.5	34.0	32.4	34.6	34.6	33.2
Orbital index	75.58	79.03	78.50	82.80	83.00	78.8
Nasal height	48.5	49.5	48.4	50.6	49.4	47.3
Nasal breadth	25.0	25.5	25.7	26.8	25.0	24.0
Nasal index	51.55	52.80	54.20	52.70	50.70	50.50

BIBLIOGRAPHY

Abbott, J., *The Keys of Power*, London and New York, 1932.

Albright, W. F., "A Set of Egyptian Playing Pieces and Dice from Palestine," *Mizraim*, Vol. I, 1933. New York, London.

Allen, J., "Ancient Indian Coins," *Catalogue British Museum, 1936.*

Ancient Egypt and the East, 1933-35.

Andrae, A. W., *Die Archaischen Ischtar-Temple in Assur*, Leipzig Berlin, 1922.

Andrews, F. H., "Neolithic Pottery in Sistān," *Burlington Magazine*, 1925.

Annual Bibliography of Indian Archaeology for 1932, Leyden, 1934.

Anthropos, 1933, Vienna.

Antiquaries Journal, Society of Antiquaries, London. Vols. II, VIII, X, XII, XIII.

Antiquity, Vols. I, IX, X. Gloucester.

Archaeologia, published by the Society of Antiquaries, London. Vol. LXXIX.

Arkell, A. J., "Cambay and the Bead Trade," *Antiquity*, Vol. X.

Annual Report of the Archaeological Survey of India, 1926-1929.

Beck, H., "Notes on Glazed Stones (Glazed Steatite)," *Ancient Egypt and the East*, 1934.

Biometrika, 1920-24, 1933. Cambridge, England.

Bosanquet and Dawkins, "Palaikastro Excavations," *Journal British School, Athens:* Suppl. Paper, No. 1.

Brunton, G., *Mostagedda*. London, 1937.

Brunton, G., and G. Caton-Thompson, *The Badarian Civilization*, London, 1928.

Burlington Magazine, London, 1925.

Buxton, L. H. D., "Report on the Human Remains at Kish," *Journal Royal Anthropological Institute*, 1931.

Catalogue, Devizes Museum, Devizes, Eng.

Caton-Thompson, G. and G. Brunton, *The Badarian Civilization*, London, 1928.

Childe, V. G., *Ancient Egypt and the East*, London, 1933.

———, *The Aryans*, New York, London, 1926.

———, *Danube in Prehistory*, Oxford, 1929.

———, *New Light on the Most Ancient East*, New York, London, 1934.

Contenau, G. and G. Ghirshman, *Fouilles du Tépé Giyan*, Paris, 1935.

Cowell, E. B., The Vātaka or stories of the Buddha's former births (Mittavinda-Vātaka).

Crooke, W., *Religion and Folk-lore of Northern India*, London, 1896.

Delaporte, L., *Catalogue des Cylindres Orientaux*, Musée du Louvre, Paris.

Dixon, R. B., *The Racial History of Man*, New York, London, 1923.

Dumont, P. E., *Journal American Oriental Society*, Vol. 53.

Durai, H. G., *Man*, 1929.

Ebert, M., *Reallexikon der Vorgeschichte*. Berlin, 1924-1932.

Evans, Sir A., *Palace of Minos*. London, 1921-35.

"Evil Eye Brands," *Illustrated Weekly of India*, April, 1931.

Fleure, H., and H. Peake, *Journal Royal Anthropological Institute*, 1930.

Frankfort, H., in *Illustrated London News*, 1932.

———, *Oriental Institute Communications*, Chicago, Nos. 16, 19, 20.

———, "The Indus Civilization and the Near East," *Annual Bibliography of Indian Archaeology*, 1932. Leyden, 1934.

Friederichs, H. F., *Der Alte Orient*, 1933.

———, and H. W. Muller, "Die Rassenelemente in Indus-Tal während des 4 und 3 vorchristlichen Jahrtausends und ihre Verbreitung," *Anthropos*, 1933. Wien.

Further Excavations at Mohenjo-daro (F. E. M.), by E. J. H. Mackay, Government of India Press, New Delhi, 1938.

Gadd, C. J., "Seals of Ancient Indian Style found at Ur," *Proceedings of the British Academy*, Vol. XVIII.

Ghirshman, R., *Fouilles de Sialk*, Musée du Louvre, Vol. I, 1938.

Guha, B. S., Census of India, 1931. Vol. I, *India*. Part III, *Ethnographical*. A. *Racial Affinities of the Peoples of India*. Government of India Press, Simla, 1935.

Guha, B. S., *Racial Affinities of the People of India* (Abst.), C. R. Congrès Internat. des Sciences Anthrop. et Ethnol., 1934.

Guide to the Antiquities of the Bronze Age, British Museum, 1920.

Hall, H. R., *A Season's Work at Ur*, London, 1930.

———, *Babylonian and Assyrian Sculpture in the British Museum*, Paris and Brussels, 1928.

———, *Bronze Age of Greece*, New York, 1927; London, 1928.

———, and C. L. Woolley, *Ur Excavations*, Vol. I. London and Philadelphia, 1928.

Hamilton, R. W., "Excavations at Tell Abu Hawām," *Quarterly of the Department of Antiquities in Palestine*, Vol. IV, 1934.

Hargreaves, H., "*Excavations in Balūchistān (Memoir of the Archaeological Survey of India, No. 35)*, 1929.

Harrison, H. S., *Pots and Pans* (The Beginning of Things Series). London, 1928.

Hawes, H. B., *Gournia. Univ. of Pennsylvania Museum Trans.*, Vol. 1, 1904.

Heine-Geldern, R., "Archaeological Traces of the Vedic Aryans," *Journal of the Indian Society of Oriental Art*, Vol. IV, 1936.

Hemmy, A. S., "Statistical Treatment of Ancient Weights," *Ancient Egypt and the East*, 1935.

Herzfeld, E., *Die Ausgrabungen von Samarra, V.*, 1930.

Herzfeld, E., in *Illustrated London News*, 1929.

Hilzheimer, M., "The Evolution of the Domestic Horse," *Antiquity*, Vol. IX.

Hopkins, E. W., *The Religions of India*, Boston, 1895.

Hrozny, B., *O Nejstarším Stěhování Národů A O Problému Civilisace Proto-Indické*, Prague, 1939.

Hume, R. E., *The Thirteen Principal Upanishads*.

Hutton, J. H., *Racial and Cultural History of India* (Abst.), C. R. Congrès Internat. des Sciences Anthrop. et Ethnol., 1934.

Illustrated London News, 1929, 1931, 1932, 1939.

Illustrated Weekly of India, 1931. Bombay.

Iraq, Vols. III, VII. London.

Jordan, J., Abhandlungen der Preussischen Akademie der Wissenschaften. Phil.-Hist. Klasse (*Ausgrabungen in Uruk-Warka*), 1929.

Journal American Oriental Society, Vols. 53, 57.

Journal British School at Athens: Suppl. Paper No. 1.

Journal of Egyptian Archaeology, 1928. London.

Journal of the Indian Society of Oriental Art, Vol. IV, 1936.

Journal of the Royal Anthropological Institute, 1930, 1931, 1934.

Journal of the Royal Asiatic Society, 1930, 1933.

Kappers, C. U. A., *The Anthropology of the Near East* (with Chapter by L. W. Parr), Amsterdam, 1934.

Kitson, E., and G. M. Morant, "A Study of the Nāga Skull," *Biometrika*, 1933.

Koldewey, R., *Excavations at Babylon*, 1914.

Krogman, W. M., *Cranial Types from Alisar Hüyük, and their Relations to Other Racial Types, Ancient and Modern of Europe and Western Asia*. in *The Alishar Hüyük, Seasons* 1930-32 (*Oriental Institute Publications, Chicago*, Vol. XXX), 1938.

Langdon, S., *Oxford Editions of Cuneiform Texts*, Vol. VII.

Legrain, L., *Culture of the Babylonians*, Philadelphia, 1925.

———, *Ur Excavations*, Vol. III.

Liverpool Annals of Archaeology and Anthropology, Vol. VIII.

Lucas, A., *Ancient Egyptian Materials*. London, 1934.

Mackay, E., *Anthropology Memoirs*, Field Museum, Chicago, Vol. I.
———, "Bead Making in Ancient Sind," *Journal American Oriental Society*, Vol. 57.
———, "Decorated Carnelian Beads," *Man*, Vol. XXXIII.
———, "Excavations at Chanhu-daro by the American School of Indic and Iranian Studies and the Museum of Fine Arts, Boston: Season 1935-36," *Bulletin of the Museum of Fine Arts, Boston*, November, 1936.
———, *Further Excavations at Mohenjo-daro* (F. E. M.), Government of India Press, New Delhi, 1938.
———, "Painted Pottery in Modern Sind," *Journal of the Royal Anthropological Institute*, 1930.
Majumdar, N. G., "Explorations in Sind" (*Memoir Archaeological Survey of India*, No. 48), 1934.
Mallowan, M. E. L., "Excavations at Tall Chagar Bazar," *Iraq*, Vol. III.
———, M. E. L., in *Illustrated London News*, 1939.
Mallowan, M. E. L., and J. Cruikshank Rose, *Prehistoric Assyria*, 1935.
Man, 1925, 1929, 1933, 1939.
Marshall, Sir J. (edited by). *Mohenjo-daro and the Indus Civilization* (M. I. C.), 1931. London.
Martin, R., *Lehrbuch der Anthropologie* (2nd Edit.), Vol. II, 1928. Jena.
Mémoires de la Mission Archéologique en Perse, Vols. I, VIII, XIII, XX.
Memoirs of the Archaeological Survey of India, Nos. 35, 37, 43, 48.
Mizraim, New York, Vol. I, 1933.
Moore, *Carthage of the Phoenicians*. London, 1905.
Morant, G. M., "A First Study of the Tibetan Skull," *Biometrika*, 1922-23.
Morant, G. M., "A Study of certain Oriental Crania including the Nepalese and Tibetan Series in the British Museum (Natural History)," *Biometrika*, 1924.
Morgan, J. de, *La Préhistoire Orientale*. Paris, 1925-1927.
Museum Journal, University Museum, University of Pennsylvania, 1933, 1937.
Myres, J. L., "The Structure and Origin of the Minoan Body-shield." *Man*, 1939.
Noetling, *Zeitschrift für Ethnologie*, 1898.
Oppenheim, Baron Max von, *Tell Halaf*. Leipzig, 1931; London and New York, 1933.
Oppert, G., *On the Original Inhabitants of Bharatavarsa or India*, 1893. Madras, 1889.
Oriental Institute Communications, Chicago. Nos. 16, 19, 20.
Peet, T. E., *Stone and Bronze Ages in Italy and Sicily*, Oxford, 1909.
Petrie, Sir F., *Ancient Gaza*, IV. London, 1931-34.
———, *Buttons and Design Scarabs*. London, 1925.
———, *Decorative Patterns of the Ancient World*, London, 1930.
———, *Egyptian Decorative Art*, London, 1895.
———, *Illahun, Kahun and Gurob*, London, 1891.
———, *The Making of Egypt*, London and New York, 1939.
———, *Shabtis*, London, 1935.
———, and J. E. Quibell, *Nagada and Ballas*, London, 1896.
Preusser, C., *Tell Asmar and Khafaje*, Oriental Institute of Chicago, Chicago, 1932.
Pumpelly, R., *Explorations in Turkestān, 1904: Prehistoric Civilizations of Anau*, Carnegie Institute of Washington, 1908.
Quarterly of the Department of Antiquities in Palestine, Vol. IV.
Quibell, J. E., and F. W. Green, *Hierakonpolis*, London, 1900-1902.
Rostovtzeff, M., *History of the Ancient World*, Oxford, 1926-7.
Schliemann, H., *Ilios*, New York, 1881.
———, *Troja*, Waren, Gwandt, 1875.
———, *Troy and Its Remains*, London, 1875.
Schmidt, E. F., "Tepe Hissar Excavations, 1931," *The Museum Journal*, University Museum, Philadelphia, Vol. XXIII, 1933.
Sewell, R. B. S., and B. S. Guha, "Human Remains found at Mohenjo-daro," *Mohenjo-daro and the Indus Civilization*, 1931.

———, ———, "Report on the Bones excavated at Nāl," in *Memoir of the Archaeological Survey of India*, No. 35, 1929.

Sergi, G., "Description of some Skulls from the North Kurgan, Anau," in *Explorations in Turkestān*, Vol. II, 1908.

Smith, S., *Alalakh and Chronology*, 1940.

Speiser, E. A., *Excavations at Tepe Gawra*, Vol. I. American Schools of Oriental Research, Philadelphia, 1935.

———, "The Pottery of Tell Billa," *The Museum Journal*, University Museum, Philadelphia, Vol. XXIII, 1933.

Stein, Sir A., *Archaeological Reconnaissances in North-Western India and South-Eastern Irān*, New York, 1937.

———, *An Archaeological Tour in Gedrosia* (*Memoir Archaeological Survey of India*, No. 43), 1931.

———, *An Archaeological Tour in Wāziristān and Northern Balūchistān* (*Memoir Archaeological Survey of India*, No. 37), 1929.

———, "The Indo-Iranian Borderlands: their Prehistory in the Light of Geography and Recent Explorations," *Journal Royal Anthropological Institute*, 1934.

———, in *Iraq*, Vol. III.

Streeter, E. W., *Precious Stones and Gems*, London, 1877.

Swindler, M. H., *Ancient Painting*, New Haven and London, 1929.

Thompson, C., *Archaeologia*, Vol. LXXIX.

———, and M. Mallowan, *Illustrated London News*, 1931.

Tildesley, M. L., "A First Study of the Burmese Skull," *Biometrika*, 1920-21.

Ur Excavations, Vols. I, II, III, V. London and Philadelphia, 1927, 1934, 1936, 1939.

Ward, W. H., *The Seal Cylinders of Western Asia*, Washington, 1910.

Watelin, L. Ch., *Excavations at Kish*, IV.

Woodward, F. L., *The Book of Gradual Sayings* (Anguttara-Nikaya).

Woolley, Sir L., *Antiquaries Journal*, Vol. XII.

———, *The Development of Sumerian Art*, London, 1935.

———, *Royal Cemetery, Ur Excavations*, Vol. II, London and Philadelphia, 1934.

———, *The Ziggurat and its Surroundings, Ur Excavations*, Vol. V.

Zervos, C., *L'Art Mesopotamie*, Paris, 1935.

CATALOGUE OF ILLUSTRATED OBJECTS

[Plates: Frontispieces: XXIII–XCVI]

All measurements are in inches and decimals of inches.
Abbreviations: A. = America (where objects so marked were sent).

Ag. Agate
Ameth. Amethyst
Bar. Barrel-shaped
Bf. Buff
Bl. Black
Blu. Blue
Br. Brown or Bronze
Brec. Breccia
Car. Carnelian
Ch. Chert
Chal. Chalcedony
Cop. Copper
Cr. Cream-coloured
Cry. Crystal
Cyl. Cylindrical
Dec. Decoration
Di. Diameter
Dp. Deep
Dr. Drab
Drk. Dark
Fai. Faience
Gl. Glaze
Gr. Grey
Gre. Green
Hi. High
Hnd. mde. Hand-made
Hor. Hornblende
Iv. Ivory
Jas. Jasper
Lap.-laz. Lapis-lazuli
Lev. Level
Lg. Long
Lim. Limestone
Loc. Locus
Lt. Light (of hue)
Mar. Marble
Pas. Paste
Perf. Perforated
Pla. Plasma
Pnk. Pink
Pot. Pottery
Pt. Paint
Purp. Purple
Rd. Red
San. Sandstone
Sect. Section
Sh. Shell
Slp. Slip
Sq. Square
St. Stone
Steat. Steatite
Th. Thick
Unfin. Unfinished
Vitr. Vitreous paste
Wde. Wide
Wh. White
Yell. Yellow

Frontispiece (a). Painted Jar (Harappā Culture). Chapter VI. (No. 503). 21.2 hi. Trench B(3), lev. – 6.5 ft.

Frontispiece (b). Painted Pottery (Jhukar Culture). Chapter VII

(1). (No. 4731). Pnk. pas. Cr. slp. Bl. & Rd. pts. 3.23 lg. Cut., sq. 10/G, loc. 477, lev. + 0.8 ft. A
(2). (No. 5164). Pnk. pas. Pnk. slp. Bl. & Rd. pts. 2.5 hi. Cut., sq. 10/F, loc. 484, lev. — 1.4 ft. A
(3). (No. 4746). Pnk. pas. Cr. slp. Br. & Rd. pts. 2.62 lg. Cut., sq. 10/F, loc. 464, lev + 1.3 ft. A
(4). (No. 2111). Pnk. pas. Cr. slp. Purp. & Rd. pts. Sq. 8/E, loc. 91. lev. + 13.5 ft. A
(5). (No. 2086). Pnk. pas. Rd. slp. Bl. pt. 2.75 lg. Sq. 8/E, loc. 146, lev. + 15.0 ft.
(6). (No. 2086). Pnk. pas. Rd. slp. Bl. pt. Sq. 8/E, loc. 146, lev. + 15.0 ft. A
(7). (No. 2015). Pnk. pas. Pnk. slp. Bl. & Rd. pts. Sq. 9/E, loc. 127, lev. + 13.3 ft. A
(8). (No. 2111). Pnk. pas. Cr. slp. Purp. & Rd. pts. Sq. 8/E, loc. 91, lev. + 13.5 ft. A
(9). (No. 1849). Pnk. pas. Cr. slp. Bl. & Rd. pts. 2.42 lg. Sq. 9/E, loc. 123, lev. + 17.5 ft. A
(10). (No. 1754). Pnk. pas. Rd. & Cr. slps. Rd. & Br. pts. 3.62 lg. Sq. 8/D, loc. 84, lev. + 20.7 ft. A

Plate XXIII. Painted Pottery (Harappā Culture). Chapter VI.

(1). (No. 5373). Pnk. pas. Rd. slp. Bl. pt. Cut., sq. 10/G, loc. 478, lev. — 9.4 ft. A
(2). (No. 3702). Pnk. pas. Rd. slp. Bl. pt. 2.5 hi. Trench B(5), loc. 43, lev. — 5.9 ft. A
(3). (No. 4935). Pnk. pas. Rd. slp. Bl. pt. Mound I, sq. 12/K, loc. 20, lev. + 13.5 ft. A
(4). (No. 5393). Pnk. pas. Rd. slp. Bl. pt. 7.7 di. Cut., sq. 9/F, loc. 469, lev. — 11.0 ft. A
(5). (No. 3754). Pnk. pas. Rd. slp. Bl. pt. 5.28 lg. Trench F(2), loc. 66, lev. — 6.6 ft.
(6). (No. 3011, A). Pnk. pas. Rd. slp. Bl. pt. Sq. 9/C, loc. 208, lev. + 9.6 ft. A

Plate XXIV. Storage Jars (Harappā Culture). Chapter VII

(1). (No. 3323). Pnk. pas. Sq. 9/C, loc. 296, lev. + 7.2 ft. A
(2). (No. 3209). Incised pan. Pnk. pas. Rd. slp. Sq. 9/B, loc. 442, lev. + 6.7 ft.
(3). (No. 3489). Pnk. pas. Sq. 7/C, loc. 461, lev. + 9.1 ft.
(4). (No. 3324, A). Pnk. pas. Cr. slp. Sq. 7/E, loc. 324, lev. + 9.2 ft. A
(5). (No. 3047). Pnk. pas. Cr. slp. Sq. 8/E, loc. 87, lev. + 8.7 ft.
(6). (No. 3491). Pnk. pas. Rd. slp. Bl. pt. Sq. 8/C, loc. 289, lev. + 8.6 ft. A
(7). (No. 3321). Pnk. pas. Cr. slp. Sq. 6/F, loc. 159, lev. + 8.8 ft. A
(8). (No. 3153, A). Pnk. pas. Rd. slp. Sq. 7/F, loc. 110, lev. + 8.7 ft. A
(9). (No. 3490). Pnk. pas. Sq. 7/C, loc. 461, lev. + 9.1 ft.

Plate XXV. Pottery Vessels (Harappā Culture). Chapter VI

(1). (No. 4411). Dish of food-stand. Pnk. pas. Rd. slp. Sq. 7/D, loc. 271, lev. + 7.2 ft.
(2). (No. 3958). Dish of food-stand. Pnk. pas. Rd. slp. Cut., sq. 10/F, loc. 423, lev. + 7.7 ft. A
(3). (No. 2815). Dish of food-stand. Pnk. pas. Rd. slp. Sq. 9/C, loc. 213, lev. + 10.4 ft.
(4). (No. 5330). Dish of food-stand. Pnk. pas. Rd. slp. Bl. pt. Cut., sq. 9/F, loc. 468, lev. — 3.7 ft.
(5). (No. 1558). Dish of food-stand. Pnk. pas. Rd. slp. Bl. pt. Trench J(1), lev. — 3.4 ft. A
(6). (No. 2913). Dish of food-stand. Pnk. pas. Rd. slp. Sq. 7/F, loc. 158, lev. + 9.6 ft.
(7). (No. 718). Dish of food-stand. Pnk. pas. Rd. slp. Trench C(3), lev. — 5.4 ft.
(8). (No. 431). Dish of food-stand. Pnk. pas. Trench D(1), lev. — 2.0 ft. A
(9). (No. 5332). Dish of food-stand. Gr. pas. Bl. slp. Cut., sq. 9/F, loc. 420, lev. — 4.6 ft.
(10). (No. 813). Dish of food-stand. Pnk. pas. Rd. slp. Trench F(1), lev. — 1.6 ft. A
(11). (No. 764). Incised base of food-stand. Pnk. pas. Rd. & Cr. slps. Bl. pt. Trench B(5), lev. — 6.6 ft. A
(12). (No. 1241). Base of food-stand. Pnk. pas. Rd. & Cr. slps. Bl. pt. Trench H(1), lev. — 7.5 ft.
(13). (No. 4187). Bowl of food-stand. Pnk. pas. Rd. slp. Bl. pt. Sq. 8/E, loc. 104, lev. + 9.2 ft.
(14). (No. 4920). Bowl of food-stand. Pnk. pas. Rd. & Cr. slps. Bl. pt. Sq. 9/E, loc. 111, lev. + 7.8 ft.
(15). (No. 811). Stem of food-stand. Pnk. pas. Rd. slp. Bl. pt. Trench G(1), lev. — 1.0 ft.
(16). (No. 3789). Incised stem of food-stand. Gr. pas. Gr. slp. Trench A(4), lev. — 7.8 ft.
(17). (No. 5439). Incised stem of food-stand. Pnk. pas. Rd. slp. Cut., sq. 10/G, loc. 481, lev. — 22.0 ft.
(18). (No. 2506). Bowl of food-stand. Gr. pas. Sq. 8/F, loc. 144, lev. + 11.4 ft.
(19). (No. 4787). Stem of food-stand. Pnk. pas. Rd. slp. Cut., sq. 10/G, loc. 481, lev. + 1.7 ft. A
(20). (No. 3704). Food-stand. Pnk. pas. Rd. pt. Trench B(5), loc. 55, lev. — 1.7 ft. A
(21). (No. 470). Stem and base, food-stand. Pnk. pas. Rd. slp. Trench C(3), lev. — 5.8 ft. A
(22). (No. 4928). Base of food-stand. Pnk. pas. Mound I, sq. 12/K, loc. 32, lev. + 12.7 ft.
(23). (No. 1811). Food-stand. Pnk. pas. Rd. & Cr. slps. Bl. pt. Trench A(4), loc. — 4.9 ft. A
(24). (No. 3747). Food-stand. Dr. pas. Hnd-mde. Trench B(5), lev. — 1.8 ft. A
(25). (No. 2246). Food-stand. Pnk. pas. Rd. slp. Bl. pt. Trench A(4), lev. — 3.5 ft. A
(26). (No. 5069). Bowl of food-stand. Pnk. pas. Cr. slp. Mound I, sq. 12/K, loc. 21, lev. + 14.3 ft.
(27). (No. 4197). Stem and base of food-stand. Pnk. pas. Rd. slp. Sq. 8/E, loc. 155, lev. + 8.8 ft. A
(28). (No. 3272). Dish of food-stand. Pnk. pas. Cr. slp. Sq. 7/C, loc. 237, lev. + 11.0 ft.
(29). (No. 4854). Food-stand. Pnk. pas. Rd. slp. Bl. pt. Trench F(1), loc. 42, lev. — 4.0 ft. A
(30). (No. 3843). Cup. Pnk. pas. Hnd-mde. Sq. ?, loc. ?, lev. + 3.2 ft. A
(31). (No. 5113). Frag. dish. Pnk. pas. Rd. slp. Bl. pt. Mound I, sq. 13/J, loc. 5, lev. + 13.3 ft.

(32). (No. 3375). Frag. dish. Pnk. pas. Rd. slp. Sq. 8/E, loc. 155, lev. + 11.5 ft.
(33). (No. 5163). Frag. dish. Pnk. pas. Rd. slp. Bl. pt. Cut., sq. 9/F, loc. 428, lev. — 1.0 ft.
(34). (No. 2913). Frag. dish. Pnk. pas. Rd. slp. Sq. 7/F, loc. 158, lev. + 9.6 ft. A
(35). (No. 3370). Frag. dish. Pnk. pas. Rd. slp. Sq. 8/E, loc. 155, lev. + 11.5 ft.
(36). (No. 2913). Frag. dish. Pnk. pas. Rd. slp. Sq. 7/F, loc. 158, lev. + 9.6 ft. A
(37). (No. 5446). Frag. dish. Pnk. pas. Rd. slp. Cut., 10/G, loc. 481, lev. — 18.6 ft.
(38). (No. 5436). Frag. dish. Pnk. pas. Rd. slp. Bl. pt. Cut., 10/G, loc. 481, lev. — 20.5 ft.
(39). (No. 5191). Frag. dish. Pnk. pas. Rd. slp. Bl. pt. Cut., sq. 9/F, loc. 473, lev. — 12.3 ft.
(40). (No. 5192). Frag. dish. Pnk. pas. Rd. slp. Bl. pt. Cut., sq. 9/F, loc. 469, lev. — 6.7 ft.
(41). (No. 5444). Frag. dish. Pnk. pas. Rd. slp. Bl. pt. Cut., sq. 10/G, loc. 481, lev. — 22.0 ft.
(42). (No. 1469). Frag. dish. Pnk. pas. Rd. slp. Bl. pt. Trench F(2), lev. — 4.6 ft. A
(43). (No. 5011). Jar. Pnk. pas. Cr. slp. Rd. pt. Sq. 7/F, loc. 147, lev. + 7.2 ft.
(44). (No. 4944). Jar. Pnk. pas. Rd. & Cr. slp. Cut., sq. 9/F, loc. 407, lev. + 0.6 ft.
(45). (No. 3758). Jar. Pnk. pas. Rd. slp. Trench F(2), lev. — 6.6 ft.
(46). (No. 4976). Jar. Pnk. pas. Cr. slp. Rd. pt. Sq. 7/F, loc. 298, lev. + 8.0 ft. A
(47). (No. 4087). Cup. Pnk. pas. Rd. Slp. Sq. 8/E. loc. 114, lev. + 9.1 ft.
(48). (No. 2966). Jar. Pnk. pas. Rd. pt. Sq. 10/D, loc. 339, lev. + 7.0 ft. A
(49). (No. 4877). Cup. Pnk. pas. Rd. slp. Hnd-mde. Sq. 6/F, loc. 436, lev. + 9.2 ft. A
(50). (No. 5384). Bowl. Pnk. pas. Rd. slp. Rd. pt. Cut., sq. 9/F, loc. 469, lev. — 19.0 ft.
(51). (No. 4682). Pnk. pas. Sq. 9/D, loc. 209, lev. + 6.8 ft. A
(52). (No. 4509). Cup. Pnk. pas. Hnd. mde. Sq. 7/C, loc. 240, lev. + 7.0 ft.
(53). (No. 4362). Pnk. pas. Rd. pt. Hnd. mde. Sq. 8/C, loc. 152, lev. + 8.3 ft. A
(54). (No. 203). Handled cup. Pnk. pas. Cr. slp. Hnd. mde. Trench C(2), lev. — 5.0 ft. A
(55). (No. 670). Handled cup. Pnk. pas. Cr. slp. Trench I(1), loc. 61, lev. — 6.5 ft.
(56). (No. 4351). Feeding-cup. Pnk. pas. Rd. & Br. slps. Sq. 8/D, loc. 311, lev. + 7.2 ft.
(57). (No. 4503). Incised bowl. Pnk. pas. Cr. slp. Sq. 9/F, loc. 468, lev. + 3.8 ft.
(58). (No. 3700). Handled cup. Pnk. pas. Hnd. mde. Sq. 7/D, loc. 321, + 7.1 ft.
(59). (No. 3787). Handled cup. Pnk. pas. Hnd. mde. Trench A(4), lev. — 7.9 ft. A
(60). (No. 4074). Feeding-cup. Pnk. pas. Sq. 8/F, loc. 116, lev. + 6.7 ft. A

Plate XXVI. Pottery Vessels (Harappā Culture). Chapter VI

(1). (No. 5151). Perforated ware. Pnk. pas. Mound I, sq. 12/J, loc. 35, lev. + 13.6 ft.
(2). (No. 4384). Perforated jar. Pnk. pas. Cut., sq. 10/F, loc. 423, lev. + 0.5 ft.
(3). (No. 4073). Perforated jar. Pnk. pas. Cr. slp. Rd. pt. Sq. 8/F, loc. 116, lev. + 6.6 ft. A
(4). (No. 2665). Jar-stand. Pnk. pas. Cr. slp. Sq. 8/C, loc. 167, lev. + 10.9 ft. A
(5). (No. 1795). Jar-stand. Pnk. pas. Sq. 8/D, loc. 311, lev. + 7.2 ft.
(6). (No. 4241). Jar-stand. Pnk. pas. Cr. slp. Mound I, sq. 13/J, loc. 3, lev. + 16.3 ft.
(7). (No. 4295). Jar-stand. Pnk. pas. Cr. slp. Sq. 7/F, loc. 158, lev. + 8.5 ft. A
(8). (No. 4296). Jar-stand. Pnk. pas. Rd. slp. Sq. 7/F, loc. 158, lev. + 8.6 ft.
(9). (No. 3855). Jar-stand. Pnk. pas. Trench F(2), lev. — 8.9 ft.
(10). (No. 1922). Jar-stand. Pnk. pas. Sq. 9/D, loc. 216, lev. + 11.8 ft. A
(11). (No. 4999). Jar-stand. Pnk. pas. Mound I, sq. 12/J, loc. 18, lev. + 14.3 ft.
(12). (No. 5005). Jar-cover. Pnk. pas. Mound I, sq. 13/K, loc. 34, lev. + 14.3 ft. A
(13). (No. 5062). Jar-cover. Pnk. pas. Cr. slp. Cut. sq. 10/G, loc. 485, lev. — 0.5 ft.
(14). (No. 200). Jar-cover. Pnk. pas. Trench C(2), lev. — 6.0 ft.
(15). (No. 5229). Jar-cover. Pnk. pas. Cr. slp. Mound I, sq. 13/K, loc. 37, lev. + 13.1 ft.
(16). (No. 4583). Jar-cover. Pnk. pas. Cr. pls. Mound I, sq. 12/K, loc. 20, lev. + 16.7 ft. A
(17). (No. 5327). Jar-cover. Pnk. pas. Cr. slp. Mound I, sq. 13/K, loc. 34, lev. + 12.0 ft.
(18). (No. 5070). Jar-cover. Pnk. pas. Cr. slp. Mound I, sq. 12/K, loc. 21, lev. + 14.2 ft.
(19). (No. 89). Jar-cover. Pnk. pas. Trench B(1), lev. — 6.1 ft. A
(20). (No. 116). Jar-cover. Pnk. pas. Cr. slp. Trench C(2) lev. — 5.2 ft.
(21). (No. 90). Jar-cover. Pnk. pas. Trench B(1), lev. — 5.2 ft.

(22). (No. 5255). Jar-cover. Pnk. pas. Rd. pt. Mound I, sq. 13/K, loc. 37, lev. + 13.0 ft.
(23). (No. 2817). Jar-cover. Pnk. pas. Cr. slp. Sq. 8/C, loc. 297, lev. + 10.1 ft.
(24). (No. 5228). Jar-cover. Pnk. pas. Cr. slp. Mound I, sq. 13/K, loc. 37, lev. + 13.1 ft.
(25). (No. 873). Jar-cover. Pnk. pas. Cr. slp. Trench H(1), lev. — 5.2 ft.
(26). (No. 4044). Jar-cover. Pnk. pas. Sq. 8/E, loc. 425, lev. + 6.8 ft.
(27). (No. 3936). Jar-cover. Pnk. pas. Trench E(1), lev. — 3.8 ft. A
(28). (No. 1373). Jar-cover. Pnk. pas. Trench F(2), lev. — 3.1 ft. A
(29). (No. 1046). Jar-cover. Gr. pas. Trench H(1), lev. — 1.8 ft.
(30). (No. 4485). Jar-cover. Pnk. pas. Sq. 7/E, loc. 306, lev. + 7.7 ft.
(31). (No. 3851). Jar-cover. Pnk. pas. Trench B(5), lev. — 9.9 ft.
(32). (No. 4927). Jar-cover. Pnk. pas. Rd. slp. Mound I, sq. 12/J, loc. 28, lev. + 14.5 ft. A
(33). (No. 1363). Jar-cover. Gr. pas. Trench E(1), lev. — 6.4 ft.
(34). (No. 2832). Pnk. pas. Sq. 7/F, loc. 346, lev. + 8.5 ft.
(35). (No. 2699). Jar-cover. Pnk. pas. Cr. slp. Sq. 9/D, loc. 139, lev. + 9.7 ft.
(36). (No. 3514). Jar-cover. Pnk. pas. Hnd. mde. Sq. 7/D, loc. 273, lev. + 8.1 ft. A
(37). (No. 3514). Jar-cover. Pnk. pas. Hnd. mde. Sq. 7/D, loc. 273, lev. + 8.1 ft.
(38). (No. 4998). Jar-cover. Pnk. pas. Mound I, sq. 12/K, loc. 29, lev. + 14.9 ft. A
(39). (No. 3906). Jar-cover. Pnk. pas. Rd. pt. Hnd. mde. Trench D(1), lev. — 4.3 ft. A
(40). (No. 2765). Jar-cover. Pnk. pas. Hnd. mde. Sq. 8/B, loc. 234, lev. + 9.9 ft.
(41). (No. 2357). Jar-cover. Pnk. pas. Rd. slp. Sq. 8/C, loc. 109, lev. + 10.7 ft.
(42). (No. 2912). Jar-cover. Pnk. pas. Hnd. mde. Sq. 9/D, loc. 130, lev. + 9.7 ft.
(43). (No. 3514). Jar-cover. Pnk. pas. Hnd. mde. Sq. 7/D, loc. 273, lev. + 8.1 ft. A
(44). (No. 2986). Jar-cover. Pnk. pas. Sq. 10/E, loc. 251, lev. + 7.2 ft. A
(45). (No. 4277). Jar-cover. Pnk. pas. Sq. 7/F, loc. 299, lev. + 7.4 ft. A
(46). (No. 5328). Jar-cover. Pnk. pas. Mound I, sq. 13/K, loc. 34, lev. + 17.8 ft.
(47). (No. 1855). Jar-cover. Pnk. pas. Rd. slp. Sq. 7/E, loc. 99, lev. + 11.0 ft.
(48). (No. 5221). Jar-cover. Gr. pas. Mound I, sq. 13/J, loc. 10, lev. + 13.9 ft.
(49). (No. 4284). Jar-cover. Pnk. pas. Rd. slp. Sq. 7/F, loc. 299, lev. + 7.4 ft. A
(50). (No. 4879). Jar-cover. Pnk. pas. Sq. 7/F, loc. 440, lev. + 6.7 ft.
(51). (No. 4662). Jar-cover. Pnk. pas. Rd. slp. Sq. 8/D, loc. 281, lev. + 7.6 ft.
(52). (No. 4372). Jar-cover. Pnk. pas. Sq. 8/B, loc. 452, lev. + 7.6 ft.
(53). (No. 2780). Jar-cover. Pnk. pas. Rd. slp. Sq. 8/B, loc. 234, lev. + 11.1 ft. A
(54). (No. 4810). Jar-cover. Pnk. pas. Sq. 7/F, loc. 331, lev. + 7.5 ft.
(55). (No. 5249). Jar-cover. Pnk. pas. Rd. slp. Mound I, sq. 13/K, loc. 12, lev. + 13.9 ft.
(56). (No. 4140). Partitioned tray. Pnk. pas. Hnd. mde. Sq. 10/D, loc. 341, lev. + 6.6 ft. A
(57). (No. 4730). Jar-cover. Pnk. pas. Cr. slp. Mound I, sq. 12/J, loc. 17, lev. + 15.8 ft.
(58). (No. 4229). Jar. Pnk. pas. Rd. slp. Bl. pt. Sq. 9/C, loc. 291, lev. + 7.0 ft. A
(59). (No. 4016). Jar. Pnk. pas. Rd. slp. Cut., 9/F, loc. 404, lev. + 4.9 ft. A
(60). (No. 2816). Cup. Pnk. pas. Cr. slp. Sq. 9/C, loc. 228, lev. + 10.3 ft.
(61). (No. 565). Sherd. Pnk. pas. Trench B(2), lev. — 10.1 ft. A
(62). (No. 3658). Jar. Pnk. pas. Rd. pt. Trench G(1), lev. — 3.8 ft.
(63). (No. 3973). Jar. Pnk. pas. Rd. slp. Sq. 8/E, loc. 114, lev. + 7.2 ft. A
(64). (No. 728). Jar. Pnk. pas. Cr. slp. Trench D(1), lev. — 0.9 ft. A
(65). (No. 434). Jar. Pnk. pas. Cr. slp. Trench D(1), lev, — 1.5 ft.
(66). (No. 2516). Jar. Sq. 9/D, loc. 192, lev. + 14.3 ft.
(67). (No. 4989). Sherd. Pnk. pas. Cr. slp. Cut., sq. 10/F, loc. 421, lev. + 0.5 ft. A
(67, a). (No. 2886). Sherd. Pnk. pas. Cr. slp. Sq. 8/D, loc. 290, lev. + 9.9 ft. A
(68). (No. 3969). Jar. Pnk. pas. Cr. slp. Trench C(3), lev. — 5.6 ft.
(69). (No. 2988). Jar. Pnk. pas. Cr. slp. Sq. 9/D, loc. 264, lev. + 8.5 ft.
(70). (No. 4297). Jar. Pnk. pas. Cr. slp. Sq. 7/E, loc. 300, lev. + 6.1 ft. A
(71). (No. 5275). Jar. Pnk. pas. Rd. slp. Bl. pt. Cut., sq. 10/G, loc. 477, lev. — 2.9 ft.
(72). (No. 4406). Jar. Pnk. pas. Rd. & Br. slps. Sq. 9/D, loc. 264, lev. + 10.0 ft.
(73). (No. 2224). Jar. Pnk. pas. Cr. slp. Sq. 9/E, loc. 85, lev. + 20.0 ft. A

(73, a). (No. 5098). Jar. Pnk. pas. Mound I, sq. 13/J, loc. 11, lev. + 14.2 ft.
(74). (No. 1180). Cup. Pnk. pas. Cr. slp. Trench G(1), lev. — 4.3 ft.
(75). (No. 5118). Jar. Pnk. pas. Cut., sq. 9/F, loc. 428, lev. —2.3 ft.
(76). (No. 4563). Cup. Pnk. pas. Rd. slp. Sq. 7/C, loc. 238, lev. + 7.5 ft.
(77). (No. 5099). Bowl. Pnk. pas. Cr. slp. Mound I, sq. 13/J, loc. 11, lev. + 14.2 ft.
(78). (No. 3793). Bowl. Pnk. pas. Trench A(4), lev. — 6.1 ft. A
(79). (No. 4404). Bowl. Pnk. pas. Cr. slp. Rd. pt. Sq. 10/E, loc. 230, lev. + 8.8 ft.
(80). (No. 5409). Bowl. Pnk. pas. Cr. slp. Cut., 10/G, lev. — 18.6 ft.
(81). (No. 5367). Jar. Dr. pas. Cr. slp. Cut., sq. 10/G, loc. 477, lev. — 10.1 ft.
(82). (No. 4975). Jar. Pnk. pas. Rd. slp. Bl. pt. Sq. 7/F, loc. 298, lev. + 8.1 ft.
(83). (No. 3801). Jar. Gr. pas. Gr. slp. Trench B(5), lev. — 10.2 ft.
(84). (No. 4694). Jar. Pnk. pas. Cr. slp. Sq. 7/F, loc. 147, + 6.9 ft. A
(85). (No. 987). Cup. Pnk. pas. Trench E(1), lev. — 5.2 ft. A
(86). (No. 635). Cup. Pnk. pas. Trench A(3), lev. — 1.8 ft.
(87). (No. 2786). Pnk. pas. Sq. 9/D, loc. 194, lev. + 10.9 ft.
(88). (No. 5094). Bowl. Pnk. pas. Cut., sq. 10/G, loc. 481, lev. — 2.2 ft.
(89). (No. 2821). Jar. Pnk. pas. Sq. 8/C, loc. 241, lev. + 10.6 ft.
(90). (No. 5210). Jar. Pnk. pas. Cr. slp. Cut., sq. 10/G, loc. 481, lev. — 1.0 ft.
(91). (No. 5334). Jar. Pnk. pas. Cut., sq. 9/F, loc. 408, lev. — 5.4 ft.

Plate XXVII. Pottery Vessels (Harappā Culture). Chapter VI

(1). (No. 5432). Dish. Pnk. pas. Hnd. mde. Cut., sq. 9/F, loc. 469, lev. — 18.3 ft.
(2). (No. 5438). Dish. Pnk. pas. Hnd. mde. Cut., sq. 10/G, loc. 481, lev. — 24.8 ft.
(3). (No. 3905). Dish. Pnk. pas. Trench D(1), lev. — 4.3 ft. A
(4). (No. 4805). Dish. Dr. pas. Cut., sq. 10/G, loc. 480, lev. — 0.3 ft. A
(5). (No. 2161). Dish. Pnk. pas. Hnd. mde. Trench J(1), lev. — 7.8 ft.
(6). (No. 4527). Dish. Pnk. pas. Cr. slp. Sq. 7/E, loc. 278, lev. + 7.5 ft.
(7). (No. 5092). Dish. Pnk. pas. Cut., sq. 10/G, loc. 481, lev. — 2.2 ft.
(8). (No. 3751). Bowl. Pnk. pas. Rd. pt. Trench B(5), lev. — 10.2 ft.
(9). (No. 3805). Bowl. Pnk. pas. Trench A(3), lev. — 7.8 ft. A
(10). (No. 4267). Bowl. Dr. pas. Hnd. mde. Cut., sq. 10/G, loc. 478, lev. + 0.9 ft.
(11). (No. 4671). Bowl. Dr. pas. Cut., sq. 10/G, loc. 478, lev. + 0.9 ft.
(12). (No. 2833). Bowl. Pnk. pas. Hnd. mde. Sq. 7/F, loc. 346, lev. + 8.8 ft.
(13). (No. 600). Cup. Pnk. pas. Trench C(2), lev. — 4.9 ft.
(14). (No. 2888). Cup. Pnk. pas. Sq. 8/F, loc. 260, lev. + 10.0 ft.
(15). (No. 5308). Cup. Pnk. pas. Hnd. mde. Mound I, sq. 13/K, loc. 34, lev. + 12.7 ft.
(16). (No. 2996). Cup. Pnk. pas. Sq. 8/D, loc. 108, lev. + 8.6 ft. A
(17). (No. 2316). Cup. Pnk. pas. Hnd. mde. Sq. 9/E, loc. 131, lev. + 11.2 ft. A
(18). (No. 1161). Cup. Pnk. pas. Rd. slp. Rd. pt. Trench D(1), lev. — 4.6 ft.
(19). (No. 306). Cup. Pnk. pas. Rd. pt. Trench B(3), loc. — 4.9 ft. A
(20). (No. 2707). Bowl. Gr. pas. Sq. 7/D, loc. 273, lev. + 9.6 ft.
(21). (No. 3391). Bowl. Gr. pas. Hnd. mde. Sq. 9/E, loc. 124, lev. + 16.1 ft.
(22). (No. 5244). Dish. Pnk. pas. Mound I, sq. 13/J, loc. 8, lev. + 14.1 ft.
(23). (No. 3015). Cup. Pnk. pas. Sq. 9/E, loc. 254, lev. + 9.3 ft. A
(24). (No. 2163). Dish. Pnk. pas. Rd. slp. Bl. pt. Sq. 7/E, loc. 120, lev. + 12.0 ft. A
(25). (No. 4945). Bowl. Gr. pas. Bl. & Gr. slps. Cut., sq. 9/F, loc. 408, lev. + 0.8 ft. A
(26). (No. 5197). Bowl. Pnk. pas. Cr. slp. Rd. pt. Mound I, sq. 13/K, loc. 51, lev. + 12.8 ft.
(27). (No. 3870). Dish. Pnk. pas. Trench K(1), lev. — 6.9 ft.
(28). (No. 4613). Bowl. Dr. pas. Hnd. mde. Cut., sq. 10/F, loc. 378, lev. + 5.5 ft. A
(29). (No. 2112). Bowl. Pnk. pas. Cr. slp. Hnd. mde. Sq. 8/E, loc. 92, lev. + 13.7 ft. A
(30). (No. 2775). Bowl. Pnk. pas. Pnk. slp. Sq. 9/C, loc. 208, lev. + 9.1 ft.
(31). (No. 3298). Dish. Pnk. pas. Rd. slp. Sq. 7/E. loc. 97, lev. + 9.4 ft.
(32). (No.5055). Bowl. Dr. pas. Br. slp. Cut., sq. 9/F, loc. 407, lev. + 0.8 ft. A

(33). (No. 4468). Oval dish. Pnk. pas. Hnd. mde. Sq. 7/C, loc. 102, lev. + 6.8 ft.
(34). (No. 204). Bowl. Pnk. pas. Trench C(2), lev. — 4.3 ft. A
(35). (No. 27). Bowl. Pnk. pas. Trench C(1), lev. —3.2 ft. A
(36). (No. 3968). Dish of food-stand. Pnk. pas. Rd. slp. Trench C(3), loc. 36, lev. — 5.6 ft. A
(37). (No. 432). Dish. Pnk. pas. Rd. slp. Trench D(1), lev. — 1.5 ft.
(38). (No. 154). Bowl. Pnk. pas . Cr. slp. Trench B(1), lev. — 5.8 ft.
(39). (No. 1155). Bowl. Pnk. pas. Pnk. slp. Rd. pt. Trench D(1), lev. — 0.0 ft.
(40). (No. 5325). Bowl. Pnk. pas. Mound I, sq. 13/K, loc. 34, lev. + 12.0 ft.
(41). (No. 729). Bowl. Pnk. pas. Cr. slp. Rd. pt. Trench D(1), lev. — 1.3 ft. A
(42). (No. 531). Bowl. Pnk. pas. Rd. slp. Trench B(3), lev. — 5.7 ft.
(43). (No. 2265). Bowl. Pnk. pas. Cr. slp. Sq. 7/C, loc. 98, lev. + 12.0 ft. A
(44). (No. 341). Bowl. Pnk. pas. Cr. slp. Rd. pt. Trench C(2), lev. — 9.7 ft. A
(45). (No. 29). Bowl. Pnk. pas. Trench A(1), lev. — 3.0 ft.
(46). (No. 5385). Bowl. Pnk. pas. Cut., sq. 10/F, loc. 466, lev. — 6.9 ft.
(47). (No. 3603). Bowl. Gr. pas. Trench I(1), lev. + 0.7 ft.
(48). (No. 2977). Bowl. Pnk. pas. Hnd. mde. Sq. 9/E, loc. 137, lev. + 14.3 ft. A
(49). (No. 4403). Bowl. Pnk. pas. Hnd. mde. Sq. 8/B, loc. 232, lev. + 9.7 ft. A
(50). (No. 5115). Bowl. Pnk. pas. Pnk. slp. Purp. pt. Mound I, sq. 13/K, loc. 37, lev. + 13.1 ft.
(51). (No. 3109). Bowl. Pnk. pas. Pnk. & Cr. slps. Sq. 7/F, loc. 147, lev. + 10.0 ft.
(52). (No. 5390). Bowl. Pnk. pas. Rd. slp. Cut., sq. 10/G, loc. 478, lev. — 7.2 ft.
(53). (No. 2528). Bowl. Pnk. pas. Rd. slp. Bl. pt. Sq. 8/C, loc. 297, lev. + 10.1 ft.
(54). (No. 1090). Bowl. Pnk. pas. Pnk. slp. Trench F(1), lev. — 9.5 ft.
(55). (No. 3073). Bowl. Pnk. pas. Hnd. mde. Sq. 8/E, loc. 156, lev. + 14.5 ft.
(56). (No. 4402). Bowl. Pnk. pas. Cr. slp. Sq. 9/E, loc. 254, lev. + 9.6 ft.
(57). (No. 4932). Bowl. Pnk. pas. Rd. slp. Cut., sq. 10/G, loc. 481, lev. + 1.7 ft. A
(58). (No. 3287). Bowl. Pnk. pas. Rd. & Cr. slps. Sq. 7/E, loc. 97, lev. + 10.6 ft. A
(59). (No. 3702). Bowl. Pnk. pas. Rd. slp. Bl. pt. Trench B(5), loc. 43, lev. — 5.9 ft. A
(60). (No. 2829). Bowl. Pnk. pas. Cr. slp. Sq. 7/F, loc. 147, lev. + 8.7 ft. A
(61). (No. 930). Bowl. Pnk. pas. Rd. slp. Rd. pt. Trench A(3), lev. — 4.1 ft.
(62). (No. 1129). Bowl. Pnk. pas. Rd. slp. Trench I(1), lev. + 1.5 ft.
(63). (No. 825). Bowl. Pnk. pas. Cr. slp. Trench C(3), loc. 26, lev. — 5.0 ft. A
(64). (No. 3490, B). Bowl. Gr. pas. Sq. 7/C, loc. 461, lev. + 9.1 ft. A
(65). (No. 4571). Bowl. Pnk. pas. Rd. slp. Sq. 8/C, loc. 394, lev. + 7.5 ft. A
(66). (No. 3345). Bowl. Pnk. pas. Rd. & Cr. slps. Sq. 8/C, loc. 151, lev. + 12.0 ft. A
(67). (No. 2694). Bowl. Pnk. pas. Rd. & Cr. slps. Sq. 9/C, loc. 205, lev. + 9.3 ft.
(68). (No. 2225). Jar. Pnk. pas. Rd. & Pnk. slps. Bl. pt. Sq. 9/E, loc. 112, lev. + 13.4 ft.
(69). (No. 2337). Cosmetic jar. Pnk. pas. Hnd. mde. Sq. 9/E, loc. 162, lev. + 15.2 ft.
(70). (No. 3302). Cos. jar. Pnk. pas. Sq. 7/F, loc. 443, lev. + 6.7 ft. A
(71). (No. 852). Cos. jar. Pnk. slp. Rd. pt. Trench B(5), loc. 56, lev. — 1.7 ft.
(72). (No. 4093). Cos. jar. Pnk. pas. Rd. slp. Sq. 8/F, loc. 115, lev. + 8.0 ft.
(73). (No. 5199). Cos. jar. Pnk. pas. Cr. slp. Bl. pt. Mound I, sq. 13/K, loc. 34, lev. + 12.9 ft.
(74). (No. 1301). Cos. jar. Pnk. pas. Rd. pt. Trench J(1), lev. — 5.9 ft. A
(75). (No. 5049). Cos. jar. Pnk. pas. Rd. pt. Cut., sq. 9/F, loc. 409, lev. + 0.5 ft.
(76). (No. 499). Cos. jar. Pnk. pas. Rd. pt. Trench E(1), loc. 33, lev. — 2.7 ft. A
(77). (No. 3380). Cos. jar. Pnk. pas. Rd. slp. Trench D(1), lev. — 7.5 ft.
(78). (No. 4232). Cos. jar. Pnk. pas. Cr. slp. Rd. pt. Sq. 10/C, loc. 385, lev. + 6.9 ft. A
(79). (No. 4230). Insect cage. Pnk. pas. Rd. pt. Hnd. mde. Sq. 9/C, loc. 291, lev. + 7.1 ft.
(81). (No. 1875). Cos. jar. Pnk. pas. Rd. pt. Trench G(1), loc. 49, lev. — 1.0 ft.
(82). (No. 786). Cos. jar. Pnk. pas. Cr. slp. Rd. pt. Trench B(5), lev. — 3.2 ft.
(83). (No. 3264). Cos. jar. Pnk. pas. Pnk. slp. Bl. & Rd. pts. Sq. 9/C, loc. 190, lev. + 13.7 ft. A
(84). (No. 472). Cos. jar. Pnk. pas. Hnd. mde. Trench C(3), lev. — 9.0 ft. A
(85). (No. 2916). Cos. jar. Pnk. pas. Sq. 7/F, loc. 299, lev. + 9.5 ft.

(86). (No. 3459). Cos. jar. Pnk. pas. Br. slp. Sq. 9/C, loc. 244, lev. + 6.9 ft. A
(87). (No. 2271). Cos. jar. Pnk. pas. Sq. 8/C, loc. 153, lev. + 14.1 ft. A
(88). (No. 4360). Cos. jar. Pnk. pas. Sq. 8/D, loc. 311, lev. + 7.2 ft.
(89). (No. 5126). Cos. jar. Pnk. pas. Cut., sq. 10/G, loc. 477, lev. — 1.0 ft.
(90). (No. 4909). Cos. jar. Pnk. pas. Rd. slp. Bl. pt. Mound I, sq. 13/K, loc. 12, lev. + 13.1 ft.
(91). (No. 1023). Cos. jar. Pnk. pas. Cr. slp. Trench A(2), lev. — 8.6 ft.
(92). (No. 3484). Cos. jar. Gr. pas. Hnd. mde. Sq. 9/C, loc. 291, lev. + 7.1 ft.

Plate XXVIII. Pottery and Pottery Groups (Harappā Culture). Chapter VI.

(1). (No. 2349). Jar. Pnk. pas. Cr. slp. Sq. 7/C, loc. 98, lev. + 12.4 ft.
(2). (No. 2711). Jar. Pnk. pas. Sq. 9/C, loc. 205, lev. + 10.0 ft. A
(3). (No. 3271). Jar. Pnk. pas. Rd. slp. Bl. pt. Sq. 7/C, loc. 166, lev. + 10.9 ft.
(4). (No. 2698). Incised jar. Pnk. pas. Cr. slp. Sq. 9/D, loc. 139, lev. + 9.7 ft.
(5). (No. 2243). Jar. Pnk. pas. Sq. 9/D, loc. 209, lev. + 11.7 ft. A
(6). (No. 4919). Incised jar. Pnk. pas. Cr. slp. Sq. 7/E, loc. 301, lev. + 7.9 ft. A
(7). (No. 4869). Jar. Pnk. pas. Cr. slp. Sq. 7/F, loc. 445, lev. + 6.7 ft.
(8). (No. 4861). Jar. Pnk. pas. Sq. 8/E, loc. 280, lev. + 7.0 ft.
(9). (No. 125). Jar. Pnk. pas. Cr. slp. Trench A(1), lev. — 3.4 ft.

* * * * * * * * * *

(10). (No. 3047, D). Jar. Pnk. pas. Cr. slp. Sq. 8/E, loc. 87, lev. + 6.8 ft. A
(11). (No. 3047, F). Jar. Pnk. pas. Cr. slp. Sq. 8/E, loc. 87, lev. + 6.8 ft. A
(12). (No. 3047, D). Jar. Pnk. pas. Cr. slp. Sq. 8/E, loc. 87, lev. + 6.8 ft. A
(13). (No. 3047, B). Jar. Pnk. pas. Rd. & Cr. slp. Sq. 8/E, loc. 87, lev. + 6.8 ft.
(14). (No. 3047, C). Jar. Pnk. pas. Cr. slp. Sq. 8/E, loc. 87, lev. + 6.8 ft. A
(15). (No. 3047, I). Cup. Pnk. pas. Cr. slp. Sq. 8/E, loc. 87, lev. + 6.8 ft. A
(16). (No. 3047, G). Cup. Pnk. pas. Cr. slp. Sq. 8/E, loc. 87, lev. + 6.8 ft. A
(17). (No. 3047, H). Jar. Pnk. pas. Cr. slp. Sq. 8/E. loc. 87, lev. + 6.8 ft. A

* * * * * * * * * *

(18). (No. 3283, B). Jar. Pnk. pas. Rd. slp. Bl. pt. Sq. 7/E, loc. 276, lev. + 9.4 ft.
(19). (No. 3283, A). Jar. Pnk. pas. Sq. 7/E, loc. 276, lev. + 9.4 ft.
(20). (No. 3283, D). Jar. Pnk. pas. Sq. 7/E, loc. 276, lev. +9.4 ft. A
(21). (No. 3283, C). Jar. Pnk. pas. Sq. 7/E, loc. 276, lev. +9.4 ft. A
(22). (No. 3283, G). Jar. Pnk. pas. Cr. slp. Sq. 7/E, loc. 276, lev. + 9.4 ft.
(23). (No. 3283, F). Jar. Pnk. pas. Cr. slp. Sq. 7/E. loc. 276, lev. + 9.4 ft.

* * * * * * * * * *

(24). (No. 866, B). Jar. Pnk. pas. Trench F(1), loc. 42, lev. — 10.5 ft.
(25). (No. 866, F). Cup. Pnk. pas. Trench F(1), loc. 42, lev. — 10.5 ft. A
(26). (No. 866, E). Cup. Pnk. pas. Trench F(1), loc. 42, lev. — 10.5 ft.
(27). (No. 866, C). Cup. Pnk. pas. Trench F(1), loc. 42, lev. — 10.5 ft. A
(28). (No. 866, A). Jar. Pnk. pas. Trench F(1), loc. 42, lev. — 10.5 ft.
(29). (No. 866, D). Jar. Pnk. pas. Trench F(1), loc. 42, lev. — 10.5 ft.

* * * * * * * * * *

(30). (No. 3489, D). Cup. Pnk. pas. Sq. 7/C, loc. 461, lev. + 9.1 ft.
(31). (No. 3489, B). Bowl of food-stand. Pnk. pas. Rd. & Pnk. slps. Sq. 7/C, loc. 461, lev. + 9.1 ft. A
(32). (No. 3489, C). Bowl. Pnk. pas. Rd. slp. Sq. 7/C, loc. 461, lev. + 9.1 ft.

* * * * * * * * * *

(33). (No. 1844). Cup. Pnk. pas. Cr. slp. Hnd. mde. Jhukar. Sq. 8/E, loc. 86, lev. + 17.5 ft.
(34). (No. 1843). Jar. Pnk. pas. Jhukar. Sq. 8/E, loc. 86, lev. + 17.5 ft. A

* * * * * * * * * *

(35). (No. 3150, B). Jar. Pnk. pas. Sq. 7/E, loc. 306, lev. + 8.0 ft.
(36). (No. 3150, D). Jar. Pnk. pas. Sq. 7/E, loc. 306, lev. + 8.0 ft.
(37). (No. 3150, C). Jar. Pnk. pas. Sq. 7/E, loc. 306, lev. + 8.0 ft.

* * * * * * * * * *

(38). (No. 2594, N). Jar. Pnk. pas. Rd. slp. Bl. pt. Sq. 9/C, loc. 228, lev. + 9.9 ft. A
(39). (No. 2594, M). Jar. Pnk. pas. Rd. pt. Hnd. mde. Sq. 9/C, loc. 228, lev. + 9.9 ft. A
(40). (No. 2594, O). Cup. Pnk. pas. Hnd. mde. Sq. 9/C, loc. 228, lev. + 9.9 ft.
(41). (No. 2594, P). Cup. Pnk. pas. Rd. slp. Hnd. mde. Sq. 9/C, loc. 228, lev. + 9.9 ft. A

* * * * * * * * * *

(42). (No. 995). Cup. Pnk. pas. Rd. slp. Trench B(5), lev. — 2.0 ft.
(43). (No. 996). Cup. Pnk. pas. Cr. slp. Rd. pt. Trench B(5), lev. — 2.0 ft. A
(44). (No. 997). Cup. Pnk. pas. Rd. pt. Trench B(5), lev. — 2.0 ft. A

* * * * * * * * * *

(45). (No. 4657, A). Jar. Pnk. pas. Sq. 9/D, loc. 209, lev. + 5.9 ft.
(46). (No. 4657, B). Jar. Pnk. pas. Sq. 9/D, loc. 209, lev. + 5.9 ft.
(47). (No. 4657, C). Jar. Pnk. pas. Sq. 9/D, loc. 209, lev. + 5.9 ft. A
(48). (No. 4657, D). Bowl. Gr. pas. Sq. 9/D, loc. 209, lev. + 5.9 ft.

* * * * * * * * * *

(49). (No. 3011, A). Jar. Pnk. pas. Rd. slp. Bl. pt. Sq. 9/C, loc. 208, lev. + 9.6 ft. A
(50). (No. 3011, C). Jar. Gr. pas. Sq. 9/C, loc. 208, lev. + 9.6 ft.

* * * * * * * * * *

(51). (No. 3009, D). Cup. Pnk. pas. Cr. slp. Sq. 8/F, loc. 149, lev. + 8.9 ft.
(52). (No. 3009, C). Cup. Pnk. pas. Sq. 8/F, loc. 149, lev. + 8.9 ft.
(53). (No. 3009, B). Jar. Pnk. pas. Cr. slp. Sq. 8/F, loc. 149, lev. + 8.9 ft. A
(54). (No. 3009, A). Jar. Pnk. pas. Cr. slp. Sq. 8/F, loc. 149, lev. + 8.9 ft. A

* * * * * * * * * *

(55). (No. 2728). Jar. Pnk. pas. Pnk. slp. Sq. 9/E, loc. 162, lev. + 10.0 ft.
(56). (No. 3988). Jar. Pnk. pas. Rd. pt. Sq. 9/F, loc. 427, lev. + 7.0 ft.
(57). (No. 4779). Jar. Pnk. pas. Rd. pt. Cut., sq. 9/F, loc. 428, lev. — 1.0 ft.
(58). (No. 4777). Jar. Pnk. pas. Cut., sq. 9/F, loc. 409, lev. — 1.1 ft.
(59). (No. 3654). Jar. Pnk. pas. Bl. & Rd. pts. Trench E(1), loc. 32, lev. — 2.3 ft.
(60). (No. 3783). Bowl. Pnk. pas. Rd. & Purp. slps. Sq. 8/C, loc. 289, lev. + 7.5 ft. A
(61). (No. 5398). Perforated jar. Pnk. pas. Hnd. mde. Cut., sq. 10/G, loc. 481, lev. — 13.4 ft.
(62). (No. 3536). Perforated jar. Pnk. pas. Sq. 8/C, loc. 295, lev. + 7.4 ft. A
(63). (No. 1782). Perforated jar. Pnk. pas. Sq. 8/F, loc. 163, lev. + 14.1 ft.
(64). (No. 4666). Bowl. Pnk. pas. Rd. pt. Sq. 10/D, loc. 248, lev. + 6.9 ft.
(65). (No. 3241). Jar. Pnk. pas. Rd. slp. Hnd. mde. Sq. 8/F, loc. 83, lev. + 7.1 ft. A
(66). (No. 5090). Jar-cover. Pnk. pas. Rd. slp. Hnd. mde. Sq. 9/F, loc. 474, lev. + 0.9 ft.
(67). (No. 4095). Bowl. Pnk. pas. Sq. 8/E, loc. 94, lev. + 7.7 ft.
(68). (No. 5079). Bowl. Pnk. pas. Mound I, sq. 12/K, loc. 21, lev. + 14.5 ft.
(69). (No. 4362). Jar. Pnk. pas. Rd. pt. Sq. 8/C, loc. 152, lev. + 8.5 ft.

Plate XXIX. Pottery and Other Objects (Harappā Culture). **Chapters VI; VIII; XIII**

(1). (No. 3343). Jar. Pnk. pas. Sq. 9/E, loc. 125, lev. + 10.4 ft. A
(2). (No. 4390). Jar. Pnk. pas. Sq. 8/D, loc. 178, lev. + 6.9 ft.
(3). (No. 4500). Jar. Gr. pas. Bl. slp. Mound I, sq. 13/J, loc. 3, lev. + 16.3 ft. A
(4). (No. 4398). Jar. Pnk. pas. Cr. slp. Sq. 7/C, loc. 102, lev. + 9.6 ft.
(5). (No. 3003). Cup. Pnk. pas. Sq. 7/C, loc. 313, lev. + 10.0 ft.
(6). (No. 4801). Cup. Pnk. pas. Cut., sq. 9/G, loc. 483, lev. — 0.9 ft.
(7). (No. 4528). Cup. Pnk. pas. Cr. slp. Sq. 7/C, loc. 102, lev. + 9.6 ft. A
(8). (No. 4922). Cup. Pnk. pas. Sq. 7/E, loc. 301, lev. + 7.9 ft. A
(9). (No. 868). Cup. Pnk. pas. Trench A(1), lev. — 5.6 ft.

(10). (No. 680). Cup. Pnk. pas. Trench D(1), lev. — 4.7 ft.
(11). (No. 3966). Cup. Pnk. pas. Sq. 9/E, loc. 171, lev. + 7.6 ft. A
(12). (No. 3960). Cup. Pnk. pas. Sq. 9/E, loc. 171, lev. + 7.6 ft. A
(13). (No. 5410). Cup. Pnk. pas. Hnd. mde. Cut., sq. 10/G, loc. 481, lev. — 23.8 ft.
(14). (No. 982). Cup. Pnk. pas. Trench F(1), lev. — 4.6 ft.
(15). (No. 5046). Cup. Pnk. pas. Cut., sq. 9/F, loc. 407, lev. + 0.8 ft.
(16). (No. 2515). Cup. Pnk. pas. Br. slp. Sq. 9/C, loc. 212, lev. + 11.0 ft. A
(17). (No. 3759). Cup. Pnk. pas. Trench F(2), lev. — 6.6 ft.
(18). (No. 5387, B). Cup. Pnk. pas. Cut., sq. 9/F, loc. 468, lev. — 6.8 ft.
(19). (No. 2784). Cup. Pnk. pas. Sq. 8/E, loc. 156, lev. + 9.7 ft. A
(20). (No. 2968). Cup. Pnk. pas. Sq. 10/D, loc. 363, lev. + 6.8 ft.
(21). (No. 2744). Cup. Pnk. pas. Sq. 8/B, loc. 235, lev. + 9.9 ft.
(22). (No. 2731). Cup. Pnk. pas. Pnk. slp. Sq. 10/D, loc. 246, lev. + 9.6 ft. A
(23). (No. 3595). Cup. Pnk. pas. Trench H(1), lev. — 8.5 ft. A
(24). (No. 5045). Cup. Pnk. pas. Cut., sq. 9/F, loc. 407, lev. + 10.8 ft.
(25). (No. 5215). Cup. Pnk. pas. Cr. slp. Mound I, sq. 12/K, loc. 27, lev. + 13.5 ft.
(26). (No. 5057). Cup. Pnk. pas. Cr. slp. Mound I, sq. 12/K, loc. 15, lev. + 14.1 ft. A
(27). (No. 5326). Cup. Pnk. pas. Mound I, sq. 13/K, loc. 34, lev. + 11.7 ft.
(28). (No. 4811). Cup. Pnk. pas. Br. slp. Sq. 7/F, loc. 299, lev. + 8.1 ft. A
(29). (No. 5003). Cup. Pnk. pas. Mound I, sq. 12/J, loc. 18, lev. + 14.9 ft. A
(30). (No. 4156). Cup. Pnk. pas. Sq. 9/C, loc. 207, lev. + 7.7 ft. A
(31). (No. 3100). Cup. Pnk. pas. Cr. slp. Sq. 9/E, loc. 201, lev. + 9.5 ft. A
(32). (No. 5411). Cup. Pnk. pas. Rd. slp. Hnd. mde. Cut., sq. 9/F, loc. 469, lev. — 22.4 ft.
(33). (No. 851). Cup. Pnk. pas. Pnk. slp. Trench I(1), lev. — 6.7 ft.
(34). (No. 3004). Cup. Pnk. pas. Sq. 8/C, loc. 309, lev. + 9.7 ft.
(35). (No. 424). Cup. Pnk. pas. Rd. slp. Trench D(1), lev. — 1.1 ft.
(36). (No. 2976). Cup. Pnk. pas. Cr. slp. Sq. 9/E, loc. 137, lev. + 14.0 ft.
(36, a). (No. 4617). Jar. Pnk. pas. Cr. slp. Mound I, sq. 13/J, loc. 10, lev. + 16.2 ft.
(37). (No. 2596). Pan. Pnk. pas. Cr. slp. Sq. 8/C, loc. 297, lev. + 9.3 ft.
(38). (No. 3959). Jar. Pnk. pas. Rd. slp. Sq. 9/E, loc. 171, lev. + 7.7 ft. A
(39). (No. 2697). Jar. Dr. pas. Rd. slp. Sq. 9/D, loc. 215, lev. + 9.4 ft.
(40). (No. 2700). Jar. Pnk pas. Rd. slp. Sq. 9/D, loc. 139, lev. + 9.7 ft.
(41). (No. 2708). Jar. Pnk. pas. Sq. 7/D, loc. 272, lev. + 9.4 ft.
(42). (No. 2709). Jar. Pnk. pas. Cr. slp. Sq. 7/D, loc. 272, lev. + 9.6 ft. A
(43). (No. 3275). Bowl. Pnk. pas. Rd. slp. Bl. pt. Sq. 9/D, loc. 95, lev. + 9.5 ft. A
(43, a). (No. 5007). Jar. Pnk. pas. Cr. slp. Sq. 7/F, loc. 188, lev. + 7.9 ft. A
(44). (No. 2239). Jar. Pnk. pas. Sq. 8/F, loc. 149, lev. + 10.2 ft. A
(45). (No. 5078). Jar. Pnk. pas. Mound I, sq. 12/K, loc. 21, lev. + 14.2 ft.
(46). (No. 3419). Jar. Pnk. pas. Cr. slp. Sq. 9/E, loc. 171, lev. + 6.5 ft.
(47). (No. 2984). Dish. Gr. san. Sq. 8/C, loc. 308, lev. + 10.0 ft.
(48). (No. 2245). Dish. Gr. san. Sq. 9/D, loc. 191, lev. + 11.6 ft. A
(49). (No. 1721). Jar-cover. Pnk. pas. Hnd. mde. Sq. 8/E, loc. 104, lev. + 14.9 ft.
(50). (No. 2176). Jar-cover. Pnk. pas. Hnd. mde. Sq. 8/E, loc. 94, lev. + 12.1 ft. A
(51). (No. 1617). Jar-cover. Pnk. pas. Hnd. mde. Sq. 8/F, loc. 144, lev. + 12.9 ft. A
(52). (No. 1980). Jar-cover. Pnk. pas. Hnd. mde. .Sq. 8/D, loc. 108, lev. + 14.6 ft.
(53). (No. 3080). Jar-cover. Pnk. pas. Rd. slp. Hnd. mde. Sq. 8/E, loc. 425, lev. + 6.8 ft. A
(54). (No. 4720). Neck and mouth of jar. Fai. Lt. gre. gl. 2.09 hi. Mound I, sq. 12/J, loc. 35, lev. + 13.6 ft.
(55). (No. 1487). Cosmetic jar. Fai. Lt. gre. gl. 1.3 hi. Sq. 8/C, loc. 109, lev. + 17.7 ft.
(56). (No. 4743). Cosmetic jar. Fai. Lt. gre. gl. Mound I, sq. 12/J, loc. 18, lev. + 13.9 ft.
(57). (No. 5109). Jar-cover. Pnk. pas . Hnd. mde. Cut., sq. 10/F, loc. 421, lev. — 1.0 ft.
(58). (No. 2054). Jar-cover. Pnk. pas. Hnd. mde. Trench G(1), lev. ?.
(59). (No. 2054). Jar-cover. Pnk. pas. Hnd. mde. Trench G(1), lev ?. A

(60). (No. 1035). Jar-cover. Pnk. pas. Hnd. mde. Trench F(1), lev. — 5.2 ft.
(61). (No. 1163). Jar-cover. Pnk. pas. Hnd. mde. Trench D(1), lev. — 2.5 ft. A
(62). (No. 2756). Jar-cover. Pnk. pas. Rd. slp. Hnd. mde. Sq. 10/D, loc. 362, lev. + 6.7 ft.
(64). (No. 1828). Jar-cover. Sh. 1.32 di. Sq. 8/F, loc. 116, lev. + 11.5 ft.
(65). (No. 2333). Jar-cover. Sh. 1.28 di. Sq. 8/C, loc. 241, lev. + 11.0 ft.
(66). (No. 3409). Jar-cover. Sh. 1.27 di. Sq. 10/E, loc. 261, lev. + 7.5 ft.
(67). (No. 1671). Head-cone. Fai. Lt. gre. gl. 2.3 hi. 1.3 di. Sq. 9/E, loc. 132, lev. + 16.5 ft. A
(68). (No. 1600). Head-cone. Fai. Lt. gre. gl. Now 2.8 hi, 1.3 di. Sq. 9/E, loc. 150, lev. + 16.7 ft.
(69). (No. 4844). Jar-stopper. Pnk. pas. Cut., sq. 10/G, loc. 481, lev. — 2.2 ft.
(70). (No. 1376). Jar-cover. Pnk. pas. Hnd. mde. Trench F(2), loc. 65, lev. — 3.0 ft.
(71). (No. 1794). Jar-cover. Gr. pas. Hnd. mde. Sq. 7/F, loc. 119, lev. + 11.7 ft.
(72). (No. 377). Jar-cover. Pnk. pas. Hnd. mde. Trench F(1), lev. — 4.3 ft.
(73). (No. 2897). Jar-stopper. Pnk. pas. Rd. slp. Hnd. mde. Sq. 8/E, loc. 155, lev. + 9.8 ft.

Plate XXX. Painted Sherds (Harappā Culture). Chapter VI

(1). (No. 3592). Pnk. pas. Rd. slp. Bl. pt. 7.1 lg. Trench I(1), lev. — 5.8 ft.
(2). (No. 776). Pnk. pas. Rd. slp. Bl. pt. Trench F(1), lev. — 4.6 ft. A
(3). (No. 3472). Pnk. pas. Rd. slp. Bl. pt. 6.1 lg. Sq. 7/D, loc. 271, lev. + 9.2 ft.
(4). (No. 776). Pnk. pas. Rd. slp. Bl. pt. Trench F(1), lev. — 8.7 ft. A
(5). (No. 3581). Pnk. pas. Rd. slp. Bl. pt. 3.7 lg. Trench E(1), lev. — 0.2 ft. A
(6). (No. 780). Pnk. pas. Rd. slp. Bl. pt. Trench B(5), lev. — 3.9 ft.
(7). (No. 541). Pnk. pas. Rd. slp. Bl. pt. 2.84 lg. Trench B(3), lev. — 6.1 ft. A
(8). (No. 906). Pnk. pas. Rd. slp. Bl. pt. 3.9 lg. Trench B(3), lev. — 4.2 ft. A
(9). (No. 3580). Pnk. pas. Rd. slp. Bl. pt. Trench E(1), lev. — 0.2 ft. A
(10). (No. 2895). Pnk. pas. Rd. slp. Bl. pt. 3.4 lg. Sq. 8/E, loc. 113, lev. + 10.1 ft.
(11). (No. 975). Pnk. pas. Rd. slp. Bl. pt. Trench H(1), lev. — 2.1 ft.
(12). (No. 5163). Pnk. pas. Rd. slp. Bl. pt. Cut., sq. 9/F, loc. 428, lev. — 1.0 ft. A
(13). (No. 3402). Pnk. pas. Rd. slp. Bl. pt. 2.01 lg. Sq. 9/F, loc. 184, lev. + 14.3 ft.
(14). (No. 1330). Pnk. pas. Rd. slp. Bl. pt. 4.0 lg. Trench D(1), lev. — 3.4 ft. A
(15). (No. 3281). Pnk. pas. Rd. slp. Bl. pt. 3.7 lg. Sq. 8/C, loc. 168, lev. + 11.1 ft. A
(16). (No. 3611). Pnk. pas. Rd. slp. Bl. pt. 4.2 lg. Trench K(1), lev. — 2.7 ft. A
(17). (No. 1466). Pnk. pas. Rd. slp. Bl. pt. Trench F(2), lev. — 4.6 ft.
(18). (No. 1331). Pnk. pas. Rd. slp. Bl. pt. Trench D(1), lev. ?.
(19). (No. 4736). Pnk. pas. Rd. slp. Bl. pt. Cut., loc. ?, lev. ?.
(20). (No. 4655). Pnk. pas. Rd. slp. Bl. pt. 3.61 lg. Sq. 8/F, loc. 163, lev. + 11.5 ft. A
(21). (No. 5117). Pnk. pas. Rd. slp. Bl. pt. Cut., sq. 9/F, loc. 474, lev. — 2.3 ft.
(22). (No. 1679). Pnk. pas. Rd. slp. Bl. pt. Trench H(1), lev. ?.
(23). (No. 3338). Pnk. pas. Rd. slp. Bl. pt. Sq. 8/F, loc. 145, lev. + 9.9 ft.
(24). (No. 5373). Pnk. pas. Rd. slp. Bl. pt. Cut., sq. 10/G, loc. 478, lev. — 9.4 ft.

Plate XXXI. Painted Sherds (Harappā Culture). Chapter VI

(1). (No. 1556). Pnk. pas. Rd. slp. Bl. pt. 4.9 lg. Trench H(1), lev. — 3.2 ft. A
(2). (No. 5440). Pnk. pas. Rd. & Cr. slps. Bl. pt. Cut., sq. 9/F, loc. 469, lev. — 18.3 ft.
(3). (No. 5440). Pnk. pas. Rd. & Cr. slps. Bl. pt. Cut., sq. 9/F, loc. 469, lev. — 18.3 ft.
(4). (No. 1244). Pnk. pas. Rd. slp. Bl. pt. 5.93 lg. Trench K(1), lev. — 4.8 ft. A
(5). (No. 5442). Pnk. pas. Rd. slp. Bl. pt. Cut., sq. 9/F, loc. 469, lev. — 18.3 ft.
(6). (No. 5175). Pnk. pas. Rd. slp. Bl. pt. Cut., sq. 9/F, loc. 428, lev. — 1.2 ft.
(7). (No. 5436). Pnk. pas. Rd. slp. Bl. pt. Cut., sq. 10/G, loc. 481, lev. — 20.5 ft.
(8). (No. 4848). Pnk. pas. Rd. slp. Bl. pt. Sq. 8/D, loc. 176, lev. + 8.1 ft.
(9). (No. 5216). Pnk. pas. Bf. slp. Bl. pt. Mound I, sq. 13/K, loc. 22, lev. + 13.3 ft.
(10). (No. 5201). Pnk. pas. Bl. pt. Cut., sq. 10/G, loc. 478, lev. — 9.3 ft.

(11). (No. 5442). Pnk. pas. Rd. slp. Bl. pt. Cut., sq. 9/F, loc. 469, lev. — 18.3 ft.
(12). (No. 5445). Pnk. pas. Rd. slp. Bl. pt. Cut., sq. 10/G, loc. 481, lev. — 18.6 ft.
(13). (No. 3922). Pnk. pas. Rd. & Bf. slps. Bl. pt. Trench B(3), lev. — 10.3 ft.
(14). (No. 2280). Pnk. pas. Rd. slp. Bl. pt. 5.4 lg. Sq. 7/C, loc. 134, lev. + 12.2 ft. A
(15). (No. 4047). Pnk. pas. Rd. slp. Bl. pt. 4.4 lg. Sq. 9/D, loc. 174, lev. + 8.0 ft. A
(16). (No. 3284). Pnk. pas. Rd. & Cr. slps. Bl. pt. Trench B(5), lev. — 6.7 ft. A
(17). (No. 4640). Pnk. pas. Rd. slp. Bl. pt. Mound I, sq. 13/J, loc. 1, lev. + 15.8 ft.
(18). (No. 975). Pnk. pas. Rd. slp. Bl. pt. Trench H(1), lev. — 2.1 ft.
(19). (No. 3668). Pnk. pas. Rd. slp. Bl. pt. Trench F(2), lev. — 4.2 ft.
(20). (No. 3575). Pnk. pas. Rd. & Cr. slps. Bl. pt. 5.53 lg. Trench K(1), lev. — 2.7 ft. A
(21). (No. 3902). Pnk. pas. Rd. slp. Bl. pt. Trench A(4), lev. — 4.2 ft.
(22). (No. 4525). Pnk. pas. Rd. & Cr. slps. Bl. pt. Sq. 7/F, loc. 346, lev. + 6.9 ft. A
(23). (No. 5329). Pnk. pas. Rd. slp. Bl. pt. Sq. 10/E, loc. 348, lev. — 3.7 ft.

Plate XXXII. Painted Sherds (Harappā Culture). Chapter VI

(1). (No. 3922). Pnk. pas. Rd. slp. Bl. pt. Trench B(3), lev. — 10.3 ft.
(1, a). (No. 3922). Pnk. pas. Rd. slp. Bl. pt. Trench B(3), lev. — 10.3 ft.
(2). (No. 4299). Pnk. pas. Rd. slp. Bl. pt. Sq. 8/C, loc. 151, lev. + 12.5 ft.
(3). (No. 1557). Pnk. pas. Rd. slp. Bl. pt. 5.1 lg. Trench F(2), lev. — 4.5 ft.
(4). (No. 5113). Pnk. pas. Rd. slp. Bl. pt. Mound I, sq. 13/J, loc. 5, lev. + 13.3 ft.
(5). (No. 5448). Pnk. pas. Rd. slp. Bl. pt. Cut., sq. 10/G, loc. 481, lev. — 18.0 ft.
(6). (No. 5372). Pnk. pas. Rd. slp. Bl. pt. Cut., sq. 9/F, loc. 473, lev. — 12.5 ft.
(7). (No. 4740). Pnk. pas. Pnk. slp. Br. pt. Mound I, sq. 12/K, loc. 26, lev. + 15.7 ft. A
(8). (No. 3284). Pnk. pas. Rd. & Cr. slps. Bl. pt. Trench B(5), lev. — 6.7 ft.
(9). (No. 3745). Pnk. pas. Rd. slp. Bl. pt. 4.23 lg. Trench K(1), lev. — 4.4 ft. A

Plate XXXIII. Painted Sherds (Harappā Culture). Chapter VI

(1). (No. 1069). Pnk. pas. Rd. slp. Bl. pt. Trench D(1), lev. — 6.5 ft.
(2). (No. 3797). Pnk. pas. Rd. slp. Bl. pt. 5.0 lg. Trench B(5), lev. — 6.8 ft. A
(3). (No. 3621). Pnk. pas. Rd. slp. Bl. pt. 4.1 lg. Trench F(1), lev. — 4.5 ft. A
(4). (No. 907). Pnk. pas. Rd. slp. Bl. pt. 2.3 di. Trench B(3), lev. — 7.8 ft.
(5). (No. 966). Pnk. pas. Rd. slp. Bl. pt. 3.9 lg. Trench B(5), lev. ? A
(6). (No. 3671). Pnk. pas. Yell. & Wh. slps. Bl. Rd. & Wh. pts. 2.99 lg. Sq. 10/E, loc. 250, lev. + 6.8 ft.
(7). (No. 5280). Pnk. pas. Rd. slp. Bl. pt. Cut., sq. 9/F, loc. 475, lev. — 3.1 ft.
(8). (No. 4656). Pnk. pas. Rd. slp. Bl. pt. Sq. 9/D, loc. 195, lev. + 7.0 ft.
(9). (No. 3583). Pnk. pas. Rd. slp. Bl. pt. Trench E(1), lev. — 4.8 ft.
(10). (No. 4656). Pnk. pas. Rd. slp. Bl. pt. Sq. 9/D, loc. 195, lev. + 7.0 ft. A
(11). (No. 1467). Pnk. pas. Rd. slp. Bl. pt. Trench F(2), lev. — 4.6 ft.
(12). (No. 3878). Pnk. pas. Rd. slp. Bl. pt. 7.6 lg. Trench B(5), lev. — 3.3 ft. A
(13). (No. 0). Pnk. pas. Rd. slp. Bl. pt.
(14). (No. 3872). Pnk. pas. Rd. slp. Bl. pt. 5.1 lg. Trench H(1), lev. — 8.1 ft. A
(15). (No. 1558). Pnk. pas. Rd. slp. Bl. pt. Trench J(1), loc. 73, lev. — 3.4 ft. A
(16). (No. 3516). Pnk. pas. Rd. slp. Bl. pt. 3.9 lg. Trench E(1), lev. — 5.8 ft. A
(17). (No. 4474). Pnk. pas. Rd. slp. Bl. pt. Sq. 7/C, loc. 269, lev. + 6.7 ft. A

Plate XXXIV. Painted Sherds. (Harappā and Jhukar Cultures). Chapters VI; VII

Harappā Sherds.

(1). (No. 1469). Pnk. pas. Rd. slp. Bl. pt. Trench F(2), lev. — 4.6 ft. A
(2). (No. 100). Pnk. pas. Rd. slp. Bl. pt. 2.42 lg. Trench B(1), lev. — 4.2 ft. A
(3). (No. 3419). Inscription on jar (Pl. XXXIX, 24). Pnk. pas. Cr. slp. Sq. 9/E, loc. 171, lev. + 6.8 ft.

(4). (No. 2288). Pnk. pas. Bl. & Rd. pts. Sq. 9/D, loc. 195, lev. + 11.0 ft.
(5). (No. 1876). Pnk. pas. Rd. slp. Bl. pt. Trench G(1), lev. — 7.9 ft. A
(6). (No. 5443). Pnk. pas. Pnk. slp. Rd. pt. Cut., sq. 9/F, loc. 469, lev. — 21.3 ft.
(7). (No. 5441). Pnk. pas. Rd. & Cr. slps. Bl. pt. Cut., sq. 10/G, loc. 481, lev. — 22.0 ft.
(8). (No. 776). Pnk. pas. Rd. slp. Bl. pt. Trench F(1), lev. — 4.6 ft. A
(9). (No. 5373). Pnk. pas. Rd. slp. Bl. pt. Cut., sq. 10/G, loc. 478, lev. — 9.4 ft.
(10). (No. 1090). Pnk. pas. Pnk. slp. Bl. pt. Trench F(1), lev. — 9.5 ft.
(11). (No. 876). Pnk. pas. Rd. slp. Bl. pt. 4.0 lg. Trench H(1), lev. — 0.2 ft. A
(12). (No. 991). Pnk. pas. Rd. slp. Bl. pt. 3.12 lg. Trench E(1), lev. — 5.9 ft. A
(13). (No. 4286). Pnk. pas. Rd. slp. Bl. pt. 4.9 lg. Mound I, sq. 12/J, loc. 18, lev. + 15.6 ft. A
(14). (No. 1381). Pnk. pas. Rd. slp. Bl. pt. 6.2 lg. Trench A(4), lev. + 1.0 ft. A
(15). (No. 776). Pnk. pas. Rd. slp. Bl. pt. Trench F(1), lev. — 4.6 ft. A
(16). (No. 3668). Pnk. pas. Rd. slp. Bl. pt. Trench F(2), lev. — 4.2 ft. A

Jhukar Sherds.

(17). (No. 1869). Pnk. pas. Rd. & Cr. slps. Bl. pt. 3.2 lg. Sq. 8/E, loc. 104, lev. + 18.5 ft. A
(18). (No. 1938. Pnk. pas. Pnk. slp. Bl. & Rd. pts. 7.1 lg. Sq. 8/C, loc. 153, lev. + 16.0 ft.
(19). (No. 2373). Pnk. pas. Cr. slp. Purp. & Rd. pts. 4.3 lg. Sq. 9/D, loc. 180, lev. + 14.8 ft. A
(20). (No. 2269). Pnk. pas. Cr. slp. Purp. pt. 3.3 lg. Sq. 9/E, loc. 173, lev. + 15.8 ft. A
(21). (No. 1755). Pnk. pas. Rd. & Cr. slps. Bl. & Rd. pts. 4.82 lg. Sq. 7/E, loc. 99, lev. + 17.7 ft. A
(22). (No. 1155). Pnk. pas. Pnk. slp. Rd. pt. Trench D(1), lev. — 0.0 ft.
(23). (No. 2282). Pnk. pas. Cr. slp. Purp. & Rd. pts. 4.9 lg. Sq. 8/F, loc. 182, lev. + 13.7 ft. A
(24). (No. 1507). Pnk. pas. Cr. slp. Bl. pt. 6.9 lg. Sq. 8/E, loc. 90, lev. + 17.0 ft.

Plate XXXV. Storage Jars (Harappā Culture). Chapter VI

(1). (No. 503). Pnk. pas. Rd. slp. Bl. pt. 21.2 hi. Trench B(3), lev. — 6.5 ft. A
(2). (No. 3153, A). Pnk. pas. Br. & Rd. slps. 29.0 hi. Sq. 7/F, loc. 110, lev. + 8.7 ft. A
(3). (No. 3491). Pnk. pas. Rd. slp. Bl. pt. 30.75 hi. Sq. 8/C, loc. 289, lev. + 8.6 ft. A
(4). (No. 4656). Pnk. pas. Rd. slp. Bl. pt. 21.75 hi. Sq. 9/D, loc. 195, lev. + 7.0 ft. A

Plate XXXVI. Painted Sherds (Harappā Culture). Chapter VI

(1). (No. 5372). Pnk. pas. Rd. slp. Bl. pt. Cut., sq. 9/F, loc. 473, lev. — 12.5 ft.
(2). (No. 5417). Pnk. pas. Rd. slp. Bl. pt. Cut., sq. 10/G, loc. 481, lev. — 15.7 ft.
(3). (No. 4363). Pnk. pas. Rd. slp. Bl. pt. 4.12 lg. Sq. 7/D, loc. 321, lev. + 7.1 ft.
(4). (No. 662). Pnk. pas. Rd. slp. Bl. pt. Trench D(1), lev. — 8.1 ft.
(5). (No. 3668). Pnk. pas. Rd. slp. Bl. pt. Trench F(2), lev. — 4.2 ft.
(6). (No. 3785). Pnk. pas. Rd. slp. Bl. pt. Trench A(2), lev. — 7.8 ft.
(7). (No. 612). Pnk. pas. Rd. slp. Bl. pt. Trench B(3), lev. — 7.7 ft
(8). (No. 4502). Pnk. pas. Rd. slp. Bl. pt. Mound I, sq. 13/J, loc. 3, lev. + 15.9 ft.
(9). (No. 3668). Pnk. pas. Rd. slp. Bl. pt. Trench F(2), lev. — 4.2 ft. A
(10). (No. 1237). Pnk. pas. Rd. slp. Bl. pt. 2.8 lg. Trench B(5), lev. —3.7 ft.
(11). (No. 5300). Pnk. pas. Bl. pt. Cut., sq. 9/G, loc. 483, lev. — 4.9 ft.
(12). (No. 3381). Pnk. pas. Rd. slp. Bl. pt. 5.42 lg. Trench D(1), lev. — 7.5 ft. A
(13). (No. 5205). Pnk. pas. Rd. slp. Bl. pt. Cut., sq., 10/G, loc. 481, lev. — 11.4 ft.
(14). (No. 5192). Pnk. pas. Rd. slp. Bl. pt. Cut., sq. 9/F, loc. 469, lev. — 6.7 ft.
(15). (No. 5114). Pnk. pas. Rd. slp. Bl. pt. Mound I, sq. 13/J, loc. 5, lev. + 13.4 ft. A
(16). (No. 1216). Pnk. pas. Rd. slp. Bl. pt. 6.52 lg. Trench A(4), lev. — 0.3 ft.
(17). (No. 5191). Pnk. pas. Rd. slp. Bl. pt. Cut., sq. 9/F, loc. 473, lev. — 12.3 ft.
(18). (No. 3668). Pnk. pas. Rd. slp. Bl. pt. Trench F(2), lev. — 4.2 ft.

(19). (No. 2710). Pnk. pas. Rd. slp. Bl. pt. 6.23 lg. Sq. 7/D, loc. 272, lev. + 9.0 ft.
(20). (No. 713). Pnk. pas. Rd. slp. Bl. pt. 5.1 lg. Trench D(1), lev. — 2.5 ft.
(21). (No. 3667). Pnk. pas. Rd. slp. Bl. & Rd. pts. 4.7 lg. Trench K(1), lev. — 4.4 ft.
(22). (No. 3280). Pnk. pas. Rd. slp. Bl. pt. 8.49 lg. Sq. 8/C, loc. 152, lev. + 10.9 ft.
(23). (No. 3671). Pnk. pas. Yel. & Wh. slps. Bl. & Rd. & Wh. pts. 1.99 lg. Sq. 10/E, loc. 250, lev. + 6.8 ft.
(24). (No. 3213). Pnk. pas. Br. slp. Bl. pt. Sq. 7/F, loc. 331, lev. + 6.9 ft.
(25). (No. 3668). Pnk. pas. Rd. slp. Bl. pt. Trench F(2), lev. — 4.2 ft.
(26). (No. 3710). Pnk. pas. Rd. slp. Bl. pt. 6.58 lg. Trench B(5), lev. — 1.7 ft.
(27). (No. 3380). Pnk. pas. Bl. pt. Trench D(1), lev. — 7.5 ft.
(28). (No. 5362). Pnk. pas. Rd. slp. Bl. pt. Sq. 8/E, loc. 425, lev. — 9.1 ft.
(29). (No. 3790). Pnk. pas. Rd. & Cr. slps. Bl. pt. 5.1 lg. Trench A(4), lev. — 8.2 ft.
(30). (No. 3873). Pnk. pas. Rd. & Cr. slps. Bl. pt. 4.4 lg. Trench H(1), lev. — 8.1 ft.
(31). (No. 3877). Pnk. pas. Rd. slp. Bl. pt. 5.93 lg. Trench B(5), lev. — 3.3 ft. A
(32). (No. 4401). Pnk. pas. Rd. slp. Bl. pt. Sq. 7/C, loc. 135, lev. + 11.3 ft.
(33). (No. 1168). Pnk. pas. Rd. slp. Bl. pt. 4.21 lg. Trench B(5), lev. — 4.7 ft. A
(34). (No. 4973). Pnk. pas. Rd. slp. Bl. pt. 5.2 lg. Sq. 8/F, loc. 83, lev. + 11.6 ft.
(35). (No. 5371). Pnk. pas. Rd. slp. Bl. pt. Cut., sq. 9/F, loc. 473, lev. — 12.5 ft.
(36). (No. 4791). Pnk. pas. Rd. slp. Bl. pt. 3.52 lg. Cut., sq. 9/F, loc. 475, lev. + 0.6 ft.
(37). (No. 662). Pnk. pas. Rd. & Cr. slps. Bl. pt. Trench D(1), lev. — 8.1 ft.
(38). (No. 5436). Pnk. pas. Rd. slp. Bl. pt. Cut., sq. 10/G, loc. 481, lev. — 20.5 ft.
(39). (No. 1470). Pnk. pas. Rd. slp. Bl. pt. Trench F(2), lev. — 4.6 ft. A
(40). (No. 3650). Pnk. pas. Rd. slp. Bl. pt. Trench E(1), lev. — 2.3 ft.
(41). (No. 3668). Pnk. pas. Rd. slp. Bl. pt. Trench F(2), lev. — 4.2 ft.

Plate XXXVII. Painted Sherds (Harappā Culture). Chapter VI

(1). (No. 5298). Pnk. pas. Rd. slp. Bl. pt. Cut., sq. 9/G, loc. 483, lev. — 4.9 ft.
(2). (No. 4996). Pnk. pas. Rd. slp. Bl. pt. 4.19 lg. Mound I, sq. 12/K, loc. 31, lev. + 14.9 ft.
(3). (No. 5201). Pnk. pas. Bl. slp. Cut., sq. 10/G, loc. 478, lev. — 9.3 ft. A
(4). (No. 5313). Pnk. pas. Rd. & Cr. slps. Bl. pt. Cut., sq. 9/F, loc. 469, lev. — 4.9 ft.
(5). (No. 2288). Pnk. pas. Bl. & Rd. pts. 3.32 lg. Sq. 9/D, loc. 195, lev. + 11.0 ft.
(6). (No. 608). Pnk. pas. Rd. slp. Bl. pt. Trench D(1), lev. — 4.9 ft. A
(7). (No. 4935). Pnk. pas. Rd. slp. Bl. pt. Mound I, sq. 12/K, loc. 20, lev. + 13.5 ft. A
(8). (No. 3254). Pnk. pas. Rd. slp. Bl. pt. Sq. ?, lev. ? A
(9). (No. 4298). Pnk. pas. Rd. slp. Bl. pt. Sq. 8/C, loc. 151, lev. + 12.5 ft. A
(10). (No. 5260). Pnk. pas. Rd. slp. Bl. pt. Cut., sq. 9/G, loc. 479, lev. — 5.0 ft.
(11). (No. 5302). Pnk. pas. Rd. slp. Bl. pt. Cut., sq. 9/F, loc. 468, lev. — 5.3 ft.
(12). (No. 544). Pnk. pas. Rd. slp. Bl. pt. 5.8 lg. Trench B(3), lev. — 7.7 ft. A
(13). (No. 3277). Pnk. pas. Rd. slp. Bl. pt. 3.91 lg. Sq. 8/E, loc. 93, lev. + 12.6 ft.
(14). (No. 5418). Pnk. pas. Rd. slp. Bl. pt. Cut., sq. 10/G, loc. 481, lev. — 15.7 ft.
(15). (No. 4938). Pnk. pas. Rd. slp. Bl. pt. 3.22 lg. Mound I, sq. 12/K, loc. 30, lev. + 13.7 ft.
(16). (No. 1162). Pnk. pas. Rd slp. Bl. pt. 2.16 lg. Trench D(1), lev.?
(17). (No. 3434). Pnk. pas. Rd. slp. Bl. pt. 4.22 lg. Sq. 8/E, loc. 185, lev. + 9.8 ft. A
(18). (No. 3432). Pnk. pas. Rd. slp. Purp. pt. 7.9 lg. Trench D(1), lev. — 7.0 ft.
(19). (No. 3183). Pnk. pas. Rd. slp. Purp. pt. 3.52 lg. Sq. 7/F, loc. 119, lev. + 10.6 ft. A
(20). (No. 662). Pnk. pas. Rd. & Cr. slps. Bl. pt. Trench D(1), lev. — 8.1 ft.
(21). (No. 4798). Pnk. pas. Rd. slp. Bl. pt. 6.26 lg. Cut., sq. 9/F, loc. 469, lev. + 0.6 ft.
(22). (No. 3435). Pnk. pas. Rd. slp. Bl. pt. 9.22 lg. Sq. 9/F, loc. 265, lev. + 10.1 ft. A
(23). (No. 3597). Pnk. pas. Rd. slp. Bl. pt. Trench H(1), lev. — 8.5 ft.
(24). (No. 5361). Pnk. pas. Rd. slp. Bl. pt. 6.28 lg. Cut., sq. 9/F, loc. 475, lev. — 9.0 ft.
(25). (No. 5430). Pnk. pas. Rd. slp. Bl. pt. Cut., sq. 10/G, loc. 481, lev. — 22.0 ft.
(26). (No. 1689). Pnk. pas. Rd. slp. Bl. pt. Trench H(1), lev. — 3.2 ft.
(27). (No. 5026). Pnk. pas. Bf. slp. Bl. pt. Mound I, sq. 12/K, loc. 32, lev. + 12.3 ft.

(28). (No. 3720). Pnk. pas. Rd. slp. Bl. pt. 5.79 lg. Trench F(2), lev. — 3.6 ft. A
(29). (No. 3395). Pnk. pas. Rd. slp. Bl. pt. 4.7 lg. Trench B(5), lev. — 6.8 ft.
(30). (No. 743). Pnk. pas. Rd. slp. Bl. pt. 2.23 lg. Trench B(5), lev. — 0.9 ft. A
(31). (No. 3133). Pnk. pas. Rd. slp. Purp. pt. 4.0 lg. Sq. 8/D, loc. 176, lev. + 13.9 ft. A
(32). (No. 409). Pnk. pas. Rd. slp Bl. pt. 4.38 lg. Trench E(1), lev. — 3.5 ft. A
(33). (No. 4677). Pnk. pas. Rd. slp. Bl. pt. 6.9 lg. Sq. 8/D, loc. 176, lev. + 8.0 ft.
(34). (No. 5314). Pnk. pas. Rd. slp. Bl. pt. Cut., sq. 9/F, loc. 469, lev. — 5.0 ft.
(34, a). (No. 4410). Pnk. pas. Rd. slp. Bl. pt. Sq. 7/D, loc. 271, lev. + 7.2 ft.
(35). (No. 3725). Pnk. pas. Rd. & Cr. slps. Bl. pt. 4.92 lg. Trench H(1), lev. — 7.6 ft.
(36). (No. 5312). Pnk. pas. Rd. slp. Bl. pt. Cut., sq. 9/F, loc. 469, lev. — 4.9 ft.
(37). (No. 5392). Pnk. pas. Rd. & Cr. slps. Bl. pt. Cut., sq. 10/G, loc. 478, lev. — 13.4 ft.
(38). (No. 3140). Pnk. pas. Rd. slp. Bl. pt. 2.8 lg. Sq. 8/D, loc. 202, lev. + 12.8 ft.
(39). (No. 749). Pnk. pas. Rd. slp. Bl. pt. 7.3 lg. Trench D(1), lev. — 7.4 ft. A
(40). (No. 3754). Pnk. pas. Rd. slp. Bl. pt. 5.28 lg. Trench F(2), lev. — 6.6 ft. A
(41). (No. 3709). Pnk. pas. Rd. slp. Bl. pt. 6.2 lg. Trench B(5), lev. — 1.7 ft. A
(42). (No. 4301). Pnk. pas. Rd. slp. Bl. pt. 5.58 lg. Sq. 8/C, loc. 289, lev. + 7.4 ft.
(43). (No. 5427). Pnk. pas. Cr. slp. Rd. pt. Cut., sq. 10/G, loc. 481, lev. — 22.0 ft.
(44). (No. 5429). Pnk. pas. Bl. pt. Sq. 9/D, loc. 95, lev. + 6.7 ft.
(45). (No. 5271). Pnk. pas. Rd. slp. Bl. pt. Mound I, sq. 13/K, loc. 23, lev. + 13.2 ft.
(46). (No. 538). Pnk. pas. Cr. slp. Rd. pt. 2.2 lg. Trench B(3), lev. — 7.7 ft.
(47). (No. 5393). Pnk. pas. Rd. slp. Bl. pt. 7.7 di. Cut., sq. 9/F, loc. 469, lev. — 11.0 ft.
(48). (No. 4798). Pnk. pas. Rd. slp. Bl. pt. 6.26 lg. Sq. 9/F, loc. 469, lev. + 0.6 ft.

Plate XXXVIII. Incised Sherds (Harappā Culture). Chapter VI

(1). (No. 3048). Pnk. pas. 2.82 di. Sq. 9/F, loc. 258, lev. + 7.0 ft. A
(2). (5036). Pnk. pas. Cr. slp. 7.01 lg. Cut., sq. 10/G, loc. 480, lev. — 1.4 ft.
(3). (No. 5032). Pnk. pas. 6.6 lg. Cut., sq. 10/G, loc. 480, lev. — 1.4 ft.
(5). (No. 4789). Pnk. pas. Br. slp. Trench F(1), loc. 42, lev. — 3.1 ft. A
(6). (No. 4749). Pnk. pas. 4.02 lg. Cut., sq. 10/F, loc. 464, lev. + 1.3 ft.
(7). (No. 4036). Pnk. pas. Cr. slp. 5.2 lg. Sq. 9/E, loc. 201, lev. + 8.4 ft. A
(8). (No. 564). Pnk. pas. Trench B(3), lev. — 7.7 ft. A
(9). (No. 5042). Pnk. pas. Cr. slp. Mound I, sq. 12/K, loc. 15, lev. + 14.0 ft. A
(10). (No. 935). Pnk. pas. 2.9 lg. Trench C(2), lev. — 4.2 ft. A
(11). (No. 4340). Pnk. pas. Br. slp. 3.8 lg. Sq. 9/D, loc. 133, lev. + 6.9 ft.
(12). (No. 5342). Dish of food-stand. Gr. pas. Bl. slp. Cut., sq. 9/F, loc. 475, lev. — 6.9 ft.
(13). (No. 1247). Dish of food-stand. Pnk. pas. Rd. slp. 4.62 lg. Trench K(1), lev. — 4.8 ft.
(14). (No. 143). Dish of food-stand. Pnk. pas. Rd. slp. 9.27 lg Trench B(1), lev. — 6.2 ft.
(15). (No. 5403). Dish of food-stand. Gr. pas. Bl. slp. 5.1 lg. Cut., sq. 10/G, loc. 481, lev. — 15.1 ft.
(16). (No. 4504). Dish of food-stand. Pnk. pas. Rd. slp. 6.73 lg. Cut., sq. 9/F, loc. 468, lev. + 3.8 ft. A
(17). (No. 3875). Dish of food-stand. Pnk. pas. Rd. slp. 4.91 lg. Trench H(1), lev. — 8.1 ft. A
(18). (No. 4414). Dish of food-stand. Pnk. pas. Rd. slp. 4.84 lg. Sq. 9/D, loc. 192, lev. + 4.2 ft. A
(19). (No. 4465). Dish of food-stand. Pnk. pas. Rd. slp. Bl. pt. Sq. 9/E, loc. 111, lev. + 7.5 ft.
(20). (No. 5356). Dish of food-stand. Pnk. pas. Rd. slp. Cut., sq. 9/F, loc. 469, lev. — 8.2 ft.
(21). (No. 1258). Dish of food-stand. Pnk. pas. Rd. slp. 4.5 lg. Trench H(1), lev. —7.7 ft. A
(22). (No. 5416). Pnk. pas. Rd. & Cr. slps. Cut., sq. 10/G, loc. 481, lev. — 15.1 ft. A
(23). (No. 1042). Pnk. pas. Rd. slp. Bl. pt. 4.88 lg. Trench D(1), lev. — 4.5 ft. A
(24). (No. 5447). Pnk. pas. Cr. slp. 4.2 lg. Cut., sq. 10/G, loc. 481, lev. — 18.0 ft.
(25). (No. 4272). (Dish of food-stand. Pnk. pas. Cr. slp. 3.2 lg. Sq. 7/C, loc. 134, lev. + 6.8 ft. A

(26). (No. 3566). Pnk. pas. Pnk. slp. 3.62 lg. Trench C(3), lev. — 7.9 ft. A
(27). (No. 5318). Pnk. pas. Dk. Gr. & Lt. Gr. slps. Cut., sq. 10/G, loc. 477, lev. — 15.2 ft.
(28). (No. 5378). Pnk. pas. Cut., sq. 10/G, loc. 478, lev. — 8.2 ft.
(29). (No. 5404). Pnk. pas. Purp.-bl. & Cr. (?) slps. Cut., sq. 10/G, loc. 481, lev. — 15.1 ft.

Plate XXXIX. Pottery (Jhangar, Jhukar and Harappā Cultures). Chapters VI; VII; VIII

Jhangar Pottery.

(1). (No. 1816). Gr. pas. Hnd, mde. 6.91 lg. Sq. 9/D, loc. 95. lev. + 19.3 ft.
(2). (No. 1422). Gr. pas. 2.4 hi. Sq. 8/D, loc. 82, lev. + 22.0 ft.
(3). (No. 1832). Gr. pas. Hnd. mde. 8.65 hi. Sq. 8/E, loc. 87, lev. + 21.9 ft. A
(4). (No. 1448). Gr. pas. Hnd. mde. 2.36 hi. Sq. 9/D, loc. 95, lev. + 19.3 ft.
(5). (No. 1229). Gr. pas. Hnd. mde. 3.77 hi. Sq. 8/D, loc. 82, lev. + 22.0 ft.
(6). (No. 1831). Gr. pas. Hnd. mde. 3.4 hi. Sq. 9/D, loc. 95, lev. + 22.2 ft.
(7). (No. 1411). Gr. pas. Hnd. mde. 3.47 hi. Sq. 8/E. loc. 93. lev. + 18.9 ft. A
(7, a). (No. 4732). Gr. pas. Hnd. mde. 2.3 lg. Cut., sq. 10/G, loc. 477, lev. + 0.9 ft. A
(8). (No. 1796). Gr. pas. Hnd. mde. 3.0 hi. Sq. 9/D, loc. 95, lev. + 22.2 ft. A

Jhukar Pottery.

(9). (No. 5068). Jar-cover. Pnk. pas. Pnk. slp. Br. pt. 2.4 di. Mound I, sq. 13/K, loc. 21, lev. + 14.3 ft.
(10). (No. 3182). Pnk. pas. Cr. slp. Purp. & Rd. pts. 6.5 hi. Sq. 10/E, loc. 251, lev. + 7.2 ft.
(11). (No. 4802). Pnk. pas. Hnd. mde. 2.2 hi. Cut., sq. 10/F, loc. 465. lev. + 1.1 ft. A
(12). (No. 5035). Pnk. pas. Cr. slp. Hnd mde. 2.1 hi. Cut., sq. 10/G, loc. 480, lev. — 1.4 ft.
(13). (No. 4742). Pnk. pas. Hnd. mde. 2.9 hi. Mound I, sq. 12/J, loc. 25, lev. + 15.9 ft.
(14). (No. 1988). Lamp. Dr. pas. Hnd. mde. 1.8 hi. Sq. 8/D, loc. 108, lev. + 14.4 ft.
(15). (No. 2666). Pnk. pas. Cr. slp. Bl. & Rd. pts. 5.01 hi. Sq. 8/E, loc. 142, lev. + 9.4 ft.

Harappā Pottery.

(16). (No. 3481). Tumbler. Pnk. pas. 3.4 hi. Sq. 8/E, loc. 103, lev. + 7.9 ft. A
(17). (No. 4140). Partitioned dish. Pnk. pas. Hnd. mde. 4.3 lg. Sq. 10/D, loc. 341, lev. + 6.6 ft. A
(18). (No. 4468). Oval dish. Pnk. pas. Hnd. mde. 4.7 lg. Sq. 7/C, loc. 102, lev. + 6.8 ft.
(19). (No. 3064). Jar-cover. Pnk. pas. Pnk. slp. Rd. pt. Sq. 8/E, loc. 114, lev. + 12.6 ft. A
(20). (No. 4074). Feeding-cup. Pnk. pas. 5.12 lg. Sq. 8/F, loc. 116, lev. + 6.7 ft. A
(21). (No. 4880). Feeding-cup. Pnk. pas. Rd. slp. 3.0 lg. Sq. 7/F, loc. 440, lev. + 7.7 ft.
(22). (No. 3484). Kohl-jar. Gr. pas. Hnd. mde. 3.45 hi. Sq. 9/C, loc. 291, lev. + 7.1 ft.
(23). (No. 3011, A). Jar. Pnk. pas. Rd. slp. Bl. pt. Sq. 9/C, loc. 208, lev. + 9.6 ft. A
(24). (No. 3419). Inscribed jar. Pnk. pas. Cr. slp. Bl. pt. 6.1 hi. Sq. 9/E, loc. 171, lev. + 6.8 ft.
(25). (No. 5214). Pnk. pas. Rd. & Cr. slps. Bl. pt. 2.82 hi. Mound I, sq. 13/J, loc. 10, lev. + 14.0 ft.
(26). (No. 5199). Kohl-jar. Pnk. pas. Cr. slp. Bl. pt. 2.24 hi. Mound I, sq. 13/K, loc. 34, lev. + 12.9 ft.
(27). (No. 1004). Insect cage. Pnk. pas. Cr. slp. Rd. pt. Hnd. mde. 3.2 hi. Trench A(3), lev. — 4.4 ft. A

Plate XL. Pottery (Muhammedan, Harappā, Jhangar and Jhukar Cultures). Chapters VI; VII; VIII

Muhammadan

(1). (No. 2231). Pnk. pas. Cr. slp. Bl. & Rd. pts. Sq. 7/E, loc. 88, lev. + 15.0 ft.
(2). (No. 2230). Pnk. pas. Cr. slp. Rd. pt. Sq. 7/E, loc. 88, lev. + 15.0 ft.
(3). (No. 2232). Pnk. pas. Sq. 7/E, loc. 88, lev. + 15.0 ft.

Late Harappā(?)

(4). (No. 3810). Pnk. pas. Incis. Mound I, sq. 13/J, loc. 3, lev. + 16.0 ft.

Jhangar.

(5). (No. 1797). Gr. pas. Hnd. mde. Sq. 9/D, loc. 95, lev. + 19.3 ft.
(6). (No. 4289). Gr. pas. Bl. slp.(?). Hnd. mde. Sq. 10/E, loc. 387, lev. + 7.0 ft.
(7). (No. 1833). Gr. pas. Bl. slp.(?). Hnd. mde. Sq. 8/E, loc. 87, lev. + 18.9 ft. A
(7, a). (No. 1943). Gr. pas. Bl. slp.(?). Hnd. mde. Sq. 8/E, loc. 86, lev. + 20.0 ft. A
(8). (No. 1796). Gr. pas. Hnd. mde. Sq. 9/D, loc. 95, lev. + 22.3 ft. A
(9). (No. 1832). Gr. pas. Hnd. mde. Sq. 8/E, loc. 87, lev. +21.9 ft. A
(9, a). (No. 5206). Gr. pas. Hnd. mde. Cut., sq. 10/G, loc. 488, lev. — 1.4 ft.
(10). (No. 1831). Gr. pas. Hnd. mde. Sq. 9/D, loc. 95, lev. + 22.7 ft. A
(11). (No. 1816). Gr. pas. Hnd. mde. Sq. 9/D, loc. 95, lev. + 19.7 ft.

Jhukar Pottery.

(12). (No. 2058). Pnk. pas. Cr. slp. Rd. pt. Trench G(1), lev. — 9.0 ft.
(13). (No. 2153). Dr. pas. Cr. slp. Sq. 8/E, loc. 113, lev. + 13.2 ft.
(14). (No. 2065). Pnk. pas. Sq. 8/D, loc. 82, lev. + 21.4 ft.
(15). (No. 4476). Dr. pas. Hnd. mde. Cut., loc. ?, lev. ?.
(16). (No. 4478). Dr. pas. Hnd. mde. Cut., loc. ?, lev. ?. A
(17). (No. 3670). Incised jar-cover. Pnk. pas. Cr. slp. Sq. 8/F, loc. 145, lev. + 8.4 ft.
(18). (No. 4742). Pnk. pas. Hnd. mde. Mound I, sq. 12/J, loc. 25, lev. + 15.9 ft.
(19). (No. 2510). Pnk. pas. Cr. slp. Purp. pt. Sq. 9/E, loc. 137, lev. + 17.6 ft.
(20). (No. 2130). Pnk. pas. Pnk. & Cr. slps. Purp. pt. Sq. 7/E, loc. 88, lev. + 14.3 ft. A
(21). (No. 2066). Dr. pas. Hnd. mde. Sq. 8/D, loc. 82, lev. + 20.8 ft. A
(22). (No. 3057). Pnk. pas. Rd. slp. Purp. pt. Sq. 9/E, loc. 128, lev. + 11.5 ft. A
(23). (No. 4802). Pnk. pas. Hnd. mde. Cut., sq. 10/F, loc. 465, lev. + 1.1 ft. A
(24). (No. 1788). Dr. pas. Hnd. mde. Sq. 8/C, loc. 109, lev. + 14.0 ft. A
(25). (No. 1563). Dr. pas. Hnd. mde. Sq. 8/E, loc. 86, lev. + 18.0 ft.
(26). (No. 2334). Pnk. pas. Pnk. & Cr. slps. Bl. & Rd. pts. Sq. 8/C, loc. 151, lev. + 13.1 ft.
(27). (No. 1425). Pnk. pas. Hnd. mde. Sq. 8/E, loc. 90, lev. + 15.5 ft. A
(28). (No. 4033). Pnk. pas. Pnk. slp. Bl. pt. Sq. 8/E, loc. 185, lev. + 12.9 ft.
(29). (No. 2244). Pnk. pas. Sq. 9/E, loc. 85, lev. + 18.2 ft. A
(30). (No. 4788). Incised jar-stand. Pnk. pas. Sq. 8/D, loc. 82, lev. + 22.6 ft.
(31). (No. 1861). Pnk. pas. Rd. slp. Bl. pt. Sq. 9/E, loc. 126, lev. + 18.9 ft. A
(32). (No. 1553). Pnk. pas. Hnd. mde. Sq. 8/E, loc. 90, lev. + 15.6 ft. A

Plate XLI. Pottery (Jhukar Culture). Chapter VII

(1). (No. 2612). Frag. storage jar. Pnk. pas. Cr. slp. Purp. & Rd. pts. Sq. 8/F, loc. 182, lev. + 13.7 ft. A
(2). (No. 3135). Frag. of dish. Pnk. pas. Rd. & Pnk. slps. Bl. & Rd. pts. Sq. 8/D, loc. 176, lev. + 13.9 ft.
(3). (No. 3134). Frag. storage jar. Pnk. pas. Cr. slp. Bl. & Rd. pts. Sq. 8/D, loc. 176, lev. + 14.4 ft. A
(4). (No. 4743). Frag. of dish. Pnk. pas. Cr. slp. Rd. & Br. pts. Mound I, sq. 12/J, loc. 16, lev. + 16.0 ft.
(5). (No. 3096). Frag. of dish. Pnk. pas. Rd. slp. Bl. & Rd. pts. Sq. 8/E, loc. 185, lev. + 11.4 ft.
(6). (No. 3066). Frag. storage jar. Pnk. pas. Pnk. slp. Bl. & Rd. pts. Sq. 8/D, loc. 108, lev. + 14.4 ft. A
(7). (No. 3127). Frag. storage jar. Pnk. pas. Cr. slp. Bl. & Rd. pts. Sq. 9/D, loc. 130, lev. + 13.9 ft. A

(8). (No. 5061). Frag. storage jar. Pnk. pas. Cr. slp. Purp. & Rd. pts. Cut., sq. 10/G, loc. 486, lev. — 1.3 ft.
(9). (No. 3136). Frag. storage jar. Pnk. pas. Cr. slp. Bl. & Rd. pts. Sq. 9/D, loc. 136, lev. + 13.0 ft.
(10). (No. 3143). Pnk. pas. Cr. slp. Sq. 9/E, loc. 161, lev. + 14.4 ft. A
(11). (No. 1850). Pnk. pas. Cr. slp. Bl. & Rd. pts. Sq. 9/E, loc. 123, lev. + 18.8 ft. A
(12). (No. 1758). Frag. of dish. Pnk. pas. Rd. & Cr. slps. Bl. & Rd. pts. Sq. 8/E, loc. 90, lev. + 15.3 ft.
(13). (No. 3429). Pnk. pas. Pnk. slp. Bl. & Rd. pts. Sq. 8/D, loc. 82, lev. + 17.2 ft. A
(14). (No. 3059). Frag. of dish. Pnk. pas. Rd. & Cr. slps. Purp. & Rd. pts. Sq. 8/D, loc. 108, lev. + 11.7 ft.
(15). (No. 1902). Pnk. pas. Pnk. & Cr. slps. Purp. & Rd. pts. Sq. 7/E, loc. 121, lev. + 15.9 ft.
(16). (No. 1903). Pnk. pas. Cr. slp. Bl. & Rd. pts. Sq. 7/E, loc. 121, lev. + 15.9 ft. A
(17). (No. 2266). Pnk. pas. Purp. pt. Sq. 9/E, loc. 112, lev. + 14.0 ft. A
(18). (No. 2099). Pnk. pas. Cr. slp. Hnd. mde. Sq. 8/E, loc. 93, lev. + 18.0 ft. A
(19). (No. 3175). Pnk. pas. Pnk. slp. Bl. & Rd. pts. Sq. 8/D, loc. 178, lev. + 15.0 ft.
(20). (No. 3176). Pnk. pas. Pnk. slp. Bl. & Rd. pts. Sq. 8/D, loc. 178, lev. + 15.0 ft. A
(21). (No. 2712). Pnk. pas. Cr. slp. Purp. pt. Sq. 7/E, loc. 277, lev. + 9.6 ft. A
(22). (No. 2995). Pnk. pas. Rd. slp. Bl. pt. Sq. 8/E, loc. 104, lev. + 15.5 ft. A
(23). (No. 2766). Pnk. pas. Hnd. mde. Sq. 8/E, loc. 94, lev. + 9.9 ft.
(24). (No. 4152). Pnk. pas. Rd. & Cr. slps. Rd. & Purp. pts. Sq. 9/E, loc. 123. lev. + 9.9 ft.
(25). (No. 1863). Pnk. pas. Rd. & Cr. slps. Bl. & Rd. pts. Sq. 8/E, loc. 90, lev. + 14.0 ft. A
(26). (No. 4257). Pnk. pas. Sq. 9/F, loc. 408, lev. + 2.8 ft.
(27). (No. 2960). Pnk. pas. Pnk. slp. Sq. 9/E, loc. 200, lev. + 13.1 ft.
(28). (No. 2091). Pnk. pas. Rd. & Cr. slps. Sq. 8/D, loc. 82, lev. + 22.7 ft.
(29). (No. 2242). Pnk. pas. Rd. slp. Bl. pt. Sq. 9/F, loc. 184, lev. + 13.0 ft.
(30). (No. 3285). Pnk. pas. Cr. slp. Sq. 7/C, loc. 135, lev. + 11.3 ft.
(31). (No. 2104). Pnk. pas. Sq. 8/E, loc. 104, lev. + 15.2 ft. A
(32). (No. 2253). Pnk. pas. Cr. slp. Hnd. mde. Sq. 9/E, loc. 124, lev. + 11.6 ft. A
(33). (No. 2155). Dr. pas. Cr. slp. Hnd. mde. Sq. 8/E, loc. 114, lev. + 15.9 ft.
(34). (No. 1867). Pnk. pas. Rd. slp. Sq. 8/E, loc. 104, lev. + 18.6 ft. A
(35). (No. 5068). Pnk. pas. Pnk. slp. Br. pt. Mound I, sq. 13/K, loc. 21, lev. + 14.3 ft.
(36). (No. 4294). Pnk. pas. Rd. & Cr. slps. Bl. pt. Sq. 7/F, loc. 445, lev. + 6.6 ft.
(37). (No. 1817). Pnk. pas. Sq. 9/D, loc. 95, lev. + 19.8 ft. A
(38). (No. 3182). Pnk. pas. Cr. slp. Purp. & Rd. pts. Sq. 10/E, loc. 251, lev. + 7. 2 ft.
(39). (No. 4610). Pnk. pas. Rd. slp. Cut., sq. 10/F, loc. 471, lev. + 2.8 ft.
(40). (No. 1868). Pnk. pas. Rd. slp. Sq. 8/E, loc. 104, lev. + 19.0 ft. A
(41). (No. 2240). Pnk. pas. Rd. slp. Purp. pt. Sq. 7/C, loc. 102, lev. + 15.5 ft. A
(42). (No. 3937). Pnk. pas. Cr. slp. Purp. & Rd. pts. Sq. 9/E, loc. 124, lev. + 17.0 ft. A
(43). (No. 2129). Pnk. pas. Hnd. mde. Sq. 8/F, loc. 83, lev. + 21.2 ft.
(44). (No. 2098). Pnk. pas. Sq. 8/E, loc. 104, lev. + 17.5 ft.
(45). (No. 2534). Pnk. pas. Pnk. slp. Sq. 9/F, loc. 258, lev. + 9.3 ft. A
(46). (No. 4729). Pnk. pas. Rd. slp. Cut., sq. 10/G, loc. 477, lev. + 0.8 ft.
(47). (No. 1798). Pnk. pas. Cr. slp. Sq. 7/C, loc. 102, lev. + 14.1 ft.
(48). (No. 2074). Pnk. pas. Rd. & Cr. slps. Sq. 8/E, loc. 146, lev. + 17.7 ft. A
(49). (No. 1799). Pnk. pas. Yell. slp. Purp. & Rd. pts. Sq. 8/D, loc. 82, lev. + 16.4 ft.
(50). (No. 1779). Pnk. pas. Cr. slp. Purp. & Rd. pts. Sq. 9/E, loc. 127, lev. + 16.7 ft.

Plate XLII. Painted Sherds (Jhukar Culture). Chapter VII

(1). (No. 1722). Pnk. pas. Cr. slp. Bl. & Rd. pts. 5.43 lg. Sq. 8/E, loc. 87, lev.+ 18.8 ft. A
(2). (No. 4582). Pnk. pas. Rd. slp. Bl. pt. 3.9 lg. Cut., sq. 10/G, loc. 481, lev. + 0.4 ft. A
(3). (No. 4191). Pnk. pas. Cr. slp. Bl. pt. Sq. 9/F, loc. 401, lev. + 8.3 ft.

(4). (No. 2086). Pnk. pas. Rd. slp. Bl. pt. 2.75 lg. Sq. 8/E, loc. 146, lev. + 15.0 ft. A
(5). (No. 4191). Pnk. pas. Cr. slp. Bl. pt. Sq. 9/F, loc. 401, lev. + 8.3 ft.
(6). (No. 4747). Pnk. pas. Cr. slp. Br. & Rd. pts. 7.8 lg. Sq. 10/F, loc. 464, lev. + 1.3 ft.
(7). (No. 1871). Pnk. pas. Cr. slp. Rd. pt. 6.35 lg. Sq. 9/E, loc. 123, lev. + 18.8 ft.
(8). (No. 1848). Pnk. pas. Pnk. slp. Bl. & Rd. pts. 3.9 lg. Sq. 8/E, loc. 114, lev. + 17.7 ft. A
(9). (No. 2068). Pnk. pas. Cr. slp. Bl. & Rd. pts. 3.91 lg. Sq. 8/D, loc. 82, lev. + 20.7 ft.
(10). (No. 4191). Pnk. pas. Cr. slp. Bl. pt. Sq. 9/F, loc. 401, lev. + 18.3 ft.
(11). (No. 4573). Pnk. pas. Cr. slp. Bl. & Rd. pts. 6.11 lg. Cut., sq. ?, lev. ? A
(12). (No. 1509). Pnk. pas. Pnk. slp. Bl. & Rd. pts. Sq. 9/E, loc. 85, lev. + 19.1 ft. A
(13). (No. 4746). Pnk. pas. Cr. slp. Br. & Rd. pts. 2.62 lg. Cut., sq. 10/F, loc. 464, lev. + 1.3 ft. A
(14). (No. 1505). Pnk. pas. Cr. slp. Bl. & Rd. pts. 6.02 lg. Sq. 9/E, loc. 85, lev. + 19.1 ft. A
(15). (No. 4287). Pnk. pas. Cr. slp. Bl. & Rd. pts. 2.1 lg. Mound I, sq. 12/J, loc. 18, lev. + 15.9 ft. A
(16). (No. 1849). Pnk. pas. Cr. slp. Bl. & Rd. pts. 2.42 lg. Sq. 9/E, loc. 123, lev. + 17.5 ft. A
(17). (No. 4731). Pnk. pas. Cr. slp. Bl. & Rd. pts. 3.23 lg. Cut., sq. 10/G, loc. 477, lev. + 0.8 ft. A
(18). (No. 2920). Pnk. pas. Cr. slp. Bl. & Rd. pts. 4.93 lg. Sq. 9/E, loc. 131, lev. + 13.7 ft.
(19). (No. 1873). Pnk. pas. Pnk. slp. Bl. & Rd. pts. 2.6 lg. Sq. 8/E, loc. 87, lev. + 18.7 ft. A
(20). (No. 1872). Pnk. pas. Cr. slp. Rd. pt. 2.2 lg. Sq. 8/E, loc. 87, lev. + 18.6 ft.
(21). (No. 4585). Pnk. pas. Rd. slp. Bl. pt. 2.2 lg. Mound I, sq. 12/J, loc. 14, lev. + 16.1 ft.
(22). (No. 4498). Pnk. pas. Cr. slp. Bl. pt. Mound I, sq. 13/J, loc. 3, lev. + 15.9 ft. A
(23). (No. 4792). Pnk. pas. Rd. slp. Bl. pt. 2.2 lg. Cut., sq. 9/F, loc. 475, lev. + 0.6 ft. A
(24). (No. 1861). Pnk. pas. Rd. slp. Bl. pt. 7.0 lg. Sq. 9/E, loc. 126, lev. + 18.9 ft. A
(25). (No. 1774). Pnk. pas. Rd. & Cr. slps. Bl. pt. 4.7 lg. Sq. 8/E, loc. 87, lev. + 17.6 ft. A
(26). (No. 1862). Pnk. pas. Rd. slp. Bl. pt. 4.33 lg. Sq. 8/E, loc. 94, lev. + 17.1 ft. A

Plate XLIII. Painted Sherds (Jhukar Culture). Chapter VII

(1). (No. 4567). Pnk. pas. Cr. slp. Purp. & Rd. pts. 9.8 lg. Cut., sq. 10/F, loc. 466, lev. + 2.4 ft.
(2). (No. 1757). Pnk. pas. Cr. slp. Bl. & Rd. pts. 4.09 lg. Sq. 7/E, loc. 99, lev. + 18.0 ft. A
(3). (No. 1756). Pnk. pas. Cr. slp. Bl. & Rd. pts. 7.62 lg. Sq. 7/C, loc. 102, lev. + 14.9 ft.
(4). (No. 1904). Pnk. pas. Rd. & Cr. slps. Bl. & Rd. pts. 4.92 lg. Sq. 8/E, loc. 113, lev. + 17.2 ft. A
(5). (No. 3599). Pnk. pas. Cr. slp. Bl. & Rd. pts. 9.85 lg. Sq. 8/D, loc. 84, lev. + 19.3 ft. A
(6). (No. 1759). Pnk. pas. Pnk. slp. Bl. & Rd. pts. 7.58 lg. Sq. 8/E, loc. 87, lev. + 19.4 ft. A
(7). (No. 1758). Pnk. pas. Rd. & Cr. slps. Red. & Bl. pts. 7.82 lg. Sq. 8/E, loc. 90, lev. + 15.3 ft.
(8). (No. 1767). Pnk. pas. Rd. & Cr. slps. Bl. & Rd. pts. 7.4 lg. Sq. 7/E, loc. 88, lev. + 10.9 ft.
(9). (No. 5153). Pnk. pas. Pnk. slp. Rd. pt. Mound I, sq. 13/K, loc. 34, lev. + 13.8 ft.
(10). (No. 1935). Pnk. pas. Rd. & Cr. slps. Bl. pt. 7.2 lg. Sq. 9/D, loc. 133, lev. + 16.7 ft. A
(11). (No. 1866). Pnk. pas. Rd. slp. Bl. pt. 4.2 lg. Sq. 9/D, loc. 130, lev. + 18.9 ft. A
(12). (No. 2612). Pnk. pas. Cr. slp. Purp. & Rd. pts. 10.3 lg. Sq. 8/F, loc. 182, lev. + 13.7 ft. A

Plate XLIV. Painted Sherds (Jhukar Culture). Chapter VII

(1). (No. 1516). Pnk. pas. Rd. slp. Bl. pt. 3.6 lg. Sq. 8/E, loc. 87, lev. + 18.0 ft. A
(2). (No. 4637). Pnk. pas. Rd. slp. Purp. pt. 3.8 lg. Cut., sq. ?, lev. ?, A
(3). (No. 4185). Pnk. pas. Rd. slp. Bl. pt. 4.84 lg. Sq. 9/E, loc. 172, lev. + 8.2 ft. A
(4). (No. 1939). Pnk. pas. Cr. slp. Bl. & Rd. pts. 4.7 lg. Sq. 8/C, loc. 153, lev. + 16.5 ft. A
(5). (No. 2146). Pnk. pas. Rd. slp. Rd. pt. 4.4 lg. Sq. 8/C, loc. 109, lev. + 15.0 ft. A

(6). (No. 1845). Pnk. pas. Purp. pt 5.5 lg. Sq. 8/D, loc. 82, lev. + 17.7 ft. A
(7). (No. 1940). Pnk. pas. Cr. slp. Bl. & Rd. pts. Sq. 8/C, loc. 109, lev. + 20.0 ft.
(8). (No. 4309). Pnk. pas. Rd. slp. Bl. pt. 5.6 lg. Sq. 9/D, loc. 209, lev. + 12.4 ft.
(9). (No. 4193). Pnk. pas. Rd. slp. Bl. pt. 6.7 lg. Sq. 9/F, loc. 401, lev. + 8.3 ft.
(10). (No. 3600). Pnk. pas. Pnk. & Cr. slps. Bl. pt. 7.6 lg. Sq. 8/D, loc. 84, lev. + 19.3 ft. A
(11). (No. 1937). Pnk. pas. Cr. slp. Bl. & Rd. pts. 7.2 lg. Sq. 8/C, loc. 152, lev. + 16.6 ft. A
(12). (No. 1777). Pnk. pas. Rd. & Pnk. slps. Bl. pt. 6.02 lg. Sq. 8/E, loc. 87, lev. + 17.6 ft.
(13). (No. 3142). Pnk. pas. Rd. & Cr. slps. Bl. & Rd. pts. Sq. 8/E, loc. 114, lev. + 12.6 ft. A
(14). (No. 1933). Pnk. pas. Cr. slp. Purp. & Rd. pts. 7.78 lg. Sq. 7/C, loc. 101, lev. + 16.5 ft.
(15). (No. 1723). Pnk. pas. Rd. & Pnk. slps. Bl. Purp. & Rd. pts. 5.37 lg. Sq. 8/E, loc. 90, lev. + 16.2 ft. A

Plate XLV. Painted Sherds (Trihni and Jhukar Cultures). Chapters VII; VIII

Trihni Pottery.

(1). (No. 4551). Pnk. pas. Cr. slp. Br. & Rd. pts. 4.04 lg. Cut., sq. 10/G, loc. 486, lev. — 1.3 ft.
(2). (No. 815). Pnk. pas. Cr. slp. Rd. pt. 5.73 lg. Trench F(1), lev. — 1.6 ft.
(3). (No. 107). Pnk. pas. Cr. slp. Bl. pt. 1.72 lg. Trench B(1), lev. — 3.8 ft.
(4). (No. 217). Pnk. pas. Pnk. slp. Bl. & Rd. pts. 3.82 lg. Trench B(1), lev. — 3.8 ft. A
(5). (No. 226). Pnk. pas. Cr. slp. Bl. & Rd. pts. 2.9 lg. Trench B(2), lev. — 5.3 ft.
(6). (No. 219). Pnk. pas. Cr. slp. Purp. & Rd. pts. 5.4 lg. Trench B(3), lev. — 2.1 ft. A
(7). (No. 201). Pnk. pas. Cr. slp. Purp. & Rd. pts. 5.26 lg. Trench C(2), lev. — 5.8 ft. A
(8). (No. 138). Pnk. pas. Bl. pt. 1.95 lg. Trench B(1), lev. — 6.8 ft. A
(9). (No. 148). Pnk. pas. Bl. & Rd. pts. 4.2 lg. Trench B(1), lev. — 6.3 ft.
(10). (No. 145). Pnk. pas. Pnk. slp. Bl. & Rd. pts. 2.9 lg. Trench B(1), lev. — 5.6 ft. A
(11). (No. 225). Pnk. pas. Pnk. slp. Bl. & Rd. pts. 2.75 lg. Trench B(2), lev. — 4.6 ft.
(12). (No. 384). Pnk. pas. Yell. slp. Bl. & Rd. pts. 3.3 lg. Trench B(2), lev. — 6.6 ft. A
(13). (No. 298). Pnk. pas. Pnk. slp. Rd. pt. 2.15 lg. Trench B(3), lev. — 4.7 ft.
(14). (No. 214). Pnk. pas. Yell. slp. Bl. pt. 1.62 lg. Trench B(3), lev. — 4.2 ft. A
(15). (No. 99). Pnk. pas. Cr. slp. Bl. & Rd. pts. 2.77 lg. Trench B(1), lev. — 4.9 ft. A
(16). (No. 1145). Pnk. pas. Yell. slp. Bl. & Rd. pts. 1.92 lg. Trench G(1), lev. — 1.5 ft. A
(17). (No. 221). Pnk. pas. Pnk. slp. Br. pt. 6.0 lg. Trench B(3), lev. — 3.2 ft.
(18). (No. 75). Pnk. pas. Cr. slp. Bl. & Rd. pts. 6.31 lg. Trench B(1), lev. — 3.5 ft. A

Jhukar Pottery.

(19). (No. 3258). Pnk. pas. Cr. slp. Purp.-Bl. pt. 5.71 lg. Loc. ?, lev. ?
(20). (No. 1754). Pnk. pas. Rd. & Cr. slps. Br. & Rd. pts. 3.62 lg. Sq. 8/D, loc. 84, lev. + 20.7 ft. A
(21). (No. 4934). Pnk. pas. Cr. slp. Purp. pt. 4.85 lg. Mound I, sq. 12/J, loc. 13, lev. + 14.2 ft.
(22). (No. 2060). Pnk. pas. Rd. & Pnk. slps. Purp. & Rd. pts. 6.11 lg. Sq. 9/D, loc. 130, lev. + 16.8 ft.
(23). (No. 2251). Pnk. pas. Bl. & Rd. pts. 3.44 lg. Sq. 8/C, loc. 152, lev. + 14.8 ft.
(24). (No. 2015). Pnk. pas. Pnk. slp. Bl. & Rd. pts. 4.9 lg. Sq. 9/E, loc. 127, lev. + 13.3 ft. A
(25). (No. 3102). Pnk. pas. Rd. & Cr. slps. Bl. & Rd. pts. 6.42 lg. Sq. 10/E, loc. 218, lev. + 11.1 ft. A
(26). (No. 2164). Pnk. pas. Rd. & Cr. slps. Purp. pt. 4.26 lg. Sq. 9/D, loc. 130, lev. + 16.8 ft. A
(27). (No. 3132). Pnk. pas. Pnk. & Cr. slps. Bl. & Rd. pts. 4.7 lg. Sq. 8/D, loc. 176, lev. + 15.0 ft. A
(28). (No. 2116). Pnk. pas. Pnk. slp. Bl. & Rd. pts. 6.1 lg. Sq. 8/E, loc. 146, lev. + 14.2 ft.
(29). (No. 3260). Pnk. pas. Pnk. slp. Bl. pt. 6.02 lg. Sq. 9/C, loc. 190, lev. + 14.4 ft. A

(30). (No. 2284). Pnk. pas. Gr. slp. (?). Bl. & Rd. pts. 5.1 lg. Sq. 9/E, loc. 125, lev. + 14.5 ft.
(31). (No. 3387). Pnk. pas. Rd. & Pnk. slps. Bl. & Rd. pts. 5.0 lg. Sq. 9/D, loc. 133, lev. + 14.1 ft. A
(32). (No. 4795). Pnk. pas. Rd. slp. Bl. pt. Cut., sq. 10/F, loc. 464, lev. + 0.1 ft.
(33). (No. 3058). Pnk. pas. Rd. & Pnk. slps. Purp. pt. 4.0 lg. Sq. 8/D, loc. 108, lev. + 11.7 ft. A
(34). (No. 1945). Pnk. pas. Cr. slp. Bl. & Rd. pts. Sq. 9/D, loc. 136, lev. + 18.3 ft.
(35). (No. 3424). Pnk. pas. Cr. slp. Bl. & Rd. pts. Loc. ?, lev. + 14.3 ft.
(36). (No. 4942). Pnk. pas. Rd. slp. Br. pt. Cut., sq. 10/F, lev. 472, lev. + 0.6 ft. A
(37). (No. 2167). Pnk. pas. Pnk. & Cr. slps. Bl. & Rd. pts. 4.4 lg. Sq. 9/D, loc. 130, lev. + 16.8 ft.
(38). (No. 1847). Pnk. pas. Cr. slp. Purp. & Rd. pts. 5.61 lg. Sq. 8/E, loc. 104, lev. + 17.5 ft.
(39). (No. 1936). Pnk. pas. Rd. slp. Bl. pt. 8.5 lg. Sq. 9/E, loc. 152, lev. + 16.6 ft.
(40). (No. 3276). Pnk. pas. Cr. slp. Purp. pt. 3.72 lg. Sq. 8/E, loc. 114, lev. + 11.4 ft. A
(41). (No. 2134). Pnk. pas. Gr. slp. (?). Bl. pt. 5.92 lg. Sq. 9/E, loc. 162, lev. + 15.7 ft.
(42). (No. 2117). Pnk. pas. Pnk. slp. Purp. & Rd. pts. 2.42 lg. Sq. 8/E, loc. 91, + 13.7 ft.

Plate XLVI. Painted Pottery (Jhukar Culture). Chapter VII

(1). (No. 2610). Pnk. pas. Rd. & Pnk. slps. Bl. & Rd. pts. 5.67 lg. Sq. 8/D, loc. 107, lev. + 14.3 ft.
(2). (No. 5132). Pnk. pas. Rd. slp. Purp. pt. 7.86 lg. Cut., sq. 10/F, loc. 466, lev. — 1.2 ft.
(3). (No. 3842). Pnk. pas. Pnk. slp. Bl. pt. 3.71 lg. Mound I, sq. 13/J, loc. 4, lev. + 17.8 ft. A
(4). (No. 2139). Pnk. pas. Rd. & Pnk. slps. Bl. & Rd. pts. 5.36 lg. Sq. 7/E, loc. 99, lev. + 13.4 ft. A
(5). (No. 4611). Pnk. pas. Pnk. & Cr. slps. Br. & Rd. pts. 3.88 lg. Cut., sq. 9/F, loc. 475, lev. + 3.8 ft. A
(6). (No. 3251). Pnk. pas. Rd. & Cr. slps. Bl. & Rd. pts. 4.87 lg. Sq. 9/E, loc. 199, lev. + 13.4 ft.
(7). (No. 3177). Pnk. pas. Rd. & Pnk. slps Bl. & Rd. pts. 9.83 lg. Sq. 9/D, loc. 192, lev. + 15.0 ft. A
(8). (No. 4814). Pnk. pas. Rd. & Cr. slps. Purp. & Rd. pts. 7.59 lg. Cut., sq. 10/F, loc. 472, lev. + 1.9 ft.
(9). (No. 4576). Pnk. pas. Pnk. & Cr. slps. Purp. pt. 5.3 lg. Mound I, sq. 13/J, loc. 6, lev. + 16.5 ft.
(10). (No. 5265). Pnk. pas. Rd. slp. Bl. pt. Sq. 7/E, loc. 99, lev. + 16.1 ft.
(11). (No. 4302). Pnk. pas. Rd. slp. Purp. pt. 5.9 lg. Cut., sq. 10/F, loc. 466, lev. + 2.9 ft. A
(12). (No. 2121). Pnk. pas. Rd. & Cr. slps. Purp. pt. 4.4 lg. Sq. 8/D, loc. 89, lev. + 15.3 ft. A
(13). (No. 1945). Pnk. pas. Cr. slp. Bl. & Rd. pts. Sq. 9/D, loc. 136, lev. + 18.3 ft.
(14). (No. 3130). Pnk. pas. Rd. slp. Purp. pt. 3.7 lg. Cut., sq. 10/F, loc. 472, + 2.8 ft.
(15). (No. 4808). Pnk. pas. Cr. slp. Bl. & Rd. pts. 6.15 lg. Cut., sq. 10/F, loc. 464, lev. + 1.3 ft. A
(16). (No. 2119). Pnk. pas. Rd. & Cr. slps. Purp. & Rd. pts. 6.2 lg. Sq. 8/E, loc. 146, lev. + 13.4 ft.
(17). (No. 2275). Pnk. pas. Rd. & Pnk. slps. Bl. pt. 6.61 lg. Sq. 9/D, loc. 95, lev. + 14.8 ft.
(18). (No. 2335). Pnk. pas. Rd. slp. Bl. pt. 3.7 lg. Sq. 8/C, loc. 169, lev. + 12.7 ft. A
(19). (No. 4475). Pnk. pas. Rd. slp. Bl. pt. 3.9 lg. Cut., loc. (?), lev. (?).
(20). (No. 5061). Pnk. pas. Cr. slp. Purp. & Rd. pts. Cut., sq. 10/G, loc. 486, lev. — 1.3 ft.
(21). (No. 3140). Pnk. pas. Rd. slp. Bl. pt. 2.8 lg. Sq. 8/D, loc. 202, lev. + 12.8 ft.
(22). (No. 4512). Pnk. pas. Rd. slp. Bl. pt. 5.76 lg. Cut., sq. 10/F, loc. 379, lev. + 2.7 ft. A
(23). (No. 5295). Pnk. pas. Pnk. slp. Br. pt. Cut., sq. 10/G, loc. 477, lev. — 4.6 ft.

(24). (No. 2132). Pnk. pas. Cr. slp. Bl. & Rd. pts. 1.97 lg. Sq. 9/E, loc. 161, lev. + 15.2 ft.
(25). (No. 3070). Pnk. pas. Rd. slp. Bl. pt. 4.38 lg. Sq. 8/E, loc. 185, lev. + 13.9 ft. A
(26). (No. 3054). Pnk. pas. Cr. slp. Br. pt. 3.72 lg. Sq. 9/E, loc. 172, lev. + 11.4 ft.
(27). (No. 3107). Pnk. pas. Rd. & Cr. slp. Bl. & Rd. pts. Sq. 8/E, loc. 177, lev. + 12.3 ft.
(28). (No. 3068). Pnk. pas. Pnk. slp. Bl. & Rd. pts. 5.62 lg. Sq. 8/E, loc. 185, lev. + 14.0 ft.
(29). (No. 4577). Pnk. pas. Cr. slp. Purp. pt. 5.31 lg. Mound I, sq. 13/J, loc. 11, + 16.3 ft.
(30). (No. 4745). Pnk. pas. Cr. slp. Br. & Rd. pts. 9.45 lg. Cut., sq. 10/F, loc. 464, lev. + 1.3 ft.
(31). (No. 5131). Pnk. pas. Cr. slp. Bl. & Rd. pts. Cut., sq. 10/F, loc. 466, lev. — 1.2 ft. A
(32). (No. 1420). Pnk. pas. Cr. slp. Bl. & Rd. pts. 5.85 lg. Sq. 8/E, loc. 86, lev. + 20.9 ft.
(33). (No. 2111). Pnk. pas. Cr. slp. Purp. & Rd. pts. Sq. 8/E, loc. 91, lev. + 13.5 ft.
(34). (No. 2111). Pnk. pas. Cr. slp. Purp. & Rd. pts. Sq. 8/E, loc. 91, lev. + 13.5 ft. A
(35). (No. 5311). Pnk. pas. Cr. slp. Bl. & Rd. pts. Cut., sq. 10/G, loc 477, lev. — 5.8 ft.
(36). (No. 1279). Pnk. pas. Cr. slp. Bl. & Rd. pts. Sq. 8/E, loc. 87, lev. + 21.2 ft. A
(37). (No. 0). Pnk. pas. Rd. & Cr. slps. Bl. & Rd. pts. Loc. (?), lev. (?).
(38). (No. 4269). Dr. pas. Cr. slp. Purp. & Rd. pts. Cut., sq. 10/F, loc. 467, lev. + 4.0 ft.
(39). (No. 3056). Pnk. pas. Pnk. & Rd. slps. Bl. & Rd. pts. 4.0 lg. Sq. 9/E, loc. 199, lev. + 11.4 ft.
(40). (No. 5266). Pnk. pas. Cr. slp. Rd. pt. Sq. 8/D, loc. 89, lev. + 18.5 ft.
(41). (No. 2145). Pnk. pas. Rd. & Cr. slps. Bl. & Rd. pts. 5.56 lg. Sq. 7/E, loc. 154, lev. + 16.7 ft.
(42). (No. 2084). Pnk. pas. Cr. slp. Bl. & Rd. pts. 7.48 lg. Sq. 8/E, loc. 92, lev. + 16.7 ft.
(43). (No. 2113). Pnk. pas. Rd. & Pnk. slps. Bl. & Rd. pts. 6.93 lg. Sq. 8/E, loc. 91, lev. + 14.3 ft. A
(44). (No. 2172). Pnk. pas. Cr. slp. Purp. & Rd. pts. 6.3 lg. Sq. 9/E, loc. 132, lev. + 16.5 ft.
(45). (No. 4941). Pnk. pas. Cr. slp. Bl. & Rd. pts. 7.22 lg. Cut., sq. 10/F, loc. 472, lev. + 0.4 ft. A

Plate XLVII. Painted Pottery (Jhukar Culture). Chapter VII

(1). (No. 3065). Pnk. pas. Rd. slp. Bl. pt. 7.1 lg. Sq. 8/D, loc. 84, lev. +13.7 ft.
(2). (No. 2136). Pnk. pas. Rd. & Cr. slps. Bl. pt. 4.9 lg. Sq. 9/E, loc. 127, lev. + 16.8 ft. A
(3). (No. 3055). Pnk. pas. Gr. slp. (?). Bl. pt. 3.22 lg. Sq. 9/E, loc. 172, lev. + 11.4 ft.
(4). (No. 2168). Pnk. pas. Cr. slp. Bl. & Rd. pts. 6.4 lg. Sq. 8/F, loc. 165, lev. + 14.0 ft. A
(5). (No. 3111). Pnk. pas. Rd. & Pnk. slps. Bl. & Rd. pts. Sq. 7/F, loc. 118, lev. + 10.0 ft. A
(6). (No. 4422). Pnk. pas. Cr. slp. Bl. & Rd. pts. Sq. 10/G, loc. 480, lev. + 0.4 ft.
(7). (No. 2366). Pnk. pas. Pnk. & Cr. slps. Br. & Rd. pts. 6.5 lg. Sq. 8/E, loc. 177, lev. + 12.9 ft. A
(8). (No. 2272). Pnk. pas. Pnk. slp. Bl. & Rd. pts. 4.82 lg. Sq. 8/C, loc. 152, lev. + 14.6 ft. A
(9). (No. 3033). Pnk. pas. Cr. slp. Br. & Rd. pts. 6.5 lg. Sq. 9/E, loc. 172, lev. + 11.4 ft. A
(10). (No. 3260). Pnk. pas. Pnk. slp. Bl. pt. 6.02 lg. Sq. 9/C, loc. 190, lev. + 14.4 ft. A
(11). (No. 3095). Pnk. pas. Cr. slp. Bl. & Rd. pts. 6.87 lg. Sq. 9/E, loc. 162, lev. + 12.5 ft. A
(12). (No. 1965). Pnk. pas. Rd. slp. Bl. & Rd. pts. 9.18 lg. Sq. 8/D, loc. 108, lev. + 16.4 ft.
(13). (No. 1846). Pnk. pas. Pnk. slp. Rd. & Bl. pts. 5.72 lg. Sq. 9/E, loc. 123, lev. + 18.1 ft.
(14). (No. 2107). Pnk. pas. Cr. slp. Purp. & Rd. pts. Sq. 9/E, loc. 123, lev. + 15.7 ft.
(No. 2083). Pnk. pas. Cr. slp. Purp. & Rd. pts. Sq. 8/E, loc. 91, lev. + 15.7 ft.
(15). (No. 3141). Pnk. pas. Cr. slp. Bl. pt. 8.3 lg. Sq. 8/E, loc. 114, lev. + 12.9 ft. A
(16). (No. 2250). Pnk. pas. Rd. & Pnk. slps. Bl. & Rd. pts. 9.4 lg. Sq. 8/D, loc. 89, lev. + 13.0 ft. A
(17). (No. 3264). Pnk. pas. Pnk. & Cr. slps. Bl. & Rd. pts. 3.83 lg. Sq. 9/C, loc. 190, lev. + 13.7 ft. A
(18). (No. 2149). Pnk. pas. Cr. slp. Bl. & Rd. pts. 2.0 lg. Sq. 8/E, loc. 104, lev. + 15.6 ft. A

(19). (No. 1504). Pnk. pas. Cr. slp. Bl. & Rd. pts. 5.4 lg. Sq. 9/E, loc. 85, lev. + 18.9 ft. A
(20). (No. 3108). Pnk. pas. Rd. slp. Bl. pt. 3.7 lg. Sq. 8/D, loc. 108, lev. + 12.8 ft.
(21). (No. 3249). Pnk. pas. Rd. slp. Purp. pt. 5.12 lg. Sq. 7/E, loc. 120, lev. + 13.8 ft.
(22). (No. 2279). Pnk. pas. Rd. slp. Purp. pt. 3.7 lg. Sq. 9/E, loc. 126, lev. + 15.8 ft. A
(23). (No. 3255). Pnk. pas. Cr. slp. Bl. & Rd. pts. 4.6 lg. Loc. (?), lev. (?).
(24). (No. 2367). Pnk. pas. Bl. & Rd. pts. 6.6 lg. Sq. 8/E, loc. 177, lev. + 12.9 ft. A
(25). (No. 2121). Pnk. pas. Rd. & Cr. slps. Bl. & Purp. pts. 4.4 lg. Sq. 8/D, loc. 89, lev. + 15.3 ft. A
(26). (No. 2166). Pnk. pas. Rd. slp. Purp. pt. 4.91 lg. Sq. 8/D, loc. 84, lev. + 16.9 ft. A
(27). (No. 1280). Pnk. pas. Bl. & Rd. pts. 3.04 lg. Sq. 8/D, loc. 82, lev. + 20.0 ft.
(28). (No. 5264). Pnk. pas. Rd. slp. Bl. pt. Sq. 7/E, loc. 99, lev. + 16.8 ft.
(29). (No. 3139). Pnk. pas. Cr. slp. Bl. pt. 5.28 lg. Sq. 8/D, loc. 138, lev. + 13.1 ft. A
(30). (No. 2250). Pnk. pas. Rd. & Pnk. slps. Bl. & Rd. pts. 9.4 lg. Sq. 8/D, loc. 89, lev. + 13.0 ft. A
(31). (No. 1965). Pnk. pas. Rd. slp. Bl. & Rd. pts. 9.18 lg. Sq. 8/D, loc. 108, lev. + 16.4 ft.
(32). (No. 2615). Pnk. pas. Cr. slp. Bl. & Rd. pts. 7.2 lg. Sq. 8/E, loc. 105, lev. + 11.5 ft.
(33). (No. 2045). Pnk. pas. Cr. slp. Rd. pt. Sq. 8/E, loc. 91, lev. + 17.9 ft. A
(34). (No. 1799). Pnk. pas. Yell. slp. Purp. & Rd. pts. Sq. 8/D, loc. 82, lev. + 16.4 ft.
(35). (No. 1779). Pnk. pas. Cr. slp. Purp. & Rd. pts. Sq. 9/E, loc. 127, lev. + 16.7 ft.

Plate XLVIII. Incised Pottery (Jhukar Culture). Chapter VII

(1). (No. 5281). Pnk. pas. Cut., sq. 9/F, loc. 475, lev. — 2.5 ft.
(2). (No. 3918). Pnk. pas. Hnd. mde. 2.7 hi. Cut., sq. 10/F, loc. 424, lev. + 3.2 ft.
(3). (No. 1776). Pnk. pas. Cr. slp. 4.62 lg. Sq. 8/D, loc. 84, lev. + 20.0 ft.
(4). (No. 5000). Pnk. pas. 4.1 lg. Mound I, sq. 12/J, loc. 18, lev. + 14.5 ft.
(5). (No. 2717). Dr. pas. Cr. slp. 3.13 lg. Sq. 9/E, loc. 200, lev. + 8.5 ft.
(6). (No. 2273). Pnk. pas. Cr. slp. 4.7 lg. Sq. 8/C, loc. 153, lev. + 14.1 ft. A
(7). (No. 2137). Pnk. pas. Bl. pt. 3.7 lg. Sq. 9/D, loc. 95, lev. + 14.7 ft. A
(8). (No. 3268). Pnk. pas. Cr. slp. 7.2 lg. Sq. 8/D, loc. 176, lev. + 12.5 ft. A
(9). (No. 3266). Pnk. pas. Sq. 9/C, loc. 190, lev. + 13.2 ft. A
(10). (No. 3385). Pnk. pas. Cr. slp. Sq. 8/E, loc. 94, lev. + 16.2 ft.
(11). (No. 4489). Knob of jar cover. Pnk. pas. Cr. slp. 3.7 di. Sq. 9/E, loc. 111, lev. + 7.9 ft. A
(12). (No. 2369). Pnk. pas. 6.3 lg. Sq. 8/C, loc. 168, lev. + 12.3 ft.
(13). (No. 2808). Knob of jar cover. Pnk. pas. Cr. slp. Sq. 10/E, loc. 252, lev. + 9.3 ft.
(14). (No. 3125). Pnk. pas. Cr. slp. 6.44 lg. Sq. 9/E, loc. 200, lev. + 13.1 ft. A
(15). (No. 2268). Pnk. pas. Cr. slp. Sq. 9/E, loc. 181, lev. + 14.6 ft. A
(16). (No. 4148). Dr. pas. Bf. slp. 6.83 lg. Sq. 9/E, loc. 173, lev. + 6.8 ft.
(17). (No. 3422). Knob. of jar cover. Pnk. pas. Sq. 7/F, loc. 119, lev. + 11.8 ft.
(18). (No. 4575). Pnk. pas. Cr. slp. 4.1 lg. Cut., loc. (?), lev. (?). A
(19). (No. 2103). Pnk. pas. 8.93 lg. Sq. 7/F, loc. 158, lev. + 11.0 ft.
(20). (No. 3143). Pnk. pas. Cr. slp. Sq. 9/E, loc. 161, lev. + 14.4 ft. A
(21). (No. 3399). Pnk. pas. Cr. slp. 6.0 lg. Sq. 7/E, loc. 100, lev. + 14.6 ft.
(22). (No. 4925). Knob of jar cover. Pnk. pas. Mound I, sq. 12/J, loc. 14, lev. + 16.1 ft.
(23). (No. 4799). Pnk. pas. Rd. & Cr. slps. Cut., sq. 9/G, loc. 483, lev. — 0.9 ft.
(24). (No. 3390). Pnk. pas. Sq. 9/E, loc. 162, lev. + 15.8 ft.
(25). (No. 5256). Pnk. pas. Cr. slp. Mound I, sq. 13/K, loc. 12, lev. + 13.9 ft.

Plate XLIX. Seal-amulets and Impressions of the Jhukar Period. Chapter IX

(1). (No. 1652). Type III. Gr. pot. 1.0 di. × 0.63 th. Two animals (oxen?), one placed above the other. Vertical markings above. Sq. 7/E, loc. 121, lev. + 13.2 ft.
(2). (2604). Type III. Fai., cr. surf. 0.98 di. × 0.05 th. Sq. 9/E, loc. 219, lev. + 9.6 ft.

(3). (No. 1946). Type III. Lt. rd. pot. 0.92 di. × 0.7 th. Roughly incised parallel lines and rough prickings. Sq. 9/F, loc. 184, lev. + 13.7 ft.

(4). (No. 1918). Type III. Fai., lt. gre. 1.18 di. × 0.6 th. Back ornamented with oblique incised lines close to edge. Unintelligible design on slightly rounded face. Sq. 9/D, loc. 179, lev. + 14.9 ft.

(5). (1426). Type III. Fai., cr. surf. 1.3 di. × 1.2 th. Solar motif on flat face. Sq. 8/E, loc. 103, lev. + 15.4 ft.

(6). (No. 3819). Type III. Bl. steat. 0.68 lg. × 0.62 wde. × 0.28 th. Notched bevelled edges. Mound I, sq. 13/K, loc. 34, lev. + 13.6 ft.

(7). (4213). Type I. Lt. rd. pot. 1.2 di. × 0.6 th. Rounded faces back and front ornamented with deep prickings. Cut., sq. 10/F, loc. 470, lev. + 0.3 ft.

(8). (4203). Type III. Cop. or br. 0.81 di. × 0.42 th. Flat face bearing lightly incised conventional tree. Presumably cast. Cut., sq. 9/F, loc. 468, lev. + 1.3 ft.

(9). (1266). Type I. Lt. rd. pot. 1.2 di. × 0.52 th. Back rounded & plain. Impression of animal on face, with head to left and two indistinct marks above. Sq. 8/F, loc. 83, lev. + 12.9 ft.

(10). (1582). Type III. Dr. pot. 1.23 di. × 0.31 th. Handle now missing from back. Two couchant animals, one above the other, but no further details. Sq. 8/E, loc. 92, lev. + 17.9 ft.

(11). (1726). Type I. Lt. rd. pot. 1.21 di. × 0.62 th. Back rounded and much abraded. Design on face unintelligible. Sq. 6/F, loc. 159, lev. + 16.6 ft.

(12). (3768). Type I. Lt. rd. pot. 1.34 di. × 0.68 th. Face nearly flat and plain rounded back. Cut., sq. 10/F, loc. 465, lev. + 2.7 ft.

(13). (2011). Type I. Lt. rd. pot. 1.34 di. × 0.51 th. Both faces rounded and much abraded. Roughly hatched pattern visible only on one side. Sq. 8/E, loc. 185, lev. + 11.5 ft.

(14). (3917). Type III. Lt. rd. pot. 1.32 di. × 0.7 th. Almost flat face bearing a linear design. Cut., sq. 10/F, loc. 470, lev. + 3.2 ft.

(15). (1993). Type III. Lt. rd. pot. 1.6 di. × 1.4 th. Sq. 9/E, loc. 150, lev. + 12.8 ft.

Plate L. Seal-amulets and Impressions of the Jhukar Period. Chapter IX

(1). (4227) (see also Pl. LXXXVII, 20). Type II. Wh. steat. 0.78 di. × 0.38 th. The circumference of this amulet is ornamented with three well-cut grooves giving it a fluted appearance. Cut., sq. 10/F, loc. 484, lev. — 0.1 ft.

(2). (2680). Type I. Lt. rd. pot. 1.02 di. × 0.62 th. Both faces rounded; lightly incised crossed irregular lines. Sq. 9/E, loc. 201, lev. + 9.5 ft.

(3). (1575). Type IV. Fai., lt. gre. gl. 0.97 lg. × 0.61 wde. × 0.31 th. Slightly rounded faces. Designs cut with sharp instrument. Sq. 8/E, loc. 86, lev. + 17.3 ft.

(4). (3497) (see Pl. LXXXVII, 1). Type I. Hard cr. st. 0.79 di. × 0.31 th. Faces very rounded. Edge milled and 0.17 th. Very carefully made. Cut., sq. 10/F, loc. 464, lev. + 2.5 ft.

(5). (1911). Type II. Yell. pas.; gre. gl. 1.15 di. × 0.4 th. Two grooves round circumference. Sq. 9/E, loc. 220, lev. + 14.6 ft.

(6). (1801). Br. steat. 0.6 lg. × 0.57 wde. × 0.32 th. Back unfinished, with rectangular handle measuring 0.39 × 0.29 × 0.14 ins., and pierced by small hole. Sq. 7/C, loc. 135, lev. + 10.4 ft.

(7). (1453) (see Pl. LXXXVII, 23). Type II. Fai., blu. gl. 0.92 di. × 0.23 th. Flat faces. Frag. of copper wire in hole. Sq. 8/E, loc. 90, lev. + 16.8 ft.

(8). (1886). Type II. Fai., gre. gl. 0.9 di. × 0.4 th. Three rough grooves round circumference. Sq. 9/D, loc. 136, lev. + 15.6 ft.

(9). (1574). Type I. Lt. rd. pot. 1.0 di. × 0.7 th. Faces very rounded. Back plain. Svastika impressed on obverse. Sq. 8/E, loc. 91, lev. + 17.9 ft.

(10). (4003). Type II. Fai., gl. wh. 1.2 di. × 0.43 th. Flat faces. Cut., sq. 10/F, loc. 472, lev. + 2.6 ft.

(11). (2928). Type I. Dr. pot. 0.98 di. × 0.41 th. Faces slightly convex. Sq. 10/E, loc. 252, lev. + 7.1 ft.
(12). (1815). Type I. Gr. pot. 1.25 di. × 0.43 th. One side only impressed; two parallel lines. Sq. 9/E, loc. 124, lev. + 14.9 ft.
(13). (2488). Type III. Lt. rd. pot. 1.23 di. × 0.64 th. Slightly convex face, back plain. Sq. 8/D, loc. 82, lev. + 14.9 ft.
(14). (3840). Type I. Lt. red. pot. 1.27 di. × 0.6 th. Slightly rounded faces. Same design on both sides. Sq. 10/F, loc. 465, lev. + 2.3 ft.
(15). (2289). Type I. Lt. rd. pot. 1.2 di. × 0.62 th. Faces slightly convex. Sq. 10/E, loc. 225, lev. × 10.3 ft.
(16). (1594). Type I. Dk. gr. st. 1.2 di. × 0.4 th. Bi-conical hole through edge. Sq. 8/C, loc. 109, lev. + 16.5 ft.

Plate LI. Seal-amulets of the Harappā Period. Chapter IX

(1). (3198). Yell. steat. 0.65 × 0.6 × 0.32 ins. Sq. 7/E, loc. 121, lev. + 8.8 ft.
(2). (3052). Gr. steat. 1.07 × 1.07 × 0.4 ins. Sq. 7/E, loc. 121, lev. + 7.8 ft.
(3). (594). Br. steat. 0.87 × 0.84 × 0.49 ins. Trench B(5), loc. 56, lev. — 5.7 ft.
(4). (518). Gr. steat. 1.64 × 1.5 × 0.32 ins. Trench B(5), loc. 56, lev. + 0.8 ft.
(5). (4770). Gr. steat. 0.9 × 0.9 × 0.6 ins. Cut., sq. 9/F, loc. 410, lev. — 1.1 ft.
(6). (3737). Gr. steat. 0.62 × 0.67 × ? ins. Sq. 7/C, loc. 459, lev. + 7.0 ft.
(7). (3200). Wh. steat. 0.68 × 0.7 × 0.6 ins. Sq. 8/F, loc. 344, lev. + 6.9 ft.
(8). (3159). Gr. steat. 1.05 × 1.0 × 0.4 ins. Sq. 7/E, loc. 121, lev. + 7.8 ft.
(9). (2000). Gr. st. 0.78 × 0.78 × 0.47 ins. Sq. 8/D, loc. 223, lev. + 12.2 ft.
(10). (4767). Wh. steat. 0.72 × 0.72 × 0.32 ins. Mound I, sq. 12/K, loc. 47, lev. + 13.1 ft.
(11). (3485, b). Wh. steat. 0.91 × 0.91 × 0.41 ins. Sq. 8/C, loc. 231, lev. + 7.2 ft.
(12). (3493). Gr. steat. 0.75 × 0.75 × 0.42 ins. Sq. 7/C, loc. 240, lev. + 7.0 ft.
(13). (3148). Wh. steat. 1.41 × 1.38 × 0.73 ins. Sq. 8/E, loc. 113, lev. + 6.8 ft.
(14). (3215). Wh. steat. 0.75 × 0.78 × 0.43 ins. Sq. 9/B, loc. 283, lev. + 6.9 ft.
(15). (2285). Wh. steat. 1.04 × 1.04 × 0.5 ins. Sq. 9/D, loc. 215, lev. + 10.4 ft.
(16). (3049). Wh. steat. 1.47 × 0.35 × 0.55 ins. Sq. 8/F, loc. 115, lev. + 6.5 ft.
(17). (3495). Wh. steat. 0.95 × 0.92 × 0.5 ins. Sq. 7/C, loc. 98, lev. + 7.5 ft.
(18). (926). Wh. steat. 0.92 × 0.96 × 0.5 ins. Trench E(1), loc. 34, lev. — 7.1 ft.
(19). (2845). Wh. steat. 1.1 × ? × ? ins. Sq. 9/F, loc. 405, lev. + 8.0 ft.
(20). (2594, h). Wh. steat. 1.09 × 1.08 × 0.51 ins. Sq. 9/C, loc. 228, lev. + 9.9 ft.
(21). (1269). Wh. steat. 0.94 × 0.94 × 0.5 ins. Trench F(2), loc. 65, lev. — 4.1 ft.
(22). (3207). Wh. steat. 0.83 × 0.82 × 0.39 ins. Sq. 9/B, loc. 442, lev. + 7.7 ft.
(23). (2532). Wh. steat. 1.28 × 0.52 ins. Sq. 7/E, loc. 122, lev. + 9.4 ft.
(24). (3051). Wh. steat. 1.5 × 1.5 × ? ins. Sq. 9/D, loc. 211, lev. + 8.1 ft.
(25). (3817). Bl. steat. 2.02 × 1.49 × 0.1 ins. Mound I, sq. 12/K, loc. 26, lev. + 14.1 ft.
(26). (3043). Wh. steat. 1.05 × 1.05 × 0.55 ins. Sq. 8/E, loc. 430, lev. + 7.3 ft.
(27). (3045). Wh. steat. 1.1 × 1.09 × 0.61 ins. Sq. 8/E, loc. 177, lev. + 7.6 ft.
(28). (2293). Wh. steat. 1.4 × 1.36 × 0.73 ins. Sq. 10/E, loc. 261, lev. + 9.3 ft.
(29). (2297). Wh. steat. 1.1 × 1.1 × 0.41 ins. Sq. 9/D, loc. 174, lev. + 10.0 ft.
(30). (3485, a). Yell. steat. 1.24 × 1.24 × 0.6 ins. Sq. 8/C, loc. 231, lev. + 7.2 ft.
(31). (1293). Bl. steat. 1.5 × 1.5 × 0.76 ins. Sq. 7/E, loc. 97, lev. + 14.9 ft.
(32). (2361). Wh. steat. 1.3 × 1.3 × 0.52 ins. Sq. 9/C, loc. 227, lev. + 10.9 ft.
(33). (2462). Wh. steat. 1.44 × 1.44 × 0.75 ins. Sq. 8/D, loc. 82, lev. + 9.5 ft.

Plate LII. Seal-amulets of the Harappā Period. Chapter IX

(1). (2597). Wh. steat. 1.37 × 1.33 × 0.68 ins. Sq. 9/D, loc. 192, lev. + 8.9 ft.
(2). (2848). Wh. steat. 0.82 × 0.83 × 0.4 ins. Sq. 8/E, loc. 425, lev. + 8.0 ft.
(3). (3359). Wh. steat. 0.7 × 0.71 × 0.42 ins. Sq. 7/F, loc. 110, lev. + 7.1 ft.

(4). (3168). Wh. steat. 1.17 × 1.17 × 0.42 ins. Sq. 9/D, loc. 211, lev. + 8.1 ft.
(5). (4852). Wh. steat. 1.13 × 1.13 × 0.51 ins. Cut., sq. 9/F, loc. 469, lev. — 2.8 ft.
(6). (2390). Wh. steat. 1.18 × 1.2 × 0.7 ins. Sq. 8/B, loc. 235, lev. + 9.9 ft.
(7). (4327). Wh. steat. 0.52 × 0.9 × 0.39 ins. Mound I, sq. 12/K, loc. 20, lev. + 14.8 ft.
(8). (3886). Gr. steat. 1.1 × 1.13 × 0.33 ins. Mound I, sq. 13/J, loc. 6, lev. + 16.8 ft.
(9). (950). Wh. steat. 0.45 × 0.45 × 0.3 ins. Trench J(1), loc. 73, lev. — 0.1 ft.
(10). (3326). Wh. steat. 0.62 × 0.61 × 0.34 ins. Sq. 10/C, loc. 385, lev. + 6.9 ft.
(11). (3206). Wh. steat. 0.5 × 0.5 × 0.37 ins. Sq. 9/D, loc. 204, lev. + 6.9 ft.
(12). (2558). Wh. steat. 1.03 × 0.55 × 0.35 ins. Sq. 9/D, loc. 106, lev. + 8.8 ft.
(13). (2603). Wh. steat. 0.75 × 0.75 × 0.23 ins. Sq. 10/D, loc. 362, lev. + 6.8 ft.
(14). (2426). Wh. steat. 0.91 × 0.91 × 0.42 ins. Sq. 9/E, loc. 199, lev. + 9.0 ft.
(15). (2531). Wh. steat. 1.01 × 1.01 × 0.47 ins. Sq. 8/D, loc. 178, lev. + 9.6 ft.
(16). (1393). Bl. steat. 0.88 × 0.88 × 0.32 ins. Sq. 8/F, loc. 83, lev. + 15.4 ft.
(17). (4960). Gr. steat. 0.9 × 0.9 × 0.42 ins. Mound I, sq. 13/J, loc. 9, lev. + 13.5 ft.
(18). (3154). Wh. steat. 0.88 × 0.89 × 0.41 ins. Sq. 9/C, loc. 395, lev. + 7.7 ft.
(19). (2428). Br. steat. 1.0 × 1.0 × 0.49 ins. Sq. 9/D, loc. 286, lev. + 9.7 ft.
(20). (2559). Wh. steat. 1.0 × 1.0 × 0.52 ins. Sq. 9/C, loc. 296, lev. + 9.5 ft.
(21). (2358). Wh. steat. 1.0 × 1.0 × 0.58 ins. Sq. 8/C, loc. 152, lev. + 11.1 ft.
(22). (2595). Br. steat. 0.8 × 0.78 × 0.42 ins. Sq. 7/E, loc. 164, lev. + 9.3 ft.
(23). (2529, CC). Wh. steat. 0.82 × 0.81 × 0.43 ins. Sq. 8/C, loc. 297, lev. + 10.4 ft.
(24). (2605). Wh. steat. 1.09 × 1.1 × 0.51 ins. Sq. 6/F, loc. 159, lev. + 8.4 ft.
(25). (4596). Wh. steat. 1.01 × 1.01 × 0.5 ins. Mound I, sq. 13/J, loc. 2, lev. + 14.4 ft.
(26). (2467). Wh. steat. 1.12 × 1.12 × 0.6 ins. Sq. 8/C, loc. 151, lev. + 10.5 ft.
(27). (2468). Wh. steat. 1.1 × 1.09 × 0.55 ins. Sq. 7/F, loc. 189, lev. + 9.8 ft.
(28). (3318). Wh. steat. 1.65 × 1.65 × 0.8 ins. Sq. 10/F, loc. 423, lev. + 6.7 ft.
(29). (3811). Gr. steat. 1.2 × 1.2 × 0.64 ins. Cut., sq. 9/F, loc. 468, lev. + 3.8 ft.
(30). (2389). Gr. steat. 1.25 × 1.25 × 0.69 ins. Sq. 7/C, loc. 240, lev. + 9.2 ft.
(31). (2530). Wh. steat. 1.02 × 1.02 × 0.5 ins. Sq. 7/E, loc. 300, lev. + 9.5 ft.
(32). (3492). Gr. steat. 1.07 × 1.08 × 0.55 ins. Sq. 8/C, loc. 289, lev. + 8.6 ft.

Plate LIII. Figurines. Chapter X

(1). (2039). Pot., cr. slp. 3.75 hi. Hollow body with walls averaging 0.35 th. Open base. Found with jar-stand in Pl. XXVI, 10. Sq. 9/D, loc. 216, lev. + 11.2 ft.

(2). (4070). Pot. 3.1 hi. Hollow body & base; the roughly oval hole in the latter measuring 0.75 × 0.63 ins. Sq. 7/E, loc. 88, lev. + 7.9 ft.

(3). (1602). Pot. 2.6 hi. Hollow body and base; hole in latter measuring 0.24 di. Sq. 7/E, loc. 121, lev. + 13.5 ft.

(4). (3585). Pot. 2.4 hi. Hollow body and open base. No legs unless they were attached to two breaks in front, in which case it would have been a seated figure. Trench E(1), loc. 38, lev. — 4.8 ft.

(5). (3584). Pot., rd. slp. 1.7 hi. Hole for peg in base, 0.12 in di. Scarf round neck broken away with head, ends showing. Trench E(1), lev. — 4.8 ft.

(6). (3190). Pot., rd. slp. 2.18 hi. Arms and lower part of body missing. Sq. 8/E, loc. 280, lev. + 7.1 ft.

(7). (2423). Pot. 3.53 hi. Hollow body & open base; hole in latter 0.7 di. Sq. 7/F, loc. 118, lev. + 9.8 ft.

(8). (2257). Pot. 4.24 hi. Nostrils indicated by holes. Solid body. Sq. 7/C, loc. 314, lev. + 10.8 ft.

(9). (3706). Pot., rd. slp. 1.21 hi. Solid. Vertical hole running down from back of shoulders. Trench B(5), lev. — 1.7 ft.

(10). (621). Pot. rd. slp. 2.39 hi. Solid. Vertical hole at back, 0.1 di. Trench B(5), loc. 56; lev. — 4.8 ft.

(11). (2427). Pot. 1.75 hi. Solid. Sq. 7/C, loc. 238, lev. + 10.4 ft.

(12). (3347). Pot., cr. slp. 2.82 hi. Solid. Sq. 8/B, loc. 284, lev. + 9.2 ft.
(13). (2527). Pot. 3.97 hi. Solid. Sq. 9/C, loc. 227, lev. + 10.1 ft.

Plate LIV. Figurines. Chapter X

(1). (3201). Pot. 2.61 hi. Solid. Sq. 7/F, loc. 440, lev. + 7.6 ft.
(2). (2683). Pot. 2.42 hi. Solid. Sq. 8/E, loc. 91, lev. + 10.0 ft.
(3). (3186). Pot. 2.37 hi. Solid. Sq. 8/E, loc. 280, lev. + 7.0 ft.
(4). (3454). Pot. 1.7 hi. Solid. Sq. 7/E, loc. 324, lev. + 7.5 ft.
(5). (3205). Pot. 2.9 hi. Solid. Hole in base to set figure on pin. Sq. 8/E, loc. 155, lev. + 7.0 ft.
(6). (3334). Pot. 3.48 hi. Solid. Sq. 7/E, loc. 164, lev. + 6.9 ft.
(7). (465). Pot. 3.39 hi. Solid. Trench C(3), lev. — 7.9 ft.
(8). (3418). Pot. 2.63 hi. Solid. Sq. 10/C, loc. 381, lev. + 6.8 ft.
(9). (4069). Pot. 2.62 hi. Solid. Vertical hole in base, 0.09 di.; 0.52 dp. Sq. 7/F, loc. 445, lev. + 6.7 ft.
(10). (3366). Pot., cr. slp. 2.6 hi. Solid. Sq. 7/F, loc. 331, lev. + 7.0 ft.
(11). (3739). Pot. 2.9 hi. Solid. Sq. 7/F, loc. 240, lev. + 7.0 ft.
(12). (3619). Pot. 2.8 hi. Solid. Trench F(1), lev. — 4.1 ft.

Plate LV. Model Animals. Chapter X

(1). (3743). Pot. 2.52 hi. Trench K(1), lev. — 4.4 ft.
(2). (487). Pot. 2.99 lg. Trench B(5), lev. — 0.7 ft.
(3). (337). Pot. rd. slp. bl. pt. 4.47 lg. Trench B(5), lev. — 4.2 ft.
(4). (3839). Pot. 1.9 lg. Cut., sq. 10/F, loc. 466, lev. + 2.3 ft.
(5). (3957). Pot. 2.71 lg. Cut., sq. 10/F, loc. 378, lev. + 5.3 ft.
(6). (533). Pot. cr. slp. rd. pt. 2.2 lg. Trench B(3), lev. — 7.7 ft.
(7). (2721). Pot. 2.23 lg. Sq. 6/C, loc. 266, lev. + 9.0 ft.
(8). (3513). Pot. 5.4 lg. Sq. 7/D, loc. 319, lev. + 8.0 ft.
(9). (3838). Pot., rd. slp. 2.03 lg. Cut., sq. 10/F, loc. 466, lev. + 2.3 ft.
(10). (952). Pot., cr. slp. 2.4 lg. Trench J(1), loc. 79, lev. — 0.5 ft.
(11). (4718). Pot. 1.83 lg. Cut., sq. 9/F, loc. 475, lev. — 0.6 ft.
(12). (4175). Pot., rd. slp. 2.2 lg. Cut., sq. 10/F, loc. 464, lev. + 0.2 ft.
(13). (3852). Pot. 2.23 lg. Trench B(5), loc. 43, lev. — 10.2 ft.
(14). (3120). Pot., rd. slp. 2.3 lg. Sq. 9/F, loc. 407, lev. + 6.4 ft.
(15). (1971). Pot. 2.83 lg. Sq. 8/F, loc. 149, lev. + 10.7 ft.

Plate LVI. Model Animals. Chapter X

(1). (2583). Pot. 2.87 lg. Sq. 8/C, loc. 109, lev. + 9.4 ft.
(2). (2658). Pot. 2.5 lg. Sq. 8/D, loc. 178, lev. + 9.6 ft.
(3). (4252). Pot., cr. slp. 2.6 lg. Sq. 9/D, loc. 133, lev. + 7.0 ft.
(4). (1418). Pot., cr. slp. 2.51 lg. Trench G(1), loc. 67, lev. — 6.1 ft.
(5). (882). Pot. 1.9 lg. rd. pt. Trench C(1), loc. 50, lev. — 5.3 ft.
(6). (883). Pot. 2.79 lg. rd. pt. Trench F(2), loc. 65, lev. — 3.4 ft.
(7). (3989). Pot. 1.9 lg. Sq. 8/F, loc. 259, lev. + 7.0 ft.
(8). (2701). Pot., cr. slp. 3.72 lg. Sq. 9/C, loc. 212, lev. + 10.2 ft.
(9). (3483). Pot. rd. pt. 4.72 lg. Sq. 8/D, loc. 196, lev. + 10.1 ft.
(10). (2652). Pot., cr. slp. rd. pt. 2.58 lg. Sq. 7/C, loc. 315, lev. + 9.3 ft.
(11). (3234). Pot., rd. slp. 3.9 lg. Sq. 8/E, loc. 146, lev. + 6.9 ft.
(12). (3781). Pot. 2.9 lg. Sq. 8/C, loc. 289, lev. + 7.4 ft.

Plate LVII. Model Animals. Chapter X.

(1). (948). Wh. pas. 1.88 lg. Trench J(1), loc. 79, lev. + 0.5 ft.
(2). (2396). Pot. 1.37 lg. Sq. 8/B, loc. 284, lev. + 9.9 ft.
(3). (2892). Pot. rd. pt. 2.65 lg. Sq. 8/C, loc. 295, lev. + 9.4 ft.
(4). (2020). Wh. pas. gl. nil. 1.29 hi. Sq. 7/E, loc. 204, lev. + 12.9 ft.
(5). (5027). Pot. 3.03 lg. Sq. 9/F, loc. 408, lev. — 5.3 ft.
(6). (1402). Pot. 3.1 lg. Trench G(1), loc. 47, lev. — 6.1 ft.
(7). (3804). Pot. rd. pt. 3.2 lg. Trench A/3. lev. — 7.8 ft.
(8). (889). Pot., pnk. slp. 3.3 lg. Trench K(1), loc. 77, lev. — 1.5 ft.
(9). (1276). Pot. rd. pt. 3.1 lg. Trench E(1), lev. — 3.2 ft.
(10). (1912). Pot., yel. slp. rd pt. 2.36 hi. Sq. 9/E, loc. 171, lev. + 14.6 ft.
(11). (3204). Pot. rd. pt. 2.91 lg. Sq. 7/C, loc. 101, lev. + 7.6 ft.
(12). (757). Pot., cr. slp. 3.8 lg. Trench A(3), loc. 40, lev. — 6.7 ft.
(13). (4929). Pot. 2.6 hi. Mound I, sq. 12/J, loc. 17, lev. + 14.3 ft.
(14). (1912). As No. 10.
(15). (5395). Pot. 3.9 lg. Cut., sq. 10/G, loc. 477, lev. — 12.5 ft.

Plate LVIII. Toys and Playthings. Chapter XI

(1, 1a). (2463). Model cart. Br. 2.93 lg. × 1.2 wde. × 1.73 hi. End bent upwards and small portions missing. Wheels, one with the axle, revolved inside two eyelets cast with the framework. Sq. 7/C, loc. 101, lev. + 9.7 ft.

(2). (2291). Model cart. Br. 2.4 pres. hi. × 1.1 wde. × 1.7 lg. Holes for axle, 0.14 di. Sq. 9/C, loc. 213, lev. + 10.3 ft.

(3). (3802). Model cart-wheel. Pot. no. slp. 3.3 di. × 0.52 th. at hub; 0.3 th. at rim. Hole 0.22 di. and acentric. Trench B(5), loc. 44, lev. — 10.2 ft.

(4). (4990). Model cart-frame. Pot. no slp. 2.92 lg. × 1.9 wde. Pair of holes on each side of lower surface for axle-pins. Hole at end to take shaft. Sq. 9/F, loc. 408, lev. + 0.9 ft.

(5). (5008). Model cart. Pot. no slp. 3.0 lg. × 1.6 wde. × 1.2 hi. with peak. Practically complete, except for small portion at end. Hole for axle, 0.13 di., hole for shaft 0.13 di. Reverse slightly hollow. Sq. 8/F, loc. 115, lev. + 6.6 ft.

(6). (3708). Model cart. Pot. no slp. Turned up tip missing and part gone at the right end in photograph. Axle-hole 0.12 di., shaft hole smaller. Concave base roughly finished. Trench B(5), loc. 55, lev. — 1.7 ft.

(7). (1206). Model draught-ox. Pot. no slp. 3.98 lg. Each pair of legs joined together. Hole through neck for yoke, 0.11 di. Trench H(1), loc. 52, lev. — 4.1 ft.

(8). (3568). Model draught-ox. Pot. rd. slp. 2.83 lg. Legs joined in pairs. Eyes, round discs of clay with slightly oblique incisions for pupils; mouth a gash; two indentations for nostrils. Dewlap barely indicated. Hole to take yoke, 0.16 di. Trench C(3), lev. — 7.9 ft.

(9). (5159). Model four-wheeled cart or chariot. Pot. no slp. 5.0 lg. × 2.53 wde. × 3.19 hi. Roughly made. Holes 0.18 di. to take two pairs of wheels, one pair larger than the other. Part of canopy in front missing. Cut. Sq. 9/F, loc. 475, lev. — 0.6 ft.

(10). (723). Model cart. Pot. no slp. 4.12 lg. × 2.21 wde. × 1.28 hi. Hollowed-out base. Portion missing from tail and from upper portion close to shaft-hole. Trench D(1), lev. — 4.1 ft.

(11). (2937). Model ram. Pot. no slp. 4.3 lg. × 3.28 hi. Fleece roughly represented by crossed dk. rd. lines. Hole for axle 0.38 di. Round pellets for eyes with incision in centre. Mouth mere cut; two holes for nostrils. Horns only just recognizable. Hollow body, triangular in section. No tail and flat hind-quarters. Wheels not found with this animal. Sq. 8/D, loc. 288, lev. + 8.7 ft.

(12). (4134). Model ram. Pot. no slp. 5.13 lg. × 3.0 hi. Hollow body, somewhat triangular in section. Fleece represented by cross lines of lt. rd. pt. Horns reddened, and some of this colour on muzzle. Eyes, oval pellets with prickings in centres. Nostrils, shallow holes; mouth a slight cut. Part of one horn missing. No trace of tail. Sq. 7/C, loc. 267, lev. + 7.2 ft.

(13). (4533). Model cart or chariot body. Pot. no slp. 6.1 lg. × 2.8 wde. × 2.7 hi. Middle of sides, 1.46 hi. Two small holes each side for axles, 0.11 di. Flat, even base. Sq. 7/E, loc. 121, lev. + 6.9 ft.

(14). (5204). Model cart. Pot. no slp. 2.9 lg. × 1.92 wde. × 0.83 hi. Two compartments. Two holes for axle-pins on each side of partition. Over-baked, blistered and distorted on one side. Cut. Sq. 10/G, loc. 481, lev. — 6.9 ft.

(15). (3301). Model ram. Pot. Cr. slp. 5.12 lg. × 2.62 hi. Hollow body. Round pellets for eyes. Slight cut for mouth. Narrow, lt. rd. lines cover body vertically and horizontally, forming a series of squares. Axle-hole, 0.3 di. No hole for draw-cord. Sq. 7/F, loc. 443, lev. + 6.7 ft.

(16). (4271). Model ram's head. Pot. Cr. slp. 2.37 hi. Red. markings on tightly curled horns and tip of muzzle. Crossed red lines on breast and round neck. Sq. 7/D, loc. 271, lev. + 6.8 ft.

(17). (3714). Model animal. Pot. no slp. 4.4 lg. Minute round pellets for eyes. Traces of horn in middle of forehead. Narrow, vertical cuts for insertion of ears. Legs joined in pairs, with axle-holes, 0.17 di. Small lateral hole through neck for string. Ornamented with dk. rd. pt. Trench F(2), lev. — 3.6 ft.

(18). (5282). Frag. cart-frame. Pot. Cr. slp. Now 3.4 lg. × 2.98 wde. × 0.62 th. Upper surface ornamented with dk. rd. lines to imitate netting. Cut. Sq. 9/F, loc. 473, lev. — 3.2 ft.

(19). (1000). Model cart. Pot. Pnk. slp. 4.2 lg. × 3.1 wde. × 1.9 hi. Walls average 0.2 th. and 1.4 dp. inside. Drilled holes for shaft and axle-pins. Base flat and covered with thick deposit of sand and mica. Toy has been much played with; sides scraped by the wheels found with this cart which average 2.0 di × 0.36 th. Lt. rd. lines on body to imitate wickerwork or netting. Trench A(3), lev. — 3.8 ft.

(20). (2723). Wheel. Pot. no slp. 4.49 di. × 0.8 th. including hub. Hole 0.3 di., tyre 0.24 th. Broad band of dk. rd. pt., 2.3 wde. on each side to indicate that a wheel of three pieces of wood is meant. Obverse has hub, 1.45 di., projecting 0.28 inch. Sq. 7/E, loc. 154, lev. + 9.5 ft.

(21). (2318). Model cart-frame. Pot. no slp. 7.1 lg. × 3.32 wde. × 0.85 th. Ends slightly curved upwards. Sq. 7/C, loc. 98, lev. + 12.1 ft.

(22). (591, 859, 1429, 1880; see also No. 26). Model cart drawn by oxen. Frame, pot, no slp. 2.9 lg. × 1.9 wde. × 0.6 th. Wheels average 2.05 di × 0.45 th. Bulls average 3.08 lg. One bears traces of a rd. wash, other coated with a cr. slp. Trench E(1), lev. — 2.2 ft. Trench G(1), loc. 49, lev. — 8.0 ft.

(23). (5059). Wheel. Pot. no slp. 1.92 di. × 0.8 th. Both faces convex. Shows signs of paring with sharp instrument. Axle-hole, 0.2 di., very askew. Mound I. Sq. 12/J, loc. 14, lev. + 14.1 ft.

(24). (1062). Wheel. Pot. no slp. 2.5 di. × 0.31 th. Axle-hole 0.22 di. Both sides coated with thick deposit of sand and mica. Edges worn by friction against frame of cart or chariot. Trench A(3), lev. — 4.2 ft.

(25). (607, 1005, 1028). Model cart and wheels. Cart, pot. pnk. slp. 7.6 lg. × 3.83 wde. × 0.86 th. Trench C(2), lev. — 5.0 ft. Wheels, pot. no slp. Average 3.01 di. Sides thickly coated with sand and mica. Trenches A(3), F(1), levels — 3.7 ft.

(26). (591). Model cart. Pot. no slp. Same as No. 22.

Plate LIX. Toys and Playthings. Chapter XI.

(1). (1013). Model bull. Pot. Cr. slp. 3.5 lg. without head. Two perforated flanges in front of shoulders to take head. Hole through shoulders, hump and rump for cord or fibre to move head. Trench A(4), loc. 67, lev. — 6.1 ft. Head, not found with body. Pot. no slp.

1.38 lg. Hole at back of head to swing on pin and a second through mouth and forehead for pull-string. Trench A(4), loc. 67, lev. — 6.1 ft.

(2). (3303). Toy with movable arms. Pot. Cr. slp. 3.07 hi. Hole for missing arms 0.11 di. Remains of dk. rd. band round neck. Sq. 7/E, loc. 300, lev. + 7.6 ft.

(3). (4352, 3509, 1127, from left). Balls. Ch. lim. No. 4352 1.38 di. Sq. 9/C, loc. 294, lev. + 7.2 ft. No. 3509 1.3 di. Sq. 7/D, loc. 273, lev. + 8.1 ft. No. 1127 1.4 di. Trench A(2), loc. 81, lev. — 8.9 ft.

(4). (1219). Ball. Pot. no slp. 1.02 di. Pricked over with small holes. Trench A(4), loc. 67, lev. — 0.7 ft.

(5). (467). Whistle. Pot. Cr. slp. 2.71 hi. Concave base to pedestal. Trench C(3), loc. 26, lev. — 12.1 ft.

(6). (1970). Whistle. Pot. Cr. slp. 2.46 hi. Lt. rd. markings. Sq. 7/F, loc. 118, lev. + 11.1 ft.

(7). (1008). Rattle (see Pl. LXI, 1). Pot. no slp. 1.43 di. Decorated with rd. pt. Trench A(3), lev. — 3.6 ft.

(8). (1599). Rattle (see Pl. LXI, 4). Pot. no. slp. 1.81 di. Decorated with dk. rd. lines. Sq. 8/F, loc. 149, lev. + 11.0 ft.

(9). (1074). Rattle. Pot. Cr. slp. 1.91 di. Decorated with dk. rd. lines. Found with No. 7 in Pl. LXI. Trench F(2), loc. 65, lev. — 7.2 ft.

(10). (1074). Rattle (see Pl. LXI, 7). Pot. Cr. slp. 2.2 di. Dk. rd. lines. Found with No. 9.

(11). (Upper register from left, 870, 615, 724). No. 870. Pellet. Pot. no slp. 1.09 di. Decorated with rd. spots. Trench A(1), lev. — 3.8 ft. No. 615. Pellet. Pot. Cr. slp. 1.12 di. Irregular rd. spots. Trench B(5), lev. — 6.9 ft. No. 724. Pellet. Pot. Cr. slp. 1.01 di. Decorated with rd. spots. Trench D(1), lev. — 4.6 ft.

(12). (3724). Pellet. Pot. no slp. 1.4 di. Trench H(1), lev. — 7.6 ft.

(13). (5020). Pellet. Fai. 1.1 di. Decorated with incised circles. Cut. Sq. 9/F, loc. 408, lev. — 5.3 ft.

(14). (2556). Ball. Sh. 1.2 di. Incised concentric circles. Sq. 8/C, loc. 297, lev. + 10.4 ft.

(15). (2050). Ball. Sh. 1.3 di. Incised concentric circles. Sq. 9/D, loc. 215, lev. + 12.8 ft.

(16). (4916). Ball. Pot. no slp. 1.51 di. Irregular in shape. Impressed with thumb nail. Cut. Sq. 10/F, loc. 484, lev. + 0.1 ft.

(17). (2030). Ball. Pot. no slp. 1.78 di. Impressed with thumb nail. Sq. 8/D, loc. 108, lev. + 12.7 ft.

(18). (4355). Whistle. Dr. pot no slp. 1.71 hi. Sq. 8/C, loc. 170, lev. + 7.3 ft.

(19). (4680). Whistle. Pot. no slp. 1.81 hi. Sq. 7/F, loc. 158, lev. + 7.2 ft.

(20). (4646). Whistle. Pot. no slp. 1.82 hi. Sq. 9/C, loc. 389, lev. + 6.7 ft.

(21). (1780). Draughtsman. Pot. rd. slp. 0.82 di. × 0.18 th. Base coated with thick deposit of sand and mica. Sq. 7/E, loc. 88, lev. + 10.8 ft.

(22). (95). Draughtsman. Pot. no slp. 1.21 di. × 0.35 th. Trench B(1), lev. — 5.1 ft.

(23). (1735). Ball. Pot. Cr. slp. Fragment measuring 2.1 lg. Sq. 9/D, loc. 106, lev. + 16.6 ft.

(24). (4916). Ball. Pot. no slp. 1.9 di. Found with No. 16. Cut. Sq. 10/F, loc. 484, lev. + 0.1 ft.

(25). (784). Gamesman. Pot. no slp. 0.55 across. Trench B(5), lev. — 4.4 ft.

(26). (1334). Gamesman. Pot. no slp. 0.5 each way. Trench K(1), loc. 77, lev. — 3.4 ft.

(27). (1181). Gamesman. Pot. no slp. 1.3 × 1.18 × 0.41. Sq. 8/E, loc. 90, lev. + 14.1 ft.

(28). (783). Gamesman. Pot. no slp. 0.55 across each way. Trench B(5), lev. — 4.4 ft.

(29). (978). Gamesman. Pot. no slp. 0.61 each way. Trench H(1), lev. — 2.9 ft.

(30). (1324). Gamesman. Pot. no slp. 0.62 each way. Trench D(1), loc. 31, lev. — 5.2 ft.

(31). (1481). Draughtsman. Pot. no slp. 1.3 × 1.19 × 0.41 ins. Sq. 8/E, loc. 90, lev. + 14.1 ft.

(32). (1450). Draughtsman. Dr. pot; no slp. 1.1 × 1.08 × 0.57 ins. Sq. 8/E, loc. 86, lev. + 18.8 ft.

(33). (1535). Bobbin or gamesman. Gr. pot. 1.2 hi. × 0.7 di. Slightly rounded ends and does not stand well. Pierced by vertical hole. Sq. 9/D, loc. 133, lev. + 16.5 ft.

(34). (1548). Bobbin or gamesman. Gr. pot. 0.96 hi × 0.52 di. Both ends rounded and will not stand. No hole. Sq. 7/C, loc. 101, lev. + 16.2 ft.

(35). (1551). Bobbin or gamesman. Gr. pot. 0.61 hi. × 0.4 di. One end rounded, stands with difficulty on other. Pierced by oblique hole. Sq. 9/D, loc. 133, lev. + 16.1 ft.
(36). (3919). Bobbin or gamesman. Gr. pot. 1.1 hi. × 0.6 di. Both ends fairly flat. Pierced by vertical hole. Cut. Sq. 10/F, loc. 424, lev. + 3.2 ft.
(37). (2004). Knuckle-bone. 1.28 lg. Shows polish of much use. Sq. 9/F, loc. 187, lev. + 12.8 ft.
(38). (773). Draughtsman. Pot. Cr. slp. 1.73 di. × 0.3 th. Trench B(1), lev. — 4.7 ft.
(39). (1197). Draughtsman. Pot. no slp. 1.83 di. × 0.56 th. Trench D(1), loc. 41, lev. — 5.1 ft.
(40). (1292). Bobbin or gamesman. Gr. pot. 1.5 hi. × 0.8 di. One end rounded, other flat. Pierced by oblique hole. Sq. 8/E, loc. 83, lev. + 17.9 ft.
(41). (2095). Bobbin or gamesman. Gr. pot. 1.4 hi. × 0.9 di. One end flat, other rounded. Pierced by vertical hole. Trench I(1), lev. — 2.1 ft.
(42). (1638). Bobbin or gamesman. Gr. pot. 1.35 lg. × 1.0 di. Oval in section, both ends concave. Pierced by vertical hole. Sq. 8/E, loc. 142, lev. + 14.7 ft.
(43). (2070). Knuckle-bone. 0.91 lg. Sq. 8/D, loc. 82, lev. + 21.0 ft.

Plate LX. Toys and Playthings. Chapter XI

(1). (5307). Gamesman. Pot. no slp. 1.0 hi. × 0.9 di. Mound I. Sq. 13/K, loc. 67, lev. + 13.0 ft.
(2). (5435). Gamesman. Pot. no slp. 1.03 di. × 0.67 th. Edges well rounded. Cut. Sq. 10/G, loc. 481, lev. — 23.8 ft.
(3). (3694). Gamesman. Pot. no slp. 1.11 di. × 0.3 th. Top convex; base concave. Sq. 8/C, loc. 308, lev. + 7.5 ft.
(4). (5024). Gamesman. Sh. 0.59 × 0.5 × 0.22 ins. Cut. Sq. 9/F, loc. 469, lev. — 4.9 ft.
(5). (2573). Gamesman. Cr. col. ch. lim. 0.92 hi. × 0.45 di. Sq. 8/C, loc. 170, lev. + 10.3 ft.
(6). (3871). Gamesman. Pot. no slp. 0.68 each way. Trench H(1), loc. 51, lev. — 8.1 ft.
(7). (2326, i). Gamesman. Fai. lt. blu. 1.0 each way. Carefully made with acute edges and slightly rounded points. Sq. 9/D, loc. 215, lev. + 10.3 ft.
(8). (2177). Gamesman. Fai. cr. col. 1.5 hi. × 1.15 di. Well made with flat top and base. Sq. 8/D, loc. 217, lev. + 12.0 ft.
(9). (4430). Gamesman. Hrd. bl. st. 0.82 hi. × 0.63 di. Mound I. Sq. 12/J, loc. 14, lev. + 14.1 ft.
(10). (2400). Gamesman. Fai. Cr. col. 0.42 hi. × 0.4 di. Sq. 8/B, loc. 285, lev. + 9.6 ft.
(11). (2419). Gamesman. Fai. Lt. gr. 0.61 hi. Depression 0.22 di. on top for inlay. Sq. 9/D, loc. 287, lev. + 9.9 ft.
(12). (275). Die. Iv. Now 1.8 lg. × 0.32 × 0.27. One end missing. Trench B(5), lev. + 0.3 ft.
(13). (4707). Bobbin or gamesman. Gr. pot. 1.0 lg. × 0.5 di. Oblique hole. Cut. Sq. 10/F, loc. 464, lev. — 1.5 ft.
(14). (4212). Bobbin or gamesman. Gr. pot. 0.92 hi. × 0.76 di. Pierced by vertical hole. Cut. Sq. 10/F, loc. 464, lev. + 0.1 ft.
(15). (4174). Bobbin or gamesman. Pnk. pot. 0.84 hi. × 0.6 di. Pierced by oblique hole. Cut. Sq. 10/G, loc. 482, lev. + 0.3 ft.
(16). (2670). Die. Iv. drk. br. Now 2.3 lg. × 0.3 × 0.3. One end missing. Partially burnt. Sq. 10/E, loc. 359, lev. + 7.1 ft.
(17). (4154). Bobbin or gamesman. Pnk. pot. 1.7 hi. × 0.92 di. Pierced half-way with vertical hole. Sq. 8/E, loc. 185, lev. + 9. 8 ft.
(18). (5041). Bobbin or gamesman. Dr. pot. 1.4 hi. × 1.0 di. Pierced by vertical hole. Cut. Sq. 10/G, loc. 482, lev. — 1.4 ft.
(19). (1281). Bobbin or gamesman. Gr. pot. 1.49 hi. × 0.8 di. Pierced by oblique hole. Sq. 8/D, loc. 82, lev. + 21.8 ft.
(20). (1345). Bobbin or gamesman. Dr. pot. 1.2 hi. × 0.7 di. Narrow hole at one end. Sq. 8/E, loc. 87, lev. + 19.0 ft.

(21). (3795). Cone. Pot. drk. br. slp. Now 1.62 hi. × 1.3 di. Two grooves round lower portion. Trench A(4), loc. 67, lev. — 6.1 ft.
(22). (806). Cone. Pot. purp. bl. slp. over a rd. slp. Now 1.5 hi. × 1.2 di. Conical hole in base. Spiral grooving round lower portion. Trench B(5), lev. — 3.9 ft.
(23). (3707). Cone. Pot. drk. rd. slp. Now 2.53 hi. Trench B(5), loc. 55, lev. — 2.2 ft.
(24). (3262, b). Cone. Sh. Now 1.92 hi. Found with No. 30. Sq. 7/E, loc. 121, lev. + 6.9 ft.
(25). (1178). Cone. Pot. red slp. 2.26 hi. Hard-baked, surface smooth and almost polished. Trench I(1), lev. — 3.2 ft.
(26). (4520). Cone. Pot. cr. slp. 2.51 hi. Sq. 9/F, loc. 258, lev. + 8.6 ft.
(27). (3461). Cone. Pot. 2.13 hi. Sq. 9/D, loc. 283, lev. + 6.8 ft.
(28). (1395). Cone. Gre. pot. Hard baked. Sq. 9/D, loc. 95, lev. + 19.1 ft.
(29). (1157). Cone. Pot. 2.5 hi. Point re-trimmed. Trench D(1), lev. — 2.1 ft.
(30). (3262, a). Cone. Sh. 2.93 hi. Incised pattern round base. Found with No. 24. Sq. 7/E, loc. 121, lev. + 6.9 ft.
(31). (3533). Cone. Sh. 3.7 hi. Incised decoration at base. Sq. 9/C, loc. 208, lev. + 7.0 ft.
(32). (5242). Cone. Pot. 3.1 hi. Semi-rounded base with remains of white substance inset. Signs of accidental burning. Mound I. Sq. 13/J, loc. 3, lev. + 14.3 ft.
(33). (3933). Cone. Dr. pot. 2.7 hi. Hard baked. Four lines of pricking at base. Trench E(1), loc. 38, lev. — 3.8 ft.
(34). (3715). Cone. Pot. 2.6 hi. Decorated with five roughly painted broad, red bands. Red paint on base. Trench F(2), lev. — 3.6 ft.
(35). (3414). Cone. Pot. 2.7 hi. Sq. 7/E, loc. 302, lev. + 7.7 ft.
(36). (2401). Cone. Sh. 3.61 hi. Has been burnt and is now a black colour. Sq. 9/D, loc. 215, lev. + 9.3 ft.
(37). (1928). Cone. Sh. 2.79 hi. Sq. 9/D, loc. 174, lev. + 14.3 ft.
(38). (1190). Cone. Pot. Drk. gr. slp. 2.42 hi. Trench C(3), lev. — 4.0 ft.
(39). (1354). Cone. Pot. Now 2.4 hi. Semi-polished surface, decorated with thin lines of light red. Trench J(1), loc. 73, lev. — 7.8 ft.

Plate LXI. Toys and Playthings. Chapter XI

(1). (1008). Rattle. See also Pl. LIX, 7.
(2). (4300). Rattle. Pot. Approx. 1.65 di. Light red lines arranged about four poles. Sq. 7/C, loc. 267, lev. + 7.2 ft.
(3). (4978). Rattle. Pot. Approx. 1.51 di. Light red lines arranged about two poles not opposite. Sq. 9/C, loc. 395, lev. + 7.3 ft.
(4). (1599). Rattle. See also Pl. LIX, 8.
(5). (5065). Rattle. Pot. Approx. 2.02 di. Divided into four quarters by two thick, dark red lines. Mound I. Sq. 13/J, loc. 5, lev. + 14. 2 ft.
(6). (4737). Rattle. Pot. Approx. 2.1 di. Light red lines arranged about four poles. Cut. Sq 9/F, loc. 409, lev. + 3.1 ft.
(7). (1074). Rattle. See also Pl. LIX, 10.

Plate LXII. Copper and Bronze Group (No. 2529). Chapter XII

(1). (No. 2529, V). Jar. 3.03 hi. × 2.28 di. Sq. 8/C, loc. 297, lev. + 10.4 ft.
(2). (No. 2529, W). Scale-pan. 0.17 hi. × 2.23 di.
(3). (No. 2529, S). Scale-pan. 0.27 hi. × 2.2 di.
(4). (No. 2529, R). Scale-pan. 0.32 hi. × 2.24 di.
(5). (No. 2529, X). Bangle. 2.0 di. × 0.2 × 0.2 in sect.
(6). (No. 2529, X). Bangle. 1.85 di. × 0.11 × 0.2 in sect.
(7). (No. 2529, Y). Tube-drill. 1.6 lg. 0.21-0.35 di.
(8). (No. 2529, AA). Scale-pan. 0.25 hi. × 2.26 di.
(9). (No. 2529, D). Awl. 3.43 lg. × 0.2 di.

(10). (No. 2529, P). Scale-pan. 0.2 hi. × 2.22 di.
(11). (No. 2529, H). Knife. 3.61 lg. × 1.28 wde. × 0.11 th.
(12). (No. 2529, C). Chisel. 6.58 lg. × 0.88 wde. × 0.45 th.
(13). (No. 2529, Q). Chisel. 5.92 lg. × 0.33 wde. × 0.9 th.
(14). (No. 2529, K). Awl. 5.2 lg. × 0.22 sq.
(15). (No. 2529, A). Chisel. 2.31 lg. × 0.52 wde. × 0.3 th.
(16). (No. 2529, L). Knife. 1.95 wde. × 0.12 th.
(17). (No. 2529, HH). Knife. 5.92 lg. × 1.82 wde. × 0.12 th.
(18). (No. 2529, B). Chisel. 3.24 lg. × 0.73 wde. × 0.21 th.
(19). (No. 2529, L). Chisel. 5.91 lg. × 0.42 wde. × 0.13 th.
(20). (No. 2529, F). Port. of axe. 5.35 lg. × 2.10 wde. × 0.18 th.
(21). (No. 2529, GG). Adze. 8.11 lg. × 1.83 wde. × 0.20 th.
(22). (No. 2529, BB). Port. of axe. 5.85 lg. × 3.7 wde. × 0.46 th.
(23). (No. 2529, E). Adze. 8.13 lg. × 1.54 wde. × 0.16 th.

Plate LXIII. Copper and Bronze Groups (Nos. 2529, 2525, 2384). Chapter XII

(1). (No. 2529, DD). Saw. 10.73 lg. × 3.53 wde. × 0.14 th.
(2). (No. 2529, U). Spear-head. 9.22 lg. × 3.15 wde. × 0.14 th.
(3). (No. 2529, G). Axe. 8.0 lg. × 3.25 wde. × 0.32 th.
(4). (No. 2529, HH). Spear-head. 10.55 lg. × 3.05 wde. × 0.12 th.
(5). (No. 2529, J). Spear-head. 10.93 lg. × 2.8 wde. × 0.05 th.

* * * * * * * * *

(6). (No. 2525, A). Chisel. 5.25 lg. × 0.83 wde. × 0.1 th. Sq. 9/C, loc. 227, lev. + 9.4 ft.
(7). (No. 2525, E). Chisel. 4.3 lg. × 0.3 wde. × 0.28 th.
(8). (No. 2525, D). Chisel. 3.2 lg. × 0.5 wde. × 0.22 th.
(9). (No. 2525, F). Scale-pan. 0.14 hi. × 2.85 di.
(10). (No. 2525, C). Knife. 2.61 lg. × 0.7 wde. × 0.3 th.
(11). (No. 2525, G). Scale-beam. 3.95 lg. × 0.2 di.

* * * * * * * * *

(12). (No. 2384, D). Chisel. 7.13 lg. × 0.37 wde. × 0.12 th. Sq. 9/D, loc. 215, lev. + 9.3 ft.
(13). (No. 2384, B). Scale-pan. 0.15 hi. × 2.24 di.
(14). (No. 2384, F). Knife. 3.8 lg. × 0.83 wde. × 0.2 th.

Plate LXIV. Copper and Bronze Group (No. 2593). Chapter XII

(1). (No. 2593, W). Knife. 8.62 lg. × 2.72 wde. × 0.12 th. Sq. 9/C, loc. 212, lev. + 9.1 ft.
(2). (No. 2593, FF). Knife. 8.96 lg. × 2.86 wde.
(3). (No. 2593, Z). Knife. 9.2 lg. × 2.6 wde. × 0.19 th.
(4). (No. 2593, FF). Knife. 10.0 lg. × 2.39 wde.
(5). (No. 2593, V). Knife. 8.69 lg. × 1.8 wde. × 0.11 th.
(6). (No. 2593, GG). Knife. 6.33 lg. × 2.5 wde. × 0.1 th.
(7). (No. 2593, BB). Port. of knife. 7.2 lg. × 0.4 wde.
(8). (No. 2593, N). Adze. 6.92 lg. × 1.8 wde. × 0.31 th.
(9). (No. 2593, C). Dish. 0.65 hi. × 4.97 di.
(10). (No. 2593, P). Adze. 3.9 lg. × 1.7 wde.
(11). (No. 2593, Q). Adze. 4.75 lg. × 1.57 wde. × 0.23 th.

Plate LXV. Copper and Bronze Group (No. 2593). Chapter XII

(1). (No. 2593, EE). Spear-head. 7.83 lg. × 3.61 wde. × 0.11 th. Sq. 9/C, loc. 212, lev. + 9.1 ft.
(2). (No. 2593, Y). Knife. 10.4 lg. × 3.21 wde. × 0.11 th.
(3). (No. 2593, U). Knife. 9.35 lg. × 2.5 wde. × 0.2 th.

(4). (No. 2593, X). Knife. 9.93 lg. × 2.63 wde. × 0.15 th.
(5). (No. 2593, AA). Knife. 8.11 lg. × 1.94 wde. × 0.1 th.
(6). (No. 2593, FF). Knife. 7.92 lg. × 1.85 wde.
(7). (No. 2593, CC). Knife. 6.88 lg. × 1.97 wde. × 0.08 th.
(8). (No. 2593, HH). Knife, 4.53 lg. × 1.87 wde.
(9). (No. 2593, DD). Casting. 5.7 lg. × 1.81 wde. × 0.3 th.

Plate LXVI. Copper and Bronze Groups (Nos. 2593, 2199). Chapter XII

(1). (No. 2593, F). Handled dish. 7.57 lg. × 4.92 di. × 0.6 hi. Sq. 9/C, loc. 212, lev. + 9.1 ft.
(2). (No. 2593, G). Bangle. 1.63 di. × 0.2 round in sect.
(3). (No. 2593, S). Axe. 7.25 lg. × 3.33 wde. × 0.43 th.
(4). (No. 2593, O). Axe. 6.01 lg. × 2.4 wde. Sq. 9/C, loc. 212, lev. + 9.1 ft.
(5). (No. 2593, R). Axe. 5.05 lg. × 3.4 wde.

* * * * * * * * *

(6). (No. 2199, M). Jar-cover. 0.6 hi. × 3.14 di. Sq. 9/C, loc. 227, lev. + 11.3 ft.
(7). (No. 2199, D). Dish. 0.3 hi. × 2.65 di.
(8). (No. 2199, O). Bangle. 2.06 di. × 0.23 round in sect.
(9). (No. 2199, M). Bangle. 1.87 di. × 0.23 round in sect.
(10). (No. 2199, E). Bangle. 1.81 di. × 0.18 round in sect.
(11). (No. 2199, G). Bangle. 1.63 di. × 0.18 round in sect.
(12). (No. 2199, C). Scale-pan. 0.32 hi. × 2.35 di.
(13). (No. 2199, H). Chisel. 2.73 lg. × 0.39 wde. × 0.25 th.
(14). (No. 2199, L). Awl. 3.2 lg. × 0.2 di.
(15). (No. 2199, A). Axe. 6.6 lg. × 3.4 wde. × 0.26 th.
(16). (No. 2199, M). Knife. 5.62 lg. × 1.62 wde. × 0.09 th.
(17). (No. 2199, J). Chisel. 4.55 lg. × 0.55 wde. × 0.1 th.
(18). (No. 2199, K). Chisel. 4.15 lg. × 0.5 wde. × 0.03 th.
(19). (No. 2199, H). Chisel. 2.7 lg. × 0.42 wde.
(20). (No. 2199, F). Chisel. 2.8 lg. × 0.52 wde.
(21). (No. 2199, B). Awl. 4.91 lg. × 0.11 di.

Plate LXVII. Copper and Bronze Groups (Nos. 2596, 2360, 2382). Chapter XII

(1). (No. 2596, O). Razor. 2.61 lg. × 1.4 wde. Sq. 8/C, loc. 297, lev. + 9.3 ft.
(2). (No. 2596, F). Scale-pan. 0.19 hi. × 1.96 di.
(3). (No. 2596, H). Chisel. 1.16 lg. × 0.4 wde. × 0.3 th.
(4). (No. 2596, M). Bangle. 1.99 di. × 0.8 × 0.12, half-round in sect.
(5). (No. 2596, O). Bangle. 1.7 di. × 0.2 × 0.12, half-round in sect.
(6). (No. 2596, L). Chisel. 3.73 lg. × 1.11 wde. × 0.21 th.
(7). (No. 2596, C). Razor. 4.11 lg. × 0.51 wde. × 0.07 th.
(8). (No. 2596, O). Spatula (?). 2.72 lg. × 0.49 wde. × 0.08 th.
(9). (No. 2596, O). Chisel. 2.23 lg. × 0.4 wde. × 0.21 th.
(10). (No. 2596, G). Chisel. 2.2 lg. × 0.8 wde. × 0.26 th.
(11). (No. 2596, D). Chisel. 5.53 lg. × 0.43 wde. × 0.15 th.
(12). (No. 2596, N). Knife. 8.0 lg. × 2.32 wde. × 0.03 th.

* * * * * * * * *

(13). (No. 2360, C). Pin. 3.83 lg. × 0.11 di. Sq. 9/C, loc. 213, lev. + 10.4 ft.
(14). (No. 2360, A). Knife. 9.45 lg. × 2.62 wde. × 0.08 th. Sq. 9/C, loc. 213, lev. + 10.4 ft.
(15). (No. 2360, A). Knife. 8.4 lg. × 2.1 wde. × 0.05 th.
(16). (No. 2360, E). Knife. 7.9 lg. × 1.8 wde.
(17). (No. 2360, G). Pin. 3.87 lg. × 0.1 di.

(18). (No. 2360, D). Chisel. 4.07 lg. × 0.25 wde. × 0.11 th.
(19). (No. 2360, B). Chisel. 4.31 lg. × 0.6 wde. × 0.4 th.

* * * * * * * * *

(20). (No. 2382, B). Knife. 9.7 lg. × ? × 0.02 th. Sq. 9/C, loc. 213, lev. + 10.1 ft.
(21). (No. 2382, A). Axe. 6.37 lg. × 2.96 wde. × 0.21 th.

Plate LXVIII. Copper and Bronze Group (No. 2365). Chapter XII

(1). (No. 2365, B). Jar. 6.9 hi. × 5.9 di. Sq. 8/B, loc. 284, lev. + 9.5 ft.
(2). (No. 2365, H). Handled-pan. 4.7 lg. × 2.9 wde. × 0.54 hi.
(3). (No. 2365, A). Jar. 7.62 hi. × 9.5 di.
(4). (No. 2365, E). Staff-head. 2.4 hi. × 2.2 di.
(5). (No. 2365, D). Staff-head. 2.4 hi. × 2.2 di.
(6). (No. 2365, M). Arrow-head. 1.08 lg. × 0.06 th.
(7). (No. 2365, C). Staff-head. 0.67 hi. × 0.84 di.
(8). (No. 2365, K). Knife. 3.19 lg. × 0.8 wde. × 0.05 th.
(9). (No. 2365, I). Pin. 4.0 lg. × 0.15 di.
(10). (No. 2365, G). Knife. 5.36 lg. × 1.72 wde. × 0.1 th.
(11). (No. 2365, Q). Adze. 13.12 lg. × 1.5 wde. × 0.29 th.
(12). (No. 2365, F). Adze. 6.23 lg. × 1.64 wde. × 0.21 th.
(13). (No. 2365, L). Dagger (?). 10.0 lg. × 2.65 wde. × 0.13 th.
(14). (No. 2365, P). Frag. of Fillet. 3.45 lg. × 0.4 wde. × 0.05 th. (see note 8[a] in chapter XIII).
(15). (No. 2365, N). Dagger (?). 8.62 lg. × 2.63 wde. × 0.13 th.
(16). (No. 2365, L). Knife. 8.62 lg. × 2.45 wde.

Plate LXIX. Copper and Bronze Groups (Nos. 2290, 3145, 3324). Chapter XII

(1). (No. 2290, A). Knife. 8.42 lg. × 2.84 wde. Sq. 9/D, loc. 215, lev. + 10.1 ft.
(2). (No. 2290, B). Knife. 9.27 lg. × ? × 0.17 th.

* * * * * * * * *

(3). (No. 3145, A). Handled-pan. 5.38 lg. × 0.51 hi. Sq. 8/F, loc. 417, lev. + 7.2 ft.
(4). (No. 3145, B). Knife. 7.32 lg. × 2.16 wde.

* * * * * * * * *

(5). (No. 1919). Pin. 3.52 lg. 0.09 di. Sq. 9/D, loc. 179, lev. + 15.6 ft.
(6). (No. 2294, A). Pin. 4.58 lg. × 0.18 di. Sq. 9/D, loc. 215, lev. + 10.3 ft.
(7). (No. 2294, B). Pin. 3.95 lg. × 0.15 di. Sq. 9/D, loc. 215, lev. + 10.3 ft.
(8). (No. 2193). Pin. 4.32 lg. × 0.16 di. Sq. 9/D, loc. 95, lev. + 12.1 ft.
(9). (No. 1859). Pin. 4.82 lg. × 0.15 di. Sq. 8/D, loc. 107, lev. + 12.6 ft.
(10). (No. 4381). Pin. 4.55 lg. × 0.09 di. Cut., sq. 10/F, loc. 379, lev. + 0.05 ft.

* * * * * * * * *

(11). (No. 3324, H). Bangle. 1.15 di. × 0.13, round in sect. Sq. 7/E, loc. 324, lev. + 9.2 ft.
(12). (No. 3324, E). Chisel. 3.0 lg. × 0.72 wde. × 0.2 th.
(13). (No. 3324, D). Frag. of axe. 3.82 lg. × 2.0 wde. × 0.21 th.
(14). (No. 3324, B). Axe. 7.25 lg. × 3.25 wde. × 0.32 th.
(15). (No. 3324, C). Axe. 8.5 lg. × 3.3 wde. × 0.34 th.

Plate LXX. Copper and Bronze Tools and Implements. Chapter XII

(1). (No. 2465). Chisel. 1.92 lg. × 0.81 wde. × 0.21 th. Sq. 9/C, loc. 292, lev. + 8.6 ft.
(2). (No. 3938). Chisel. 1.8 lg. × 0.41 wde. × 0.3 th. Cut., sq. 9/F, loc. 410, lev. + 2.1 ft.
(3). (No. 339). Chisel. 1.23 lg. × 0.51 wde. × 0.27 th. Trench D(1), lev. — 1.9 ft.
(4). (No. 4063). Chisel. 0.8 lg. × 0.6 wde. × 0.2 th. Cut., sq. 9/F, loc. 420, lev. + 2.9 ft.

(5). (No. 3949). Chisel. 1.21 lg. × 0.63 wde. × 0.27 th. Cut., sq. 9/F, loc. 410, lev. + 3.6 ft.
(6). (No. 2842). Chisel. 1.83 lg. × 0.55 wde. × 0.42 th. Sq. 8/E, loc. 114, lev. + 9.1 ft.
(7). (No. 2642). Chisel. 0.87 lg. × 0.61 wde. × 0.17 th. Sq. 9/D, loc. 174, lev. + 8.3 ft.
(8). (No. 3494). Chisel. 4.85 lg. × 0.78 wde. × 0.1 th. Sq. 7/C, loc. 238, lev. + 7.5 ft.
(9). (No. 2469). Chisel. 4.41 lg. × 0.19 wde. × 0.19 th. Sq. 9/C, loc. 294, lev. + 8.9 ft.
(10). (No. 3211). Chisel. 5.8 lg. × 0.37 wde. × 0.34 th. Sq. 8/F, loc. 117, lev. + 6.9 ft.
(11). (No. 3152). Chisel. 6.52 lg. × 0.9 wde. × 0.4 th. Sq. 9/G, loc. 439, lev. + 7.5 ft.
(12). (No. 1805). Chisel. 5.11 lg. × 0.26 wde. × 0.18 th. Sq. 8/E, loc. 104, lev. + 13.4 ft.
(13). (No. 3149). Chisel. 6.62 lg. × 0.89 wde. × 0.29 th. Sq. 7/F, loc. 119, lev. + 8.0 ft.
(14). (No. 5019). Chisel. 4.84 lg. × 0.72 wde. × 0.41 th. Mound I, sq. 13/K, loc. 34, lev. + 13.9 ft.
(15). (No. 2575). Chisel. 5.43 lg. × 0.6 wde. × 0.12 th. Sq. 8/C, loc. 297, lev. + 10.4 ft.
(16). (No. 2287). Rod. 5.12 lg. × 0.22 di. Sq. 9/D, loc. 215, lev. + 10.3 ft.
(17). (No. 1989). Chisel. 5.01 lg. × 0.31 wde. × 0.19 th. Sq. 8/E, loc. 142, lev. + 12.5 ft.
(18). (No. 4176). Awl. 6.47 lg. × 0.18 di. Cut., sq. 10/F, loc. 484, lev. + 10.3 ft.
(19). (No. 1660). Chisel. 3.9 lg. × 0.39 wde. × 0.33 th. Sq. 8/E, loc. 141, lev. + 15.0 ft.
(20). (No. 1634). Chisel. 2.9 lg. × 0.22 wde. × 0.12 th. Sq. 8/E, loc. 122, lev. + 15.3 ft.
(21). (No. 592). Knife. 4.62 lg. × 1.4 wde. × 0.12 th. Trench G(1), loc. 49, lev. — 3.1 ft.
(22). (No. 1348). Knife. 3.55 lg. × 1.11 wde. × 0.11 th. Trench G(1), loc. 67, lev. — 2.3 ft.
(23). (No. 2028). Knife. 2.34 lg. × 0.45 wde. × 0.06 th. Sq. 8/D, loc. 138, lev. + 13.2 ft.
(24). (No. 2408). Knife. 2.57 lg. × 0.67 wde. ×0.07 th. Sq. 9/D, loc. 215, lev. + 9.4 ft.
(25). (No. 2931). Knife. 2.95 lg. × 0.48 wde. × 0.06 th. Sq. 8/B, loc. 285, lev. + 8.2 ft.
(26). (No. 1891). Plumb-bob (?). 1.1 lg. × 0.61 di. Sq. 9/E, loc. 173, lev. + 15.8 ft.
(27). (No. 2495). Casting. 1.04 lg. × 0.69 di. × 0.08 th. Sq. 9/C, loc. 208, lev. + 9.9 ft.
(28). (No. 1810). Razor. 4.35 lg. × 1.35 wde. × 0.06 th. Sq. 7/C, loc. 135, lev. + 13.6 ft.
(29). (No. 4313). Axe. 3.3 lg. × 2.35 wde. × 0.03 th. Cut., sq. 10/F, loc. 466, lev. + 0.05 ft.
(30). (No. 1994). Axe. 4.85 lg. × 2.75 wde. × 0.38 th. Sq. 9/E, loc. 201, lev. + 11.2 ft.
(31). (No. 1803). Lance-head. 4.13 lg. × 1.41 wde. × 0.04 th. Sq. 7/C, loc. 165, lev. + 11.8 ft.

Plate LXXI. Copper and Bronze Tools and Implements. Chapter XII

(1). (No. 2601). Scale-beam. 11.06 lg. × 0.47 di. Sq. 6/E, loc. 330, lev. + 9.2 ft.
(2). (No. 2490). Scale-beam. 3.32 lg. × 0.19 di. Sq. 8/F, loc. 115, lev. + 10.9 ft.
(3). (No. 2964). Scale-beam. 4.7 lg. × 0.12 di. Sq. 9/E, loc. 171, lev. + 6.9 ft.
(4). (No. 3697). Axe. 4.86 lg. × 1.78 wde. Sq. 9/C, loc. 205, lev. + 7.1 ft.
(5). (No. 4898). Axe. 5.7 lg. × 1.95 wde. Mound I, sq. 13/J, loc. 10, lev. + 12.9 ft.
(6). (No. 2296). Axe. 6.34 lg. × 2.9 wde. × 0.3 th. Sq. 9/C, loc. 263, lev. + 10.2 ft.
(7). (No. 835). Knife. 5.21 lg. × 1.14 wde. × 0.1 th. Trench B(5) loc. 63, lev. — 6.0 ft.
(8). (No. 3322). Knife. 7.02 lg. × 1.6 wde. Sq. 8/C, loc. 297, lev. + 8.0 ft.
(9). (No. 2843). Adze. 10.52 lg. × 1.95 wde. Sq. 9/E, loc. 171, lev. + 7.7 ft.
(10). (No. 2200). Adze. 9.7 lg. × 1.58 wde. Sq. 9/C, loc. 228, lev. + 11.1 ft.
(11). (No. 2847). Adze. 8.97 lg. × 2.61 wde. × 0.3 th. Sq. 8/E, loc. 92, lev. + 7.0 ft.
(12). (No. 2602). Spear-head. 12.83 lg. × 4.17 wde. × 0.12 th. Sq. 9/E, loc. 137, lev. + 8.3 ft.

Plate LXXII. Copper and Bronze Objects. Chapter XII

(1). (No. 3486). Knife. 9.3 lg. × 2.4 wde. × 0.16 th. Sq. 9/C, loc. 291, lev. + 7.1 ft.
(2). No. 2523, A). Knife, 9.56 lg. × 2.32 wde. × 0.1 th. Sq. 9/C, loc. 227, lev. + 10.3 ft.
(3). (No. 3147). Knife. 6.1 lg. × 2.18 wde. × 0.1 th. Sq. 8/F, loc. 260, lev. + 6.2 ft.
(4). (No. 3496). Knife. 6.93 lg. × 2.7 wde. × 0.12 th. Sq. 7/C, loc. 238, lev. + 8.8 ft.
(5). (No. 2663). Knife. 7.43 lg. × 1.8 wde. × 0.1 th. Sq. 7/F, loc. 189, lev. + 8.8 ft.
(6). (No. 5383). Awl. 1.52 lg. × 0.12 wde. × 0.07 th. Cut., sq. 9/F, loc. 469, lev. — 15.1 ft.
(7). (No. 636). Awl. 1.9 lg. × 0.15 wde. × 0.15 th. Trench B(5), loc. 56, lev. — 3.1 ft.
(8). (No. 1926). Awl. 2.68 lg. × 0.17 wde. × 0.17 th. Sq. 8/E, loc. 141, lev. + 13.7 ft.

(9). (No. 197). Awl. 2.12 lg. × 0.17 wde. × 0.14 th. Trench B(3), loc. 22, lev. — 4.3 ft.
(10). (No. 637). Awl. 1.5 lg. × 0.17 wde. × 0.17 th. Trench B(5), loc. 56, lev. — 4.8 ft.
(11). (No. 2197). Rod. 7.62 lg. × 0.26 wde. × 0.3 th. Sq. 9/E, loc. 224, lev. + 12.5 ft.
(12). (No. 3736). Awl. 4.42 lg. × 0.26 wde. × 0.26 th. Sq. 8/C, loc. 394, lev. + 8.6 ft.
(13). (No. 2441). Awl. 4.66 lg. × 0.2 wde. × 0.2 th. Sq. 9/D, loc. 215, lev. + 9.5 ft.
(14). (No. 2196). Awl. 4.74 lg. × 0.3 wde. × 0.2 th. Sq. 7/E, loc. 154, lev. + 11.8 ft.
(15). (No. 2332). Awl. 3.58 lg. × 0.25 wde. × 0.2 th. Sq. 9/C, loc. 212, lev. + 11.1 ft.
(16). (No. 2362, E). Awl. 4.04 lg. × 0.07 di. Sq. 9/D, loc. 215, lev. + 9.4 ft.
(17). (No. 1835). Awl. 5.7 lg. × 0.13 di. Sq. 7/C, loc. 166, lev. + 14.1 ft.
(18). (No. 1958). Pin. (Jhukar?). 6.38 lg. × 0.3 wde. × 0.27 th. Sq. 9/F, loc. 187, lev. + 13.7 ft.
(19). (No. 1982). Pin (Jhukar?). 4.34 lg. × 0.23 sq. at head. Shank, 0.1 di. Sq. 8/D, loc. 196, lev. + 14.5 ft.
(20). (No. 3816). Pin. (Jhukar?). 4.97 lg. × 0.61 × 0.6 wde. & th. at head. Shaft, 0.25 di. Cut., sq. 10/F, loc. 379, lev. + 0.05 ft.
(21). (No. 1630). Pin. (Jhukar?). 4.86 lg. × 0.13 di. Sq. 9/D, loc. 130, lev. + 16.7 ft.
(22). (No. 1659). Pin. (Jhukar?). 5.20 lg. × 0.16 di. Sq. 8/E, loc. 92, lev. + 16.3 ft.
(23). (No. 1610). Chisel (Jhukar?). 3.16 lg. × 0.32 wde. × 0.23 th. Sq. 8/E, loc. 91, lev. + 17.2 ft.
(24). (No. 108). Arrowhead. Iron. (Jhangar?). 2.32 lg. × 1.1 wde. × 0.22 th. Trench B(1), lev. — 2.7 ft.
(25). (No. 1655). Axe. (Jhukar?). 3.95 lg. × 1.94 wde. × 1.21 th. Oval socket, 0.71 × 0.82. Edge 1.94 wde. Sq. 9/E, loc. 112, lev. + 17.6 ft.

Plate LXXIII. Copper and Bronze Objects. Chapter XII

(1). (No. 1666). Arrow-head. 1.53 lg. × 0.51 wde. × 0.11 th. Sq. 8/E, loc. 87, lev. + 15.7 ft.
(2). (No. 3444, A). Arrowhead. 1.11 lg. × 0.08 th. Sq. 8/B, loc. 447, lev. + 7.0 ft.
(3). (No. 3446, B). Arrowhead. 1.4 lg. × 0.07 th. Sq. 8/B, loc. 447, lev. + 7.0 ft.
(4). (No. 2540). Arrow-head. 0.65 lg. × 0.57 wde. × 0.06 th. Sq. 9/C, loc. 208, lev. + 9.1 ft.
(5). (No. 2943). Fish-hook. 1.12 lg. × 0.08 in sect. Sq. 9/D, loc. 264, lev. + 7.0 ft.
(6). (No. 488, A). Fish-hook. 0.43 lg. × 0.06 in sect. Trench B(5), loc. 44, lev. — 0.7 ft.
(7). (No. 3038). Fish-hook. 1.22 lg. × 0.09 in sect. Sq. 9/D, loc. 139, lev. + 6.9 ft.
(8). (No. 3812). Fish-hook. 1.28 lg. × 0.12 in sect. Cut, sq. 9/F, loc. 469, lev. + 2.8 ft.
(9). (No. 5146). Ring. Coiled wire. 0.8 di. × 0.27 wde. Cut., sq. 10/G, loc. 478, lev. — 6.6 ft.
(10). (No. 3411). Ring. Coiled wire. 0.75 di. × 0.1 wde. Sq. 6/F, loc. 434, lev. + 7.1 ft.
(11). (No. 4312). Ring. Coiled wire. 0.71 di. × 0.77 wde. Mound I, sq. 13/J, loc. 11, lev. + 14.1 ft.
(12). (No. 3167). Ring. Coiled wire. 0.7 di × 0.32 wde. Sq. 9/D, loc. 211, lev. + 8.1 ft.
(13). (No. 364). Arrow-head. 3.8 lg. × 0.54 wde. × 0.15 th. Trench B(5), lev. — 3.9 ft.
(14). (No. 3309). Arrow-head. 1.5 lg. × 0.8 wde. × 0.02 th. Sq. 7/F, loc. 346, lev. + 6.7 ft.
(15). (No. 2571). Arrow-head. 1.1 lg. × 0.05 th. Sq. 8/D, loc. 129, lev. + 9.6 ft.
(16). (No. 3208). Arrow-head. 1.7 lg. × 0.04 th. Sq. 9/D, loc. 209, lev. + 7.6 ft.
(17). (No. 3641). Fish-hook. 1.68 lg. × 0.11 th. Sq. 8/D, loc. 311, lev. + 7.1 ft.
(18). (No. 3487). Fish-hook. 1.87 lg. × 0.15 th. Sq. 9/C, loc. 292, lev. + 7.0 ft.
(19). (No. 3458). Bangle. 2.0 di. × 0.27 di. in sect. Sq. 9/C, loc. 244, lev. + 7.1 ft.
(20). (No. 1621). Ring. 0.85 di. × 0.12 di. in sect. Sq. 7/F, loc. 147, lev. + 11.2 ft.
(21). (No. 1908). Ring. 0.93 di. × 0.12 di in sect. Sq. 8/E, loc. 114, lev. + 14.0 ft.
(22). (No. 3214). Razor. 1.89 lg. × 1.99 wde. Sq. 8/F, loc. 148, lev. + 6.8 ft.
(23). (No. 1959). Bangle. 2.18 di. × 0.18 di. in sect. Sq. 9/F, loc. 187, lev. + 13.7 ft.
(24). (No. 2487). Bangle. 2.38 di. × 0.22 di. in sect. Sq. 8/D, loc. 178, lev. + 9.5 ft.
(25). (No. 2608). Razor. 4.62 lg. × 1.9 wde. Sq. 9/E, loc. 126, lev. + 8.5 ft.
(26). (No. 2846). Razor. 1.72 lg. × 1.48 wde. Sq. 9/E, loc. 224, lev. + 6.9 ft.
(27). (No. 2850). Razor. 3.47 lg. × 2.43 wde. Sq. 8/E, loc. 177, lev. + 8.0 ft.

(28). (No. 496). Razor. 2.46 lg. × 2.05 wde. Trench B(5), loc. 55, lev. — 0.5 ft.
(29). (No. 2596, B). Bangle. 2.06 di. × 0.23 di. in section. Sq. 8/C, loc. 297, lev. + 9.3 ft.
(30). (No. 3210). Bangle. 2.8 di. × 0.2-0.21 di. in sect. Sq. 7/F, loc. 299, lev. + 7.3 ft.
(31). (No. 525). Razor. 2.8 across × 0.1 th. Trench A(3), loc. 36, lev. — 2.7 ft.
(32). (No. 3319). Razor. 2.82 lg. × 2.55 wde. × 0.1 th. Sq. 6/F, loc. 434, lev. + 7.1 ft.
(33). (No. 2359). Razor. 3.08 lg. × 2.6 wde. Sq. 9/C, loc. 227, lev. + 10.0 ft.
(34). (No. 172). Jar. 1.14 hi. × 1.3 di. Trench B(3), loc. 22, lev. — 4.3 ft.
(35). (No. 2844). Dish. 1.04 hi. × 10.18 di. Sq. 9/E, loc. 171, lev. + 7.2 ft.
(36). (No. 2522). Jar-cover. 0.47 hi. × 2.41 di. Sq. 8/D, loc. 290, lev. + 9.8 ft.
(37). (No. 2449). Canister. 4.4 hi. × 5.1 di. Sq. 9/D, loc. 215, lev. + 9.5 ft.
(38). (No. 1800). Jar. 3.57 hi. × 5.41 di. Sq. 8/D, loc. 138, lev. + 16.5 ft.
(39). (No. 1977). Kohl-jar. 3.6 hi. × 1.81 di. Sq. 9/E, loc. 201, lev. + 13.1 ft.

Plate LXXIV. Copper and Bronze Tools and Implements (Groups 2529, 2593). Chapter XII

(1, 1, a). (No. 2596, A). Port. of axe. Inscribed both sides. 3.43 lg. × 2.67 wde. × 0.28 th. Sq. 8/C, loc. 297, lev. + 9.3 ft.

* * * * * * * * *

(2). (No. 2529, H). Ingot. 13.75 lg. × aver. 1.4 di. Sq. 8/C, loc. 297, lev. + 10.4 ft.
(3). (No. 2529, E). Adze. 8.13 lg. × 1.54 wde. × 0.16 th.
(4). (No. 2529, DD). Saw. 10.73 lg. × 3.53 wde. × 0.14 th.
(5). (No. 2529, AA). Scale-pan. 0.25 hi. × 2.26 di.
(6). (No. 2529, A). Chisel. 2.31 lg. × 0.52 wde. × 0.3 th.
(7). (No. 2529, V). Jar. 3.03 hi. × 2.28 di.
(8). (No. 2529, G). Axe. 8.00 lg. × 3.25 wde. × 0.32 th.
(9). (No. 2529, GG). Adze. 8.11 lg. × 1.83 wde. × 0.2 th.

* * * * * * * * *

(10). (No. 2593, C). Platter. 1.07 hi. × 10.02 di. Sq. 9/C, loc. 212, lev. + 9.1 ft.
(11). (No. 2593, S). Axe. 7.25 lg. × 3.33 wde. × 0.43 th.
(12). (No. 2593, X). Knife. 9.93 lg. × 2.62 wde. × 0.15 th.
(13). (No. 2593, D). Shovel. 16.3 lg. × 8.62 wde. × 1.2.
(14). (No. 2593, R). Axe. 5.05 lg. × 3.4 wde.
(15). (No. 2593). Group as found.
(16). (No. 2593, DD). Casting. 5.7 lg. × 1.81 wde. × 0.3 th.
(17). (No. 2593, V). Knife. 8.69 lg. × 1.8 wde. × 0.11 th.

Plate LXXV. Copper and Bronze Implements and Utensils (Groups 2365, 2199). Chapter XII

(1). (No. 2365). Group as found. Sq. 8/B, loc. 284, lev. + 9.5 ft.
(2). (No. 2365, B). Jar. 6.9 hi. × 5.9 di.
(3). (No. 2365, A). Jar. 7.62 hi. × 9.5 di.
(4). (No. 2365, D). Staff-head. 2.4 hi. × 2.2 di.
(5). (No. 2365, Q). Adze. 13.12 lg. × 1.5 wde. × 0.29 th.
(6). (No. 2365, I). Pin. 4.0 lg. × 0.15 di.
(7). (No. 2365, H). Handled-pan. 0.54 hi. × 4.7 lg. × 2.9 wde.
(8). (No. 2365, F). Adze. 6.23 lg. × 1.64 wde. × 0.21 th.
(9). (No. 2365, L). Knife. 8.62 lg. × 2.45 wde.
(9). (No. 2365, L). Dagger(?). 10.0 lg. × 2.65 wde. × 0.13 th.
(10). (No. 2365, R). Platter. 1.28 hi. × 9.75 di.
(10). (No. 2365, R). Platter. 1.28 hi. × 10.21 di.

* * * * * * * * *

(11). (No. 2199, M). Knife. 5.62 lg. × 1.62 wde. × 0.09 th. Sq. 9/C, loc. 227, lev. + 11.3 ft.
(11). (No. 2199, M). Jar-cover. 0.6 hi. × 3.14 di.

(11). (No. 2199, M). Bangle. 1.87 di. × 0.23 di. in sect. Sq. 9/C, loc. 227, lev. + 11.3 ft.
(12). (No. 2199, E). Bangle. 1.81 di. × 0.18 di. in sect.
(13). (No. 2199, B). Awl. 4.91 lg. × 0.11 di.

* * * * * * * * *

(14). (No. 2844). Platter. 1.04 hi. × 10.18 di. Sq. 9/E, loc. 171, lev. + 7.2 ft.
(15). (No. 2449). Canister. 4.4 hi. × 5.1 di. Sq. 9/D, loc. 215, lev. + 9.5 ft.
(16). (No. 1800). Jar. 3.57 hi. × 5.41 di. Sq. 8/D, loc. 138, lev. + 16.5 ft.

Plate LXXVI. Copper and Bronze Implements and Tools. Chapter XII

(1). (No. 3145, B). Knife. 7.32 lg. × 2.16 wde. Sq. 8/F, loc. 417, lev. + 7.1 ft.
(2). (No. 3145, A). Handled pan. 5.38 lg. × 0.51 hi.

* * * * * * * * *

(3). (No. 3152). Chisel. 6.52 lg. × 0.9 wde. × 0.4 th. Sq. 9/G, loc. 439, lev. + 7.5 ft.
(4). (No. 1994). Axe. 4.85 lg. × 2.75 wde. × 0.38 th. Sq. 9/E, loc. 201, lev. + 11.2 ft.

* * * * * * * * *

(5). (No. 3324, B). Axe. 7.25 lg. × 3.25 wde. 0.32 th. Sq. 7/E, loc. 324, lev. + 9.2 ft.
(6). (No. 3324, C). Axe. 8.5 lg. × 3.3 wde. × 0.34 th.

* * * * * * * * *

(7). (No. 2290, B). Knife. 9.27 lg. × ? × 0.17 th. Sq. 9/D, loc. 215, lev. + 10.3 ft.
(8). (No. 835). Knife. 5.21 lg. × 1.14 wde. × 0.1 th. Trench B(5), loc. 63, lev. — 6.0 ft.
(9). (No. 3149). Chisel. 6.62 lg. × 0.89 wde. × 0.29 th. Sq. 7/F, loc. 119, lev. + 8.0 ft.
(10). (No. 2295). Chisel. 4.65 lg. × 0.39 wde. × 0.36 th. Sq. 9/D, loc. 262, lev. + 10.7 ft.
(11). (No. 1989). Chisel. 5.0 lg. × 0.31 wde. × 0.19 th. Sq. 8/E, loc. 142, lev. + 12.5 ft.
(12). (No. 2642). Chisel. 0.87 lg. × 0.61 wde. × 0.17 th. Sq. 9/D, loc. 174, lev. + 8.3 ft.
(13). (No. 2842). Chisel. 1.83 lg. × 0.55 wde. × 0.42 th. Sq. 8/E, loc. 114, lev. + 9.1 ft.
(14). (No. 2384, D). Chisel. 7.13 lg. × 0.37 wde. × 0.12 th. Sq. 9/D, loc. 215, lev. + 9.3 ft.
(15). (No. 3487). Fish-hook. 1.87 lg. × 0.15 di. Sq. 9/C, loc. 292, lev. + 7.0 ft.
(16). (No. 2847). Adze. 8.97 lg. × 2.61 wde. × 0.3 th. Sq. 8/E, loc. 92, lev. + 7.0 ft.
(17). (No. 2602). Spear-head. 12.83 lg. × 4.17 wde. × 0.12 th. Sq. 9/E, loc. 137, lev. + 8.3 ft.
(18). (No. 2601). Scale-beam. 11.06 lg. × 0.47 di. Sq. 6/E, loc. 330, lev. + 9.2 ft.
(19). (No. 2596, B). Bangle. 2.06 di. × 0.23 di. in sect. Sq. 8/C, loc. 297, lev. + 9.3 ft.
(20). (No. 1959). Bangle. 2.18 di. × 0.18 di. in sect. Sq. 9/F, loc. 187, lev. + 13.7 ft.
(21). (No. 3210). Bangle. 2.8 di. × 0.2 × 0.21 in sect. Sq. 7/F, loc. 299, lev. + 7.3 ft.
(22). (No. 4381). Pin. 4.55 lg. × 0.09 di. Cut., sq. 10/F, loc. 379, lev. + 0.05 ft.
(23). (No. 2193). Pin. 4.32 di. × 0.16 di. Sq. 9/D, loc. 95, lev. + 12.1 ft.
(24). (No. 1859). Pin. 4.82 lg. × 0.15 di. Sq. 8/D, loc. 107, lev. + 12.6 ft.
(25). (No. 2365, K). Knife. 3.19 lg. × 0.8 wde. × 0.05 th. Sq. 8/B, loc. 284, lev. + 9.5 ft.
(26). (No. 2028). Knife. 2.34 lg. × 0.45 wde. × 0.06 th. Sq. 8/D, loc. 138, lev. + 13.2 ft.
(27). (No. 2931). Knife. 2.95 lg. × 0.48 wde. × 0.06 th. Sq. 8/B, loc. 285, lev. + 8.2 ft.
(28). (No. 3319). Razor. 2.82 lg. × 2.55 wde. × 0.1 th. Sq. 6/E, loc. 434, lev. + 7.1 ft.

* * * * * * * * *

(29). (No. 2594, G). Knife. 7.22 lg. × 2.1 wde. Sq. 9/C, loc. 228, lev. + 9.8 ft.
(30). (No. 2594, F). Dagger(?). 12.12 lg. × 2.2 wde. × 0.24 th.
(31). (No. 2594, C). Knife. 5.82 lg. × 1.62 wde. × 0.07 th.

* * * * * * * * *

(32). (No. 1977). Kohl-jar. 3.6 hi. × 1.81 di. Sq. 9/E, loc. 201, lev. + 13.1 ft.
(33). (No. 2359). Razor. 3.08 lg. × 2.6 wde. Sq. 9/C, loc. 227, lev. + 10.0 ft.
(34). (No. 2850). Razor. 3.47 lg. × 2.43 wde. Sq. 8/E, loc. 177, lev. + 8.0 ft.
(35). (No. 2608). Razor. 4.62 lg. × 1.9 wde. Sq. 9/E, loc. 126, lev. + 8.5 ft.

(36). (No. 2846). Razor. 1.72 lg. × 1.48 wde. Sq. 9/E, loc. 224, lev. + 6.9 ft.
(37). (No. 1655). Axe. 3.95 lg. × 1.94 wde. × 1.21 th. Sq. 9/E, loc. 112, + 17.6 ft.

Plate LXXVII. Pottery, Faience, and Shell Bangles. Chapter XIII

(1). (No. 4166). Sealing. Pottery. 1.45 di. × 0.61 th. Face impressed by square seal 0.71 × 0.71. Cut., sq. 10/F, loc. 465, lev. + 1.1 ft. See Pl. LII, 36.
(2). (No. 1841). Frag. Bangle. Fai. Lt. gre. 1.5 across; 0.15 × 0.21 in sect. Sq. 7/C, loc. 101, lev. + 14.1 ft.
(3). (No. 1851). Frag. bangle. Fai. Lt. gre. 1.28 across; 0.15 × 0.17 in sect. Sq. 7/E, loc. 121, lev. + 11.2 ft.
(4). (No. 4126). Frag. bangle. Fai. Lt. gre. 0.21 × 0.15 in sect. Cut., sq. 10/G, loc. 480, lev. + 0.4 ft.
(5). (No. 1961). Frag. bangle. Fai. Lt. gre. 1.9 across; 0.13 × 0.12 in sect . Sq. 8/F, loc. 117, lev. + 9.9 ft.
(6). (No. 954). Frag. bangle. Sh. 1.3 lg. × 0.5 × 0.25 in sect. Trench A(4), loc. 69, lev. — 3.5 ft.
(7). (No. 3722). Frag. bangle. Sh. 0.35 × 0.13 in sect. Trench F(2), lev. — 3.6 ft.
(8). (No. 1987). Frag. bangle. Fai. Lt. gre. 1.52 across; 0.18 × 0.2 in sect. Sq. 9/D, loc. 175, lev. + 13.3 ft.
(9). (No. 1687). Frag. bangle. Pot., Cr. slp. 2.41 across; 0.43 × 0.44 in section. Trench G(1), lev. — 4.2 ft.
(10). (No. 4429). Frag. bangle. Fai., Ltd blue. 2.41 across; 0.4 × 0.29 in sect. Mound I, sq. 12/K, loc. 15, lev. + 14.0 ft.
(11). (No. 2747). Frag. bangle. Pot. Pnk. slp. Dk. rd. dec. 0.35 × 0.12-0.26 in sect. Sq. 9/E, loc. 128, lev. + 8.3 ft.
(12). (No. 1699). Frag. bangle. Pot. Lt. rd. dec. 1.9 across; 0.6 × 0.12-0.18 in sect. Trench E(1), lev. ?.
(13). (No. 121). Frag. bangle. Pot. Pnk. slp. Dk. rd. stripes. 0.32 di. in sect. Trench C(1), lev. — 5.8 ft.

Plate LXXVIII. Buttons and Other Ornaments. Chapter XIII

(1). (No. 2385). Ornament. Cop. & steat. 1.61 hi. × 1.31 wde. × 0.62 th. Sq. 9/C, loc. 263, lev. + 10.4 ft.
(2). (No. 2596, O). Ornament. Cop. Now 3.82 lg. × 0.31 wde. × 0.65 th. Sq. 8/C, loc. 297, lev. + 9.3 ft.
(3). (No. 2194). Frag. button. Fai. Lt. gre. 1.34 di. × 0.43 th. Sq. 7/C, loc. 102, lev. + 13.5 ft.
(4). (No. 1406). Button. Fai. 1.1 di. × 0.42 th. Sq. 8/E, loc. 90, lev. + 16.2 ft.
(5). (No. 4764). Button. Fai. Lt. gre. 0.9 di. × 0.4 th. Mound I, sq. 13/J, loc. 11, lev. + 14.0 ft.
(6). (No. 4387). Button. Fai. Lt. gre. 1.02 di. × 0.41 th. Mound I, sq. 13/J, loc. 21, lev. + 14.4 ft.
(7). (No. 5015). Button. Fai. Lt. gre. 0.75 di. × 0.13 th. Mound I, sq. 13/K, loc. 67, lev. + 13.0 ft.
(8). (No. 4838). Nose or ear-plug. Fai. Lt. gre. 0.8 di. × 0.31 th. Mound I, sq. 12/J, loc. 35, lev. + 13.2 ft.
(9). (No. 3673). Button, Steat. Wh. 0.44 di. × 0.21 th. Sq. 8/B, loc. 233, lev. + 7.6 ft.
(10). (No. 4055). Nose or ear-plug. Fai. Wh. 0.59 di. × 0.59 lg. Cut., sq. 10/F, loc. 465, lev. + 2.3 ft.
(11). (No. 3884). Nose or ear-plug. Fai. Lt. gre. 0.57 lg. × 0.53 di. Cut., sq. 10/F, loc. 424, lev. + 2.9 ft.
(12). (No. 1748). Button. Fai. Cr. 0.6 lg. × 0.59 di. Sq. 8/E, loc. 146, lev. + 13.5 ft.

(13). (No. 3685). Ornament. Sh. 1.2 di. × 0.25 th. Sq. 7/C, loc. 461, lev. + 7.5 ft.
(14). (No. 4217). Button. Steat. Wh. 1.0 di. × 0.2 th. Mound I, sq. 12/K, loc. 29, lev. + 15.6 ft.
(15). (No. 1957). Button. Fai. Wh. 0.8 lg. × 0.55 di. Sq. 8/D, loc. 183, lev. + 15.3 ft.
(16). (No. 2190). Nose or ear-plug. Fai. Lt. gre. 0.84 di. × 0.55 th. Sq. 8/C, loc. 152, lev. + 12.8 ft.

Plate LXXIX. Decorated Carnelian Beads. Chapter XIII

(1). (No. 258). Wh. on rd. 0.5 lg. × 0.51 wde. × 0.11 th. Trench D(1), loc. 31, lev. — 2.3 ft.
(2). (No. 2434). Wh. on rd. 0.43 lg. × 0.43 wde. × 0.12 th. Sq. 9/D, loc. 215, lev. + 9.4 ft.
(3). (No. 2485). Wh. on rd. 0.53 lg. × 0.4 wde. × 0.18 th. Sq. 7/E, loc. 278, lev. + 9.8 ft.
(4). (No. 223). Wh. on rd. 0.39 lg. × 0.2 wde. × 0.06 th. Trench B(3), lev. — 4.6 ft.
(5). (No. 511). Wh. on rd. 0.7 lg. × 0.4 wde. × 0.2 th. Trench F(1), loc. 46, lev. — 5.5 ft.
(6). (No. 3354). Bl. on wh. 1.0 lg. × 0.59 wde. × 0.2 th. Sq. 7/E, loc. 278, lev. + 7.5 ft.
(7). (No. 3999). Wh. on rd. Now 0.42 lg. × 0.51 wde. × 0.13 th. Sq. 9/F, loc. 473, lev. + 3.2 ft.
(8). (No. 4320). Wh. on rd. 0.54 lg. × 0.21 wde. 0.13 th. Mound I, sq. 12/K, loc. 20, lev. + 13.8 ft.
(9). (No. 590). Wh. on rd. 0.3 lg. × 0.2 di. Trench E(1), loc. 35, lev. — 3.8 ft.
(10). (No. 2797). Bl. on wh. 0.23 lg. × 0.33 di. Sq. 9/E, loc. 125, lev. + 9.7 ft.
(11). (No. 3506). Wh. on rd. 0.26 lg. × 0.32 di. Sq. 8/B, loc. 451, lev. + 7.5 ft.
(12). (No. 368). Bl. on wh. Formerly 0.74 lg. × 0.58 wde. × 0.17 th. Trench E(1), lev. — 1.4 ft.
(13). (No. 2326, Q). Wh. on rd. Formerly 0.4 lg. × 0.28 wde. × 0.16 th. Sq. 9/D, loc. 215, lev. + 10.4 ft.
(14). (No. 2513). Bl. on wh. 0.5 lg. × 0.35 wde. × 0.2 th. Sq. 8/C, loc. 226, lev. + 9.6 ft.
(15). (No. 373). Wh. on rd. Formerly 0.64 lg. × 0.46 wde. × 0.15 th. Trench B(5), loc. 43, lev. — 3.9 ft.
(16). (No. 943). Wh. on rd. 0.6 lg. × 0.31 wde. × 0.18 th. Trench D(4), loc. 41, lev. — 4.4 ft.

Plate LXXX. Beads and Bead-tools. Chapter XIII

(1). (No. 4226). Bead-tool. Cop. or Br. 1.9 lg. × 0.2-0.29 di. Cut., sq. 9/F, loc. 468, lev. + 1.3 ft.
(2). (No. 4226). Bead-tool. Cop. or Br. 1.65 lg. × 0.2-0.3 di. Point 0.1. di. Cut., sq. 9/F, loc. 468, lev. + 1.3 ft.
(3). (No. 2375). Bead-tool. Cop. or Br. 1.15 lg. × 0.2 di. Point 0.19 lg. Sq. 9/D, loc. 215, lev. + 10.3 ft.
(4). (No. 2326, C). Bead-tool. Cop. or Br. 1.05 lg. × 0.2-0.28 di. Sq. 9/D, loc. 215, lev. + 10.4 ft.
(5). (No. 2326, C). Bead-tool. Cop. or Br. 1.02 lg. × 0.19 di. Sq. 9/D, loc. 215, lev. + 10.4 ft.
(6). (No. 2304). Bead-tool. Cop. or Br. 0.93 lg. × 0.18 di. Point now 0.25 lg. × 0.08 di. Sq. 9/D, loc. 215, lev. + 10.2 ft.
(7). (No. 2304). Bead-tool. Cop. or Br. Sq. 9/D, loc. 215, lev. + 10.2 ft.
(8). (No. 2202). Bead-tool. Cop. or Br. 1.2 lg. × 0.19 di. Head 0.26 di. Sq. 9/D, loc. 215, lev. + 9.1 ft.
(9). (No. 2596, O). Tube-drill. Cop. or Br. 1.37 lg. × 0.25-0.32 di. Sq. 8/C, loc. 297, lev. + 9.3 ft.
(10). (No. 3364). Spacer. Cop. or Br. 0.65 × 0.32 × 0.05. Sq. 10/C, loc. 343, lev. + 6.9 ft.
(11). (No. 3122). Spacer. Cop. or Br. 1.31 × 0.3 × 0.07. Sq. 9/C, loc. 263, lev. + 7.4 ft.

(12). (No. 2541). Spacer. Cop. or Br. 1.52 lg. Sq. 9/C, loc. 291, lev. + 9.6 ft.
(13). (No. 3032). Spacer. Cop. or Br. 0.7 × 0.32. Sq. 9/E, loc. 126, lev. + 7.1 ft.
(14). (No. 3678). Spacer. Cop. or Br. 1.0 × 0.25 × 0.09. Sq. 8/B, loc. 233, lev. + 7.6 ft.
(15). (No. 4961). Spacer. Wh. steat. 0.73 lg. × 0.7 wde. × 0.18 th. Mound I, sq. 12/K, loc. 20, lev. + 11.2 ft.
(16). (No. 2326, V). Spacer. Wh. steat. Sq. 9/D, loc. 215, lev. + 10.4 ft.
(17). (No. 644). Spacer. Wh. pas. 0.43 × 0.36 × 0.11. Trench G(1), loc. 48, lev. — 3.6 ft.
(18). (No. 2414, C). Spacer. Vitr. pas. Lt. blue. 0.62 × 0.8 × 0.2. Sq. 9/D, loc. 179, lev. + 9.9 ft.
(19). (No. 2414, B). Spacer. Vitr. pas. Lt. blue. 0.72 × 0.81 × 0.2. Sq. 9/D, loc. 179, lev. + 9.9 ft.
(20). (No. 2452). Spacer. Vitr. pas. Lt. blue. Sq. 9/D, loc. 215, lev. + 8.6 ft.
(21). (No. 2512). Terminal. Fai. Cr. 0.65 lg. × 0.25-0.5 di. Sq. 7/E, loc. 276, lev. + 9.5 ft.
(22). (No. 5017). Terminal. Fai. Lt. gre. 0.79 × 0.41 × 0.15. Mound I, sq. 13/K, loc. 34, lev. + 13.0 ft.
(23). (No. 1972). Terminal. Pot. 2.6 × 1.18 × 0.5. Sq. 7/F, loc. 119, lev. + 10.6 ft.
(24). (No. 2526). Terminal. Fai. Lt. gre. 1.28 × 1.03 × 0.12. Sq. 9/C, loc. 227, lev. + 10.0 ft.
(25). (No. 4377). Terminal. Fai. Lt. blue. 0.71 × 0.34 × 0.19. Mound I, sq. 12/J, loc. 18, lev. + 13.8 ft.
(26). (No. 3123). Pendant. Steat. Dk. gr. 0.23 hi. × 0.42 di. Sq. 9/C, loc. 263, lev. + 7.4 ft.
(27). (No. 1943). Pendant. Hor. Bl. 0.83 hi. × 0.31 di. Groove 0.01 wde. × 0.02 dp. Sq. 7/F, loc. 119, lev. + 10.8 ft.
(28). (No. 3362). Pendant. Hor. Bl. 0.72 lg. × 0.29 di. Sq. 7/F, loc. 298, lev. + 6.8 ft.
(29). (No. 3316). Pendant. Lt. gr. st. 0.61 hi. × 0.39 di. Groove 0.15 wde. and dp. Sq. 7/E, loc. 97, lev. + 6.6 ft.
(30). (No. 4059). Pendant. Hor. Bl. 0.74 hi. × 0.28 di. Cut., sq. 9/F, loc. 405, lev. + 3.1 ft.
(31). (No. 3226). Pendant. Hor. Bl. 0.3 hi. × 0.25 di. Sq. 7/E, loc. 121, lev. + 6.9 ft.
(32). (No. 4173). Pendant. Hor. Bl. 0.41 hi. × 0.19 di. Mound I, sq. 12/K, loc. 26, lev. + 15.7 ft.
(33). (No. 4957). Pendant. Hor. Bl. 0.48 × 0.27. Mound I, sq. 13/K, loc. 51, lev. + 12.8 ft.
(34). (No. 3193). Pendant. Car. 0.78 hi. × 0.28 di. Sq. 7/F, loc. 147, lev. + 8.6 ft.

Plate LXXXI. Beads. Chapter XIII

(1). (No. 2433). Cyl. Steat. Wh. Sq. 9/D, loc. 215, lev. + 9.4 ft.
(2). (No. 886). Cyl. Cop. 0.28 lg. × 0.22 di. Trench I(1), loc. 73, lev. — 1.02 ft.
(3). (No. 2619). Cyl. Pas. Lt. yel. 0.31 lg. × 0.39 di. Sq. 8/C, loc. 167, lev. + 10.2 ft.
(4). (No. 1082). Cyl. Steat. Wh. Trench B(5), loc. 43, lev. — 9.8 ft.
(5). (No. 836). Cyl. Lap.-laz. 0.45 lg. × 0.15 di. Trench D(1), loc. 42, lev. — 7.4 ft.
(6). (No. 3330). Cyl. Pas. Yell. 0.43 lg. × 0.21 di. Sq. 7/F, loc. 299, lev. + 8.1 ft.
(7). (No. 2653). Cyl. Pas. Wh. 0.6 lg. × 0.23 di. Sq. 7/F, loc. 158, lev. 9.1 ft.
(8). (No. 2946, A). Cyl. Pas. Wh. 0.63 lg. × 0.09 di. Sq. 9/D, loc. 174, lev. + 6.8 ft.
(9). (No. 550). Cyl. Pas. Wh. 0.59 lg. × 0.12 di. Trench D(1), loc. 41, lev. — 2.4 ft.
(10). (No. 3698). Cyl. Fai. Lt. gre. 0.62 lg. × 0.12 di. Sq. 8/C, loc. 236, lev. + 7.5 ft.
(11). (No. 551). Cyl. Pas. Wh. 0.7 lg. × 0.1 di. Trench D(1), loc. 56, lev. — 1.7 ft.
(12). (No. 2049). Cyl. Pot. 0.75 lg. × 0.21 di. Sq. 9/D, loc. 133, lev. + 12.4 ft.
(13). (No. 2946, A). Cyl. Pas. Wh. 0.63 lg. × 0.09 di. Sq. 9/D, loc. 174, lev. + 6.8 ft.
(14). (No. 4379). Lap.-laz. 0.49 lg. × 0.1 sq. Cut., sq. 9/F, loc. 409, lev. + 0.6 ft.
(15). (No. 2624, C). Tube-drill. Cop. 1.62 lg. × 0.25-0.32 di. Sq. 9/C, loc. 228, lev. + 10.1 ft.
(16). (No. 4741). Cyl. Pot. 1.91 lg. × 0.22 di. Cut., sq. 9/F, loc. 475, lev. — 0.6 ft.
(17). (No. 4226, B). Jas. and Br. Dk. rd. veined with wh. Sq. 9/F, loc. 468, lev. + 1.3 ft.
(18). (No. 4226, C). Jas. and Br. Sq. 9/F, loc. 468, lev. + 1.3 ft.

(19). (No. 2640). Cyl., oval sect. Br. 0.68 lg. × 0.4 wde. × 0.3 th. Sq. 8/C, loc. 167, lev. + 8.9 ft.
(20). (No. 4834). Lap.-laz. 0.82 lg. × 0.32 wde. × 0.29 th. Cut., sq. 10/G, loc. 481, lev. — 2.2 ft.
(21). (No. 4226, A). Jas. and Br. Cut., sq. 9/F, loc. 468, lev. + 1.3 ft.
(22). (No. 2562). Fai. Cr. 0.61 × 0.53 × 0.16. Sq. 9/C, loc. 227, lev. + 10.0 ft.
(23). (No. 2940). Lap.-laz. 0.9 × 0.3 × 0.27. Sq. 9/E, loc. 85, lev. + 7.4 ft.
(24). (No. 2938). Amazon st. Lt. gre. 0.62 lg. × 0.3 di. Sq. 9/D, loc. 136, lev. + 6.6 ft.
(25). (No. 1200). Lg.-bar. cyl. Pot, rd. slp. 3.61 × 0.4. Trench D(1), loc. 58, lev. — 7.2 ft.
(26). (No. 3024, C). Lg.-bar. cyl. Pot. 2.6 lg. × 0.31 di. Sq. 9/D, loc. 139, lev. + 6.9 ft.
(27). (No. 3996). Lg.-bar. cyl. Pot., rd. slp. 4.1 lg. × 0.39 di. Cut., sq. 9/F, loc. 409, lev. + 3.5 ft.
(28). (No. 3688). Lg.-bar. cyl. Pot., rd. slp. 2.02 lg. × 0.15 di. Sq. 9/D, loc. 133, lev. + 6.9 ft.
(29). (No. 3086). Lg.-bar. cyl. Pot., rd. slp. 3.83 lg. × 0.4 di. Sq. 9/C, loc. 213, lev. + 7.3 ft.
(30). (No. 1049). Lg.-bar. cyl. Pot., rd. slp. 2.0 lg. × 0.41 di. Trench H(1), lev. — 3.1 ft.
(31). (No. 2673). Lg.-bar. cyl. Car. 2.27 lg. × 0.41 di. Sq. 9/E, loc. 131, lev. + 8.2 ft.
(32). (No. 2623). Lg.-bar. cyl. Car. 2.12 lg. × 0.35 di. Sq. 8/D, loc. 183, lev. + 9.6 ft.
(33). (No. 2630). Lg.-bar. cyl. Ag.-car. Yell. & Rd. 1.42 lg. × 0.32 di. Sq. 9/D, loc. 139, lev. + 8.7 ft.
(34). (No. 2298). Lg.-bar. cyl. Ag.-car. Yell. & Rd. 2.7 lg. × 0.38 di. Sq. 9/D, loc. 215, lev. + 9.1 ft.
(35). (No. 625). Lg.-bar. cyl. Ag. Lt. yell. 1.7 lg. × 0.47 di. Trench F(1), lev. — 4.7 ft.
(36). (No. 2750). Lg.-bar. cyl. Car. Burnt wh. 1.4 lg. × 0.39 di. Sq. 10/E, loc. 352, lev. + 7.2 ft.

Plate LXXXII. Stone and Glazed Beads. Chapter XIII

(1). (No. 3231). Bead. Bar.-cyl. Pas. Wh. 1.09 lg. × 0.39 di. Sq. 8/F, loc. 117, lev. + 7.0 ft.
(2). (No. 1975). Bar.-cyl. Ag. Lt. br. 1.08 lg. × 0.42 di. Sq. 8/D, loc. 129, lev. + 14.2 ft.
(3). (No.1423). Bar.-cyl. Fai. Cr. 0.94 lg. × 0.37 di. Sq. 8/E, loc. 103, lev. + 15.1 ft.
(4). (No. 669). Bar.-cyl. Dk. gr. veined with Lt. gr. 1.17 lg. × 0.5 di. Trench F(2), loc. 65, lev. — 0.4 ft.
(5). (No.2452). Bar-cyl. Banded jas. Dk. br., rd. and dk. gre. 1.05 lg. × 0.37 di. Sq. 9/D, loc. 215, lev. + 8.6 ft.
(6). (No. 672). Bar-cyl. Mar.(?). Pnk. 1.14 lg. × 0.45 di. Trench B(5), loc. 55, lev. — 5.7 ft.
(7). (No. 520). Bar-cyl. Gr-br. st. 0.88 lg. × 0.25 th. Trench B(5), loc. 55, lev. — 1.3 ft.
(8). (No. 2621). Bar-cyl. Amason st. Lt. gre. 0.8 lg. × 0.3 di. Sq. 7/E, loc. 304, lev. +9.5 ft.
(9). (No. 937). Bar.-cyl. Pas. Wh. 0.71 lg. × 0.37 di. Trench F(2), loc. 66, lev. — 4.6 ft.
(10). (No. 4902). Bar.-cyl. Fai. Lt. gre. Mound I, sq. 13/K, loc. 12, lev. + 13.0 ft.
(11). (No. 1208). Bar.-cyl. Pas. Cr. 0.85 lg. × 0.28 di. Trench L(1), lev. + 8.2 ft.
(12). (No. 582). Bar.-cyl. Pas. Wh. 0.92 lg. × 0.4 di. Trench D(1), level ?.
(13). (No. 2326, W). Bar.-cyl. Pas. Wh. Moulded. 0.49 lg. × 0.29 di. Sq. 9/D, loc. 215, lev. + 10.4 ft.
(14). (No. 272). Bar.-cyl. Fai., Br. and Wh. 1.07 lg. × 0.3 di. Trench B(5), lev. — 0.7 ft.
(15). (No. 1125). Bar.-cyl. Pas. Wh. with purp. band. 0.93 lg. × 0.33 di. Trench K(1), loc. 76, lev. — 7.8 ft.
(16). (No. 2945). Bar.-cyl. Pas., wh. Dk. br. band. Sq. 9/D, loc. 264, lev. + 7.0 ft.
(17). (No. 2945). Bead. Br.-cyl. Pas. Wh. Dk. br. band. Sq. 9/D, loc. 264, lev. + 7.0 ft.
(18). (No. 2259). Bar.-cyl. Pas. Wh. Lt. gre. band. 0.7 lg. × 0.31 di. Sq. 9/E, loc. 137, lev. + 11.3 ft.
(19). (No. 380). Bar.-cyl. Pas. Wh. Purp.-bl. band. 0.85 lg. × 0.29 di. Trench D(1), loc. 41, lev. + 1.0 ft.
(20). (No. 3020). Bar.-cyl. Pas. Wh. Br. band. Sq. 9/D, loc. 136, lev. + 6.8 ft.

(21). (No. 2646). Bar.-cyl. Pas. Wh. Br. band. 1.03 lg. × 0.3 di. Sq. 8/D, loc. 82, lev. + 8.2 ft.
(22). (No. 2945). Bar. Pas. Wh. Br. band. Sq. 9/D, loc. 264, lev. + 7.0 ft.
(23). (No. 3681). Bar. Quartz. Lt. gr. 0.75 lg. × 0.29 di. Sq. 7/C, loc. 461, lev. + 7.3 ft.
(24). (No. 1108). Fai. Lt. gre. 0.65 lg. × 0.29 wde. × 0.09 th. Trench G(1), loc. 49, lev. — 8.8 ft.
(25). (No. 2458). Jas. Dk. rd. & gr. 0.73 lg. × 0.48 wde. × 0.2 th. Sq. 9/C, loc. 190, lev. + 9.8 ft.
(26). (No. 2326, V). Jas. Dk. gre. Sq. 9/D, loc. 215, lev. + 10.4 ft.
(27). (No. 2452). Jas. Sq. 9/D, loc. 215, lev. + 8.6 ft.
(28). (No. 1808). Ag. Gr. & Br. bands. 0.8 lg. × 0.47 di. Sq. 9/E, loc. 171, lev. + 18.2 ft.
(29). (No. 1606). Banded ag. Br. & Wh. 0.5 lg. × 0.25 di. Sq. 9/E, loc. 96, lev. + 16.0 ft.
(30). (No. 2961). Ag. Yell. veined Wh. 0.65 lg. × 0.4 di. Sq. 10/F, loc. 378, lev. + 7.3 ft.
(31). (No. 292). Ag. Gr. 0.49 lg. × 0.3 di. Trench B(4), lev. — 5.6 ft.
(32). (No. 1595). Lim.(?). Lt. br. Fossil of creature with scaly carapace and sternum. 0.52 lg. × 0.33 di. Sq. 8/C, loc. 109, lev. + 16.5 ft.
(33). (No. 1940). Onyx. Wh. with Br. ends. 0.59 lg. × 0.3 di. Sq. 7/F, loc. 119, lev. + 10.5 ft.
(34). (No. 2326, V). Ag. Br. & Wh. Sq. 9/D, loc. 215, lev. + 10.4 ft.
(35). (No. 4494). St. Wh. veined with rd. & bl. 0.7 lg. × 0.43 wde. × 0.2 th. Cut., sq. 10/G, loc. 488, lev. — 1.2 ft.
(36). (No. 2581). Steat. Wh. Stained rd. in patches. 0.5 lg. × 0.33 wde. × 0.22 th. Sq. 8/C, loc. 295, lev. + 9.6 ft.
(37). (No. 1609). Plas. Dk. gre. 0.48 lg. × 0.35 wde. × 0.18 th. Sq. 8/E, loc. 92, lev. + 17.0 ft.
(38). (No. 1651). St. Gr. mottled with Wh. 0.6 lg. × 0.4 wde. × 0.21 th. Sq. 9/D, loc. 136, lev. + 17.0 ft.
(39). (No. 2201). Steat. Wh., stained with red. 1.0 lg. × 0.71 wde. × 0.43 th. Sq. 9/D, loc. 215, lev. + 9.1 ft.
(40). (No. 2420, B). Vitr. pas. Blue. Sq. 9/D, loc. 215, lev. + 9.3 ft.
(41). (No. 2326, L). Vitr pas. Blue. 0.68 lg. × 0.55 wde. × 0.25 th. Sq. 9/D, loc. 215, lev. + 10.4 ft.
(42). (No. 2352). Brec. Gr., dk. br. & wh. 0.98 lg. × 0.73 wde. × 0.3 th . Sq. 10/E, loc. 261, lev. + 9.5 ft.
(43). (No. 3083). Pas. Cr. 0.53 lg. × 0.53 wde. × 0.13 th. Sq. 9/E, loc. 126, lev. + 7.1 ft.

Plate LXXXIII. Stone and Faience Beads. Chapter XIII

(1). (No. 5305). Pot. 0.52 lg. × 0.8 di. Cut., sq. 9/F, loc. 408, lev. — 5.3 ft.
(2). (No. 4396). Pot. 0.73 lg. × 1.14 di. Sq. 9/C, loc. 292, lev. + 6.9 ft.
(3). (No. 4524). Pot., cr. slp. 0.7 lg. × 1.51 di. Sq. 9/E, loc. 162, lev. + 7.5 ft.
(4). (No. 3570). Pot. 0.8 lg. × 1.3 di. Trench C(3), lev. — 7.9 ft.
(5). (No. 3576). Pot. 0.4 lg. × 0.89 di. Trench K(1), lev. — 2.7 ft.
(6). (No. 2754). Pot. 0.45 lg. × 0.92 di. Sq. 9/E, loc. 96, lev. + 8.3 ft.
(7). (No. 3770). Fai. 0.41 lg. × 0.48 di. Sq. 7/C, loc. 268, lev. + 7.1 ft.
(8). (No. 2477). Pas. Wh. Sq. 7/E, loc. 99, lev. + 9.8 ft.
(9). (No. 2192). Sh. 0.21 lg. × 0.45 di. Sq. 7/C, loc. 102, lev. + 12.8 ft.
(10). (No. 369). Pas. Wh. 0.35 lg. × 0.51 di. Trench C(3), lev. — 9.0 ft.
(11). (No. 4163). Lap.-laz. 0.19 lg. × 0.27 di. Cut., sq. 9/G, loc. 483, lev. + 0.9 ft.
(12). (No. 4118). Car. 0.21 lg. × 0.25 di. Mound I, sq. 13/K, loc. 23, lev. + 15.5 ft.
(13). (No. 3997). Car. 0.3 lg. × 0.3 di. Cut., sq. 9/F, loc. 409, lev. + 3.2 ft.
(14). (No. 513). Pas. Wh. 0.38 lg. × 0.49 di. Trench F(1), loc. 46, lev. — 5.3 ft.
(15). (No. 3682). Pot., Lt. rd. slp. 0.55 lg. × 0.87 di. Sq. 8/C, loc. 241, lev. + 7.8 ft.
(16). (No. 1893). Onyx. Bl. & Wh. 0.18 lg. × 0.25 di. Sq. 8/C, loc. 153, lev. + 14.1 ft.
(17). (No. 4901). Quartz. Milky Wh. 0.25 lg. × 0.31 di. Cut., sq. 10/G, loc. 477, lev. — 2.9 ft.

(18). (No. 3455). Chal. 0.27 lg. × 0.32 di. Sq. 9/C, loc. 244, lev. + 6.9 ft.
(19). (No. 2493). Pas. Wh. Sq. 7/E, loc. 154, lev. + 9.8 ft.
(20). (No. 2206). Car. 0.3 lg. × 0.32 di. Sq. 9/E, loc. 171, lev. + 13.0 ft.
(21). (No. 2565). Car. 0.28 lg. × 0.31 di. Sq. 8/E, loc. 143, lev. + 9.5 ft.
(22). (No. 3505). Pas. Cr. 0.3 lg. × 0.31 di. Sq. 8/B, loc. 449, lev. + 7.6 ft.
(23). (No. 3549). Pas. Wh. 0.22 lg. × 0.3 di. Sq. 8/C, loc. 393, lev. + 13.6 ft.
(24). (No. 4699). Steat. Wh. Mound I, sq. 12/J, loc. 35, lev. + 13.6 ft.
(25). (No. 1656). Car. 0.4 lg. × 0.4 di. Sq. 8/D, loc. 84, lev. + 16.9 ft.
(26). (No. 1078). Pas. Wh. 0.35 lg. × 0.53 di. Trench J(1), loc. 73, lev. + 0.1 ft.
(27). (No. 3331). Pas. Yell. 0.2 lg. × 0.35 di. Sq. 7/F, loc. 331, lev. + 7.8 ft.
(28). (No. 1103). Pas. Wh. Trench G(1), loc. 49, lev. — 7.9 ft.
(29). (No. 1010). Pas. Wh. Trench D(1), loc. 41, lev. — 6.9 ft.
(30). (No. 3346). Pot. Rd. slp. 0.2 lg. × 0.31 di. Sq. 8/B, loc. 284, lev. + 6.6 ft.
(31). (No. 4065). Pot. Rd. slp. 0.21 lg. × 0.31 di. Cut., sq. 9/F, loc. 408, lev. + 3.1 ft.
(32). (No. 2500). Pot. Rd. slp. 0.28 lg. × 0.33 di. Sq. 8/C, loc. 226, lev. + 9.5 ft.
(33). (No. 2856). Pot. Rd. slp. 0.14 lg. × 0.3 di. Mound II.
(34). (No. 1211). Pas. Wh. Trench I(1), loc. 73, lev. — 3.2 ft.
(35). (No. 561). Steat. Wh. 0.19 lg. × 0.58 di. Trench A(3), loc. 40, lev. — 6.7 ft.
(36). (No. 1305). Steat. Wh. Trench J(1), loc. 78, lev. — 4.5 ft.
(37). (No. 515). Steat. Wh. Trench F(1), loc. 42, lev. — 7.6 ft.
(38). (No. 515). Steat. Wh. Trench F(1), loc. 42, lev. — 7.6 ft.
(39). (No. 581). Steat. Wh. Trench D(1), loc. 41, lev. — 5.3 ft.
(40). (No. 2433). Steat. Wh. 0.1 lg. × 0.13 di. Sq. 9/D, loc. 215, lev. + 9.4 ft.
(41). (No. 2433). Steat. Wh. Sq. 9/D, loc. 215, lev. + 9.4 ft.
(42). (No. 4117). Pot. 0.4 lg. × 1.3 di. Mound I, sq. 12/K, loc. 21, lev. + 15.8 ft.
(43). (No. 2326, V). Steat. Wh. Sq. 9/D, loc. 215, lev. + 10.4 ft.
(44). (No. 501). Steat. Trench F(1), loc. 46, lev. — 5.4 ft.
(45). (No. 3217). Pas. Wh. 0.11 lg. × 0.5 di. Sq. 8/E, loc. 103, lev. + 6.8 ft.
(46). (No. 290). Fai., Lt. gre. 0.09 lg. × 0.3 di. Trench B(5), lev. — 1.8 ft.
(47). (No. 2326, V). Fai. Lt. gre. Sq. 9/D, loc. 215, lev. + 10.4 ft.
(48). (No. 522). Fai. Wh. 0.09 lg. × 0.31 di. Trench B(5), loc. 55, lev. — 2.2 ft.
(49). (No. 2077). Steat. Wh. 0.48 lg. × 0.9 di. Sq. 9/E, loc. 137, lev. + 13.2 ft.
(50). (No. 2645). Steat. Wh. 2.4 lg. × 0.3 di. Sq. 9/D, loc. 174, lev. + 8.2 ft.
(51). (No. 4066). Steat. Wh. 2.5 lg. × 0.55-0.7 di. Cut., sq. 9/F, loc. 407, lev. + 2.9 ft.
(52). (No. 4116). Fai. Yell. 0.38 lg. × 0.13 di. Mound I, sq. 13/K, loc. 23, lev. + 15.5 ft.
(53). (No. 4427). Fai. Lt. blue. 0.35 lg. × 0.2 di. Mound I, sq. 12/K, loc. 15, lev. + 19.0 ft.
(54). (No. 521). Pot. Rd. slp. 0.73 lg. × 0.8 wde. 0.27 th. Trench B(5), loc. 55, lev. — 1.3 ft.
(55). (No. 630). Pot. Rd. slp. 0.72 lg. × 0.59 wde. × 0.26 th. Trench F(1), lev. — 4.4 ft.
(56). (No. 3196). Pot. Rd. slp. 0.62 lg. × 0.57 wde. × 0.27 th. Sq. 9/D, loc. 211, lev. + 6.7 ft.
(57). (No. 2546). Ag. Yell. veined with Wh. Unfinished. 1.61 lg. × 1.33 wde. × 0.35 th. Sq. 9/C, loc. 208, lev. + 9.1 ft.

Plate LXXXIV. Stone and Pottery Beads. Chapter XIII

(1). (No. 1020). Pas. Wh. 1.2 lg. × 0.7 wde. × 0.21 th. Trench F(2), loc. 65, lev. — 5.5 ft.
(2). (No. 2422, B). Vitr. pas. Blue. Sq. 9/D, loc. 215, lev. + 9.3 ft.
(3). (No. 3079). Pas. Wh. 0.62 lg. × 0.37 wde. × 0.12 th. Sq. 8/D, loc. 129, lev. + 6.9 ft.
(4). (No. 665). Ag. Br. 0.88 lg. × 0.82 wde. × 0.15 th. Trench F(2), loc. 64, lev. — 0.2 ft.
(5). (No. 494). Ag. Wh. (calcined). 0.76 lg. × 0.52 wde. × 0.21 th. Trench E(1), loc. 33, lev. — 6.0 ft.
(6). (No. 2566). Sh. 0.7 lg. × 0.8-0.88 di. Sq. 8/C, loc. 297, lev. + 10.4 ft.
(7). (No. 3889). Sh. 0.63 lg. × 0.58-0.63 di. Cut., sq. 9/F, loc. 474, lev. + 5.2 ft.
(8). (No. 1333). St. Dk. gr. 0.89 lg. × 0.31-0.58 di. Trench D(1), loc. 31, lev. — 3.5 ft.

(9). (No. 2647). Pas. Lt. Yell. 0.5 lg. × 0.62 di. Sq. 9/D, loc. 174, lev. + 8.2 ft.
(10). (No. 5145). Pot. Rd. slp. 0.6 lg. × 0.7 wde. × 0.29 th. Sq. 10/F, loc. 471, lev. + 6.3 ft.
(11). (No. 4703). Pot. Rd. slp 0.52 lg. × 0.61 wde. × 0.23 th. Mound I, sq. 13/K, loc. 37, lev. + 13.7 ft.
(12). (No. 2567). St. Rd. with Wh. vein. 0.44 lg. × 0.5 wde. × 0.21 th. Sq. 9/C, loc. 243, lev. + 9.0 ft.
(13). (No. 2420, A). Ag. Yell. veined with Rd. 2.11 lg. × 0.35-0.72 di. Sq. 9/D, loc. 215, lev. + 9.3 ft.
(14). (No. 2684). Pot. 0.37 lg. × 1.01 di. Sq. 7/F, loc. 346, lev. + 8.7 ft.
(15). (No. 5317). Pot. 0.51 lg. × 1.11 di. Cut., sq. 9/F, loc. 469, lev. — 4.9 ft.
(16). (No. 4966). Pot. 0.68 lg. × 1.0 di. Cut., sq. 9/F, loc. 408, lev. — 5.4 ft.
(17). (No. 2022). Pot. 0.54 lg. × 1.1 di. Sq. 9/E, loc. 199, lev. + 13.1 ft.
(18). (No. 2852). Pot. 0.7 lg. 1.07 di. Sq. 10/D, loc. 339, lev. + 6.6 ft.
(19). (No. 1916). Pot. 0.66 lg. × 1.22 di. Sq. 9/D, loc. 136, lev. + 15.6 ft.
(20). (No. 3946). Pot. Rd. marks. 0.72 lg. × 1.15 di. Cut., sq. 9/F, loc. 469, lev. + 4.0 ft.
(21). (No. 3846). Pot. 1.0 lg. × 1.32 di. Cut., sq. 9/F, loc. 409, lev. + 2.4 ft.
(22). (No. 1009). Pot. 0.9 lg. × 1.4 di. Trench A(3), lev. — 3.2 ft.
(23). (No. 3225). Pot. 0.7 lg. × 1.2 di. Sq. 8/E, loc. 103, lev. + 7.0 ft.
(24). (No. 4050). Pot. 0.85 lg. × 0.96 di. Cut., sq. 9/F, loc. 409, lev. + 2.6 ft.
(25). (No. 5304). Pot. Rd. slp. 0.93 lg. × 1.0 di. Cut., sq. 9/F, loc. 408, lev. — 5.3 ft.
(26). (No. 2221). Pot. Gr. 1.21 lg. × 1.43 di. Sq. 9/D, loc. 192, lev. + 11.7 ft.
(27). (No. 3995). Pot. Rd. slp. 0.89 lg. × 1.1 di. Mound I, sq. 12/J, loc. 16, lev. + 18.3 ft.
(28). (No. 1396). Pot. 0.9 lg. × 1.1 di. Trench I(1), loc. 73, lev. — 8.4 ft.
(29). (No. 2851). Pot. Rd. slp. 1.0 lg. × 1.01 di. Sq. 10/D, loc. 339, lev. + 6.6 ft.
(30). (No. 1473). Pot. 0.82 lg. × 1.1 di. Sq. 8/E, loc. 87, lev. — 18.2 ft.

Plate LXXXV. Beads and Other Objects. Chapter XIII

(1). (No. 3945). Fai. Lt. yell. 0.55 lg. × 1.2 di. Cut., sq. 9/F, loc. 410, lev. + 3.0 ft.
(2). (No. 1598). Fai. Lt. gre. 0.44 lg. × 0.88 di. Locus and level ?.
(3). (No. 1948). Fai. Lt. gr. 0.37 lg. × 0.8 di. Sq. 9/E, loc. 124, lev. + 14.3 ft.
(4). (No. 2354). Fai. Cr. 0.39 lg. × 0.93 di. Sq. 10/E, loc. 252, lev. + 9.2 ft.
(5). (No. 4172). Fai. Lt. gr. 0.5 lg. × 0.1 di. Mound I, sq. 12/K, loc. 26, lev. + 15.7 ft.
(6). (No. 2314). Fai. Lt. gr. 0.39 lg. × 0.88 di. Sq. 9/E, loc. 161, lev. + 12.1 ft.
(7). (No. 2023). Fai. Lt. gre. 0.4 lg. × 0.98 di. Sq. 9/E, loc. 200, lev. + 13.2 ft.
(8). (No. 1852). Fai. Cr. 0.29 lg. × 0.53 di. Locus and level ?.
(9). (No. 2402). Fai. Lt. gre. 0.55 lg. × 0.9 di. Sq. 9/E, loc. 201, lev. + 9.5 ft.
(10). (No. 1739). Fai. Lt. gre. 0.41 lg. × 1.1 di. Sq. 7/C, loc. 101, lev. + 15.4 ft.
(11). (No. 2299). Fai. Lt. gre. 0.72 lg. × 1.09 di. Sq. 7/E, loc. 154, lev. 11.3 ft.
(12). (No. 1913). Fai. Lt. gre. 0.8 lg. × 1.0 di. Sq. 8/D, loc. 84, lev. + 15.5 ft.
(13). (No. 2403). Fai. Lt. gre. 0.98 lg. × 1.0 di. Sq. 9/F, loc. 256, lev. + 10.0 ft.
(14). (No. 2036). Fai. Lt. gre. 0.82 lg. × 1.04 di. Sq. 8/D, loc. 108, lev. + 12.0 ft.
(15). (No. 1889). Fai. Lt. blue. 1.19 lg. × 1.04 di. Sq. 9/D, loc. 136, lev. + 15.7 ft.
(16). (No. 2958). Fai. Lt. gr. 1.0 lg. × 1.1 di. Sq. 9/E, loc. 254, lev. + 7.0 ft.
(17). (No. 1729). Fai. Rd. 1.3 lg. × 1.19 di. Sq. 8/E, loc. 92, lev. + 13.7 ft.
(18). (No. 2205). Fai. Cr. 0.92 lg. × 1.02 di. Sq. 9/E, loc. 200, lev. + 11.6 ft.
(19). (No. 1479). Fai. Lt. yell. 0.56 lg. × 1.35 di. Sq. 7/E, loc. 97, lev. + 14.1 ft.
(20). (No. 2312). Fai. Lt. purp. 0.48 lg. × 0.98 di. Sq. 8/F, loc. 145, lev. + 10.4 ft.
(21). (No. 2552). Fai. Lt. yell. 0.46 lg. × 0.98 di. Sq. 8/E, loc. 105, lev. + 9.7 ft.
(22). (No. 562). Terminal. Lap.-laz. 0.21 lg. × 0.32 wde. × 0.11 th. Trench A/3, loc. 40, lev. — 6.7 ft.
(23). (No. 846). Lap.-laz. 0.47 lg. × 0.61 di. Trench I(1), loc. 62, lev. — 6.8 ft.
(24). (No. 2430). Fai. Lt. gr. 0.93 lg. × 1.02 di. Sq. 7/F, loc. 118, lev. + 9.9 ft.

(25). (No. 2755). Fai. Lt. gre. 1.1 lg. × 1.15 di. Sq. 9/E, loc. 219, lev. + 8.3 ft.
(26). (No. 2009). Fai. Cr. 1.1 lg. × 1.2 di. Sq. 9/E, loc. 124, lev. + 13.1 ft.
(27). (No. 492). Amulet. Pot. 1.63 lg. × 1.12 wde. × 0.11 th. Trench B/5, loc. 44, lev. — 0.79 ft.
(28). (No. 1664). Fai. Lt. gre. 0.62 lg. × 1.2 di. Sq. 7/C, loc. 135, lev. + 12.3 ft.
(29). (No. 900). Pendant. Sh. 1.3 lg. × 0.32 di. Trench I(1), loc. 78, lev. — 0.1 ft.
(30). (No. 238). Cop. 0.29 di. × 0.15 wde. Trench D(1), lev. — 2.3 ft.
(31). (No. 278). Cop. 0.36 di. × 0.18 wde. Sq. 7/E, loc. 278, lev. + 9.8 ft.
(32). (No. 1960). Terminal. Amazon st. Lt. gr. 0.44 lg. × 0.24 di. Sq. 9/E, loc. 162, lev. + 14.3 ft.
(33). (No. 2689). Cop. 0.2 lg. × 0.3 di. Sq. 8/D, loc. 197, lev. + 8.7 ft.
(34). (No. 2078). Fitting. Sh. 0.75 hi. × 0.7 di. Sq. 8/D, loc. 138, lev. + 13.1 ft.

Plate LXXXVI, a. Beads and Micro-photographs. Chapter XIII

(1). (No. 2307). Unfinished disc-beads. Car. Aver. 0.33 di. Sq. 9/D, loc. 215, lev. + 10.2 ft.
(2). (No. 2307). Unfinished disc-beads. Car. Aver. 0.58 di. × 0.21 th. Sq. 9/D, loc. 215, lev. + 10.2 ft.
(3, a). (No. 3161). Unfinished disc-bead. Car. Mag. × 3 times. Sq. 8/F, loc. 259, lev. + 7.0 ft.
(3, b). (No. 3161). Same.
(4). (No. 3686). End of broken bead. Car. Mag. × 9 times. Sq. 8/C, loc. 394, lev. + 7.9 ft.
(5). (No. 4758). End of drill. Ch. Mag. × 12 times. Sq. 9/F, loc. 428, lev. — 1.0 ft.
(6). (No. 2447). Unfinished bead. Br. steat. Mag. × 25 times. Sq. 9/D, loc. 215, lev. + 9.3 ft.
(7). (No. 3686). End of bead. Car. Mag. × 9 times. Sq. 8/C, loc. 394, lev. + 7.9 ft.

Plate LXXXVI, b. Beads and Bead-drills. Chapter XIII

(1). (No. 4205). Perf. sh. Cr. Now 1.05 lg. Sq. 9/F, loc. 475, lev. + 0.6 ft.
(2). (No. 747). Cowrie. Perf. Cr. 1.51 lg. Trench D(1), lev. — 3.2 ft.
(3). (No. 67). Cowrie. Unperf. Pnk. dappled with yell. 1.9 lg. Trench C(1), lev. — 3.5 ft.
(4). (No. 1185). Cowrie. Unperf. Cr. 1.0 lg. Trench G(1), lev. — 4.1 ft.
(5). (No. 276). Cowrie. Unperf. Lt. yell. 1.02 lg. Trench E(2), lev. — 5.4 ft.
(6). (No. 4603). Sh. Perf. Cr. 1.01 lg. Cut., sq. 10/G, loc. 488, lev. — 1.4 ft.
(7). (No. 1417). Jhangar bead. Dk.-gr. clay, no slp. 1.57 di. × 1.62 lg. Sq. 8/E, loc. 93, lev. + 18.6 ft.
(8, a). (No. 3526, A). Drill. Bl. ch. 1.15 lg. × 0.11 di. Sq. 9/C, loc. 293, lev. + 7.0 ft.
(8, b). (No. 3551). Drill. Bl. ch. 0.74 lg. × 0.13 di. Sq. 8/c, loc. 450, lev. + 7.5 ft.
(8, c). (No. 3174). Drill. Bl. ch. 1.1 lg. × 0.12 di. Sq. 8/E, loc. 103, lev. + 7.9 ft.
(8, d). (No. 3448). Drill. Bl. ch. 1.05 lg. × 0.11 di. Sq. 8/D, loc. 108, lev. + 7.4 ft.
(8, e). (No. 3173). Drill. Bl. ch. 1.5 lg. × 0.12 di. Sq. 8/E, loc. 105, lev. + 7.6 ft.
(8, f). (No. 3172, A). Drill. Bl. ch. 1.23 lg. × 0.12 di. Sq. 8/E, loc. 141, lev. + 7.7 ft.
(8, g). (No. 3551, A). Drill. Bl. ch. 1.28 lg. × 0.11 di. Sq. 8/C, loc. 450, lev. + 7.7 ft.
(8, h). (No. 3172, B). Drill. Bl. ch. 0.73 lg. × 0.11 di. Sq. 8/E, loc. 141, lev. + 7.7 ft.
(8, i). (No. 259). Drill. Bl. ch. 0.58 lg. × 0.12 di. Trench D(1), loc. 31, lev. — 2.3 ft.
(9). Brought in by carrier. 3.3 long.
(10). (No. 117). Unfinished drill. Bl. ch. 1.5 lg. × 0.29 wde. × 0.22 th. Trench C(1), lev. — 5.7 ft.
(11). (No. 4739). Brick. End missing. 5.2 wde. × 2.32 th. Mound I, sq. 13/J, loc. 11, lev. + 13.3 ft.

Plate LXXXVII. Beads and Other Ornaments (Jhukar Culture). Chapter XIII

(1). (No. 3497). Bead-amulet. Hard st. Cr. 0.79 di. × 0.31 th. Cut., sq. 10/F, loc. 464, lev. + 2.5 ft.

(2). (No. 1267). Fai. Lt. gre. 1.02 lg. Sq. 8/D, loc. 84, lev. + 22.7 ft.
(3). (No. 3915). Fai. Wh. 1.02 lg. Cut., sq. 10/F, loc. 423, lev. + 3.8 ft.
(4). (No. 4218). Fai. Gr. 0.81 lg. Mound I, sq. 12/K, loc. 29, lev. + 15.6 ft.
(5). (No. 2005). Fai. Lt. gre. 0.88 lg. Sq. 9/C, loc. 190, lev. + 16.7 ft.
(6). (No. 1289). Fai. Lt. gre. 1.0 lg. Sq. 8/D, loc. 84, lev. + 21.2 ft.
(7). (No. 1718). Fai. Lt. gre. 1.47 lg. Sq. 9/D, loc. 95, lev. + 17.0 ft.
(7, a). (No. 1601). Fai. Lt. gre. 0.9 lg. Sq. 9/E, loc. 150, lev. + 16.7 ft.
(8). (No. 1284). Fai. Cr. 0.7 di. × 0.45 lg. Sq. 8/E, loc. 86, lev. + 23.4 ft.
(9). (No. 3833). Fai. Lt. gre. 0.73 di. × 0.57 lg. Cut., sq. 10/F, loc. 465, lev. + 2.3 ft.
(10). (No. 1274). Fai. Yell. gl. 0.8 di. × 0.58 lg. Sq. 7/E, loc. 88, lev. + 15.0 ft.
(11). (No. 1288). Gr. pot.; bl. slp. Polished. 1.6 lg. × 1.2 di. Sq. 8/D, loc. 89, lev. + 21.5 ft.
(12). (No. 1415). Gr. pot. 0.96 lg. × 1.32 di. Sq. 8/E, loc. 87, lev. + 17.6 ft.
(13). (No. 1445). Gr. pot. Semi-polished. 0.9 lg. × 1.22 di. Sq. 9/D, loc. 95, lev. + 19.4 ft.
(14). (No. 1906). Gr. pot.; bl. slp. 1.15 lg. × 1.35 di. Sq. 9/D, loc. 95, lev. + 14.7 ft.
(15). (No. 1577). Gr. pot. Polished surf. 2.1 lg. × 1.5 di. Sq. 8/E, loc. 86, lev. + 17.1 ft.
(16). (No. 1573). Gr. pot. 1.38 lg. × 1.02 di. Sq. 8/E, loc. 86, lev. + 17.5 ft.
(17). (No. 3039). Gr. pot. Semi-polished. 0.84 lg. × 1.05 di. Cut., sq. 10/F, loc. 377, lev. + 7.2 ft.
(18). (No. 3955). Gr. pot. 0.69 lg. × 0.82 di. Cut., sq. 10/F, loc. 471, lev. + 2.8 ft.
(19). (No. 1650). Dr. pot. 0.7 lg. × 1.3 di. Sq. 9/E, loc. 137, lev. + 16.6 ft.
(20). (No. 4227). Bead-amulet. Wh. steat. 0.78 di. × 0.38 th. Cut., sq. 10/F, loc. 484, lev. — 0.1 ft.
(21). (No. 2902). Gr. pot. 1.03 lg. × 1.18 di. Sq. 10/E, loc. 252, lev. + 7.2 ft.
(22). (No. 1417). Jhangar bead. Gr. pot. 1.62 lg. × 1.57 di. Sq. 8/E, loc. 93, lev. + 18.6 ft.
(23). (No. 1453). Bead-amulet. Fai. Lt. blu. 0.92 di. × 0.23 lg. Sq. 8/E, loc. 90, lev. + 16.8 ft.
(24). (No. 1268). Bead-amulet. Fai. Lt. gre. 1.8 di. (estimated) × 0.56 th. Sq. 8/F, loc. 83, lev. + 20.2 ft.

Plate LXXXVIII. Miscellaneous Objects. Chapter XIV

(1). (No. 2633). Bulla. Pot. Rd. slp. 1.5 di. × 0.22 th. Sq. 7/D, loc. 274, lev. + 9.6 ft.
(2). (No. 3779). Bulla. Pot. 1.36 di. × 0.22 th. Sq. 7/D, loc. 271, lev. + 6.7 ft.
(3). (No. 1895). Bulla. Pot. 1.23 di. × 0.2 th. Sq. 7/C, loc. 98, lev. + 12.0 ft.
(4). (No. 5320). Cone. Pot. 1.2 hi. × 0.95 di. Mound I, sq. 13/K, loc. 51, lev. + 12.6 ft.
(5). (No. 3907). Button. Pot. 1.8 di. × 0.7 th. Trench D(1), lev. — 0.7 ft.
(6). (No. 5408). Handle. Pot. 3.68 lg. × 2.67 wde. × 1.06 th. Cut., sq. 10/G, loc. 481, lev. — 20.5 ft.
(7). (No. 4196). Tube. Pot. 4.2 lg. × 1.22 di. Sq. 9/F, loc. 401, lev. + 8.2 ft.
(8). (No. 3374). Tube. Pot. 6.01 lg. × 2.0 di. Sq. 8/E, loc. 155, lev. + 11.5 ft.
(9). (No. 5405). Tube. Pot. 5.62 lg. × 2.03 di. Cut., sq. 10/G, loc. 477, lev. — 16.2 ft.
(10). (No. 4804). Tube. Pot. 3.25 lg. × 1.22 di. Cut., sq. 10/F, loc. 464, lev. + 1.3 ft.
(11). (No. 2012). Mould. Pot. 3.0 di. × 1.41 hi. Sq. 9/F, loc. 184, lev. + 13.0 ft.
(12). (No. 4238). Tube. Pot. 8.0 lg. × 1.22 di. Sq. 8/B, loc. 449, lev. + 7.6 ft.
(13). (No. 2517). Tube. Pot. 5.23 lg. × 2.91 di. Sq. 7/C, loc. 134, lev. + 11.6 ft.
(14). (No. 1991). Drain-pipe. Pot. 18.82 lg. × 6.36 di. Sq. 9/C, loc. 212, lev. + 11.2 ft.
(15). (No. 1991). Drain-pipe. Pot. 18.6 lg. × 7.2 di. Sq. 9/C, loc. 212, lev. + 11.2 ft.
(16). (No. 3464). Drain-pipe. Pot. 18.9 lg. × 5.64 di. Sq. 9/D, loc. 95, lev. + 9.5 ft.
(17). (No. 2720). Drain-pipe. Pot. 12.25 lg. × 5.29 di. Sq. 6/C, loc. 266, lev. + 8.5 ft.
(18). (No. 2236). Drain-pipe. Pot. 19.0 lg. × 6.4 di. Trench H(1), lev. — 10.8 ft.

Plate LXXXIX. Miscellaneous Objects. Chapter XIV

(1). (No. 2188). Amulet. Fai. 1.2 lg. × 0.8 wde. × 0.61 hi. Sq. 8/D, loc. 82, lev. + 13.4 ft.
(2). (No. 2936). Jar. Fai. Lt. gre. 1.5 hi. × 1.35 di. Sq. 9/E, loc. 224, lev. + 6.9 ft.

(3). (No. 1547). Model head-rest. Pot. 1.3 lg. × 1.2 wde. × 1.3 hi. Sq. 7/E, loc. 121, lev. + 16.1 ft.
(4). (No. 5029). Pedestal. Pot. 3.9 hi. × 7.43 di. Mound I, sq. 12/K, loc. 15, lev. + 14.0 ft.
(5). (No. 1618). Pin. Ivory. 1.7 lg. × 0.13 di. Sq. 9/E, loc. 123, lev. + 18.0 ft.
(6). (No. 4005). Pendant. Gr. steat. 1.14 lg. × 0.5 wde. × 0.3 th. Cut., sq. 10/F, loc. 421, lev. + 4.3 ft.
(7). (No. 2405). Peg. Ivory. 1.72 lg. × 0.55 di. Sq. 9/D, loc. 215, lev. + 9.3 ft.
(8). (No. 1278). Ring. Pot. 0.91 di. × 0.11 th. Trench E(1), loc. 33, lev. — 4.9 ft.
(9). (No. 4317). Weight. Ag. 1.28 di. × 0.11 hi. Cut., sq. 10/F, loc. 423, lev. + 0.15 ft.
(10). (No. 3822). Weight. Ag. 1.14 di. × 0.75 hi. 27.36 gms. Mound I, sq. 13/J, loc. 3, lev. + 15.8 ft.
(11). (No. 3882). Weight. Ag. 0.75 di. × 0.52 hi. Mound I, sq. 13/J, loc. 6, lev. + 16.4 ft.
(12). (No. 3488). Comb. Ivory. 1.79 lg. × 2.4 wde. × 0.2 th. Sq. 9/C, loc. 205, lev. + 7.1 ft.
(13). (No. 2626). Jar-stopper. Sh. 0.63 lg. × 0.88 di. Sq. 8/D, loc. 310, lev. + 10.1 ft.
(14). (No. 3409). Frag. of cover. Sh. 1.27 di. × 0.2 th. Sq. 8/D, loc. 281, lev. + 7.5 ft.
(15). (No. 2351). Object. Ivory. 1.59 lg. × 0.26 wde. × 0.34 th. Sq. 9/C, loc. 190, lev. + 10.5 ft.
(16). (No. 5198). Mace-head. Purp.-gr. sand. 4.1 di. × 0.77 th. Mound I, sq. 13/K, loc. 51, lev. + 12.8 ft.
(17). (No. 5219). Mace-head. Wh. lim. 3.78 di. × 1.21 th. Mound I, sq. 12/J, loc. 18, lev. + 13.3 ft.
(18). (No. 2003). Pendant. Sh. 2.45 lg. × 0.52 di. Sq. 9/F, loc. 184, lev. + 13.0 ft.
(19). (No. 5218). Mace-head. Wh. lim. 1.89 di. × 1.71 hi. Mound I, sq 12/K, loc. 38, lev. + 13.0 ft.
(20). (No. 4775). Mace-head. Cr. lim. 2.3 di. × 1.9 hi. Mound I, sq. 13/K, loc. 37, lev. + 13.1 ft.
(21). (No. 3693). Whetstone. Gre.-gr. st. 7.37 lg. × 0.53 wde. × 0.8 hi. Sq. 8/D, loc. 311, lev. + 7.1 ft.
(22). (No. 3684). Mace-head. Cr. lim. 2.09 di. × 1.71 hi. Sq. 8/C, loc. 394, lev. + 7.9 ft.
(23). (No. 1126). Mace-head. Gr. lim. 2.4 di. × 2.3 hi. Trench A(4), loc. 69, lev. — 5.3 ft.
(24). (No. 1860). Model axe. Pot. 2.21 lg. × 1.4 wde. × 0.3 th. Sq. 8/E, loc. 113, lev. + 11.6 ft.
(25). (No. 3608). Mace-head. Cr. lim. 1.81 di. × 1.61 hi. Trench H(1), loc. 51, lev. — 8.0 ft.
(26). (No. 2838). Mace-head. Cr. lim. 1.59 di. × 1.4 hi. Sq. 9/D, loc. 139, lev. + 8.4 ft.
(27). (No. 3721). Rubber. Dk. gr. st. 6.2 lg. × 2.38 wde. × 3.97 hi. Trench F(2), lev. — 3.6 ft.
(28). (No. 4537). Drill-head. Cr. lim. 2.41 di. × 1.9 hi. Sq. 7/E, loc. 121, lev. + 6.9 ft.
(29). (No. 3660). Mace-head. Cr. lim. Unfin. 1.51 di. × 1.64 hi. Trench G(1), lev. — 3.8 ft.
(30). (No. 3170). Model axe. Pot. 2.68 lg. × 1.77 wde. × 0.37 th. Sq. 8/F, loc. 418, lev. + 7.0 ft.

Plate XC. Miscellaneous Objects. Chapter XIV

(1). (No. 2991). Shell. Sq. 9/D, loc. 215, lev. + 9.3 ft.
(2). (No. 2408). Feeding-cup. Sh. 4.82 lg. × 0.67 wde. × 0.07 hi. Sq. 9/D, loc. 215, lev. + 9.4 ft.
(3). (No. 2973). Dish. Sh. 3.01 lg. × 2.77 wde. × 0.6 hi. Sq. 8/D, loc. 197, lev. + 8.9 ft.
(4). (No. 4359). Dish. Sh. 3.1 lg. × 2.18 wde. × 0.53 hi. Sq. 7/D, loc. 321, lev. + 7.1 ft.
(5). (No. 2587). Part of cone. Sh. Sq. 8/C, loc. 151, lev. + 10.2 ft.
(6). (No. 4308). Ladle. Sh. Unfin. 9.61 lg. × 6.11 wde. × 3.2 hi. Sq. 9/D, loc. 211, lev + 11.6 ft.
(7). (No. 4831). Inlay. Sh. 1.5 lg. × 0.11 wde. × 0.2 th. Mound I, sq. 13/J, loc. 5, lev. + 13.4 ft.
(8). (No. 4602). Inlay. Sh. 1.36 lg. × 0.1 wde. × 0.14 th. Mound I, sq. 13/J, loc. 5, lev + 14.2 ft.

(9). (No. 4366). Dish. Sh. 2.91 lg. × 2.14 wde. × 0.8 hi. Sq. 8/C, loc. 153, lev. + 6.9 ft.
(10). (No. 2624, A). Dish. Sh. 2.32 lg. × 2.27 wde. × 0.6 hi. Sq. 9/C, loc. 228, lev. + 10.1 ft.
(11). (No. 2587). Part of cone. Sh. Sq. 8/C, loc. 151, lev. + 10.2 ft.
(12). (No. 2587). Part of cone. Sh. Sq. 8/C, loc. 151, lev. + 10.2 ft.
(13). (No. 2453). Ladle. Sh. 1.23 lg. × 0.4 hi. Sq. 9/D, loc. 179, lev. + 9.8 ft.
(14). (No. 4698). Ladle. Sh. 2.51 lg. × 2.0 wde. × 0.7 hi. Mound I, sq. 13/J, loc. 11, lev. + 14.1 ft.
(15). (No. 2871). Bangles. Sh. Sq. 9/E, loc. 181, lev. + 8.0 ft.
(16). (No. 2379). Object. Sh. 3.41 lg. across. Sq. 9/C, loc. 228, lev. + 10.1 ft.
(17). (No. 4046). Ladle. Sh. Unfin. 3.2 lg. × 3.2 wde. × 0.98 hi. Sq. 9/E, loc. 171, lev. + 7.2 ft.
(18). (No. 2326, K). Object. Sh. 2.51 lg. × 0.75 wde. × 0.51 hi. Sq. 9/D, loc. 215, lev. + 10.3 ft.
(19). (No. 5450). Carved object. Sh. 2.37 hi. × 3.20 wde. Cut., sq. 10/G, loc. 481, lev. — 25.1 ft.
(20). The same.
(21). The same.
(22). (No. 3155). Dish. Sh. 5.71 lg. × 4.42 wde. × 1.9 hi. Sq. 8/E, loc. 103, lev. + 12.0 ft.
(23). (No. 3031). Paddle. Bone. Now 14.23 lg. × 2.22 wde. × 0.36 th. Sq. 7/F, loc. 110, lev. + 8.7 ft.
(24). (No. 4238). Tube. Pot. 8.0 lg. × 1.22 di. Sq. 8/B, loc. 449, lev. + 7.6 ft.
(25). (No. 4564). Tube. Pot. 7.1 lg. × 1.4 di. Sq. 8/D, loc. 89, lev. + 7.5 ft.
(26). (No. 1441). Bangle. Pot. 2.7 × 2.51 di. × 0.47 th. Sq. 7/E, loc. 88, lev. + 11.2 ft.
(27). (No. 1100). Bangle. Pot. 2.7 × 2.5 di. × 0.4 th. Trench F(1), lev. — 3.4 ft.
(28). (No. 967). Bangle. Pot. 2.3 di. × 0.34 th. Trench B(5), lev. — 4.9 ft.
(29). (No. 968). Bangle. Pot. 2.3 di. × 0.23 th. Trench B(5), lev. — 2.7 ft.
(30). (No. 2236). Drain-pipe. Pot. 19.0 lg. × 5.39-7.42 di. Trench H(1), lev. — 10.8 ft.
(31). (No. 2234). Drain-pipe. Pot. 19.5 lg. × 5.49-7.24 di. Trench H(1), lev. + 10.8 ft.
(32). (No. 2198). Drain-pipe. Pot. 16.7 lg. × 3.75-5.0 di. Sq. 8/C, loc. 226, lev. + 11.7 ft.
(33). (No. 2292). Drain-pipe. Pot. 16.75 lg. × 3.86-5.02 di. Sq. 9/D, loc. 216, lev. + 10.2 ft.
(34). (No. 3002). Bangle. Pot. 2.26 lg. × 2.7 di. Sq. 9/D, loc. 139, lev. + 9.1 ft.
(35). (No. 2007). Bangle. Fai. Cr. glaze. 2.3 across, 0.15 × 0.19 sect. Sq. 9/C, loc. 212, lev. + 11.7 ft.
(36). (No. 1974). Bangle. Fai. Lt. gre. 2.4 across, 0.14 × 0.18 sect. Sq. 8/D, loc. 129, lev. + 13.8 ft.
(37). (No. 2924). Bangle. Fai. Lt. blue. 2.05 across, 0.13 × 0.18 sect. Sq. 9/E, loc. 198, lev. + 6.8 ft.
(38). (No. 4429). Bangle. Fai. Lt. blu. 2.41 across, 0.29 × 0.4 sect. Mound I, sq. 12/K, loc. 15, lev. + 14.0 ft.
(39). (No. 3865). Bangle. Pot. 2.36 across, 0.25 × 0.28 sect. Trench H(1), loc. 53, lev. — 1.7 ft.
(40). (No. 1687). Bangle. Pot. Cr. slp. 2.41 across, 0.43 × 0.44 sect. Trench G(1), lev. — 4.2 ft.

Plate XCI. Miscellaneous Objects. Chapter XIV

(1). (No. 87). Table. Pot. 6.0 lg. × 3.56 wde. × 2.9 hi. Trench B(1), lev. — 4.7 ft.
(2). (No. 3740). Table. Pot. Cr. slp, dk. rd. pt. 2.61 lg. × 1.66 wde. × 1.09 hi. Sq. 7/C, loc. 98, lev. + 7.2 ft.
(3). (No. 2466). Ink-pot. Pot. 1.89 hi. × 1.68 × 1.75 sq. at top. Sq. 8/E, loc. 141, lev. + 9.8 ft.
(4). (No. 3488). Comb. Ivory. 1.79 lg. × 2.4 wde. × 0.2 th. Sq. 9/C, loc. 205, lev. + 7.1 ft.
(5). (No. 2457). Pulley. Bone. 3.5 lg. × 1.42-1.48 di. Sq. 10/E, loc. 230, lev. + 8.8 ft.
(6). (No. 998). Table. Pot. Cr. slp. Lt. rd. dec. 5.7 lg. × 4.19 wde. × 1.9 hi. Trench A(3), lev. — 3.7 ft.

(7). (No. 5316). Table. Pot. Cr. slp. Lt. rd. dec. 2.55 lg. × 1.5 wde. × 0.37 hi. Cut., sq. 9/F, loc. 469, lev. — 4.9 ft.
(8). (No. 5193). Table. Pot. Cr. slp. Dk. rd. dec. Now 5.93 lg. × 3.31 wde. × 1.42 hi. Cut., sq. 9/F, loc. 469, lev. — 8.5 ft.
(9). (No. 4844). Stopper. Pot. 1.56 lg. × 1.02 di. Cut., sq. 10/G, loc. 481, lev. — 2.2 ft.
(10). (No. 5408). Handle. Pot. 3.68 lg. × 2.67 wde. × 1.06 th. Cut., sq. 10/G, loc. 481, lev. — 20.5 ft.
(11). (No. 157). Plumb-bob. Yell. st. 2.0 lg. Trench B(1), lev. — 6.6 ft.
(12). (No. 3579). Cyl. Pas. 3.55 lg. × 1.52-1.58 di. Trench E(1), surface.
(13). (No. 355). Cyl. Pas. 3.0 lg. × 1.22 di. Trench C(2), lev. — 2.5 ft.
(14). (No. 5060). Door-socket. Brick. Now 4.7 × 3.42 × 2.57. Mound I, sq. 13/K, loc. 23, lev. + 14.1 ft.
(15). (No. 4971). Cut brick. 9.75 × 2.45 × 2.2. Sq. 7/F, loc. 147, lev. + 11.2 ft.
(16). (No. 3171). Net-sinker. Pot. 2.5 × 0.8 × 1.0. Sq. 8/F, loc. 115, lev. + 6.8 ft.
(17). (No. 4608). Runnel. Brick. 11.6 × 5.6 × 2.7. Sq. 9/F, loc. 410, lev. + 9.5 ft.
(18). (No. 4609). Runnel. Brick. 9.8 × 5.3 × 2.7. Sq. 8/F, loc. 414, lev. + 4.2 ft.
(19). (No. 1545). Gutter. Pot. 22.0 × 5.1 × 3.2. Trench H(1), loc. 51, lev. — 10.8 ft.
(20). (No. 4776). Cyl. Pas. Tr. gre. gl. 3.9 lg. × 1.69 di. Cut., sq. 9/F, loc. 428, lev. — 1.1 ft.
(21). (No. 1039). Plaque. Pas. 4.2 × 0.9 ×0.4. Trench D(1), lev. — 8.1 ft.
(22). (No. 1187). Plaque. Pas. 2.76 × 0.97 × 0.4. Trench G(1), lev. — 2.9 ft.
(23). (No. 881). Pebble weight. Dk. gr. st. 1.37 × 1.1 × 0.68. 27.19 gms. Trench G(1), loc. 49, lev. — 5.6 ft.
(24). (No. 1072). Pebble weight. Amphibole-schist. Wh. & Bl. 1.74 × 0.01 × 0.6. 30.28 gms. Trench G(1), loc. 49, lev. — 7.2 ft.
(25). (No. 3169). Pebble weight. Dk. gr.-gre. st. 1.4 × 0.9 × 0.8. 27.68 gms. Sq. 9/C, loc. 213, lev. — 4.7 ft.
(26). (No. 1095). Pebble weight. Amphibole-schist. Wh. & bl. 1.3 × 1.06 × 0.58. 21.39 gms. Trench F(2), loc. 65, lev. — 4.7 ft.
(27). (No. 2016). Weight. Rd. quartzite. 2.11 hi. × 2.25 di. 273.59 gms. Sq. 9/F, loc. 187, lev. + 12.7 ft.
(28). (No. 2075). Weight. Gr. san. 2.4 hi. × 2.84 di. 544.77 gms. Sq. 8/E, loc. 92, lev. + 17.0 ft.
(29). (No. 3189). Weight. Ch. 1.0 × 0.98 × 0.76. 27.53 gms. Sq. 8/E, loc. 280, lev. + 7.0 ft.
(30). (No. 2760). Weight. Ag. 1.0 × 1.0 × 0.77. 27.66 gms. Sq. 8/F, loc. 115, lev. + 8.8 ft.
(31). (No. 2867). Weight. Ch. 1.11 × 1.11 ×0.6. 27.14 gms. Sq. 9/E, loc. 127, lev. + 8.3 ft.
(32). (No. 3164). Weight. Ag. 0.9 × 0.9 × 0.9. 27.34 gms. Sq. 6/E, loc. 431, lev. + 10.1 ft.
(33). (No. 1496). Curry-stone. Br.-gr. san. 18.7 × 7.2 × 6.0. Trench A(3), loc. 36, lev. — 3.4 ft.
(34). (No. 4335). Palette. Dk. br. st. 4.91 × 1.9 × 0.23. Cut., sq. 9/F, loc. 408, lev. + 0.9 ft.
(35). (No. 2012). Mould. Pot. 1.41 hi. × 3.0 di. Sq. 9/F, loc. 184, lev. + 13.0 ft.
(36). (No. 3563). Hone. Purp.-gr. san. 4.99 × 1.62 × 1.11. Sq. 8/C, loc. 393, lev. + 7.3 ft.
(37). (No. 3278). Hone. Cr.-col. san. 4.59 × 1.76 × 0.82. Sq. 9/F, loc. 184, lev. + 10.7 ft.
(38). (No. 2157). Hone. Dk. gr. st. 4.4 × 2.0 × 1.08. Sq. 8/F, loc. 145, lev. + 11.9 ft.
(39). (No. 714). Hone. Purp. san. 5.87 × 2.4 × 1.63. Trench D(1), lev. — 2.6 ft.
(40). (No. 1496). Curry-stone. Br.-gr. 18.7 × 7.2 × 6.0. Trench A(3), loc. 36, lev. — 3.4 ft.
(41). (No. 2158). Rubber. Br. ch. 3.61 × 1.81 × 1.61. Sq. 8/E, loc. 90, lev. + 13.1 ft.
(42). (No. 3187). Palette. Lt. yell. st. Now 4.08 × 1.63 × 0.3. Sq. 8/E, loc. 280, lev. + 7.0 ft.
(43). (No. 1122). Palette. Yell.-br. st. 4.21 × 1.54 × 0.5. Trench J(1), loc. 79, lev. — 2.5 ft.
(44). (No. 5095). Hone. Dk. gr. san. 9.28 × 2.72 × 1.2. Cut., sq. 10/G, loc. 481, lev. — 2.2 ft.
(45). (No. 4754). Round st. Ch.-lim. 5.22 hi. × 15.4 di. Mound I, sq. 12/K, loc. 15, lev. + 14.0 ft.
(46). (No. 4544). Round st. Ch.-lim. 6.5 hi. × 12.62 di. Sq. 9/F, loc. 419, lev. + 4.6 ft.

(47). (No. 1139). Rolling-pin. Pot. 4.29 lg. × 1.29 di. Trench G(1), lev. — 2.9 ft.
(48). (No. 1140). Rolling-pin. Pot. 3.3 lg. × 1.1 di. Trench G(1), loc. 49, lev. — 2.9 ft.
(49). (No. 1056). Rolling-pin. Pot. 3.18 lg. × 1.47 di. Trench A(3), loc. 35, lev. — 5.9 ft.

Plate XCII. Miscellaneous Objects. Chapter XIV

(1). (No. 4450). Bricks forming water-chute. 10.75 × 4.75 × 2.5 & 11 × 5.5 × 2.25. Sq. 10/D, loc. 246, lev. + 7.0 ft.
(2). (No. 135). Drill-head. Wh. ch.-lim. 1.5 hi. × 1.71 di. Trench A(1), lev. — 5.5 ft.
(3). (No. 4687). Drill-head. Hard st. Bl. & wh. 2.13 hi. × 1.13 di. Sq. 9/C, loc. 206, lev. + 6.8 ft.
(4). (No. 4383). Whorl. Pot. 1.5 di. × 0.52 th. Cut., sq. 10/F, loc. 421, lev. + 0.5 ft.
(5). (No. 4222). Whorl. Pot. 1.51 di. × 0.63 th. Cut., sq. 9/F, loc. 474, lev. + 0.8 ft.
(6). (No. 5048). Bobbin. Pot. 1.9 di. × 0.7 th. Cut., sq. 9/F, loc. 409, lev. + 0.5 ft.
(7). (No. 5071). Whorl. Pot. 2.01 di. × 0.8 th. Mound I, sq. 13/K, loc. 34, lev. + 14.2 ft.
(8). (No. 4021). Cut brick. 5.73 × 5.36 × 2.5. Sq. 9/F, loc. 406, lev. + 8.0 ft.
(9). (No. 4367). Net-weight. Pot. 3.1 × 2.75 × 1.32. Sq. 8/B, loc. 235, lev. + 7.7 ft.
(10). (No. 4990). Drill-socket. Hard cr. col. st. 1.82 di. × 0.93 hi. Cut., sq. 10/F, loc. 421, lev. + 0.5 ft.
(11). (No. 4872). Mace-head. Unfin. Ch.-lim. 2.6 di. × 1.95 hi. Mound I, sq. 12/J, loc. 16, lev. + 18.3 ft.
(12). (No. 3128). Rubber. Ch.-lim. 2.72 di. × 3.7 hi. Sq. 9/E, loc. 173, lev. + 13.0 ft.
(13). (No. 4589). Pedestal. Dk. rd. san. 2.03 hi. × 1.22 × 1.22 at base. Mound I, sq. 13/J, loc. 2, lev. + 14.3 ft.
(14). (No. 4565). Net-weight. Pot. 2.6 × 1.5 × 0.9. Sq. 7/C, loc. 463, lev. + 6.4 ft.
(15). (No. 4984). Triangular plaque. Purp. san. 2.93 lg. × 1.18 th. Sq. 8/F, loc. 83, lev. + 11.4 ft.
(16). (No. 3144). Rubber. Dk. br. san. 2.07 hi. × 2.03 di. Sq. 9/E, loc. 161, lev. + 14.2 ft.
(17). (No. 2377). Coiled object. Pot. 1.4 across × 0.38 th. Sq. 9/D, loc. 264, lev. + 10.0 ft.
(18). (No. 3500). Round plaque. Pot. 3.76 di. × 2.1 th. Sq. 9/D, loc. 287, lev. + 7.1 ft.
(19). (No. 188). Pestle. Dk. gr. igneous st. 4.72 hi. × 2.86 di. Trench B(2), loc. 22, lev. — 5.3 ft.
(20). (No. 5030). Grating. Pot. Now 5.8 lg. × 3.7 wde. × 0.71 th. Mound I, sq. 12/K, loc. 26, lev. + 14.0 ft.
(21). (No. 3588). Triangular plaque. Pot. 2.53 lg. × 0.78 th. Trench E(1), lev. — 4.8 ft.
(22). (No. 1308). Round stone. Gr.-br. col. 11.85 di. × 4.51 hi. Trench H(1), loc. 51, lev. — 4.4 ft.
(23). (No. 4541). Round plaque. Pot. 2.9 di. × 0.42 th. Sq. 9/E, loc. 111, lev. + 7.2 ft.
(24). (No. 2308). Jar-cover(?). Pot. 2.7 di. × 1.72 hi. Sq. 8/C, loc. 170, lev. + 11.9 ft.
(25). (No. 1357). Spoon. Pot. 4.6 lg. × 2.89 wde. Sq. 8/F, loc. 83, lev. + 13.5 ft.
(26). (No. 4521). Triangular plaque. Pot. 4.7 lg. × 1.09 th. Sq. 9/F, loc. 258, lev. + 8.5 ft.
(27). (No. 2690). Stick. Rd. oxide. Now 1.75 lg. × 0.58 × 0.39. Sq. 8/D, loc. 176, lev. + 11.2 ft.
(28). (No. 1963). Awl. Bone. 4.37 lg. Sq. 9/D, loc. 106, lev. + 14.9 ft.
(29). (No. 2079). Awl. Bone. 4.08 lg. × 0.47 wde. × 0.36 th. Sq. 9/E, loc. 181, lev. + 13.1 ft.
(30). (No. 1962). Awl. Bone. 3.73 lg. Sq. 9/D, loc. 130, lev. + 15.0 ft.
(31). (No. 2018). Awl. Bone. 3.4 lg. × 0.45 wde. × 0.31 th. Sq. 9/D, loc. 106, lev. + 13.5 ft.
(32). (No. 2052). Awl. Bone. 3.3 lg. × 0.31 wde. × 0.28 th. Sq. 8/D, loc. 89, lev. + 12.3 ft.
(33). (No. 1394). Awl. Bone. 3.0 lg. × 0.5 wde. × 0.35 th. Sq. 9/D, loc. 95, lev. + 19.3 ft.
(34). (No. 4310). Cut brick. 10.85 lg. × 5.4 hi. × 2.5 th. Sq. 7/C, loc. 134, lev. + 6.9 ft.
(35). (No. 2027). Unknown object. Pot. Cr. slp. 2.4 lg. 2.2 hi. × 1.03 wde. Sq. 8/D, loc. 138, lev. + 15.1 ft.
(36). (No. 5029). Pedestal. Pot. No slp. 7.43 di. × 3.9 hi. Mound I, sq. 12/K, loc. 15, lev. + 14.0 ft.

(37). (No. 1550). Unknown object. Pot. Cr. slp. 4.05 lg. × 1.4 wde. × 0.73 th. Sq. 7/C, loc. 134, lev. + 16.1 ft.

(38). (No. 3498). Head-rest. Pot. Purp.-bl. pt. on cherry rd. slp. 12.3 lg. × 7.1 hi. × 1.6-2.4 th. Cut., sq. 10/F, loc. 465, lev. + 2.9 ft.

Plate XCIII. Miscellaneous Objects. Chapter XIV

(1). (No. 2326, E). Lump of wh., trans. cry. 2.0 lg. Sq. 9/D, loc. 215, lev. + 10.4 ft.

(2). (No. 2865). Lump of Ameth. 1.9 × 1.5 × 1.3. Sq. 9/E, loc. 124, lev. + 9.9 ft.

(3). (No. 2381). Lump of Car. 1.92 lg. Sq. 7/C, loc. 237, lev. + 11.0 ft.

(4). (No. 2189). Lump of Car. 2.9 lg. Sq. 9/D, loc. 139, lev. + 11.6 ft.

(5). (No. 2391, B). Mass of beads. Wh. steat. Sq. 9/D, loc. 215, lev. + 9.4 ft.

(6). (No. 2326, F). Drill. Lt. gr. ch. 2.43 lg. × 0.4 wde. Sq. 9/D, loc. 215, lev. + 10.4 ft.

(7). (No. 2941). Drill. Lt. gr. ch. 1.4 lg. × 0.4 wde. × 0.14 th. Sq. 9/E, loc. 85, lev. + 7.4 ft.

(8). (No. 2957). Drill. Lt. br. ch. 1.5 lg. × 0.4 wde. × 0.12 th. Sq. 9/F, loc. 255, lev. + 6.9 ft.

(9). (No. 3564). Bead-hone. Lt. gr. san. 9.01 lg. × 3.95 wde. × 0.2 th. Sq. 8/C, loc. 393, lev. + 7.3 ft.

(No. 2496). Bead. Car. Unfin. 2.48 lg. × 0.39 di. Sq. 9/C, loc. 208, lev. + 9.7 ft.

(10). (No. 4728). Bead-hone. Dk. gr. san. 12.25 lg. × 4.2 wde. × 3.6 th. Sq. 8/D, loc. 178, lev. + 11.1 ft.

(11). (No. 3013). Bead-hone. Dk. gr. san. 9.45 lg. × 4.03 hi. Sq. 9/C, loc. 208, lev. + 9.7 ft.

(12). (No. 4226, A). Bead-tool. Cop. or Br. 1.9 lg. × 0.2-0.29 di. See Pl. LXXX, 1. Sq. 9/F, loc. 468, lev. + 1.3 ft.

(13). (No. 4226, B). Bead-tool. Cop. or br. 1.65 lg. × 0.2-0.3 di. Weighted at end by flange 0.19 lg. × 0.3 di. Point 0.1 di. Sq. 9/F, loc. 468, lev. + 1.3 ft.

(14, e). (No. 2479). Unfin. bead. Ag. Yell. mottled with br. 3.06 lg. × 0.69 wde. × 0.66 th. Ends show cortex. Sq. 9/F, loc. 184, lev. + 10.2 ft.

(14, d). (No. 3084). Unfin. bead. Ag. Yell. 2.87 lg. × 0.4 wde. × 0.39 th. Sq. 9/E, loc. 150, lev. + 7.3 ft.

(14, c). (No. 2857). Unfin. bead. Ag. Yell. 3.63 lg. × 0.4 wde. × 0.35 th. Sq. 6/F, loc. 160, lev. + 8.4 ft.

(14, b). (No. 249). Unfin. bead. Ag. Yell. 3.0 lg. × 0.4 di. Trench D(1), loc. 31, lev. — 2.3 ft.

(14, a). (No. 2673). Bead. Car. Clear rd. 2.27 lg. × 0.41 di. Sq. 9/E, loc. 131, lev. + 8.2 ft.

(15). (No. 1561). Bead-hone. Dk. gr. san. 3.2 lg. × 2.4 wde. × 1.31 th. Sq. 7/E, loc. 120, lev. +13.5 ft.

(16). (No. 3151). Bead-hone. Dk. gr. san. 9.6 lg. Sq. 7/F, loc. 439, lev. + 7.5 ft.

(17). (No. 2326, U). Car. nodule. 3.6 lg. Sq. 9/D, loc. 215, lev. + 10.4 ft.

(18). Same number and position.

(19). Same number and position.

(20). Same number and position.

(21). (No. 2128). Fossil shell. Cr. col. ch.-lim. 2.71 lg. Sq. 8/F, loc. 83, lev. + 16.3 ft.

(22). (No. 4619). Fossil shell. Dk. gr. st. 1.63 lg. Mound I, sq. 13/K, loc. 12, lev. + 16.2 ft.

(23). (No. 3844). Fossil shell. Cr. col. ch. 2.13 lg. × 2.02 di. Cut., sq. 10/F, loc. 465, lev. + 2.4 ft.

(24). (No. 918). Ribbon flake. Lt. gr. ch. 4.6 × 0.6 × 0.28. Trench B(3), lev. — 4.2 ft.

(25). (No. 1031). Ribbon flake. Gr.-br. ch. 4.7 × 0.58 × 0.19. Trench F(1), lev. — 5.1 ft.

(26). (No. 804). Ribbon-flake. Lt. gr. ch. 5.0 × 0.5 × 0.21. Trench B(5), lev. — 3.2 ft.

(27). (No. 3162). Saw. Lt. gr. ch. 4.07 × 0.6 × 0.11. Sq. 8/F, loc. 115, lev. + 6.4 ft.

(28). (No. 3012). Core as burnisher. Gr. ch. 3.68 × 1.3 × 0.9. Sq. 9/D, loc. 215, lev. + 6.4 ft.

(29). (No. 2862, A). Core. Lt. br. ch. 3.27 × 1.09 × 0.46. Sq. 9/E, loc. 96, lev. + 8.4 ft.

(30). (No. 2178). Frag. of dish. Dk. gr. steat. 2.55 lg. × 0.23 th. Sq. 8/E, loc. 104, lev. + 12.5 ft.

(31). Bali girl carrying food-stand upon her head.

(32). (No. 4950). Mace-head. Wh. lim. 2.2 di. × 0.97 hi. Cut., loc. 407, lev. + 0.6 ft.
(33). (No. 2693). Mace-head. Lt. gr. lim. 3.88 di. × 1.28 hi. Sq. 9/C, loc. 228, lev. + 10.8 ft.
(34). (No. 2972). Mace-head. Dk. gre. st. 3.88 di. × 1.1 hi. Sq. 9/E, loc. 201, lev. + 9.6 ft.
(35). (No. 1126). Mace-head. Lt. gr. lim. 2.4 di. × 2.3 hi. Trench A(4), loc. 69, lev. — 5.3 ft.
(36). (No. 5198). Mace-head. Purp.-gre. san. 4.1 di. × 0.77 hi. Mound I, sq. 13/K, loc. 51, level + 12.8 ft.

Plate XCIV. Skull Burial (Harappā Culture). Chapter XVI

(1-3). Views of jar containing skull copper and bronze implements, and conch shell. Mound II, square 7/E, loc. 324, lev. + 9.2 feet. [E. M.]

Plate XCV. Skull Burial (Harappā Culture). Chapter XVI

(4). Right lateral view of skull as received for study. [W. H. S.]
(5-9). Photographs of skull in facial, left lateral, vertical, ocipital, and basilar views. [W. H. S.]

Plate XCVI. Skull Burial (Harappā Culture). Chapter XVI

(10-12). Craniographic drawings in facial left lateral, and vertical views. [W. M. K.]

INDEX

PLATES

PLATE I

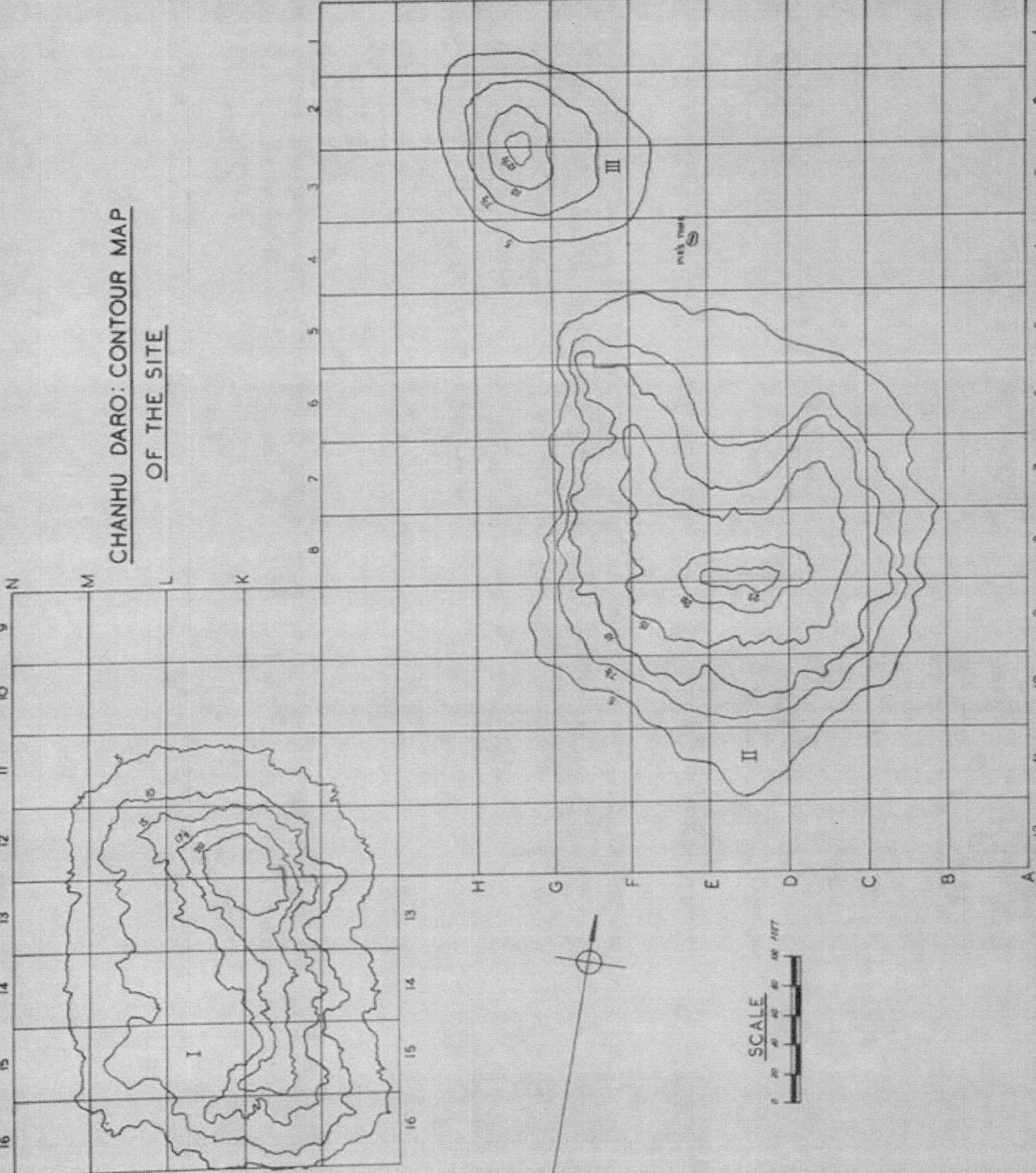

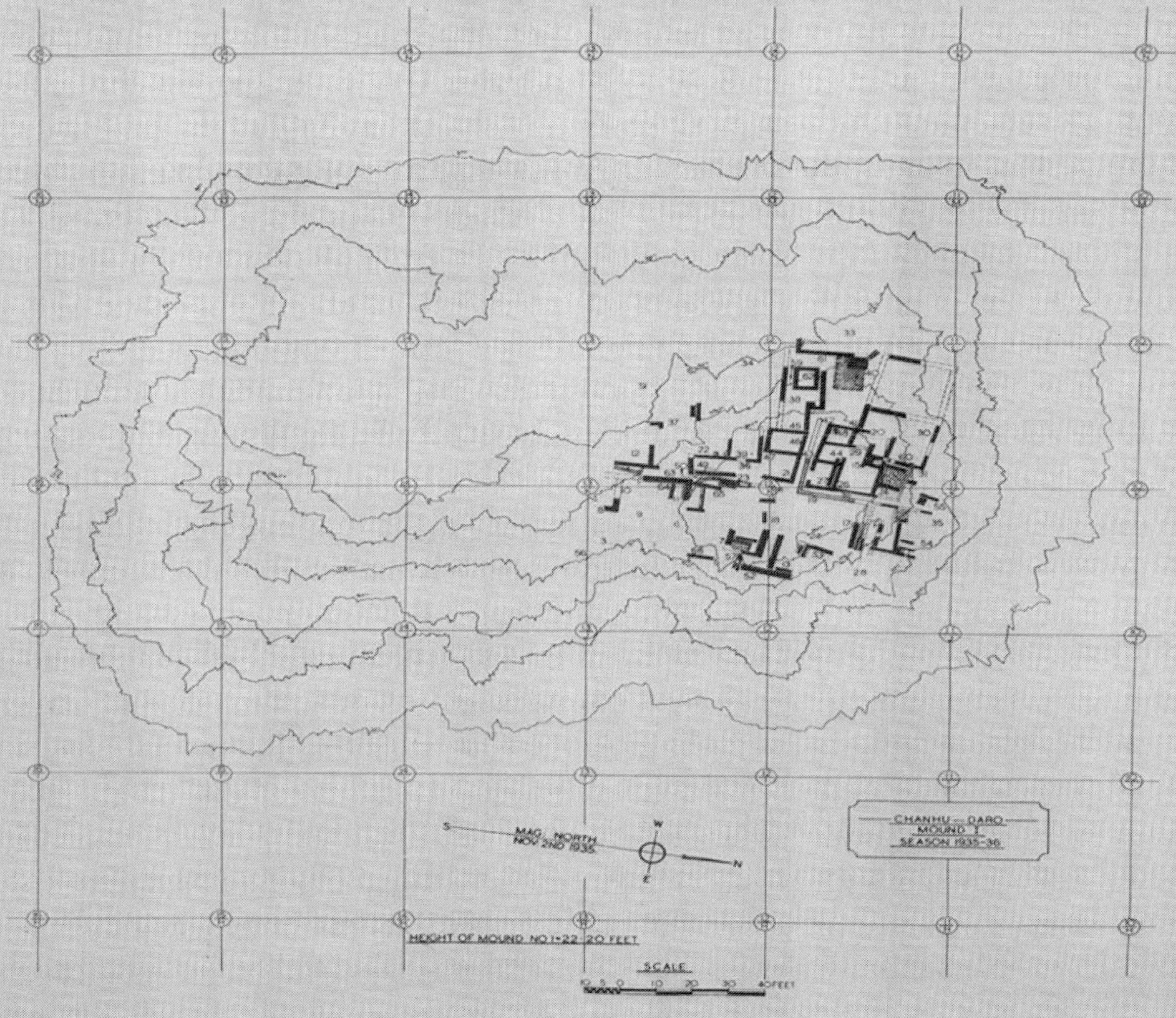
CHANHU – DARO
MOUND I
SEASON 1935–36
MAG. NORTH
NOV 2ND 1935
S
N
W
E
HEIGHT OF MOUND NO I = 22·20 FEET
SCALE
10 5 0 10 20 30 40 FEET

CHANHU-DARO: MOUNDS II AND III

PLATE III

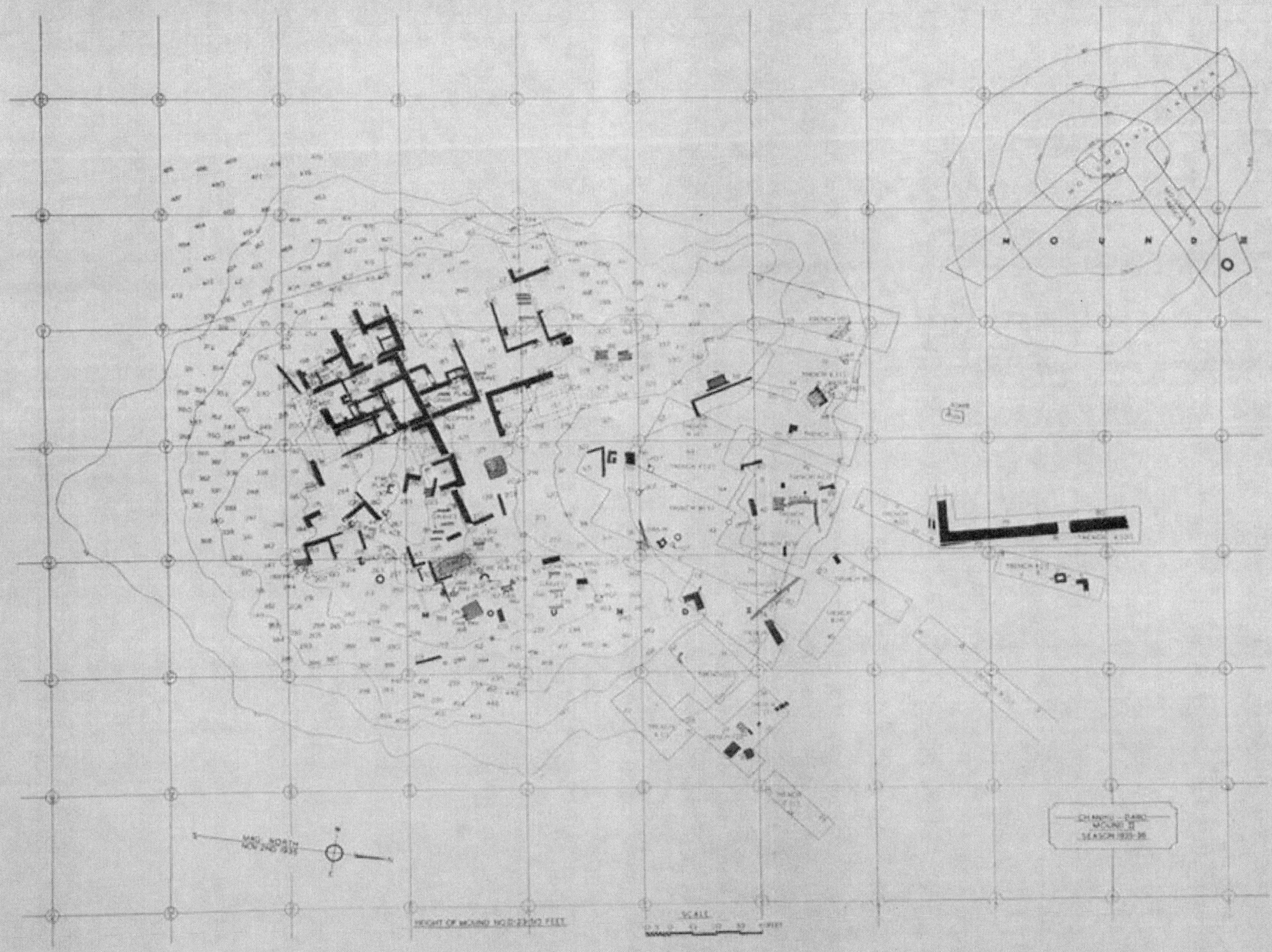

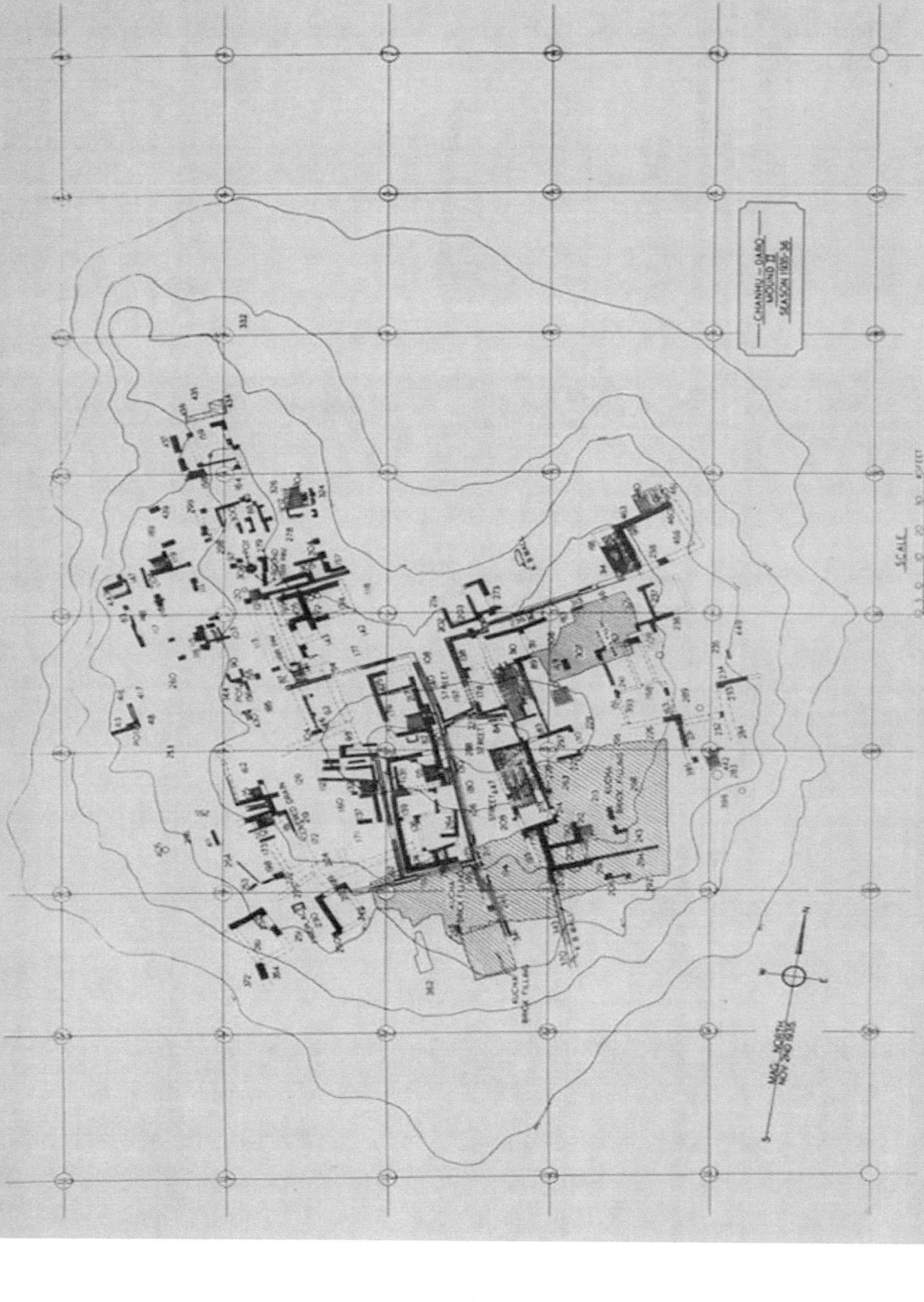

CHANHU-DARO: SECTIONS OF MOUND II

PLATE V

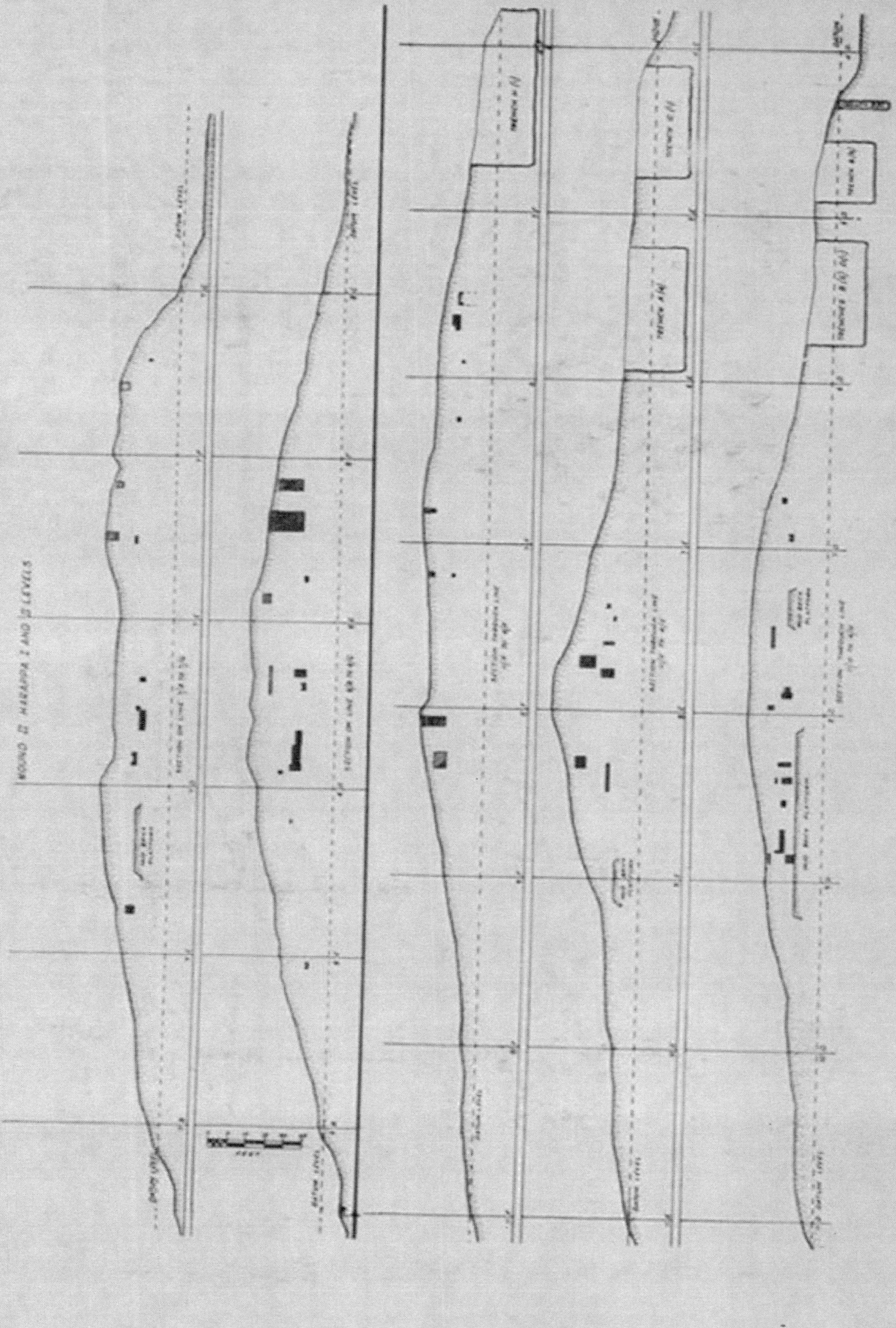

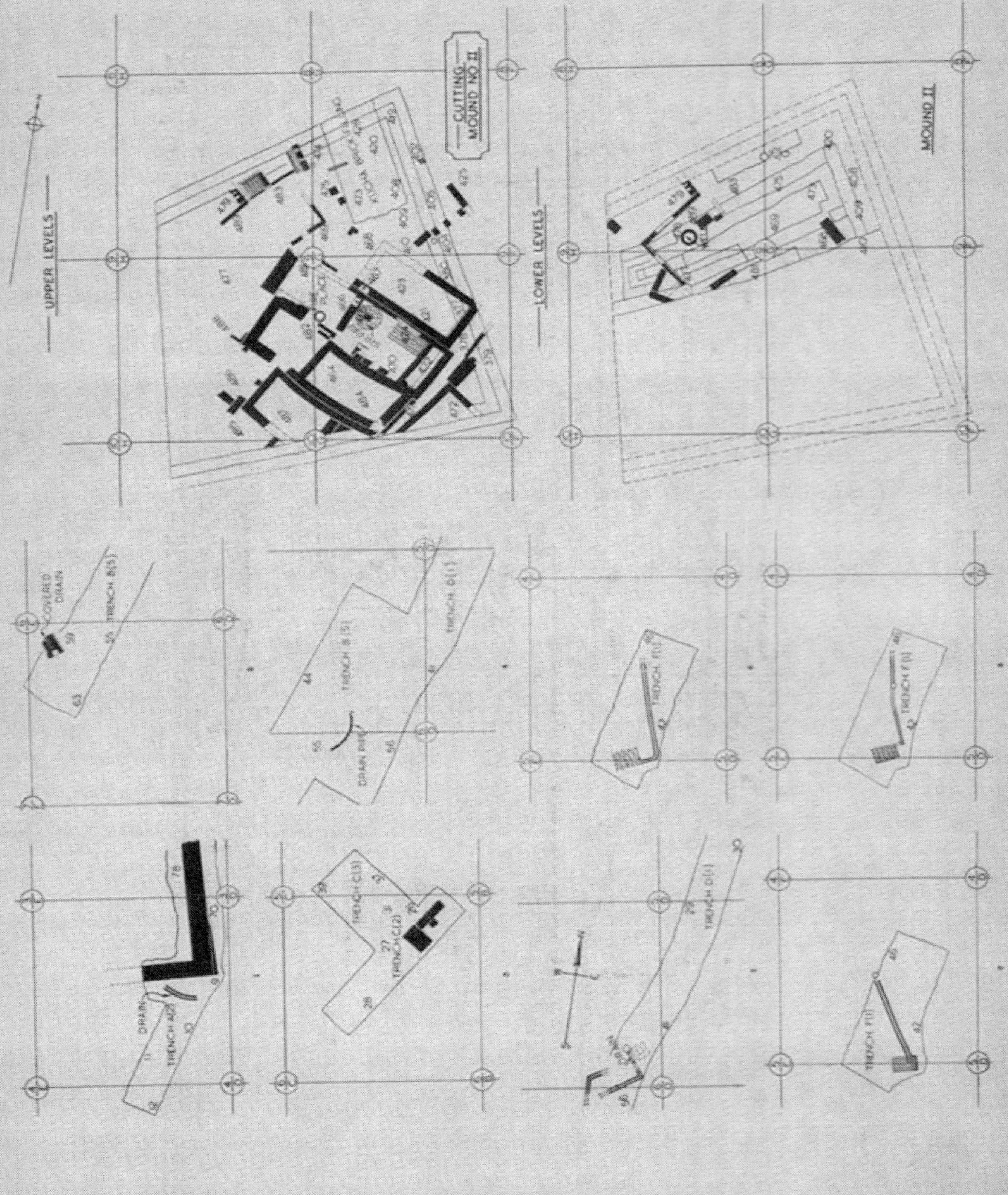
UPPER LEVELS
CUTTING
MOUND NO II
LOWER LEVELS
MOUND II
COVERED DRAIN
TRENCH B(5)
TRENCH D(1)
DRAIN
TRENCH C(3)
TRENCH C(2)
TRENCH F(1)

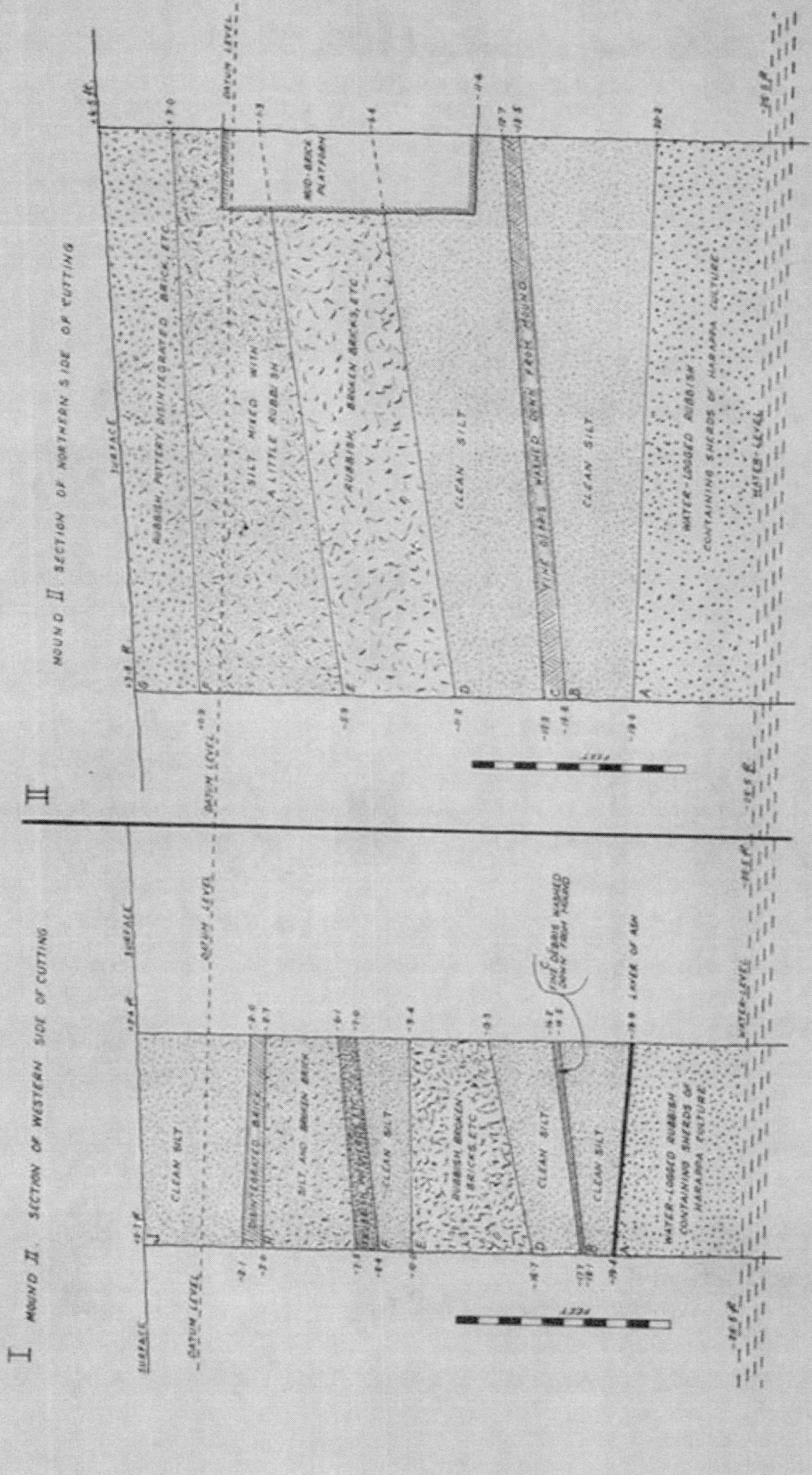
I
MOUND II. SECTION OF WESTERN SIDE OF CUTTING
SURFACE
DATUM LEVEL
CLEAN SILT
DISINTEGRATED BRICK
SILT AND BROKEN BRICK
CLEAN SILT
RUBBISH BROKEN BRICKS, ETC.
CLEAN SILT
FINE DÉBRIS WASHED DOWN FROM MOUND
CLEAN SILT
LAYER OF ASH
WATER-LOGGED RUBBISH CONTAINING SHERDS OF HARAPPA CULTURE
WATER-LEVEL
FEET
II
MOUND II SECTION OF NORTHERN SIDE OF CUTTING
SURFACE
DATUM LEVEL
RUBBISH, POTTERY, DISINTEGRATED BRICK, ETC.
SILT MIXED WITH A LITTLE RUBBISH
RUBBISH, BROKEN BRICKS, ETC.
MUD-BRICK PLATFORM
CLEAN SILT
FINE DÉBRIS WASHED DOWN FROM MOUND
CLEAN SILT
WATER-LOGGED RUBBISH CONTAINING SHERDS OF HARAPPA CULTURE
WATER-LEVEL
FEET

CHANHU-DARO: MOUND II, FURNACE PLATE VIII

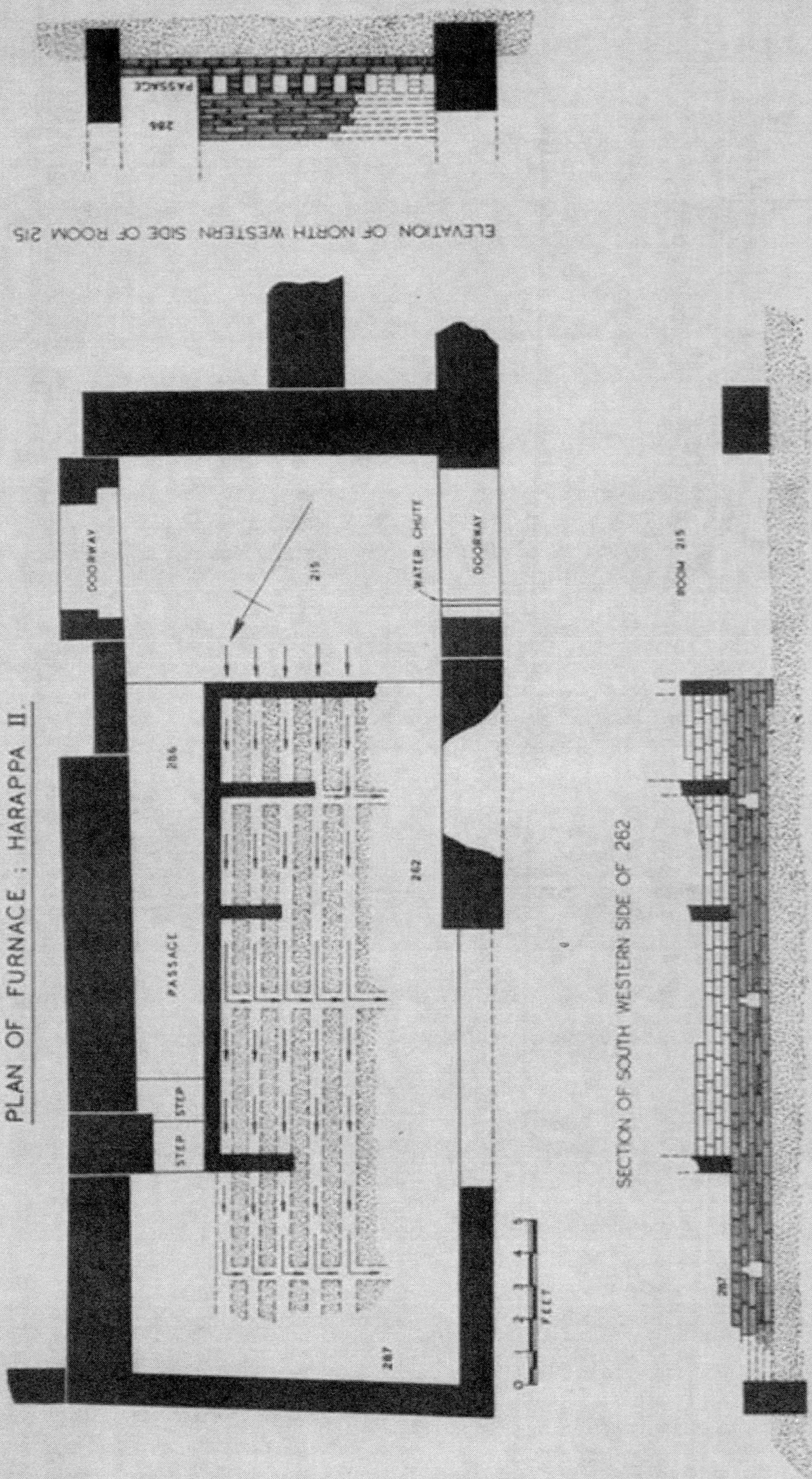

(a) Mound II, from north-north-west.

(b) Mound II, from south.

(c) Mound II, from north-west.

(d) Mound II, from north-east.

(e) Mound III, from Pir's tomb in foreground, from east.

(f) Mound I, from north-east.

(a) Trench F(1), from north-east.

(b) Trench H(1), from north.

(c) Trench A(1), showing great wall, from south.

(d) Trench A(1), great wall, from north.

(a) Early stages in trenching, from south.

(b) Trench B(5), from north-east.

(c) Trench E(1), from north-north-west.

(d) Trench B(5), from east.

(e) Trench F(1), from south.

(f) Trench F(1), from north.

(a) Work in progress in Cutting, from north-east.

(b) Cutting, showing Harappā IV masonry on left, from west.

(c) Harappā III masonry in upper part of Cutting, from south.

(d) Southern end of Cutting, from south-west. Well in foreground.

(e) Harappā III masonry in upper levels of Cutting, from west.

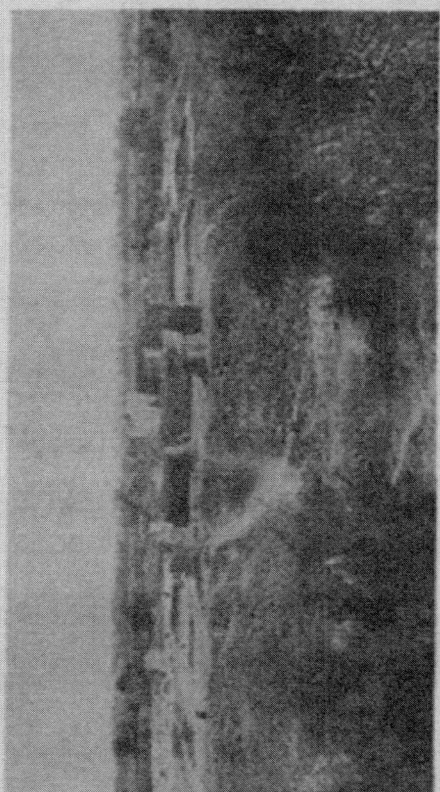

(a) Harappā I occupation, from north-west.

(b) Harappā I occupation (fully cleared), from north-west.

(c) Harappā II occupation (partially cleared), from north-west.

(d) Harappā II occupation (fully cleared), from north-west.

(a) Harappā I occupation, from south-west.

(b) Harappā II occupation, from south-west.

(c) Harappā II occupation (fully cleared), from south-west.

(a) Buildings of Harappā I occupation, from north-east.

(b) Buildings of Harappā II occupation, from north-east.

(a) Mound II. Sq. 9/B, from west. Pan at locus 442. Harappā II level.

(b) Mound II. Sq. 8/C, from east. Jhukar fire-place at locus 307.

(c) Mound II. Sq. 9/E, from south-south-east. Jar and drain at locus 181. Harappā II level.

(d) Mound II. Cutting, sq. 10/F, from north-west. Tusk in room 470. Harappā III level.

(e) Mound II. Sq. 9/C, from north-west. Drain-pipes at locus 212. Harappā II level.

(f) Mound II. Sq. 7/E, from east. End of drain at locus 157. Harappā II level.

(g) Mound I. Sq. 12/J, from south. Circular bin at locus 54.

(h) Mound II. Sq. 7/E, from north. Circular pavement at locus 306. Harappā II level.

(a) Sq. 8/E, from south-south-east. Drainage jar at locus 87. Harappā II level.

(b) Sq. 8/D, from south-west. Drainage jar at locus 84. Harappā II level.

(c) Sq. 7/C, from west. Drainage jar at locus 98. Harappā I.

(d) Sq. 8/D, from north-west. Late burial (No. 83).

(e) Sq. 8/D, from north-west. Late burial (No. 83) with covering removed.

(f) Sq. 8/E, from north-east. Fireplace of Jhukar period in room 91.

(g) Sq. 7/E, from east. Drainage jar containing skull at locus 324. Harappā II level.

(h) Sq. 7/E, from south-east. Skull and shell in jar. Harappā II level.

(i) Sq. 9/D, from south-west. Drainage jars at locus 209. Harappā II level.

(a) Sqs. 9/D, 9/E, 10/D, with locus 246 in foreground, from east-south-east, Harappā I and II levels.

(b) Sqs. 8/D, 8/E, loci 86, 140 in foreground, from south-east. Harappā I buildings.

(c) Sq. 8/E, from north. Entrance to room 104, Harappā I level.

(d) Sq. 8/D, from east-south-east. Harappā I structures at back, Harappā II buildings and drain in foreground.

(e) Sq. 9/E, from south-west. Pavements of rooms 220, 221 in foreground. Harappā I.

(f) Sqs. 8/D, 9/D, loci 106, 180, from north-east. Harappā I and II occupations.

(a) Sqs. 8/C, 8/D, from west-south-west, Jhukar pavements in background.

(b) Sq. 8/E, from north. Harappā I rooms 142, 143, in foreground.

(c) Sq. 9/E, from south-west. Room 219, before final clearance in foreground. Harappā I.

(d) Sqs. 7/E, 8/E, from south-west. Rooms 125, 162 (partially cleared) in foreground. Harappā I.

(e) Sq. 9/D, from north-north-east. Junction of drains at locus 211 Harappā II.

(f) Sq. 9/E, from west-north-west. Pavement at locus 125 in foreground. Harappā II.

(a) Sq. 7/E, from north-east. Privy and drain at locus 121.

(b) Sq. 7/E, from north-west. Stairway outside room 88.

(c) Sq. 9/E, from north-west. Furnace in main street.

(d) Sq. 9/E, from south-west. Furnace in main street.

(e) Sqs. 8/D, 9/D, from east-south-east. Room 183 in foreground.

(f) Sq. 9/D, from east. Privy in room 95.

(a) Sq. 7/C, from north-north-east. Pavement at locus 240 in foreground. Walls of Harappā I level at back.

(b) Sqs. 7/D, 8/D, from west. Room 203 in foreground.

(c) Sq. 9/C, from south-south-east. Dump in distance.

(d) Sq. 9/D, from south-west. Corner of building at locus 192.

(e) Sqs. 8/D, 8/F, from north-west. Main street.

(f) Sqs. 9/D, 10/D, from south-east. Main street.

(a) Mound I. View of excavations, from north-east. Locus 25 in foreground.

(b) Mound I. Northern side of excavations, from east. Locus 54 in foreground.

(c) Mound I. Southern side of excavations, from south-south-east. Room 64 in foreground.

(d) Mound I. Unusual masonry in room 39, from west.

(e) Mound I. South-eastern side of excavations, from south-south-west. Loci 4, 66 in foreground.

(f) Mound I. Northern side of excavations, from north-north-west. Loci 31, 35, 54, 55, in foreground.

1

2

3

4

5

6

Painted by Nina de Garis Davies and Suzanne E. Chapman

STORAGE JARS: HARAPPĀ CULTURE

PLATE XXIV

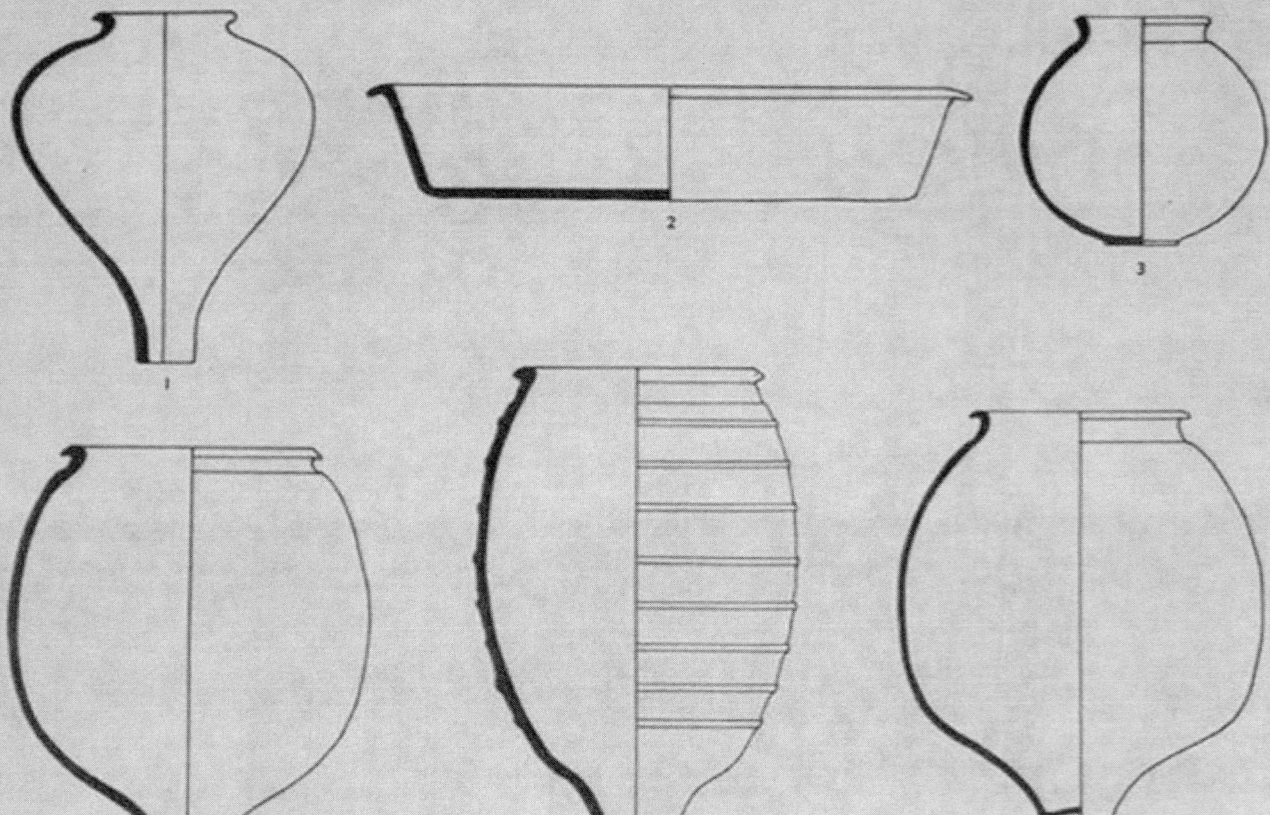

Scale 1:12

POTTERY: HARAPPĀ CULTURE

PLATE XXV

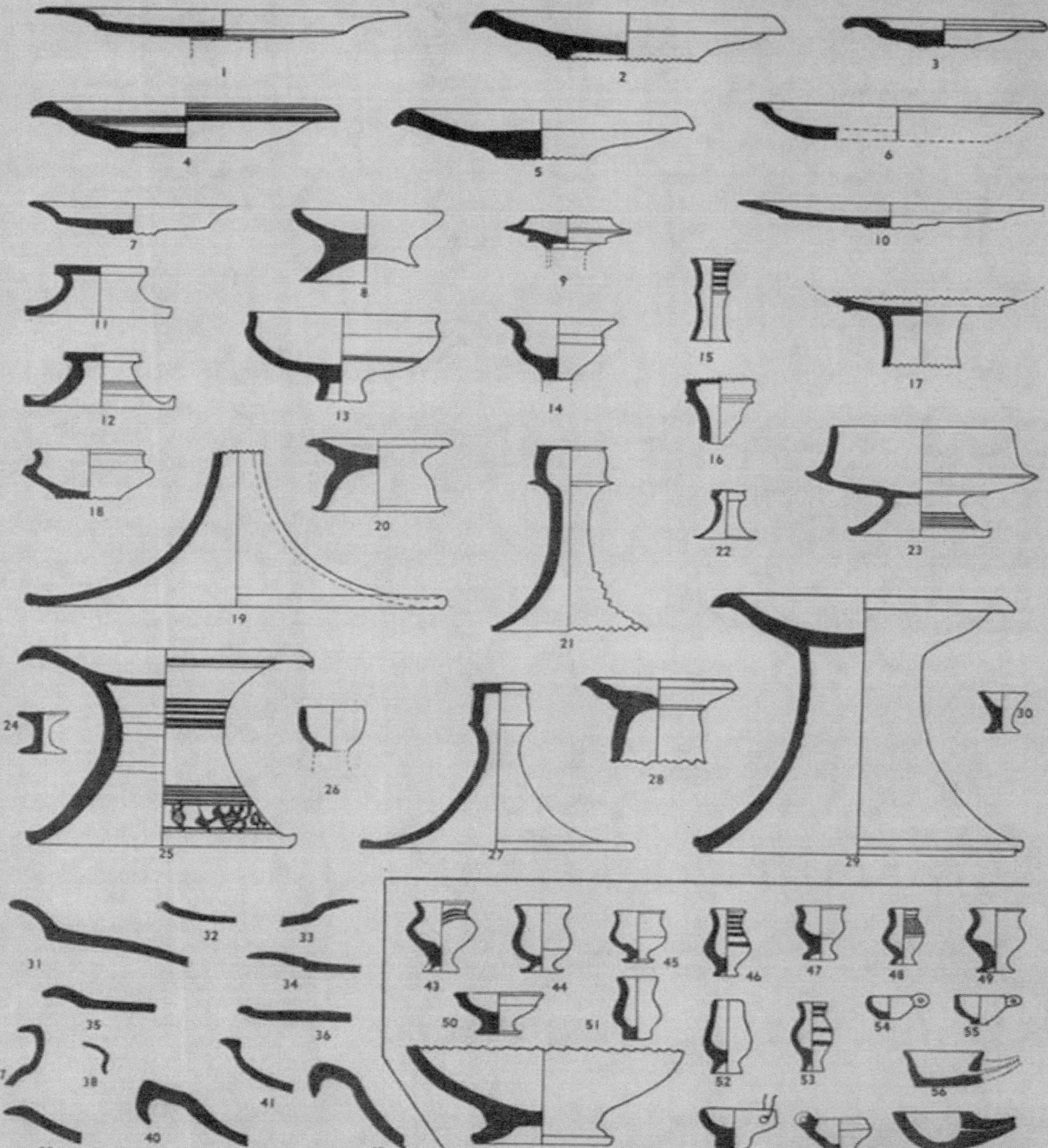

Scale 1:6

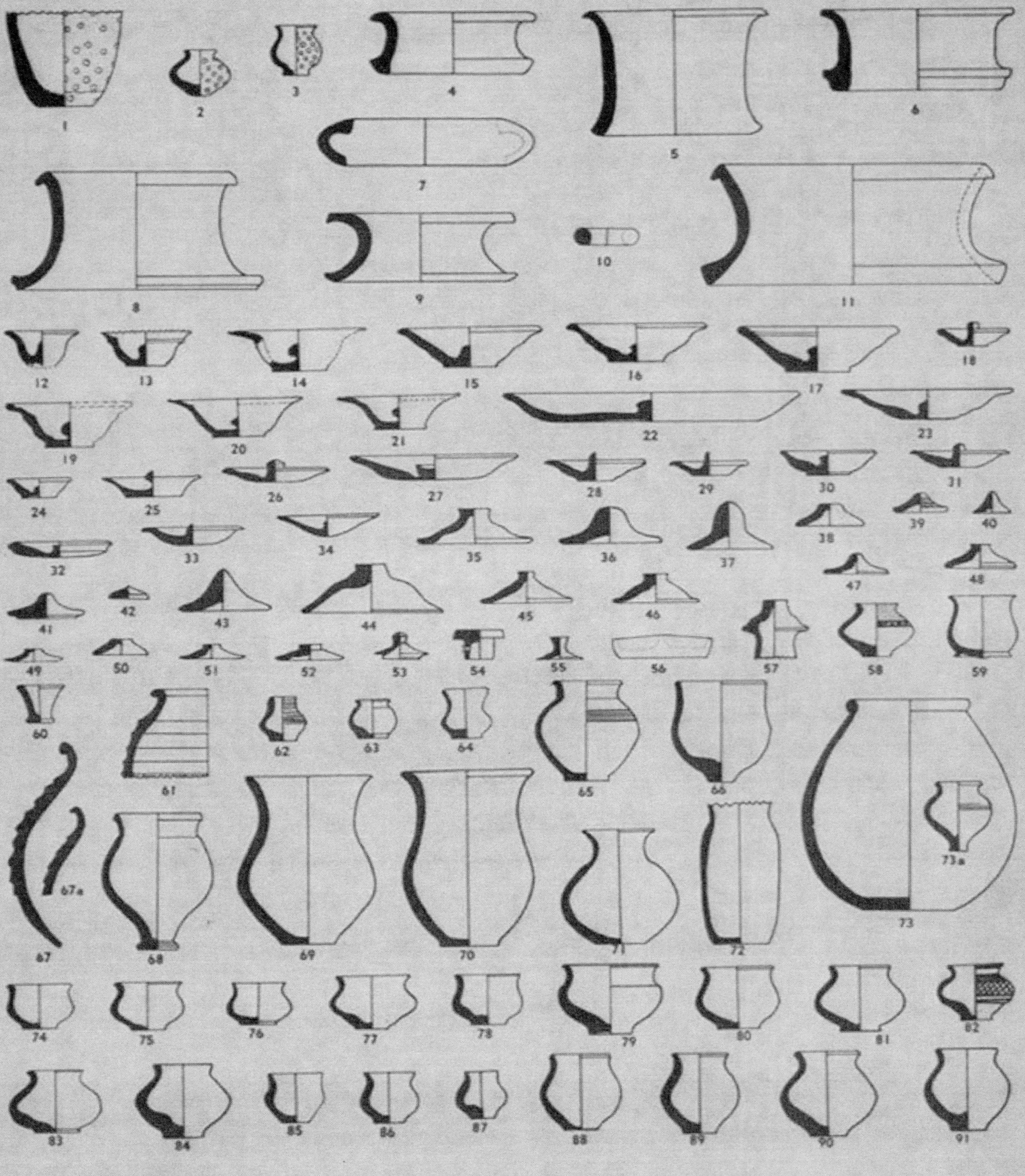
1
2
3
4
5
6
7
8
9
10
11
12
13
14
15
16
17
18
19
20
21
22
23
24
25
26
27
28
29
30
31
32
33
34
35
36
37
38
39
40
41
42
43
44
45
46
47
48
49
50
51
52
53
54
55
56
57
58
59
60
61
62
63
64
65
66
67
67a
68
69
70
71
72
73
73a
74
75
76
77
78
79
80
81
82
83
84
85
86
87
88
89
90
91

Scale 1:16

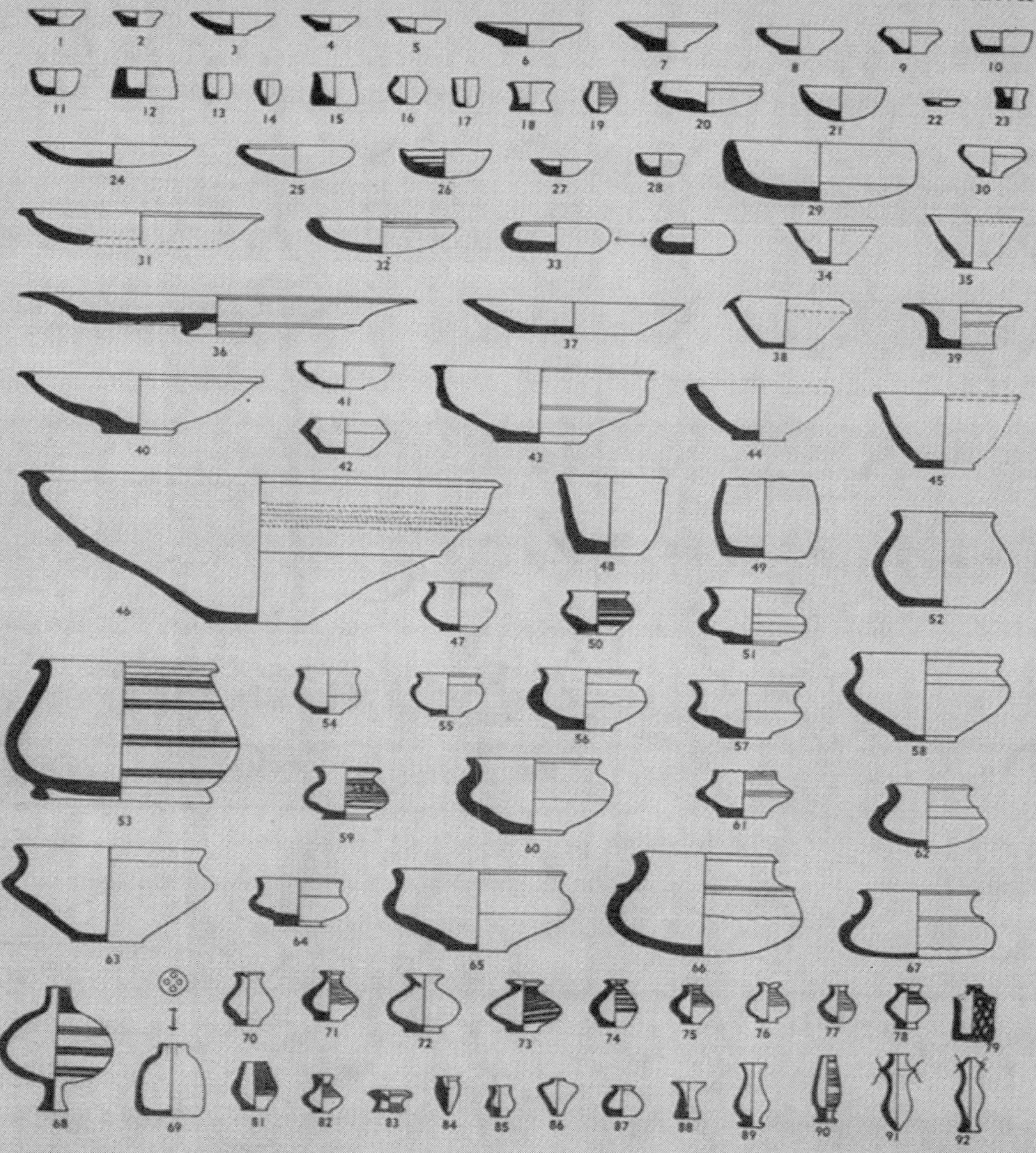
1
2
3
4
5
6
7
8
9
10
11
12
13
14
15
16
17
18
19
20
21
22
23
24
25
26
27
28
29
30
31
32
33
34
35
36
37
38
39
40
41
42
43
44
45
46
47
48
49
50
51
52
53
54
55
56
57
58
59
60
61
62
63
64
65
66
67
68
69
70
71
72
73
74
75
76
77
78
79
81
82
83
84
85
86
87
88
89
90
91
92

Scale 1:6

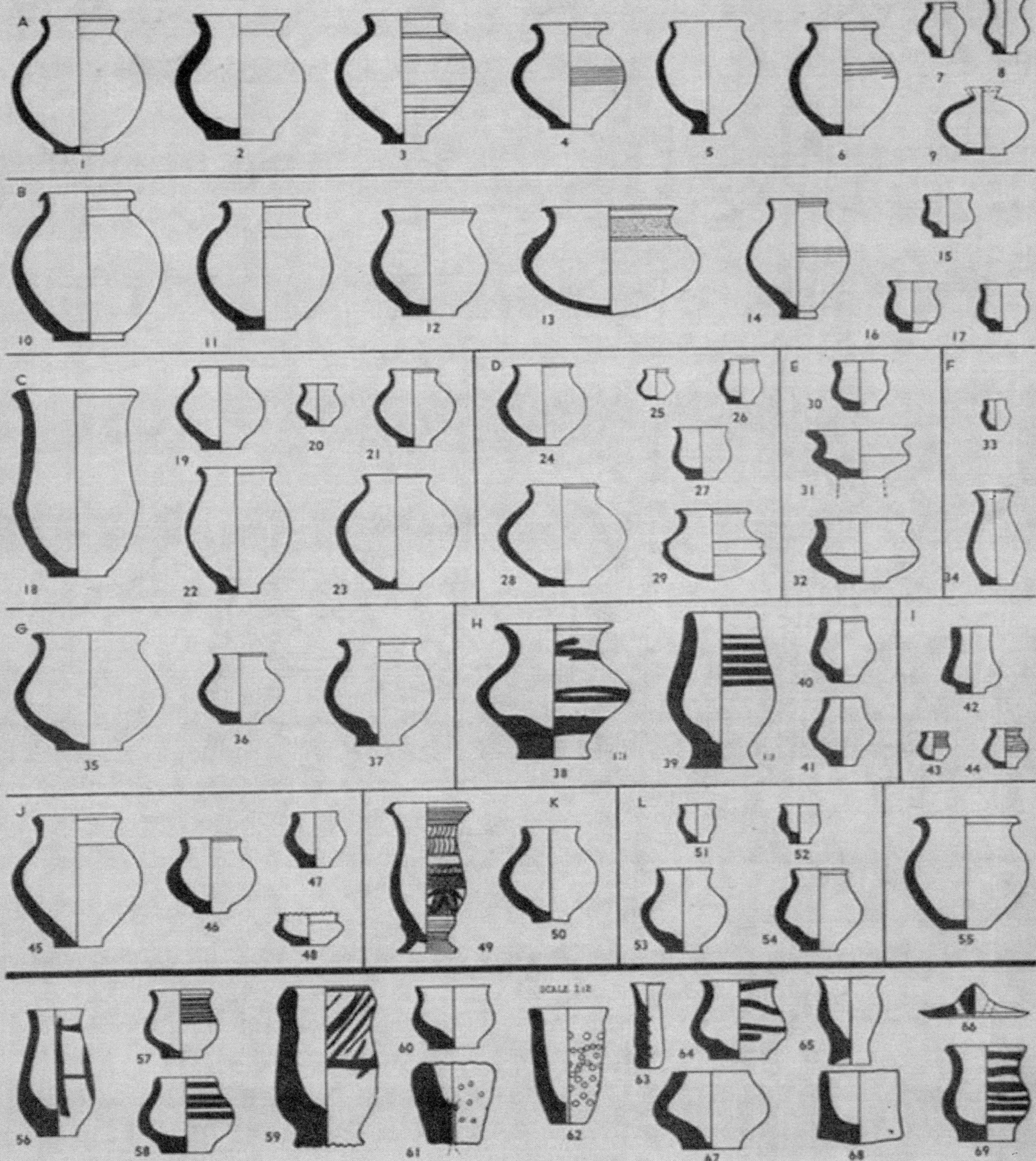

Scale 1:6

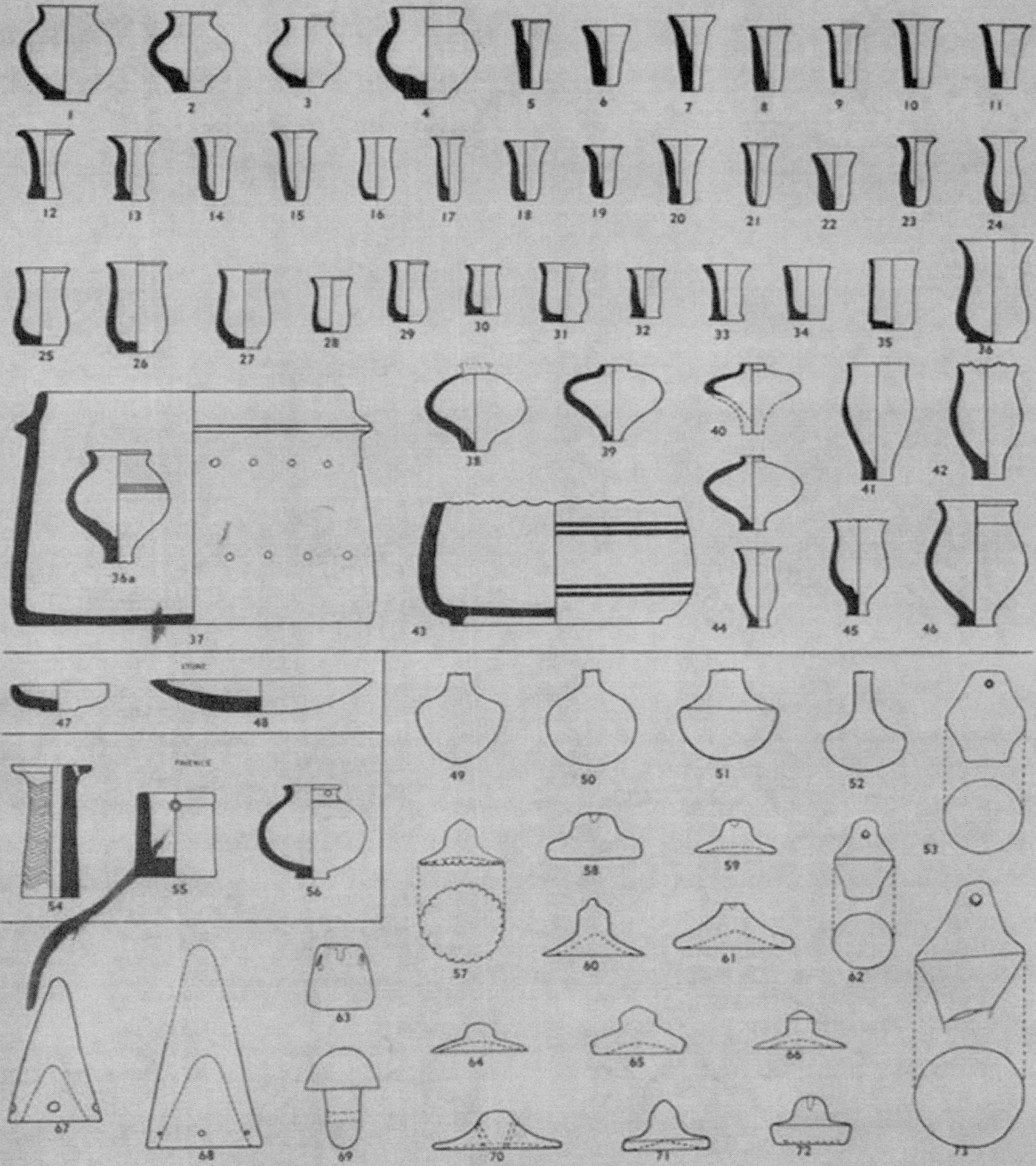

Scale 1:6

Scale 1:3

Scale 1:3

PAINTED POTTERY: HARAPPĀ CULTURE

PLATE XXXII

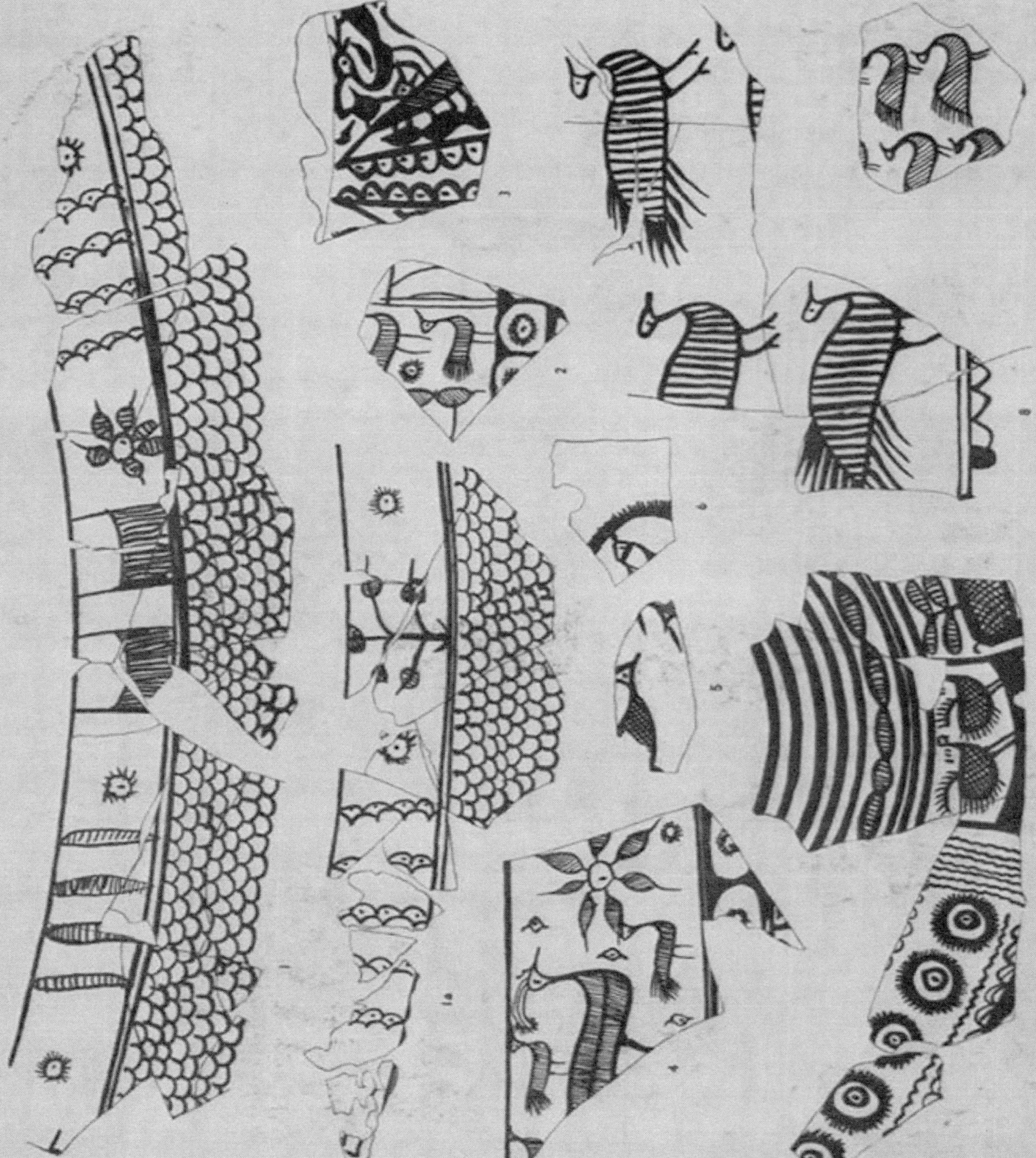

Scale 1:3

PAINTED POTTERY: HARAPPĀ CULTURE

PLATE XXXIII

Scale 1:3

JHUKAR

Scale 1:3

1

2

3

4

1
2
3
4
5
6
7
8
9
10
11
12
13
14
15
16
17
18
19
20
21
22
23
24
25
26
27
28
29
30
31
32
33
34
35
36
37
38
39
40
41

Approx. Scale 1:4

INCISED WARE: HARAPPĀ CULTURE

PLATE XXXVIII

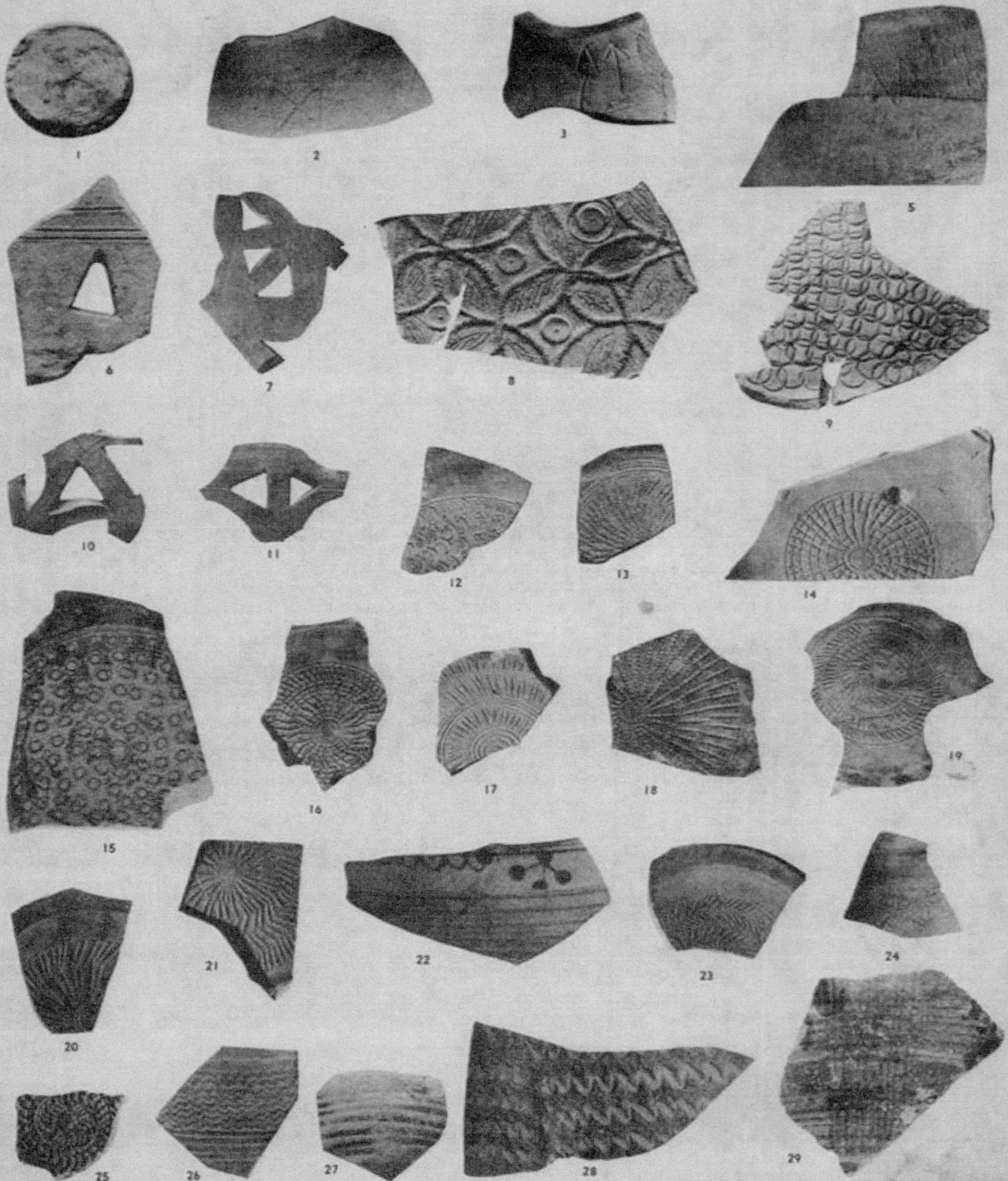

POTTERY: JHANGAR, JHUKAR AND HARAPPĀ CULTURES

PLATE XXXIX

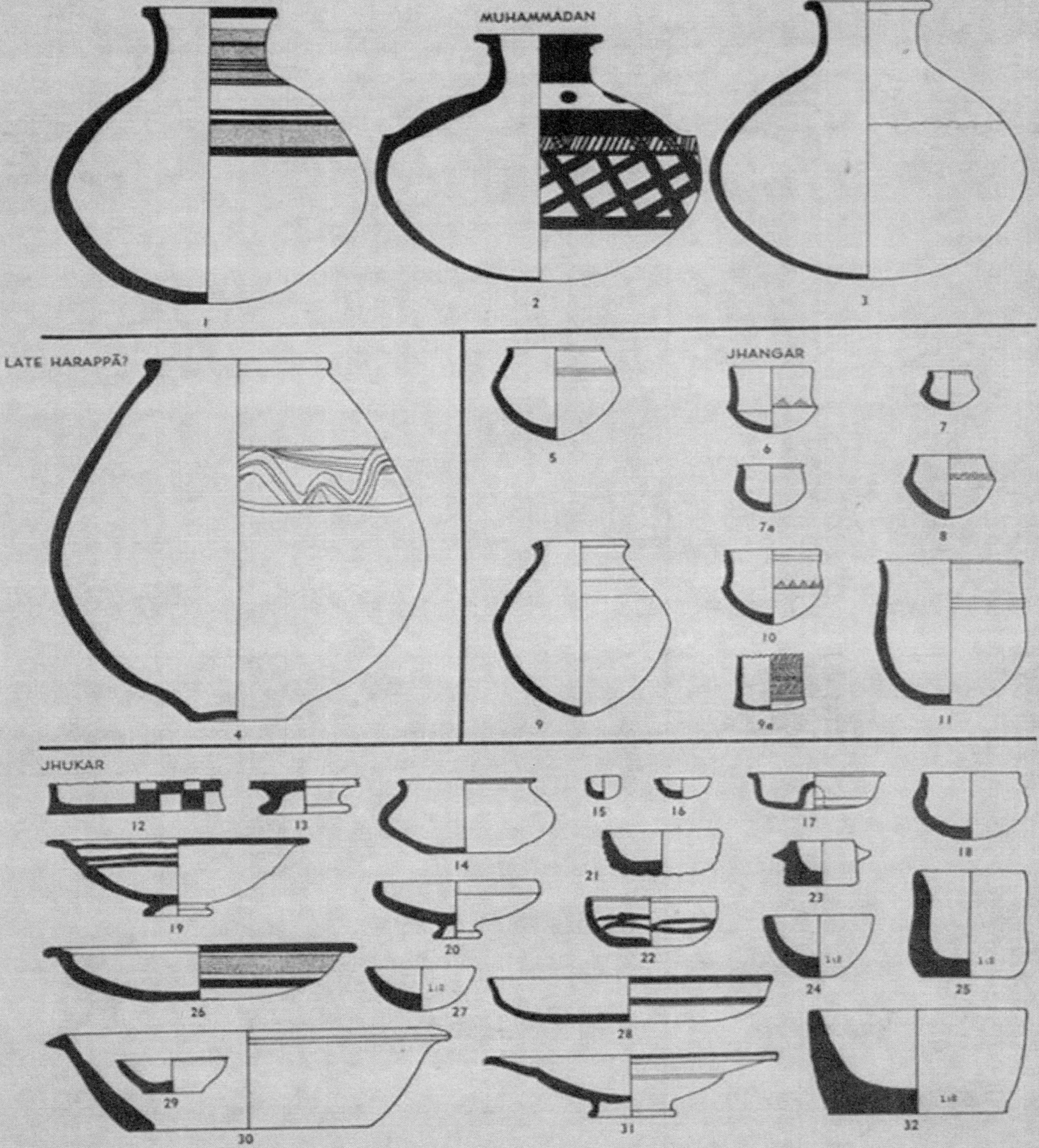
MUHAMMADAN
1
2
3
LATE HARAPPĀ?
4
JHANGAR
5
6
7
7a
8
9
9a
10
11
JHUKAR
12
13
14
15
16
17
18
19
20
21
22
23
24
25
26
27
28
29
30
31
32

Scale 1:6

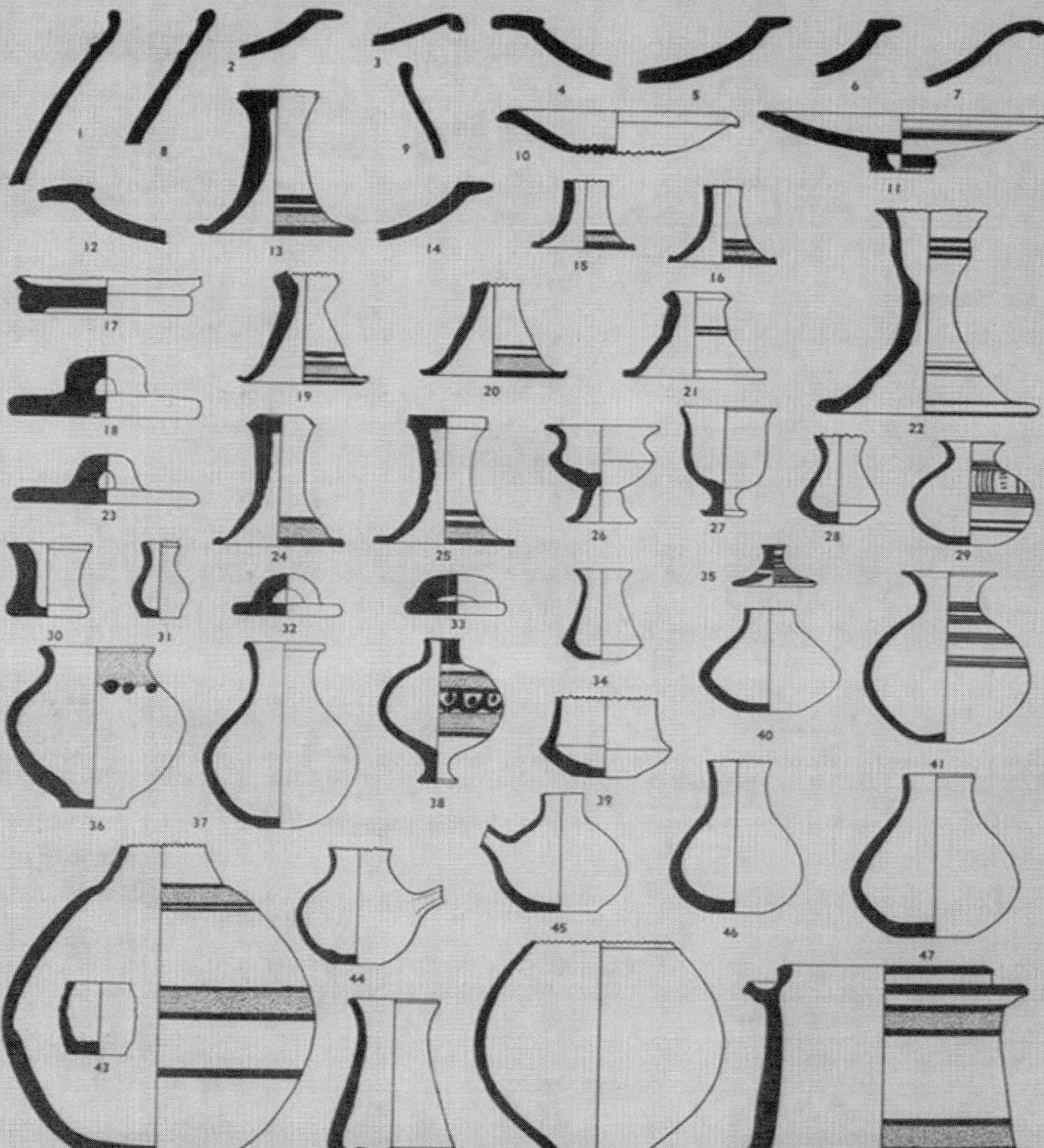
1
2
3
4
5
6
7
8
9
10
11
12
13
14
15
16
17
18
19
20
21
22
23
24
25
26
27
28
29
30
31
32
33
34
35
36
37
38
39
40
41
42
43
44
45
46
47
48
49
50

Scale 1:6

Scale 1:3

Scale 1:3

Scale 1:3

Approx. Scale 1:4

Approx. Scale 1:4

Approx. Scale 1:4

1
2
3
4
5
6
7
8
9
10
11
12
13
14
15
16
17
18
19
20
21
22
23
24
25

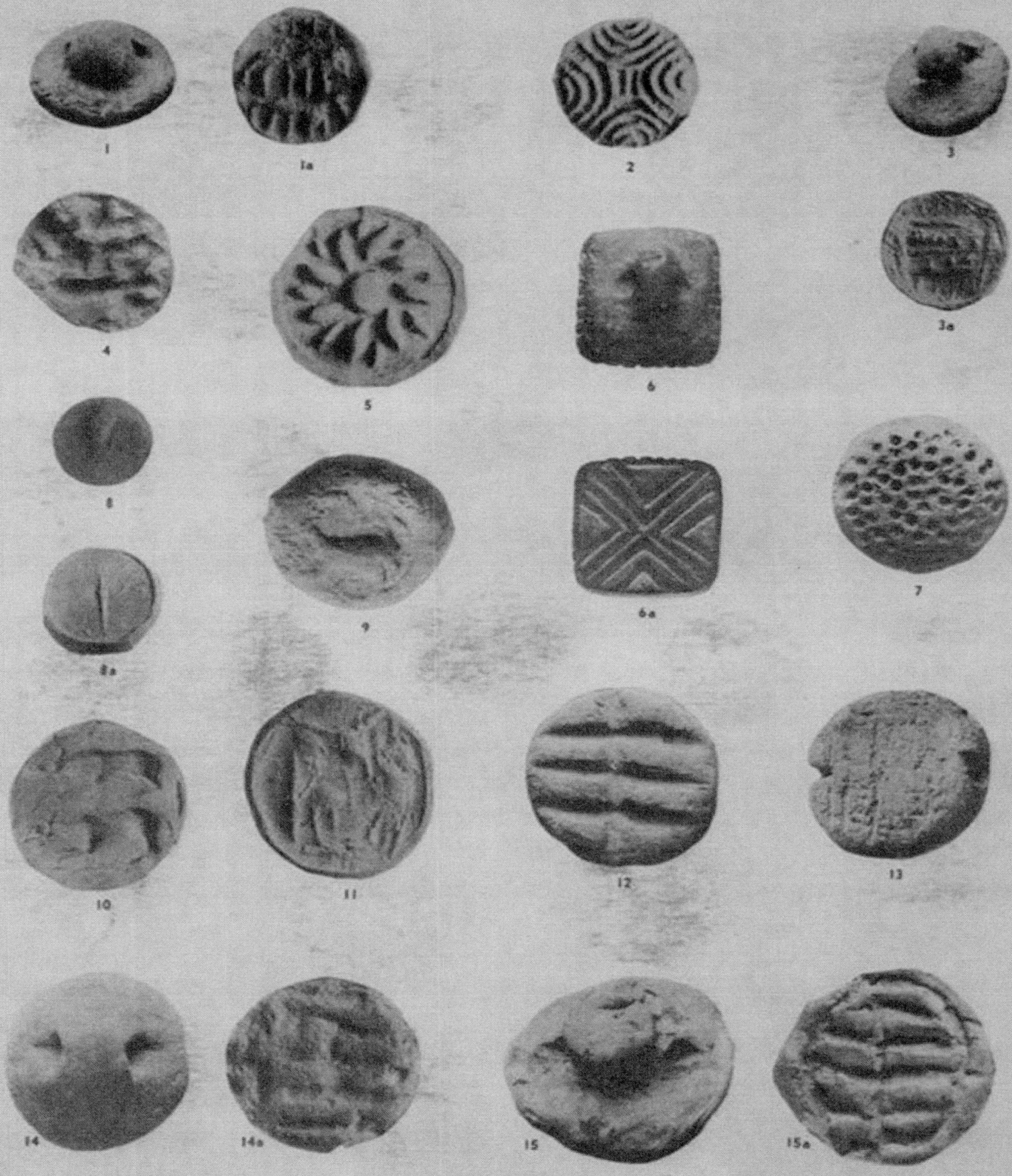
1
1a
2
3
4
5
6
3a
8
9
6a
7
8a
10
11
12
13
14
14a
15
15a

1
1a
2
3
3a
2a
4
4a
5
5a
6
7
8
10
11
7a
8a
9
10a
11a
12
14
15
16
13
14a
15a
16a

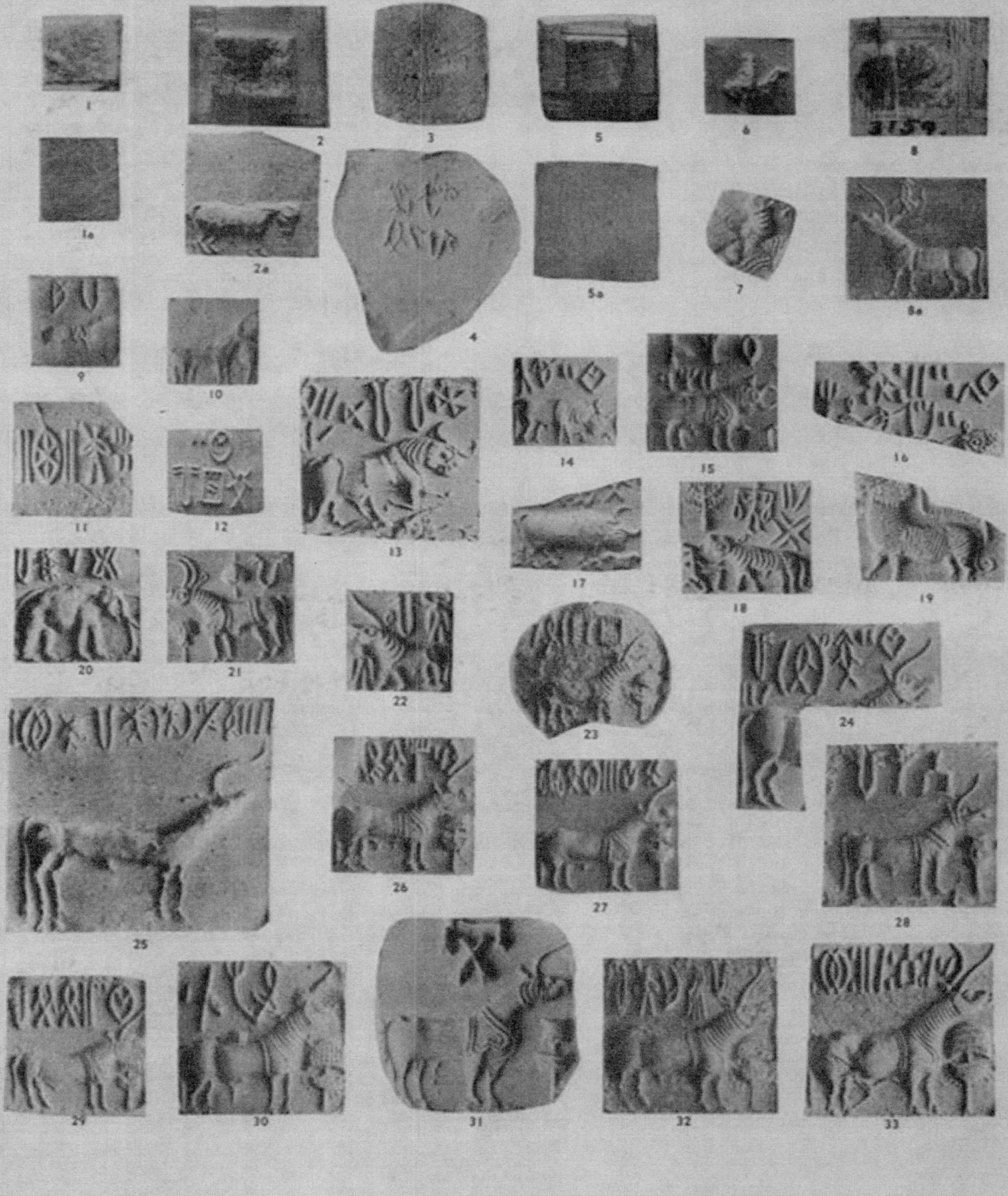

1
2
3
4
5
6
7
8
9
10
11
12
13
14
15
16
17
18
19
20
21
22
23
24
25
26
27
28
29
30
31
32
33
33a
34
35
36

1
2
3
4
5
6
7
8
9
10
11
11a
12
13

1
2
3
4
4a
5
6
7
8
9
10
11
12

PLATE LV

MODEL ANIMALS IN POTTERY PLATE LVI

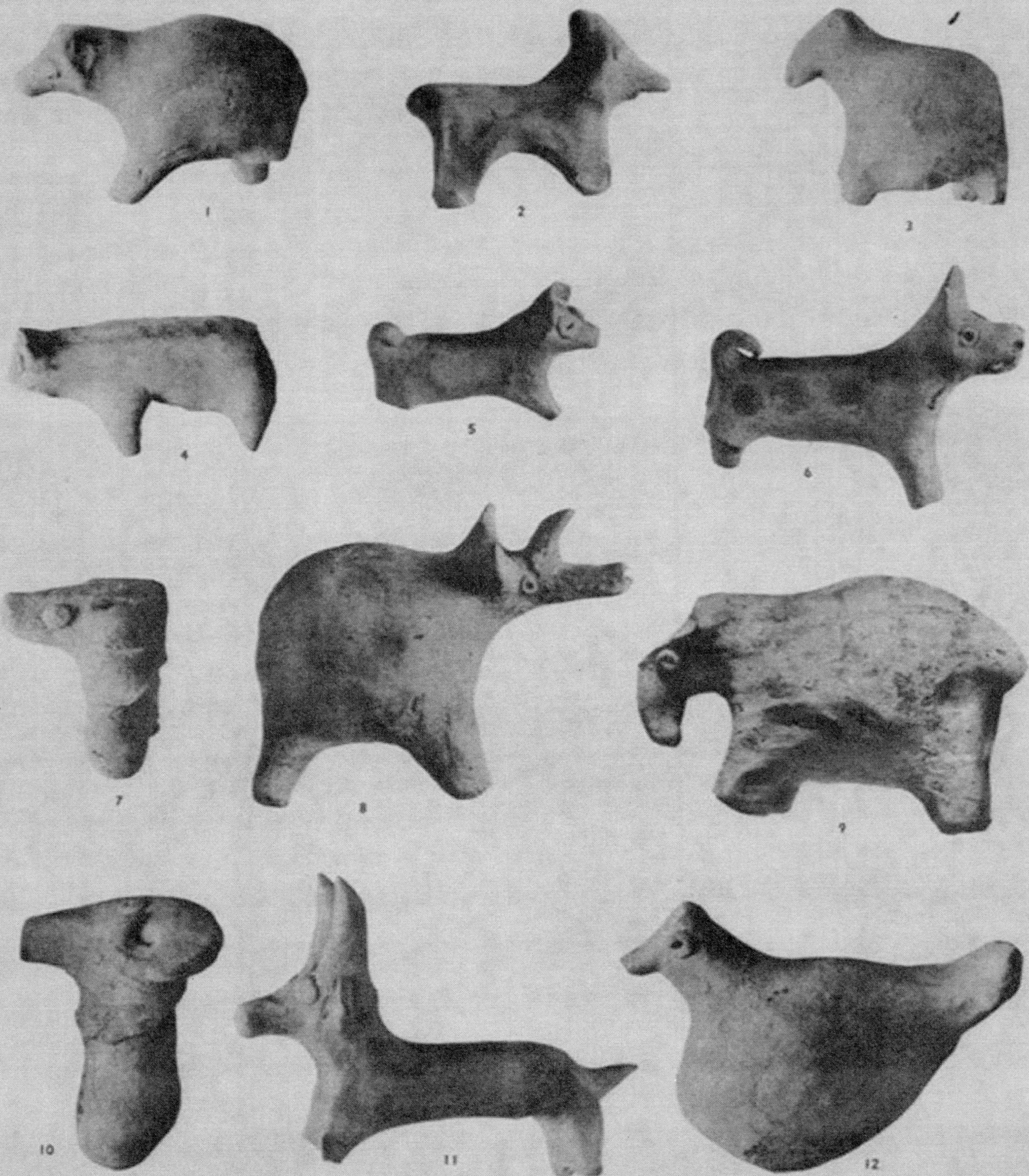

MODEL ANIMALS IN PASTE AND POTTERY

PLATE LVII

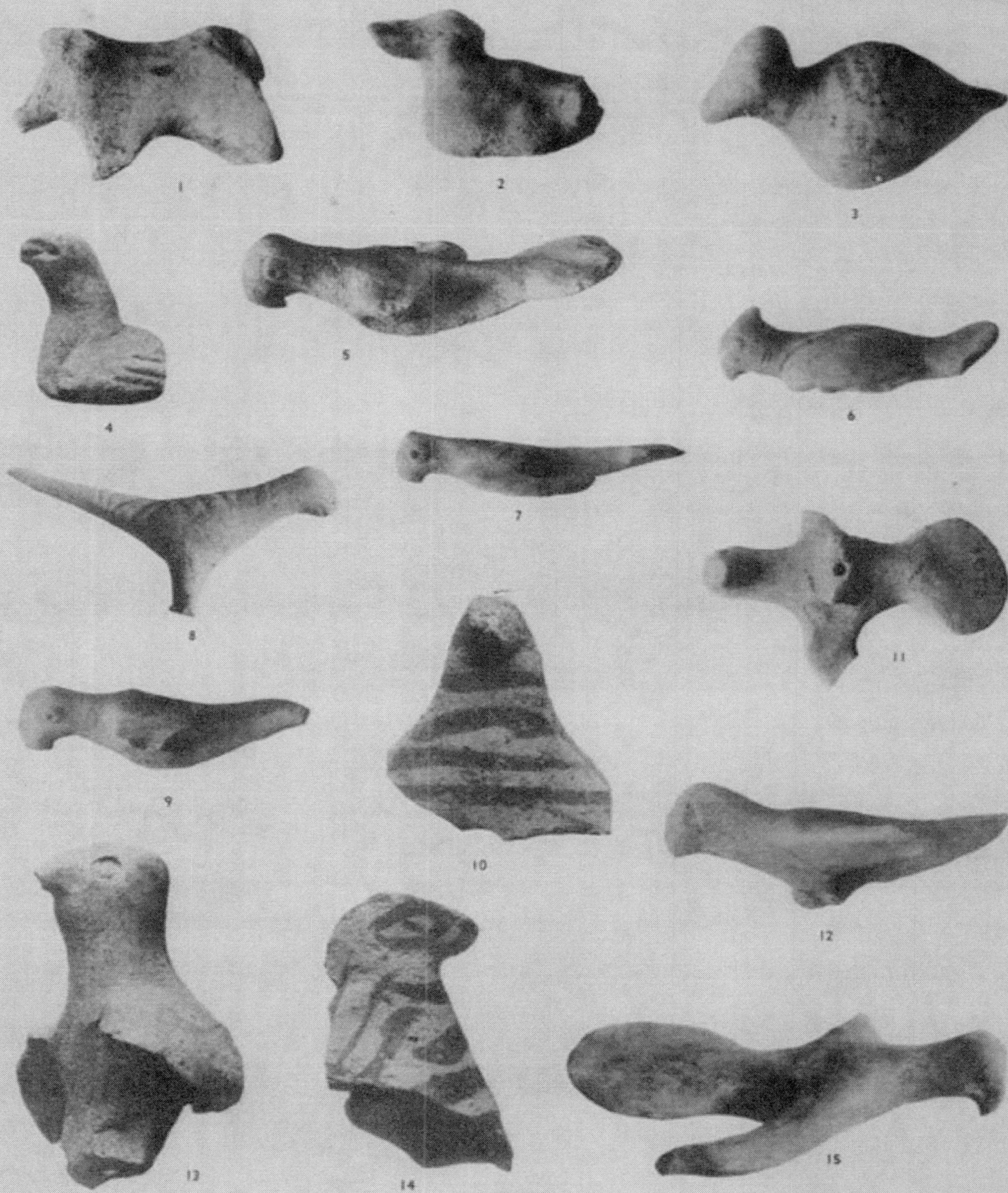

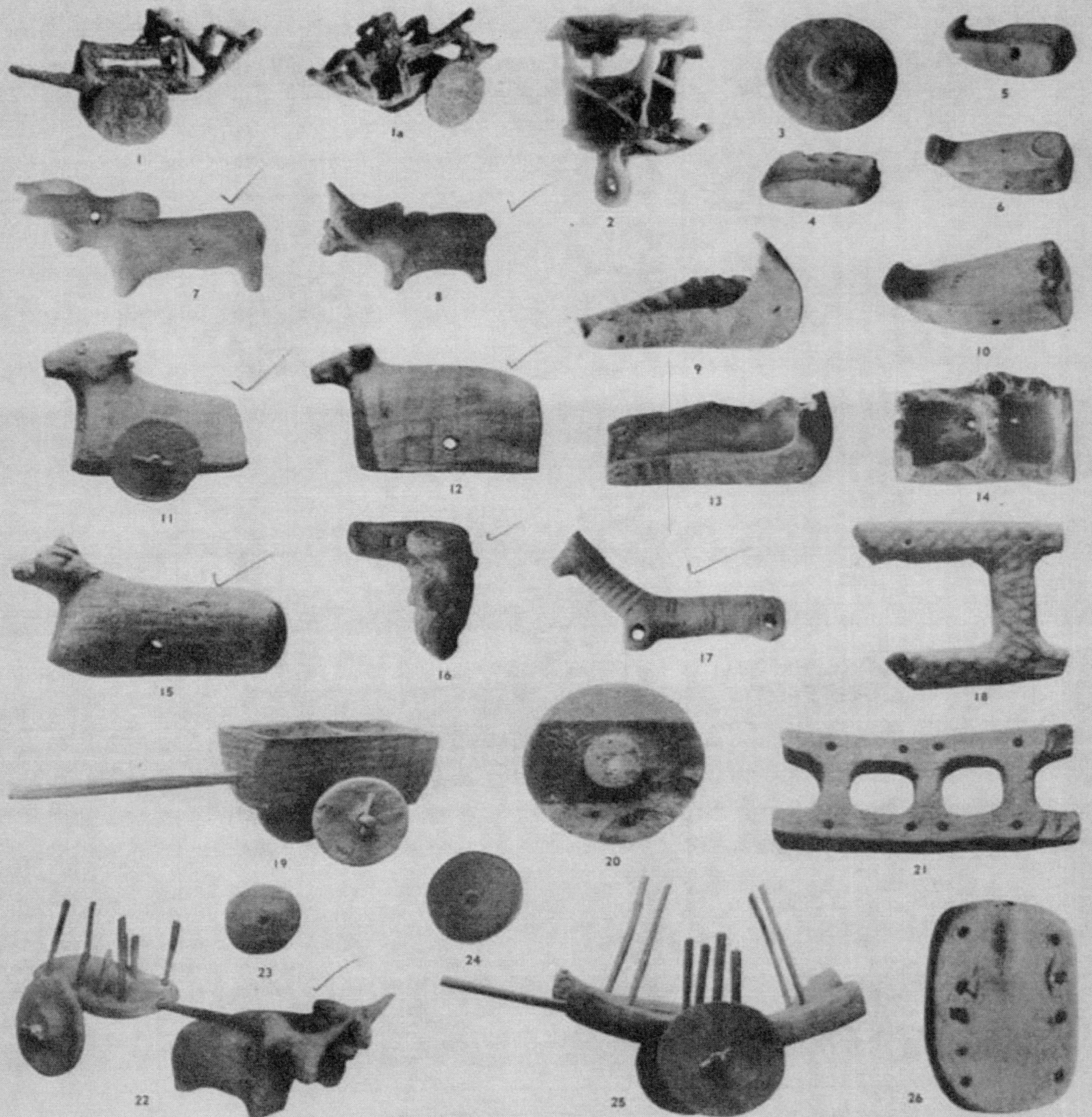
1
1a
2
3
4
5
6
7
8
9
10
11
12
13
14
15
16
17
18
19
20
21
22
23
24
25
26

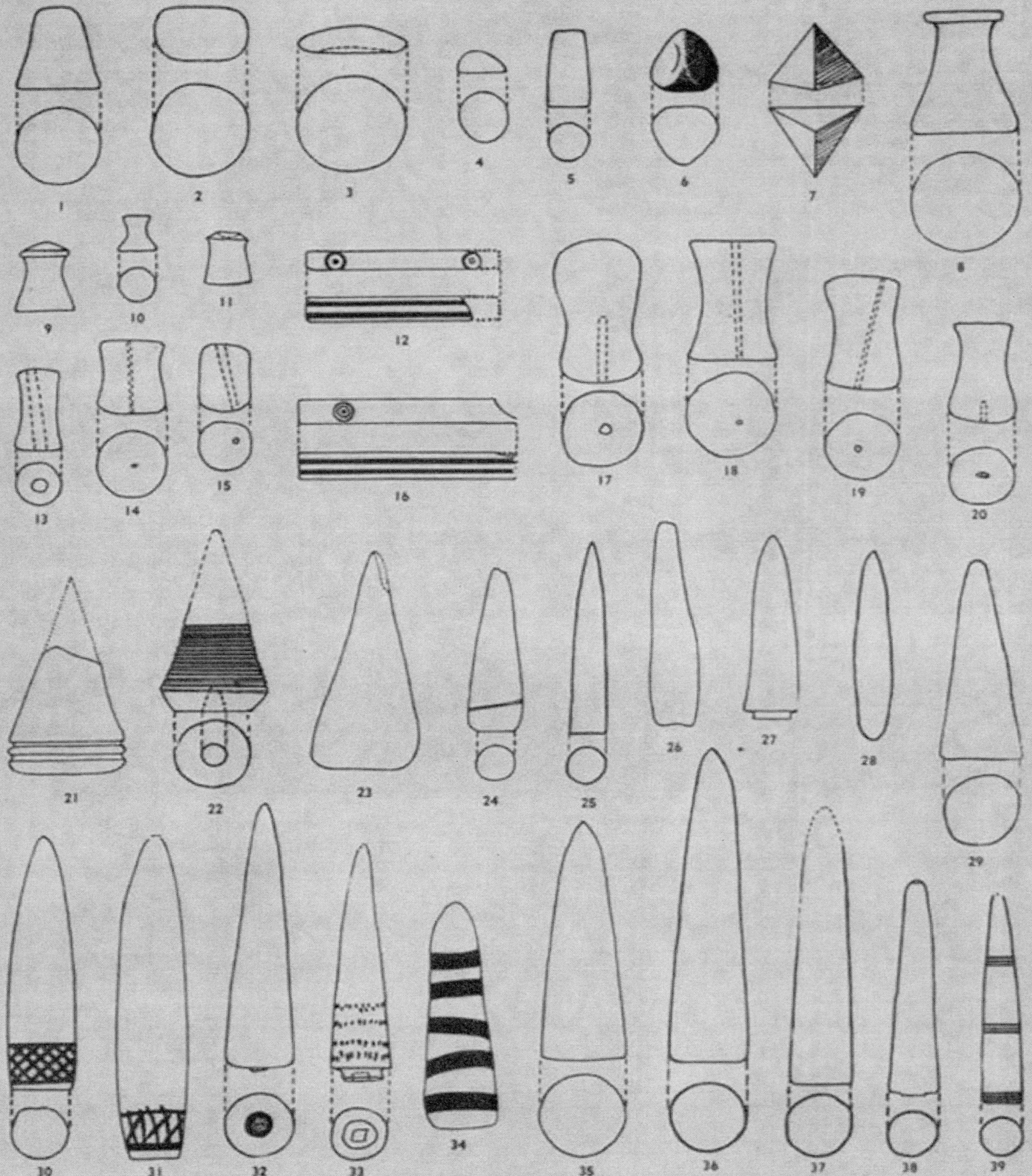
1
2
3
4
5
6
7
8
9
10
11
12
13
14
15
16
17
18
19
20
21
22
23
24
25
26
27
28
29
30
31
32
33
34
35
36
37
38
39

Scale 1:1½

Scale 1:1

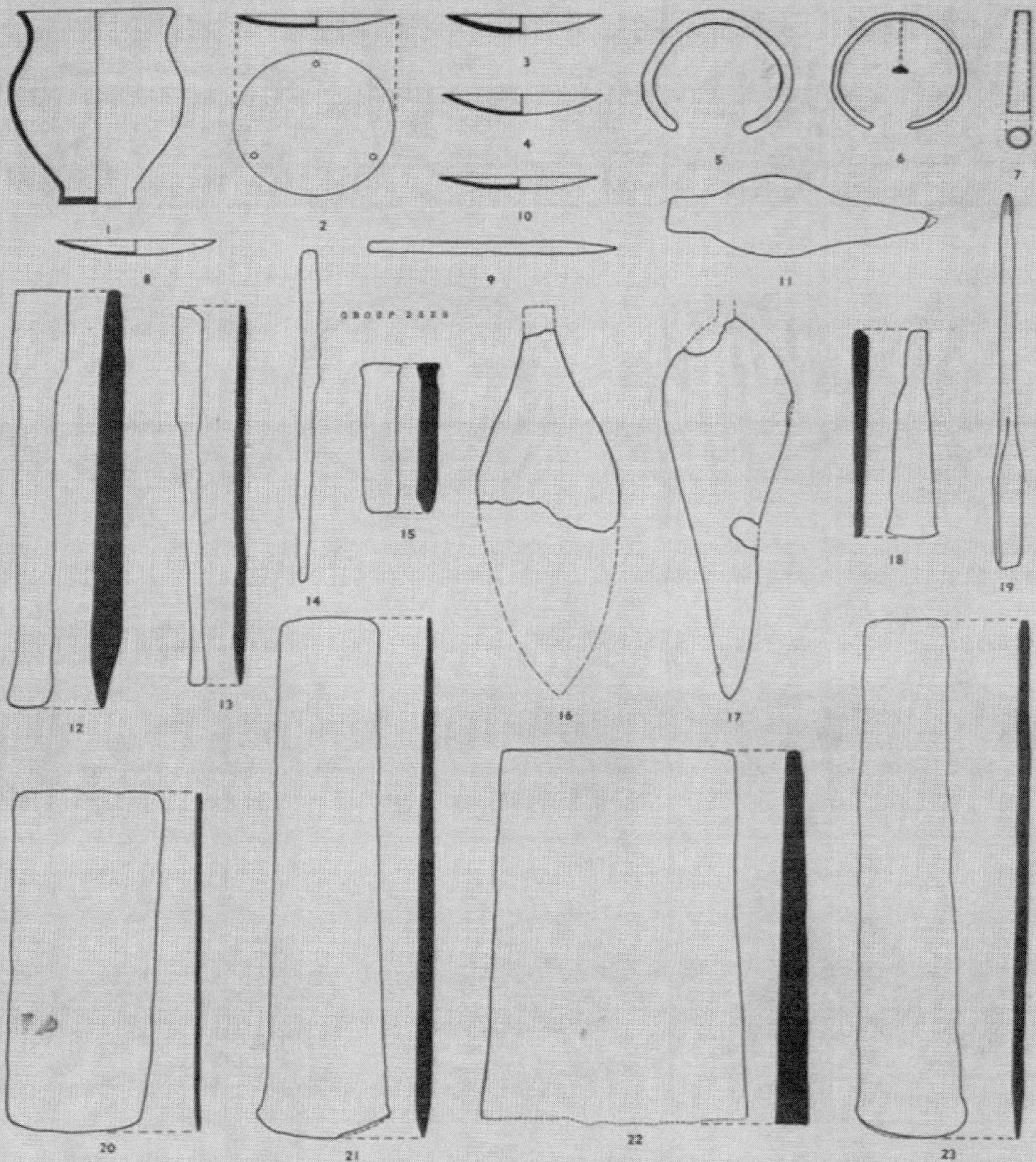

Scale 1:2

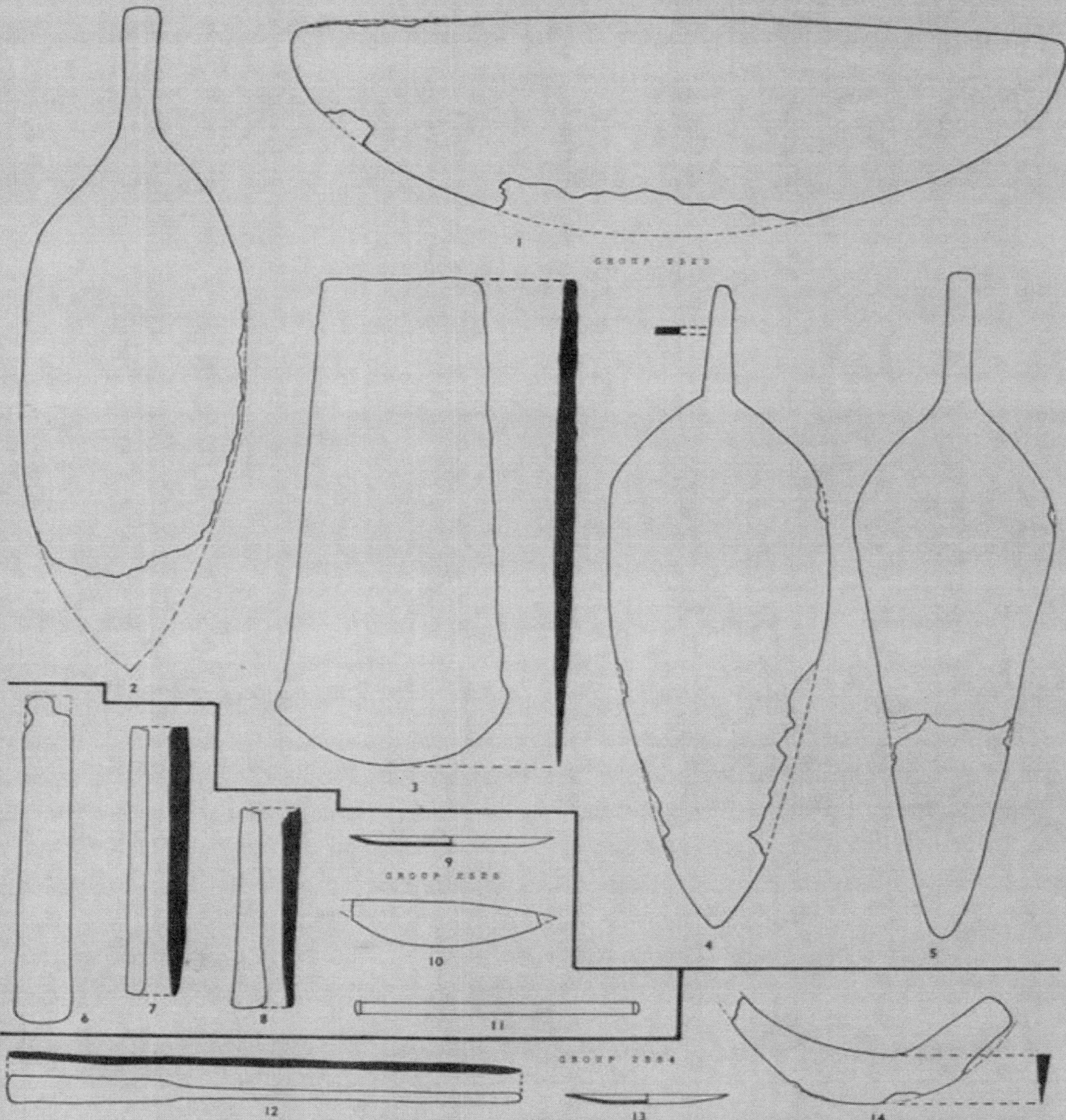

Scale 1:2

COPPER AND BRONZE GROUP (No. 2593): HARAPPĀ CULTURE PLATE LXIV

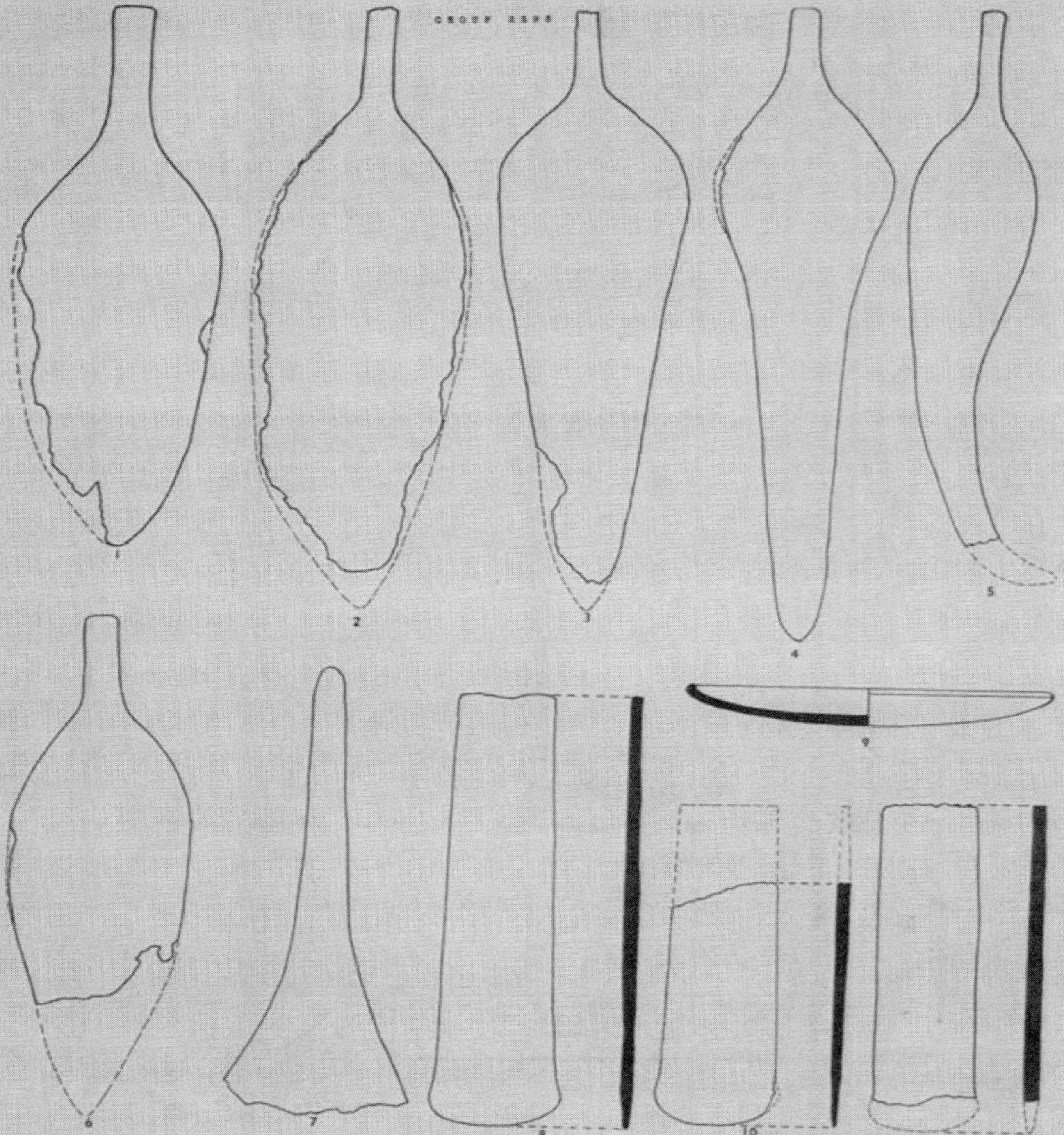

Scale 1:2

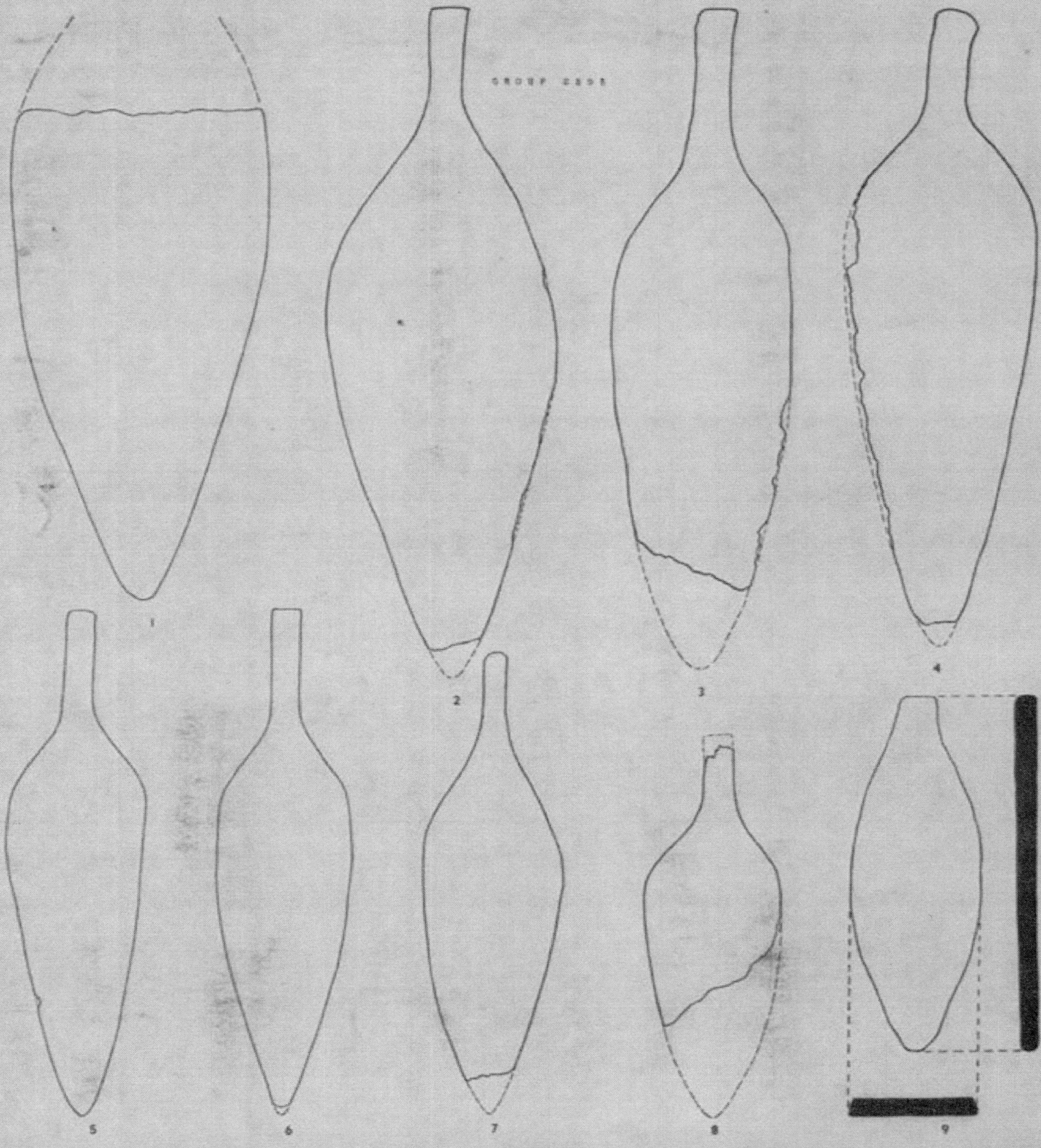

Scale 1:2

COPPER AND BRONZE GROUPS (Nos. 2593, 2199): HARAPPĀ CULTURE PLATE LXVI

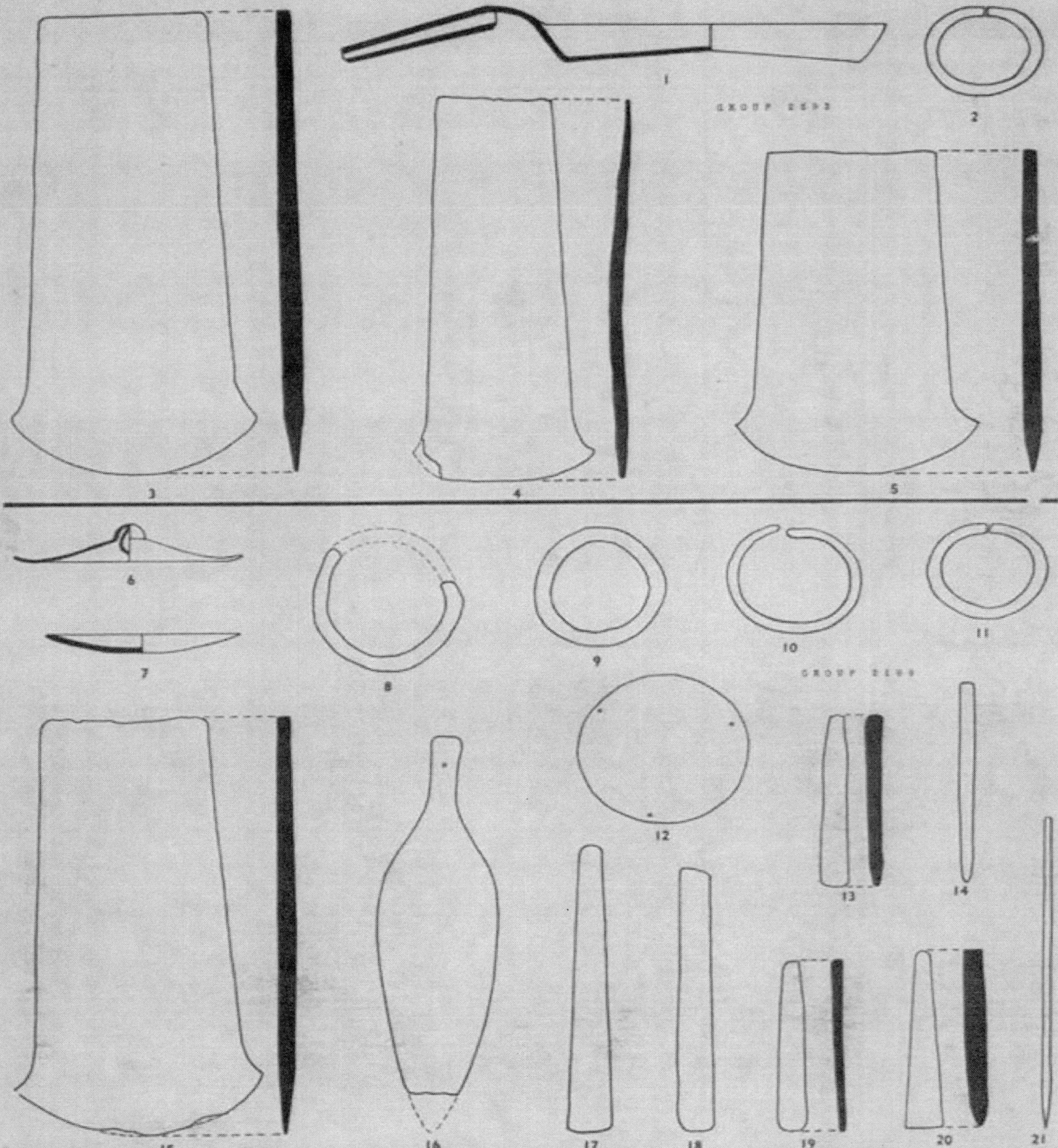

Scale 1:2

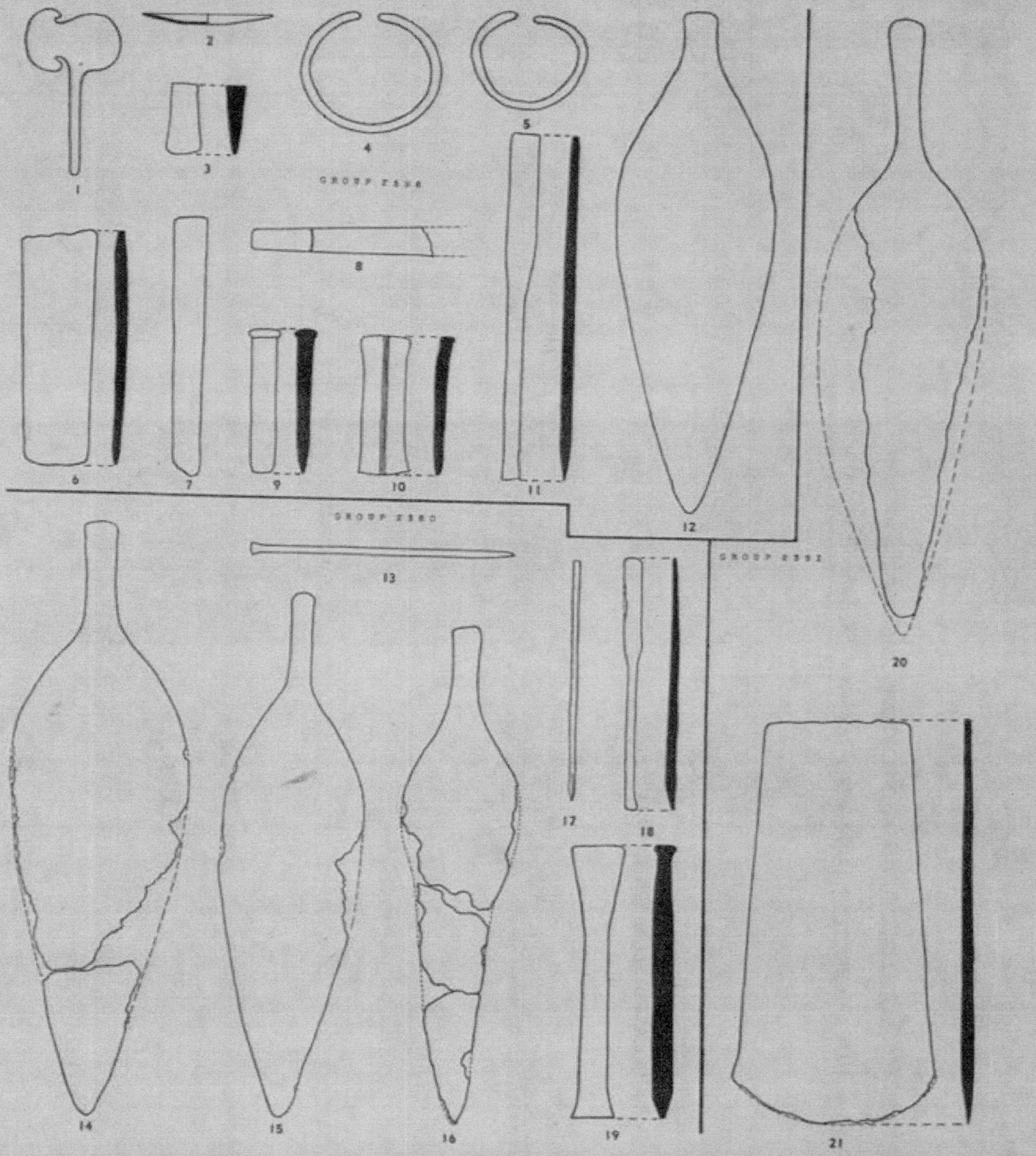

Scale 1:2

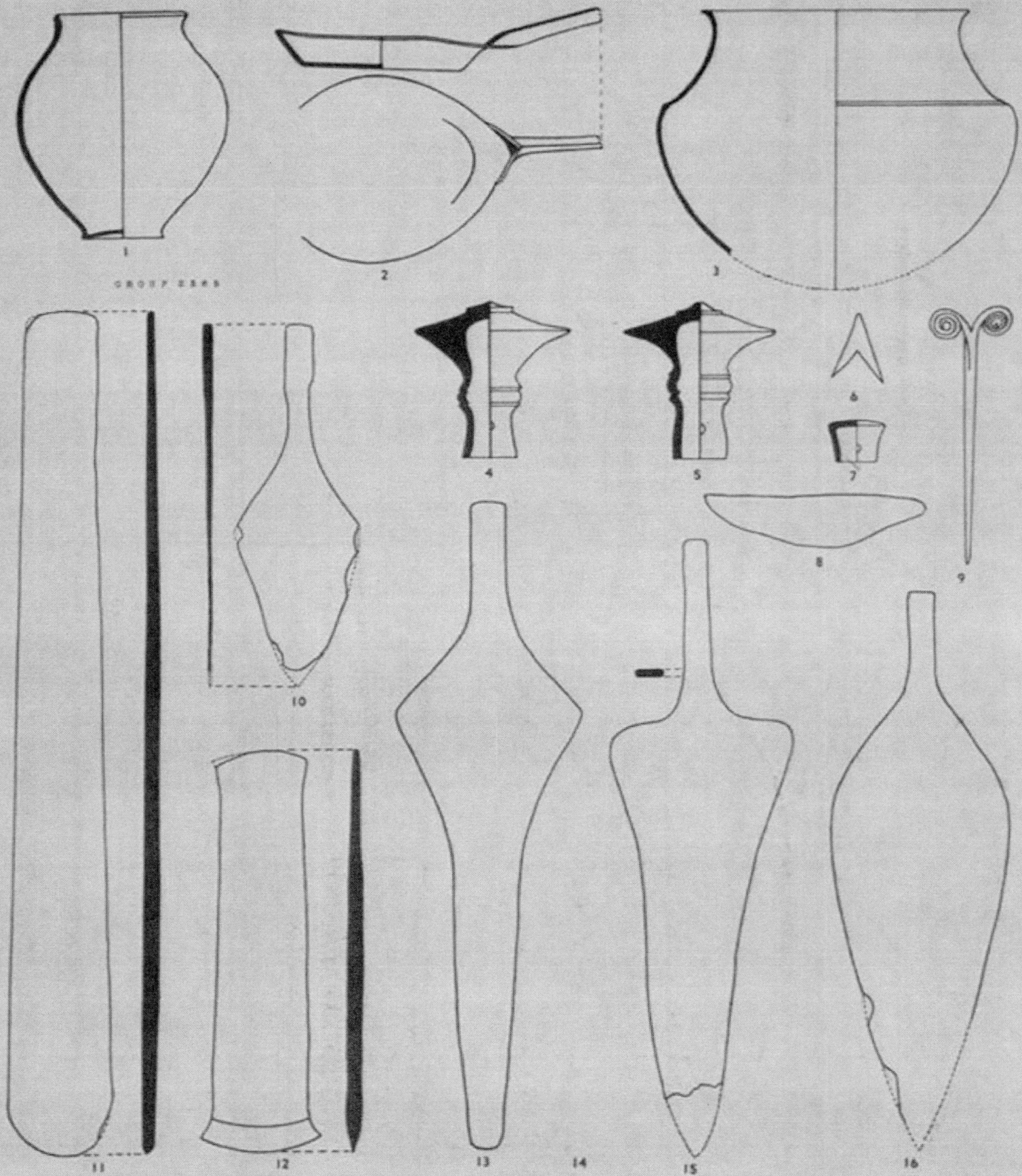

Scales—Utensils 1:4
Tools 1:2

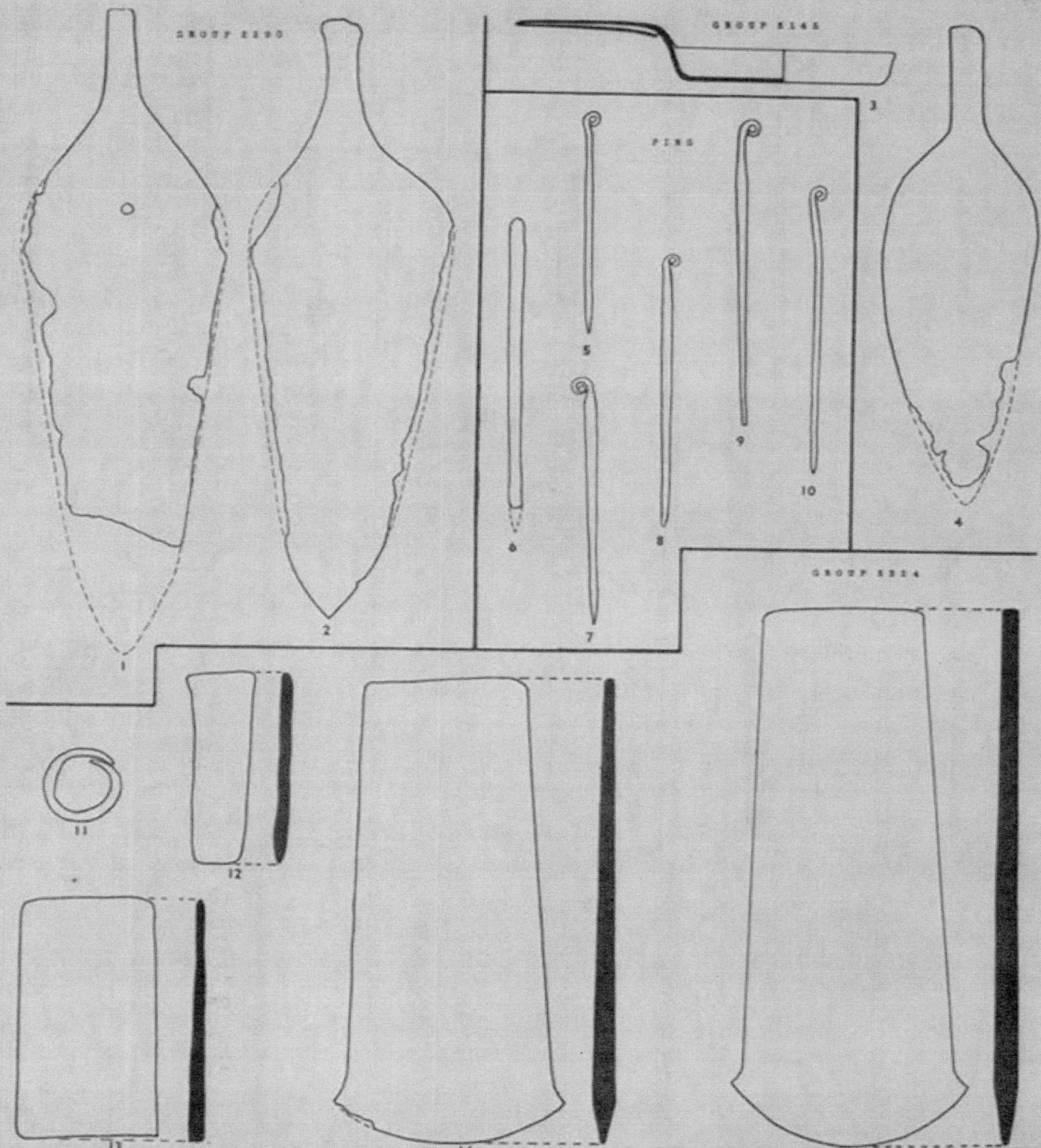
GROUP 2290
GROUP 3145
PINS
GROUP 3324
1
2
3
4
5
6
7
8
9
10
11
12
13
14
15

Scale 1:2

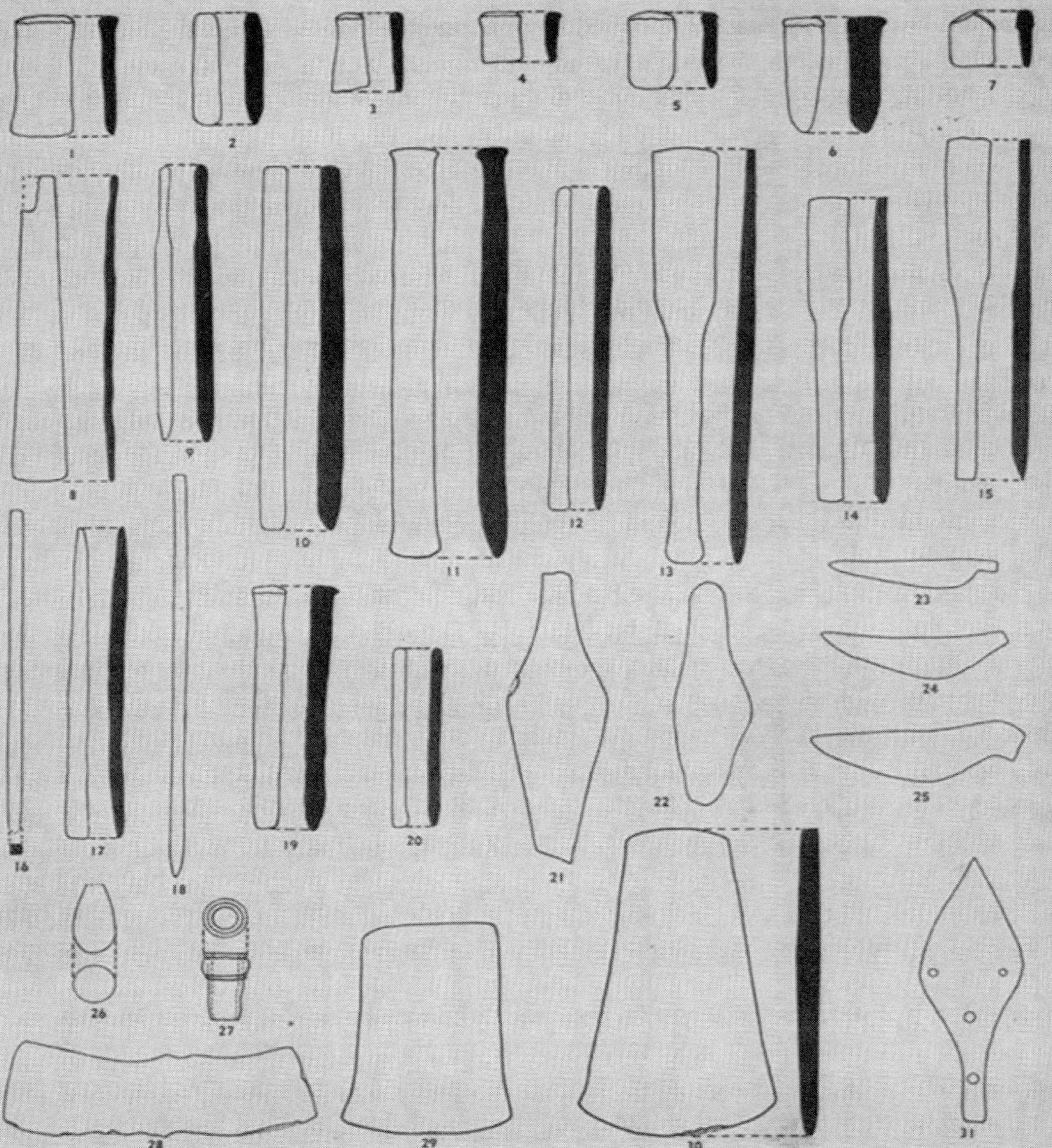
1
2
3
4
5
6
7
8
9
10
11
12
13
14
15
16
17
18
19
20
21
22
23
24
25
26
27
28
29
30
31

Scale 1:2

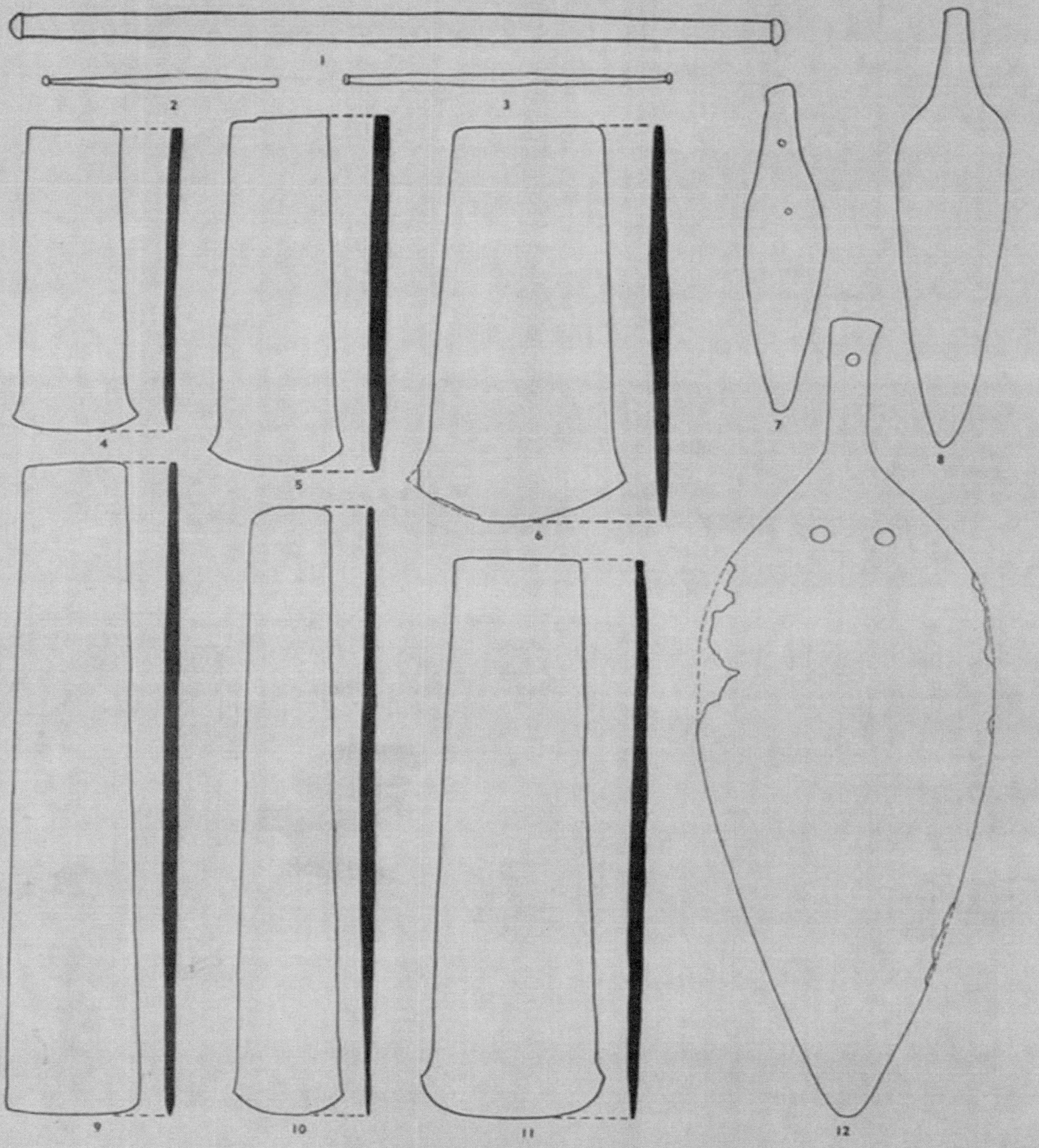

Scale 1:2

COPPER AND BRONZE OBJECTS: HARAPPĀ AND JHUKAR (?) CULTURES PLATE LXXII

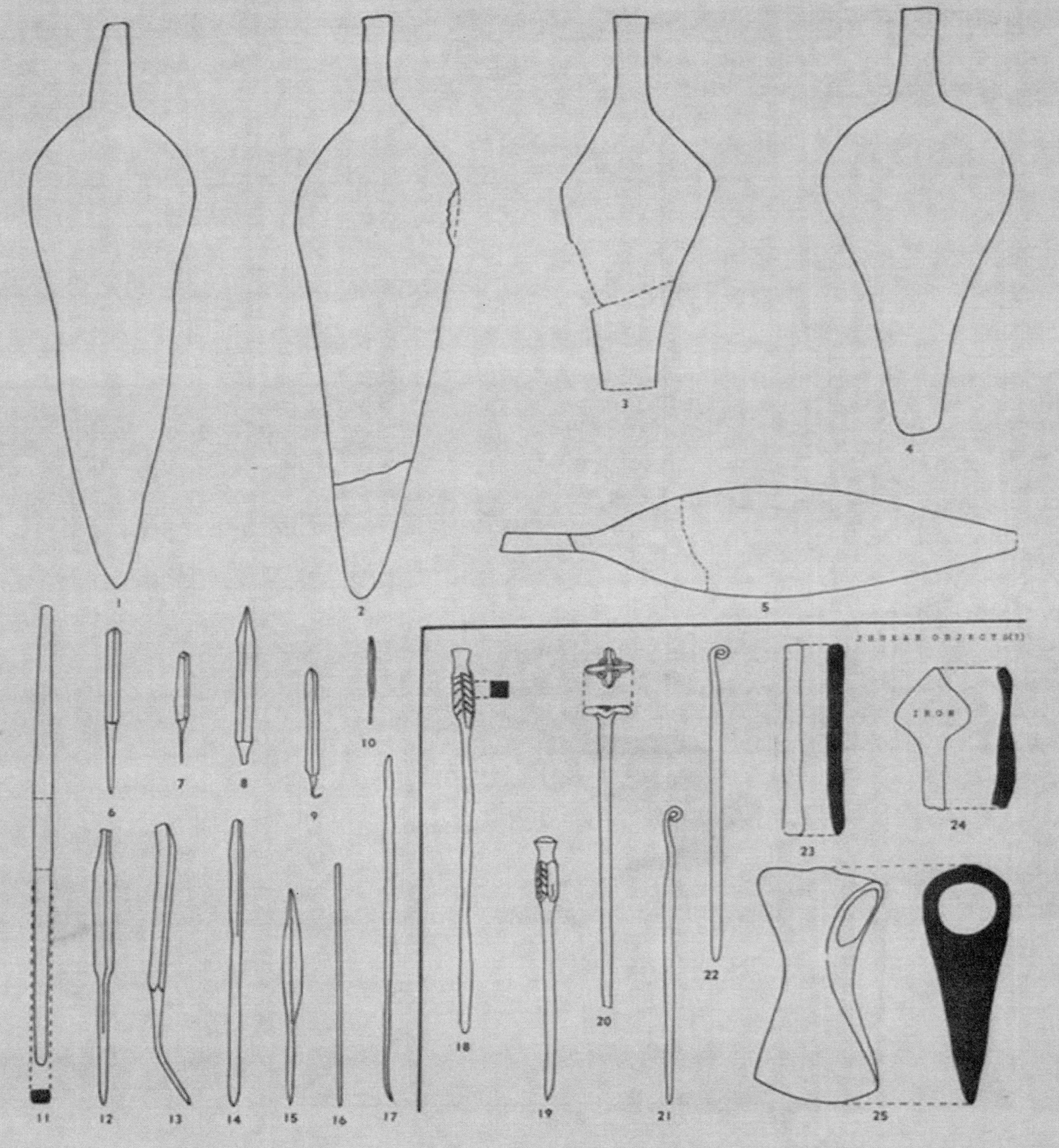

Scale 1:2

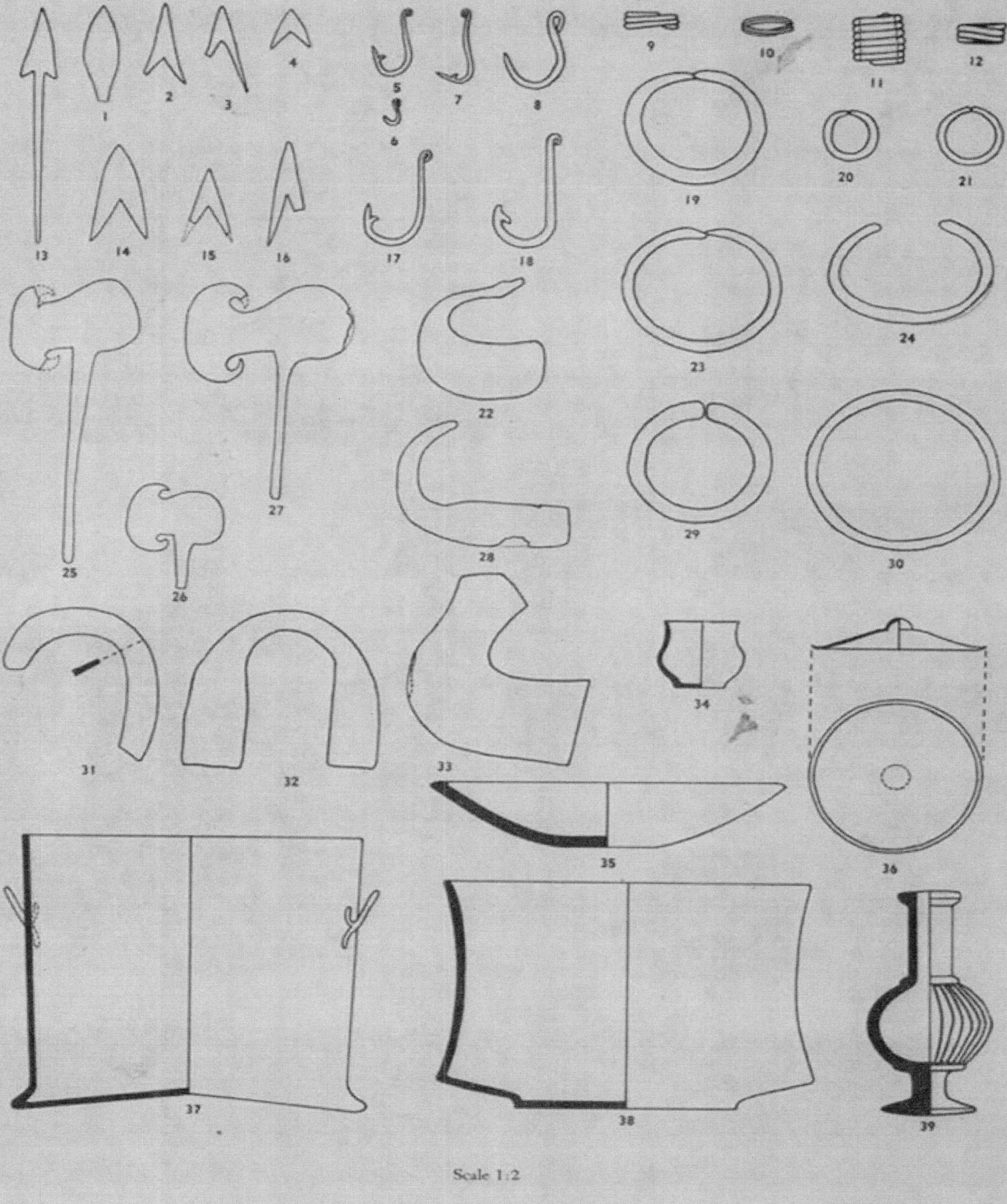
1
2
3
4
5
6
7
8
9
10
11
12
13
14
15
16
17
18
19
20
21
22
23
24
25
26
27
28
29
30
31
32
33
34
35
36
37
38
39

Scale 1:2

1
1a
2
3
4
5
6
7
8
9
10
11
12
13
14
15
16
17

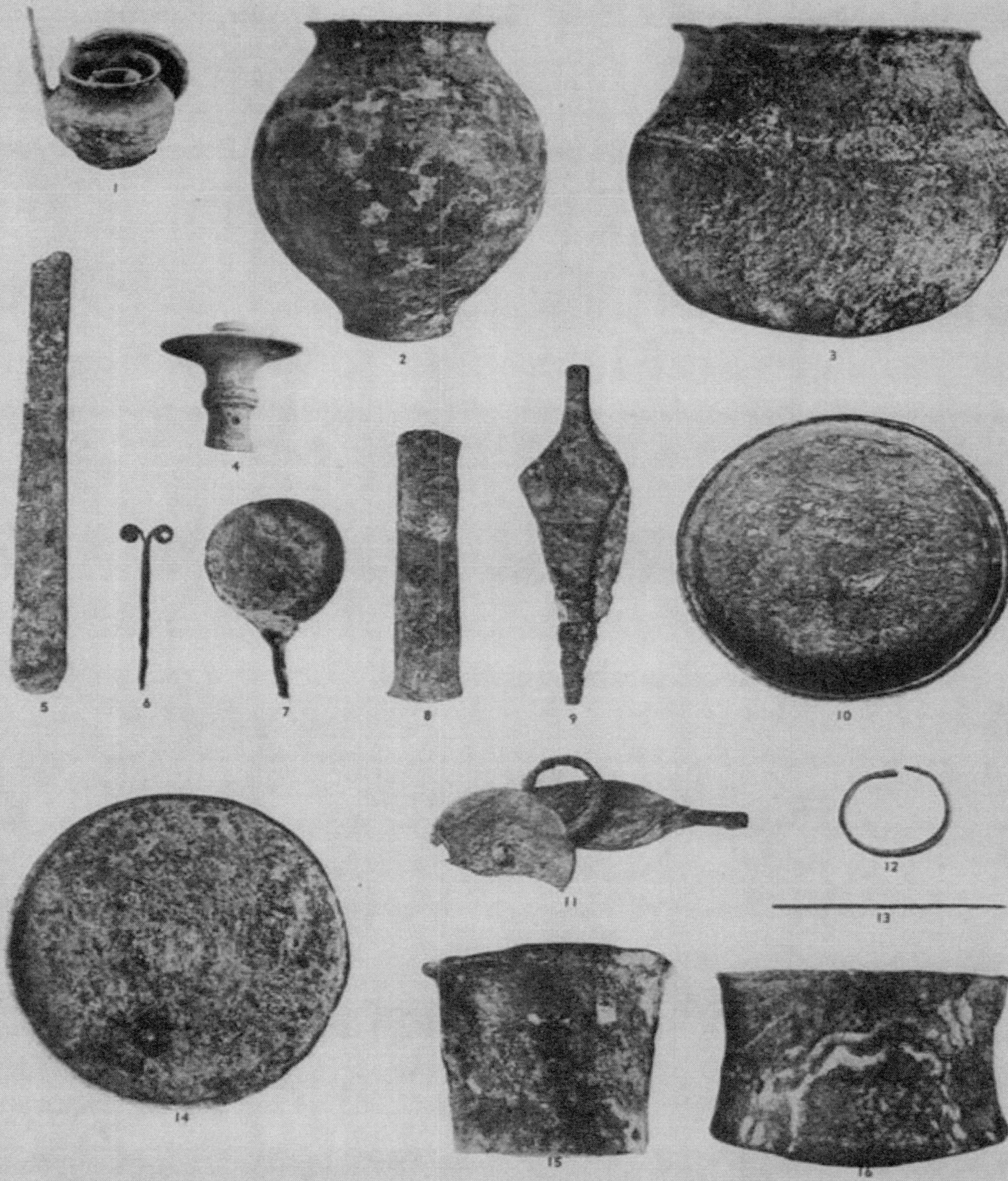
1
2
3
4
5
6
7
8
9
10
11
12
13
14
15
16

COPPER AND BRONZE IMPLEMENTS AND TOOLS: HARAPPĀ CULTURE PLATE LXXVI

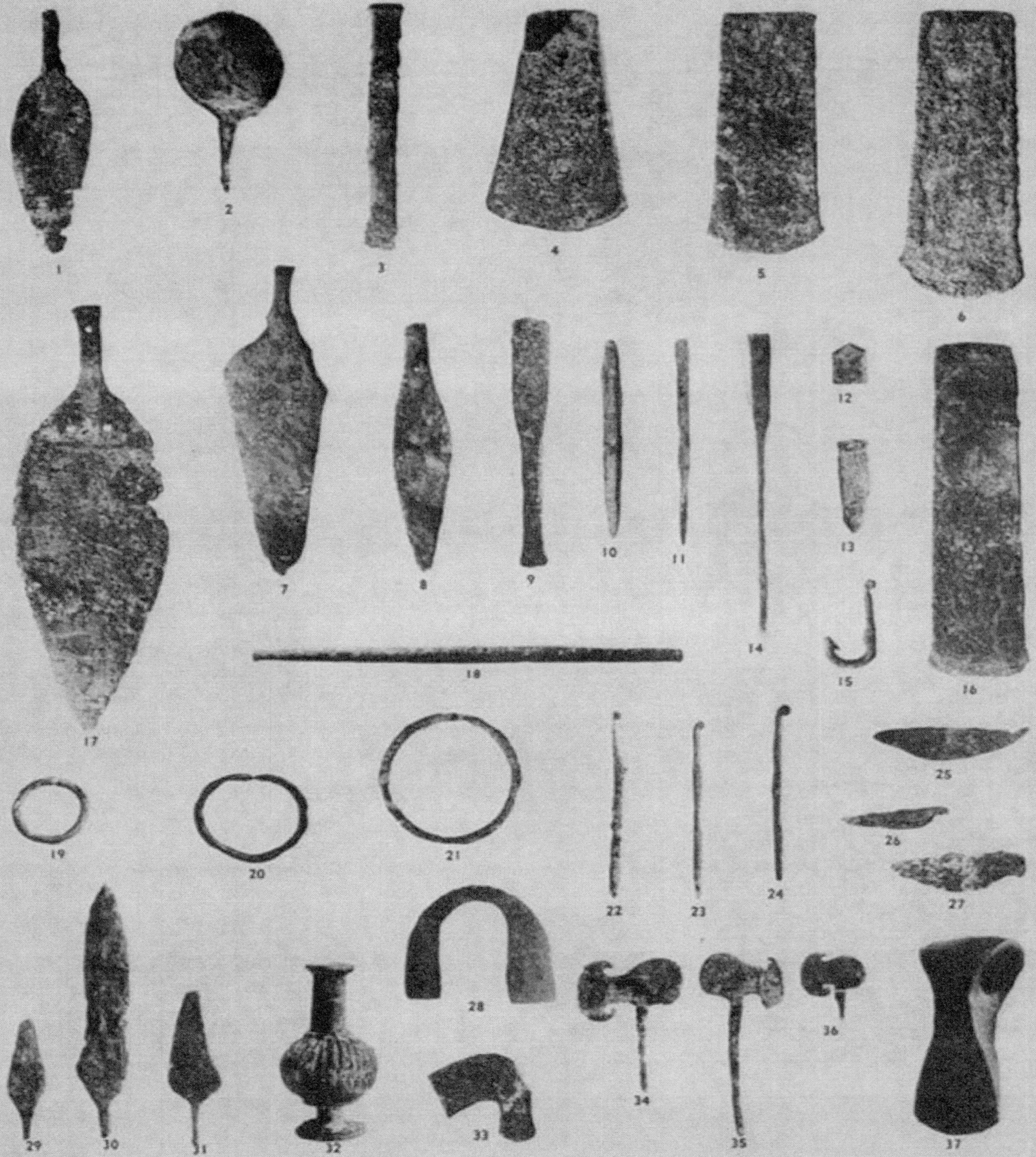

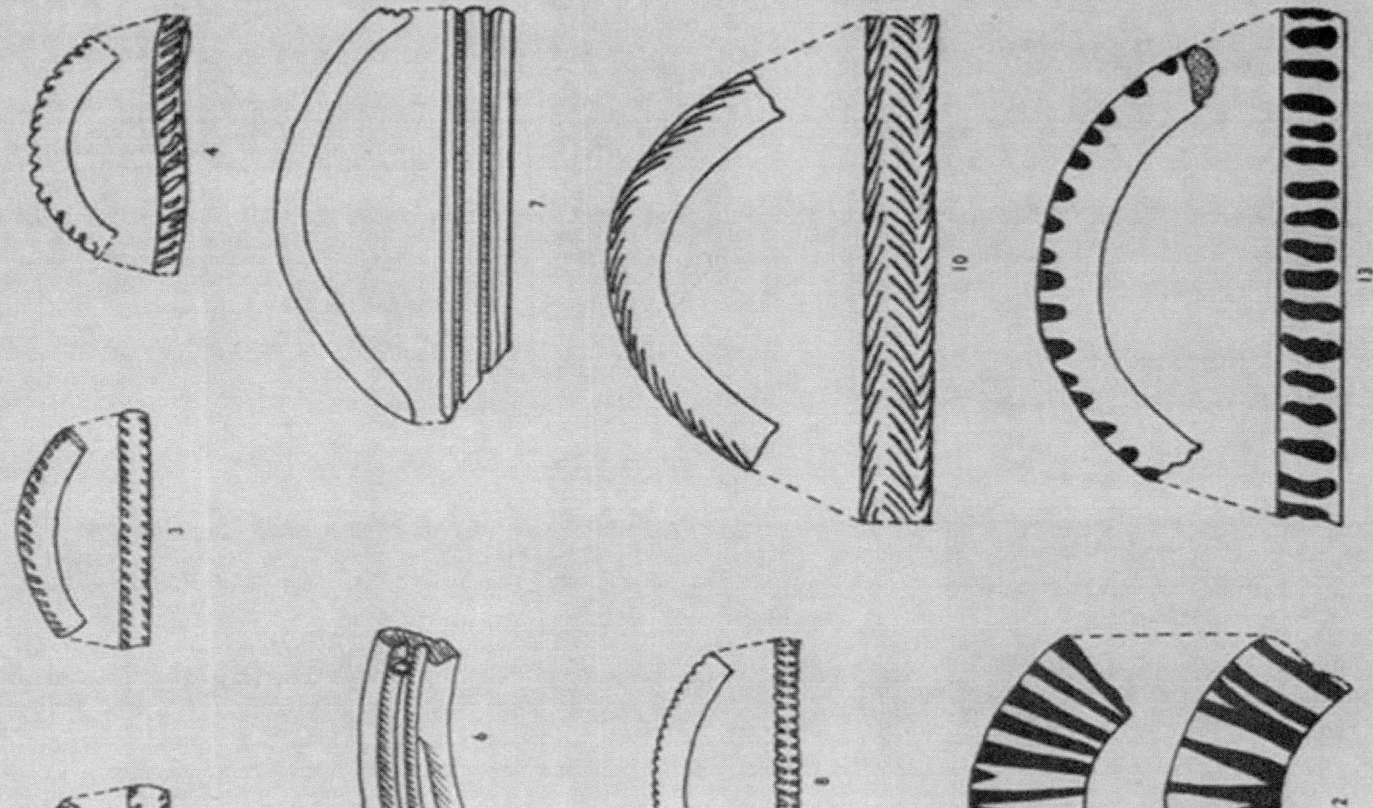

Scale 1:1

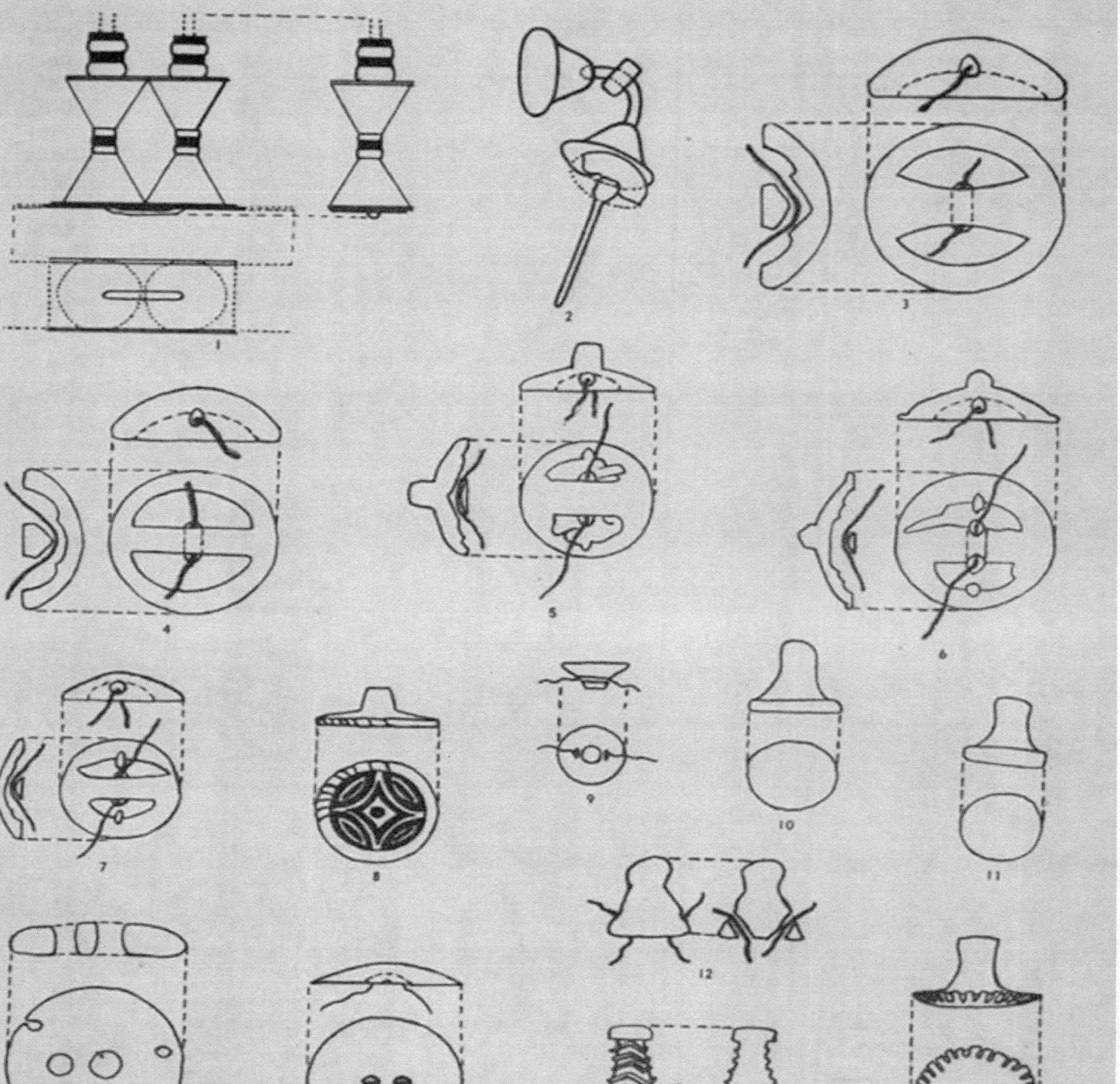

Scale 1:1

Scale 2:1

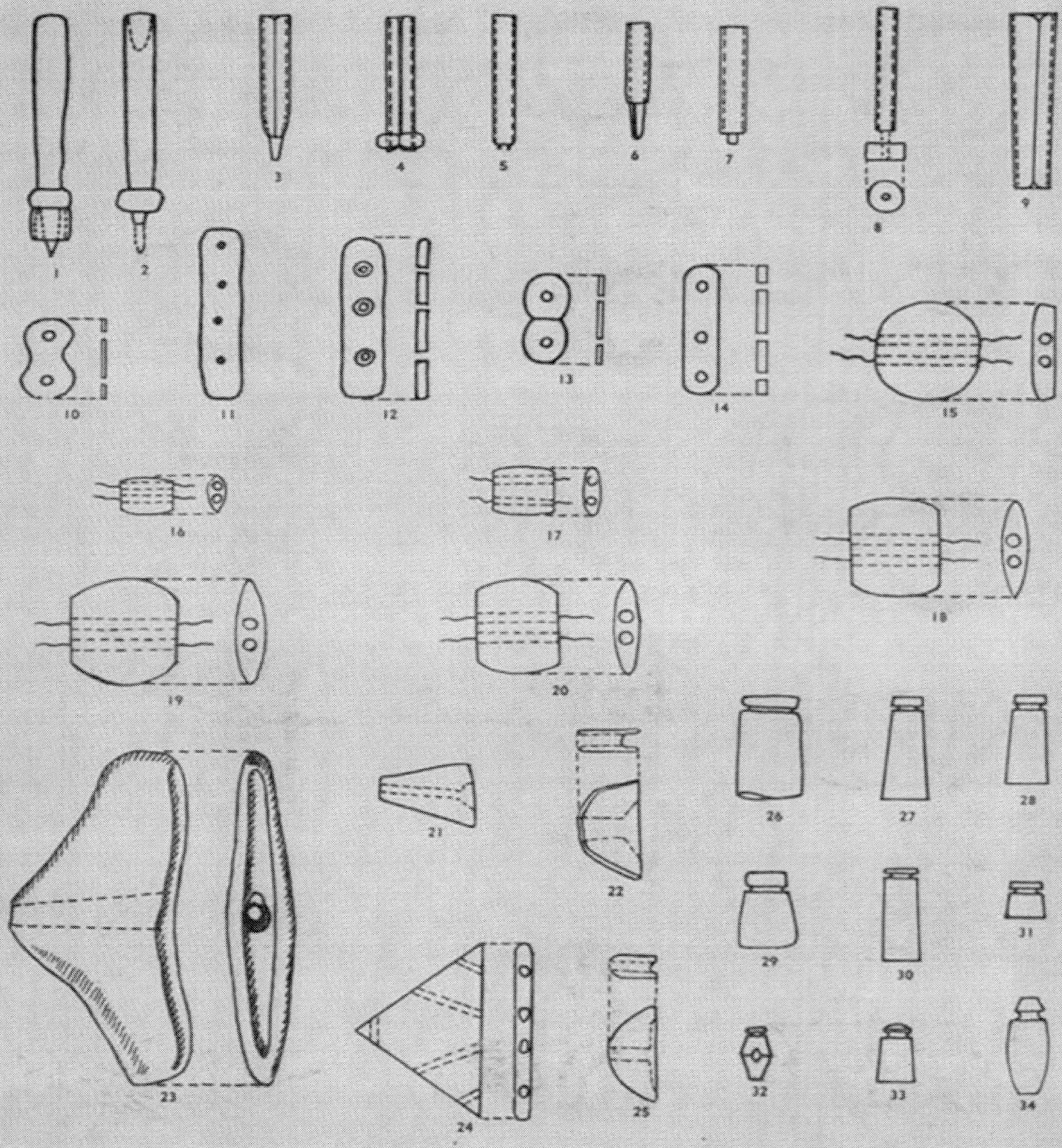
1
2
3
4
5
6
7
8
9
10
11
12
13
14
15
16
17
18
19
20
21
22
23
24
25
26
27
28
29
30
31
32
33
34

Scale 1:1

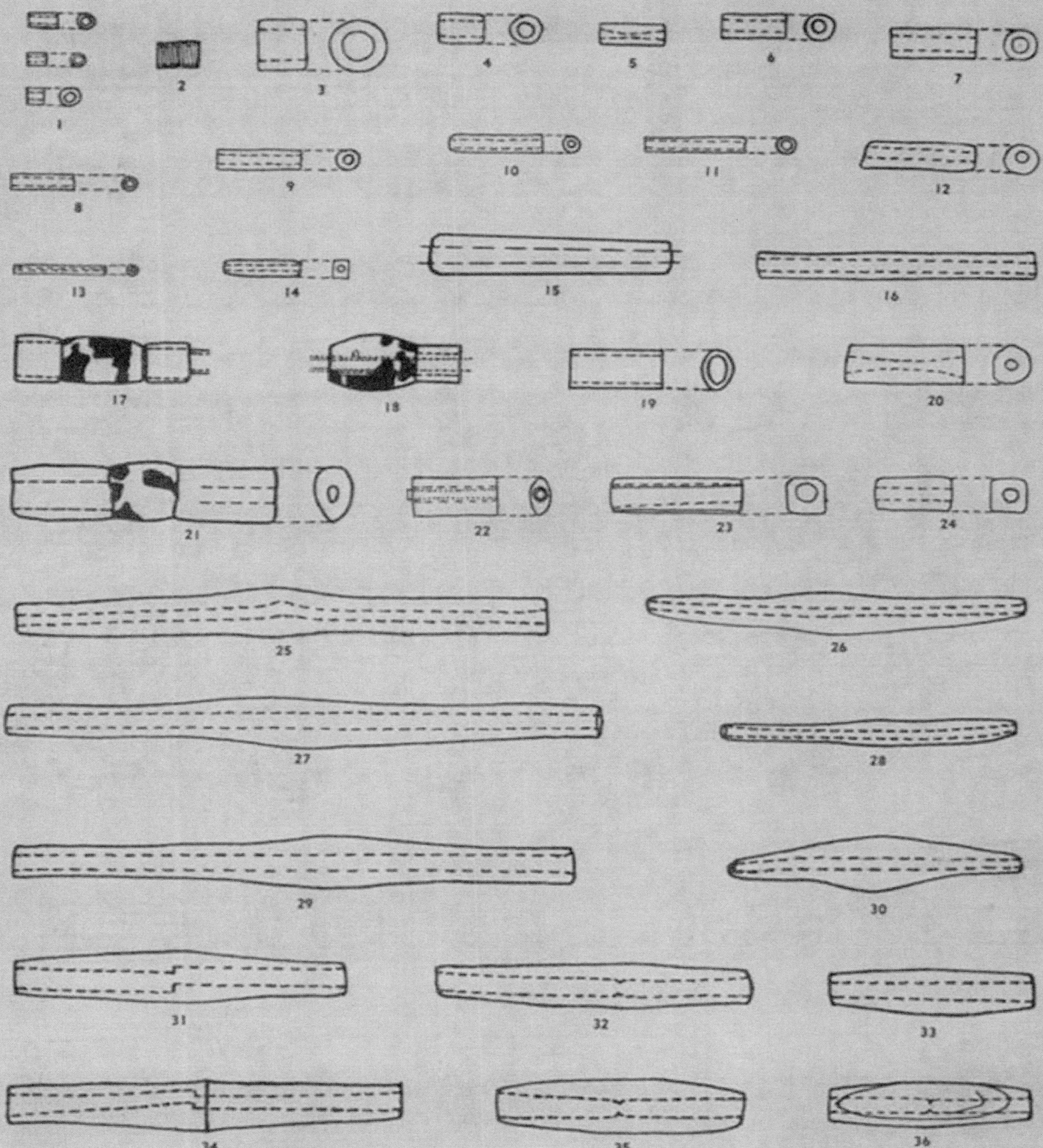
1
2
3
4
5
6
7
8
9
10
11
12
13
14
15
16
17
18
19
20
21
22
23
24
25
26
27
28
29
30
31
32
33
34
35
36

Scale 1:1

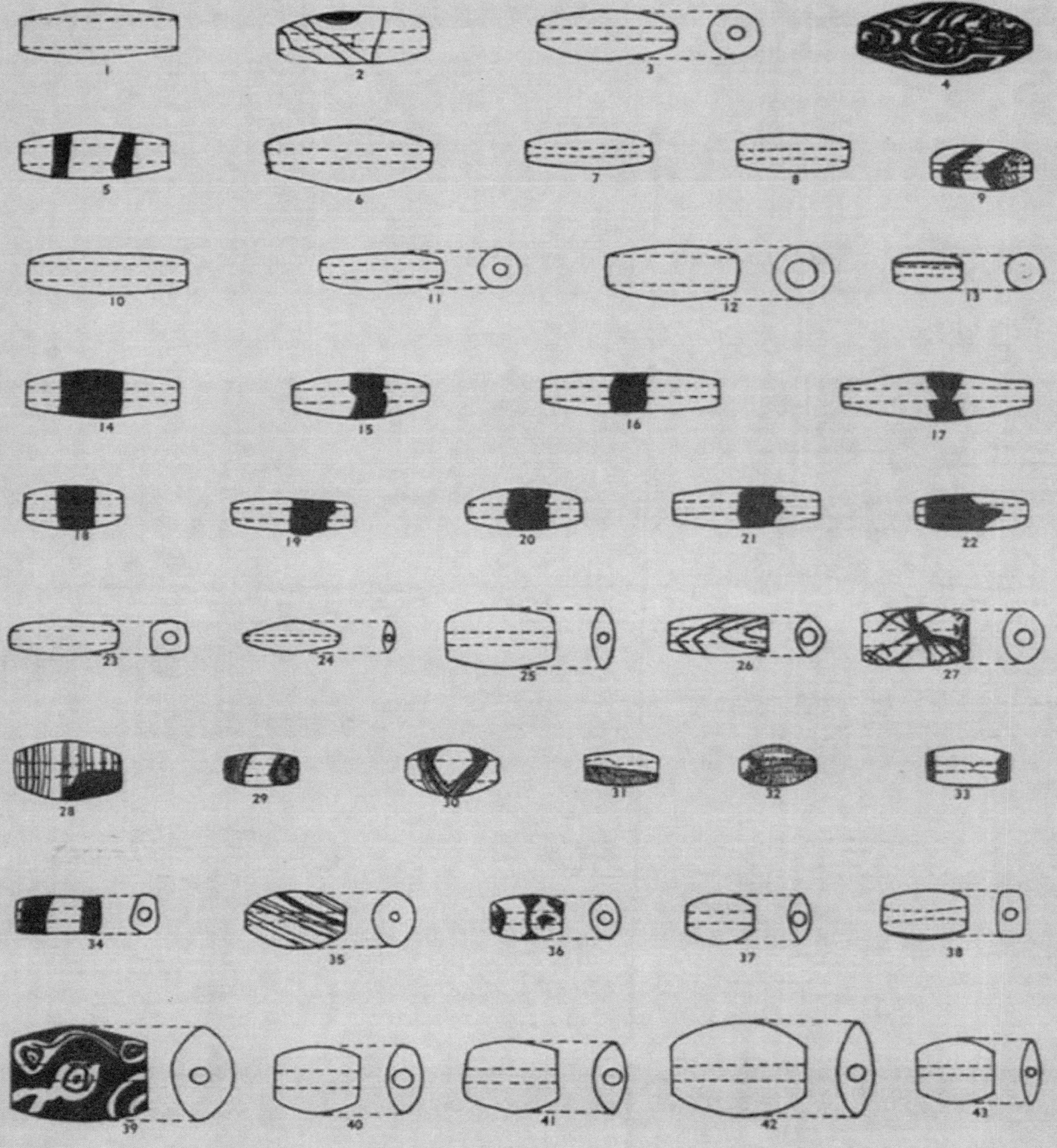
1
2
3
4
5
6
7
8
9
10
11
12
13
14
15
16
17
18
19
20
21
22
23
24
25
26
27
28
29
30
31
32
33
34
35
36
37
38
39
40
41
42
43

Scale 1:1

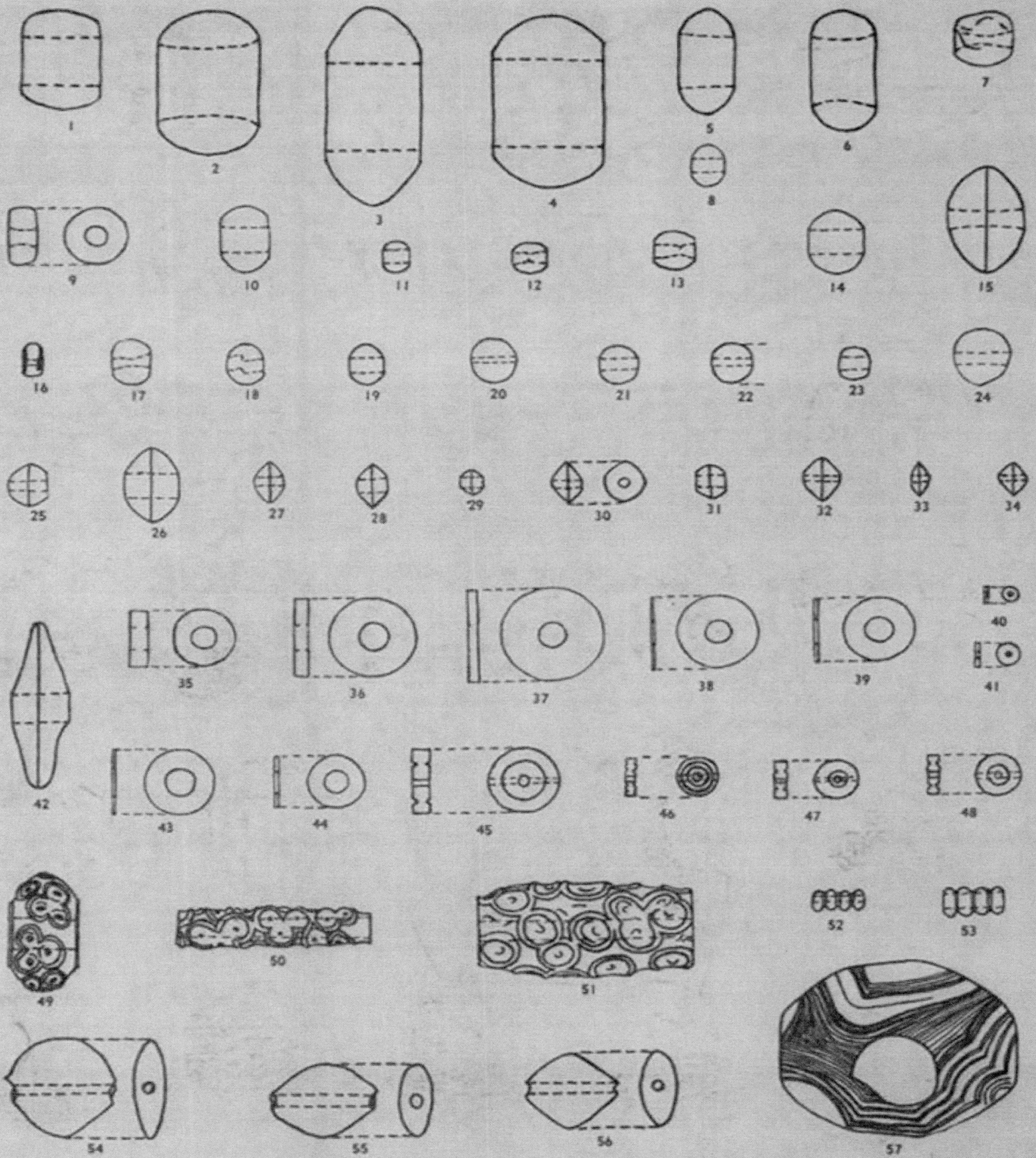
1
2
3
4
5
6
7
8
9
10
11
12
13
14
15
16
17
18
19
20
21
22
23
24
25
26
27
28
29
30
31
32
33
34
35
36
37
38
39
40
41
42
43
44
45
46
47
48
49
50
51
52
53
54
55
56
57

Scale 1:1

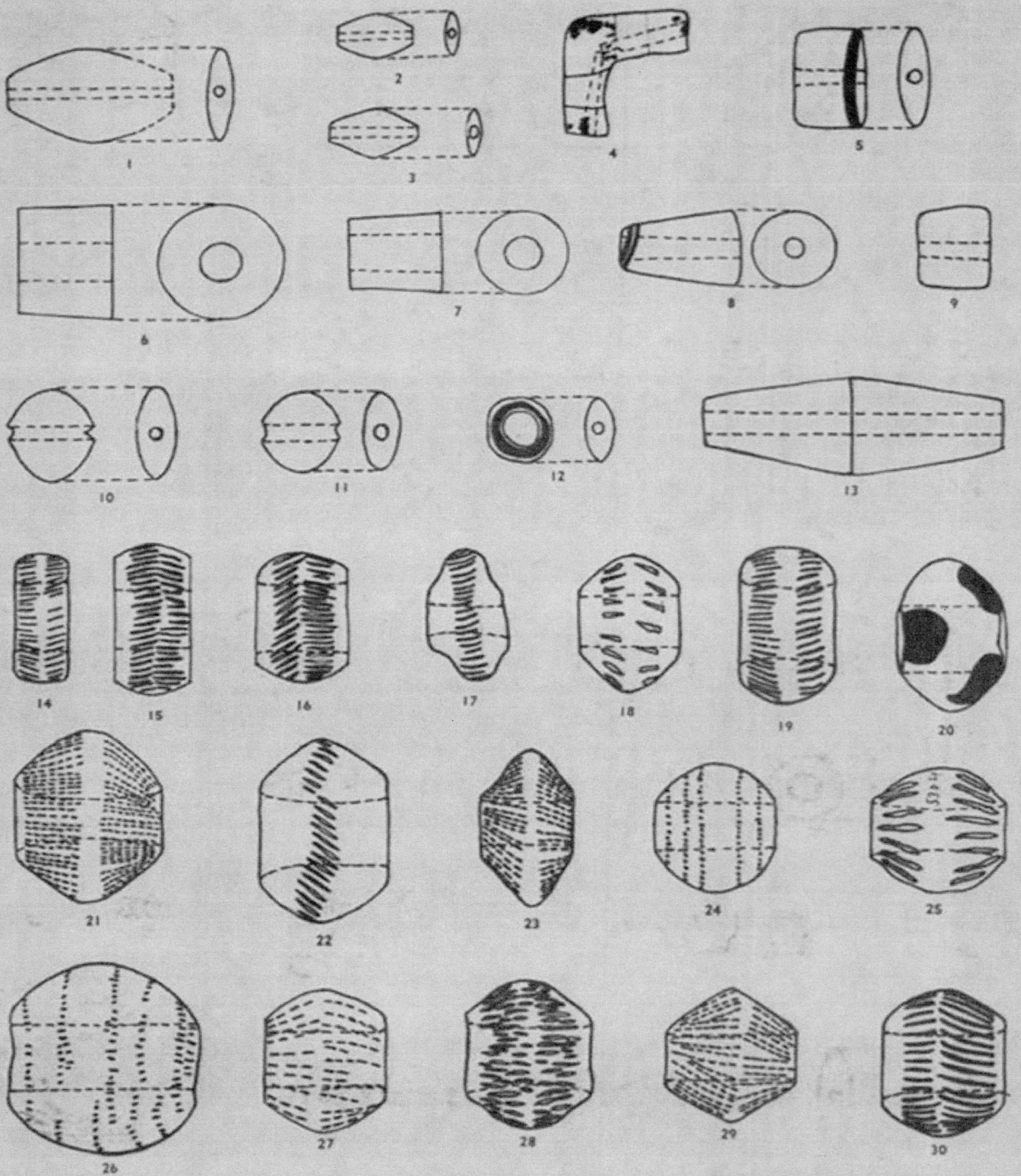
1
2
3
4
5
6
7
8
9
10
11
12
13
14
15
16
17
18
19
20
21
22
23
24
25
26
27
28
29
30

Scale 1:1

1
2
3
4
5
6
7
8
9
10
11
12
13
14
15
16
17
18
19
20
21
22
23
24
25
26
27
28
29
30
31
32
33
34

Scale 1:1

BEADS AND MICRO-PHOTOGRAPHS (HARAPPĀ CULTURE) PLATE LXXXVI, a

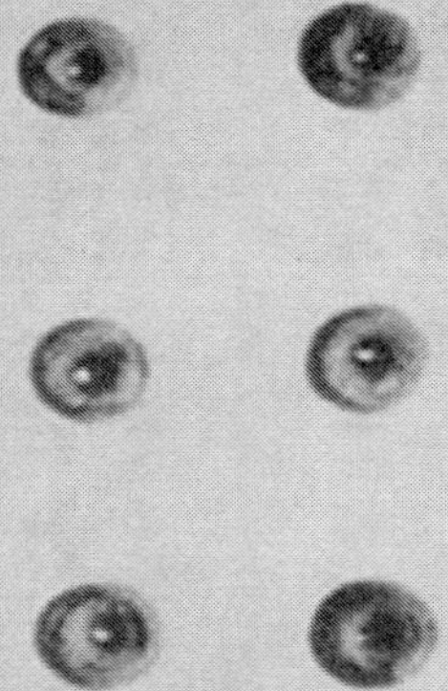

1

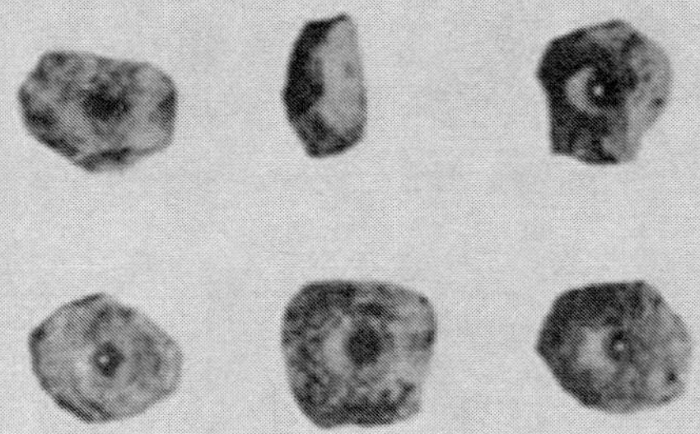

2

3a

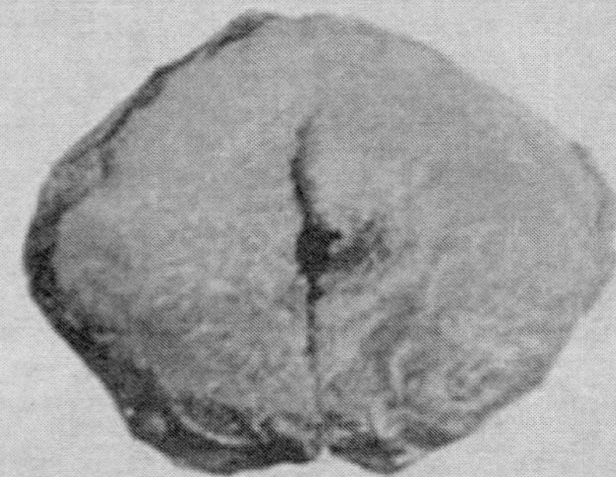

3b

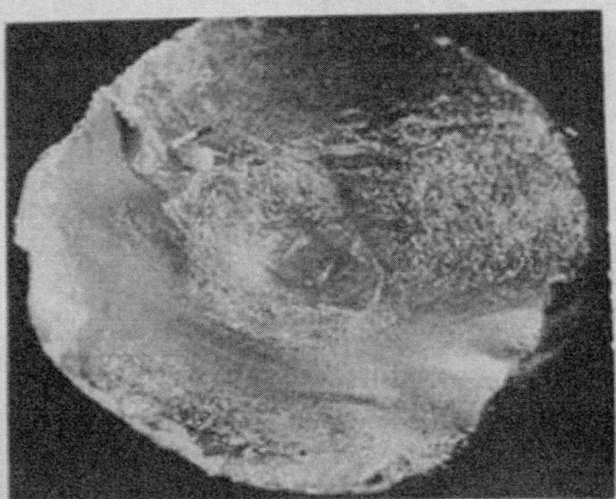

4

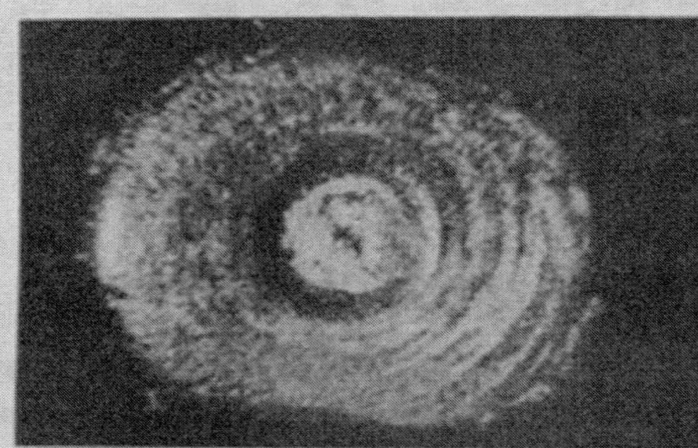

5

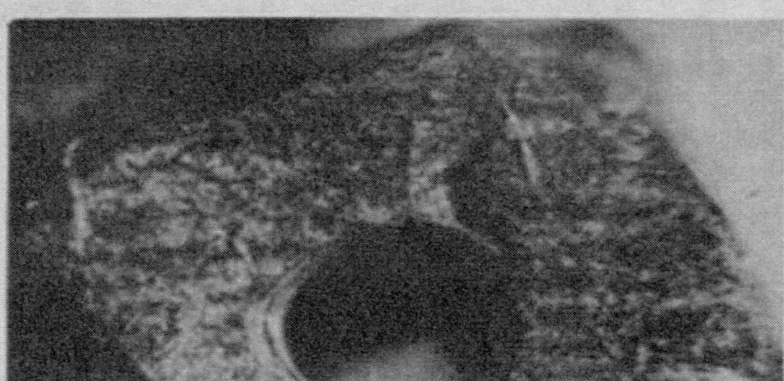

6

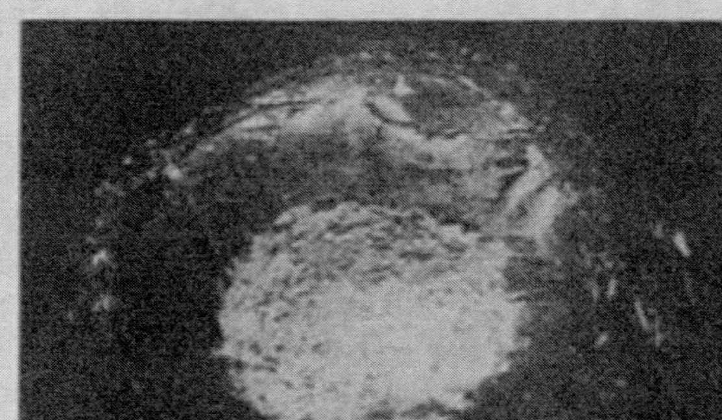

7

SHELLS, BEADS, BEAD-DRILLS, AND BRICK — PLATE LXXXVI, b

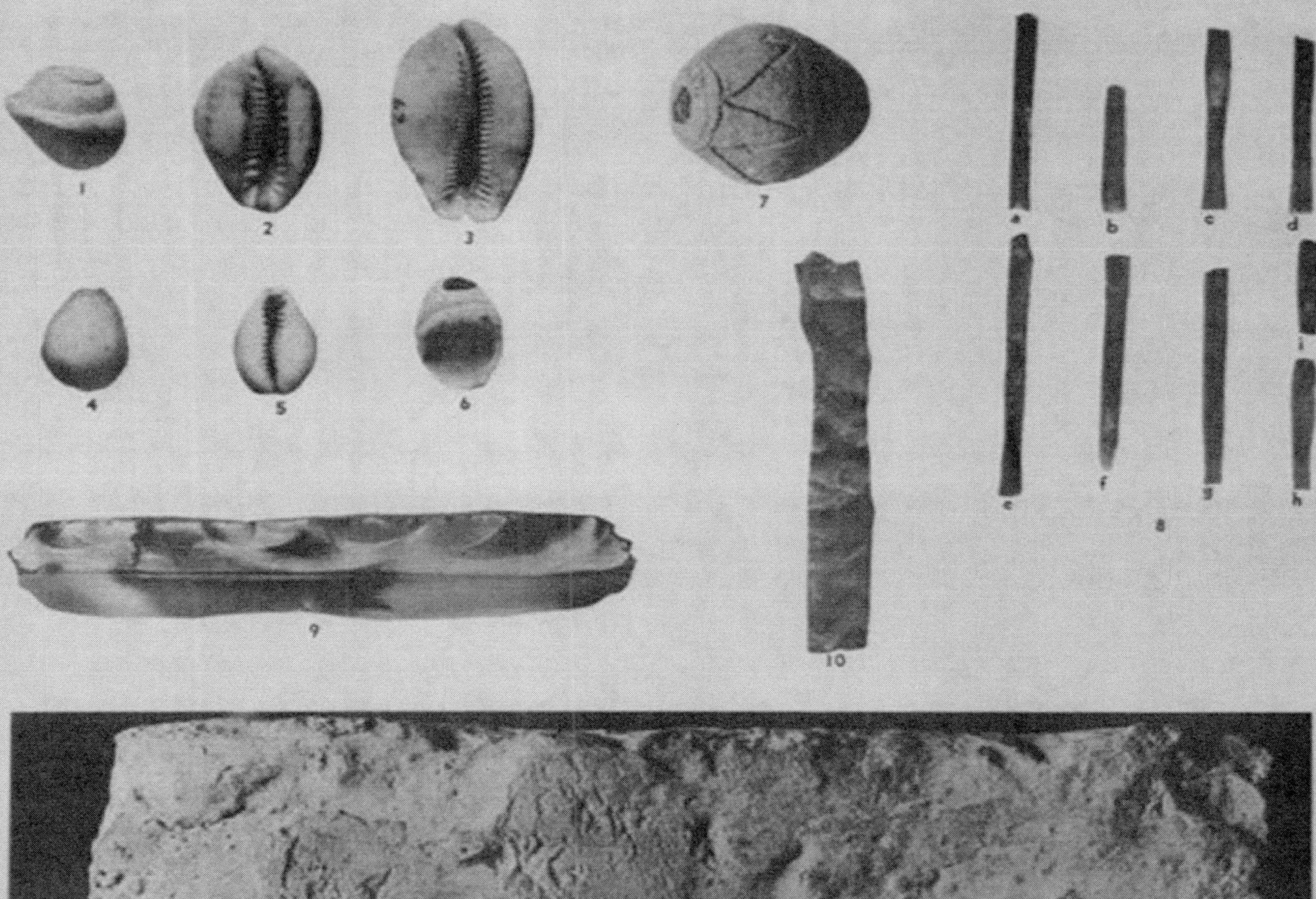

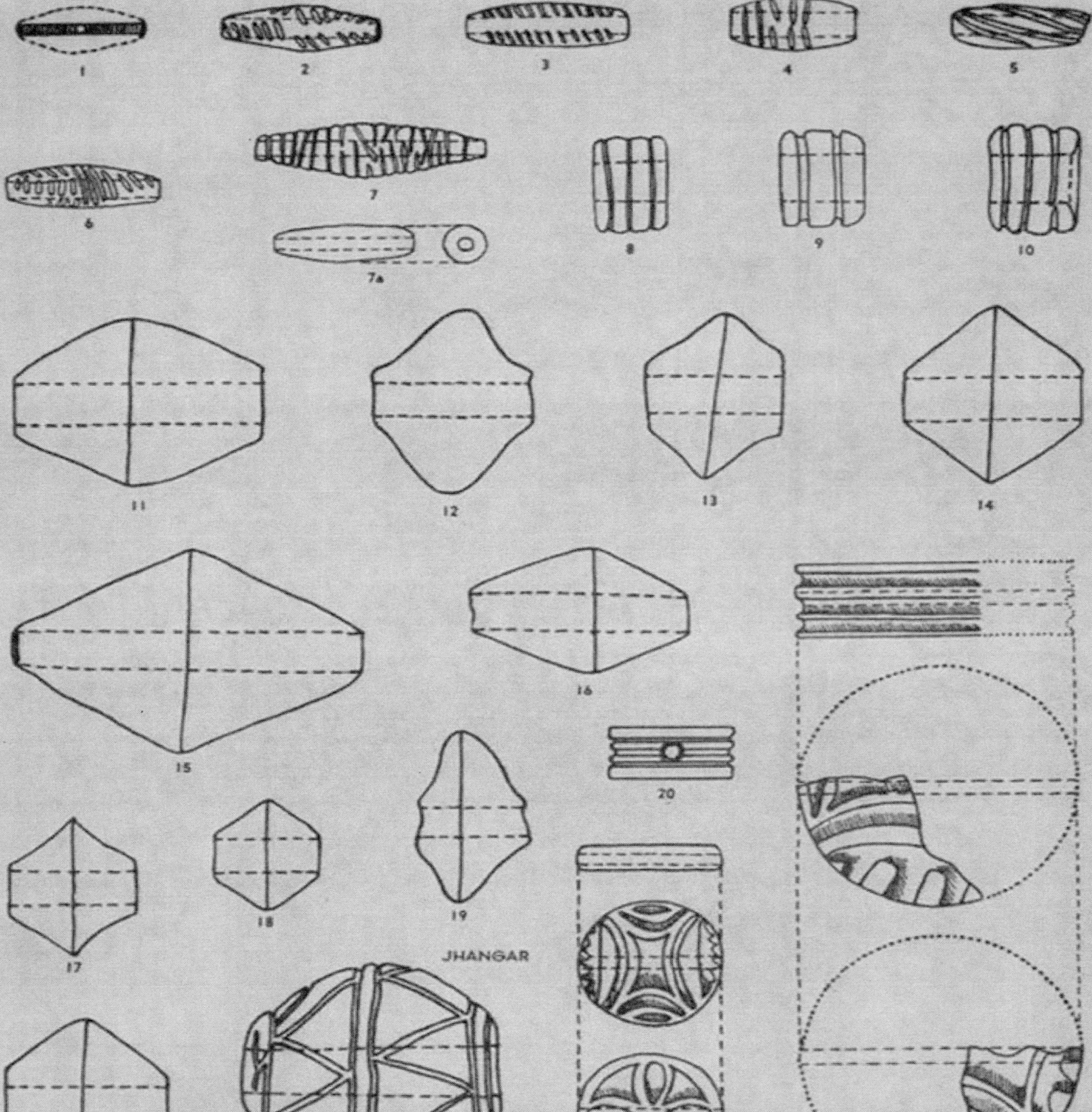

Scale 1:1

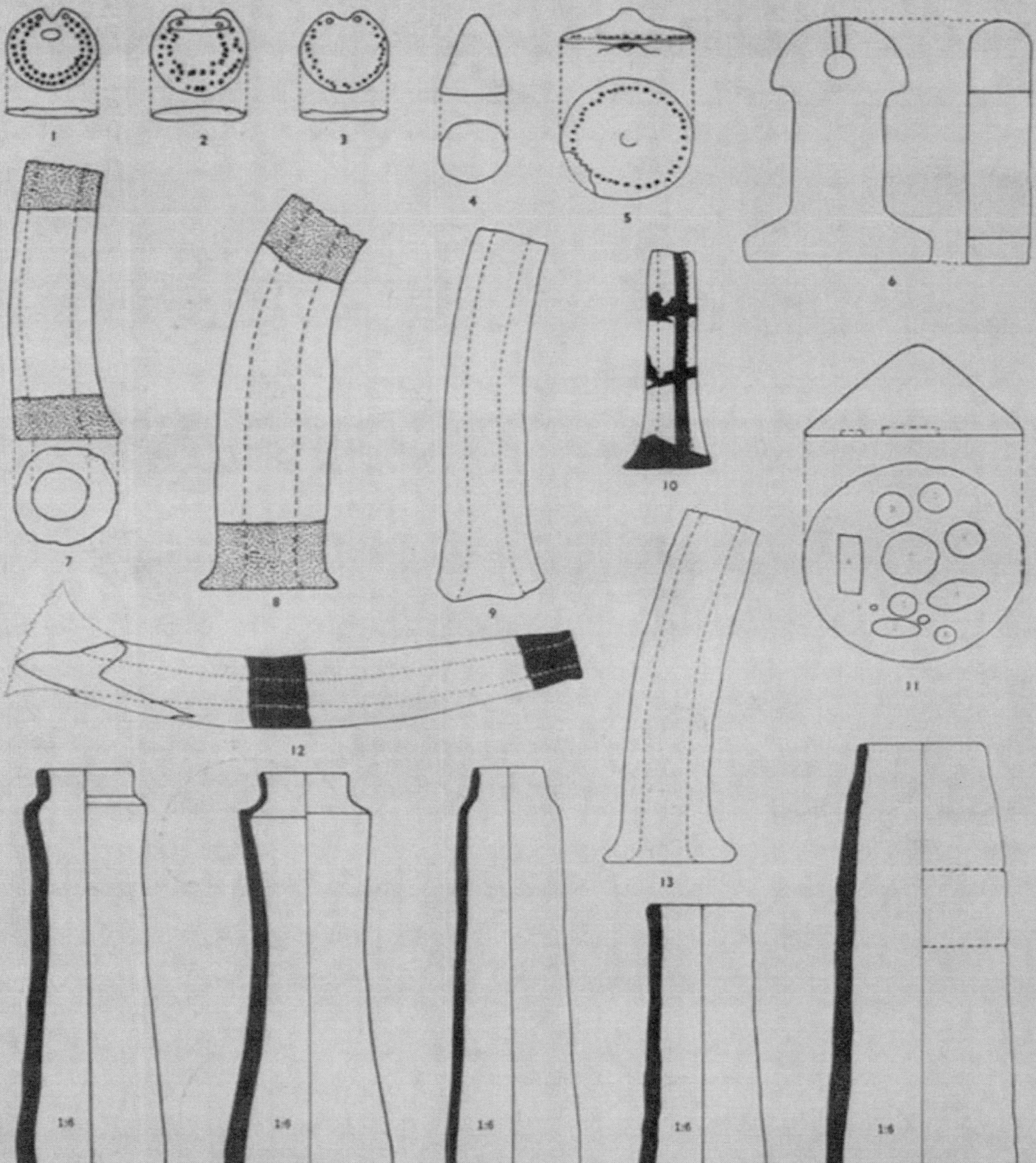

Scale 1:2

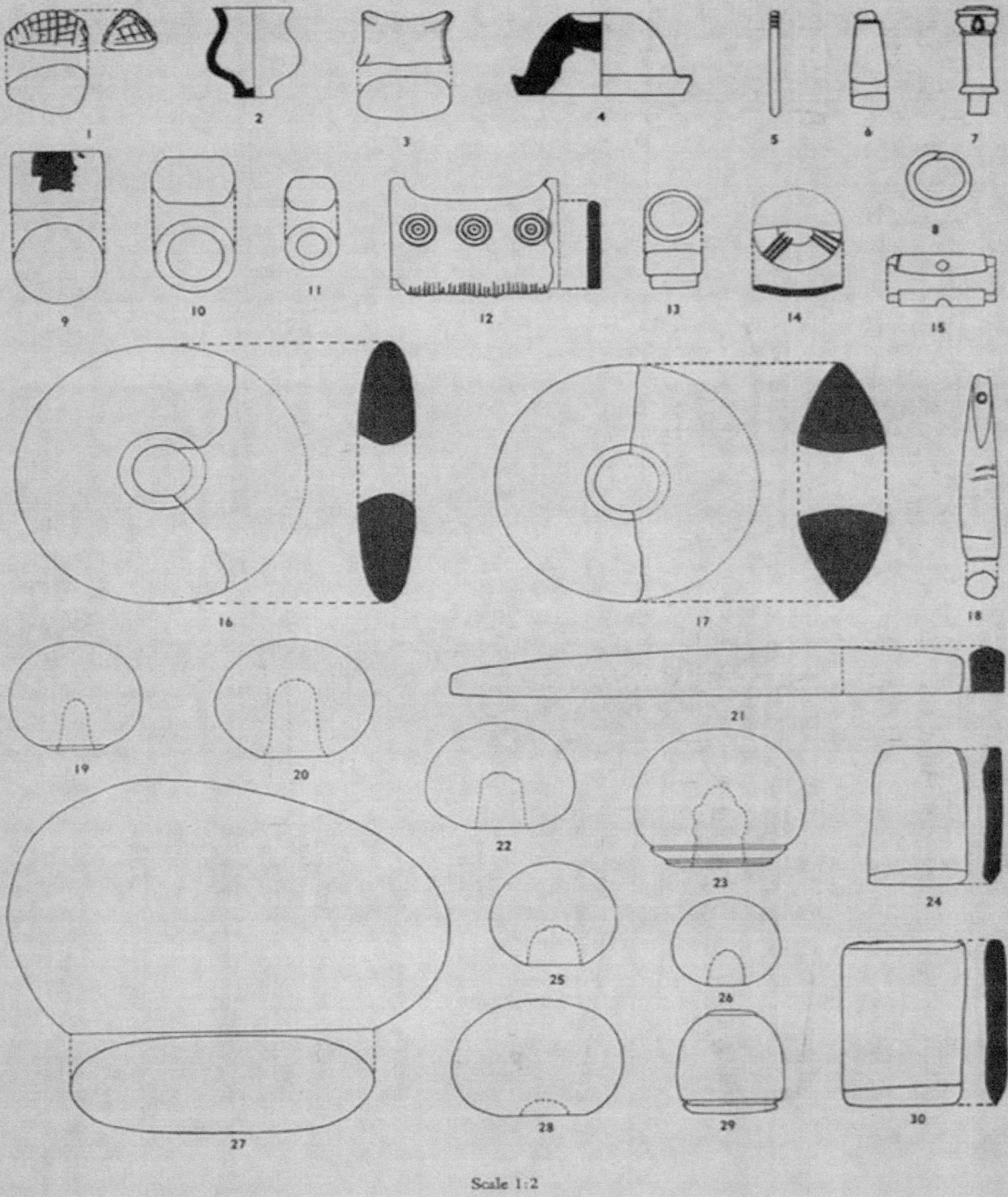
1
2
3
4
5
6
7
8
9
10
11
12
13
14
15
16
17
18
19
20
21
22
23
24
25
26
27
28
29
30

Scale 1:2

MISCELLANEOUS OBJECTS (HARAPPĀ CULTURE)

PLATE XC

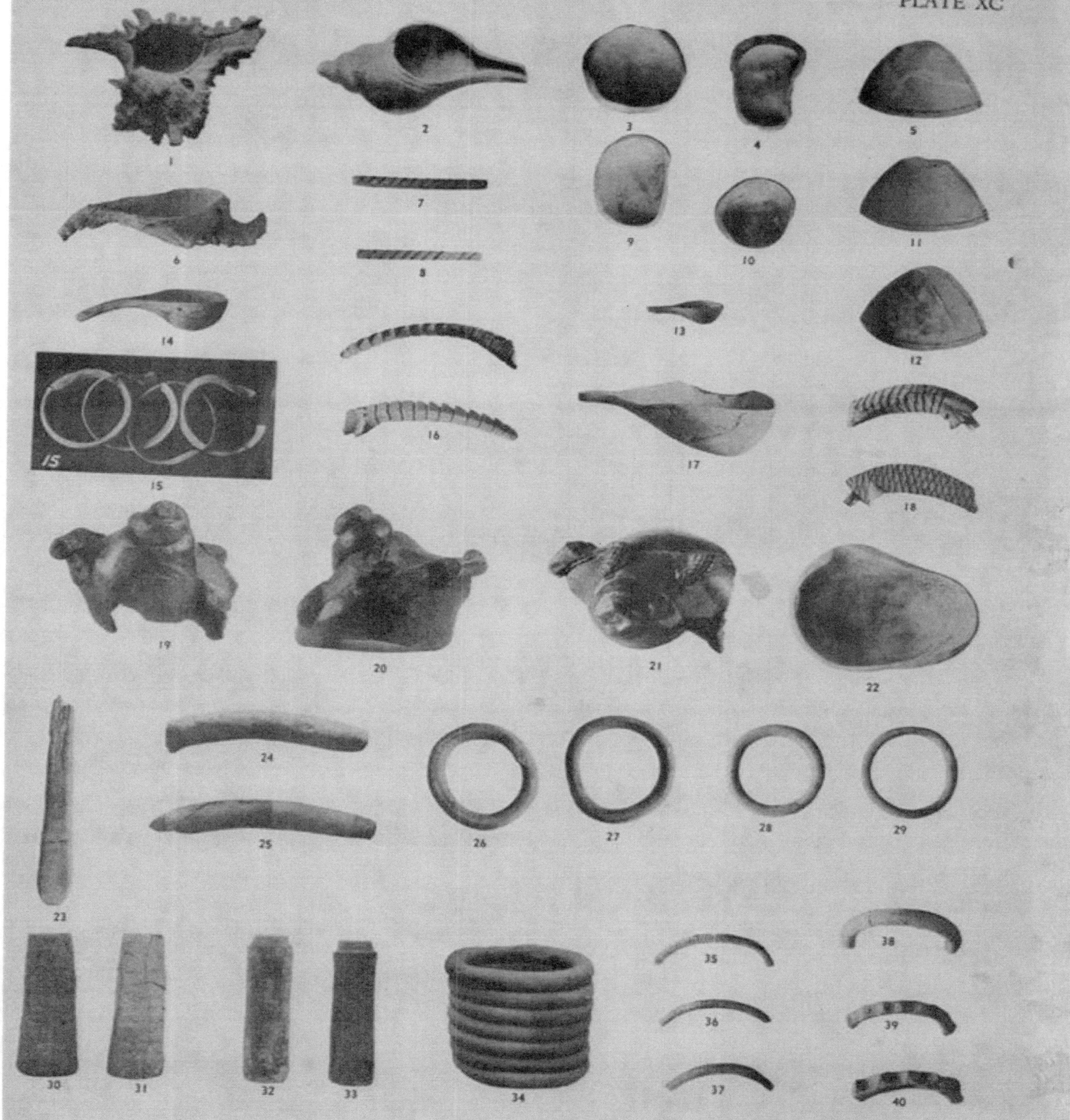

MISCELLANEOUS OBJECTS (HARAPPĀ CULTURE)

PLATE XCI

1
2
3
4
5
6
7
8
9
10
11
12
13
14
15
16
17
18
19
20
21
22
23
24
25
26
27
28
29
30
31
32
33
34
35
36
37
38

BEADS, TOOLS AND MISCELLANEOUS OBJECTS: HARAPPĀ CULTURE

PLATE XCIII

Fig. 1. Jar containing skull, copper and bronze implements and shell. Mound II, Sq. 7/E, loc. 324, lev. + 9.2 ft.

Fig. 2. Upper part of jar removed to show contents.

Fig. 3. Close up of Fig. 2, from slightly different angle.

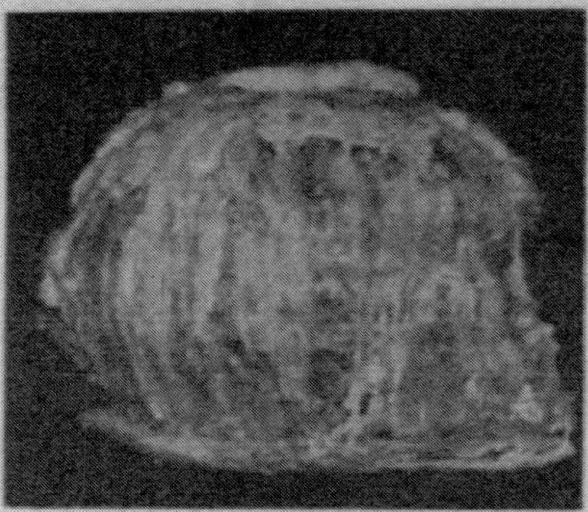

Fig. 4. Right lateral view of skull as received for study.

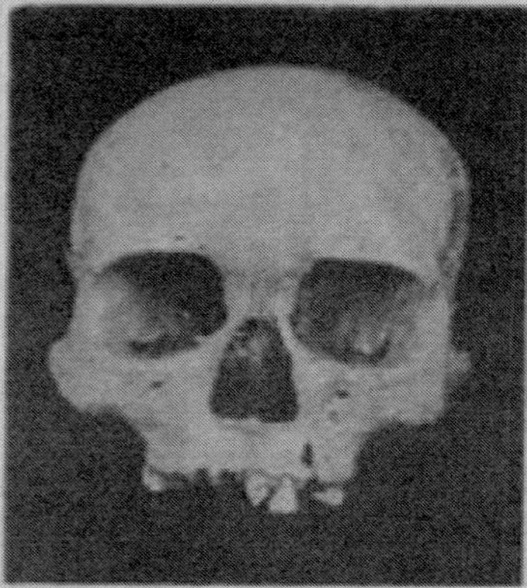

Fig. 5. Facial view.

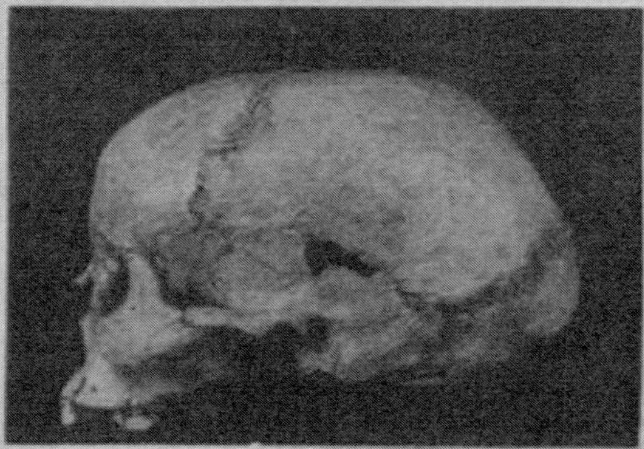

Fig. 6. Left lateral view.

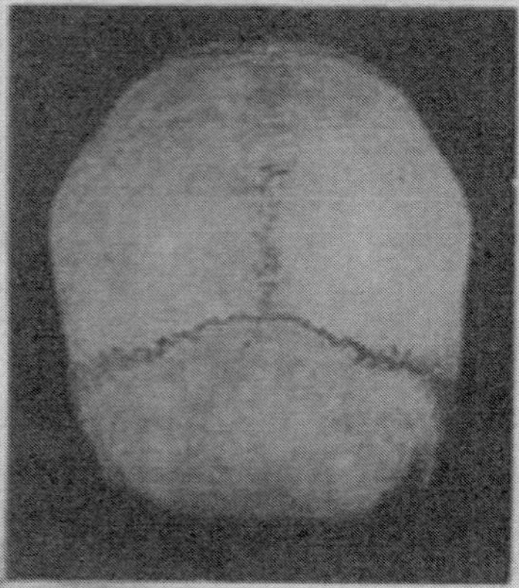

Fig. 7. Vertical view.

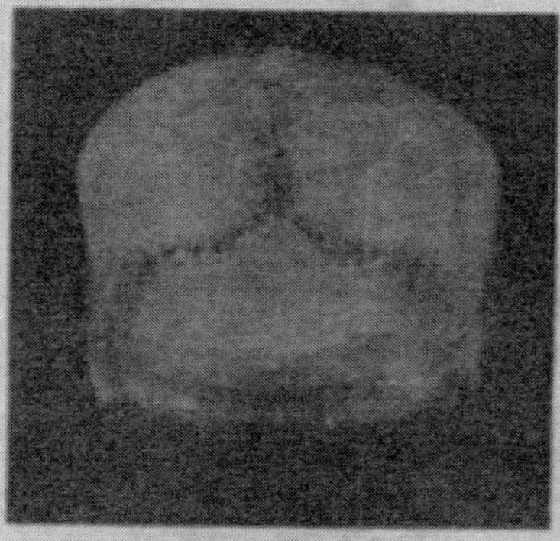

Fig. 8. Occipital view.

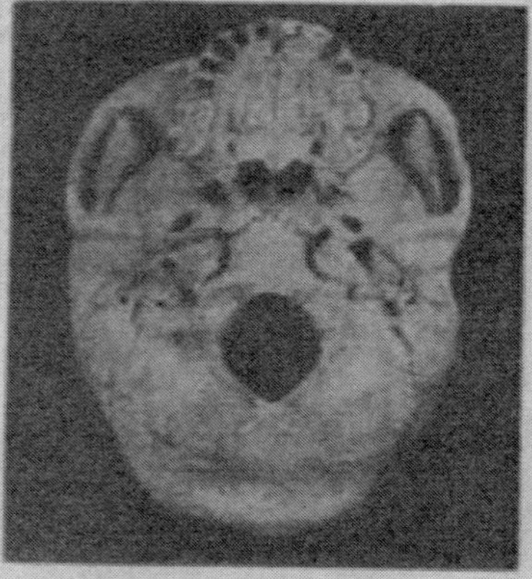

Fig. 9. Basilar view.

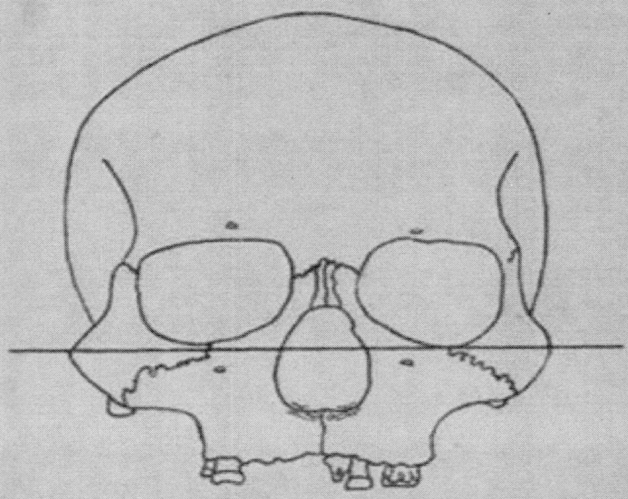

Figure 10

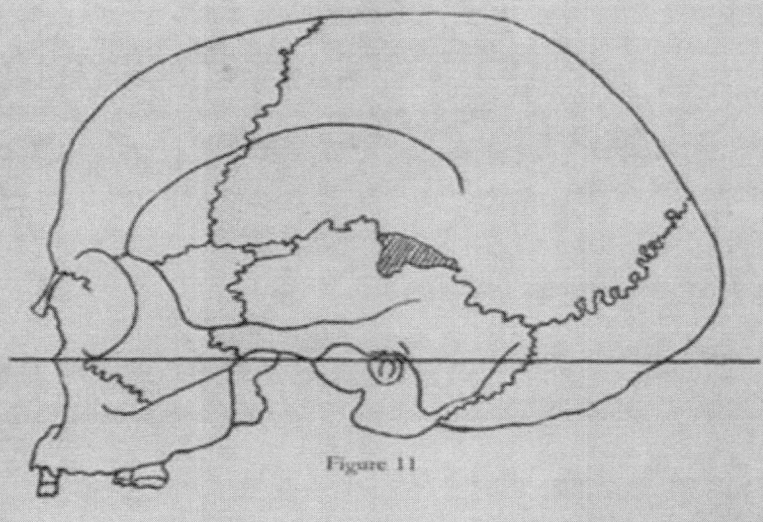

Figure 11

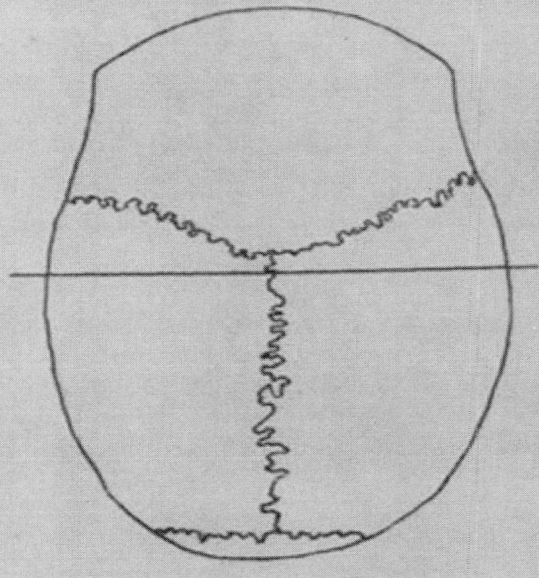

Figure 12

Scale 1:2